CANTUAR

# CANTUAR
## The Archbishops in their Office

EDWARD CARPENTER

CASSELL · LONDON

CASSELL & COMPANY LTD
35 Red Lion Square, London WC1
*Sydney, Auckland*
*Toronto, Johannesburg*

First published 1971

I.S.B.N.   0 304 93850 5

*Printed in Great Britain by*
*The Camelot Press Ltd, London and Southampton*

I dedicate this book with continuing affection to my parents; and to my daughter Louise in the hope that when she gets older she may read it.

# CONTENTS

*after page 322*

Thomas Tenison (*National Portrait Gallery*)
William Wake*
Thomas Secker*
Addington Palace (*John Maltby Ltd.*)
John Moore*
William Howley (*National Portrait Gallery*)
John Bird Sumner*
Charles Longley (*National Portrait Gallery*)
The First Lambeth Conference, 1867 (*by kind permission of the United
    Society for the Propagation of the Gospel*)
Archibald Campbell Tait*
A Punch cartoon arising out of the Irish Church question, 1868
Edward White Benson*

*after page 450*

Frederick Temple*
The Archbishop's Palace, Canterbury (*Walter Scott, Bradford*)
Randall Thomas Davidson (*National Portrait Gallery*)
Cosmo Gordon Lang (*reproduced by kind permission of the Archbishop of
    York and the Church Commissioners: copyright reserved to the Church
    Commissioners*)
William Temple*
Geoffrey Francis Fisher*
Archbishop Fisher crowns Queen Elizabeth II (*Fox Photos Ltd.*)
Arthur Michael Ramsey
Lambeth Palace
Cardinal Heenan, Dr. Immanuel Jakobovits, the Chief Rabbi, and
    Dr. Ramsey, 1971 (*Daily Telegraph*)

When I was invited to write *Cantuar* I was fully aware of the hazards which await the general historian. Of necessity he must invade the specialisms of others without their years of intensive application; and at a time when, for example in the medieval period, a more disciplined approach to manuscript sources has led to many a revised judgement. He cannot acquire the kind of sensitivity which only first-hand intimacy with primary material over long years can hope to give. What W. F. Hook attempted in his 12-volume *Lives of the Archbishops*, published between the years 1860–76, would now be undertaken only by a team of scholars. Yet there are compensations, if not advantages, in the longer view implicit in a more general study —the wide reading which it entails; the attractive byways into which it encourages entry; the sense of historic continuity which it engenders; the charity, if not maturity, of judgement which it can breed when the perspective is lengthened.

My intention in this study is to illustrate across the centuries the outreach of an office, together with the character and aptitudes of those who have discharged it; to trace how the Archbishop, in his unique office, has helped to condition, and in his turn been conditioned by, the continuing life of the English people. For me the personal interest has been dominant throughout, and where possible I have allowed Archbishops to speak for themselves and be their own advocates. It will be seen, however, that the method of treatment has varied. Prior to the Norman Conquest the approach, on the whole, is chronological. In dealing with the Middle Ages it appeared more fitting and convenient to handle separately the various aspects of the Archbishop's many-sided responsibilities. The period from the Reformation to the Bloodless Revolution of 1688, during which time the Archbishop was intimately involved with the developing political life of the English nation, lent itself naturally to a chronological presentation. A different approach was required to catch the ethos of the XVIIIth century, when the Church's history ceased to be bound up with that of the nation. With the achievement of such a history of its own in the XIXth and XXth centuries, return to a chronology seemed appropriate.

As the method of treatment has varied, so has the allocation of space to particular periods. The four hundred years of Anglo-Saxon England are restricted to forty pages, the longer period of the Middle Ages to eighty. Yet the subsequent five hundred years occupy two-thirds of the book, within which the last hundred years have been allocated nearly two hundred pages. This seeming lack of proportion is deliberate, and illustrates the selective character of the work.

In addition to general histories and more specialized studies, I have been particularly dependent upon recent biographies of Arch-bishops, culled from original and hitherto untapped sources. The official records of Convocation, Church Assembly, and Parliament are of course indispensable. For the XVIIIth century the Newcastle manuscripts, among others at the British Museum, are important; while there is no better way of getting the 'feel' of the emerging pre-occupations of an Archbishop in the latter half of the XIXth century than by browsing through the Longley, Tait, Benson and Temple papers at Lambeth.

Perhaps it should be added that the spelling of some direct quota-tions has been modernized for the convenience of the general reader.

The number of people I should thank for helping me during the course of writing this book is legion. The tendency has been to bore one's friends. I would, however, particularly express my apprecia-tion to Miss Christine Zochonis for not only enduring the labour of much typing but assisting me throughout; to Miss G. I. Drake, for ransacking the Church House Library in search of possible material; and to the Reverend Harold Goodwin, Fellow of the Institute of Journalists, a friend of long standing, for his professional skill in looking over the manuscript and reading the proofs. I should also like to thank my publishers for their forbearance, advice and assistance.

*June 1971*                                   EDWARD CARPENTER

# ACKNOWLEDGEMENTS

I should like to thank the following for permission to reprint copyright material:

The Benson Estate and Longmans Green:
*As We Were* by E. F. Benson
Cambridge University Press:
*Magna Carta* by J. C. Holt
Clarendon Press:
*Bede's Ecclesiastical History of the English People* (trs. and ed. Colgrave and Mynors)
*Thomas Cranmer* by Jasper Ridley
*Lanfranc* by A. J. Macdonald
Hodder and Stoughton:
*Cosmo Gordon Lang* by J. G. Lockhart
Hodder and Stoughton and the author:
*Fisher of Lambeth* by William Purcell
Thomas Nelson & Sons:
*The Lordship of Canterbury* by F. R. H. Du Boulay

I am also indebted to Macmillan's biographies of *A. C. Tait* (Davidson and Benham), *E. W. Benson* (A. C. Benson), and *Frederick Temple* (ed. Sandford), and to the Oxford University Press's *Randall Davidson* (Bell)—all of which proved invaluable.

# PART I

# ANGLO-SAXON ENGLAND:
# THE FORMATIVE YEARS

*Archbishops*

| | |
|---|---|
| AUGUSTINE | *597 |
| LAURENTIUS | 604 |
| MELLITUS | 619 |
| JUSTUS | 624 |
| HONORIUS | 627 |
| DEUSDEDIT | 655 |
| THEODORE | 668 |
| BEORHTWEALD | 693 |
| TATWINE | 731 |
| NOTHELM | 735 |
| CUTHBEORHT | 740 |
| BREGUWINE | 761 |
| JAENBEORHT | 765 |
| AETHELHEARD | 793 |
| WULFRED | 805 |
| FEOLOGILD | 832 |
| CEOLNOTH | 833 |
| AETHELRED | 870 |
| PLEGMUND | 890 |
| AETHELHELM | 914 |
| WULFHELM | 923 |
| ODA | 942 |
| AEFSIGE | 959 |
| BEORHTHELM | 959 |
| DUNSTAN | 960 |
| ATHELGAR | c988 |
| SIGERIC SERIO | 990 |
| AELFRIC | 995 |
| AELFHEAH | 1005 |
| LYFING | 1013 |
| AETHELNOTH | 1020 |
| EADSIGE | 1038 |
| ROBERT OF JUMIÈGES | 1051 |
| STIGAND | 1052 |

*Year of Accession

# 1

## AUGUSTINE AND THE ROMAN MISSION

The British monarchy can trace its descent from William of Normandy, the vanquisher of Harold, and beyond him to Cerdic the Saxon. The Archbishop of Canterbury has played a significant national role since St. Augustine landed in Kent at the end of the VIth century. Augustine came from Rome, and thus links up the office of his successors with the Christian Church of near apostolic days and the secular Empire which gave unity to western Europe. When Dr. Michael Ramsey was enthroned as the hundredth Archbishop on Tuesday, 27 June 1961, he did not enter into his estate as a Melchizedek without ancestry. Not the least moving moment of the historic ceremony was his swearing to preserve the rights of 'this Cathedral and Metropolitical Church of Christ, Canterbury', on a book of the Gospels sent over to England, so tradition asserts, as early as 601. In this ancient oath, the past became contemporary.

*Cantuar* will trace how the Archbishop, in his unique office, has helped to condition, and in his turn has been conditioned by, the continuing life of the English people. This developing theme finds its point of departure in Rome. It was in this ancient city, and under the impetus of Pope Gregory the Great, that the mission of St. Augustine was conceived. Without his initiative and fostering care the enterprise would have foundered in its early days. Behind St. Gregory lay the resources and the administrative experience of the Roman Church, which, in days when the Empire was in the process of disintegrating, carried over into a new age some of the cultivation of the old.

Gregory, in whom a simple but informed Christian faith blended with the best in contemporary culture, was himself the outstanding ecclesiastical statesman of his day. Missionary enterprise was dear to his heart, and in a well-known story the Venerable Bede testifies to Gregory's interest in the 'lost province' of Britain. Walking one day through the slave market in Rome, he was struck by a group of boys paraded for sale. He was told that they were Angles from the Kingdom of Deira ruled by Aelle. His reply, expressed in a series of puns, is too familiar to need repetition. Soon after this encounter, Gregory himself set out ostensibly upon a mission to this distant land, but was recalled by the people of Rome. The opportunity for such personal evangelism never returned. However, his election to the papacy in 590 gave him an opportunity to realize his ambition through the agency of others.

It was not only missionary ardour which prompted this concern, for the condition of the Roman Church itself gave cause for anxiety. Dependent upon the Eastern Empire and under threat of attack from the Lombards, its authority won little respect from the Churches of Gaul and Spain. In such circumstances to recall Britain to a lost allegiance might well serve to buttress up a declining morale. Piety and policy thus went hand in hand.

Gregory's choice of missionaries for so hazardous an expedition may seem somewhat curious, since it was into the hands of monks from his own monastery of Clevum Scauri, led by their *praepositus* Augustine and not secular priests, that he committed this trust. Doubtless it was dictated by his belief that for such a pioneering task order and discipline were essential. Monks through their vocation as slaves of God were linked together in common obedience to their abbot, and by the very nature of their calling were required to live sacrificially.

Thus Augustine and a party of forty, mostly monks, but including a number of English youths bought by Gregory in the slave markets of Marseilles, departed from Rome, probably in June 596. None of them could have expected to see Italy again. The journey was to test both their endurance and courage. They had not long set out when, according to the Venerable Bede, author of that remarkable piece of historical writing *The Ecclesiastical History of the English People*, they panicked, and 'paralysed with terror . . . began to contemplate returning home rather than going to a barbarous, fierce and unbelieving nation whose language they did not even understand'.

Augustine retraced his footsteps, but Gregory sent him back to his post, rallying his followers by making it clear that the mission had behind it the unequivocal support of his apostolic office. At the same time he increased Augustine's authority by making him an abbot. Recovering their nerve, the party finally reached the Channel coast where, taking ship northward, they sailed past the old Roman fort at Dover into the mouth of the Stour. They were now about twelve miles from the town of Durovernum, modern Canterbury, this being situated at the point where Watling Street forded the river.

Durovernum was already distinguished by a long history. When Julius Caesar came to Britain, he found the site already in occupation by Belgic invaders, and the Roman surveyors erected there the capital city of Eastern Kent. Modern archaeology has made possible the reconstruction of its main outlines, which reveal the conventional grid-iron pattern with a forum, amphitheatre, a large market square and a basilica. Despite the subsequent destruction by the Jutish invaders, occupation of the city, if not organized civic life, continued.

Durovernum, at the time when the Roman mission arrived in Thanet, was the governmental seat of the Kentish king Aethelberht. Augustine wisely decided not to advance direct to the city, but to dispatch a messenger proclaiming that he had come from Rome bearing good news which offered to those who received it the assured promise of eternal joys in an endless kingdom. The King responded by ordering that the monks be kindly treated by the local inhabitants until he came to consult with them personally.

So far, Augustine and his followers had been preoccupied with the dangers of their arduous journey. What they could not fully appreciate, though doubtless they had acquired some information whilst in Gaul, was that there were certain factors favourable to the success of their enterprise. Eastern Kent was more closely linked to Gaul than any other part of England. Indeed the Romano-British Church— that is, the Church established during the Roman occupation—had maintained administrative and doctrinal connexions with the Continent until as late as 455; and some of its 'plant' had survived the havoc wrought by the invading Teutons. In Canterbury there still stood at least three churches, built under the Romans. The oldest of the Anglo-Saxon settlements could now boast an indigenous history of some 150 years, and though at first the invaders preferred to eschew the advantages of Roman civilization they were yet forced to recognize that transit across the seas, by weakening tribal loyalties, had broken long-established patterns of behaviour. A local priesthood, dedicated to Thor and Wodin, still discharged a traditional function; but its hold was less constraining. The Germanic tribes were ready for a change to something more adequate to their new condition. Augustine came as the representative of a mature faith, challenging to a higher moral code and equipped to handle the mysterious themes of death and judgment. Equally significant, he brought with him the aura of a great Empire which even in decline witnessed to an advanced standard of public duty and a severe social discipline.

More immediately to Augustine's advantage, the King of East Kent, Aethelberht, had already been some thirty years on the throne, during which time he had won the confidence of his people. Nor was his prestige confined to his own territory. All the kingdoms south of the Humber recognized him as *Bretwalda* or leading ruler. He had married Bertha, the Christian daughter of Charibert, Frankish King of Paris. The treaty which regulated this union stipulated that she should be free to exercise her own religion, and for this purpose she

4

brought with her the aged Luidhard, formerly Bishop of Senlis. Though Aethelberht does not seem to have acquainted himself at first hand with her faith, his marriage undoubtedly helped him in his relations with the Roman mission. Certainly his sagacity shines through the story, which Bede records, of his first encounter with Augustine, an encounter fraught with tremendous consequences for more than just the religious history of Britain. Archbishops and monarchs were frequently to confront one another in the days to come; but never with greater import than on the marshy island of Thanet. One thing is certain: had Aethelberht proved hostile, the task of Christian evangelism could not for the moment have gone forward.

The King, perhaps accompanied by his Queen, travelled from his capital city for the meeting. Augustine, supported by his followers bearing a silver cross and a picture of the crucifixion, advanced in procession chanting a litany. The King preferred that they should remain in the open air lest any magical art be practised upon him. Augustine, through his interpreter, explained the reason for his coming, and Aethelberht replied: 'We do not wish to do you harm; on the contrary, we will receive you hospitably and provide what is necessary for your support; nor do we forbid you to win all you can to your faith and religion by your preaching.'[1]

Thus encouraged, the monks proceeded on their way to Durovernum, which they entered ceremonially.

The early days of the mission, in the nature of the case, were critical, and the King must have awaited anxiously the general reaction of his people. He himself showed a helpful initiative in making available a dwelling-house and two churches, one of which was later to become the Cathedral of Christ Church.

A truly catholic church demanded a local episcopate. To secure this, not long after his landing in Britain, Augustine crossed over to Arles where he was consecrated 'Bishop of the English' by the metropolitan Vergilius, the only notable Gallican ecclesiastic in full communion with Rome.

Meanwhile the conversion of the Kingdom of Kent proceeded, apparently so rapidly that Pope Gregory, writing to the Eastern Emperor, speaks of a mass baptism of some ten thousand people on Christmas Day 597. Most significant of all, particularly in a society just emerging from an earlier tribalism, Aethelberht submitted himself to Christian initiation. Such an example served to offset the prejudice of the more conservative thegns, who tended to regard the new religion as distinctive of a subject people, since they knew of it only through the Celtic Christians whom they had forced into slavery. Miss Deanesly, in her biography of St. Augustine, writes of this royal baptism:

5

It marks . . . the point when the waters of the Tiber began to flow into the Kentish Stour, and a Mediterranean civilisation to influence a Germanic society.[2]

The task before Augustine and his companions was now two-fold: to continue with, and consolidate, the work of evangelism, and to lay down some pattern of order for the infant Church.

As to the first, the overriding need was for reinforcements, since Augustine's *familia*, or household, was wholly insufficient, the more so as it included monks who were not of a calibre to be raised to the priesthood. A native clergy would take time to train, and Augustine could not turn to the Gallic or ancient British Churches. The first was in part heretical; the second geographically remote, and hostile. Only Pope Gregory was able and willing to meet the need.

As to ordering the Church's life, Augustine felt that he must seek guidance from the same quarter. This need not be seen as indicating irresolute leadership. Gregory's judgement was universally respected, and his interest in the mission remained constant. It was natural, therefore, to consult him on the eve of laying down long-term plans. Lawrence, the priest, and Peter, the monk, accordingly went off to Rome and returned with new recruits, including two future Archbishops of Canterbury, Mellitus and Justus, as well as Paulinus, later Bishop of York. They brought with them sacred vessels, vestments, relics, and a number of service books; also, a letter addressed to Augustine, significantly conferring on him the *pallium*.

The *pallium* was an ecclesiastical garment of lamb's wool, once peculiar to the Pope but now bestowed upon metropolitans, primates, and archbishops, as a symbol of their delegated authority. In the case of Augustine, its use was to be limited, as Gregory was careful to point out, to the 'performance of the solemnities of the Holy Mass'. As to the ecclesiastical organization which Augustine was required to establish, Gregory's instructions were fraught with such great significance for the future that they are best quoted in his own words:

> We wish to send as bishop to the city of York one whom you yourself shall decide to consecrate; yet, always provided that if this city together with the neighbouring localities should receive the Word of the Lord, he is also to consecrate twelve bishops and enjoy the honourable rank of a metropolitan: for it is our intention, God willing, if we live, to give him the *pallium* too; nevertheless, brother, we wish him to be subject to your authority: but, after your death, he should preside over the bishops he has consecrated, being in no way subject to the authority of the bishop of London. There is, however, to be this distinction in honour, in future, between the bishops of London

6

and York, that he who was first consecrated is to be reckoned senior. But let them agree to do whatever has to be done, taking counsel together and acting out of zeal for Christ. Let them judge rightly and with one mind and so carry out their decisions without disagreement.[3]

There was nothing exceptional about these instructions. Ecclesiastical order followed closely the pattern of the Empire, and originally there had been two provinces in Britain, one centred on London the other on York. Gregory doubtless drew upon his own experience in Aquileia and Ravenna as well as in Gaul.

In matters of detail, Gregory's knowledge of Britain was confined to the lingering traditions of an imperial past—he may have consulted an old *notitia* of Septimus Severus—and such scraps of information as percolated to Rome through traffickers in the slave trade. To transfer the seat of St. Augustine's see from Canterbury to London, even if politically possible, was quite impracticable until the conversion of the East Saxons. It was made more difficult by the fact that a rudimentary form of ecclesiastical government was already growing out of Augustine's *familia* based on the capital city of Kent.

Gregory's injunctions as to York were to prove a continuing embarrassment to successive Archbishops of Canterbury, and were to lead, in 735, to the setting up of an independent northern archbishopric.

Gregory's letter also contained answers to the specific questions which Augustine had put to him concerning the management of his composite *familia*; a correct liturgical use; the punishment of crime; marriage discipline; consecration of bishops; and relations with the Churches of Gaul and Britain.

Here Gregory's answers were instinct with a wise liberality, mixed with a shrewd common sense, even where his advice showed that he was ignorant of Anglo-Saxon tribal customs. As to the Archbishop's household, which included lay and clerical monks as well as young men under training, Gregory believed that its integrity could no longer be maintained. Those not in orders who felt themselves unable to remain celibate must live outside its rule and receive stipends.

The time had also come to differentiate between those members of the *familia* whose vocation was the daily discharge of their monastic obedience and for whom the monastery church of St. Peter and St. Paul was to be built; and those more immediately associated with Augustine in his wider responsibilities as a missionary bishop. Augustine often had to be at the disposal of the King, to travel throughout Kent, and to appear in the moot or public assembly. He had to preach, to baptize and to confirm; to perform the liturgy, and in particular to celebrate the Mass in his cathedral church. Neither he nor those who attended him in his apostolic labours could strictly fulfil the rule of their order, though they continued to live communally.

Concerning relations with the Churches of Gaul and Britain, it is best again to quote Gregory's own words. Of Gaul he writes:

> We give you no authority over the Bishops of Gaul because the Bishop of Arles received the *pallium* long ago in the days of my predecessors, and we must on no account deprive him of the authority he has received. . . . You have no right to judge the Bishops of Gaul, who are outside your jurisdiction.[4]

But of Britain, however,

> We commit to you, my brother, all the Bishops of Britain that the unlearned may be instructed, the weak strengthened by your counsels.[5]

The latter somewhat ambiguous injunction may serve to introduce what is often regarded as Augustine's greatest failure, namely his inability either to exercise authority over, or to enter into co-operative relations with, the old Church of Britain. This failure was the more regrettable because both Gregory and Augustine wished to enlist its support in the conversion of the English. Blame cannot be apportioned.

The bare facts are these: St. Augustine was present at two con-ferences, the first possibly in Gloucestershire attended by the bishops and the doctors of the nearest province of Britain; the second further north, maybe along Watling Street, near Chester, with seven bishops drawn from the great monastery near Bangor. An old tradition asserts that at the second conference Augustine failed to rise to greet the Welsh bishops—to have done so might be thought to prejudice his claim to authority—and that this led to the breakdown of negotiations. What seems certain is that the Welsh bishops would not agree to accept the Roman dating of Easter. Disappointed and angry, Augustine pronounced sentence of doom on those who would not join with him.

Such differences, however, point to causes of division lying far deeper, and for these Augustine was not responsible, nor could tact overcome them. Two worlds, separated by a great divide, met, and neither was knowledgeable about the character of the other, nor sensitive to it. The British Church, monastic in its structure and distinguished by its own forms of piety, did not organize its life around a hierarchical or geographical episcopate. Cut off from western Christendom by a solid wedge of paganism, the Irish

Channel and not the Mediterranean constituted its inland sea. Celtic suspicion, moreover, had a more immediate cause than the clash of cultures. To Christians of the Celtic Church, the Teutonic invaders were an implacable foe who had ravaged their land and driven them westwards. Augustine had come to terms with the enemy and the very negotiations were possible only through the goodwill of a Kentish king. It was one thing to receive, in friendly converse, an itinerant missionary from distant Rome; quite another to accept his authority, particularly when his episcopal seat was in the capital city of a Kentish kingdom. Augustine may not have been as discreet as these delicate talks demanded. Perhaps he felt his hands tied by Gregory's instructions; but it is difficult to see how the final outcome could have been different. The breakdown was not fortuitous; and for some time to come the Celtic Church remained aloof from the Roman mission. Laurentius, Augustine's successor, also failed to persuade the British bishops to conform to the customs of the Roman Church. Equally non-co-operative were Celtic Christians in Ireland (*Scotti*), as is illustrated in a letter which Laurentius sent jointly with the Bishops of London and Rochester 'to our most dear brethren the Lords Bishops and Abbots throughout the kingdom of the Scots':

> The apostolic see, according to its custom in all parts of the world, directed us to preach to the heathen in these western regions, and it was our lot to come to this island of Britain; before we knew them we held the holiness both of the Britons and of the Irish in great esteem, thinking that they walked according to the customs of the universal Church: but on becoming acquainted with the Britons, we still thought that the Irish would be better. But now we have learned from Bishop Dagan when he came to this island and from Abbot Columban when he came to Gaul that the Irish did not differ from the Britons in their way of life. For when Bishop Dagan came to us he refused to take food, not only with us but even in the very house where we took our meals.[6]

This letter was presumably meant to be conciliatory, but its tone is indicative of that claim to authority which both Augustine and Laurentius saw as necessarily belonging to the Roman see.

The failure of the talks with the British Church meant that for the time being the task of converting the English remained with the Roman mission, drawing its inspiration and resources from Canterbury. The result was to bestow a unique prestige upon the metropolitan see—a prestige which was to stand it in good stead when later in difficulty. Gregory was insistent that the missionary enterprise should go forward, and since such a work of evangelism was essentially apostolic, this implied that new bishops, with their *familiæ* around them, must labour in other parts of the country. Such an increase in the episcopate was impossible without royal support, for it entailed in each instance the building of a cathedral church and the provision of an income. Aethelberht once again proved willing to discharge the responsibility imposed upon him as a Christian ruler. Augustine was thereby enabled to consecrate two bishops, Justus to the Church of St. Andrew in Rochester, situated at the point where Watling Street crossed the Medway; and, once Essex was converted, Mellitus, 'Abbot of the Gauls', to St. Paul's, built on the site of the old Roman forum in London, a city which Bede describes as on the banks of the Thames, 'an emporium for many nations who come to it by land and sea'.[7]

Augustine was no missionary pioneer, if by this we mean a man acting on his own initiative. He was the agent of Pope Gregory, and without the imperious command of that great churchman, he would never have left his monastery in Rome. Yet, if a little unimaginative, he was a man of solid worth who proved loyal to his instructions.

Certain aspects of Augustine's ministry reveal the limitations within which many future archbishops would be required to work. From the beginning he was in practice dependent upon the goodwill of the king, no matter how much he saw the source of his authority as emanating from the Apostolic See. His day-to-day labours had more than a purely religious outreach, since his mission was as much to civilize as to convert. Christian faith brought with it learning, literacy, and written documentation. It is significant that the laws of Aethelberht were the first to be written down. Moreover, Augustine's *familia* was the embryo from which, in the course of time, an intricate administrative system emerged, which influenced English constitutional development.

Once arrived in Britain, Augustine must have accepted that thenceforth the 'lost province' was to be his homeland. Psychologically this encouraged him to integrate the new religion into the social life of the English people. It was not long before the Archbishop acquired his own wergild, or legal evaluation.

Augustine died some time between the years 604 and 609 and was buried in the monastery grounds of the half-finished church of St. Peter and St. Paul, later known as St. Augustine's. When the church was completed, his body was interred in the north portico, and the following epitaph was later engraved on his tomb:

Here lies the most reverend Augustine, first archbishop of

Canterbury, who was formerly sent hither by St. Gregory, bishop of Rome; being supported by God in the working of miracles he led King Aethelberht and his nation from the worship of idols to a faith in Christ and ended the days of his office in peace; he died on the twenty-sixth day of May, during the reign of the same king.[8]

Shortly before his death Augustine, with the consent of Aethelberht, consecrated Laurentius, a member of the original band, as his successor, an uncanonical act which may account for there being no reference to his ever receiving the *pallium*. Doubtless this irregularity was dictated by the necessity of avoiding an interregnum, and as such was accepted by his two episcopal colleagues of London and Rochester.

England was at this time divided into several kingdoms struggling against each other, a situation which made the evangelistic task of the Roman mission difficult; particularly when initial enthusiasm had cooled. It was further complicated in that Aethelberht had already lost the *Bretwalda*-ship to Raedwald, King of the East Angles, before his death in February 616 led to a crisis in the Kentish Church.

The fact was that after some twenty years Christianity had hardly penetrated East Anglia, although its King, Raedwald, underwent a half-hearted conversion. In the rest of the Anglo-Saxon territories evangelism had hardly begun. Even in Kent, Christianity was resisted by the more conservative of the thegns, and Aethelberht's successor, his son Eadbald, undeterred by the protest of Laurentius, refused to be baptized and reverted to heathenism. A more extreme situation developed in Essex, upon the death in 616 of Saeberht, who, to quote from Bede, had been 'cleansed in . . . the font of salvation', when his three sons, all pagans, inherited the kingdom. This reaction in south-east England brought with it severe consequences. Mellitus and Justus fled to Kent and then withdrew to Gaul. Bede records that Laurentius contemplated following them. However, on the eve of his departure, as he kept vigil at the tomb of Augustine in the monastery church, he fell asleep, and dreamed that he was being scourged by St. Peter for deserting his flock. 'Have you forgotten my example?' asked the Apostle. 'For the sake of the little ones whom Christ himself entrusted to me as a token of his love, I endured chains, blows, imprisonment, and every affliction. Finally I suffered death, even the death of the cross at the hands of infidels and enemies of Christ that I might be crowned with him.'[9]

'Who has dared to inflict scourging on so great a man?' inquired the King, on seeing his miraculously inflicted wounds in the morning.

The exiled bishops were recalled. Eadbald abandoned his heathenism forthwith and was baptized.

Laurentius was succeeded by Mellitus, who suffered from gout, but according to Bede guided 'the English Church with great care and energy. . . . He was noble by birth but nobler still in loftiness of spirit.' Such was his fame that his prayers were said to have saved Canterbury from destruction by fire.

Mellitus was followed by Justus, Bishop of Rochester, who had come over to England with the second missionary band. It was during his archiepiscopate that Eadbald, in consenting to the marriage of his sister, Princess Ethelberga, to Edwin, the powerful pagan king of Northumbria, insisted that she be allowed to continue the practice of her own Christian religion. To ensure this, Justus consecrated Paulinus to accompany her northwards—a fortunate choice since the Northumbrian King had already made his acquaintance when in exile at the court of Raedwald, King of East Anglia. Paulinus proceeded to show great missionary zeal, with the result that Edwin with his counsellors received baptism.

Meanwhile, the death in 627 of Justus, the first Archbishop after Augustine to receive the *pallium*, led to the nomination of Honorius, a former pupil of Gregory, though it is not certain whether he was one of the original companions of Augustine. With his death in 653, the succession of bishops who retained personal memories of the great Roman pontiff ceased.

Honorius was faced with the initial difficulty that there was no bishop in southern England to whom he could go for consecration, the sees of London and Rochester being vacant. Such was the sad plight of the Christian mission. It was a matter of going to Gaul, or travelling north to Paulinus. Honorius preferred the latter, and was consecrated in about 627 in a small stone church in Lincoln. In 634 *pallia* were sent over from Rome for Honorius and Paulinus, the Pope expressly specifying that each Archbishop should have equal status, with a mutual right of appointment on a vacancy. The conferring of two *pallia* was a papal attempt to implement Gregory's original intention; but nothing came of it since Paulinus, then a fugitive in Kent, was never able to return to York.

The progress of the Christian mission continued to be hindered by strife between the kingdoms with, as a consequence, spasmodic relapses into heathenism. In 633 Edwin was killed in battle at Hatfield, and Northumbria was thus exposed to the savagery of Penda (*ob.* 655), the heathen King of Mercia, and Cadwalla, the last British king of any importance. Paulinus and Queen Ethelberga fled to Kent, the former to become Bishop of Rochester, the latter Abbess of the convent at Lyminge.

Northumbria was now beyond the reach of Canterbury, and it remained so even with the accession of the Christian Oswald in 634—later killed in battle with Penda in 642. It was with the devoted labours of Aidan, a Celtic monk who owed no allegiance to Canterbury and Rome, that the kingdom was brought back to Christian faith.

In this early story of thrust forward and retrogression, so inextricably interwoven with tribal jealousies going back to the days of settlement, the role of the several kings was of supreme importance. For example, it was King Sigeberht, 'devout Christian and a very learned man' (ob. 637?) who brought East Anglia back to Christianity and co-operated with Felix of Burgundy, its first Bishop, whom Archbishop Honorius 'sent . . . to preach the word of life to this nation of the Angles'. Wessex, however, was evangelized by Birinus (ob. 650), a Benedictine monk from Rome, who was made a bishop by Asterius of Genoa. His signal triumph was to baptize Cynegils, King of Wessex, in the presence of King Oswald of Northumbria. Under Birinus's successor, Agilberht, the see of Winchester was founded.

This outburst of missionary enterprise was in the main independent of Canterbury, and this in spite of the fact that in Kent Eadbald's successor, Earconberht, was well-disposed to Christianity, even to the extent of ordering the destruction of idols. The death of Honorius in 653 marks the end of a decisive period both in the history of the *Ecclesia Anglorum* and of the office which he held. Assuming that he was only eighteen when he made the journey with Augustine—and it is unlikely that he could have been so young—he must have been forty-five at the time of his appointment to Canterbury and over seventy at his death. Probably he was older; indeed, with the exception of St. Augustine, the early archbishops were well advanced in years. The physical strain imposed upon them must have been severe. Their duties were manifold. They travelled extensively on horseback along rough Roman roads no longer kept in repair. They preached often; they regularly performed the liturgy; they baptized catechumens; they consecrated bishops; they frequented the king's court and offered him counsel. The bishop, in Latin Christianity, was the hub around which ecclesiastical administrative machinery revolved. The time of the archdeacon was not yet.

The death of Archbishop Honorius was followed by a vacancy of some eighteen months. The situation thus created was serious, the more so since communication with Rome had become spasmodic, and there was possibly a feeling in Italy that the Canterbury mission had failed. Certainly its authority extended only to Kent and East Anglia—and possibly Wessex.

From 633, after the death of King Edwin, a major role in the conversion of the English was taken over by Celtic monks from Iona, in particular by those settled at Lindisfarne. Indeed, until 664 the whole of Christian England except Kent, East Anglia, Wessex, and Sussex remained attached to the Celtic communion, and even Wessex was still under bishops ordained on the Continent and in communion with the Celtic Church. Sussex remained heathen. To an objective observer it must have seemed doubtful whether the future of England lay with Europe, centred in Rome and under obedience to Canterbury, or with the far different ethos, political and religious, of Celtic Christianity centred in the western islands. The choice of an Archbishop of Canterbury, in circumstances such as these, was never more important though it might seem to have little other than a local interest. Feeling the significance of the occasion the clergy and monks of the Archbishop's *familia* took the initiative, and in co-operation with King Earconberht, proposed a West Saxon named Frithonas (Deusdedit), perhaps converted to Christianity by the mission of Birinus, and the first native-born Englishman to sit in the Chair of Augustine. His consecration in Canterbury on 26 March 655 was presided over by Ithamar, Bishop of Rochester, the first ever English-born bishop. Apart from scanty references in the Anglo-Saxon Chronicle, little is known of Deusdedit's activities, except that he went at the invitation of Wulfhere, King of Mercia, to consecrate a new monastery at Medeshamstede. What is significant is that out of the six or seven bishops elected while he was at Canterbury, only one, Damianus, received consecration at his hands, for the greater part of England was subject to the Celtic Church. These years were therefore critical, not only for the Church in England but for the office of Archbishop. The general situation was made worse by a plague, which swept across Europe and led to serious depopulation. The impact of such a natural disaster on a tribal community painfully emerging from a more primitive religious pattern and half-fearful of the effects of its own apostasy may help to account for the recrudescence of heathenism.

Just before Deusdedit died an event took place which owed nothing to his initiative but proved significant for the future of the Archbishopric. This was the Synod of Whitby in 664, one of the immediate causes of which was the zeal of that remarkable churchman Wilfrid, at that time Abbot of Ripon. Educated in a Celtic monastery, he yet became passionately convinced of the superior culture of the Latin Church which he had come to know at first-hand in both Rome and at Lyons. With his patron, Alchfrid, under-king of Deira (the southern part of Northumbria) he formed the nucleus of a growing Roman party in the Celtic North, which campaigned fervently against the Celtic usages. As the dissensions increased, the prudent Oswy, King of Northumbria (whose wife followed the Roman ways) decided to call a conference to decide the issues between the two Churches. This was held at the monastery of Strenaeshalc (Whitby). On the Celtic side there attended Cedd, Bishop of the East Saxons, and Colman, Bishop of Lindisfarne; on the Roman side Wilfrid and Agilberht, sometime Bishop of Dorchester. Bede tells us that it was the eloquence of Wilfrid that finally won the day, appealing as he did to Peter as the foundation of the authority of the Roman Church and rounding off his argument with Matthew xvi, 18–19: 'Thou art Peter; and upon this rock I will build my church; and the gates of hell shall not prevail against it. And I will give unto thee the keys of the kingdom of heaven.' The result was decisive. Colman withdrew from Northumbria. The Celts who remained conformed to Roman practices.

The decision had important long-term consequences. It ensured that the future of England, both religious and political, would be bound up with western Europe, whose culture and political forms owed much to the Roman brand of Christian faith. The Celtic Church had its own distinctive piety and monasticism, but it was not integrated into the main stream of European life and thought; nor was it 'structured' so as to direct from within the historic life of a nascent and energetic people. Had the decision at Whitby gone the other way, leaving large areas of England with a Church looking to Lindisfarne and Iona, then the Church in England might well have developed along other lines, in which case the Archbishop of Canterbury would have become a different kind of person. Certainly without Whitby Theodore's work would have been impossible, and the extension of the authority and influence of the Archbishop of Canterbury over the Church in England might have been long delayed.

# THEODORE, THE ARCHITECT

In July 664, Earconberht, King of Kent, and Deusdedit both died. The appointment of a successor was now all-important. Fortunately, though the influence of Canterbury was then at its lowest, the traditional link with St. Augustine served to prevent the nomination from being treated as of only local interest. Oswy of Northumbria, no longer bound by Celtic loyalties, and Egberht, the new King of Kent, decided, doubtless supported by responsible ecclesiastical opinion, that on this occasion the authority of the papacy must be called in to give the new archbishop added status and prestige. Consecration by any bishop in Britain or Gaul was not, in this crisis, politically expedient. Their choice fell on Wighard, an Englishman, who had been educated in the monastery at Canterbury, and had served as a chaplain in Deusdedit's *familia*.

Wighard immediately set off for Rome, but had not been there long before, with many of his companions, he fell a victim to the plague. The unexpected situation created by his death persuaded Pope Vitalian that for political reasons—the Roman See was itself passing through a period of difficulty—he must now take the matter into his own hands. He turned first to Hadrian, a learned monk of African origin who was destined to play an important part in the developing life of the Church in England. Feeling himself inadequate, however, Hadrian suggested Andrew, head of a neighbouring monastery. Andrew also declined, and Vitalian finally nominated Theodore, already sixty-six years of age.

Little is known of Theodore before his appointment. Born somewhere about the year 602 in a Byzantine city, he studied at Athens and became a fine classical scholar, being known in Rome, where he came as a refugee from Islam, as 'the philosopher'.[10]

The Pope was at first sceptical as to Theodore's fitness, largely because his formative years had been spent in the Orthodox Church, and at that moment there was acrimonious disagreement between East and West arising out of the heresy of the Monothelites. The Pope insisted that Hadrian should therefore accompany Theodore to Britain.

It is a curious thought that Theodore, among the greatest of all the Archbishops of Canterbury, should have been fourth on the list; that he was already a comparatively old man when nominated, and utterly unfamiliar with conditions in Britain. Sir Frank Stenton well writes: 'Superficially there can have been little to suggest that this aged scholar from Asia Minor was fitted for the task of restoring Roman order in a distracted northern Church.'[11] Doubtless Vitalian knew him to have energy, strength of will and administrative ability.

After waiting some four months for his hair to grow in accordance with the requirements of the western tonsure, and being consecrated bishop by Vitalian on 26 March 668, Theodore set out from Rome with Hadrian, taking with him, among others, a Northumbrian monk, Benedict Biscop, as interpreter, later Abbot both of St. Augustine's and of the famous centre of scholarship at Jarrow. The journey on which Theodore now embarked was to become familiar to successive generations of archbishops who went to Rome in person to receive their *pallia*. It could often prove dangerous for men no longer young, because of robbers, political hostility and austere weather. Theodore avoided the perils of the Alps, which later proved fatal to Archbishop Aefsige, by taking the sea route to Marseilles and proceeding to Arles, to whose Archbishop the Pope had commended him. From there he went on to Paris, where he lived with Agilberht, the former bishop of Dorchester, doubtless using the opportunity to become more intimately acquainted with the conditions of the Church throughout Britain: but Egberht, King of Kent, grew impatient and dispatched his reeve to escort him across the Channel. At long last, after an illness at Etaples, he reached Canterbury on 27 May 669, exactly a year after he had set out. Hadrian was to join him later.

A new era in the life of the Church in Britain was about to begin.

When Theodore arrived in Kent there had already been a vacancy in the see of Canterbury for some five years. This could well have proved disastrous. Time was not on the new Archbishop's side.

Theodore saw his overall task as that of restoring, indeed of imposing, order and fostering Christian living. He realized that there was a need for more bishops, who were the linchpin of Latin ecclesiastical administration; and that large dioceses, coextensive with the kingdoms, must be divided. Such reform was beset with political difficulties and could only be effected through royal support, which meant in practice exploiting his position as direct representative of the Roman see. His immediate concern was to make himself known throughout the country, for which purpose he set out with Hadrian on an extensive fact-finding tour of the areas where the Anglo-Saxon tribes had settled. He found that all dioceses were without bishops except London, whose occupant had bought his see, and

Northumbria, which was in dispute between Chad and Wilfrid. The result was general lawlessness. Theodore determined to meet this situation by insisting upon an unequivocal conformity to a Roman obedience. He refused to recognize bishops who had been consecrated either by Britons or Scots, unless they agreed to reconsecration. Of this first journey Bede writes:

> Theodore journeyed to every district, consecrating bishops in suitable places, and, with their help, correcting whatever he found imperfect.[12]

He restored Wilfrid to York, re-ordained Chad to Lichfield, and sent Putta to Rochester.

By 673, Theodore felt that his work of reorganization had gone far enough to enable him to call together a council of bishops and 'other teachers of the Church'. It met at Hertford on 24 September. This assembly was remarkable in many respects, not least because at a time when Britain was divided by warfare between the separate kingdoms, the Church was able to transcend frontiers and to embody a visible if incomplete unity. At this council there were present, as well as Theodore, who described himself as 'the unworthy bishop of Canterbury appointed by the apostolic see', Bisi, Bishop of the East Angles; Putta of Rochester; Eleutherios of the West Saxons; and Winfrith of the Mercians. Wilfrid did not himself attend, but was represented by proxies.

Theodore proposed a set of canons which, with one exception, were accepted unanimously. They are worth listing as showing how the Archbishop understood his priorities:

1. That the Roman dating of Easter should be observed.
2. That bishops should not interfere in each other's dioceses.
3. That monasteries should be free from episcopal interference.
4. That monks should not wander from monastery to monastery, or
5. Clergy from diocese to diocese.
6. That clergy should obtain permission of the bishop to officiate within his jurisdiction.
7. That synods should be held once, possibly twice, a year at Cloveshoe (probably in Kent or on the borders of Mercia).
8. That bishops should take precedence in accordance with the date of their consecration.
9. That as conversions went forward new dioceses should be created.
10. That divorce should be confined to the rules laid down in the Scriptures.

For the first time a standard of discipline had been set for the whole Church in Britain.

The canon that did not secure unanimous support was that requiring the creation of additional dioceses. This could only be brought about by the division of existing ones, and here the bishops demurred. The effect of this opposition was to convince Theodore that he must act on his own responsibility as opportunity offered. Thus he secured the consecration of two bishops for East Anglia, and one each for the Mercians, the East Saxons (with the cathedral in London), and the West Saxons. In 678 events in Northumbria, arising out of King Eagfrid's unrelenting hostility to Bishop Wilfrid, led to Theodore being summoned to go north. The result was the division of the kingdom into four dioceses, Bernicia, Deira, Lindsey, and York, Wilfrid's authority being confined to the last. Understandably, since he had not been consulted, Wilfrid determined to seek redress of grievances, and to do so in a way which was to set a precedent for centuries. He appealed to Rome and left for Italy, where he found, however, that a letter to Pope Agatho from Theodore had forestalled him. The Pope's decision was a mediating one: that Wilfrid's jurisdiction should be confined to York, but that he should nominate, for consecration by Theodore, the bishops for the other three Northumbrian sees, those already holding them by Theodore's appointment to be deprived. The Pope's orders, however, were never carried out. In the end Wilfrid had to be content with the bishopric of York and Hexham, and even this he did not enjoy until after the death of King Eagfrid in 685, so great was the royal hostility.

Theodore could not have been happy at the setting aside of a papal mandate, since respect for Roman authority was one of the guiding principles of his life. For this reason, doubtless, he interceded on Wilfrid's behalf with Aethelred, the Mercian King; and also with Aldfrid, King of Northumbria. Whether Eddius Stephanus, Wilfrid's biographer, is right in suggesting that the Archbishop later confessed himself partly in the wrong and intimated that, in reparation, he would nominate Wilfrid as his successor, is another matter. Respect for Roman authority led Theodore to summon a second council at Hatfield, where, in the presence of the papal envoy, Abbot John, the bishops declared against the Monothelite heresy, at the same time maintaining their firm adherence to the Catholic faith.

There may well be significance in the fact that, whereas at the first council Theodore appears in Bede's transcription as 'bishop of the church of Canterbury', at the second he is delineated as 'archbishop of the island of Britain and of the city of Canterbury'. This is in line with the description of Theodore at a Council in Rome in 679 as 'archbishop and philosopher of the Island of Great Britain'. It was a designation which, in implying claims for Canterbury, Gregory I would never have allowed; and Bede's use of it earlier than the late VIIth century is an anachronism. It became accepted in the VIIIth century and Beorhtweald, Theodore's successor, was the first Archbishop to be referred to as 'primate'.

The determination with which Theodore persisted in his policy of dividing dioceses certainly caused difficulty between him and his suffragans. Though his methods were at times somewhat arbitrary— he deprived Winfrith, Bishop of Mercia, and Lothare of the West Saxons—he was successful in exercising authority in both north and south. His solid achievement is seen in that whereas at his coming, effective episcopal control was almost non-existent, his archiepiscopate saw the establishment of three bishops in Northumbria, four in Mercia, two each in Anglia and Wessex, as well as the two long established in Kent. Concerning Theodore's relations with these dioceses, Bede remarks somewhat cryptically:

> He was the first of the archbishops whom the whole English Church consented to obey.[13]

This is substantially true, certainly of the first fifteen years of his archiepiscopate: but with the death of King Eagfrid of Northumbria in 685 his authority in the north began to decline, and the disturbed state of Kent made it impossible for him to do anything about it. At the time of his death he had only one suffragan bishop, Putta of Rochester. So firmly, however, did he build, that apart from the removal of some diocesan seats to the larger towns at the Conquest, and four creations by Henry VIII, no sees were added to the southern province till the XIXth century.

Theodore, when in Rome, had gained a reputation for scholarship. It is to his credit that he remained true to this interest amidst the preoccupations of his administrative labours. Indeed, integral with his policy was the encouragement of learning. With his usual practical common sense, he founded a school in the monastery at Canterbury which became famous throughout Europe. Among the subjects of instruction were Latin, Greek, music, theology, astronomy, and medicine, he himself teaching from time to time. Many of the scholars trained here rose to become responsible leaders in the Church, some embarking upon missionary enterprises on the Continent. Hadrian, whose counsel was ever at Theodore's disposal, followed the great Benedict Biscop as Abbot of St. Augustine's.

The Archbishop himself left no written works behind him. The well-known *Penitential of Theodore* is a collection of practical answers given by him to pastoral questions. It represents an attempt to introduce Christian teaching into everyday life, the sections on marriage being particularly illuminating. Clearly Theodore recognized many causes of breakdown, and was liberal in his attitude to remarriage. Here we find the essential humanity of a man who has known many countries, many customs, and many Churches.

Nor was his influence by any means confined to matters connected with the life of the Church. In 679 he succeeded in reconciling Eagfrid and Ealfrid whose kingdoms of Northumbria and Mercia had long been ravaged by internecine strife.

At his death in 690, the see of St. Augustine was within a few years of celebrating its centenary. Theodore was without doubt the first outstanding personality, in terms of strength of will, clarity of vision and sustained energy, to enter into the responsibilities of the archbishopric. He came at a time of crisis so severe that the future of the Roman Church in Britain, and with it the see of Canterbury, was uncertain. He left behind him a Christianity rooted in a Roman obedience, a diocesan structure firmly established, and a metropolitan of greater authority and increased prestige.

# 3

## THE ARCHBISHOPRICS OF YORK AND
## LICHFIELD

I

Our task now is to trace how the see of Canterbury, given a new direction by Theodore, fared in Anglo-Saxon England up to the time of the Norman conquest. This will mean tracing its reaction to other centres of power, in particular to the monarchies of the several kingdoms, and its influence on the developing life of the nation.[14]

In the immediate future it was to suffer a severe setback when an archbishop was placed in York and, for a short time, another in Lichfield.

Gregory's original intention for the future organization of the Church in Britain, was, as we have seen, that there should be two metropolitans, each receiving his *pallium* from Rome. They were to be independent of each other, with their respective cathedrals in London and York, and each province was to consist of twelve dioceses. Precedence, after Augustine died, was to go to the senior bishop, determined by the date of his consecration, but this was a seniority of courtesy; it had nothing to do with jurisdiction. However, this scheme was never, in its entirety, realized. Tradition and growing reverence for Augustine, whose body rested there, apart from political considerations, prevented transfer from Canterbury to London. Also Boniface V confirmed Canterbury as the seat of the metropolitical see.

Relations between Canterbury and York, however, were never easy. Beorhtweald, who made two journeys northwards in connexion with Bishop Wilfrid, exercised only a minimal jurisdiction outside his own Province. Eddius, a monk at Ripon, confirms this by referring to him as 'archbishop of the Kentishmen and almost all Britain'. Relations between Canterbury and the north were complicated for many years by the activities of that brilliant, wayward and yet dedicated Christian evangelist, Bishop Wilfrid, to whom reference has already been made. His precise motives are obscure. How far he definitely stood for the ecclesiastical independence of Northumbria is doubtful. Certainly, in his appeal to the Pope he made no reference to Gregory's instructions, which would powerfully have supported such a claim. However, in practice his long struggles had the effect of keeping alive the dream of an independent province, the drive behind which drew its inspiration from the fierce independence of the northern kingdom. There were, however, other practical reasons behind this demand, such as Bede sets out at some length in a letter to Egberht, who later became the first Archbishop. The Church in the north was in a sad condition of decline. There was a need for more clergy and the creation of more dioceses. Only a metropolitan at York could deal effectively with this situation. Bede therefore advised that with the support of Ceolwulf, King of Northumbria, the Pope be petitioned to confer the *pallium* on Eagberht and for the dioceses in the northern province to be increased to twelve. Such an application was in fact made, and in 734(?) Gregory III sanctioned the request.

Archbishop Eagberht had the advantage of being a cousin of Ceolwulf, and brother of Eadberht, both Kings of Northumbria; but his policy of reform never got under way. This was due not simply to local hostility, but to the disorder into which the Kingdom of Northumbria was plunged, and the consequent failure to find adequate royal endowments. In fact the northern province continued with only four dioceses throughout Anglo-Saxon England, though Canterbury obtained its twelve.

Yet the creation of a second independent and autonomous province certainly had short-term benefits. Eagberht's great school at York promoted an indigenous scholarship and helped to civilize the clergy of Northumbria. Moreover its vitality led to that great missionary activity on the Continent which is such a remarkable feature of the history of the Church in England in the later VIIIth century. Indeed, when under Jaenbeorht, Archbishop of Canterbury, the Church in the south fell into a state of decline, York held the foremost place in power and esteem. Yet its long-term results were not so uniformly beneficial. An independent northern see rekindled the fire of Northumbrian independence, thus delaying the final union of the kingdom, and it broke up the constitutional integrity of the *Ecclesia Anglorum*. By doing this it weakened the authority of the southern Primate and enabled both Pope and monarch to play off one archbishop against the other. Not until the creation of the National Synod in 1970 was the division finally transcended, though the autonomy of the northern province, with its own Synod, remains to this day.

II

The establishment of a third archbishopric at Lichfield arose out of the shift of power away from Kent to Mercia.

Penda (*ob.* 655) welded the Mercians into a powerful people, and identified them with militant paganism. After a period of decline, their fortunes revived under Aethelbald (716–755) and reached their peak under the Christian Offa (755–796), the one King in England who corresponded on terms of equality with the Emperor Charlemagne. Offa's objective was the extinction of the independent kingdoms comprising the heptarchy, and during his reign the dynasties of Kent, Sussex, and the Hwicca either disappeared or gave up their kingly titles. Such a changing political situation was bound to have its repercussions on the status of the Archbishop of Canterbury. No king struggling to establish his own supremacy could be indifferent to so important an ecclesiastical person possessing more than a Kentish significance. The word of the Archbishop, like that of a king, was received in courts of justice as equivalent to his oath; he had authority to grant nine days' grace to an offender whose life was sought by the murdered man's family; he owned extensive estates, and on these he could hold court, try offenders, and execute thieves; he possessed the right to coin money and to emboss his own image upon it. Inevitably kings, not only in Kent, involved themselves directly in his appointment; and realistic archbishops recognized that they could not function effectively without royal support.

It was understandable, therefore, that Offa, with his vast political ambitions, should view the position of the Archbishop of Canterbury with suspicion. The Archbishop, though a national figure, was established in a kingdom which, if for the time being subdued, might at any time erupt into rebellion. Moreover, he was nominated to his office by a rival, and himself represented a focal point for Kentish resistance.

Signs of positive action to deal with this potentially dangerous situation soon appeared. An obvious means of counteracting it was for Mercian power to secure the appointment of a friendly archbishop. It was therefore not without significance that Archbishop Cuthbeorht (740–758), formerly Bishop of Hereford, to which diocese he was nominated through the influence of Aethelbald, King of Mercia, was a native of that kingdom. On his return from Rome, where the pomp and splendour of the papacy made a great impression on him, Cuthbeorht held a council at Cloveshoe, which again, significantly, the King of Mercia attended.

It was not always possible, however, for Mercia to get its way.

Cuthbeorht's successor, Breguwine (761–764), a native of old Saxony and educated in one of the schools founded by Theodore, owed his appointment to King Aethelberht of Kent. When Breguwine was followed by Jaenbeorht (765–792), Abbot of St. Augustine's, Offa prudently saw the need to establish friendly relations with Canterbury. His policy in the early days was therefore conciliatory, as exemplified in his grant to the metropolitical see of land at Higham. But Jaenbeorht, deeply rooted in a Kentish loyalty, was a strong supporter of the naïve King Egberht II, and as such determined to resist increasing Mercian pressure. Though the story that he corresponded with Charlemagne, inviting him over to fight Mercia on behalf of the southern kingdom, may be apocryphal, yet it is in character. His loyalty was to Kent and not to Mercia. Thus Offa saw Jaenbeorht as a political danger, the more so since as Archbishop of Canterbury he enjoyed spiritual jurisdiction over Mercia and the other kingdoms subject to Offa's overlordship.

The King decided to deal with the problem by tackling it at its root, that is, by establishing a third archbishopric in his own territory at Lichfield, thereby limiting Canterbury's jurisdiction and weakening both its prestige and authority.

A case for such an innovation could easily be made even if it ran counter to Gregory's original instructions. The Kingdom of Northumbria now had its own Archbishop at York. Few, if any, archbishoprics in Gaul consisted of as many as twelve sees, and Charlemagne, at the time of his death, left behind some twenty-one metropolitans most of which he had himself established.

Such a project of course needed papal sanction. Offa therefore petitioned Pope Adrian II at what proved a favourable time since he was anxious to re-establish the ancient Roman connexion with the English Church. The result was that he sent two papal legates to Britain: George, Bishop of Ostia, and Theophylact, Bishop of Todi— the first of their kind to arrive on these shores since the time of Theodore. They came ostensibly to renew the traditional friendship and Catholic faith which Pope Gregory had brought to Britain through the 'blessed Augustine'. The moral decline in England during the latter part of the VIIIth century was only too evident, and the best minds of the day, including Boniface, the English Archbishop of Mainz, saw the need for reform.

Landing in Kent, the legates first proceeded to Canterbury, where they were received by Jaenbeorht in a manner appropriate to their high station. They then went on to 'Offa's hall' and gave to the King a personal letter from the Pope. Bishop George then proceeded northwards to be entertained by the King of Northumbria, and to hold in conjunction with the Archbishop of York a synod at Finchale, near Durham, in 787, which enacted a number of canons dealing with faith, baptism and episcopal duties. Finally the two legates attended a great Council at Cealchyth (Chelsea?) where were assembled Offa, Jaenbeorht, twelve bishops of his province, and a number of clergy. The decrees of the northern council were re-affirmed, this being the first occasion when the Archbishops of Canterbury and York subscribed to the same document; and the royal proposal for the creation of an archbishopric centred on Lichfield inevitably came up for discussion. After what the Anglo-Saxon Chronicle describes as a 'stormy debate', Offa finally had his way. Before the end of 788(?), Hygebeorht, Bishop of Lichfield, received his *pallium* from the Pope as Metropolitan and Archbishop; and the jurisdiction of the see of Canterbury was cut down to the dioceses south of the Thames—Rochester, London, Selsey, Winchester, and Sherborne. Precedence between the two Archbishops was to be determined by the date of consecration, which gave it for the time being to Canterbury, though at a subsequent council the Archbishop of Canterbury's name appears under that of Hygebeorht. Jaenbeorht, however, does not seem to have made any formal protest to Rome either against the division of his province, or later when Offa despoiled him of some of his estates. Certainly Mercian power became particularly evident when, on the death of Jaenbeorht in 792, Offa secured as his successor Aethelheard, Abbot of Louth, of whom very little is known prior to his nomination, though his subsequent history shows him to have been devoted to Mercian interests, without, however, abandoning the rights of his own see. So enraged were the men of Kent by his appointment that they refused to allow him to enter his own cathedral in Canterbury, an exclusion which raised acutely the problem of his consecration, whether it should be in York or in Rome. Offa sought the advice of Alcuin, and the probability is that he was consecrated by Hygebeorht in the cathedral at Lichfield.

Hygebeorht, during the early years of his archiepiscopate, undoubtedly used his metropolitical power to further the work of the Church throughout the whole of his province, an important contribution to the life of the nation, since Jaenbeorht's suspected disloyalty made Canterbury ineffective.

Offa now seems to have had second thoughts, and his policy changed to that of building up the status of Aethelheard, Jaenbeorht's successor, granting him lands north of the Thames and situated in the newly created archbishopric of Lichfield. Aethelheard, on his part, began to invade Hygebeorht's jurisdiction by consecrating bishops from his Province, with the result that by the close of the VIIIth century a majority of bishops owed canonical obedience to

Canterbury. Aethelheard, however, still had his difficulties. When Cenwulf followed Offa Kent rebelled, and the Archbishop, universally disliked as the representative of an alien rule, against the advice of Alcuin fled the country.

Such political uncertainties made Cenwulf determined to reverse the policy of his great predecessor so far as concerned the Lichfield archbishopric. The result was a petition to Pope Leo III for the restoration of the integrity of the original southern province. At the same time Cenwulf expressed surprise that the Pope should have acquiesced in the violation of Gregory's original plan to establish only one southern province with its seat in London. Leo, in reply, made it clear that Pope Adrian had acted as he had only on Offa's categorical assurance that his request had the unanimous support of his own advisers, who were emphatic that the southern province was too vast to be manageable. What Cenwulf himself knew, and indeed admitted in a subsequent letter to the Pope, was that the driving force behind the Mercian King's request was his hatred for the men of Kent and, not least among them, for Archbishop Jaenbeorht.

Cenwulf's desire to end the division of the southern province did not mean that he wished the Archbishop's seat to remain permanently in Canterbury. Rather he was considering its transference to London in view of a political situation which might at any time exclude him from Kent, and where at the moment rebellion was raging. By this means Cenwulf sought to secure all that Offa had hoped for from his third archbishopric at Lichfield. Cenwulf's petition to the Pope on this score was the more urgent because Aethelheard had already written to Rome asking for the restitution of the rights of his see.

The Pope's position was certainly not easy, for he himself was a fugitive at the court of Charlemagne, and could not easily reverse so recent a decision decreed by one of his predecessors. His reply to Cenwulf, therefore, avoided a positive decision on the Lichfield archbishopric, though he condemned the Kentish rebels and affirmed in general terms that 'the Primacy of Canterbury should be venerated and honoured as the archiepiscopal see in all things'.

The political situation which was the *fons et origo* of Cenwulf's, as it had been of Offa's, request, changed again. The revolt in Kent was soon suppressed, and Aethelheard was back in Canterbury. Hence that part of Cenwulf's proposals which concerned the transference to London was not relevant. In this complex and changing political situation Aethelheard, having consulted the Archbishop of York, now decided to set out for Italy. Upon his arrival in Rome, he forcefully put his case, and Pope Leo investigated the records relating to the establishment of the archbishopric of Lichfield. His judgment was decisive. Though he could not accommodate Cenwulf by removing the metropolitical see to London—the reverence felt for Canterbury, where the bones of St. Augustine rested, was already too great for this to be done without protest—he confirmed Aethelheard in the rights of his primacy. As to the dioceses and the monasteries which he 'formerly held and of which he has been illegally deprived . . . we have restored them to him in their entirety as they were in former times'. Armed with this explicit judgment, Aethelheard returned to England, and at the Council of Cloveshoe in October 803, when there were present, as well as the Archbishop and Cenwulf, the bishops and abbots of the two provinces of Lichfield and Canterbury, the archbishopric of Lichfield was brought to an end and its dioceses merged once more into the province of Canterbury. The words of the Pope were read out:

> We give this in charge, and sign it with the sign of the cross, that the see archiepiscopal from this time forward never be in the monastery of Lichfield, nor in any other place but in the city of Canterbury where Christ's Church is; and where the Catholic faith first shone forth in this island; and where holy baptism was first established by St. Augustine.[15]

The synod then proceeded, with doubtful canonicity, to go further than the Pope, and pronounce the charter and *pallium* conferred on Archbishop Hygebeorht to be of no validity on the grounds that they were obtained by deception.

No person could less have merited such treatment than the Archbishop of Lichfield himself. He had acquiesced in the gradual reassertion by Aethelheard of his ancient jurisdiction; and resigned his see, retiring into a monastery, on the eve of Aethelheard's journey to Rome.

Archbishop Aethelheard, who died in 805 and was buried in his cathedral church of Canterbury, may well have felt that he had come out of a challenging political situation with credit. He had secured the suppression of the archbishopric of Lichfield after only a few years of its existence. He had seen Cenwulf's scheme for removing the Archbishop of Canterbury to London founder.

The collapse of the Lichfield archbishopric had other and more solid results. It led to a clear pronouncement by the papacy safeguarding for the future the status of the see of Canterbury, subject of course to there being another metropolitan see at York. It also caused Aethelheard, when consecrating bishops in the Province of Lichfield, to insist on a profession of obedience to himself and his successors together with a profession of orthodoxy. This had come to stay.

Aethelheard's successor was Wulfred (805–832), his archdeacon—the first appearance of such an office in Anglo-Saxon England—of whose early life little else is known apart from contemporary charters showing him to own large properties in Kent. This doubtless gave him considerable local influence, a fact which is reflected in the minting of his coins, the reverse of which no longer bear the name of the King of Mercia, but simply *Durovernis Civitas* together with the designation of the moneyer. It was Wulfred who, in 813, restored Christ Church, and gave permission for the clergy to live in the houses which they themselves had built, and to bequeath them to inmates of the monastery. Some two years after his consecration, and upon the death of Cuthred who had ruled Kent as an underling of Mercia, Wulfred seems, from a letter of Pope Leo III to Charlemagne, to have fallen out of favour with Cenwulf. True, there was, for a time, no public rupture, and at a Witanagemot held in London in 811 the King sold Wulfred land in West Kent to the value of 126 mancuses—a mancus being worth about thirty pence. But a journey to Rome in 814 undertaken with Wigbert, Bishop of Sherborne, to negotiate on behalf of the English Church, was probably prompted by his strained relations with Mercia. Yet both Monarch and Archbishop were present at a council at Cealchyth, the last great assembly of its kind during the Mercian supremacy. Their joint attestation of charters till 817 witnesses to continued co-operation, if with occasional strain.

A serious quarrel, however, arose when the Mercian King claimed certain possessions belonging to the see of Canterbury, and proceeded to seize the monasteries of South Minster and Reculver. The Archbishop resisted strongly, and the King retaliated by bringing charges against him before the Pope. Whatever the rights or wrongs of this unhappy business, the practical result, according to a contemporary chronicle, was that 'the whole nation was deprived of the benefits "of the primordial [*sic*] authority and of the ministry of holy baptism" for six years',[16] from 817 to 822. This 'strange' and 'unprecedented' event can hardly mean what it might seem to imply, that an interdict was imposed upon Britain; rather that the Archbishop, in the face of such implacable royal hostility, found it almost impossible to exercise his office. To be *persona grata* with the King was a *sine qua non* of being effective. The dispute dragged on, finally ending in a way that was humiliating to the Archbishop personally and to the dignity of his office. In 821 Cenwulf, probably as a result of intervention by the Pope and the Emperor, summoned Wulfred to appear before his council in London. There he ordered that the Archbishop should surrender thirty hides of land and submit to a large fine. Wulfred had no alternative but to comply, whereupon

Cenwulf promised to restore him to his full rights, and to clear him of the charges brought against him to the Pope.

This extraordinary episode must have been extremely damaging at the time to the authority of the Archbishop, and illustrates what will become apparent later in differing contexts, that it was difficult for him to stand up successfully against royal power when ruthlessly exercised. True, there were limitations to such power, for the successor of St. Augustine, particularly when backed up by a strong Pope, always counted for much. Still, King and Archbishop were usually unequal contestants. If for 'King' we read 'State' in post-Reformation England, the same will be found to apply.

Fortunately for Archbishop Wulfred, the confiscated estates in Kent, after passing on Cenwulf's death to his daughter, the Abbess of Cwenthritha, were largely restored to the archbishopric, though at the cost of a great deal of litigation.

So did the metropolitical see of Canterbury weather the storms which gathered around it during the years of the Mercian supremacy—a supremacy which finally collapsed when in 827 Mercia itself came under the dominion of Egberht, King of Wessex, who ruled England south of the Humber and was acknowledged as lord over Northumbria. Though in succeeding centuries Canterbury was frequently under fire, and for some sixteen years suppressed by Parliament, never again until the XXth century would the creation of new provinces come up for serious discussion. London still awaits its metropolitan.

# 4

I

The rise of Wessex saw the emergence of a unifying monarchy and therefore a new political climate in which all Archbishops of Canterbury must perforce live. Equally, Kings of Wessex, in seeking to establish a national hegemony, could not remain indifferent to the metropolitan of southern England. His national status gave him a unique significance. They expected, as the condition of any possible *modus vivendi*, to have the decisive voice in his appointment. The Archbishop, on his part, recognized a responsibility to advance the dignity of Christian kingship and to assist the monarch, by counsel and sometimes by solemn warning, to approach more nearly to its austere demands. Indeed, the very monotheism for which the Christian faith stood, in contrast to the polytheism of northern paganism, helped in subtle ways to build up the unique character of the single sovereign, and to weaken the concept of the heptarchy. The relentless incursions of the Danes added to the need for political unity, if only of military command. Here the Church pointed the way.

The importance which an ambitious monarchy in Wessex gave to right relations with Canterbury can be seen in the deliberations of a council called by Eagberht to meet at Kingston in 838. Here a perpetual treaty of reconciliation and alliance was entered into between the metropolitical see and the West Saxon kings. Under its terms, Archbishop Ceolnoth obtained the restoration of his lands at Malling, of which his Church had been unjustly deprived. On the accession of Ethelwulf, Eagberht's son, this agreement was solemnly confirmed at a council of bishops held at Astran in 839.

It now became the usual custom for Kings of Wessex to be crowned by the Archbishop of Canterbury, and for a Christian significance to be introduced into the ancient ceremony used on these occasions. This ritual went back to the time when

> the ruler, upon his election, was raised on a shield, and, standing upon it, was borne on the shoulders of certain of the chief men

of the tribe or nation round the assembled people. . . . At its conclusion a spear was placed in the King's hand, and the diadem, a richly wrought band of silk or linen, which must not be confused with the crown, was bound round his forehead, as a sign of regal authority.[17]

The Church wisely added its own benediction to this venerable custom and introduced into it a more rigorous moral demand. From the Old Testament it took over the ceremony of anointing, which became the central element in the king's sacring.

The most ancient coronation ritual is the pontifical of Egberht, Archbishop of York, in which the whole ceremony is framed within the Mass. Alfred the Great (870–901) did more than any other monarch to hold aloft the ideal of Christian kingship, and it was probably his example which stamped a unique significance upon the coronation rite. His son, Edward the Elder, was crowned in 901 by Archbishop Plegmund at Kingston.

The precise form does not seem to have become fixed until the coronation of Edgar by Archbishop Dunstan in 973. The importance which the Archbishop ascribed to the occasion may be seen in two experimental drafts of the service, both of which centre around the solemn anointing. It has been suggested that Edgar, who delayed his coronation until he was thirty years of age, below which no man could canonically be consecrated to the episcopate, saw the rite as analogous to such a consecration. The view that the anointing gave the monarch a *quasi*-religious character persisted till after the Conquest, and doubtless was encouraged by Dunstan; but it was specifically repudiated by the time of Archbishop Lanfranc. Referring to this question in one of his letters he writes that the king is not anointed to the ministry but to the service of the Church.

Apart from Edmund, Matilda, Edward V and Edward VIII, none of whom was ever crowned, coronations of English and British monarchs have been maintained in an unbroken succession; and the Archbishop of Canterbury has regarded it as his customary right to perform the ceremony. True, the Archbishop of York assisted in the case of Aethelred and Edgar, and, since Stigand, Archbishop of Canterbury (1052–1070), was under condemnation, crowned both Harold and William.

Coronations gave to the Church a unique opportunity, not only of exercising influence but of subsequently calling monarchs to account. It was no light thing that kings pledged themselves to protect God's Church and people, to forbid iniquity and to rule with justice and mercy. Moreover, coronations at times involved archbishops in competing dynastic claims.

Mention has already been made of the significance of Alfred, a monarch of genius capable of standing comparison with the great Charlemagne. In the centuries which preceded this most notable of all Anglo-Saxon kings, the Church had been the leaven in the lump, a humanizing ingredient working within the tribal life of the various kingdoms, and introducing Roman administrative techniques into Germanic customary procedures. Alfred, however, who with Edgar was a 'better bishop than the bishops', inaugurated the tendency for England to become more of a theocracy. This meant that the Church assumed a positive role; and as power moved steadily towards Wessex, so were ecclesiastics inexorably drawn into the business of government. Church and royal councils began to merge into each other; Witanagemots and ecclesiastical synods to fuse. Archbishops and bishops mixed with *ealdormen* in the King's councils. When Alfred promulgated his great 'dooms', quotations from the Ten Commandments and the Gospels did not seem incongruous.

Alfred's rule was important also because its background was the marauding aggression of the Danes leading to unsettlement, lawlessness and the revival of heathenism. The fact was that a culture which flowered in the IXth century had not penetrated deeply enough to withstand the unsettlement of invasion. What Alfred achieved by his military victories was to buy time until the Danes were Christianized, and were thus able to provide the nation with Oda, Archbishop of Canterbury, appointed by Edmund I in 942, and some seventy-five years later with Canute, a responsible king. Of Oda, who crowned both Eadred and Eadwy and held office for some seventeen years, Bishop Stubbs writes:

> It is, however, certain that he did nothing to thwart the policy of Dunstan, and enough of his legislation remains to show that, in a determination to enforce the observance of both monastic vows and laws of marriage, he came in no degree behind his more famous successor.[18]

Upon Oda's death, Eadwy's first choice fell upon Aefsige of Winchester, who, however, died of cold in the Alps *en route* to receive his *pallium* in Rome. The King then turned to Beorhthelm, Bishop of Wells, but the accession of Edgar in 959 created a new situation. The strength of the monarchy was now seen when the King set aside Beorhthelm's election on the ground that he was not adequate to exercise so heavy a responsibility, and ordered him back to his diocese of Wells. He was replaced in 960 by Dunstan, who was then Bishop of London, having previously held the See of Worcester.

Dunstan's earlier life—he was born into a family related to the royal house—is important. After being taught by the Irish monks at Glastonbury, where he gained a reputation for scholarship, he was introduced early to the disturbed life of the King's household, in particular to the companionship of Edmund and Eadred, step-brothers to King Aethelstan. Banishment from court led to a period of acute mental distress, followed by a return to Glastonbury where he adopted the life of a hermit. Restored to favour by Edmund on his becoming King, he was made Abbot of Glastonbury in 945. For the next eleven years he remained there, vigorously restoring an organized community life after the lapse of two generations—an achievement of incalculable importance against the background of disorder into which England had fallen, and from which it never fully recovered before the Conquest.

Dunstan recognized that any reform in Church and nation could only be brought about through strong royal support. He did not disdain, therefore, to become the friend of princes, while at the same time preserving his own independence. Edmund was followed on the throne by Eadred, and Eadred by his young brother Eadwy, at whose coronation there took place an extraordinary incident which later chroniclers delighted to embellish. On the day after his crowning, according to Dunstan's biographer, Eadwy left the feast to dally with a noble lady and her daughter, both of whom were seeking to entice him into marriage. Such a royal departure could only be regarded as a studied insult to the guests. Dunstan, together with the Bishop of Lichfield, sought out the absentee monarch, and after a somewhat violent altercation brought him back to the solemn festivities.

A further period of exile followed in the monastery of St. Peter in Ghent, which proved fortunate in that Dunstan was introduced at first hand to the reformed movement on the Continent, a useful preparation for one who was to be Archbishop of Canterbury for some twenty-seven years, and at a time of general decline.

With Dunstan's appointment to Canterbury there began a partnership between King and Archbishop which has its closest and perhaps only parallel in that of William the Conqueror and Lanfranc. In both cases the relationship led to the reform of the Church and a united endeavour to establish law and order in days of change and near-crisis. Dr. Stenton writes:

> Kings and Archbishops have often co-operated in a programme of ecclesiastical reform; but there are few parallels in any country to the enthusiasm with which Edgar brought the whole power of the English state to the furtherance of Dunstan's

Ceolnoth

Aelfheah.
From an illuminated MS.
in the British Museum

Stigand.
From the Bayeux Tapestry

*The murder of Thomas à Becket*

*The seal of Boniface*

*Simon Langham.*
*From his tomb in Westminster Abbey*

*Thomas Arundel*

*Henry IV being crowned by Archbishop Arundel*

*Henry Chichele's tomb in Canterbury Cathedral*

*William Warham. By Hans Holbein*

*Canterbury Cathedral*

*Thomas Cranmer*

*Cardinal Pole*

religious policy. Ancient scholars who inherited the traditions of the monastic revival naturally regarded Edgar with veneration, and modern historians, realizing the significance of the ideals to which he gave his patronage, have tended to include him among the greatest of old English rulers. In part their praise is justified.[19]

It is no exaggeration to say that in every department of Edgar's government, the influence of Dunstan was apparent, whether in securing civil order or external peace, or adopting a wise and liberal policy towards the Danes. Bishop Stubbs's verdict is equally impressive:

> There can be no doubt that the glories of Edgar's reign were largely due to Dunstan's abilities and industry;

and

> The true mark of Dunstan's mind must be looked for in Edgar's legislation . . . throughout the reign he was the King's closest friend and adviser, the chief of his witan, the ecclesiastical head of the nation.[20]

The Archbishop was thus frequently about the court where his precedence as the chief member of the King's council was taken for granted. Long experience and the *charisma* of his compelling personality added to his authority. With a highly strung temperament which brought with it bouts of nervous disorder, Dunstan combined marked administrative ability. His consistent policy was to raise the standard of the nation's life by promoting a general reform in the Church. In conjunction with the King he hoped, through conciliating the Danes, to heal past animosities and to create in the country one people. Contemporary Popes, a thousand miles away, tended to see things somewhat differently, believing that the English bishops might have done more to promote resistance to the pagan Scandinavian invader.

Such a general policy, Dunstan believed, could only be brought about by recalling the religious in monasteries to a proper obedience, particularly in relation to their vows of chastity; parochial clergy to celibacy; cathedral chapters to communal living; schools to a disciplined scholarship such as had given lustre to Canterbury, York, Jarrow, Wearmouth, and, more recently, Glastonbury. To achieve these objectives royal support was essential, since they could only be realized by endowment of land, and, on occasions, invasion of lay rights. Yet in the implementation of such a policy, Dunstan showed marked moderation, although determined to carry it forward. Often he was content to work through others. Thus he did not expel the secular clergy from Canterbury as at Winchester, nor himself endow a single Benedictine house. There was no harrying of married clergy as such.

Yet his earlier work at Glastonbury and his appointments of Aethelwold to Winchester and Oswald to Worcester have for ever, and properly, associated his name with monastic reform.

The death of Edgar, in 975, caused the general issue of reform to be caught up in the struggle for power between the rival houses of Mercia and Wessex. Civil war seemed imminent. National unity was further threatened by a dynastic struggle within Wessex which involved both Edward, the elder son of Edgar, and Aethelred, his brother, who had the support of the Western shires. The authority which an archbishop could exercise was now asserted in an almost dramatic fashion. Dunstan had every reason to take sides. Edward was known to support the policy of monastic reform, and had in fact been designated as his successor by Edgar himself. Also, if Aethelred were to be raised to the throne of Wessex, a long minority would ensue, thus incurring the risk of the reactionary West Saxons gaining the ascendancy. Taking the initiative, and in co-operation with Oswald, Archbishop of York, Dunstan declared firmly for Edward at a Witan held (probably) in Winchester. This intervention proved decisive, and the two Archbishops crowned Edward at Kingston. This success, however, was short-lived, for in March 978, he was assassinated at Corfe Castle on the order of his stepmother, and Aethelred ascended the throne. Dunstan and Oswald again realistic-ally co-operated in crowning the new King: but if that doubtful authority, Florence of Worcester, is to be trusted, Dunstan's unease was reflected in the course of the ceremony, for he required the young King to read a pledge that he would govern well, and then himself delivered a short exhortation on the obligations of Christian kingship. His concluding words were full of doom:

> Because thou hast been raised to the throne by the death of thy brother, whom thy mother has slain, hear now the word of the Lord; The sword shall not depart from thy house, but shall rage against thee, all the days of thy life, cutting off thy seed, until thy kingdom become the kingdom of an alien, whose customs and tongue the nation which thou rulest knows not.[21]

The credibility of this prophecy is somewhat weakened by the fact that Florence of Worcester recorded it in 1018.

Almost the last public act of Dunstan was to provide for the burial at Shaftesbury of the late King. His remaining years at Canterbury, disturbed by the increasing depredations of the Danes, were given to the quiet discharge of his diocesan and provincial duties.

So distinguished an archiepiscopate was bound to have repercussions on the office which he held, particularly in relation to the emergent national monarchy. Dunstan was an intimate adviser to successive kings, and in this capacity showed great independence, personal and official. He did not hesitate to rebuke Edgar for his frequent bouts of profligacy, though the story that he forbade the King to wear his crown as a penance for having carried off a nun from Wilton Abbey is a fabrication, if in character. The more likely version of the story is that Monica, a lady who had borne a daughter to Edgar, and who refused to marry him, entered Wilton Abbey as a nun—a not uncommon step for ladies of rank. Monica in time became Abbess of Wilton, as did her daughter, St. Edith, after her. Dunstan well illustrates in practice the words of Liebermann, in his *The National Assembly in the Anglo-Saxon Period*:

> As soon as Canterbury became subject to the supreme power of England, the primate is scarcely ever absent from her witenage-mots. He is the king's chief counsellor. He alone shares with the king the honour of being personally named in some laws . . . it is the nation itself in whose name he makes the king swear the coronation oath.

II

The remaining period of Anglo-Saxon England up to the Norman Conquest produced no archbishop comparable in stature. On the Continent new life and vigour were being brought into the Church through the reform movement initiated from Cluny, which culminated in placing Gregory VII in the papal chair. In England, however, the Church was finding it difficult to maintain a sense of direction, as the Danes increasingly threatened law and order. In 1009 a fleet under Earl Thurkill ravaged the shores of Britain. Later a larger armament under Heming and Eglaf stormed Canterbury. In September 1011 the Danes returned to besiege the city, and a priest betrayed the citadel to the invader. Florence of Worcester relates that there followed the most terrible butchery, but this is not borne out by the more sober narrative in the Anglo-Saxon Chronicle. However, the Cathedral of Christ Church was burned; the city sacked; and the Danes made off in their ships, taking Archbishop Aelfheah with them, and keeping him a prisoner for several months,

37

while they tried to extract an extremely large ransom. On Easter Day, 19 April 1012, the Archbishop was paraded before the Danes as they were feasting in their hall at Greenwich. He was pelted with stones, until finally Thrum, whom Aelfheah had confirmed the day before, compassionately brought his sufferings to an end by killing him with an axe. So 'his holy soul was sent forth to God's Kingdom'.

The Danes soon repented of this wanton act perpetrated in a drunken orgy, and the next day they brought the Archbishop's body reverently into London to be interred in St. Paul's Cathedral in the presence of the Bishops of London and Dorchester.

The policy of Edgar and Dunstan, building upon the more than military achievements of Alfred the Great, was now to yield its long-term results. Canute, the Dane, who had been baptized at the age of six, was elected by the Witan King of all England, and was crowned by Archbishop Lyfing in 1017. On the death of the Archbishop, Canute chose his own chaplain, Aethelnoth, a son of Ealdorman Aethelmar of the Western shires, as his successor, and commanded Wulfstan, Archbishop of York, to undertake his consecration.

Aethelnoth exercised a considerable influence on the Scandinavian monarch and it was doubtless through him that in 1023 Canute, having restored the cathedral, translated Aelfheah's body in great pomp to Canterbury. When some years later, Archbishop Lanfranc consulted Anselm as to the propriety of paying devotion to the slain Archbishop, permission was granted on the ground that although he had not suffered directly on behalf of the Christian faith, he had yet died to preserve justice. Maybe it was this reassurance that led to Aelfheah's image, together with that of St. Dunstan, being lifted above the high altar. But his subsequent fame was eclipsed by the European renown of Thomas à Becket. His festival is still celebrated on 19 April, and he has the distinction of being Canterbury's first martyr and one of four Archbishops to meet death by violence.

Aethelnoth was also probably responsible for the lavish endowments which Canute gave to both English and Danish Churches. His own status, within the context of a Scandinavian Empire, can be seen in his consecrating bishops for Fionia and Scansis, although this led to a dispute with the Archbishop of Hamburg. Freeman, in his *History of the Norman Conquest*, calls in question the story that at Harold Harefoot's coronation Aethelnoth placed the crown and sceptre on the altar, declaring that the King could take them if he wished, but that while a son of Emma still lived he would crown no other. Equally doubtful is William of Malmesbury's assertion that Archbishop Eadsige, Aethelnoth's successor, assisted Edward the Confessor in securing the throne, this being probably an inference from the coronation. However, the Anglo-Saxon Chronicle relates that at this ceremony, Eadsige 'fully instructed him before all the people, clearly reminding him of his duty as king and his responsibility to the nation as a whole'.[22]

The accession of the Confessor, who had spent twenty-seven years as an exile in Normandy, led to growing division, to quote Barlow, Edward's most recent biographer, 'between the local interests which backed the local man and a court party which advanced strangers—both English and foreign'. The King's policy inevitably provoked a strong English opposition, headed by Earl Godwin, which also found a strong supporter in the Archbishop of Canterbury. When Eadsige fell ill in 1044 he contrived, in connivance with Edward and Godwin, that Siward, Abbot of Abingdon, should act as his coadjutor, consecrating him Bishop of Uppsala. He did this for fear lest somebody else whom he trusted less 'would get [the archbishopric] either by asking or by purchase'.[23] The expedient does not seem to have worked well. By 1050 most of the chief officers of state were strangers, which seemed to suggest that Edward, at the next vacancy, would appoint a Norman archbishop; particularly as he was suspected of looking to Duke William to follow him.

When news of Eadsige's death reached the monks of Canterbury they hastened, as the traditional representatives of the Archbishop's *familia*, to make a canonical election without waiting to consult the wishes of the King. Their choice fell on Aelfric, kinsman to Earl Godwin, whose good offices they sought to commend their nomination to Edward. The King, however, at such a critical moment, did not intend to abandon the political advantages of having an archbishop of his own choosing. Indeed, he had already decided on Robert, Abbot of Jumièges, his friend and counsellor in France, whom the chroniclers describe as having established over him a position of complete dominance. The story ran that if Robert told the King that a black crow was white, then white it was. The extent of this dominance, however, may well be questioned, and there is evidence to support the view that politically, on occasions, 'Edward was the complete master and Robert the servant whom he used.'[24]

Edward proceeded to set aside the election of Aelfric, and at a Witanagemot in London in 1051 nominated Robert, much to the indignation of Earl Godwin and his followers. As expected, the new Archbishop used his influence in the interests of Norman power, and in pursuit of this policy fanned the hostility between the King and the Earl, even accusing him of planning Edward's death. In particular, Robert played a prominent part in engineering the King's triumph in 1051 when Godwin and his family fled the country. Indeed, Kent may have come his way as his share in the spoils, before he was dispatched on an embassage to William in Normandy. Certainly he tried to persuade the King to follow up his success by divorcing his wife, the Earl's daughter.

By identifying himself so closely with Godwin's enemies, the Archbishop made his own position impossible when the exiles returned in September 1052, and Edward's army would not fight. Robert, in company with Ulf, Bishop of Dorchester, and William of London, took refuge abroad. The exaggerated account of their flight in the Anglo-Saxon Chronicle (not an unprejudiced authority) makes somewhat macabre reading. They fought their way through London to the eastern gate, slaying many citizens *en route*; and arriving safely at Walton-on-Naze reached Normandy in an unseaworthy fishing craft. In his haste, according to the Anglo-Saxon Chronicle, Robert forsook 'his *pallium* and all Christendom here in this land, which was God's purpose since he had obtained that dignity against His will'.

The Witan duly met; deposed the Archbishop; and declared him an outlaw, an act so uncanonical that the papacy, particularly in its new spirit of reform, felt bound to repudiate it. Robert, as was expected, went to Rome, where the Pope reinstated him, but he died shortly afterwards at Jumièges, never regaining his office.

The Witan, meanwhile, under pressure from Godwin, nominated as his successor Stigand, Bishop of Winchester, who had previously shared in the disgrace of Emma, Edward's mother, since it was alleged that she had 'acted in all things according to his counsel'. Stigand had long identified himself with the Saxon party, and was active in prosecuting Godwin's return. Not, however, until six years had passed did he receive his *pallium* from the anti-Pope, Benedict X, but the grant was annulled by his successor. Stigand lived, according to a chronicler, to be excommunicated by five Popes; to be disowned by bishops in his own province; and repudiated by his friend Harold, Godwin's son. If it be true that he engaged in a public market in bishoprics and abbacies, he was not unique in sponsoring this kind of transaction, and though the motivation might have been wrong, the practice carried with it certain advantages. He attended the death-bed of Edward the Confessor, whose piety and visions failed to impress him; and as the dying monarch indulged in an outpouring of prophetic doom, Stigand remarked quietly to Harold that old age and illness had affected his reason.

Stigand's archiepiscopate illustrates, as does that of Robert of Jumièges, the difficulties of partisan ecclesiastics in a divided kingdom. The *raison d'être* of the Primacy of Canterbury was to bring together and unify. The result was that the Church in Anglo-Saxon England, on the eve of the Conquest, was in a state of schism.

*PART II*

# THE MEDIEVAL ARCHBISHOP

*Archbishops*

LANFRANC 1070
ANSELM 1093
RALPH D'ESCURES 1114
WILLIAM DE CORBEIL 1123
THEOBALD 1139
THOMAS À BECKET 1162
RICHARD (OF DOVER) 1174
BALDWIN 1185
HUBERT WALTER 1193
STEPHEN LANGTON 1207
RICHARD LE GRANT 1229
EDMUND RICH 1234
BONIFACE OF SAVOY 1245
ROBERT KILWARDBY 1273
JOHN PECHAM 1279
ROBERT WINCHELSEY 1294
WALTER REYNOLDS 1313
SIMON MEPEHAM 1328
JOHN STRATFORD 1333
THOMAS BRADWARDINE 1349
SIMON ISLIP 1349
SIMON LANGHAM 1366
WILLIAM WHITTLESEY 1368
SIMON SUDBURY 1375
WILLIAM COURTENAY 1381
THOMAS ARUNDEL 1396
ROGER WALDEN 1398
THOMAS ARUNDEL 1399
HENRY CHICHELE 1414
JOHN STAFFORD 1443
JOHN KEMP 1452
THOMAS BOURCHIER 1454
JOHN MORTON 1486
HENRY DEAN 1501

# 1

I

How did an Archbishop come to his office—in fact as well as in theory? The qualification is important; for customary rules of procedure, later laws and canons, often gave way to the demands of power, even when protocol was seemingly respected.

In the early Church, bishops were elected by the clergy and people of the city where they were to preside. Thus they were usually already well known in their local community, and as Canon Kemp has commented, the Church of the first few centuries had no objection to 'in-breeding'.[25] Though the tendency across the years was to replace spontaneity by more regular procedures, this early tradition of appointment lingered on. Even as late as the time of Gregory VII, it was still recognized that clergy and laity had rights in the nomination of their father in God. But these rights were now exercised in a wider context. Thus in the case of some 376 bishops consecrated to office in England between the years 688 and 1050, it was by no means unusual for King, Witan and cathedral chapters to be severally involved. There does not seem to have been as yet any sustained, as apart from occasional, intervention by the Pope to secure his own candidate. Rather, the Holy See was content to protect the respective rights of those engaged in the process of election. This policy was to change later, the more so with the progressive recognition of the papacy, under the increasing development of canon law, as the universal ordinary and final court of appeal. In the XIIIth century, Innocent III quashed two elections at St. David's and issued a mandate to the Chapter of Worcester to ensure a unanimous vote. The logical development of this assertion of power was the papal 'provision', first to fill vacancies created when a bishop died in Rome, or the election was disputed; later under a decree of Urban V, in 1363, to 'provide' for all sees under any circumstances. Such claims were not accepted in England at face value, at least not to the extent of overriding chapter election or metropolitan confirmation. Indeed, to resist these claims there were passed the Statutes of Carlisle, 1307, and Provisors, 1351. Yet in spite of this legislation the archiepiscopal registers from the time of Islip (1349–66) to the Reformation, apart from two years under Archbishop Chichele, show papal provision as the canonical method of appointing bishops. Dr. Churchill writes:

> The salient fact, from the administrative point of view, is that, during this period now under review, the reception of the papal bull of provision was for the Archbishops the pivot on which their subsequent actions turned.[26]

Henceforth the normal documentation in the register was three-fold: the papal bull or provision; the mandate for the release of the spiritualities; profession of obedience to the Archbishop and the See of Canterbury.

As to the election of metropolitans, in distinction from suffragan bishops, the papacy felt that it had a more immediate concern. This was represented by the conferring of the *pallium*, signifying the bestowal of jurisdiction. Before the XIth century no oath of obedience, however, seems to have been exacted from the metropolitan on receiving it; though from earlier times he had sent a profession of faith to Rome, which historically arose out of his announcing both his election and orthodoxy to his brother bishops.

With Canterbury, Rome felt itself to have a uniquely close connexion for reasons going back into history, which have already been set out.

But it was not only the Roman See which was concerned in the choice of the Archbishop. There were diverse interests which in differing degrees felt themselves involved—the King in particular, the suffragan bishops, the lay barons, and the monks of the Cathedral of Christ Church. These severally endeavoured to secure their will, using every device from bribery to violence. As time went on, however, it was increasingly the power of the King which prevailed, even when papal provisions became common.

The King essentially wanted someone who was not likely to push the claims of the *sacerdotium* too far, and who, later in the Middle Ages, was of sufficient influence with his brother bishops to persuade them to respond generously to royal demands for money; the Pope wanted a metropolitan who, while being loyal to the interests, pecuniary and legal, of Rome, would not make things too difficult for him *vis-à-vis* the secular ruler; the bishops, a father in God not prone to interfere too much in the administration of their dioceses but able to protect them from financial exploitation either by King or Pope; the lay magnates, one who was independent enough to stand by them in the maintenance of their rights; the monks of Canterbury, a titular abbot, preferably a religious, concerned to champion their constitutional position as the electing body.

No appointment system subject to these pressures could hope to work smoothly, as will be seen in particular nominations, especially during early and formative years.

When William invaded England, the repudiated Stigand 'whom the zeal of the Apostolic See had struck with anathema',[27] so William of Poitier, the French chronicler comments, was Archbishop of Canterbury. Hence the support which the Norman Duke gained for his enterprise from the Holy See. Established in England, the Conqueror, while himself taking no initiative, waited for the Pope to heal the schism. In 1070 Alexander II sent over legates who summoned Stigand to appear before them at a council in Winchester. This resulted in his deprivation on the grounds that he had occupied the archbishopric in the lifetime of Robert of Jumièges; had worn the *pallium* of his predecessor for six years; and received his own from a schismatic Pope. It was significant that William did nothing to save him.

The appointment of a successor could never have been more important. The Anglo-Saxon Church was in decline and becoming a backwater. The two former Archbishops had discredited their office, thereby weakening its authority and lowering its prestige. Invasion, leading to land redistribution, and the eclipse of the native monarchy, inevitably brought unsettlement, though by 1070 organized resistance to Norman rule had more or less ceased. William found himself with the responsibility of filling four sees, as well as the archbishopric. In respect of the latter, it might have been thought that he would choose his half-brother, Odo of Bayeux, but he was acute enough to realize the dangers of a family appointment of this kind. By a private understanding with the Pope, he nominated Lanfranc, Abbot of Caen, the barons supporting his choice, and the monks of Christ Church giving it canonical propriety by welcoming him at Canterbury.

Lanfranc had long been a trusted adviser of Duke William, but his disinclination to accept office, although overcome by the King 'with grace and dignity', was probably genuine. A few years previously he had refused the archbishopric of Rouen, and was later to write to the Pope:

> I entreat you for God's sake and for the Lord's sake, since it was by your authority that I was involved in these difficulties, by the same authority to extricate me from them and permit me once more to return to the monastic life, which above all things I delight in.[28]

Such release was not forthcoming.

Lanfranc's nomination shows strikingly how a strong king in a favourable political situation could, without difficulty, get the man he wanted. But not all kings were so strong, the situation so favourable, or the other interested parties so conciliatory.

The appointment of his successor did not work out so well. William Rufus, 'the most secular of all medieval English kings',[29] had been some two years on the throne when Archbishop Lanfranc died. Their relations had never been easy, largely because the new King resented his dependence upon a man of European reputation who, in earlier years, had both 'nourished' and conferred upon him the order of knighthood. The King was, therefore, in no hurry to appoint a successor, since bishops and abbots were more easily controlled when without their natural leader, and the King's treasury benefited handsomely during a vacancy—an important consideration for a ruler who invaded Normandy, fought against Scotland, and bogged himself down in the marches of Wales.

The appointment of Anselm, Abbot of Bec, differed in many respects from that of his predecessor. Here was no case of a king selecting his own archbishop, but, on the contrary, accepting with reluctance an ecclesiastic presented to him by popular acclaim inspired by powerful baronial support. Eadmer, Anselm's biographer, relates that Rufus was only brought to make the nomination because he believed himself to be at death's door.

Anselm, who was unknown to Rufus personally, was himself reluctant to accept the office, pleading that he was an old man and unused to worldly affairs. For some five months he continued to hope that the King might change his mind, or that the Duke of Normandy, the Archbishop of Rouen, or his community at Bec, would withhold their consent. This did not happen, and his consecration went forward.

The death of Anselm in 1109, nine years after Rufus's accidental killing (or murder) in the New Forest, was followed by another interregnum, this time of five years. Henry I's relations with Anselm had not been such as to encourage a hasty appointment. At last, in the spring of 1114, he summoned a council to Windsor where the various interested parties confronted each other. The suffragan bishops, who were determined to assert their right to a share in electing their metropolitan, joined with the barons in objecting to Favricus, Abbot of Abingdon, the King's choice, on the ground that he was a monk. The Christ Church contingent, on the contrary, were solidly behind him. A compromise was at length arrived at. Ralph D'escures, Bishop of Rochester, at one time a monk before being driven from his monastery, was unanimously elected, and enthroned at Canterbury.

The pattern of controversy seen here continued to disfigure

elections for a long time. It prevailed in February 1123, when Henry called to Gloucester a great gathering of bishops, earls and knights, together with the monks from Christ Church, and the Papal Legate, Alberic. The deliberations were heated and lasted for several days. The secular magnates supported the religious, who wanted one of their own order. The bishops, on the other hand, were for a secular clerk. William, Bishop of Salisbury, who had the ear of the King, suggested, as a compromise, that four clerks be nominated from whom the Chapter of Christ Church be invited to choose one. The monks resisted this *via media* for two days, but finally gave way, electing William de Corbeil who, as an Augustinian canon, seemed the next best thing to a religious. Hitherto only three seculars had sat in the chair of St. Augustine. His consecration at Canterbury was performed by the bishops of his own province, since Thurstan, Archbishop of York, refused to acknowledge William as Primate of All England. When the new Archbishop arrived in Rome for his *pallium*, he found that Thurstan had lodged four objections to his election: that it was uncanonical because held in a royal court; that the Chapter of Christ Church had not canonically assented to it; that the choice of a clerk was contrary to the orders of St. Augustine; and that William had not been consecrated by his brother of York. Only the powerful intervention of Henry 'who overcame Rome by what overcomes all the world, gold and silver' secured the *pallium* from Calixtus II.

Concerning the next appointment, in 1138, the monastic chronicle records simply: 'The king made Theobald Archbishop.'[30] The fact was that Stephen, irresolute and insecure, was determined that his brother Henry, Bishop of Winchester, already the most powerful subject in England and busily engaged in seeking the Primacy through the Papal Legate, should not go to Canterbury. The Chapter bowed before the King's will, and Theobald, Abbot of Bec, was elected on 24 December, being consecrated by the Papal Legate on 8 January 1139.

The next appointment was, perhaps, the most fateful in English history. The circumstances associated with it could not have been entirely welcome to the community of Christ Church who, in 1159, had secured a papal bull maintaining its rights of election. Some twelve months after Theobald's death, the bishops of the province brought letters from the King instructing the monks to proceed to elect. The Chapter duly met, the bishops speaking first and making great play of Henry II's generosity in allowing the Chapter to act in accordance with the canons. Richard de Lucy, Chief Justiciar, whose words, perhaps written up *ex post facto*, have come down to us, reiterated the theme:

The king grants you full freedom of election provided you elect a man worthy of the office and equal to the burdens. . . .[31]

The Canterbury Chapter then proceeded to elect Thomas à Becket, Chancellor of England, the King's nominee, this being ratified in Westminster Abbey by the bishops and the clergy of the province on 23 May 1162. Since Thomas was only in deacon's orders, he was ordained priest in Canterbury Cathedral by Bishop Walter of Rochester. Referring to his consecration by the Bishop of Winchester on Trinity Sunday, Roger of Pontigny writes eloquently of 'the devotion and exultation of those who came running up to meet him . . . tears flowing from his eyes'.[32] Gilbert Foliot (vegetarian and tee-totaller), a life-long opponent of Thomas, who, as Bishop of London, tried to assist its status as a metropolitical see, viewed things somewhat differently:

> The king has worked a miracle. Out of a secular man and a soldier he has made an archbishop.[33]

Later, when estranged from some of his suffragans, Thomas, in reproaching them, recalled the successive steps of his appointment:

> Consult your consciences, look at the form of the election, the consent of all the electors, the consent of the king through his son and his envoys, the assent of the son himself as well as all the magnates of the kingdom.[34]

These words show the importance attached to a proper canonical procedure, even when it was known to mask royal nomination. No appointment could have touched Henry II more keenly than that of à Becket's successor, for he was determined not to expose himself again to an archbishop so zealously attached to the principles for which his former Chancellor had chosen to die. Yet in spite of this resolve, Henry promised the monks a free election. With the memory of the recent martyr so emotionally compelling, they desired once again, after the Abbot of Bec had declined nomination, to elect a member of their own fraternity, namely Odo, their Prior, who was devoted to the cause of Thomas; but the King's Justiciar, knowing Henry's mind, supported the bishops in favouring Richard, Prior of St. Martin's, Dover, and formerly a monk of Christ Church. As expected, it was the royal will which finally prevailed. Even then, however, there was some difficulty in securing papal confirmation, since young Prince Henry, and his father-in-law Louis VII of France, brought their influence to bear against it at Rome.

A similar situation of division ensued on the appointment of Richard's successor. At a council in Reading the monks refused to make any election acceptable to the bishops, and the bishops refused to accept any of the three candidates of the black habit put forward by the monks. The council was therefore dissolved and it was not until nine months later that the King, Henry II, called it together again in London. The bishops then took matters into their own hands and elected one of their order, Baldwin of Worcester. This was too much for the monks, who withdrew in anger to Canterbury. It is a significant recognition of their unique role that the King sought them out and after a lengthy discussion persuaded them to elect Baldwin, under promise that his previous nomination by the bishops should be declared null and void.

The monks were determined not to have a repeat performance of this stalemate at the next vacancy.

As soon as they heard in November 1191 that their Abbot, Archbishop Baldwin, had died before the walls of Acre, they met hastily, in order to forestall any action by the bishops, and elected Reginald de Bohun, Bishop of Bath. Such speed, and the exclusion of the bishops, could be defended on the authority of a papal letter secured in May 1191 forbidding the bishops of the province to infringe the electoral rights of the Cathedral Chapter. But Reginald died a few months later.

The scene now returns to Acre, where Hubert Walter, Bishop of Salisbury, after being present at the Archbishop's death, set out on a tour to the Holy Places in Jerusalem, conducted by the great Saladin himself. From there, in company with William of St. Mère Eglise, an exchequer clerk, Hubert Walter (perhaps the authentic Blondel) sought out the imprisoned Richard Cœur de Lion at Ochsenfurt, and returned home to England in April 1193, bearing letters from the captive monarch to the Queen Mother, the Justiciar, and the monks of Canterbury, requiring an election to the archbishopric.

Three candidates emerged—William Longchamp, Bishop of Ely; Savaric of Bath, a relation of Henri VI, Richard's captor; and Hubert Walter, who, having proved a brave colleague in arms, seemed best suited to raise the enormous sum needed for the King's ransom.

Meanwhile, on 30 March, the community had received a letter from Richard which, Gervase of Canterbury says, did not contain any names for fear of giving the appearance of preventing a free election. Richard's wishes were, however, made known.

In these circumstances, the Queen Mother and the Archbishop of Rouen ordered the monks to come up to London on Sunday, 29 May. Their response to this directive was to elect Hubert Walter, and then for the Prior to proceed to London. Seeking out Hubert, he presented him to the Archbishop of Rouen who, with the Queen's counsellors and the bishops, was present for the purpose of holding the election. The suffragans had no option but to admit defeat, Richard Fitz Neal, Bishop of London, remarking with some sarcasm: 'You have done well to bring us our elect,' to which Prior Geoffrey replied: 'We know nothing about your elect, or what you have done, or whether you have elected anyone. But it is clear that the election ought by right to be ours by the fact that we are presenting our elect to the royal court.'[35] The bishops' nomination followed as a formality only.

Messengers from the Monastery of Christ Church were sent to the Pope forthwith, requesting the *pallium* for Hubert, and a bull of translation. Gervase of Canterbury, as sacrist of the Cathedral, kept a meticulous record of the procedure which then unfolded itself—the dispatch by the Pope of a special Nuncio to invest Hubert Walter with the *pallium* and to receive his oath of allegiance; the presentation to Hubert at Lewisham of his archiepiscopal cross; the welcome by the Nuncio Episcopellus, and by the bishops and the monks; the enthronement in the Cathedral, when the *pallium* was placed on his shoulders—an occasion marred, alas, by a squabble between the monks and the bishops of London and Rochester as to their respective parts in the ceremony.

Hubert's appointment is interesting since it shows the tenacity with which the bishops continued to fight a losing battle. It was once again the King who got his way, even in captivity. The monks preferred it so.

The nomination of Hubert's successor, however, was not, from the King's point of view, so satisfactory.

Immediately on hearing the news of Hubert's death on 13 July 1205, John, who was now King, hastened to Canterbury, where he found the usual tensions. The monks wanted one of their own order; the bishops demurred. He himself had made up his mind firmly for John de Gray, Bishop of Norwich, upon whose 'complaisant obedience' he could rely. In these circumstances it was agreed to do nothing until December; but when the monks later heard that the King, in the interval, was using bribery to get his way at Rome, they took their courage in both hands, met secretly, and by a majority elected Reginald their sub-prior. They now had a bargaining weapon.

What happened from this point onwards grows more and more complicated. Reginald, once arrived at Rome, where agents of King, bishops and Chapter had gathered, foolishly made public his nomination as Archbishop-elect, probably through sheer vanity.

When news of the secret election reached an infuriated John, he confronted the monks and forced them into the election of his own candidate, de Gray of Norwich. The Pope's reaction to this tangled web of events was to quash both the elections; to summon a further delegation of monks to Rome; and to persuade them to elect his own candidate, Stephen Langton, probably the most distinguished churchman in Europe next to himself. In doing this, Innocent III showed himself punctilious in not by-passing the Chapter of Canterbury, understandably so because, after exhaustive inquiries, he had earlier himself confirmed the monks as the sole electors. The King's proctors, equally understandably, refused to ratify the election, and the Pope then appealed in vain to John over their heads. These rebuffs did not deter Innocent from going forward, and on 17 June 1207 Langton was consecrated at Viterbo.

The *impasse* was now complete; and it took the Pope some six years of complicated diplomacy, threats, and an interdict, to bring the King to heel. Not until Stephen Langton had spent years of exile in the great Cistercian monastery at Pontigny in the diocese of Auxerre did he set foot in Canterbury. On the monks of Christ Church the King meanwhile visited his wrath and displeasure. Except for the sick who could not be moved, they were forced into exile, taking refuge at St. Bertin until Langton managed to secure their distribution among other houses.

The hostility which the King evoked from contemporary chroniclers makes an objective judgement of this papal–monarchical conflict difficult. In nominating Stephen Langton without John's consent, Innocent was unquestionably guilty of a grave breach of custom. It was not the first time the Pope had dealt with John in this somewhat high-handed way, for a Bishop of Seez and an Archbishop of Armagh had been foisted upon him against his will. H. G. Richardson and Sayles refer to Innocent's appointment as 'deliberately provocative and politically maladroit'.[36] John could legitimately claim that Stephen Langton was unknown to him personally, and that a fruitful relationship between Crown and Archbishop demanded a degree of initial confidence.

II

The heat and intransigence with which the various interests fought each other in these archiepiscopal elections show that the stakes were high. Corporate bodies felt that they had a sacred obligation to pass on rights inviolate to their successors, and that for this stewardship they would, on the dreadful Day of Judgement, be called to render up an account. Even an other-worldly philosopher like Anselm was at one with Hubert Walter in seeing things this way; indeed more so.

The history of the appointments from the Conquest to Langton illustrates the need for an established procedure, accepted by all parties concerned, and finally guaranteed by a legal authority which could enforce its will. It was precisely these which the papacy claimed to provide. Clarification of procedure was urgently needed in respect of elections by cathedral chapters. Here the papacy had for some years been trying to solve a problem not entirely unlike that confronting Cromwell when he endeavoured to combine the democratic ideal with the rule of the saints. Did capitular election mean one man one vote, or were some voters 'more equal than others'? The Lateran Council of 1179, in its canon *Quia propter*, laid down certain guiding principles, not in themselves, however, free from ambiguity.

In future, elections were to be determined by the 'major and sanior pars', which implied that votes were to be cast individually before being assessed in terms of zeal, merit, and number. Such a method still bristled with difficulties, and could only work if, as in the case of suffragans, the metropolitan exercised his authority to quash an election, or there was a final court of appeal at Rome. It was in the latter direction that the tide was flowing.

In the enforcement of the papal will the interdict, as the ultimate deterrent, was as difficult to implement then as United Nations sanctions are now. Indeed expedients to minimize its effect were part of the necessary armoury of a XIIIth-century monarch.

The nomination of an Archbishop of Canterbury, because of his unique historic status within the kingdom, presented, as we have seen, additional difficulties. Thus, when Innocent III in 1191, because of what had happened in the two previous elections, issued a papal letter which forbade the provincial bishops to violate the rights of the monks, it was clear that he did not intend an election independent of the Crown, any more than did the Pope's explicit ruling, as a result of Langton's appointment, that in future the bishops should claim no share in elections. It just was not practical politics. In fact only royal power enabled the monks successfully to resist external pressures. 'Whatever the rights of Canterbury,' Dom Knowles comments, 'they curtsied to great kings.'[37] They did so in self-defence, as a *sine qua non* of retaining their formal status as an electoral body. Even this retention, though strengthened by the growing authority of the papacy in guaranteeing canonical procedures, demanded, on occasions, both cunning and courage, together with a frank acceptance of their becoming more of a rubber stamp: yet a rubber stamp which needed to be affixed to the final documentation. And so it has remained to this day.

Equally Langton's nomination illustrates how difficult it was even for an institution such as the papacy, with responsibilities stretching from one end of western Europe to the other, to act contrary to the royal will. The alienation of a national monarch could have serious consequences. It was the King, or whoever exercised authority in his name, who throughout the Middle Ages, before it was written into the law of the land at the Reformation, largely controlled elections to the primatial see.

It remains to notice, briefly, how the system worked until the parliament of Henry VIII brought about a constitutional change.

The struggle accompanying Langton's appointment was never to be repeated on such a grand scale, but this is far from implying that appointments to Canterbury henceforward were to become free from controversy. Stephen Langton's successor, Richard Le Grant, Chancellor of Lincoln, was not the first choice, for the Chapter of Canterbury originally elected Walter, one of their number, and sent him to Rome for confirmation. The King, however, took serious umbrage, maintaining that Walter was unfit for his office. A committee of cardinals, according to Roger of Wendover, concurred in this view, and Gregory IX wrote to the suffragan bishops of the province declaring that, with the approval of a deputation of the Chapter then in Rome, and on the recommendation of Henry III, he had annulled the election of Walter and appointed Richard Le Grant. The King and the Pope had obviously made a deal.

By and large, this somewhat devious procedure continued to be the pattern, with the royal will more fiercely predominating. Conditions prevailing at any particular moment might tilt the balance one way or another, as when, before Edmund Rich's nomination in 1234, the Pope rejected three previous candidates who had come up to him through the King and the Chapter of Canterbury. To secure the appointment of Robert Kilwardby, Pope Gregory X, on his own authority, managed to persuade Adam de Chillenden, Prior of Christ Church and elected by the Chapter, to withdraw.

John Pecham, Franciscan, scholar, poet, owed his unexpected elevation entirely to a reforming Pope, Nicholas III, who passed over Edward I's nominee, Robert Burnell, Bishop of Bath and Wells. The circumstances were not dissimilar to Innocent III's appointment of Stephen Langton, but whereas King John resisted furiously, Edward accepted Pecham with a good grace.

Yet even such bald facts as these can be deceptive, since often a private understanding between King and Pope does not find its way into the official documentation. An interesting illustration of this occurred in the reign of Edward II when, some months before the death of Archbishop Winchelsey in 1313, Pope Clement V issued a bull reserving to himself the right of appointing his successor. The suspicion of the monks was immediately aroused, with the result that on the death of the Archbishop they elected Thomas Cobham,

Archdeacon of Lewes, previously Chancellor of Cambridge. The King then intervened, and petitioned the Pope, aided, probably, by a lavish gift of money, to appoint his old friend, Walter Reynolds, Bishop of Worcester, 'a mere creature of court favour'. The Pope obliged by issuing a bull quashing the monks' election and appointing Reynolds. The nomination, with its suggestion of simony, was roundly condemned by contemporary chroniclers.

This unsuccessful resort to hasty and independent action by the monks of Christ Church was not the last example of its kind; but it was increasingly countered by the Crown's insistence that there must be no election without prior royal permission granted through a *congé d'élire*. Yet as late as 1348, the monks on the death of Archbishop Stratford elected on their own initiative Thomas Bradwardine, one of the greatest scholars of the age, and the only Archbishop, apart from Thomas à Becket, to find a mention in the pages of Chaucer. In this, however, they had overplayed their hand, and Edward III, though intending this appointment, determined to rebuke such independence. He proceeded to set aside the election, and John Ufford, Dean of Lincoln, was nominated by a papal provision; but on the latter's death before his consecration, Bradwardine was elected a second time, and the King concurred.

Such tactics were not unique to the King. Simon Islip, duly chosen by Edward III and elected by the monks, was set aside by Clement VI, acting in his capacity as Supreme Ordinary. He then reappointed him.

The main drift now was towards less heat and the adoption of accepted, if not routine, procedures. This can be seen in the full documentation and smooth working of William Courtenay's election in 1381. Here the murder of Archbishop Sudbury, at the time of the Peasants' Revolt, meant that there was a need for haste. Within three days of the vacancy, the Chapter petitioned Richard II for permission to proceed to an election. A *congé d'élire* was issued on 12 July with an injunction that the monks should choose 'a devout man of God, necessary to your church, and loyal and useful to us and our realm'. Concurrently Richard almost certainly intimated that he would expect them to elect William Courtenay, Bishop of London. This they did, the Prior duly informing the King of their compliance on 31 July and craving his approval. On the same day, the Prior notified Courtenay of his election, asking him to accept the office. On 5 August, Richard gave his formal consent, and on the next day the Prior wrote to the Pope informing him of the election and seeking his confirmation. Urban, however, does not seem to have waited for any such capitular notice, since, in a letter from Rome dated 9 September, he asserted his exclusive right as Supreme Ordinary to fill all vacancies no matter how they occurred, and stated that he had 'provided' for the See of Canterbury during Sudbury's lifetime. Any nomination other than his own was, therefore, automatically null and void. Having thus safeguarded his position he then issued a bull under the same date—it did not reach Croydon until three months later—translating Courtenay from London to Canterbury. He followed this up with a mandate to the bishops of London and Rochester, instructing them to receive, on his behalf, Courtenay's oath of obedience, and to confirm in writing that this had been done. On 10 January, Courtenay took his oath of obedience before the Bishop of Rochester, and in the presence of the new Bishop of London on the following day. The bulls of translation were published in the Cathedral, and the primatial cross was formally presented to Courtenay on 12 January by one of his own monks.

It is perhaps worth noting that the King had not waited for the Pope to confirm the election before releasing the temporalities of the see. This he had done on 23 October of the previous year, Courtenay then having 'renounced voluntarily, openly, and expressly, all words therein . . . prejudicial to the king or his crown'.[38]

This detailed account is not without interest. It shows the monks proceeding regularly to a canonical election. It shows the elaborate papal machinery unwinding itself, the King having already, in respect of the temporalities of the see, either ignored it or anticipated that it would so unwind. It shows the Archbishop paying reverent respect to the papal office. It shows, in effect, two systems working together side by side, one centred on Rome, the other on Canterbury, each taking good care to conform to the royal will. Only by such conformity could this method of precedure hope to work.

# 2

## THE REGNUM

### I

The Norman Conquest coincided with a century of significant changes in the Church of Rome, all tending to make for a closer link with the ecclesiastical hierarchies in western Europe and a greater assertion of authority over them. Symptomatic of this new situation was the fact that nine out of fourteen Archbishops of Canterbury, during the years 925 to 1066, journeyed personally to Rome for their *pallia*; and, in 1051, for the first time, the Pope refused to accept a nominee of the Crown, the Abbot of Abingdon, for the vacant bishopric of London. Integral with this movement, and finding expression in the recall of the secular clergy to celibacy and the religious to fidelity, was the concern to convert the hierarchy of the *sacerdotium* into a coherent society under papal direction. This meant an attempt to withdraw the clerical order from the jurisdiction of the secular courts of the *regnum*; to prohibit laymen from presenting to ecclesiastical benefices; and to establish the Roman *Curia*, administering an articulated body of canon law, as an effective court of final appeal.

Such withdrawal was not easy, for the things of God and the things of Caesar are not tied up in clearly distinguishable packages: each contains articles which the other might well covet and claim for his own. No ecclesiastic wished to deny to the secular authorities their legitimate rights. The dispute arose as to what these rights were, since they were bound to vary according to time, place, and circumstance. The Church in England possessed its own individuality owing to the retention of many local customs going back to the tribal practices of the Teutonic invaders. This did not mean that the *Ecclesia Anglorum* wished to be eccentric or accepted papal authority only under protest. The Church in England lived its life within Catholic Christendom and was caught up in the dilemma which found its more than life-size expression in the struggles between Pope and Emperor.

A medieval Archbishop of Canterbury could not possibly see himself in practice as an exclusively ecclesiastical figure, even at a time of ideological 'withdrawal'. The traditions of his see did not make this a practical option. To take one instance, his right, and corresponding duty, to preside at coronations introduced a highly political dimension into his office, and brought it into the complex business of 'king-making', a dangerous responsibility before the principle of hereditary succession was either fully accepted or, if accepted, worked smoothly. Even when an Archbishop, as in the case of à Becket, saw his loyalty as primarily to the *sacerdotium*, he recognized that he held an office built into the structure of the secular world around him.

This was brought home to him by the fact that he was one of the most wealthy landowners in the kingdom, at a time when social obligation was integrated into the ownership of land. The see of Canterbury had inherited lavish endowments from the days of the Saxon Kings, and it was a constant preoccupation with succeeding archbishops to keep these estates from alienation or royal encroachment. Lanfranc went to great pains to recover them at the Conquest; carefully distinguishing between lands personal to the Archbishop and those owned by the monastery of Christ Church. Even the other-worldly Anselm struggled to preserve this inheritance intact, as did à Becket. Not least of the reasons why the Crown was so often tempted to prolong the vacancy of a see—Rufus kept Canterbury without an Archbishop for five years—was its retention of the temporalities. The Archbishop collected rents from six bailiwicks in Kent, Surrey, and Sussex, where, through his officials, he exercised the social and legal responsibilities attached to land tenure, including the holding of manorial courts. Mr. Du Boulay in his carefully documented *Lordship of Canterbury* has estimated that the Archbishop's demesnes, mostly of fertile arable land, brought in an annual revenue of £1,345 in 1200, £2,128 in 1245, and £3,178 by the time of the Reformation. This made him 'one of the richest men in the realm'.

Nor must it be forgotten that these lands extended over a coast-line vulnerable to attack from the Continent. Thus the Archbishop was responsible for the upkeep of a considerable number of fortresses and for raising a large contingent of troops. Sandwich, the main channel port, was one of his Christ Church manors.

Such a tremendous stake in feudal society, requiring him to provide the Crown with scutage and knight service, of necessity reacted upon the relations of Archbishop, King, and baronage. Even as late as 1601 it was the armed retainers of Archbishop Whitgift who captured the rebellious Earl of Essex.

The immediate result of the Norman Conquest was to increase the secular responsibilities of the Archbishop of Canterbury in national affairs, and to make his discharge of them both positive in character and far-reaching in its consequences. This was largely due to the uniquely co-operative relationship between William and Lanfranc; a relationship which enabled Lanfranc to make a contribution to the life of Church and nation comparable with that of Theodore and Dunstan. King and Archbishop may ultimately have lived in different worlds, yet in their instinct for law and order, and their practical concern to see these established in England, they were at one.

The Conqueror had been familiar on the Continent with a tradition of tight control exercised by the secular ruler over the Church. There was never any question of things being different in England. Lanfranc accepted this as 'a fact of life', which meant that to implement his policy of ecclesiastical reform he must work through the King, even if the King's attitude to reform was somewhat suspicious and a little old-fashioned. Sometimes, it is true, Lanfranc deplored the frustrations of his position, and left to himself would almost certainly have preferred life in a monastery. 'I know not by what judgement of God,' he protested to the Archbishop of Rouen in a letter quoted by A. J. Macdonald, his biographer, 'I undergo incessantly so many and so great difficulties in temporal affairs.' His own position midway between King and Pope was never easy, and demanded both tact and restraint. He wisely decided never to push his principles too far. Particularly was this the case when the Pope, in order to offset the anti-papalism of the Emperor Henry IV, endeavoured to wring from William an oath of fealty. 'Homage to thee I have not chosen, nor do I choose to do,' was the crushing reply. 'I never made a promise to that effect, nor do I find that it was ever performed by my predecessors to thine.'

On no occasion did Lanfranc dispute this independence, although he prudently wrote to the Pope: 'I advised him to comply with your wishes but I did not succeed.'[39] Equally, when Odo of Bayeux, the King's brother-in-law, was arrested on suspicion of rebellion and fell back on his clerical privilege, it was the Archbishop who put the words into William's mouth: 'I do not arrest the Bishop of Bayeux, but I do arrest the Earl of Kent. I arrest my Earl whom I appointed over my kingdom, and I demand of him an account of the office I entrusted to him.'[40] Lanfranc took the same line when William of Carilef, Bishop of Durham, was brought to trial at Salisbury in 1088 on a similar charge.

Lanfranc, however, was not insensitive to the contemporary mood for ecclesiastical reform. Thus he prompted the ordinance of the Conqueror which withdrew cases coming under episcopal laws, that is those involving morals, from the judgment of laymen in the hundred court, the implication being that these should go before the bishop and his synod. Perhaps Lanfranc's most important contribution to ecclesiastical government was his decreeing that bishops, who were required to have an archdeacon, should hold such an assembly in their dioceses twice a year.

So close were Lanfranc's relations with William that in effect he became the King's 'first minister', though he held no precise executive office. Thus at the time of the abortive rebellion of 1075, when William was in Normandy, the Archbishop bore the main burden of responsibility, and it was to him that the rebels, Roger and Walter, made their submission. Dr. Macdonald writes:

> His status as archbishop, his tried experience in secular affairs, gave him a position of general supervision over the administration whenever the king left England.[41]

England was indeed fortunate in that at a critical period in her national development after the Conquest, two such men as William and Lanfranc worked together for common ends.

The Conqueror died in Normandy, but the Archbishop was privy to his nomination of Rufus as his successor. Lanfranc knew Rufus too well to be happy with the choice, and was reported as having said some years earlier: 'So long as the king lives we shall enjoy peace, but after his death who knows what evils may overtake us?' Lanfranc realized, however, that neither of Rufus's brothers, Robert or Henry, was really feasible. Thus with his usual sense of what was expedient, he gave support to Rufus, but let his unease express itself at his coronation in the 'maimed rites' to which Matthew Paris refers, and also in the promise which he extracted from Rufus to follow the Archbishop's advice in everything—a solemn oath which, if taken, was honoured more in the breach than in the observance. Whatever his own private misgivings, Lanfranc stuck firmly to his life-long, regulative principle: that of absolute loyalty to the Crown. In accord with this, during the rebellion of 1088, he rallied support for the royal cause.

Lanfranc's successor, Anselm, was temperamentally very different from his predecessor. Perhaps this is illustrated in the contrast between his theological classic *Cur Deus Homo*, and Lanfranc's legacy of a series of commentaries on legal and pastoral problems. The latter could never have written:

> I would as soon be deprived of everything as of a little, and I say this not from a love of money but from love of the justice of God.

Anselm, in his handling of everyday affairs, sought to reduce their ambiguity to a clear, self-evident principle. Not only was he 'unpractised in the ways of the world; he dissociated himself from them on principle'.[42] Therefore, Pope Urban II's desire, by forbidding lay investiture, to withdraw the Church from its entanglement in the *regnum*, appealed to him as logically consistent. He became more papalist than the Pope, particularly when the Curia, for political reasons, resorted to the kind of compromise with principle that he despised.

Such an attitude to men and affairs was bound to make relations difficult between Anselm and Rufus, even though the Archbishop was by no means blind to the necessity of working in harmony with the King for the benefit of the nation. Indeed, nowhere was the need more clearly expressed than in one of his own letters to the Pope, even if most popes understood this necessity far better than he did.

> It cannot escape your prudence that we two can do nothing unless it has been suggested to the King, so that by his assent and aid our decrees can be put into effect.

On another occasion he urged the King that they

> try together, you with your royal power and I with my pontifical authority, to make some ordinance which may be published throughout the realm to the terror and discomfiture of wrong doers.[43]

Yet the framework within which Anselm wished to construct this alliance exposed the *modus vivendi* to severe strain; the temperament of Rufus made it nearly impossible. 'You are yoking an untamed bull and a weak old sheep to the same plough,' so Anselm had commented at the time of his appointment.

The controversies between Anselm and Rufus over the recognition of Pope Urban II, which Anselm won, and the royal demand for the confirmation of certain military tenures introduced on to the Canterbury estates, which Rufus won, are not so significant as the breakdown in Anselm's relations with William's successor, Henry I, a ruler of 'great political sagacity and formidable resolution'. This quarrel, which arose from Urban's declaring anathemas on those who either received investiture from laymen, or paid homage to them, was certainly not of the Archbishop's own choosing. Such a prohibition, if made effective, would have excluded the secular ruler from any 'claim on the services, and, ultimately, on the loyalty of the bishop'.

For some three years the papacy stuck to this extreme position, but under pressure from the lawyers in the papal Curia a distinction began to be drawn between lay investiture to ecclesiastical office and homage for temporal possessions. The King must renounce the former, but might keep the latter. Henry agreed to accept this compromise, which did little to shake his control of the Church, but Anselm found the abrogation of a clear principle a bitter pill to swallow. He needed all the Pope's assurance, together with grave counsel from Hugh of Lyons, to accept it.

Anselm's single-mindedness, however, did not necessarily prevent his being politically effective. When the King went north in 1095, Anselm organized the defences with energy and stuck to his post. Some years later, when Rufus was killed, Anselm helped to rally support to Henry, preferring, as R. W. Southern comments, 'an effective ruler, however unpleasant, to an ineffective one, however recommended by his personal qualities'.

Neither of Anselm's two immediate successors was a significant political figure. Ralph D'escures served as a member of Henry I's council and entered into a wrangle with him over the wearing of his crown before the coronation of Queen Adela. William de Corbeil somewhat weakly deserted the cause of Matilda to which he had pledged himself, and crowned Henry's nephew Stephen, of whom a contemporary author and wit, Walter Map, a collection of whose anecdotes and legends was edited in 1850, wrote that he was

> of outstanding skill in arms, but in other things almost an idiot, except that he was more inclined towards evil.

Archbishop Theobald suffered the frustration of being at Canterbury during the sixteen years of a reign brought to near anarchy by a violent dynastic struggle. Fortunately he proved himself a statesman of ability. His position became particularly difficult after Stephen's capture at the battle of Lincoln; and even more so when, in spite of being forbidden by the King to leave the realm, he attended a council at Rheims, enduring a journey across a choppy sea which Eugenius III, according to Gervase of Canterbury's *Actus Pontificum*, described as 'more of a swim than a sail'. Not surprisingly, his loyalty became for a time suspect.

The effect of the lawlessness during the nineteen years of Stephen's 'troubles' was to upset the balance of jurisdiction between the ecclesiastical and civil courts, largely to the King's detriment. The accession of Henry II, whom the Archbishop crowned in 1154, led to compromise and mutual concessions, the King surrendering jurisdiction over criminous clerks, the Archbishop supporting Henry's seizure from the Bishop of Salisbury of the castle of Devizes. It was Theobald's protégé, Thomas à Becket, Henry II's Chancellor, who, by no means always to the Archbishop's liking, supported the rights of the Crown against the claims of the Church.

Thomas à Becket's appointment to Canterbury in 1162, if it must be seen retrospectively as a gross miscalculation on the part of Henry, yet showed a commendable attempt to solve the contemporary problem of two jurisdictions. Perhaps the King was influenced by the Emperor Frederick Barbarossa who had made the Archbishop of Cologne his Chancellor. It could have worked, but for the uncompromising spirit of Thomas and the equal 'absolutism' of Henry. Both were great men in whom two different ideologies came to grips and neither would give way. Gilbert Foliot, known to have opposed à Becket's nomination, summed up the situation as he saw it:

> If the king should wield the temporal sword as Becket had wielded the spiritual sword, there was no prospect of peace, no hope of compromise. [44]

The drama associated with the name of the blessed martyr must not lead us to exaggerate the difficulties resulting from secular and ecclesiastical courts working side by side. The ordinary practitioner approached matters of legal procedure without strong theological prejudice. Like his kind the world over, he tended to go to the court where he felt himself most likely to win; perhaps with a slight inbuilt preference for royal justice since, as Ranulf de Glanville, Chief Justiciar, boasted: '. . . we decide cases much more quickly than your bishops do in the Church courts'. [45] Often the King's and the bishops' courts worked together; and if the King was himself present, even the personnel might be fused. While rival theoreticians argued, practical men went on doing justice and administering the country.

The King, however, was quite unprepared for Thomas's change of front after his nomination to Canterbury, though he must have had forebodings when Thomas resigned his office of Chancellor. A head-on collision seemed inevitable, for behind the disputes about criminous clerks lay a clash between different attitudes to *sacerdotium* and *regnum*. It was Henry who in many respects was the immediate innovator in that he was concerned to reinstate the older tradition of William and Henry I by recovering lost royal rights over the Church. His misfortune was to do so against the prevailing climate.

It is within this context that the Constitutions of Clarendon, agreed with the King by the bishops in January 1164, must be interpreted. Of these, two were especially controversial: first, that clerks, once convicted and degraded by an ecclesiastical court should be handed over to the secular authority for punishment—hence à Becket's complaint that God does not punish twice for the same offence; secondly, that certain types of ecclesiastical causes should not go beyond the Archbishop's Court without the King's consent, by which Henry probably wished to restrain appeals to Rome.

Thomas's attitude to the Constitutions seems at the time to have been ambiguous; a *quasi* acceptance with mental reservations, expressed, so Gilbert Foliot recorded, in the words: 'It is my lord's will [i.e. the Pope's] that I forswear myself; for the present I submit and incur perjury—to do penitence for it later as well as I can.' Henry, however, could not reasonably have expected Thomas to agree to them.

The meeting at Clarendon was followed, in October, by another in Northampton Castle. An exasperated Henry was now prepared to take extreme measures, even to threatening violence. An apprehensive Thomas, no longer able to rely on the support of his suffragans —they had never been entirely with him—fled to France, placing himself under the protection of Louis VII. The years of exile which followed saw, among other things, two abortive meetings between Archbishop and King in Normandy; the harrying of Thomas's relatives in England; a threatened excommunication of Henry by both Thomas and the Pope; the coronation of Prince Henry by Roger, Archbishop of York, assisted by the Bishops of London, Durham, Rochester, and Salisbury; and finally, on 22 July 1170, a meaningless 'reconciliation' which proved to be no reconciliation. It did lead, however, to the Archbishop's return to England, and his landing at Sandwich on 1 December. His ride through rural Kent was one long triumphal progress. Old men on their knees vied with children along the route to receive his blessing. Clergy came at the head of their parishioners bearing garlands and banners. Choirs chanted anthems. By the time à Becket reached Canterbury it was evening. He went straight into the cathedral where, to quote a contemporary, his face shone like the face of Moses as he descended from the mount. He seated himself on his throne and the monks came, one by one, to embrace him. Tears were in everyone's eyes. 'Lord,' whispered Herbert of Bosham (*fl.* 1162–1186), who has left an account of the progress, 'now we need not care at what hour you depart from this world, since today, in you, Christ's spouse the Church has won the victory.'

By the afternoon of 29 December, Thomas lay dead, murdered in his own cathedral, crying as he died: 'I commit myself and my cause to the Judge of all men. Your swords are less ready to strike than is my spirit for martyrdom.' It was Henry's final appeal to the arbitrament of violence.

For Henry, the consequences of this assassination were not so serious as might have been expected. At the enforced settlement in Avranches which followed some two years later, Henry swore 'to abolish all customs which had been introduced against the churches of the land during his reign'; and to permit free appeals to Rome in ecclesiastical causes. The important consideration, however, was not what Henry conceded in principle, but what effect this concession had in practice. Insofar as à Becket was concerned to maintain, and Henry to prevent, appeals to Rome, the martyred Archbishop of Canterbury might seem to have won the day. Such appeals continued, indeed they increased; but in practice this often meant little more than that the Pope appointed judge–delegates who sat in England, Henry himself sometimes sitting with them. And though it is true that the King had to give way on the issue of criminous clerks, his control over the Church was in effect never really shaken, as may be seen in that the first batch of bishops elected after the death of à Becket were all 'notable opponents of the martyr'. What perhaps did change was the royal technique of persuasion, which now became more subtle, more private.

The archiepiscopate of à Becket constitutes in many respects a thing apart. As Chancellor, this 'subtle deviser of the unaccustomed or concealed judgements' had shown great administrative skill combined with legal acumen, being the first minister of state who may claim to have had a foreign policy. Yet the violent change of front from the minister maintaining the King's jurisdiction to the Archbishop denying it, represents at its worst irresponsibility, at its best a lack of realism and political sense. As Primate of All England he completely lost the confidence of the King, and by so doing impaired the effectiveness of his office. One is reminded of the words allegedly spoken by Richard of Lucy, Chief Justiciar, to the monks of Canterbury at the time of à Becket's election:

> If king and archbishop are linked by affection and cherish one another in friendship, there is no doubt that the times will be happy and the existing gladness and tranquillity of the Church will continue. But if, God forbid, things should turn out otherwise, crises and confusions, troubles and tumults, damage to property and peril to souls will follow.[46]

Unfortunately no archiepiscopal registers exist until the time of Archbishop Pecham; but if they did, doubtless they would show that for long periods direction of diocesan and metropolitan affairs lay in the hands of others. Discipline as a consequence must have suffered, and the house of bishops become divided.

Yet having said this to à Becket's discredit there is a remainder, and it is a considerable one, even if it moves in the world of imponderables. Within a matter of years à Becket's banner was being held aloft before the walls of Acre; Henry was a penitent in Canterbury; pilgrims from all over western Europe, including Innocent III as a young man, were kneeling at his shrine. In that more rarefied world of human motivation à Becket counted; and dying for the claims of the *sacerdotium* as he understood them, he witnessed to another dimension of human experience, and kept alive an ideal of a Christian society. Archbishop Warham, in the grim months which preceded his death in 1532, fortified his spirit with thoughts of the blessed martyr. Thomas More did not disdain to recall him as he stood firm against royal tyranny. T. S. Eliot entertained an instinctive feeling for his significance. It is tempting to indulge the fancy that though à Becket clouded an important constitutional issue with dramatic gestures, he was yet groping after a truth which society ignores at its peril, the dangers inherent in the omni-competent sovereign state, subject to no sanctions but its own will. But this would be to lift him out of his century.

Neither of à Becket's two successors—Richard and Baldwin—involved themselves overmuch in secular business or dramatically withdrew from it. Both of them, maybe, were overpowered by the unique prestige of an experienced monarch whose realms stretched from the Solway Firth to the Pyrenees; and, in a different way, by the knight-errantry and crusading zeal of his son and successor Richard Cœur de Lion. Archbishop Richard deserves mention for his promotion of the study of canon law, and for his deliberate refusal to follow in the footsteps of à Becket, so much so that Pope Alexander complained of his allowing elections to take place in the royal chapel, and of his advocating that murderers of clerks should be handed over to the secular courts for punishment. Let no one, protested Richard, talk of double punishment—a favourite cliché of à Becket's in relation to criminous clerks—when what was begun in one court was completed in another. The two swords of the *regnum* and the *sacerdotium* needed each other's strength.

II

With Hubert Walter (1193–1205), whom Stubbs decribes as chosen simply for secular reasons, a new phase begins in the involvement of an Archbishop of Canterbury with the politics of the nation. There was a special reason for this: the King's household, like that of the Archbishop, was differentiating itself into separate departments. Government was now growing more complicated, and needed a technical personnel. The Church could provide specialists of the kind

64

needed, because the development of canon law, with the elaboration of ecclesiastical courts, added to the number of trained clerical staff who were professional in their outlook. Secular government itself, undertaking weightier responsibilities, not unnaturally devoured them. The Archbishop's court fostered a nursery in which promising young men were equipped to hold high office in Church and State. For many such the surest way to the lucrative benefice was a legal training and service in the Archbishop's or King's court. The international contacts into which high-ranking churchmen necessarily entered made them fitted for deployment in the diplomatic field. At a time when emoluments were not affixed to offices as such, an ecclesiastical benefice provided an income; someone else could discharge its duties for a consideration.

In this general process, the Archbishop himself tended to become a new kind of person. Hitherto such administrative experience as he acquired had been gained as prior or abbot in a monastery; or in the legal schools of a foreign university. Now they were men who had been attached to the King's or the Archbishop's *curia*, and had held some form of secular office. This increasing ecclesiastical participation in secular business was not officially welcomed by those still wedded to the spirit of reform initiated by Gregory VII, formerly known as Hildebrand. The third Lateran Council of 1179 forbade clerks to act as barristers before secular courts, or to hold an office such as that of a steward or judge if preferred to it by a lay ruler. Such a prohibition was intended to prevent ecclesiastical persons becoming answerable to lay courts; but it was too late in the day to stem the tide. Churchmen were essential to the discharge of government; and could not be arbitrarily removed from it. Nor were its leaders prepared to pay the price of 'withdrawal' by surrendering extensive lands in the ownership of the Church. When withdrawal finally came, it was an enforced one because secular government had now come of age.

Hubert Walter held the office of Justiciar for three years under Richard, and the Chancellorship under John, in which capacity he acted as secretary to the King and controlled a large clerical staff. He began the practice of keeping copies of charters, so that the registers of the French royal chancery of the same period seem in comparison rudimentary, and even the papal registers incomplete. Hubert may properly claim to have played a part in the steady development which led to the creation of the justices of the peace. As with Lanfranc, his loyalty to the Crown was near absolute. When Prince John acted against his brother, the King, the Archbishop helped to frustrate him. Equally, on the death of Richard, it was Hubert's decisiveness, in co-operation with the Earl Marshal, which placed

John on the throne. At John's coronation, if Roger Wendover is to be trusted, the Archbishop enunciated the elective character of the English monarchy:

> Hear all of you and let it be known that no-one has an antecedent right to succeed another in the kingdom unless he has been unanimously elected under the guidance of the Holy Spirit, preferred for the superior merits of his character after the example and likeness of Saul:

words which he uttered lest the new monarch might 'some day bring the kingdom and crown of England to ruin and confusion.'[47]

So extensive was Hubert's preoccupation with secular affairs that his biographer, C. R. Cheney, has estimated that some two-thirds of his time was spent on the King's business. A contemporary, Gervase, summarized his achievements:

> England by the grace of God enjoyed peace and quiet under the rule of the Archbishop Hubert of Canterbury and Geoffrey Fitzpeter.[48]

Perhaps the greatest tribute to the extent of his secular concerns was the relief with which John heard of his death: 'Now at last I am King of England,' he cried.

Hubert Walter could hardly be unaware of the ambiguity of his position, though this seems to have left him undisturbed. As Justiciar, it was impossible for him to conform to all the requirements of the canon law. For example, clerics were forbidden to involve themselves in bloodshed, yet he was responsible for the execution of William Fitzosbert, after the latter had been burned out of the church of St. Mary le Bow. The third Lateran Council prohibited tournaments—Richard's favourite sport—yet the Archbishop, as Justiciar, was required to provide the knights and clerks to control them.

It is not surprising, therefore, that Hubert Walter came in for a great deal of criticism from traditional ecclesiastics who still breathed the rarer atmosphere of an earlier age. Undoubtedly the Archbishop liked power, not to mention money, and accepted the conflicts of loyalty which their possession imposed upon him. The monks of Christ Church were said to have complained of him to the Pope, who in his turn admonished the King 'that for his soul's sake he should no longer permit the archbishop to engage in secular administration'. Not surprisingly the saintly Hugh, Bishop of Lincoln, gave similar counsel. Gerald of Wales was even more severe, denouncing Hubert

Walter to the papal Curia for the 'ingrained habits' of his secular upbringing in the exchequer:

> ... this was the academy, this the school, in which he has already grown old, from which he was soon summoned to all the grades of his dignities. . . . To this day he has not known how to avoid secular cares and courts. Like a fish out of water, he cannot live without the court and secular care.[49]

If Hubert Walter illustrates the ambiguities inherent in an ecclesiastic exercising political power, so does the career of his great successor, Stephen Langton. Whereas, however, the former chose such an involvement, the latter had the burden thrust upon him.

Langton's primary concern throughout life centred on the welfare of the Church. At times he was drawn to the religious life, and he entertained a deep veneration for papal authority. Yet, as an Englishman, he wished to see justice established between the baronage and the King. Here he started, as we have seen, on a bad footing, since John vehemently resisted his appointment. This was unfortunate, for Langton well knew that as Archbishop he was brought into a unique relationship with his monarch.

The part which Langton played in the events leading up to the sealing of Magna Carta on 15 June 1215 has received a variety of interpretations, as has the character of the famous document itself, whether it was a selfish attempt to preserve feudal rights or a milestone along the extended path leading to freedom under the law. In estimating Langton's precise role, it is wiser to go to the extant documents than to the chroniclers, even if this means jettisoning the well-known story of the Archbishop producing a charter of Henry I to the assembled barons at St. Paul's on 25 August 1213. Certainly he had 'the intellectual equipment to influence the course of events in 1215 and . . . shared in the ideas from which the Great Charter drew its strength'. Professor J. C. Holt writes, with restraint:

> Even if the more dramatic features of the St. Alban's tradition are left on the shelf, there is still a great deal to substantiate his influence. First, it is certain that his absolution of King John in 1213 was associated with some formal promise of reform by the king; whether this was at Langton's instigation is less clear. Secondly, it is very likely that he intervened to prevent John taking armed action against the northerners in the autumn of 1213. . . . Thirdly, it is certain that from the autumn of 1213 onwards Langton was the chief mediator between the King and his opponents. He was present at all discussions. He was named

as go-between in most of the letters of safe conduct covering the negotiations. He was present at Runnymede, where he acted as a mediator and an arbitrator, and he continued in this role until he left the country in the autumn. All this is beyond serious question and was never in doubt at the time.[50]

The task of the mediator, however, is never easy, and Langton often became suspect on all sides. To the King, whom, with his army at Nottingham, he threatened with excommunication, he became that 'notorious and barefaced traitor'. To Innocent III, against the activities of whose legates he protested, he seemed a fitful, even disingenuous, ally. To the barons who had wrung the Magna Carta from John, he sometimes appeared as too much on the royal side. When they later came to see its terms as a strait-jacket, it was Langton who stuck to its main principles as a protection of rights and a safeguard of justice. Indeed, he later supported the Justiciar, Hubert de Burgh, against the rebellious barons who threatened to usurp the royal authority. Almost his last public action was to secure from Henry III, in 1225, a confirmation of the famous charter.

Langton's influence upon secular affairs was considerable, and continued so during the last few years of his life, when his enemies accused him—Henry III was then a minor—of being the real ruler of the land which he was bringing to ruin. The Archbishop in fact gathered around him men of great administrative experience, many of whom had been trained in the royal household or exchequer, and fired them with his own ideal of a just *regnum*.

The critical reign of John, which was followed by the tender years of Henry III, provided the opportunity for an exceptional man, through his archiepiscopal office, to give leadership. The involvement of his immediate successors was less positive.

Richard Le Grant opposed both the King and his Justiciar over the wardship of the town and castle of Tonbridge. The relations of Archbishop Edmund Rich with Henry III were never easy. On one occasion, in company with a number of barons, he appeared at Court and threatened the King with excommunication unless he dismissed the many foreigners who surrounded him. He also opposed the marriage of Eleanor, the Queen's sister, with Simon de Montfort.

Edmund's successor, Boniface of Savoy (1245–1270), a connexion of the King's, was essentially a secular figure, and was indeed detained for some years with his military duties on the Continent before coming over to England in 1249 for his enthronement at Canterbury. His secularity, however, was different from that of Hubert Walter, and was dictated by family ties which led to his associating himself with the rebellious barons in 1258, and to his membership of the council of twenty-four to whom the government of the country was entrusted. Such political activity did not derive from his archiepiscopal status, though the prestige of his office added to his influence. Essentially his interests lay with the baronage.

Very different in background were the two Archbishops who followed. Robert Kilwardby, a Black Friar, showed little interest in public affairs, though he is reputed to have excommunicated Llewellyn of Wales for refusing to pay homage to Edward I. John Pecham, a Franciscan, mediated in the same dispute, being motivated by a desire to bring the Welsh church into closer conformity with the Church in England.

Archbishop Winchelsey (1294–1313) became immersed in secular affairs, but in his case it was the interests of the *sacerdotium* rather than the *regnum* which constrained him. Thus he demurred at taking the oath of homage to Edward I for his temporalities, and complied only after protesting that he did so in the same sense as his predecessors either had, or ought to have, taken it. He also endeavoured to implement Boniface VIII's famous *Clericis laicos* (1296), by which the laity were forbidden to tax the clergy. This loyalty to the Pope, in a matter which so directly affected the Crown, prejudiced relations with the King. An open breach came when Winchelsey told a synod of bishops that they must make up their own minds whether they wished to comply with royal demands for a subsidy; for himself he preferred losing all his properties rather than obey. After a few months of estrangement there was a reconciliation, but some years later the King persuaded Clement V to suspend the Archbishop from his ecclesiastical and temporal functions, probably on suspicion of complicity in a revolt headed by the Earls of Hereford and Norfolk. The accession of the young and weak-minded Edward II changed the political scene, the effect being to increase the influence which Winchelsey was able to exert.

Walter Reynolds (1313–1327), who rose to favour through his services as Treasurer and Keeper of the Wardrobe to Edward II when Prince of Wales, was appointed Chancellor, an office which he resigned in order to accompany the King on the disastrous campaign which ended in defeat at Bannockburn. It is significant of the position which the Archbishop held—a feudal magnate in his own right as well as a royal adviser—that he was called in to mediate between Edward and his barons.

III

John Stratford (1333–1348), whose early legal experience fitted him admirably for administrative responsibility, typifies the new kind of Archbishop, for whom service to the Crown constituted a major responsibility. Adventures in France were expensive, and government was growing more costly. With a large amount of the nation's wealth in ecclesiastical hands, the implication was obvious: the clergy must be increasingly taxed; but this could only be effected legally through their own representative assembly, Convocation. The King, therefore, expected the Archbishops, and in particular the Primate of the more wealthy southern province, to persuade the clergy into a liberal compliance. In the nature of the case this was not easy, for no one likes to be mulcted. It was often made more difficult in that to grant taxes for the war with France was one thing; to vote them for swelling the pockets of corrupt officials and royal favourites another. For the Archbishop to help fill the royal treasury had precedents going back a long way. In 1266, when Henry III urgently needed money for an expedition to France, Langton had called a provincial assembly for the purpose of taxing clerical benefices. At the same time he wrote to the dioceses, suggesting a contribution of a twelfth or a fourteenth, enclosing a bull from the Pope and a royal letter. For such a purpose, however, no Archbishop could be useful to the Crown unless he enjoyed the respect of his fellow bishops. He needed

> the personality and ability to control the Church in the Crown's interests, to see that the English clergy did not get too far out of line with royal policy, and above all to see that the clergy bore a share of the heavy taxation that the French war made necessary. A royal puppet in the chair of St. Augustine would have received short shrift from a bench of bishops that was far from being composed of time servers.[51]

For this reason an Archbishop such as Walter Reynolds could not hope effectively to serve the Crown's interests. John Stratford was different. After leaving Oxford, where he studied civil law, he undertook a long and varied apprenticeship in government work. He early became an adviser to the council; was summoned to Parliament; appointed an officer in the Exchequer, a clerk in Chancery and chief judge of the Ecclesiastical Court of Arches. For a time he was ambassador at the papal court in Avignon, and is said to have crossed the channel thirty-two times in the public service. Edward III made Stratford his Chancellor, an office which, though he resigned it on going to Canterbury, he yet held again for some two years, and for a short time to April 1340. Indeed, so busy was he that not until the closing years of his life did diocesan affairs effectively engage his attention. Finally, an embittered Edward III turned against the Archbishop, and in the *Libellus Famosus* accused him of fraud. Only after a dramatic scene in Parliament did a formal reconciliation take place.

Stratford typified the 'breed' of archbishops who followed him. With few exceptions up to the time of the Reformation, they 'came up' through legal and administrative office exercised in the service of Church and Crown. Out of fourteen occupants of the primatial see, ten—either before or after their enthronement—were Chancellors of England; seven were either Vicars-General, deans of, or practitioners in, the Court of Arches; two were Treasurers.

Simon Sudbury (1375–1381), who was far more independent in outlook than the contemporary chronicler, Thomas Walsingham, will allow, had the misfortune of being at Canterbury when Edward III, at the end of his reign, was incapable of discharging the duties of government, and when Richard II, his successor, was in his minority. On his way up, Sudbury had served the Roman Curia as an auditor of causes, and was rewarded with a papal provision, over the head of the royal nominee, to the bishopric of London. In all, Sudbury spent some sixteen years on the Continent serving on various diplomatic missions, the Pope on one occasion using him to persuade the King of England to enter into peace negotiations with France. The age was that of John of Gaunt, Duke of Lancaster; of increasing anti-clericalism; and the explosion of the Peasants' Revolt. Sudbury's policy, designed to foster co-operation between Church and State, followed closely that of his three predecessors. As Bishop of London, he worked hard, after some initial difficulty, as a member of the council, and was ready to act as the King's agent for the purpose of taxing the clergy. Sudbury regarded Convocation primarily as an instrument which enabled the clergy to satisfy royal demands for money, and himself as the Crown's servant as much as the clergy's leader. Thus he would argue the King's case: divide the opposition, cajole—even browbeat—the clergy into making an adequate grant with the minimum of conditions attached. Often he had to contend with Courtenay, Bishop of London, who saw it as his duty to rally the clergy to defend the rights of their order, a matter on which they were indeed sensitive. Yet Sudbury did not lose the respect of his suffragans by his firm handling of Convocation, and it must, in fairness, be added that he was convinced of the genuine need to support the Crown. In 1379, when the Commons demanded a radical recon-struction of the administration, Sudbury offered himself as Chan-cellor—and was accepted. What he would have made of this important office at such a critical period can only be a matter of conjecture, for after holding it for some eighteen months he was

71

barbarously beheaded on Tower Hill during the Peasants' Revolt of 1381.

Sudbury as Archbishop has been consistently underrated. An unsolicited testimonial, at least to his kindness, remains in the margin of one of his registers, where an official has testified that he was 'magnanimous and does not make himself very difficult'.[52] Under his archiepiscopate the wheel had turned almost full circle since the days of à Becket, for Sudbury steadfastly refused to be embarrassed by the bogy of 'anti-clericalism'.

Much, however, still depended on the character and background of each man called to the office of Archbishop. Thus the basic approach of Courtenay was in some ways different from that of his predecessor, Sudbury. That he came from an ancient Devon family which could trace its descent back to Edward I doubtless gave him greater independence than one whose apprenticeship had been served in the Curia of King, Archbishop, or Pope.

When Courtenay came to Canterbury, the Church was clearly on the defensive against the emergent secularism. Even in his more optimistic moments, the new Archbishop could not expect to redress this balance. On the death of Sudbury he took over the office of Chancellor, but resigned it after two months, probably under pressure from John of Gaunt. Henceforward his chief association with the Crown came through his presiding over Convocation, which at the time contributed as much as Parliament to the national exchequer. This meant that the Archbishop shared with the Treasurer and Chancellor in the task of keeping the government solvent. Courtenay accepted his responsibility, but determined, so far as he could, to be more of a churchman than a Crown agent. His policy was to co-operate with the government only so far as was consistent with his ecclesiastical loyalties. Hence he refused to press royal demands if he considered them unwarrantable; nor would he permit Crown or Parliament to whittle away the few privileges which Convocation still retained in the matter of debating royal subsidies. His efforts slowed down perceptibly, but did not prevent, the drift towards a state-controlled Church. In pursuing this policy, Courtenay showed courage, thereby providing Convocation with the leadership necessary 'to avert the worst dangers threatening the Church'.[53]

The first clash over the rights of Convocation came in 1384 when, in granting a subsidy, Parliament made it contingent on the Church responding in similar fashion. Courtenay protested 'that he would never again discuss with his clergy the grant of any subsidy to the King or summon Convocation for that purpose, until [the] said condition be rejected and deleted'.[54] The immediate effect of this forthright protest was to provoke enraged demands in Parliament for the expropriation of Church properties. The King, who wisely preferred to deal with two institutions rather than one, withdrew his demand; only, however, to come back for a subsidy a month later on the pretext of an imminent French invasion. Once again Courtenay sent Richard II a vigorous and reasoned letter of complaint, as he did also to the Chancellor and Treasurer. But power was on the King's side, and he finally triumphed. It was not the last attack which the Crown was to make on the customs and rights of Convocation.

Towards Richard II, on occasions, Courtenay showed real firmness. In March 1385, after an attempt on Gaunt's life 'master William Courtenay Archbishop of Canterbury, rebuked the King for his insolent life and evil governance in the realm'—a rebuke which later led to an incident when the royal and archiepiscopal barges passed each other on the Thames, and Richard 'would have run the Archbishop through had not the Earl of Buckingham, John Devereux, and Thomas Trivet stoutly resisted him'.[55] Reconciliation soon followed, Courtenay begging pardon, to the grief of the chronicler who contrasted this seeming capitulation, strategic though it certainly was, with 'the strong constancy and strength of mind [in the] holy martyr Thomas'. Such a reconciliation, however, did not place Courtenay's relations with the Crown on a permanently easy footing. When, for example, in October 1386, a commission consisting of fourteen lords was set up to superintend affairs of state, particularly the King's household, Courtenay headed the list of its members, but protested that 'it was not proper for him to take an oath to anyone beneath the dignity of the Pope'. When the growing irritation with papal provisions was met, in 1390, by strong legislation against them, Courtenay and Arundel ordered their protest to be recorded in the rolls of Parliament. Yet the Archbishop did not push his opposition too far; and on the passing of a second Statute of Praemunire in 1393, he argued that though the Church did not question the Pope's right to translate and excommunicate, the proposed Bill would only prevent an improper use of these powers. The clergy would therefore support the King in any matter where the rights of the Crown were concerned. Such restraint shows that though his ecclesiastical policy in relation to the King was based on a clear principle, he did not press it to the point of making life unnecessarily difficult. Over large areas, Church and State, Archbishop and King, worked together as a matter of routine, not least in respect of heretics, against whom they were equally zealous, as were aristocracy and hierarchy. During the late XIVth century a *modus vivendi* between the *sacerdotium* and *regnum* could still be established, in spite of increasing royal and papal pressure, without resort to a radical solution.

A recent biographer of Courtenay writes that

two weeks after the arrival of the *pallium*, Courtenay set out upon what was to prove his greatest work—the condemnation of Lollard doctrines and suppression of Wycliffism at Oxford.[56]

In this, though he did so with tact and forbearance, he acted with more determination than did Sudbury.

Wycliffe—it was the time of the Great Schism—attacked papal abuses; condemned the monks for their 'red and fat cheeks and great bellies'; protested fiercely against pluralism and non-residence; and questioned transubstantiation. Courtenay believed that the whole basis of Catholic order was being undermined, and summoned a council to meet at Blackfriars in May 1382. Undeterred by an earth-quake, he secured the condemnation of ten heretical propositions, and the declaration that some fourteen others were 'erroneous'. He followed this up by purging Oxford of Lollardry, but so skilfully 'as to permit the Wycliffites to continue at Oxford but in the orthodox fold'.[57]

Apart from his personal gifts, only someone holding the office of Archbishop of Canterbury could hope to act so decisively. 'The morning star of the Reformation,' however, had risen and did not set with John Wycliffe's death in 1384. 'We have scotch'd the snake, not killed it.'

Courtenay's successor, Thomas Arundel, a Fitzalan and related to the royal house, shows again how much depended, even against a background of commonly accepted ideas, on the particular Arch-bishop concerned. The politics of the day were intricate, charged with intense personal emotion, and often remote from high principle. Arundel's involvement in them was less dictated by the needs of the Church than by the political ambitions of his own family whose fortunes he inevitably shared. Thus when Thomas's brother was executed by Richard II for high treason, he himself was impeached on the grounds that, while holding the chancellorship some eleven years previously, he had, through the setting up of a council of reg-ency, conspired in restricting the royal authority. It was a specious charge, but the Archbishop's property was confiscated and he him-self exiled. Roger Walden, Dean of York, replaced him at Canter-bury, Richard II regularizing this uncanonical procedure with a papal bull, and attending his enthronement on 3 February 1398. The King, however, had overplayed his hand, and the final tragedy of his life began to engulf him. The deposed Archbishop, whose own plight was desperate, decided to stake everything on the military fortunes of his nephew Thomas, Earl of Arundel, and Henry of Lancaster. He was not disappointed; their triumph made his restoration automatic.

Walden was deprived, though later created Bishop of London. Thomas was present in Westminster Hall on the dramatic occasion when a near-paranoic Richard declared himself unfit to reign and was made to read a proclamation announcing his abdication. It fell to the Archbishop to escort Henry to the vacant throne, and to preach a sermon on the text *Vir dominabitur in populo*. On 13 October 1399, he officiated at the coronation in Westminster Abbey.

Yet it must not be thought that family considerations made Thomas Arundel simply a tool of the secular authorities. In 1405 he vigorously supported the rights of the Church when, to supply the urgent necessities of Henry IV, Parliament proposed to raid the revenues of the clergy. In all, Arundel held the office of Chancellor five times.

Succeeding archbishops, until the Reformation, men such as Chichele, Stafford, Morton, and Warham, typify the professional. They were trained in the Court of Arches; used on diplomatic missions abroad; held office under the Crown, and were invaluable for the purposes of government. Henry V used the drafting skill of Chichele, and employed him as principal negotiator in the diplomatic exchanges with France, in particular to mediate between the royal armies and the conquered inhabitants. Chichele was with Henry at the siege of Rouen and negotiated the conditions of surrender. In diplomacy, prestige mattered, and the Primate of All England served as a useful foil to the renowned Goutier, Archbishop of Rouen, who acted on behalf of the French. During Henry VI's minority Chichele resorted daily to the council, where he stood next to the blood royal. As Archbishop, he could be more objective than some of his contemporaries, particularly in relation to the dynastic struggles which were beginning to tear the kingdom apart; and he was called in to arbitrate between Humphrey, Duke of Gloucester, and the other magnates. Maybe his loans to the government— over £20,000 between the years 1434 to 1443—also increased his influence.

The political archbishop had now come to stay. John Stafford was a better statesman than ecclesiastic, while Kemp, gaining experience as Chichele's Vicar-General, spent long years, when Archbishop, as Chancellor, in which capacity he negotiated peace terms with France at Arras in 1435.

Thomas Bourchier (1454–1486), closely related as he was to both sides during the Wars of the Roses, did his best to mediate, but lacked the power to be effective. He held the Great Seal, but was forced to surrender it in October 1456. He presided at three Coronations: Edward IV in 1461, to whom he gave his blessing before the decisive battle of Barnet; Richard III in 1483; and Henry VII in

1485. The last act of the Archbishop's long life was to officiate at the wedding of Henry Lancaster and Elizabeth of York, which, in uniting the white and red roses, brought peace to a divided country. Bourchier was made a Cardinal by Pope Paul II in 1467 at the request of Edward IV, but is remembered unfairly by many because of his enforced abandonment of the Princes, later murdered in the Tower. Perhaps, however, Canterbury recalls him for his entertainment of Peter II, allegedly Patriarch of Antioch, when two camels and four dromedaries paraded the streets of the city.

A patron of the arts and devoted to music, his was an eventful life lived in days of duplicity and faction, when it was not easy to steer a consistent course.

Archbishop Morton came up the hard way. Earlier in life he had risked everything in support of the Lancastrians, and suffered as a consequence. Attainted and forced to sue for pardon on the death of Henry VI and the accession of Edward IV, he was later arrested and sent to Brecknock Castle in Wales. His subsequent role was not unlike that of Thomas Arundel. With skill and subtlety he introduced himself into the counsels of Henry of Lancaster, and helped him to secure the throne. His nomination to Canterbury by Henry VII on the death of Cardinal Bourchier was a well earned recognition of services rendered.

It was more than this, however, for his financial ability induced the parsimonious Henry to appoint him Chancellor. Thus was born 'Morton's Fork'. The Archbishop used to say,

> If the persons applied to for benevolence live frugally, tell them that their parsimony must have enriched them, and that the King will therefore expect from them a liberal donation; if their method of living on the contrary be extravagant, tell them that they can afford to give largely, since the proof of their opulence is evident from their expenditure.[58]

Doubtless this stratagem constituted a technique which that shrewd Welshman, first of the Tudors, desperately in need of money for the wider purposes of government, approved.

Warham was nurtured in the same stable, but the attack on his office from Wolsey, and the approach of the Reformation, changed the whole environment within which the Primate of All England was to operate. The story of this *bouleversement* must be left to a later chapter.

# THE ARCHBISHOP'S HOUSEHOLD

The Archbishop of Canterbury was not, and never had been, a solitary figure. He lived with and among his *familia* and it was from this domestic circle that a more definite and elaborate structure of ecclesiastical administration grew. Though an Archbishop, in view of his episcopal office, exercised specialized functions, yet in many respects his household, of necessity, had much in common with other comparable establishments. Professor Southern writes of the Archbishop that his revenue, £1,500 per annum, was 'sufficient to put him in the very highest class of barons and to make him the head of a very large-scale business enterprise. This enterprise could not be carried on without a large staff.'[59] The personnel of the *familia* was both lay and clerical, though in the ecclesiastical climate of England immediately after the Norman Conquest references to the lay side are meagre.

The composite duties of the household consisted of performing the daily liturgical round; providing for the mechanics of the Archbishop's day-to-day existence; and engaging in ecclesiastical business whether diocesan, provincial or papal. There was also the burden of secular office which, increasingly, archbishops undertook, though here they would expect to use the clerks of the King's *Curia*, doubtless with some doubling up since convenience often determined procedures.

As to the performance of the liturgical round, this was the responsibility of the 'religious' in the Archbishop's household, and this in itself tended to preserve a monastic 'feel'. Occasionally popes reminded archbishops of the rock whence their predecessors had been hewn. Pope Alexander III, in 1174, told Archbishop Richard that since he was a professed, he ought to keep some monks about him and to choose one of their number to have charge of his seal. The practical exigencies of the time, however, moved steadily in another direction, and by the XIIIth century the household was becoming more secular, though traces of the monastic past lingered till late in the Middle Ages. More and more, clerks replaced monks in 'literate' posts, while at the same time the number of secular employees grew.

As to the day-to-day running of the household which bore so

closely on his general comfort, Lanfranc, the first Archbishop after the Conquest, benefited from the wise oversight of Baldwin, a remarkable man who after a distinguished lay career ended up as head of the monastery at Bec. Baldwin's function as *provisor et dispensator*, or to quote Dr. Southern's description, *factotum*, was to attend to almost everything. Under him worked Ranulf, who occupied himself with outside business. But differentiation was inevitable and the domestic side came to be in charge of the 'steward' or *dapifer*, under whose authority there functioned such officials as the butler, dispenser, chamberlain, seneschal, cook, usher, porter, and marshal, each with his own responsibility for the chamber, kitchen, stable, and particularly the hall, around which the life of a medieval household revolved. Domesday suggests that the more senior among these were tenants of the Archbishop, maybe given lands in return for their service. As men of some social standing, they soon ceased to carry out their functions in person, and only on high ceremonial occasions was their presence expected. Obviously a distinction would be drawn between, for example, the Earl of Gloucester, who became the Archbishop's hereditary butler and so acted at his enthronement banquet, and the man in charge of the weekly consumption of drink. A hierarchy thus developed early. Of the more plebeian lay staff little is known, not even their names, unless as in the case of one Adam, who worked under Baldwin, they became the *locus* of some miraculous event.

Archbishops from the Conquest till about 1200 lived on fixed revenues provided by local *firmarii*, and for their daily provisions relied upon managers on their estates, which they visited in turn; in other words they lived directly off their farms. Movement of the household from manor to manor over the rough medieval trackways, the Archbishop being jogged along on horseback, could hardly have been comfortable, and doubtless strained technical as well as physical resources. 'Pecham and Winchelsey were indefatigable travellers.'[60] Such accountancy as then existed was rudimentary.

From Archbishop Winchelsey's will it is evident that, on this side of the household, there developed three grades of officials consisting of: 'knightly figures' and 'literate laymen' who served as steward, 'our special valet', cook and marshal; the tailor, usher, a subordinate cook, and a clerical almoner; and the barber, scullion, janitor,[61] pantler, baker, and 'anonymous men of office'.

The goods and chattels of Archbishop Winchelsey's household, valued at £1,000, were listed as belonging to various departments, including the wardrobe, chapel, kitchen, chamber, almonry (housed in a separate building in Maidstone), buttery, pantry, stables, armoury, and hall. An inventory drawn up after the death of

Archbishop Stratford thirty-five years later shows that some of these departments had become amalgamated.

Equally interesting are the details which have come down to us concerning the contents of Archbishop Reynolds's chapel, which were packed into nine chests marked A to J (omitting I). This 'reservoir of liquid wealth' brought with it 'the double character of financial security and aesthetic treasure'.[62] The first three contained vestments, of which the most valuable, a white set, was estimated to be worth £26 13s. 4d., and a jewelled mitre, £10. Chest D contained fourteen books, including a three-volume Bible worth £8, as well as chronicles, a book on geometry, an ordinal, a life of Thomas the Martyr (very necessary), and a painted roll of Genesis. The next four chests housed the 'muniments, rolls, bulls and charters of the archiepiscopal liberties'. The remaining one contained ornamental knives, a pastoral staff of little or no value, and a quaternion of sermons.

Some three fragments of rolls survive to give a picture of spending in the archiepiscopal household at this time. The first shows that under Archbishop Stratford, annual revenue from lands was somewhere around the figure of £2,500, and average weekly expenditure some £46—a vast sum and approximating to £2,392 per annum. The highest single item was £14 a week spent on the kitchen—and no wonder, for every manor house had its own separate building. For a great personage constantly on the move, the kitchen alone needed one cart and up to six horses. Stabling, that is transport, including as it did the feeding of all horses, was a considerable drain on resources. In addition there was the buttery, dispensing ale and wine, which drew supplies from distant manors; the pantry, with its loaves and poultry; the hall, with its charcoal and candles; the wardrobe, spending up to £3,000 or £4,000 a year. Other miscellaneous items of expenditure, though small in themselves, give a fascinating glimpse of life at the time. There was a constant allocation of money to ecclesiastics travelling backwards and forwards to Rome, often carrying expensive presents for the Pope whom the Archbishop wished to conciliate. The boy bishop of St. Nicholas, Croydon, was granted two shillings; and a 'certain fool' half that sum.

To offer hospitality was one of the Archbishop's most onerous duties, and is reflected in an extant roll for the month of October 1459, which lists household consumption, department by department. The main accounts enumerate the supplies consumed under the headings of pantry, buttery, ale, wardrobe, kitchen, poultry, saucery, scullery, marshalcy, and oats. The scale and variety of provisions do not differ much from those of a century earlier, but a great deal more can be learned of the system of internal distribution. Every member of the household had one loaf a day, and special issues of bread were made

79

to the kitchen for breakfast and for charitable purposes. The buttery dispensed red wine for private consumption in addition to allocations for the Archbishop's chamber, the kitchen, and the senior members of the household. Large quantities of ale were drunk at breakfast and throughout the day in the kitchen and chamber, some being given as alms. Dinner and supper were served daily in the hall, at which there sat down the guests and members of the domestic household, the latter being divided into gentry and the 'others'. During the month to which the roll refers there was at dinner a daily average of twenty-two gentry and fifty-two 'others'; at supper sixteen gentry and forty-six 'others'. High ranking personages, amongst whom would be senior government officials, clerics in the Archbishop's service, as well as lords and knights (usually described as coming with two, three, or four attendants), were recorded on the roll by name. The daily average in hall was four important guests and eighteen less important, this figure being maintained on most days, even on Fridays and vigils when there was no supper.

On occasions the fare offered could be sumptuous. Thomas à Becket was said to have 'continued to serve rare and delicate dishes to his thronging guests and retainers', though he himself ate sparingly, and instead of minstrels for entertainment, provided readings from sacred books, as in a monastic refectory. Laymen sat at a separate table amusing themselves less solemnly, and being waited on by pages, since by ancient custom archbishops were allowed the service of the second sons of barons. The son of Henry II did not regard it as beneath his dignity to act in this capacity.

During the last half-century before the Reformation there seems to have been a change in the general accountancy of the household. The usual references to the 'treasurer of Canterbury' and the 'keeper of the wardrobe' disappear. The new system meant that money from the manors was paid over to the receivers, who then passed it on direct to the various officers of the household—the steward, the treasurer, the clerk of the kitchen, and (from the time of Archbishop Morton) to the Archbishop's cofferer. The tendency across the years was for long-established offices to decline in importance, and for new ones to take their places.

From his detailed researches, Dr. Du Boulay sums up the state of the household during this period:

> The general impression of the archbishop's household—and in default of continuous, detailed evidence, it can be no more than this—is of a body whose structure mirrored economic change and whose personnel reflected the archbishop's natural choice: monastic under Anselm, more clearly divided in the later

twelfth and thirteenth centuries into clerical and lay, but both halves becoming more professional as time went on, until in the fifteenth century the earlier pattern is reversed and the lay element became the socially dominant one, Lambeth a more natural focus than Canterbury, and influence in political or even polite society as a whole an apter qualification for the archbishop's household service than Kentish connexions or ecclesiastical interests. Perhaps, too, the household had become a less grave place by that afternoon in Arundel's pontificate when Margery Kempe and her husband went into the hall at Lambeth to find clerks 'and other reckless men, both squires and yeomen' cursing and swearing.[63]

One other aspect of the household remains to be noticed. Amongst its personnel must have been those who were agreeable either for the intellectual stimulus which they brought or for the companionship which they offered. At a time when universities were only in the process of developing, the household of the Archbishop became a centre for the cultivation of learning, exercising an influence upon society as a whole. For young men who entered it early and who were privileged to listen to the conversation in hall, the experience across the years must have constituted a liberal education, even if Anselm, who craved the excitement of minds as alert as his own, never succeeded in creating a body around him at Canterbury comparable with that which he had known at Bec. Anselm, unique amongst all Archbishops of Canterbury, gained, and has retained, an international reputation as a philosopher. His ontological argument for the existence of God has never proved popular with theologians, and was disowned by Aquinas; but its basic presupposition has proved germinal among subsequent philosophers who have developed and refined it. Descartes, Leibnitz, Hegel, and the English idealist Bradley bear testimony to its influence.

Archbishop Theobald brought together a group of brilliant men, mainly canonists, the nearest equivalent to a university that England then boasted. There were nurtured in his household four archbishops, six bishops, and many who held important posts in secular affairs. John of Salisbury (*ob.* 1180), the most distinguished scholar of his time, was one of them, being introduced to the Archbishop by St. Bernard of Clairvaux, and acting as archiepiscopal secretary till 1164. The library of Christ Church became stocked with legal texts. Thomas à Becket began his career as a member of this *familia* and was sent at the expense of the Archbishop to pursue his legal studies in Bologna and Auxerre. On his going to Canterbury he followed his master's example, and with such effect that Herbert of Bosham lists some twenty members belonging to his household of whom two became archbishops, five bishops, and another joined the Curia of Pope Urban II. The majority of these *alumni* were English by birth, though they included Lombards, one Welshman, and a Norman, Hugh of Nunant, subsequently Bishop of Coventry.

Hubert Walter continued the practice of gathering around him men distinguished in every branch of liberal studies, men such as Master Honorius, Thomas of Marlborough, Master Peter of Blois, and Mark Symon of Sywell.

This tradition of making Lambeth a centre of learning persisted. Morton's household put on for its Christmas dramatics *Fulgens and Lucrece*, perhaps the earliest secular play known in English. Warham, the last of the pre-Reformation archbishops, was himself devoted to scholarship, if not himself a scholar. His favourite relaxation was to sup with a group of intelligent guests, 'enjoying their wit and retorting with wit of his own'. Men of distinction were always given a welcome—sometimes there were as many as two hundred of them at a sitting—and his purse was open to their needs. It was at Lambeth that the Dutch humanist, Erasmus, whom the Archbishop was anxious to retain in England, first met the Oxford reformers More and Colet. 'From Warham none ever parted in sorrow,' was the Dutch scholar's graceful tribute. The ecclesiastical side of the Archbishop's household will be dealt with in a later chapter.

# 4

## CHRIST CHURCH AND ST. AUGUSTINE'S

I

Casual reference has already been made to the priory of Christ Church, and to the monastery of St. Augustine, both situated in the city of Canterbury. The relations of the Archbishop with these institutions consituted a preoccupation throughout a great deal of the Middle Ages, and give a vivid if somewhat unattractive picture of institutional religious life at the time. It must be remembered, of course, that, as now, the uneventful did not attract the attention of either chronicler or historian.

The community of Christ Church went back, as did its neighbouring monastery of St. Augustine, to the early days of the original Christian settlement. This antiquity gave tremendous prestige. Often Christ Church was called on to entertain important personages, including the King himself; while its position *en route* for the Continent gave it a strategic significance. Its role as an archiepiscopal electoral college, to maintain which, as we have seen, it fought with great tenacity, inevitably drew it into the vortex of national affairs. The community was in charge of liturgical arrangements at enthronements. The monastery supported Anselm in his struggles against both Rufus and Henry I and also championed the efforts of successive archbishops to wring an oath of obedience from the Metropolitan of York and the Abbot of the neighbouring community of St. Augustine's. There were special and self-regarding reasons why the monastery should thus support the Archbishop, their titular Abbot. Too often, however, relations were unfriendly and uncooperative.

For a description of the state of this community at the time of the Norman Conquest we are dependent on the memories of Eadmer, the biographer of Anselm. The period of occupation by secular priests was then gradually giving way to the re-establishment of the monks. But the intellectual vigour of the community was low; there was what Professor Southern has described as an 'insularity of taste and feeling'. When Archbishop Lanfranc arrived in 1070 he found a monastery not yet recovered from the Danish invasions, demoralized by the intervening years since Stigand, and with many of its ancient traditions weakened by a disastrous fire in 9067. The rule was not observed, for, as Eadmer testifies, the brethren lived like earls, 'in all worldly glory, with gold and silver, with changes of fine clothes and delicate food, not to speak of the various kinds of musical instruments in which they delighted, nor of the horses, dogs and hawks with which they sometimes took exercise'. Yet this very condition gave Lanfranc a unique opportunity to initiate an almost dramatic break with the past. Into this predominantly English house he proceeded to introduce recruits from Bec and Caen, most of whom he had marked out for promotion. Integration was not easy. However, in spite of his preoccupation with building the new cathedral, the Archbishop seems to have brought the parties together, though the English element maintained some kind of separate existence up to the middle of the XIIth century. Lanfranc's concern was to make Christ Church a model community, and in this he succeeded, so much so that this revitalized Benedictine house became 'a living memorial' to his own zeal, and his 'customs' (*consuetudines*) set a new standard of obedience.

No subsequent Archbishop was to exercise so strong an influence on the community. On the whole they were too busy, and when, after Hubert Walter, they found themselves less often at Canterbury, their interest also declined.

The possibility of friction between Archbishop and monks was always present. The situation could never have been easy when an incoming metropolitan was forced upon the community under pressure from the Crown. Also, as titular Abbot he enjoyed constitutional rights in the appointment to, and dismissal from, certain offices, rights which the Archbishop sometimes had to struggle to maintain. Thus Theobald deposed Jeremias the Prior, only to find that through the intervention of Bishop Henry of Winchester he was reinstated by the Pope. It took a journey to Rome in 1143, in company with Thomas à Becket, then a clerk in his household, to secure a reversal of this decision. Even then the quarrel was not over. The community reacted by accusing Theobald of appropriating part of their revenues, an accusation to which the Archbishop indignantly retaliated by imprisoning several of the monks, and packing Prior Walter off to confinement in the Abbey of Gloucester.

Visitations equally could prove fruitful occasions for dispute, since they usually began at the cathedral, which was the church of the priory. Sometimes, in order to maintain their independence, the monks encouraged the General President of the Benedictine Order to undertake a visitation. Such occurred in 1378, and led to a solemn condemnation by Archbishop Sudbury.

A head-on collision developed in the time of Archbishop Baldwin, in spite of the fact that he had refused to accept office unless freely voted into it by the monks. To Baldwin, monastic chapters were an anomaly, since in common with most bishops he saw them as inhibiting his freedom of action both in the cathedral, where the monks performed the liturgy, and in his own household where they expected to provide some of the staff. For this reason Hubert Walter preferred not to draw his domestic chaplains from the monks of his own cathedral.

Archbishop Baldwin, possibly in an effort to by-pass the monks, set about founding a collegiate church in nearby Hackington, the history of which became a talking-point throughout western Europe. Fairness to the two Archbishops involved prompts the reflexion that though no one came out of this irritating *contretemps* particularly well, they at least showed up to better advantage than the Prior and his fellow monks, whose belligerence was at times extreme.

The constitution of the proposed collegiate church was ambitious: the bishops, indeed the King himself, were to have prebendal stalls; men of learning, doubtless able to serve in the Archbishop's *familia*, were to become members; and the city of Canterbury and its churches were to provide the funds. To cause even more alarm, this grandiose establishment was to be sited within almost a stone's-throw of the monastery of Christ Church! It was natural that an ancient community, jealous of its rights and proud of its intimate association with the Archbishop, should take umbrage. They feared lest this new college should oust them from their treasured electoral privileges, and surround the Archbishop, at Canterbury, with his suffragans, in the same way as the Pope was surrounded by his cardinals in Rome. Some such hope as this may have encouraged the bishops to support the project, and it was this high-level backing which added to the monks' suspicions. Peter de Blois, a voluminous author, even suggests that the scheme was concocted by the King in order to divert the interest of bishops and Archbishop away from his own designs. The saintly Hugh of Lincoln, whom Baldwin consulted, advised against it on the practical grounds that the general effect would be to lower discipline at Christ Church and to prejudice the Archbishop's relations with Rome. But Baldwin determined to go on; and he did so with crude vigour. Members of the community were imprisoned and services in the cathedral suspended. Roger Norreys was forced on the community as Prior. Appeal to Rome in these circumstances was inevitable; but six of the monks charged with the complaint died in Italy of the plague. A compromise was at last effected, namely to transfer the college to Lambeth, and to demolish the buildings at Hackington.

In 1189 Henry II died, and a year later a disillusioned Baldwin succumbed to disease in the Holy Land. But the project did not die with the Archbishop. Building operations began at Lambeth, and the monks, in 1196, obtained a papal injunction to prevent these going forward. Baldwin's successor, Hubert Walter, a statesman of outstanding merit, immediately saw the advantage of having at his disposal lucrative and nearby canonries with which to reward a trained administrative personnel grouped around himself. Monks were not so useful as secular canons. He was therefore reluctant to abandon the scheme, but though his methods of prosecuting it, as befitted his temperament, were far more conciliatory, he was in the end no more successful. To the monks he gave the fullest possible assurances—that the college would be prohibited from having any say in the election of archbishops; that neither the body of St. Thomas nor the annual consecration of chrism would ever be removed from Canterbury; that the Prior of Christ Church would always be installed as a canon of the new college in Lambeth, with a particular voice in its affairs; that all these promises would be ratified both by the Pope and the King. But all to no avail.

It is unnecesary here to go into the subsequent intricacies of this dispute—the appeals to Rome and the charges preferred to the bishops by the monks against Hubert. Finally the community had its way, and an attempt by Edmund Rich to revive the scheme by transferring it to Maidstone proved equally abortive.

Possibly the monks' intuition was a sure one, in that the long-term effect of the college would have been to change the shape and structure of the archbishopric. Something more in the nature of a *curia* might well have emerged—for better or for worse. One solid result was that the archbishops retained Lambeth; and Canterbury, as a place of residence, became less attractive. Hubert Walter subsequently visited Canterbury on some five occasions only. The more general effect of the dispute was to isolate the prior and chapter of Christ Church still further from the Archbishop's metropolitan responsibilities. They came into the picture only during vacancies of the see and then not so significantly, in spite of their victory over the bishops.

The controversy over the proposed collegiate church at Lambeth certainly clouded relations between Archbishop and monastery. But there was other combustible material which could at any time be fanned into a blaze, even though archbishops were less frequently in Canterbury. The saintly Edmund Rich, no less given to controversy because he wore the mantle of holiness, entered into furious quarrels with the monastery, perhaps with more zeal because he regarded their moral standard as leaving a great deal to be desired. The Prior was excommunicated apparently because he had aided Henry III (whom Edmund had married to Eleanor of Provence at Canterbury) in an infringement of Magna Carta. Once again there were the usual appeals to Rome, as the dispute merged into wider political issues. In a desperate attempt to induce the Pope to support his cause, the Archbishop is said to have paid over 1,000 marks—approximately £675—to papal agents. In the end, Edmund, like many of his predecessors, sought refuge at Pontigny. Archbishop Boniface, who inherited a large debt, did not commend himself by imposing heavy fines on the monks for non-observance of their *regula* at his first visitation.

The passage of time fortunately made relations easier as the monastery became more detached from the wider interests of the Archbishop: and the Archbishop correspondingly less interested in the day-to-day life of the monastery. The very nature of his diverse responsibilities removed him psychologically from the ethos of the monastic routine: but on occasions he became of necessity embroiled with the monastery and its affairs. The reforming Archbishop, John Pecham, was called in when Thomas Ryngmere, its Prior, after eleven years of rule, brought the community, through his 'financial incompetence and litigaciousness',[64] into debt to the tune of £5,000. This led to great internal divisions ending in open rebellion, in spite of attempts by the Archbishop to secure a more truly representative form of government and stricter financial control. Finally Henry Eastry was elected Prior, but Pecham remained unpopular, although he had shown marked patience, zeal, and an honest desire for reform. When Archbishop Reynolds died at his manor in Mortlake in 1327, he was said to have been mourned only by the monks of Christ Church whom he had befriended and whose Prior became his chief adviser in later years. Upon the monastery he bestowed many privileges, giving it the manor of Caldecot for the monks' 'comfort'.

To Courtenay, in spite of his frequent peregrinations, Canterbury remained home; and throughout his archiepiscopate he managed to keep in close touch with the monastery. In September 1382 he removed for 'reasonable causes' the Sub-prior, the Cellarer, and the Chamberlain. Some eight years later he presided over the election of Prior Thomas Chillenden. But even for him all was not plain sailing. Courtenay became involved in a dispute with the monks over Canterbury College in Oxford, a foundation which Archbishop Islip had left to their joint care, thus laying up problems for his successors. On this occasion Courtenay got his way but the monks protested that they accepted his judgement only under duress and would hope to reverse it as soon as opportunity offered. The Prior's letter was certainly candid:

> After you will have left the archiepiscopal dignity by some means or another, we, the prior and chapter, shall freely nominate to your successors who will then be archbishops of Canterbury, however often and by whatever manner the office of warden of the college happens to be vacant, three monks of the Canterbury church for that office, from whom so nominated the lord archbishop will appoint one to the office of warden of said college.[65]

Yet in spite of this disagreement, Courtenay's relations with his monastery during his archiepiscopate of fifteen years were, on the whole, friendly. The bite had gone out of the customary disputes.

## II

Relations were no more easy, in the early Middle Ages, with the monastery of St. Augustine, whose traditions equally went back to the days of the first Archbishop. Though not so large as Christ Church, St. Augustine's was 'wealthy and populous'; and if it lacked some of the distinction necessarily associated with its sister foundation, it had the honour of being the burial place of Augustine, the founding father. Also it had become a nursery of letters, and housed the chief versions of the *Old English Chronicle*. Its history for some time after the Norman Conquest was stormy, and the overriding desire of the community was to establish its independence of the Archbishop, not least because of the rivalry with Christ Church. Lanfranc got into difficulty with the monks because he insisted sternly on a measure of reform, and to secure this installed Wydo as Abbot against their will. Those who refused to receive him he expelled from the monastery, and when they took refuge in the Church of St. Mildred, Lanfranc sent them a message that unless they returned they would be treated as renegades. Most of them repented of their obstinacy, and made their submission; the few who did not, along with the Prior, were imprisoned. A monk named Colomban, who later plotted the death of the new Abbot, was treated with great severity. After being tied naked to the gates of the monastery, he was flogged in the sight of the people, and then driven from the city. Doubtless this was mild treatment in days when mutilation, practised horribly by Henry II, was a common form of punishment.

Such incidents may well have added to the general demand for exemption from the Archbishop's jurisdiction, and to constant disputes as to what form of profession ought appropriately to be made, on his appointment, by the Abbot to the Archbishop. Two papal mandates failed to give definitive guidance. This was not surprising for there was a division of opinion even within the ranks of the

88

monks themselves. Whereas the elder testified on oath that they had been present when a profession of obedience had been made to Archbishop William de Corbeil, this was categorically denied by the Abbot. In the end the Abbot was required to make his profession, and this decision was embodied in an instrument to which seven bishops set their seals. The matter, however, was not yet disposed of. When Richard (1174–1184) was Archbishop, Roger, Abbot-elect, resorted to the expedient of a conditional profession by adding the words, 'saving the rights of my monastery'. In doing this Roger was suspected of having made a deal with the Pope under which, in return for a yearly tribute, St. Augustine's would become exempt from the jurisdiction of the Archbishop. This dispute came before the King's court, from which Roger appealed to Rome. Its subsequent history gives a characteristic picture of competing interests operating from within entrenched positions. The Pope espoused Roger's cause, and in 1178 summoned Richard to appear before him at a Lateran Council. The Archbishop set out, but on reaching Paris was advised to turn back. He did so, and Alexander III retaliated by instructing that in future the Archbishop should give his blessing to the Abbot without requiring a profession of obedience. Henry II, however, continued to give support to Richard, and it was later proved that the charters on which Roger based his claims to exemption, and on which the Pope had given his decision, were spurious. Although resort to forged documents was by no means unique to St. Augustine's—indeed their manufacture was a highly skilled art—the monastery as a result lost many of its privileges.

The community continued to guard its status—religious communities have long memories—and Archbishop Pecham, when visiting the King at the monastery, wisely let it be known in advance that he intended no infringement of its privileges. In 1300, Boniface VIII issued an edict exempting the monastery from all episcopal jurisdiction.

Such disputes as now continued usually centred around juridical rights over certain churches and chapels appropriated by St. Augustine's. A typical instance occurred under Archbishop Mepeham, when the monks appealed to the Pope against the Archbishop, and Icherius of Concoreto, canon of Salisbury, was appointed adjudicator. Mepeham was cited before him, but the Archbishop refused to appear, retiring to his manor of Slindon in Sussex. According to Thorne's *Chronica*[66]—Thorne was a monk of St. Augustine's—a deputation from the monks, headed by their proctor and the public notary, sought him out—he had retired to bed—for the purpose of serving a writ. There was an unseemly scuffle between the Archbishop's servants and the deputation, the notary's arm being broken and the proctor receiving a wetting. The monks appealed to John XXII; the suffragans of Canterbury united in support of their Primate; but as Mepeham refused to submit he incurred sentence of excommunication.

Over a long period, visits by the Archbishop to the monastery continued to arouse suspicion. Perhaps it was a little galling to the Primate of All England that there should be a religious house, enjoying a measure of independence, just outside the walls of the city, one of a small but proud group of monastic houses which continued to thwart the ambitions of archbishops eager to exercise unrestricted spiritual authority throughout their province. In reverse, fear of the Archbishop's status and potential claims made the monastery oversensitive. Its Chronicler was forever smelling out encroachments, often when none was intended. Two examples may be quoted.

When Archbishop Sudbury endeavoured to enter the Abbey preceded by his cross, he was resisted by armed guards, until stern protests 'gained his point'. The Abbot warned him, however, that God would intervene to protect the rights of St. Augustine, and the Chronicler saw his murder in 1381 as a divine act of retribution.

Courtenay was particularly sensitive to the claims of the monastery, maybe because he spent more time in Canterbury than most of his immediate predecessors. His touchiness showed itself in small ways. Customarily the Abbot addressed an Archbishop as 'the venerable Father in Christ and Lord X, by the Grace of God Archbishop of Canterbury, Primate of All England'. Courtenay demanded that for the future the form should be: 'the most reverend Father and Lord in Christ, the Lord William, by the Grace of God Archbishop of Canterbury, Primate of All England and Legate of the Apostolic See.' To enforce this designation, Courtenay refused to accept addresses couched in any other terms. To add insult to injury, he unloaded on the Abbot, somewhat tactlessly 'as if our abbot were subject to his rule', the unenviable task of collecting the half-tenths which Convocation had voted to be raised in the city and diocese of Canterbury. The Abbot, in great heat, hurried off to London to solicit the Council, and in particular the Duke of Lancaster; but the only concession he could wring from them was permission to act under the authority of the Council rather than under the mandate of the Archbishop.

> In those days—so the monastic Chronicler writes—the archbishop here in his own church was puffed up with arrogance over his secular power and the pre-eminence of his ecclesiastical dignity and decided to arrogate rights over exempt houses now that he had the pope on his right hand and the king was there to support his arm. . . . thinking the time opportune since our

newly appointed abbot had just arrived at the Abbey. He did not delay any longer but on the day of his installation notified him that he would be coming to see him within a few days.[67]

What happened then reads rather like comedy, though doubtless the main actors took their parts very seriously. There was an interview between the Abbot and Courtenay at the Archbishop's palace, when the former asked him to change his plans; a chance meeting next day between Courtenay and the monks who 'humbly begged him to please come to their monastery in the manner he had planned, even with his cross borne erect and publicly, and that in his charity he pardon the abbot his offence'.[68] Courtenay visited the Abbey four times that same week,

> ... under pretence of devotion he approached the tombs of his predecessors, and having washed his feet in the abbot's chamber, returned with the curse of God to his own place, with his boots on.[69]

So writes the scribe, a sure indication that old suspicions remained.

In comparison with his wider responsibilities, such internal politics at Canterbury may seem trivial, but they continued irksome long after they had lost any real political significance.

# 5

A medieval Archbishop of Canterbury had a variety of responsibilities. Among these was his position as a diocesan bishop which,
then as now, carried with it a defined jurisdiction of pastoral care.

The duties of a diocesan fell into two main categories: first, those
which only a bishop could undertake, such as confirmation, ordination of priests and consecration to the episcopate; secondly, those not
inherent in the episcopal order as such, for example, visitation of
clergy and laymen under his jurisdiction, together with the administration of justice in ecclesiastical courts, and appointments to
ecclesiastical office.

Diocesan administration in Anglo-Saxon England was simple and
less documented than it became after the Conquest. Unfortunately
the story of this development cannot be told, since the evidence to
illustrate it is lacking. When Robert Kilwardby was made Cardinal
Bishop of Portus and Sancta Rufina, thereby being forced to resign
the see of Canterbury, in 1278, he took away with him all the registers
and judicial records which up to then had been housed in the
Cathedral. His successors' repeated attempts to recover these invaluable documents failed, and they have never come to light. The
oldest register preserved at Lambeth is that of John Pecham (1279–
1292). It reveals a mature administrative and legal structure which
could only have grown up, here a little, there a little, across the
years.

The diocese of Canterbury was not large according to medieval
standards. Yet what it lacked in size it made up for in significance. Its
terrain was on the route to the Continent, and the rich farm lands of
Kent produced considerable wealth. Within the diocese there were
about 260 ecclesiastical parishes, over which the Archbishop, as
chief pastor with cure of souls, exercised a final responsibility. Also
there were the monastic houses, some of which, however, particularly
after the XIth century, had managed to place themselves directly
under the Holy See, thereby securing exemption from episcopal or
archiepiscopal jurisdiction. In addition there were the 'peculiars'.
These for the most part consisted of estates owned by the Archbishop
and situated in other dioceses. On some of them, as for example at

Otford in Kent, he possessed a residence. It was an oft-repeated injunction of Anselm that where the Archbishop had possessions he must also have jurisdiction. These peculiars were exempt from the oversight of the diocesan bishop, and came directly under the Primate.

No Archbishop, of course, could personally discharge all his administrative responsibilities, particularly as he had many secular interests, and travelled incessantly, sometimes abroad. He must perforce collect a staff around him to provide official help—that is help which was recognized as validly flowing from his own authority. More simply, he needed to delegate. As the energetic Archbishop Pecham put it:

> It is not possible personally to be present at once and always to fulfil the burden of our office wherever our authority stretches. Thus we accept the help of them in whose faithfulness and industry we can have full trust.[70]

Who were the men who gave it?

The earliest official available to help the Archbishop was the archdeacon. Although little is known of his origins he seems to have become a different person after the Conquest, acting as *oculus episcopi* over the whole diocese, and so continuing right up into the XIXth century. The office was important, and was held for a time by Stephen Langton's brother, Simon. The *Black Book* of the Archdeacon of Canterbury, a XIVth-century production, states that the archdeacon exercised jurisdiction within the city and diocese of Canterbury, except in matrimonial causes and over such churches as were in the gift of the Archbishop. Officials, however, the world over, for financial as well as for psychological reasons, tend to enlarge the scope of their activities. The archdeacon was no exception. During the archiepiscopate of Richard he was accused of 'claiming more than the Archbishop was prepared to acknowledge'. Some archdeacons even aspired to setting up an almost independent jurisdiction. To further this ambition they took advantage of combustible material close to hand, particularly during vacancies in the archiepiscopal see, when there were frequent disputes between the papacy and the monks of Christ Church. Maybe the Archdeacon of Canterbury, since the Archbishop was no ordinary bishop, regarded himself as no ordinary archdeacon. The time inevitably came when he himself acquired his own official who undertook most of the routine work, and acted for him during his absence. Later he rose to the dignity of acquiring his own seal.

As well as the archdeacon, there was another traditional officer built into the structure of diocesan administration and ready at hand to be used by the Archbishop: the rural dean. The early history of the rural deans also is obscure, though it seems probable that in the diocese of Canterbury they were appointed by the archdeacon. Dr. Churchill describes those of the XIIIth century as 'liaison officers'; the link between diocesan and parish; a 'medium for communication, for investigation or for carrying out some order'.[71] Archbishop Langham used his rural deans to secure recruits needed for the defence of the realm. Essentially local persons, they dealt at the grass roots with such explosively domestic matters as the publication of excommunications or the enforcement of dues owing to incumbents.

Such traditional and long-established officers as the archdeacon and the rural deans could not, of course, cope with all central and diocesan business. Often they needed direction. Right at the heart of the Archbishop's administrative system was his *familia*, his *concilium* or *curia Cantuariensis* as it was sometimes called, recalling the *curia regis* of the Norman and Angevin Kings. Archbishop Pecham in 1282 refers to 'our council and household'. This does not mean that all its members were councillors, but it does suggest that the origin of nearly all their offices was domestic. The chancellor (*cancellarius*) probably grew from the Archbishop's need to have a secretary and keeper of his seals, these attracting to themselves the duties of scribe and registrar. Peter of Blois terms himself 'humble chancellor of our lord of Canterbury' and continued to hold the office under the next two Archbishops, Baldwin and Hubert Walter. Such long service tended to establish precedents in ways of working. Under Hubert Walter a fleeting glimpse is given of one who seems to have discharged the duties of provincial vicar-general under the style 'official general'. A similar appointment was made under Archbishop Boniface. When Archbishop Winchelsey was absent on royal or papal business, he regularly nominated a vicar-general for both his diocese and province. Sudbury put the office into commission, the wide terms of which enabled the commission to hear and do justice in respect of all the causes which came to the Archbishop's audience. So extensive were its powers that it could admit to benefices; grant letters dimissory and licences for non-residence; prove wills, and perform judicial and administrative acts on the Archbishop's behalf. Such commissions would usually be limited to a number of years, and would anyhow lapse on the death of the particular Archbishop. In course of time the *ad hoc* commissioner tended to become a more stable ingredient in the Archbishop's household—that is, fluidity hardened into formal structures, and definite officers emerged, not without problems on the way. For example, Archbishop Pecham delegated authority to a 'Commissary General of Canterbury'—a

variant of the designation 'official'—whose sphere of operation was
the city and diocese. This led to conflicts of jurisdiction with the
archdeacon and, doubtless, to a great deal of emotional upset and
jealousy. Often, however, it was simply convenience which determined who should undertake a particular duty. The Commissary
General of Canterbury was, as his title implies, an important personage. He was responsible for communicating to the diocese orders
issued by the Archbishop, in the same way as the Bishop of London,
his Dean, did to the province. Thus Archbishop Islip used his commissary to publish a scale of chaplains' fees, and to require his
beneficed clergy to 'correct their ignorance'; Archbishop Winchelsey
to order 'prayers and processions for the state of the kingdom';
Archbishop Courtenay to promote a crusade; Simon Langham (the
only Archbishop to be buried in Westminster Abbey where he had
formerly been Abbot and is now memorialized by a window in the
nave) 'to punish canonically crimes and defects of subjects, alike
cleric and lay, of the city and diocese of Canterbury'. During the
years between Archbishops Sudbury and Warham, the considerable
powers of the commissary became more or less fixed.

Officials equally necessary to the Archbishop were the commissaries who looked after the extra-diocesan deaneries, and who
exercised an authority similar to that of the archdeacon. Their
commission was given greater definition by Archbishop Islip; and
was further rationalized by Archbishop Dean who entrusted to one
man, Ralph Haynes, jurisdiction over six deaneries, thus anticipating
post-Reformation practice. This official, known as Dean of the
Peculiars, took an oath of obedience to the Archbishop. Appeal went
from him to the Court of Canterbury; thence to the court of the
Province; and finally to the Archbishop's audience.

Reference has already been made to those responsibilities which
only one in episcopal orders could discharge. Here the Archbishop
had no option but either to perform them himself or to get another
bishop to do them for him. In respect of ordination various expedients
were open. He could issue letters dimissory which gave authority to a
named, or sometimes an un-named, Catholic bishop, to act for him
in relation to a particular person. Here it was rare for an Archbishop
to commission a suffragan from his own province; more usually he
would secure an Irish, Scottish, or refugee bishop. As to himself
ordaining, the practice varied. Archbishop Pecham did so frequently,
though never in his own Cathedral, preferring for the most part the
use of certain churches in Kent. Ill health, however, finally necessitated his securing the Bishop of Hereford to act for him. Winchelsey
began well by conducting two ordinations every year in his own
Cathedral, but probably abandoned this practice in the last seven

years of his life. Extant evidence suggests that Archbishop Reynolds, apart from the first two years of his archiepiscopate, seldom ordained personally. Archbishop Sudbury ordained six times in his Cathedral at Christ Church. Courtenay, who was meticulous in the discharge of his duties, held ordinations in the dioceses of Exeter, Bath and Wells, and Lincoln, while engaged on a metropolitan visitation; and once in Cambridge, where Parliament was assembled. Archbishop Arundel never resorted to delegation, himself conducting some five or six ordinations a year, many of them in private chapels on his manors. Archbishop Bourchier, during the whole of his thirty-two years at Canterbury, never himself ordained, an omission which was followed by Warham.

When assessing the above facts, it must be remembered that apparent slackness may mean no more than defective records.

As a diocesan, the Archbishop had a responsibility to ensure that life in the parishes was kept up to some kind of standard. Pluralism and absenteeism were certainly rife during the Middle Ages, and many of the abuses which are popularly associated with the XVIIIth century were in fact scandals which go back to that time. Against these evils Pecham, for example, waged a ceaseless war, even complaining in respect of an episcopal pluralist that if it were not for the fact that the Pope supported him, he would not remain in England.

The most powerful weapon to deal with ecclesiastical abuses was the episcopal visitation, since the *sine qua non* of any remedial action was first to discover the facts. If followed up with thoroughness, a visitation could help to bring about a measure of practical reform. The Archbishop of Canterbury had a double visitatorial responsibility: to his own diocese, and to the dioceses in his province. Most medieval archbishops undertook visitations in person, though they were often forced to leave early, in which case commissaries carried on in their name.

The procedure adopted conformed to what became an established pattern. The Archbishop first announced the proposed date of his visitation to the Prior of the cathedral church, to monastic houses, to the Archdeacon and Commissary General. At the same time he commanded the attendance of those canonically required to appear before him, and meanwhile inhibited inferior jurisdictions. The visitation began with a service and sermon, usually at the Cathedral, after which the tour of systematic interrogation around the diocese began. Inquiries were made as to residence, the condition of church and parsonage, the character of the clergy, and the state of the parish generally. This led to the publication of *detecta* and *comperta*, which contained injunctions remedying what had been found amiss.

Once again, the records for archiepiscopal visitations vary in their detail. Prior to Pecham, who in the first eight years of his archiepiscopate visited with remarkable energy every diocese in his province including the Welsh ones, they are scanty indeed; though Archbishop Boniface is known to have begun a visitation at his own Cathedral, before proceeding to the convent at Faversham, and the dioceses of Rochester and London. As to Archbishop Reynolds, there are enough references to suggest that he was not inactive in discharging this duty. He began a visitation at the Cathedral of Christ Church in 1324, but was forced to leave the deaneries of Ospringe, Sittingbourne, and the Isle of Sheppey to his deputy. There seems to have been a great advance in the organization of visitations under Archbishop Islip, at least in documentation, for his tours were carefully mapped out and recorded in his register. Archbishop Langham does not appear on a single occasion to have visited the whole of his diocese, though personally going to various monastic houses. Whittlesey embarked upon a full visitation, and after a few days spent at the Cathedral, the monastery of St. Gregory's, Faversham, and Leeds, he moved on from deanery to deanery, the order he adopted being followed up to the Reformation. Archbishop Sudbury held a visitation in 1377 and preached to the Prior and Chapter of Christ Church on the text *Simon amas me, pasce oves meas*. He examined all forty-six monks separately, but left the general visitation to his Commissary General. He visited the Cathedral again the following year, warning the monks on no account to submit to a visitation by the President of the General Chapter of the Benedictine Order.

Of Archbishop Courtenay's visitations, detailed accounts remain in his register, and it may therefore help to look more closely at that of July 1393, those of 1386 and 1387 being undertaken by his commissaries.

Courtenay began on 8 July with Mass at the parish church of Lenham in the deanery of Sutton, followed by a sermon delivered by Adam Mottrun, the Archbishop's Chancellor. The Articles of Inquiry were recited, together with the orders of the Commissary General which required procurations to be paid in 'victuals and beverages'. The Archbishop and his officials then proceeded formally to visit the clergy, deanery by deanery. The schedule was as follows:

On 9 July, the Charing Deanery at Ashford; 11 July, Lympne at Romney, having visited the Priory of Bilsingham the day before. 13 July, rest and recuperation in his own castle at Saltwood; 14 July, Elham; 15 and 16 July, Dover, including the Priory, where he was 'for two days at dinner and supper and was honourably received'; 17 July, Sandwich; 18 July, Bridge; 19, 20 and 21 July, the Prior and Chapter of Christ Church, always an 'edgy' ordeal; 21 July, the monastery of St. Gregory; 22 July, the Deanery of Ospringe; 23 July,

97

the monastery of Faversham and the nuns of Davington; 24 July, the Deanery of Sittingbourne; 25 July, the nuns of Sheppey, where he received the solemn profession of the Abbess and several nuns. On 26 July, 'he notified the official of the archdeacon from his manor at Maidstone that since he had completed his visitation of Canterbury, he could resume his office of proving wills and administering the goods of the deceased.'[72]

While Courtenay was in Canterbury during this visitation, he entered into an unfortunate controversy with its bailiff and citizens. This arose from what he regarded as an excessive display by the civic authorities who processed in state, with their maces, into the Priory. The Archbishop peremptorily summoned them to appear before him, and complained that such a display had never been seen 'through a time whereof the memory of man ran not to the contrary'. Relations were restored by an apology.

Courtenay's visitations were not necessarily more thorough than those undertaken by other archbishops of the time: perhaps the documentation was better. The distinction is important.

# 6

As Metroplitan (a style not used until after the Reformation) of the province of Canterbury, the Archbishop exercised certain rights over his suffragan bishops which came to him as the result of a long process of development, strongly influenced by the growth of canon law.

The Archbishop, as early as the XIIIth century, claimed to administer the spiritualities of a see during a vacancy created by death or translation; the temporalities passing into the hands of the King and being accounted for to the Exchequer. But this claim was not accepted without protest. Indeed, before the time of Archbishop Walter, there does not seem to have been much metropolitical interference with local officials who carried on with the administration; and it may be that it was the example of cathedral chapters on the Continent, who successfully resisted archiepiscopal pressure, which encouraged opposition in England when such pressure came. During Boniface's reign at Canterbury, there was litigation in four sees. Such resistance led to 'compositions' between the Archbishop and various cathedral chapters, as for example in the cases of London, Salisbury, Lincoln, and Worcester. The precise details of these compositions differed from diocese to diocese, but all were in the nature of a compromise. At Worcester, while the main burden of administration was placed in the hands of a member of the capitular body, chosen by the Archbishop out of those names referred to him, other responsibilities were reserved to the Prior and Chapter. Not all compositions were so favourable to the diocesan authorities, but in principle the arrangement was usually along these lines. In this assertion of metropolitical oversight during diocesan vacancies, the Archbishop could usually depend on the support of both King and Pope. Thus Alexander VI reinforced Archbishop Morton's authority with a papal bull. When there was no composition the Archbishop was free to act as he wished.

With the diocese of Rochester, the Archbishop felt himself in a special relationship arising out of a long history of mutual involvement. He claimed to be patron of the church, and as a consequence to have possession, during a vacancy, of both the spiritualities and temporalities. He also tried to assert his right to nominate the new bishop, and require the formal election by the Rochester chapter to take place at Canterbury. Successive bishops of Rochester put forward similar claims in reverse, namely that they should deputize for the Archbishop when absent, and perform certain acts during a vacancy in the see of Canterbury.

Appointment of his suffragan bishops was of necessity a matter of concern to the metropolitan of the province. Because of the difficulty of assembling the suffragans together, the right of confirming their elections had passed to the Archbishop by the time of Gregory IX. The usual practice was for the chapter to elect on a licence from the Crown, the Archbishop to confirm and, through a mandate from the Bishop of London, to summon the suffragan bishops to the consecration. It may reasonably be assumed that in this process the Archbishop had informal means of making his voice heard in the matter of selection, even if he was not directly consulted.

The right of the metropolitan to visit the dioceses of his province was recognized by the XIIIth century as a canonical obligation. Yet this, again, was not established without opposition, the bishops particularly resenting the suppression of all inferior jurisdiction while such a visitation was taking place. Metropolitan visitations developed as a corollary of the bishop's own right to visit in his diocese. The early Norman archbishops do not appear to have held provincial visitations, and Pope Honorius's order to Langton to introduce them had no immediate effect. Pope Innocent IV laid it down, in 1246, that the Archbishop must first visit his own diocese before he could assert his right to go on to others. It was obviously more convenient for the Archbishop, once he had set out on the road, accompanied by his staff, to visit as many dioceses as possible. Thus Archbishop Boniface went, in 1250, from Rochester Cathedral to London, where, incidentally, he found the gates of St. Paul's locked against him. His reception by the Augustinian canons of St. Bartholomew's Priory was equally hostile.

The reason why suffragan bishops opposed these visitations, apart from the cost to them in procurations, was the extent of the jurisdiction exercised, even to the removal of dignitaries and, occasionally, their conviction for offences which could hardly be regarded as notorious. Metropolitical visitations remained a regular feature of medieval Church life, though full accounts of them rarely found their way into the registers. Pecham, anxious to deal with such abuses as non-residence and illiteracy among the clergy, visited extensively, as did Courtenay, who met violent opposition at Exeter. By the time of Arundel, the mechanics of the operation seem to have reached a high degree of efficiency. Chichele appears to have been too engrossed in secular business to have found much time to visit as metropolitan.

Indeed the problem for most archbishops was how to get through the demands which their diverse responsibilities made upon them. Often, after beginning a visitation at the cathedral and going on to one or two deaneries, they were forced to leave their commissaries to carry on. If they did this, however, they were not free to catch up the provincial visitation later in another see—that is, not without special papal sanction.

Over his suffragans personally, the metropolitan claimed to exercise a very real authority. If a bishop was too old to be active or was permanently sick, the Archbishop could, and as the registers show on occasions did, appoint a coadjutor bishop to take over, a matter concerning which Pecham sought advice from the Pope. An Archbishop could insist that a suffragan bishop lived in his cathedral city, or at least within the diocese; and if absent for a legitimate reason but without provision being made for carrying on the affairs of the see, that a vicar-general be appointed. Sometimes the latter demand was resisted, as in the case of Bishop Richard Young of Bangor, imprisoned by the Welsh. If a bishop did not institute a man duly presented, or delayed to collate to a living in his gift, then the duty devolved upon the Archbishop: similarly, if a suffragan neglected to hear appeals these went, on complaint, to the Archbishop's Court of Audience.

The general principle was that in any area of a bishop's jurisdiction, the Archbishop had the right, indeed the duty, to intervene if there was neglect or remissness. The final responsibility rested with the metropolitan to ensure that the administration of a provincial see continued, and that no impediment in the bishop frustrated this necessary discharge of the Church's care and spiritual concern. To quote Dr. Churchill again:

> All acts which a bishop could do in his diocese could through his negligence or default, if proven, devolve on the archbishop to perform—but he could only act if there were, for some reason or another, neglect on the part of the bishop.

The sanction for exercising this authority lay in the nature of the metropolitical office itself, reinforced by the decrees of many councils, not least the Lateran Council of 1179. Sometimes in exercising authority of this kind the Archbishop, in order to remove any doubt as to its validity, would prefer to act in response to a direct papal mandate.

Independent of such canonical rights asserted formally at visitations, the Archbishop was expected, as a father in God, to advise his suffragans, to support and sustain them. The registers often show him doing this in many practical if unimportant ways. Undoubtedly then, as now, it needed tact.

Apart from the existence of certain exempt orders and monastic houses, the province was, to the Archbishop, one administrative unit. Appeals came to him from diocesan courts even if papal authority could, on occasions, short-circuit his jurisdiction. According to custom, confirmed by Innocent IV, the Archbishop communicated with the province through his Dean, the Bishop of London, or his deputy, the Bishop of Lincoln, Chancellor of the Church of Canterbury. The procedure was for the Archbishop to issue a mandate and require the Dean to make its contents known to the other suffragans. The earliest examples go back to Stephen Langton who in 1226 summoned to London bishops, deans, archdeacons, abbots, and conventual priors.

The occasions on which the Archbishop might wish to communicate to his province were numerous and diverse: for example to call the bishops and clergy together to deal with Church affairs generally; to grant and collect subsidies; to publish constitutions and decisions; to order special prayers and intercessions at times of war and national peril; to summon bishops to a consecration.

One particular aspect of his metropolitical powers demands special, if brief, mention. This was his claiming jurisdiction where a testator left goods in several dioceses. This seemed reasonable, being in the interests of executors who were thereby saved resort to a number of courts; but it was strongly resisted in the dioceses and often constituted an embarrassing responsibility for the Archbishop. Sometimes the Archbishop could not sustain his claim to the full. In the case of Lincoln, Archbishop Reynolds was forced to accept a compromise by which, though the final accounts and the formal absolution of the executors were approved by the Archbishop, the Bishop retained the probate. In 1355 a great commotion developed over the will of a certain Augustine Waley, the result being an unseemly dispute between the Archbishop and the Bishop of London. A testamentary court, separated from the Court of Arches, was established by Archbishop Stafford in 1443, probably on account of increasing business. As late as the archiepiscopate of Cardinal Morton, the Bishop of London appealed unsuccessfully to the Pope against the Archbishop's exercise of this particular jurisdiction.

The Archbishop exercised his metropolitical jurisdiction in his provincial Court of Canterbury, in his Court of Audience and Court of Arches. Owing to his *mixta persona* as metropolitan, Primate of All England, and legate, distinctions of jurisdiction were not always clear cut. As far back as the time of Thomas à Becket, Alexander III, in a bull directed to the suffragan bishops of Canterbury, expressed surprise that they had questioned the Archbishop's right to hear causes from them, either as metropolitan or legate, in the first instance or by way of appeal. By the latter half of the XIVth century, the authority of the Court of Canterbury as a provincial court of appeal was well established. Its president was the 'official' of the Court of Canterbury, and if he were not present the dean of the Archbishop's London peculiars took over. Perhaps it was natural that the suffragans of Canterbury should watch this court with a jealous eye. They did not dispute its jurisdiction as a court of appeal, but they were concerned to limit its scope and to make certain both that the citation was explicit as to the cause, and that complaint to the suffragans was not short-circuited.

Matters came to a head in the time of Archbishop Pecham, whose archiepiscopate was distracted by prolonged controversy with his suffragans, led by Thomas de Cantilupe, Bishop of Hereford, an old friend and pupil. The opposition, however, was in the main constitutional, and fundamentally it centred around 'the claim of the Court of Canterbury to exercise in England the same authority as the Roman Curia over the universal Church'.[73] At the Easter Synod in 1282 the bishops of the province presented the Archbishop with their complaints—twenty-one in all, some of which related to the conduct of visitations, others to the Archbishop's Courts of Arches and Audience, in the latter of which he exercised his legatine authority. A commission was set up at Lambeth on 17 April, and a settlement was agreed which accepted that the Archbishop could delegate his metropolitical jurisdiction to his Court of Canterbury; but that appeals arising out of his legatine powers must go to the Court of Audience.

Yet this was by no means the end of these disputes, in which the Pope tried to hold the balance. Thus Clement VI ordered that neither John Gynewell, Bishop of Lincoln, nor his official, should by pretext of metropolitical authority be excommunicated or fined. Archbishop Islip did not take such a ruling kindly, particularly since the Pope relaxed the oath of obedience taken by the suffragan.

Sometimes, however, respect for the integrity of his suffragans' rights of jurisdiction enabled the Archbishop to extricate himself from embarrassing situations. Such was the case in the complicated matter of the unsuccessful attempt by John de Warenne (b. 1286) over a number of years to secure the dissolution of his marriage with Joan de Bar, niece of Edward II. Here, Archbishop Reynolds, unlike Greenfield of York, informed the Earl that he could not comply with his request to summon Joan before him, except with the express consent of the other bishops in whose dioceses the lands of the Earl and his Countess were situated. They had shown themselves unlikely to grant it.

Archbishops and suffragans were of necessity brought into relationship through their membership of the provincial synod. Meetings of bishops to legislate and to administer, within a general context of concern for the moral witness of the Church, go far back into Christian history. In Anglo-Saxon England, many such assemblies were national in character, and Lanfranc used his authority as Archbishop of Canterbury and his influence with the King to revive them after the Conquest. But such councils, representative of the whole country, did not long survive Anselm's failure to establish an effective supremacy of Canterbury over York. Henceforward they became provincial. Throughout the Middle Ages assemblies of this character continued to be summoned regularly, and XVth-century legalists described them as held by the authority of the metropolitan. Such provincial assemblies could be called for the extirpation of error; for securing papal subsidies; for sending representatives to councils such as to Constance (1414–1418) and Ferrara (1438–1439); for supporting the Pope against the Bohemian heretics; for dealing with complaints of the clergy that many who occupied judicial posts lacked the necessary learning and training (1432)—a complaint re-echoed by Archbishop Chichele.

The procedure adopted for these councils became more or less fixed in accordance with that used in 1283, on which occasion the Bishop of London, on a mandate from the Archbishop, ordered bishops, abbots, priors, deans of collegiate churches, and selected clergy, to assembly at the New Temple on 9 May. Apart from the disappearance of the religious at the Reformation, this composition survived, in its essentials, till the XXth century. Edward I's attempts, and those of his son, to summon such assemblies before himself were resisted, and resisted successfully. The position became firmly established that it was before the Archbishop that the clergy were required to attend.

The precise nomenclature used for these councils of clergy, no matter for what purpose they were called, presents some difficulties. It is tempting to suppose that in the XIIIth century a distinction was in process of being made between the *concilium provinciale*, called to promulgate statutes, and the *convocacio*, summoned by the Archbishop in response to the King's writ, to make a grant. But right up to the Reformation, so the archiepiscopal registers indicate, *concilium provinciale* and *convocacio* are used interchangeably.

These provincial councils began with a service and sermon, at St. Paul's Cathedral. Then the clergy met in the chapter house, when the Archbishop's mandate, stating exactly why they had been called together, was laid before them. On the next day the Archbishop took the opportunity of discoursing at length on the business before them, making his own views and recommendations known. The King's envoys were also free to persuade or cajole the clergy into making the required grant. The two houses customarily split up, a procedure encouraged by Archbishop Chichele (hence the development of the office of prolocutor), and the prolocutor, on behalf of the lower, would make his report to the bishops. If it were thought necessary these could be joint sessions. Finally, decisions were promulgated on the authority of the Archbishop, with the consent of the bishops, prelates, and clergy.

The power exercised in these councils by the Archbishop, if he had both the will and capacity, must have been considerable. Convocation was his assembly, and he had precedence in every respect.

# 7

## PRIMATE OF ALL ENGLAND

The Archbishop of Canterbury, as well as being metropolitan of a province, was Primate of All England. He did not forget this, though it was not always easy to say precisely what it meant in practice. Thus Reynolds, in abandoning a visitation of the diocese of Norwich, speaks of his right to visit during a vacancy as *racione primacie sue*, while at the same time using the phrase *loci metropolitanus*. What is certain is that successive archbishops—Pecham in particular is a case in point—believed that being Primate of All England did make a difference, and that some acts could be performed only because of the increased authority which this supra-provincial status gave. The French scholar, Achille Luchaire, in his *Manuel des Institutions Françaises*, makes a distinction between an 'objective' primate who exercised authority over other archbishops, and a 'subjective' one whose authority was confined to his own province. No matter what his precise legal or canonical powers, the Archbishop of Canterbury certainly saw himself as belonging more to the former than to the latter. Thus he maintained his right to administer vacant dioceses outside his own province, inhibiting inferior jurisdiction while he did so; and to allow appeals directly to his court from those who were the subjects of his suffragans. Also the unique link with the monarchy, carrying a built-in responsibility for crowning the Sovereign, brought enormous prestige and added another dimension to the office. The supremacy of Canterbury, though difficult to define, was in fact the product of a long process of historical evolution. No man stepping into the chair of St. Augustine could be an ordinary metropolitan.

The Archbishop's claims were regularly contested by the Primate of the Northern province, who, in spite of his independence and his receiving the legation from Rome, was never regarded at Canterbury, or by and large in the nation, as an equal.

Lanfranc was convinced of the necessity to assert his supremacy for two reasons: first to maintain and stabilize the new political settlement after the Conquest; secondly to inaugurate a period of ecclesiastical reform. Lanfranc entered into a politico-religious situation in which the status of his archbishopric had fallen in public esteem, due, among other causes, to the inadequacies of both Jumièges and Stigand. The result was to increase the prestige of the Northern Primate, since Ealdred of York was called in to preside at the crowning of both Harold and William. Lanfranc decided to force into the open the issue of ecclesiastical supremacy, and when his old pupil Thomas came to him for consecration to York, he demanded both a written and a verbal profession of obedience. Thomas refused unless the antiquity of the claim could be proved; and on Lanfranc being unable to satisfy him, left Canterbury without consecration. Inevitably Thomas appealed to the King, who was at first inclined to be sympathetic until Lanfranc advised that in order to promote the unity of the kingdom, it was expedient that Britain should be subject to one primate. Otherwise it might happen that the Danes, the Norwegians, or the Scots would sail up to York, attack the realm, and one of them be made King by the fickle and treacherous Yorkshiremen. William was not slow to recognize the force of the argument.

Yet there can be no question but that Lanfranc, if politically percipient in asserting the supremacy of Canterbury over York, was wrong in pretending that he had ancient precedent on his side. William may himself have realized the weakness of the claim, for whilst ordering Thomas to make a written profession of obedience, he added that this should not be required of his successors unless, in the meantime, the matter was proved by proper testimony or by a council of bishops. On these terms, after a little prevarication, Thomas submitted to consecration. The controversy, however, was too evocative of emotional loyalties and too deeply entrenched, to be thus finally disposed of.

In the following year, both Archbishops presented their causes personally at Rome, where Alexander II wisely referred the dispute to a decision by the bishops and abbots of England. Hence the case came before a royal council at Winchester in 1072. Here Lanfranc produced his evidence, consisting of extracts from Bede's *Ecclesiastical History*, together with letters from Gregory, Boniface, Honorius, Sergius, and Leo. In placing these before the council, he expressed regret that full supporting evidence had unfortunately been destroyed in a recent fire. What Lanfranc could not prove was that either a written promise or an oath of obedience had ever been made. What is now known, though probably not known to Lanfranc, is that some of the documents he produced were forgeries, fabricated by the monks of Christ Church. Thomas, in reply, argued, not very convincingly— he did not question the validity of the documents—that such supremacy as had existed had been given to Augustine alone. Finally the council gave judgment in Lanfranc's favour, and in the midst of a very emotional scene, Thomas made a formal submission.

The Council then proceeded to draw up the terms of a settlement. The Archbishop of York, and his suffragans, must attend any council called by the Archbishop of Canterbury; and on appointment must go there for consecration. In reverse, the Southern Primate was to be consecrated by his brother of York in the Cathedral of Christ Church. Thomas's written profession—the oath was omitted at the request of the King—was drawn up as follows:

> I Thomas, already consecrated metropolitan Bishop of the Church of York, having heard and recognised the evidence, make an absolute profession of obedience to thee Lanfranc, Archbishop of Canterbury, and to thy successors and whatever by them or by thee is lawfully and canonically ordered, I promise to obey. But concerning this matter, at the time when I was consecrated by thee, I was doubtful, so I promised to obey thee without conditions, but thy successors conditionally.[74]

A report of this Council was dispatched to Pope Alexander, and to the churches of England; but the Pope, though recognizing Lanfranc's supremacy, was not prepared formally to confirm it; probably because 'it did not suit the political policy of the papacy to run the risk of creating a rival to its own hegemony in the west, especially as the character of both William and Lanfranc was known to be very independent.'[75]

Lanfranc determined to use his supremacy in order to treat the Church in England as one administrative unit under his primatial authority. To do this, he revived the ancient ecclesiastical councils, which had fallen into disuse through the unsettlement of Danish invasions and the diminution in prestige of the see of Canterbury.

Thus in 1075, as the undisputed Primate of All England, he presided over a council in London attended by the bishops of both provinces, with the exception of Durham and Rochester. It determined the order of episcopal precedence, Lanfranc having himself engaged in a great deal of research on this delicate matter. The Northern Primate was to have the honour of sitting on the Archbishop of Canterbury's right hand, while the Bishop of London was to be on his left.

The effect of such councils was to raise the lowered status of Canterbury. The tragedy was that the bitter rivalry between the Archbishops of the northern and southern provinces prevented their continuance at a national level.

Anselm was as convinced as Lanfranc of the need to maintain the supremacy of Canterbury, but his approach was far more ideological. Professor Southern writes that he saw the primacy as inheriting 'the pretensions of the Anglo-Saxon kings to a quasi imperial authority over Britain and the adjacent islands'—claims to which Henry VIII later 'warmed' and which he adopted to further the ends of his royal headship of the Church. Such claims drew a somewhat mystical sanction from ancient geographical lore which looked westwards to non-Mediterranean Britain as to another world, thus prompting Urban II's famous introduction of Anselm as 'almost our equal, being as it were Pope and Patriarch of the *alter orbis*'. In response to such a high view Anselm set out to secure the subordination of the Church in Wales, and, though without success, to follow up Lanfranc's tentative assertion of authority over the sees of Dublin and Waterford in Ireland.

Anselm's main objective, however, in asserting the authority of Canterbury, was to use it as a means of restoring the Church in England to a more ancient virtue; and it was this which led to his preoccupation with relations to the see of York. Here Lanfranc had done much; but he had been unsuccessful in securing papal confirmation. Anselm, at his own consecration, unfortunately compromised himself when he gave way to Thomas of York's request that certain offending words in reference to the primacy of the southern Primate should be withdrawn. Maybe Anselm's thoughts at the time were on other things.

Thus began a struggle which persisted for many years, though from Canterbury's point of view without spectacular success. Anselm persevered with his cause at Rome, and in 1102 Pope Pascal II confirmed his personal precedence; and in the next year ordered Gerard of York to promise obedience, an obedience which he later extended to his successors. This, comments Professor Southern, was 'the only advance made for over thirty years' and represents 'the high water mark in the Canterbury case'.[76]

Once again there was a snag in it, for the judgement was not definitive: it maintained the primacy only to the extent that it had been enjoyed by Anselm's predecessors, and it was precisely this extent which was in debate. To quote Professor Southern again:

> The privilege of 1103 is the last—and, in the sense desired in Canterbury, almost the first—papal intervention in favour of the Canterbury claims. From this moment the current of informed opinion began to run ever more strongly against Lanfranc's conception of a British patriarchate.[77]

Anselm never relaxed his efforts, and at the election of Thomas of York on the death of Gerard, he made a determined, even passionate, attempt to secure an unambiguous profession of obedience. Without such a profession, he wrote to the Pope:

the Church of England would be torn asunder and brought to desolation according to the word of the Lord that every kingdom divided against itself will be made desolate—and the vigour of the apostolic discipline would in no small measure be weakened. . . . As for myself, I could on no account remain in England, for I neither ought nor can suffer the primacy of our Church to be destroyed in my life time.[78]

Almost his last act was to suspend Thomas.

Anselm's failure to secure for Canterbury the exercise of an effective supremacy over the whole Church in England was due to a complex of causes. A primacy in the north of England gave prestige and ministered to deep-seated separatist tendencies. Also, success for Anselm demanded the backing of both King and bishops, even assuming that unequivocal papal support was forthcoming, which it was not. Both Crown and papacy preferred to deal with two authorities rather than one. Canterbury could be played off against York. For this reason such submissions as were made by the Northern Archbishop always proved to lack a vital element.

After Anselm, the controversy ceased to be really significant, and its continuance became still more ridiculous with the passage of time, often breaking out on ceremonial occasions. Archbishop Thurstan of York (1119–1140), a considerable personage, proved to be a doughty fighter on behalf of the claims of his primacy, and refused to profess obedience to Canterbury. William de Corbeil persuaded Calixtus II to make him Vicar-General and Papal Legate, which gave him authority over his rival at York—but it was not an authority vested in the office of the Archbishop of Canterbury as such. To put this to the test, Thurstan appeared the next Christmas at Windsor, dressed in his archiepiscopal robes and preceded by his cross-bearer. Thus attired, he claimed an equal right, with the Archbishop of Canterbury, to place the crown on the King's head, but was ejected from the chapel by royal order.

The rivalry between Canterbury and York was bound to flare up during the archiepiscopate of Thomas à Becket, particularly since Roger, Archbishop of York, vied with him in resolution and belligerency. Their differences began as early as Roger's refusal—for the usual reason that he was asked to make a profession of obedience—to assist at à Becket's consecration. Henry II's policy was to play off the one Archbishop against the other, thus preventing the episcopate from acting as one body. In pursuit of this aim he requested the Pope to make Roger a Legate, which would give him the same superiority over à Becket as Henry de Blois of Winchester had exercised over Theobald. The Pope in complying wrote to Roger:

It has never occurred to us, and never shall, God willing, to wish your church to be subject to any but the Roman pontiff:[79]

but he managed to hem in the grant with so many restrictions that it was in practice useless. Yet Roger of York never missed any opportunity of magnifying his office, and one soon presented itself.

Henry wished to crown his son, and to this end commanded Roger of York to perform the ceremony. Ironically it was Thomas himself, when in the King's service, who had negotiated a papal bull enabling Roger to preside at the coronation of Henry II in 1154, the archbishopric of Canterbury being at the time vacant. That such permission was felt necessary in itself constituted a tacit recognition of the unique rights of Canterbury. The King's *rationale* for this procedure was to ask disingenuously who crowned William, and his grandson Henry; a question on which it was not difficult for Thomas to put the King right. Pope Alexander felt himself involved and dispatched to the bishops in England an unambiguous mandate, affirming that 'the right of crowning and anointing the kings of England has by the ancient custom of his church been reserved to the Archbishop of Canterbury'; and at the same time forbidding any of the bishops to comply with a request from the King of such 'wickedness'.[80]

But such 'wickedness' was perpetrated, for on 14 June 1170, Roger crowned and anointed young Henry, and was assisted by the Bishops of London, Durham, Salisbury, and Rochester. It was a deliberate attack on the primacy of Canterbury as well as an affront to the Pope. In such a situation Thomas's only possible riposte was to apply to the Pope for Roger's suspension, and for the excommunication of the bishops who had assisted him. The affair proved to be fraught with tremendous significance, for it was on hearing of à Becket's attitude that Henry cried out in one of his terrible Angevin rages: 'Are there none of the cowards eating my bread who will free me of this turbulent priest?'

Roger continued his war of attrition under à Becket's successor Richard, even going so far as to maintain that the Bishops of Lincoln, Worcester, and Hereford were his suffragans. Once again there were the usual monotonous appeals by both Archbishops to Rome, resulting in the sending to England of a Papal Legate whom Henry brought to Winchester. The result was a temporary settlement, which included an agreement to defer a decision on the vexed question as to whether the Archbishop of York should carry his cross in the Southern province—a symbolic act representing independence.

This thorny problem was tackled again at a council held in St. Catherine's Chapel, Westminster, presided over by the Papal Legate. The account of what happened, as given by Gervase of

Canterbury, is dramatic. Archbishop Richard took his seat on the right hand of the papal representative, an act of implied precedence, which provoked Roger, on his arrival, 'to squeeze his buttocks between the archbishop of Canterbury and the legate', thus ending up in the Primate's lap. The Archbishop of Canterbury's servants proceeded to manhandle his brother of York, throwing him on the ground and tearing his vestments. Roger indignantly took himself off to the King, who laughed and would do nothing. Henry later held another council at Winchester in 1176 and managed to persuade both parties to a truce for five years.

Hubert Walter, like his two immediate predecessors, styled himself Primate of All England, though neither Pope nor King used this form in their letters. (Geoffrey of York was Primate of England.) When Walter attended the King at Nottingham in 1194, complete with processional cross, he replied to the protest of the Archbishop of York: 'I carry my cross throughout all England, as I ought since I am primate of all England; whereas you are not carrying yours, and perhaps you are right not to do so.'[81] Probably only the presence of the King prevented a scuffle.

It would be tedious to follow in detail this traditional dispute, which had lost real significance, yet continued to generate excessive emotion. Fairness to both parties makes it necessary to add that to contend for rights was not regarded as a selfish indulgence; but as a solemn duty imposed upon a man through the office that he held. Rights acquired an almost mystical significance: and there was felt to be something really vital at stake.

Deliverance from this increasingly farcical charade finally came in 1353. Simon Islip and John Thoresby of York each agreed to accept the other's titles, Primate of All England and Primate of England. Each was allowed to bear his cross in the other's province, subject to one condition so far as concerned the Archbishop of York. Within two months of his first entry into the Southern province, he must send to the Cathedral of Canterbury a sculpted likeness in gold of an archbishop bearing a cross in his hand and valued at some £40, or some other notable jewel of the same worth, these to be offered at the shrine of St. Thomas.

A controversy, so long drawn out, makes unhappy reading. It was characteristic of the period, yet there were some contemporaries able to rise above the contending passions. To Sampson (1096–1115), the aged Bishop of Worcester, the issue of the supremacy was not worth striving for overmuch.

If I truly knew what would be best for you and us—he wrote to Anselm—I should not hesitate to tell you. But this I may say, that it seems to me unworthy that you should be too angry over this affair.[82]

William of Newburgh wrote in somewhat similar vein.

This idle dispute about priority has involved the English metropolitan in long and costly trouble. Each utterly in vain describes himself as primate of all [sic] England, since neither holds the power signified by the title.[83]

Referring to the archiepiscopate of Hubert Walter, Professor Cheney writes of the perpetuation of a pointless struggle, and 'the low comedies of battles over pectoral crosses' which 'did not add a jot to Hubert's power in his own province'.[84]

Doubtless such observations are just; but they must not be allowed to cloud the real issues originally at stake and for which both Lanfranc and Anselm were contending. Their joint failure led to the almost complete suppression of the national councils which were a common feature of Anglo-Saxon England. The ecclesiastical division into two provinces enabled both King and Pope to play the one Archbishop off against the other—and this was not healthy. Fortunately, however, in 1462, the Northern Synod decided to incorporate with their own constitutions those of the Southern Province, thus ensuring that the churches of Canterbury and York were, as far as possible, subject to one body of law. 'Thus amicably was settled at last,' so comments W. F. Hook, 'the controversies between the two branches of the English Church, which in former times had occasionally led . . . to a personal conflict between the Metropolitans.'

# 8

# PAPAL LEGATE

## I

No Archbishop of Canterbury during the Middle Ages ever doubted that he was the Pope's man. To a realist such as Hubert Walter it was natural to write to the Supreme Pontiff—the letter is quoted by Giraldus Cambrensis (*ob.* 1220?) in his *De Invectionibus*:

> . . . plenitude of power has been given to you from on high so that the fulness of your irresistible majesty may organize and reduce to order what cannot be corrected by us, who are called to share in the responsibilities.

Temperamentally an Archbishop may have interpreted this loyalty in different ways in response to varying political circumstances: but that the Church on earth was centred in Rome and that as Primate of All England he stood in a special relationship to the Pontiff who presided there was never in doubt. Nor would it have occurred to either party to wish it otherwise. Papal sovereignty inevitably limited the extent of the Archbishop's freedom of action. It made inroads, canonically and as of right, on his jurisdiction. His courts could be by-passed and appeal made direct to the papal *curia*, even if this meant a somewhat expensive procedure which only the wealthy could afford. But archbishops recognized that they would have been even more circumscribed were not Rome there in the background.

One of the Archbishop's first acts after election was to nominate proctors to petition Rome for the *pallium*, delivery of which was usually entrusted to two or three bishops. Often it was received with considerable ceremony, as when Thomas Arundel processed to the high altar of St. Paul's Cathedral *cum canticis et organis*. Its reception was followed by a profession of obedience in some such form as the following taken by William Courtenay in the XIVth century:

> I, William, elect of Canterbury, do promise and swear from this hour forward, as long as I live, I shall be loyal and obedient to

St. Peter, and to the holy, apostolic church of Rome and to my lord Urban VI, by divine providence Pope, and to his canonically appointed successors. I shall never by counsel, consent or deed, do anything which might cause them to lose life or limb or to be captured. . . .[85]

The significance of the *pallium* may be seen in William Courtenay's anxiety at its late arrival, which led to the irregularity of his making his profession of obedience without it. The reasons for this delay are still not clear. Perhaps the Pope was uncertain of the King's approval, or the *pallium* was lost *en route*.

Could Courtenay thus deprived fully discharge his archiepiscopal duties? He himself seems to have been doubtful, and he did not, therefore, preside at the consecration of two bishops; nor at the wedding of Richard and Anne of Bohemia. However, he officiated at her coronation, an act which the Chronicler who continued Ranulf Higden's (*ob.* 1364) *Polychronicon*, felt to be somewhat improper. Before carrying his primatial cross in public he first sought the opinion of leading canonists, and assured the Pope that he meant no offence. Not until some eleven months after the primacy had become vacant did Thomas Cheyne, one of the Archbishop's proctors, arrive at Croydon with the *pallium*. Two days later Courtenay was invested with it by the Bishop of London, who again received his profession of obedience.

The acknowledgement of the Pope's position as the head of Western Christendom did not exempt individual Pontiffs from exposure to criticism: indeed such criticism tended to keep pace with the increasing financial burden which their exactions imposed. Yet not until the XVth century did this become opposition to papal authority as such. For the most part throughout the Middle Ages there was an understood, if precarious, balance of power, which could, however, be easily upset by the initiative of either *sacerdotium* or *regnum*. In England, the Archbishop of Canterbury stood in the centre of this complex of competing forces; and his effective influence could be weakened by the King withdrawing his favour and dividing the episcopate or by the Pope commissioning a Legate over his head, thus making inroads on his jurisdiction. Papal legates, however, were for some time as unpopular with Kings as with Archbishops.

William the Conqueror made it plain that he would receive no such emissaries without his own express approval, a policy which Lanfranc never questioned, and understandably so because a legate, armed with papal authority and let loose in his province could equally threaten his own position. Thus when Walter, Cardinal Archbishop of Albano, brought over Lanfranc's *pallium*, and took the opportunity of suggesting that as Papal Legate he should hold a council, the Archbishop would not hear of it. Three years later in Rome, Lanfranc spoke to the Pope concerning the Roman legation over England, which, he said, the inhabitants asserted had from ancient times been held by Canterbury; and must be so unless the Church were to suffer hurt. He did not, however, convince the Pope. In 1101, Anselm, papalist as he was, refused to receive Guy, Archbishop of Vienne, whom Paschal II designated as Papal Legate for England; but the most that his protest could effect was a promise not to dispatch a legate to England with authority over the province of Canterbury during his lifetime. As to Anselm's request that only the Archbishop of Canterbury should henceforth hold the office of legate, the Pope was adamant in refusing it. In fairness to Paschal it must be confessed that across the years the precedents on which Anselm could base such a claim were precarious. Yet the policy of successive archbishops was to press these demands; and for successive popes to resist them. William de Corbeil found himself embroiled in a controversy over the 'legation' which became further complicated by its involvement in the *contretemps* with Thurstan, Archbishop of York to which reference has already been made. During his archiepiscopate, Henry I allowed a Papal Legate, John of Crema (1125), to pass through to Scotland, and in the course of his journey to adjudicate in a dispute between Northern and Southern Archbishops. His arrival in England aroused great resentment, though in public he was received with full honours. On Easter Day he took precedence over the Archbishop of Canterbury when he celebrated Mass in the cathedral of Christ Church. At a legatine council held in Westminster Abbey on 9 September 1125—it issued seventeen decrees chiefly against simony, usury, and the marriage of priests—John of Crema took priority over both Primates, the writs of summons specifying that the council was summoned with *his* consent. William de Corbeil, however, managed in Rome to persuade Calixtus II to give him legatine authority over both England and Scotland. This was a signal triumph, and the effects of this grant were considerable. It gave William precedence over Thurstan of York; it saved England from an Italian legate; it added to the prestige of the see of Canterbury.

Archbishop Theobald, in his turn, faced an attack on his authority more serious than that of William de Corbeil from Thurstan. Theobald's election to Canterbury had been engineered by Stephen and Matilda, in spite of the known ambition of Henry of Blois, Bishop of Winchester, the King's brother, who at the time was the most powerful ecclesiastic in the country. Henry poured out his resentment at Rome, and his influence was powerful enough to induce Innocent to make him Legate instead of Theobald. It was a grave blow to the office which Theobald held, for the result was a serious division of authority, which Henry of Blois exploited to the full. As the Pope's special representative, he claimed supremacy in all ecclesiastical affairs, and encouraged the monks of Christ Church to appeal to him against their own Abbot. He also held his own courts to deal with ecclesiastical disputes, permitting no appeal from them, except to Rome. He went so far as to consecrate bishops without Theobald's consent, including, in September 1143, William Fitz-herbert to the Archbishopric of York, though Theobald had opposed his election. Smarting under the wound of his royal brother's exclud-ing him from the primacy, Henry summoned Stephen to appear before a council at Winchester on a charge of confiscating the estates of three bishops accused of treason. Henry was even said to con-template converting Winchester into a metropolitan see, complete with a *pallium* from the Pope. Theobald, wisely, in spite of extreme provocation bided his time. Release came when the death of Pope Innocent II in 1143 brought the legation to an end and the two following Popes refused to renew it. For a new parallel to this situa-tion we must turn to the attack by Cardinal Wolsey on Archbishop Warham.

What Henry of Blois had shown was that no matter how irksome a legate sent over to England for a specific purpose might be, this was infinitely preferable to the exercise of the legation by a suffragan bishop. The latter situation made impossible an effective jurisdiction exercised from Canterbury, even over the bishops of the Southern province. For this reason it must have been deeply satisfying for Theobald when the diplomatic skill of a member of his household, Thomas à Becket, secured him the legation, and equally satisfying for à Becket, who followed him in this office. In his case, however, the legatine jurisdiction did not extend to the province of York, and Alexander, in making the grant, advised that it be used with 'patience and discretion'.

Hubert Walter (1193–1205) inherited a situation of great difficulty in that William Longchamp, Bishop of Ely, Chief Justiciar and the most powerful politician in England, inveigled the Pope into granting him legatine authority over the whole country. But Hubert did not endure it long, since Richard Cœur de Lion, on his return to England after his captivity, recognized the need to build up the authority of his own newly appointed Archbishop. As a result, Longchamp was expelled from the regency government; and the King obtained from Celestine III a commission which empowered the Archbishop of Canterbury to exercise the Pope's authority throughout England, notwithstanding any privileges or exemption which might be claimed by the Archbishop of York. Hubert Walter determined to put this legatine authority to the test in the Northern province. Formal notice of visitation was served, and on 15 June 1195, as legate, he entered the cathedral church of York. Fortunately for the peace of everyone concerned, Geoffrey, the Archbishop and the King's half-brother, a quarrelsome defender of what he understood as the rights of his see, was abroad, and out of favour at the *curia*. Walter and his officials heard ecclesiastical suits, while as legate he visited the great Benedictine Abbey of St. Mary, deposing the Abbot, undeterred by the fact that he was William Longchamp's brother. For two days he held a council in the Minster, attended by cathedral clergy as well as prelates and rectors from the diocese, the deliberations concluding in the issue of canons for the whole province. Also, as the King's Justiciar, his deputy held a royal assize.

It was a massive display of power, made possible only because both King and Pope were behind him. Even when Walter's commission as legate lapsed, the Pope refrained from appointing a successor during his life-time, with the result that Hubert Walter continued to serve as papal agent throughout both Northern and Southern provinces.

For Stephen Langton, his position in relation to the papacy, particularly in the years following Magna Carta, constituted an embarrassing conflict of loyalty, since he found it difficult to reconcile his role as an Englishman with his duty to Rome. In him the sense of country was more deep-seated than his intellectual conviction, never in doubt, that the papacy possessed *plenitudo potestatis*. Langton was opposed to the recognition of the Pope as a feudal suzerain, and therefore to the authority exercised by the legates sent from Rome to superintend John's formal handing over of the kingdom. Innocent III, however, intent upon promoting a crusade against the infidel, had greater and more far-reaching preoccupations than the administration of England. Langton's attitude bemused him, and it was doubtless ignorance which led to the Archbishop's suspension—the bitterest blow in his life. There is no reason to suppose that the papacy ever regarded John's surrender of the kingdom as in itself involving the right to keep legates permanently in England. Legates normally came and went. Still, the high-water mark of papal power in England was reached under the legate Pandulf, appointed by the Pope to keep the Kingdom of England under supervision. He was a member of the Curia, and though Bishop-elect of Norwich, was exempted from any jurisdiction from Canterbury. For a time, while Henry III was a minor, Pandulf constituted the actual head of state, and as such exercised greater influence than either the Justiciar or Archbishop. It was, however, a unique situation, destined neither to last long, nor ever to recur. So far as Langton's office as Archbishop of

Canterbury was concerned, it was not until all the legates had come and gone that he was free to call a provincial council at Osney in April 1222 which, by incorporating the Lateran decrees, marked a new starting-point in the history of canon law in England.

Legates, however, were not only of use to the Pope: they could be a means by which the King, in connivance with Rome, short-circuited the Archbishop. Such was the case during the reign of Henry III, who found himself at variance with Edmund Rich, who had championed the 'national party' against the 'favourites', even appearing before the King with a group of barons and threatening excommunication if the aliens were not dismissed. Henry's reaction was to connive with the Pope for a legate to be sent over in the person of Cardinal Deacon Otho. The monks of Christ Church, for their own private reasons, received the Cardinal with enthusiasm, and at all public functions he took precedence over the Archbishop. At a council held in St. Paul's, Otho dominated the proceedings, reading a letter from the Pope which abrogated all pluralities except those held on a papal dispensation.

## II

The obvious policy for the Archbishop, though its results proved disappointing, was to establish his own position as legate, not on an *ad hoc* but a permanent basis. This in fact he achieved, but how precisely it came about is obscure. Probably the process was gradual, being influenced by the claims put forward by Anselm, and also by a letter of Alexander III to the suffragan bishops of Canterbury explaining that their Archbishop had authority over them by reason of his legatine powers. To have a *legatus natus* (i.e. *ex officio*) gave great dignity to a church: and a XIVth-century manuscript quotes Canterbury as a conspicuous example of a church so honoured. With Simon Mepeham (1328–33) the formal style *apostolice sedis legatus* first appears in official documents, and thenceforward was applied to all archbishops until renounced by them at the Reformation. This meant that the Archbishop on appointment became a legate without any specific papal commission, a status which he came to share with the Archbishop of York. It was, however, its *ex officio* character which robbed it of a great deal of its significance, for its limitations were only too obvious. Whatever its precise powers, which were uncertain, they could only be exercised in the Province of Canterbury; and the grant could always be superseded by special legates sent over from Rome.

In general, the Archbishop's relations with Rome were inevitably conditioned in part by the political realities of the day. This is well illustrated in Henry Chichele, whose tenure of office coincided with a period characterized on the one hand by a rising tide of anti-papal sentiment, on the other by a determination on the part of Martin V to recover 'the pristine liberty of the Church in that most Christian country'. The latter meant in practice reserving to himself the appointment to all churches vacant by death or translation; the recovery of the back-log of money owing from England; and above all engineering the abolition of the Statute of Provisors.

Chichele was not himself *persona grata* at Rome, in the main because of the part that he had played in championing the abortive attempts at conciliar reform during the Council of Constance. In his resentment, Martin turned for support to Henry Beaufort, Bishop of Winchester, an illegitimate son of John of Gaunt and a man of vast personal ambition who was thought at one time to have his eyes on the papacy. Henry Beaufort's agents became active in Rome, and on 18 December 1417, Martin appointed him *legatus a latere* for life, with jurisdiction over England, Wales, Ireland, and other lands in obedience to Henry V. Chichele immediately recognized that this was a deliberate attack on his own authority and designed to limit his freedom of political action. On 6 March 1418, he complained to the King that such an appointment was without precedent since there was 'no great and notable cause' to warrant it. Even if there were, there should have been mutual agreement as to the terms of the commission and the duration of its authority.

Henry was equally aggrieved at the grant of the legation, and at first refused to recognize it as 'contrary to the immemorial custom of the realm'. He further threatened Beaufort with penalties under the Statute of Provisors, and made preparations for forcing him to resign his see. Henry's financial exigencies, however—he was on the verge of war—made him settle for a compromise. Beaufort was mulcted of a large sum of money, but retained his diocese. His legation, however, was rendered largely ineffective through Chichele's vigorous opposition, but this did not prevent Martin from doggedly sticking to his policy, in the process paying scant heed to local customs in the various national churches. Open opposition manifested itself when he sent over Simon of Terana (Beaufort was no longer usable for this purpose) who on 15 May 1421 appeared before Convocation and 'especially commended to the Archbishop, his brother bishops and the whole provincial council the business of the Lord Pope and particularly of his need, to have provision in the kingdom of England'.[86] This was a matter for the King and Council, was the curt reply. By ordering the release of the spiritualities of various sees without the bishop-elect swearing obedience to his metropolitan, and by giving permission to some of Chichele's suffragans to receive

consecration from any catholic bishop, Simon deliberately undermined the authority of Canterbury. It was an attack which Chichele
could not ignore, and he dealt with it severely. In a private memorandum on the rights of the see of Canterbury, he drew attention to
this invasion of his office, and served it upon the Pope through
William Sawn, his proctor in Rome.

Instances of further tension between Chichele and Martin could
easily be multiplied. A fruitful source of mutual irritation was the
'plenary indulgence' which the Archbishop decreed in connexion
with the celebration of Thomas à Becket's jubilee. Martin declared it
to be an invasion of his own prerogative—an 'unheard of presump-
tion and reckless sacrilege'. Another storm blew up over the Pope's
provision of the Cardinal of Bologna to the archdeaconry of Lincoln. 'Our Lord [King] in no way dispenses with the statutes of
England over provisions . . . which have been issued in Parliament,'
so Chichele took care to inform the Pope.

On the death of Henry V, Beaufort's stock automatically rose; and
Martin decided that the time had now come to make one further
attempt to get rid of the obnoxious Statute of Provisors.

Preparations to promote repeal were carefully set in hand, and as a
first step, on 24 March 1426, the Pope confirmed the bestowal of the
red hat on Beaufort, a bitter pill for Chichele to swallow. It was made
more irksome by his having to receive the new Cardinal ceremonially
in London. The next step was to suspend the Archbishop from his
legatine powers. Expediency demanded submission, or at least going
through the motions of it. On 30 January 1428, together with his
suffragans, Chichele went from the Lords to the Commons, where
he vainly pleaded 'with tears' for the revocation of the anti-papal
statute. Chichele gained his reward by being restored to his legatine
office.

Such periodic manifestations of conflict must not be taken as
implying that archbishops of the period entertained any opposition
to the papacy as such. Indeed, Chichele's attitude to the proposed
reforms of the conciliar movement was moderate, and his general
approach practical rather than theoretic. He vied with the Pope in
his opposition to heresy in general and John Huss in particular.
Eugenius, on the whole, proved more understanding than his
predecessor, Martin, insisting that Louis of Luxemburg, on his
appointment to the bishopric of Ely, should swear an oath of
canonical obedience to the Archbishop. This did not prevent the
Pope taking a firm line, however, when Chichele lodged a complaint
against Kemp, Cardinal and Archbishop of York, on the grounds
that he had assumed precedence in the Parliament of 1439, in spite
of the fact that non-curial cardinals could not claim equality of

status with those of the Curia. Piero du Monte, papal collector, took a different view, and reported back to the Curia that it was Chichele himself who in Parliament had shown 'unheard of pride and unwonted elation and reckless claims to pre-eminence'. Rome's attitude was that it would have been 'far more fitting to have consulted the Pope before the position arose at all'.[87]

Chichele's relations with the papacy were typically ambiguous, and it is for this reason that they have been dealt with in some detail. Yet the general drift as the XVth century advanced was, paradoxically, for archbishops to lean more heavily upon papal authority in matters of jurisdiction. They needed such support in the new political climate of the emerging nation state, and felt more secure when acting as the Pope's man in receipt of a direct mandate from Rome. By this means the Archbishop was enabled to exercise jurisdiction over people and places which might otherwise have resisted his authority. When so authorized he acted as *judex unicus a sede apostolica legitime deputatis*.

It was only with the sanction of papal authority that Archbishops of Canterbury were able to exercise jurisdiction over the territories 'in and around Calais and in Picardy in the diocese of Therouanne', territories which since the treaties of Bretigni and Paris (1360) came formally under the protection of the English Crown. The ostensible reason for a papal grant (December 1379) was the inherent right and corresponding duty of the Pope to provide for the spiritual needs of his subjects; and the impossibility, owing to the wars between the French and English kings, for these subjects to be ministered to by their own diocesans. Percipient contemporaries recognized, however, that the grant was a *quid pro quo* for the support given to Urban VI by both Archbishop Sudbury and the King of England against the rival Pope Clement VII, elected by the French cardinals.

So, on the eve of the Reformation, it was the legation as distinct from the diocesan and metropolitan aspects of the Archbishop's authority which had become most significant, hence his rights over inferior jurisdiction were more firmly established than two centuries earlier.

# PART III

# REFORMATION; ROYAL SUPREMACY; THE ELIZABETHAN SETTLEMENT

*Archbishops*

WILLIAM WARHAM 1503
THOMAS CRANMER 1533
REGINALD POLE 1556
MATTHEW PARKER 1559
EDMUND GRINDAL 1576
JOHN WHITGIFT 1583

# 1

## WILLIAM WARHAM, LAST OF HIS LINE

William Warham was the last Archbishop of Canterbury, if we exclude Reginald Pole, who died within the ancient papal allegiance. Not surprisingly, his life is shot through with the sadness and solemnity befitting the end of an age.

Warham's way up to high office was through a legal training in the Court of Arches, followed by an intimate acquaintance with the European scene through diplomatic embassies abroad. His native skill, reinforced by wide experience, led to his becoming Master of the Rolls and Lord Chancellor. With secular office went high ecclesiastical preferment. In 1502, he was made Bishop of London: and by a bull of Pope Julius II, issued on 29 November 1503, he was translated to Canterbury. He took the oath to the Pope at St. Stephen's, Westminster, on 23 January 1504, received the *pallium* at Lambeth on 2 February, and was enthroned at Canterbury in great magnificence on 9 March. At the traditional banquet which followed, 'all the Archbishop's honours were drawn, depicted, and delineated after a strange manner, on gilded marchpane upon the banquetting dishes'.[88]

So far the story is typically medieval, but the climate was changing. In the sermon at the opening of Convocation in 1512—it may be found in full in Seebohm's *Oxford Reformers*—John Colet, Dean of St. Paul's, who exercised a great influence upon Erasmus, struck a significant note in his withering attack on contemporary ecclesiastical abuses. All Christians should unite, he urged, to secure a general reformation of the Church's estate, since nothing so disfigured it as secular and worldly living among the clergy.

The background of Warham's archiepiscopate was one of increasing tension and uncertainty. The prestige of the papacy had been weakened by 'the Babylonish captivity' (1309–1377); the great schism (1378–1439); the failure of the conciliar movement to impose reform; and the splendid profligacy of the Renaissance popes. The best minds of the day, men so diverse as Erasmus, More, Colet, and even Pole, recognized the urgent need for some drastic reform. Standards which had hitherto been accepted as normal now evoked protest: and the practical result was an increasing anti-clericalism which grew more violent as it became better informed. A new official and commercial class resented the claims of a clerical élite which seemed to contribute little to the economic wealth of the nation.

Warham's archiepiscopate was further complicated by the vast ambition of Thomas Wolsey, to whom Henry VIII, in his early years, handed over the reins of government both in Church and State, thereby anticipating his own royal supremacy. Wolsey's ultimate objective remains an enigma, whether it were to ascend the papal chair or to increase the influence of England by keeping her solvent. Whatever the end, the means to it necessitated a great increase in his personal and official power. Together with the archbishopric of York, he held the see of Bath and Wells, which he exchanged for the much richer see of Durham. In the last three years of his life he held Winchester, as well as a great abbey in France.

In September, 1515, Wolsey was made a cardinal; and at the splendid ceremony in Westminster Abbey when he received his hat, it was noticed that no cross of Canterbury was carried before Warham as he passed through the recently completed nave. Maybe to the Abbot this was right. Yet Wolsey showed himself off with two, one in his capacity as cardinal, the other as Primate of the Northern province. 'None was ever borne again before [Warham] in Wolsey's presence', when 'illuminated by Wolsey's superior lustre'.[89]

This public humiliation of the Archbishop of Canterbury was an unhappy augury of the shape of things to come. Before the year was out, Warham was forced to surrender the Great Seal, Wolsey thus becoming the last ecclesiastic to wear a cardinal's hat and at the same time to hold the office of Chancellor.

But Warham's humiliation was not yet complete. Church preferment, even at the highest level, did not bring to Wolsey that dominance in ecclesiastical affairs which he desired. To secure this, only a papal grant making him *legatus a latere* could suffice. Persistence coupled with lavish bribery at the Curia finally won even this. The first papal commission, dated 17 May 1518, was limited in its purpose and duration; but in 1524 he obtained from Clement VII a legation *a latere* for life and with greatly extended powers. 'The serious implications in the citation,' comments Professor Pollard, in his study of the Cardinal, 'can be best realised by imagining a modern British government appointing as its representative at Washington a plenipotentiary who was not only an American citizen but had never been to England and was actually the President's Secretary of State.'

The inevitable result was that Warham's position as Primate of All England became hopelessly compromised, and his office for the time being almost completely superseded. Wolsey entertained no nice scruples, and with unrestrained exuberance took full advantage of his position. He extended his jurisdiction in every direction, his simple thesis being that as the Pope's special representative in England he had, ecclesiastically, almost limitless authority. This down-grading of Canterbury became so serious that Warham was forced to take account of it. In February 1519, he had approached the Cardinal direct, complaining bitterly that his own jurisdiction, particularly as exercised in his Court of Audience, was being regularly invaded, and this in spite of a promise, given by Wolsey, that he would respect it. If this situation continued, Warham went on, his own metropolitical jurisdiction would become 'extincted'. 'Not only all mine officers of my courts of the arches and the audience, but also the commissaries of my diocese in Kent and I myself, not only in matters of suit of instance of parties, but also in cases of correction depending before me and them, be continually inhibited by your officers.' So extreme was the provocation that if Wolsey persisted in it, he would 'have nothing left for me and my officers to do; but should be as a shadow and image of an archbishop and legate, void of authority and jurisdiction, which should be to me a perpetual reproach and to my church a perpetual prejudice.'[90]

The fact was that Warham, apart from being old, was temperamentally incapable of coping with a man of Wolsey's talents, particularly when to the latter were added ruthlessness, consuming ambition, and the support of the King. The liberal man is always at a disadvantage when confronting naked power. Unwisely, so far as the authority of his own office was concerned, Warham entered into an agreement with Wolsey by which he shared his own testamentary jurisdiction.

Greater inroads on Warham's jurisdiction were to follow. In February 1523 the Convocation of Canterbury was summoned in the normal way, that is, by a writ from the King to Warham, which the latter duly referred to his dean, Tunstall, Bishop of London. That was as far as normality went, as is evident from the testimony of Edward Hall (*ob.* 1547) in his *Chronicle of the Reign of Henry VIII*: 'In this season the cardinal by his power legatine dissolved the convocation at Paul's, called by the archbishop of Canterbury, and called him and all the clergy to his convocation in Westminster which was never seen before in England.'

Whether this joint convocation of both provinces ever met is uncertain; but the attack on the metropolitan status of the Archbishop was only too apparent. In defence of Wolsey it has been claimed that he was anxious to use his legatine powers to secure councils of the whole church, such as took place in Anglo-Saxon England and under Lanfranc. But the facts do not support this view, for the criterion of membership for these 'legatine councils' was arbitrary. Of any constitutional principle in their composition there is no trace. What such assemblies did was to exalt Wolsey's own authority at the expense of that of the Archbishop. Thus Professor Pollard writes:

> . . . the cumulative effect of the series of bulls which Wolsey extorted from successive pontiffs was to establish an unprecedented ecclesiastical despotism in England, to concentrate in Wolsey's hands a monopoly of legislative, executive and judicial authority over the English Church, and to supersede its medieval constitution.

The death of Wolsey in 1530 removed the cause of a great anxiety, but by this time it had been replaced by another even more fundamental. The reference is to the increasing assault upon the Catholic faith as a body of coherent doctrine, and on the independence of the Church which guaranteed it. Luther and the national state came of age together.

Warham himself was intellectually committed to the traditional concept of a papacy, albeit reformed, exercising final spiritual authority. The bidding prayer with which medieval man was familiar laid down the priorities to which he subscribed. Here intercession was first made for the Pope and the hierarchy of the Church, and for the King, that he might rule in a manner pleasing to God. Every coronation at which the Archbishop exercised his traditional role pointed to the same truth, and this truth was independent of whether the papacy was 'lovable', as Scarisbrick terms it. It derived from the nature of society as such and the principles which alone kept that society together. 'Rome's primacy was a cold, juridical fact, obvious and necessary . . . not a central, compelling, gratifying truth in the experience of the individual Christian,'[91] writes J. J. Scarisbrick. Thomas More, humanist and critic, was prepared to go calmly, almost clinically, to his death because he saw things this way.

Such a politico-religious framework gave to the clergy as a class a status which did not arise solely from their involvement in the *regnum*. Although they might be appointed to office by lay investiture, pay homage for their temporalities to a secular ruler, and be subject to his courts, yet their role in society was not exhausted in these terms. There was another claim on their loyalty, another jurisdiction which they must obey, and to which they could appeal even if to take advantage of it was made difficult by statutes of Provisors and Praemunire. Henry VIII knew what he was saying when, holding in his hand the profession of obedience which bishops made to the Pope, he exclaimed bitterly to a parliamentary delegation: 'Well-beloved subjects, we thought that the clergy had been our subjects wholly, but now we have well perceived that they be half our subjects, yes and scarce our subjects.' He might have added that the constitution of the clergy as an estate of the realm, with Convocation claiming to make canons binding on the laity without royal assent, was a permanent expression of the inadequacy of secular society in itself. The *regnum* needed the *sacerdotium*. It could not, to quote modern jargon, be self authenticating.

Such a general view was accepted by Warham almost as second nature: and it made him witness, with alarm and despondency, the steady drift towards national independence geared to royal supremacy. His misfortune was to live at a time of revolutionary innovation, and never to know at which point to stand firm. Perhaps when in his bones he did know, he lacked courage. Not until things were near breaking point, and life for him was practically over, did he finally discharge his conscience.

The story is not a happy one. As to the 'great matter' of Henry's divorce from Catherine of Aragon, it is only fair to say that Warham had always entertained doubts about the validity of the marriage, in spite of the fact that he himself was one of those who negotiated the papal dispensation which alone made it possible. He could, therefore, with integrity, support Henry's attempt at an annulment on the grounds of the Pope's inability to dispense from a divine (i.e. Biblical) prohibition. Doubtless in company with most responsible people he deplored the precise circumstances—Henry's infatuation with Anne Boleyn—which precipitated the crisis. In May 1529 Warham assisted Cardinal Wolsey at the 'extraordinary tribunal' called in to investigate the validity of the marriage. He was also nominated a counsellor to support Catherine's cause until, understandably, she refused his ambiguous assistance, declaring him to be on the King's side and to have declared: '*Ira principis mors est.*' The Queen certainly had solid grounds for such suspicion since the Archbishop had written to the University of Oxford—he was its Chancellor—urging it to come to a speedy decision on the divorce; and also to Clement VII exhorting him to annul the King's marriage. Indeed, so partisan was the Archbishop that though Henry wished him to try the case personally as Primate, the Pope realized that he had no option but to refuse such a request.

The 'King's matter' became an increasing embarrassment to Warham, the more so as Henry's inability to drive the Pope into submission led him into policies which the Archbishop could not espouse, but which temperament made him hesitate publicly to condemn. Increasingly it was clear that unless the Pope gave way, the end could only be the repudiation of an allegiance which had held sway for well-nigh a thousand years, and its replacement by the omni-competent national state expressing itself through the royal supremacy. It was significant that Henry chose to achieve this end through Parliament thereby adding both dignity and prestige to a hitherto essentially feudal and taxative assembly. The King with his shrewd insight into the signs of the times realized that it was easier to impose change upon the clergy this way than through their own Houses of Convocation. Well has it been said of Henry that he was always more concerned 'to do legally than to do justly'.

Yet Henry could not have accomplished his repudiation of Rome had he not identified himself with the contemporary anti-clericalism, which could be crude and insatiable; secular and idealistic; pious and evangelical. Nor, equally, could he have achieved his will had he not exploited religionists who sympathized with the new theological movements on the Continent, though he himself did not share their convictions.

The year 1529 may be taken as the climacteric when Henry prepared, if need be, to cross the Rubicon. Wolsey, in spite of his brilliance and his bullying, had not secured the needful divorce from Rome, and it became evident that he was not going to get it. He was peremptorily dismissed, and Henry replaced him with a lay Chancellor, Sir Thomas More. What proved to be the famous Seven-Year Parliament was summoned on 3 November 1529, an assembly which, together with the Long Parliament of a century later, may properly claim to be the most fateful in English history. Henry's questing if tortuous mind was now moving towards a conception of kingship which was to realize itself in the Acts of Annates (1532-4), the Submission of the Clergy, and the Act of Supremacy (1534). The argument ran: England is an empire, subject, under God, to no other external power. Its monarch (to quote Henry's own words) is 'not only prince and king, but set on such a pinnacle of dignity that we know no superior on earth.' At face value, this might seem to suggest that if Henry had been accommodated in the matter of the divorce, he would still have persisted in extreme measures. More likely, for the moment, this political thesis was a bargaining weapon to be used only if the Pope did not prove amenable. Thus the late summer of 1530 witnessed a concentrated warfare, on many fronts, waged by Henry against 'universal papalism'. The clergy as local representatives could hardly escape becoming a main target.

For Warham, the progressive stages of this combined assault were a galling experience. On 24 January 1531, he was summoned before a group of royal councillors in connexion with an indemnity of

£100,000 which the clergy had agreed to pay for having recognized Wolsey's legatine authority. Warham was told that the form of words attached to the grant was unacceptable, and that certain alterations needed to be made. As well as 'King and Defender of the Faith', Henry must now be styled 'Protector and only Supreme Head of the English Church'. Also he must be asked to defend only such privileges and liberties as did 'not distract from his power and the laws of the realm'. Warham realized immediately the implication of these proposed changes, and subsequently in Convocation (11 February) proposed that after the title 'supreme head' there should be added the saving if somewhat enigmatic clause 'as far as the law of Christ allows'. At first Warham found no seconder, until he broke in with the words: 'Whoever is silent means to consent.' 'Then we are silent all,' a voice cried, and so the clause was accepted in the Upper House. The account of this debate, quoted at length by T. E. Bridgett in his *Life of St. John Fisher*, makes dramatic reading.

As the tempo of the King's ecclesiastical policy increased, so more and more it was to involve Warham personally. On 8 February 1532 the Attorney-General laid indictments in the King's Bench against him, fifteen other clerics, and six laymen, concerning their exercise of such private jurisdictions as, for example, assizes of bread and ale. Though nothing came of this, Warham realized that matters were rapidly moving towards a point of no return: and he drew up a private document 'in due legal form', on 24 February 1532, which repudiated, as anti-Catholic, all that had been done by Parliament since 1529 in derogation of the rights of the Pope and of his own see of Canterbury.[92] It was a gesture, but nothing could now stem the tide. In March 1532 the Commons petitioned the King against the power of Convocation to make ordinances 'without your knowledge or royal assent and consent of any of your lay subjects'. Henry passed on the petition to Warham, and an official answer was drawn up by Gardiner, Bishop of Winchester, one passage in which, referring to an attack on the Archbishop's court, is in Warham's own handwriting. Certain matters objected to in its procedure, he claimed, had already been reformed; and as a man 'at the point to depart this world' he pleaded that the doctors of civil law, practising in the ecclesiastical courts, might continue their eminent services after his own death.

The King, however, kept up the pressure, and on 10 May 1532, a mandate was dispatched to Convocation ordering its members to subscribe to a number of articles, which if accepted would break its independence and place it entirely at the disposal of the royal will. At long last Convocation took its courage in both hands, and demurred to the King's orders. There then followed a ruthless but unequal struggle. The Upper House tried desperately to stand firm, but finally surrendered, although not without some show of protest. Eight bishops absented themselves; two refused outright; three consented but with reservations; only three gave an 'unequivocal assent'—Warham and the Bishops of Ely and Exeter. The effect of this compliance was that in future no Convocation could be summoned without a royal writ, and no new canons promulgated without royal approval. On the day of this surrender Thomas More gave up the Great Seal. The next day the Archbishop delivered the submission to the King.

Warham's reactions to these bitter, remorseful days may be seen in notes which he drew up in connexion with a threatened prosecution arising out of his consecrating Henry Standish Bishop of St. Asaph some fourteen years previously.

> I propose—he wrote—to do only that I am bound to do by the laws of God and Holy Church . . . and by mine oath that I made at the time of my profession.

If the Archbishop of Canterbury be precluded from giving the spiritualities

> to him by the pope provided as bishop until the King's own grace has granted and delivered unto him his temporalities, then the spiritual power of the archbishops should hang and depend on the temporal power of the prince and thus be of little or none effect. . . . It were, indeed as good to have no spirituality as to have it at the prince's pleasure. . . . But *Ecclesia Anglicana non habet libertates suas illaesas* when the church hath not his liberty to consecrate bishops but at Prince's pleasures, for in case it should not please princes to have any bishops consecrated so the church should cease.

In his anguish, there came into his mind thoughts of the blessed martyr St. Thomas, who

> was rewarded by God with great honour of martyrdom, which is the best death that can be . . . which thing is the example and comfort of others to speak and to do for the defence of the liberties of God's Church. . . . I think it better for me to suffer the same than in my conscience to confess this article to be a praemunire for which St. Thomas died.[93]

'Gregory VII,' comments K. Pickthorne, 'could hardly have put it more strongly'.[94] True, but Gregory VII would doubtless have done something more positive about it.

For the Archbishop it was now the end of a very long road: he died on 23 August 1532, probably over eighty.

Warham was not of the calibre of More or Fisher, both of whom were exceptional men and suffered death rather than play false to deep convictions. Certainly, he too had his scruples of conscience, but an accommodating temper made him give way little by little to a stronger will whether it was that of Wolsey or Henry. Warham's tragedy was to be called to serve the Kingdom 'at such a time as this'. Probably it would have made little difference if he had stood resolute behind his principles. Henry had the power and knew how to use it to strike down, without mercy, those who stood in his way. So it happened that Warham left behind him a primacy reduced in influence and effective power.

# 2

## THOMAS CRANMER, SENSITIVE THEOLOGIAN

I

To the King the death of Warham on 22 August 1532 must have seemed providential. Anne Boleyn was pregnant, yet Catherine was still his lawful wedded wife. It was imperative that he should now secure an archbishop who from conviction would further his cause; and having found him, persuade the Pope to confirm his election. It was better to go into schism with an archbishop appointed in accordance with long-established procedure.

The archbishopric was kept vacant for some five months, while Henry weighed the claims of possible candidates—Gardiner, Lee, Stokesley, and Fox. They were all rejected and the royal choice fell on Thomas Cranmer, then in his forty-fourth year. To contemporaries the nomination must have seemed surprising, since until the last three years, Cranmer's life had been spent as a little-noticed, indeed undistinguished, fellow of Jesus College, Cambridge. Perhaps to Henry this was part of his attraction.

These long years of academic seclusion were, however, significant in his development. They show that Cranmer was sensitive to the winds of change blowing over from protestant Germany; that he was influenced by the humanist and historical approach to the Scriptures of Erasmus and Colet; and that he conceived himself as essentially a theologian. One aspect of his thought needs special reference, namely his belief in the royal supremacy. How he arrived at this conviction is not easy to determine, although there are hints of such a doctrine in Wycliffe. What is clear is that so regulative did it become that only when faced with a painful death was he able, and then not easily, to disentangle his final commitment to a reformed faith from an uncritical obedience to his sovereign. It was not only a craven fear which made his behaviour ambiguous when Catherine of Aragon's daughter undid the work of Jane Seymour's son. To defy his prince, even when a Roman Catholic, presented a conflict of loyalties not easily resolved. Dr. J. Ridley, Cranmer's most recent biographer, writes:

Belief in royal supremacy became for Cranmer as fundamental a principle as his belief in the supremacy of Scripture. He acquiesced in every change of religious doctrine during the twenty years in which he, almost alone among the leading statesmen, survived every turn of official policy; on three occasions he granted Henry a divorce on very questionable grounds; he obeyed and glorified a cruel tyrant who repeatedly committed every one of the Seven Deadly Sins.[95]

As to Henry's first acquaintance with Cranmer, there seems little reason to doubt the story told by Morice, his secretary, in his *A Declaration Concerning the Progeny . . . of Thomas Cranmer*, that the future Archbishop came to Henry's notice in the summer of 1529, when at Waltham Cross he suggested to Fox and Gardiner, known to him from their Cambridge days, that the 'King's matter' should be submitted to the universities for their opinion; a suggestion which, when he heard of it, made Henry declare that Cranmer 'had the sow by the ear'.

This introduction to the King led to Cranmer's being sent on diplomatic missions abroad, including a spell as ambassador to the Emperor Charles V. Cranmer was at Mantua when news reached him that Henry proposed to raise him to Canterbury. That he was chosen when far away from the court intrigues which followed Warham's death shows that he had powerful backers. They almost certainly numbered among them the Boleyn family, in whose household he had lived for a short time when first coming to London.

The implications of the appointment were clear: that Henry now felt more secure; that he was determined on strong action; and that he wanted a willing instrument at Canterbury. Cranmer left Mantua on 19 November, but in spite of Thomas Cromwell's endeavour to speed his way, it was not until 10 January that he arrived in London —a dilatoriness to which he called attention at his trial many years later. Once home, his appointment soon became public and provoked considerable comment. Henry immediately advanced him £1,000 towards the expenses of entering into his office, and set about securing the necessary papal bulls, which were issued on 3 March 1533. Perhaps Clement was influenced by Henry's threatening him with the Acts of Annates if he did not comply. There was no difficulty in securing Cranmer's canonical election by the Prior and Chapter of Canterbury.

Cranmer by no means treated the process of taking up his office as a mere routine operation. His consecration in the Chapter House of Westminster Abbey on 30 March was remarkable and unprecedented. Before the ceremony began the new Archbishop, in the presence of five officials, protested that he did not intend any oath he might now take to the Pope to bind him if it were against the law of God, the interests of the illustrious King of England, the reformation of the Christian religion, or the laws and prerogatives of the realm. Having thus discharged his conscience, he moved at this point into St. Stephen's Church, with the paper in his hand on which the protestation was written. His consecration by the Bishop of Lincoln, assisted by the Bishops of Exeter and St. Asaph, then followed. According to custom Cranmer duly swore, at the high altar, to be faithful and obedient to blessed Peter, to the Holy Roman Apostolic Church, to Pope Clement VII and his successors; to defend the Roman papacy against all men; and to persecute heretics. This done, he proceeded to read his former protestation a second time, and repeated this once more, although in a shortened form, when making his profession of obedience on receiving his *pallium*. The traditional oath of allegiance to the Crown on entering into the temporalities assumed a new form, probably of his own or the King's devising. Significantly it included a promise to 'renounce and utterly forsake all such clauses, words, sentences and grants, which I have of the Pope's Holiness in his bulls of the archbishopric of Canterbury, that in any manner was, or may be hurtful or prejudicial to your Highness, your heirs, successors, estate or dignity royal; knowledging myself to take and hold the said archbishopric immediately and only of your Highness and of none other.'[96]

This 'double talk' has been both admired and condemned: admired because it was at least honest; condemned, as by Pole, because it came close to undisguised perjury. Probably Cranmer made this protestation because Henry ordered him to do so; also, perhaps, to make his own position clear and thus avoid embarrassment in the future.

The enthronement did not take place until 3 December 1533, when the occasion was marked by Cranmer's walking barefoot through the sanded streets of Canterbury. The customary banquet hardly measured up to the splendour of Warham's, yet was in its own way magnificent. Gossip reported that the Prior of Christ Church contributed so many swans and partridges that he could only afford to give Thomas Cromwell a Christmas present of apples.

Cranmer entered into the duties of the archbishopric at a time when the final breach with Rome was imminent. The door was still left slightly ajar, and neither side seemed prepared to take the responsibility of closing it once and for all.

But this uncertainty could not last much longer. One of the new Archbishop's first acts was to hold a legatine court at Dunstable, where in the company of two bishops and fortified by a declaration from Convocation, he pronounced, on 10 May, that Henry's marriage with Catherine of Aragon was null and void.

Meanwhile the anti-papal legislation in Parliament went on. The Submission of Clergy made some two years earlier in Convocation became statutory; the Act in Restraint of Annates, which laid down the procedure for the Crown's nomination of bishops, was brought into effect; papal bulls of provision were abolished; and the first Succession Statute which declared Henry's progeny by Anne Boleyn 'legitimate and heritable' was passed. Under the terms of the latter, Cranmer, together with Thomas Cromwell, the Lord Chancellor, and the Abbot of Westminster, were constituted a commission to administer the oath appended to the Act. Both More and Fisher refused to swear since, while willing to subscribe to the succession, they felt unable to take the oath in the prescribed form. It was typical of Cranmer's humanity that he urged that this offer be accepted even if only on the prudential grounds that (so he wrote to Cromwell) it would be 'a good quietation to many within the realm'. But Cranmer's common-sense did not save either More or Fisher, for they were later executed under the severe terms of the Treason Act.

All was now ready for the consummation of this progressively anti-papal legislation in the Act of Supremacy, passed in November 1534, which declared, without ambiguity, that Henry was the only 'supreme head on earth of the Church of England'. Cranmer took no initiative in these parliamentary enactments, though they certainly had his general approval. In their enforcement we may assume that he wished to ease many a troubled conscience.

While these constitutional changes were moving steadily forward, Henry's immediate concern was to build up the authority of the Archbishop's office, knowing well that it was an authority entirely dependent upon himself. Cranmer also was equally desirous that the archbishopric should suffer no diminution in its formal powers as a result of the severance from Rome. To this end he set out on a visitation of the Province of Canterbury acting under a royal mandate, although the customary inhibition restraining the jurisdiction of his suffragan bishops was issued on his own authority as metropolitan, Primate, and legate. The inclusion at this time of the legation may seem somewhat surprising, and it certainly caused difficulty. At St. Paul's Cathedral Stokesley protested against any visitation from one who styled himself a legate of the Holy See, and protested that he would take no notice of any act decreed by such a person against the Crown or the customs of the realm. Cranmer met a similar rebuff in the dioceses of Lincoln, Norwich and Exeter, and at Corpus Christi College in Oxford. It was remarkable that he should have continued to use this title some six months after the royal supremacy had been established. One thing is certain. He could not have done so, indeed would not have wished to do so, unless Henry had required it; and Henry can have required it only in order to buttress up the royal supremacy during early and tentative days. The protest of the suffragan bishops derived from a traditional dislike of any primatial interference in their own dioceses, reinforced by memories of what had happened when they recognized the legatine authority of Cardinal Wolsey. Also in 1512, suffragans had complained to Warham of his encroachment on their jurisdiction, and both Pope and King were called in to mediate. It was significant that on returning from his visitation, Cranmer announced in Convocation his abandonment of the title 'Legate of the Apostolic See'. It had obviously outlived its usefulness and the King must have acquiesced in, or insisted upon, its passing.

Cranmer never attempted to assert his authority as Primate of All England by any visitation in the Northern province, nor has any subsequent Archbishop. This did not prevent many a *fracas* with Archbishop Lee, particularly when Cranmer tried to insist on his commending the royal supremacy, even licensing Sir Francis Bigod's chaplain to preach in the cathedral on St. Peter's Day if the Archbishop of York refused to do so. Unexpectedly, York complied.

Henry, having initially 'played up' the office of Archbishop for his own purposes, now proceeded to play it down. Under the Act of Supremacy, the King was given near absolute power over the church to 'visit, repress, redress, reform, order, correct, restrain and amend all errors, heresies and abuses'. This enabled Henry to deal drastically with all aspects of the church's life—its doctrine, its worship, and its property. Henry had thus made himself, or more accurately, had persuaded Parliament to make him, another pope; but a pope living on the Archbishop's doorstep and adding to his spiritual jurisdiction the authority of secular rule. Inevitably the pre-Reformation status of the Archbishop became eroded.

Henry determined to make full use of these newly-acquired powers. At the beginning of 1535, Thomas Cromwell was appointed the King's Vicegerent or Vicar-General to exercise the royal supremacy in ecclesiastical affairs. This meant in practice that Cranmer ceased to be the 'principal minister of the King's spiritual jurisdiction' as Henry had called him in 1533. Instead Cromwell now acquired precedence over archbishops and bishops, and the prestige of Cranmer correspondingly declined. The King determined to have no rival during this critical period and during the following five years Cranmer's administrative activities were mainly confined to being a bishop in his own diocese. The ancient office of Archbishop of Canterbury had been useful in engineering the break with Rome, particularly since Cranmer had been consecrated with all the accustomed properties, even receiving the *pallium*. But Henry now had gained more confidence.

Cromwell did not prove nice or reticent in using his authority, in spite of his friendship with Cranmer. As the King's Vicar-General he, or his deputy, presided in Convocation and sent out injunctions to the clergy. But his most ambitious undertaking, taxing all the resources of his administrative genius, was the suppression of the monasteries. This was almost exclusively the Vicar-General's affair. Indeed, by an act of 1534 forbidding papal dispensations, the Archbishop of Canterbury was expressly precluded from the right to visit the monasteries. It is clear, however, that Cranmer, mild, accommodating and publicly complacent, yet resented this exclusion. Cromwell began preparations for his visitation of the monasteries in the summer of 1535 when Cranmer was still busily engaged on his own provincial visitation. A head-on clash of jurisdiction was avoided only because, on Cranmer's protesting that he would be pleased if the visitation were abandoned altogether, Cromwell postponed it until the autumn. But Cranmer dared not go further. When he received, in September, the mandate from Cromwell for the postponed visitation, neither he nor any of the bishops uttered a formal protest. On the contrary, members of the episcopate who had demurred at Cranmer's exercise of visitational powers 'submitted with a display of real enthusiasm to Cromwell'. Cynicism could hardly go further. Perhaps the most extreme assertion of royal supremacy was reached when Henry, a few weeks later, in granting new commissions to Cranmer and the bishops, made it quite clear that they exercised all their rights of ecclesiastical jurisdiction, including the ordination of priests, by licence from the Crown. Such Erastianism may find a sophisticated explanation in the need of the sovereign nation-state, as it pushed out from its moorings in Rome, to find anchorage elsewhere.

II

This attack on his office meant that such influence as Cranmer exercised on the burgeoning life of the Church of England—the paradox is that no man left the imprint of his personality more indelibly upon it—had to be achieved subtly, and in areas where the monarchical will did not wish to obtrude itself so directly. Accepting, and with a good conscience, that the royal supremacy was a necessary fact of life, Cranmer insinuated both his theological awareness and his developed liturgical interest into the religious discipline of the *Ecclesia Anglicana*. This he succeeded in doing, although Henry, except when European politics seemed to demand alignment with the reformed movement on the continent, wished for a modified catholicism with no extremes at either end. It was in matters of belief that Cranmer's own personal interests lay; and it was in his capacity as a theologian that he saw the real significance of his office. Always he sought simplicity and a true biblical insight; always he endeavoured to be eirenical and to appropriate the best wherever he could find it. Thus, while learning from Continental Protestants, he declined to jettison an older tradition where it still had value. *The Institution of a Christian Man* (1537) containing an 'Exposition' of the Creed, Seven Sacraments, and Ten Commandments (known as The Bishops' Book) which was largely his and the Bishop of Hereford's work, embodies this approach; and it was this same liberality which, in May 1539, made him for three days oppose in the Lords the reactionary Six Articles. Only a personal visit to the House by the King himself and a direct royal request that the Bill should go through, made Cranmer withdraw his opposition. When German delegates arrived in England in 1538, Cranmer, with a small group of bishops, entertained them at Lambeth and sought to reach a common understanding. Had it not been for Henry's change of front this might have proved possible. Cranmer kept up a vast correspondence with protestant theologians, Swiss as well as German. In particular he was attracted to Martin Bucer, not least in his efforts to mediate between opposing theologies, even including that of Rome.

Perhaps it is in Cranmer's developing thought in connexion with the sacraments that his essential theological position may be best discerned. He began with a belief in the Real Presence, similar to that held by Tunstall and Gardiner. But the cast of his mind made him always suggestible to new thinking, and he confessed frankly that he had been considerably influenced by Bishop Ridley to see medieval doctrine as the corruption of something more pure and primitive. Communion was essentially a corporate act in which all the faithful took part; not, as it had become, the offering of a sacrifice by the priest with the laity only occasionally partaking. He further believed that the medieval emphasis on the propitiatory nature of the Sacrament, such as in the multiplication of masses for the dead, had led to practical abuses. As to the mode of Christ's presence, Cranmer, in denying its 'corporeality', repudiated the metaphysical explanation offered in transubstantiation. On the other hand he did not, with some of the extreme reformers, see the Sacrament simply as a sign: Christ was indeed present, but spiritually; the sacraments 'effectually' conveyed grace. So far as the ordinary parishioner was concerned, Cranmer was of opinion that the Latin Mass prevented a really effective lay participation. He wanted all to communicate every Lord's day in accordance with the practice of the apostles.

There is balance and wholeness here; and it is reflected in all the Anglican formularies for which he had any responsibility. His intention in the Thirty-nine Articles (forty-two in his time) was to be deliberately mediating. When compared with professions of faith on the Continent they are certainly eirenical and moderate. The spirit is conciliatory; the Augustinianism positive; and there is evidence of a real desire to avoid negative and extreme deductions.

Cranmer cannot claim to have played a prominent role in securing a Bible in English, though he wrote the foreword to the Great Bible which in 1540 was required to be set up in every parish church.

In the ordering of a reformed worship, his own interest came to the fore and he showed a real initiative. The litany in English was his own handiwork. Its euphony, economy of expression, and general charity make it without contemporary parallel. Equally, in the first Prayer Book of Edward VI, talent and aptitude combined to encourage his genius to rise to its fullest expression. His telescoping of the traditional monastic offices into Morning and Evening Prayer for the use of lay people has proved itself, over a period of nearly four centuries, peculiarly adapted to English temperament and religious feeling. The collects which he translated from the Sarum rite, together with those of his own composition, show uniformly the right 'touch': a 'touch', however, which was lacking in his verse as he himself was the first to admit. If both the Prayer Book of 1549 and the revision of some three years later—the latter was the nearest approach made by the Church of England to a more extreme continental position—bear evident testimony to the theological ferment of the age, they yet do so within a continuing Christian tradition.

It is by his contribution in this field that Cranmer deserves well of the Church of England. The political reformation, leading to the breach with Rome, was essentially the work of the King, aided by Cromwell. The religious Reformation begun, in spite of himself, by Henry, and advanced by Somerset and Northumberland in the reign of Edward VI, took its worshipful shape from the piety of Cranmer. It was only when the royal supremacy, under Mary, ceased to come behind the Reformation settlement that his life's work ceased—and his death followed.

Perhaps the remarkable fact is not that Cranmer was put to death in 1556, but that in so violent an age he should have survived so long. Certainly there were times under Henry VIII, when contemporaries believed that his downfall was imminent. Particularly was this the case in 1543 when he was embroiled in serious differences with the newly constituted Dean and Chapter of Christ Church, and the Council had embarked upon a new persecution of heretics.

Two prebendaries from Canterbury came to London armed with articles accusing their Archbishop of heresy. Behind this attack was undoubtedly Gardiner, Bishop of Winchester. It was only Henry's humour and toughness which rescued Cranmer from the destructive intentions of the Council.

That Cranmer survived has been taken by some as indicating a sycophancy which placed personal safety as the highest *desideratum*. This is not just, for Cranmer can rightly claim to have been in many respects a brave man. Publicly, it must be admitted, he never wavered in loyalty to his master no matter how difficult on occasions this must have been for a man as inclined to mercy as Henry was to vengeance. But this did not prevent his offering critical and frank advice in private, and pleading for clemency. If in doing the latter he usually made his case on prudential grounds, in his intercession for More, Fisher, and Cromwell for example, it was because he felt that a plea of this kind was likely to be more effective. The fact is that had Cranmer been so servile as is often supposed, he would have been of less use to Henry. Still, his relations with this tyrant of a monarch remain enigmatic. We are not privileged to eavesdrop when they were alone together. Undoubtedly the King chose him to be an instrument and a tool. But it is inconceivable that the encounter between the two over the years could have been always and only at this level. True, Cranmer proved safe, unlike others who had served Henry well. Thus Cromwell once told him that he was born in a happy hour since the King would take anything at his hands. Indeed on occasions he himself had complained about him but in vain.

Cromwell was right: and it is difficult not to believe that there was genuine trust, if not affection, on the part of Henry. When at the time of his death he was asked if he wished for any spiritual ministrations, he replied that if he wanted anyone it would be Cranmer, and the Archbishop was finally brought to him. By the time he reached the bedside, Henry was already speechless, but on being asked to give some sign that he put his trust in God, he 'did wring his hand as hard as he could'.

The Archbishop's relations with Edward VI, his godson, were never so intimate as with the father. The young King was too zealously guarded by Somerset, and in his turn by Northumberland, to make this possible. With Mary, daughter of the mother whose marriage he had declared invalid, and whose religious allegiance he repudiated, it was impossible that any real relationship should exist. Anyhow this was ruled out by the Archbishop's giving way to pressure, not least from the dying King, and supporting Lady Jane Grey's claim to the Throne; an act which he described in a letter to the new Queen beseeching her pardon, as his 'heinous folly and offence'.

Why did not Cranmer follow the advice which he gave to Peter Martyr, also to his wife, and take refuge in flight? He could have claimed impeccable archiepiscopal precedent, and he certainly had both time and opportunity. Most probably it was because he felt in duty bound, by virtue of his office, to remain and to face the oncoming storm.

Cranmer's trial and execution have left an indelible impression on English Protestant history. Not many will, I suspect, be anxious to sit in judgement upon one who, partly from fear of physical pain, partly because of a life-long allegiance to an ecclesiastical supremacy vested in the Crown, forswore his Protestant faith. More and Fisher, Latimer and Ridley were made of sterner stuff, although, maybe, they were not such merciful men. Yet Cranmer's recantation in St. Mary's and his behaviour at the stake were heroic. There was ambiguity in Cranmer, and something of this has remained in the Church of England ever since. The *Ecclesia Anglicana* breeds kindly, understanding men, more prone to conciliation than to combat. Even his first marriage, at the age of twenty-five, to 'Black Joan of the Dolphin', which meant abandoning his fellowship at Cambridge, has about it the touch of a common humanity. It was fitting that during the four hundredth anniversary year of his burning, Archbishop Fisher should move a resolution

> That this Convocation do now proceed to the Chapel of Lambeth Palace, there to remember before God Thomas Cranmer, Archbishop and Martyr, with thanksgiving for all he restored and gave to the life and worship of the Catholic and Apostolic Church of this land to be our possession and the possession of the whole Anglican Communion throughout the world.

# 3

## REGINALD POLE, PUTTING THE CLOCK BACK

The death of Edward VI led to the accession of Mary, Catherine of Aragon's daughter. Her brief reign of some five years 'a disagreeable and dangerous interlude', made it certain that whatever the solution of the religious problems which confronted England, it was not to be found in a return to papal allegiance. The mark stamped upon the Church of England during the reigns of Henry VIII and Edward VI was in its political aspects to endure, although the precise character of the religious settlement remained for a long time in doubt.

Mary found herself, in the early years of her reign, in the para-doxical position of having to maintain her position as 'Supreme Head' of the Church in order to use its authority to repair the breach with Rome. Her own personal tragedy was matched only by that of her kinsman, Reginald Pole, whom she chose as Archbishop of Canterbury. Maybe it was fitting that the last of a long line at Lambeth to receive the *pallium* should be among its most selfless representatives. Papal authority went out in an aura of devotion and holiness. Yet Reginald Pole's life ended in disappointment and disillusion.

As the third son of Sir Reginald Pole and Mary, a niece of Edward IV, the young Reginald early attracted the interest of Henry VIII, who furthered his education both in England and on the Continent. Clash of temperament, coupled with the deep integrity of his religious convictions, made Pole's relations with Henry increasingly difficult. For this reason he refused both the archbishopric of York and the see of Winchester; and, on being asked by Henry for his opinion on the divorce, denounced it in forthright terms at a stormy interview, during which the King fingered his dagger. The upshot of this worsening relationship was that Pole decided to live abroad, serving the Church in a wider context, often in disguise to escape the assassins hired by Henry.

Yet he was no slavish defender of papal policy. As a delegate to the Council of Trent, he advocated reform, and was the youngest and most energetic member of a committee appointed by Pope Paul III to improve the discipline of the Church. Among his friends were such humanists as Erasmus and More. Nor was he devoid of sympathy

for certain aspects of the reformed theology; for he sought to reconcile the Lutheran doctrine of justification by faith with orthodox
Catholic teaching on works. Not surprisingly in certain quarters he
incurred the suspicion of entertaining heretical opinions. Nevertheless Pole's reputation on the Continent was high, and on two
occasions, although he did nothing to push his candidature, he was
seriously considered for the papal chair. His reluctant acceptance of a
cardinal's hat infuriated Henry, and his breach with the King
became absolute when he allowed his condemnation of the divorce to
be published at Rome in the winter of 1538–9 (*Pro Ecclesiasticae
Unitatis Defensione*). The frankness of this polemic, reproduced by
Fr. T. E. Bridgett in his *The Life of St. John Fisher*, and the violence of
its language when referring to Henry, are remarkable:

> At your age of life—Pole writes—and with all your experience of
> the world, you were enslaved by your passion for a girl. But she
> would not give you your will unless you rejected your wife, whose
> place she longed to take.

And again:

> Thou hast cast thy kingdom into miserable commotions and
> made it the spectacle of the world. Thy butcheries and horrible
> executions have made England the slaughter house of innocence.
> The holiest and most spotless men on earth have been slaughtered
> for new crimes in the most ghastly and unspeakable manner. . . .
> In their bloody deaths no torment was spared them; to religion
> no insult. All nations wept to hear of that fearful tragedy, and
> even now after so long a time, when I write of it tears burst into
> my eyes. And thou art he that argues that the Pope cannot be
> the Vicar of Christ through moral depravity! Worse art thou
> than Korah who rebelled against Aaron, worse than King
> Uzziah who usurped the priestly office, worse than Saul who
> slew the priest of Nob. Lucifer alone, who set himself against
> the Most High, may fitly be compared to thee.[97]

When, later, Reginald's brother and his aged mother, the Countess
of Salisbury, suffered death at the King's hands, Pole is said to have
exclaimed that he was now the son of a martyr, and that this was the
King's reward for her care of his daughter's education! Still he had
now one more patron in Heaven.

Pole returned to England in 1553 on the death of Edward VI, and
in the capacity of papal legate became the chosen instrument to
repair the breach with Rome. The emotion of his homecoming

recalls that of à Becket some four centuries earlier. On 20 November he sailed from Calais in the royal yacht, and when he arrived at Dover nobility and clergy, and a great company of gentlemen from all parts of the kingdom, flocked to greet him. The triumphant progress continued through Canterbury and on to Rochester where, in obedience to the royal command, he adopted the ancient pomp and insignia of a papal legate, the cross, two silver pillars and two silver pole-axes being borne before him. In London, the Queen and Philip received him with a genuine warmth.

Two days later he spoke to the Houses of Parliament at Whitehall. In a very subdued voice, not easy to hear, he told the assembly that he held from the Pope full powers to reconcile England with the Holy See, but that its exercise was dependent upon the absolute revocation of all anti-papal legislation. Next day the Houses sent a petition to Philip and Mary begging them to intercede with Pole for the removal of the interdict and promising the repeal of the noxious statutes. Then on 30 November, the members of both Houses assembled at the Palace, and kneeling with the Queen before Cardinal Pole, received solemn absolution from the guilt of schism. The Queen and many of her councillors wept aloud as they proceeded into the palace chapel where the *Te Deum* was sung and Pole pronounced the benediction.

The deprivation of Cranmer followed as a matter of course, as did Pole's election as his successor. Being still only in deacon's orders he was ordained priest on 20 March 1556, in the church of the Grey Friars in Greenwich, and on the next day—the day on which Cranmer was burnt—he celebrated his first Mass. On 22 March he was consecrated Archbishop of Canterbury by Archbishop Heath, Bishop Bonner, and five other diocesans.

Pole determined to proceed on a policy of reform for which long years had amply equipped him, and, as legate, he called together the two Convocations on 4 November 1555 to set it in hand. Every cathedral must have its own seminary, and the Catechism of Caranza was to be provided for the use of the laity. He urged bishops to use gentleness rather than violence in their dealings with heretics, and himself studiously conformed to this advice.

It must have seemed to many as if the clock had been put back some twenty years, particularly when the clergy who had been ordained according to the old rite were absolved and reinstated, while those who were ordained by the new rite were treated as laymen.

Too much water, however, had flowed under too many bridges for this to be so; nor was Pole, for all his sanctity and integrity of character, but prematurely tired and aged, the man to consolidate a revolution in reverse. To make matters more difficult for him he became *persona non grata* with Pope Paul IV, who as Cardinal Caraffa had long been his enemy.

Religion and politics were inextricably intertwined. Few rulers were as single-minded as Mary, but she was embarrassed politically by her Spanish marriage. Thus when war broke out between the Apostolic See and her husband Philip, Pole was deprived of his legatine authority by a papal bull dated 14 June 1557, and was summoned to Rome on the old charge of heresy. Only on Mary's intercession was he allowed to retain the office of *legatus natus* since it was attached to the primacy, but its powers were strictly limited. Pole's situation was now one of almost unrelieved tragedy. He was out of favour with the papacy whose sovereignty in England he had been instrumental in restoring, and whose cause, in its better interests, he had championed faithfully throughout a lifetime.

The restoration to papal allegiance was clearly precarious. Though Pole neither initiated nor supported the burnings of Mary's reign, he suffered from the effects of them. Fortunately for his own happiness, he did not live long: and as he lay dying at Lambeth on the evening of 17 November 1558, he is said to have heard the shouts which greeted the accession of Queen Elizabeth, for Mary had died earlier the same day. Gardiner was surely right when he commented of Pole: 'Seldom has any life been animated by a more single purpose.' Even his successor, Archbishop Parker, whose religious allegiance was far different, pays tribute to 'the gentleness of his disposition'. Philip Hughes, the Roman Catholic historian, in his *The Reformation in England*, describes him as 'a man in whose whole life truth was supreme . . . candid, straightforward, unworldly and entirely undiplomatic.' The story of his life in its holiness, refinement, and sadness still exhales a fragrance as he looks out upon a world whose faithlessness sickened him, in the portrait by Titian.

# MATTHEW PARKER,
# TRADITIONALIST AND REFORMER

I

The way was now open for change, even if few contemporaries were quite sure as to what would be or ought to be the road ahead. One thing may be said in advance: that in so far as the Church which emerged at the end of Elizabeth's reign, and which survived near liquidation under the Commonwealth, owed its existence and character to any one directive mind, it was that of its 'Supreme Governor' as Elizabeth preferred to describe herself. Two of her three Archbishops—the second was unceremoniously suspended by her from any effective discharge of his duties—certainly helped to condition the way forward; but they were able to do so only because the Queen, taking stock of her country's needs, gave them at least the negative support of her royal supremacy.

In considering the policy of Queen Elizabeth which affected her Archbishops so nearly, one is reminded of Kant's distinction between the phenomenal and the noumenal; the thing as it appears and the thing in itself. Elizabeth did not wear her heart on her sleeve. It is by her achievements that she must be judged, and it is in her pragmatic approach that she is distinguished from her half-sister Mary, in whom politics was made to subserve a dominating religious interest. Elizabeth had early known too many dangers, and had too often kept her life by keeping her counsel, to rush into self-revelation. Perhaps her regulative ambition was to preserve her kingdom from disruption within and from the menace of Spain and France from without. She therefore wanted a religion as inclusive as possible of the vast mass of her subjects, that is of those who were prepared to be loyal to the national idea as embodied in her own sovereignty. At first she was not quite certain what precise form this 'uniting religion' ought to take, often to the embarrassment and sometimes to the despair of her first Archbishop. What she did know from the outset was that such a religion could not be papal in allegiance; although even here the 'politique' in her determined not to break with Philip too soon. It must be some version of the reformed faith;

but this must be worked out by waiting upon events, even by watching which way the cat would jump. There must be external law and order, yet without any rigorous inquiry into deep matters of personal conviction. In XVIth-century England a pluralist society was unthinkable, and Elizabeth seems early to have convinced herself that some form of episcopal government was more congenial to the principle of monarchy than were the other variants of non-papal Christianity.

In the working out of this inclusive, enforced religion of uniformity, Elizabeth was determined to keep the initiative in her own hands. She resisted fiercely, although not successfully, any discussion of its terms in Parliament, in the same way as she did her relations with foreign states. These were her business. To Elizabeth, being Supreme Governor was not simply a status; it meant something practical; royal injunctions and visitations; courts of High Commission and Star Chamber; even the suspension of an Archbishop on her own authority. Insofar as she thought constitutionally, she saw the Crown as the *fons et origo* of both Church and State: and regarded herself as free to act religiously through Convocation and secularly through Parliament, reserving to herself the right to act independently of either when she wished to and could get away with it. Her difficulty lay not least in the fact that the XVIth century was a time of social and economic change, bringing with it the rise of a new mercantile class, which affected religious and political loyalties.

In this critical situation, the choice of her first Archbishop was important. She decided for Matthew Parker, and events proved that she could hardly have done better. By instinct and disposition, Matthew Parker was a scholar, delighting in the feel of old manuscripts, venerating the past and unwilling to squander its accumulated treasures. He was no iconoclast. Yet he had early, while at Cambridge, imbibed reformed ideas, leading him to a close study of the scriptures, although not as an alternative to the works of the Fathers. A measure of his early promise may be seen in that he was one of the Cambridge scholars—Cranmer was another—whom Wolsey tried in vain to inveigle into his new college at Oxford. In 1535 Parker was appointed chaplain to Queen Anne Boleyn, and presented to the deanery of St. John the Baptist at Stoke-by-Clare in Suffolk, then a college of secular priests. An attempt in 1539 to proceed against him for heresy on the grounds that he ridiculed the ceremonies of Easter and denied the holiness of the Cross was foiled by the good sense of Lord Chancellor Audley. This curious incident, however, did not prove detrimental to his career, for he went on to become Master of Corpus Christi College, Cambridge, where he restored order to its finances. In 1545 he was elected Vice-Chancellor of the University;

and on the suppression of Stoke College was given a pension, marrying Margaret Harlestone, the daughter of a Norfolk squire. Like Cranmer, he unwisely espoused the cause of Lady Jane Grey, and on Mary's accession was deprived of his preferments. Thenceforward he lived obscurely, moving from place to place, on one occasion falling off his horse and thereby incurring a permanent and painful injury.

Such a *curriculum vitae* may seem to suggest a lack of distinction, but those who knew Parker well were conscious of integrity, intelligence, and moderation, so much so that upon the death of Pole, William Cecil unhesitatingly advised the Queen to send him to Canterbury. Never was a man called to high office more against his own natural inclination. Parker was shy, no courtier, and only wished to be left alone to get on with his studies. 'Of all places in England,' he later confessed, 'I would wish to bestow most of my time in the university.' His first reaction to the offer was to beg release, but he could not refuse the Queen's express wish, the more so as one of the last acts of Anne Boleyn was to commend her daughter Elizabeth to his care.

Serve he did, and faithfully, sometimes without the help that he thought she ought to give him, but dared not.

Parker's enthronement and consecration—the first to be carried through without reference to Rome—were felt by him to have particular historic and religious significance. There had already been a vacancy of eight months, and he was determined that everything should be done with due form and ceremony. On 18 July 1559, royal letters for his election were issued to the Dean and Chapter of Canterbury, which complied on 1 August, and a commission, dated 9 September, was given under the Great Seal for his consecration as 'archbishop and pastor of the Cathedral and metropolitan Church of Christ at Canterbury'. But there were initial difficulties. Three bishops, originally appointed to perform the ceremony, refused. On 6 December, therefore, a new commission was issued, but this time the bishops—Barlow, Scory, Coverdale, and Hodgkins—were empowered to act collectively. The election was confirmed on 9 December at St. Mary le Bow, and the consecration finally took place in Lambeth Chapel on 17 December. Matthew Parker, for obvious reasons, was deeply concerned that his consecration should be fully documented. Its details were therefore recorded in a Latin script, which was later deposited, with other of his manuscripts, in the library of Corpus Christi College in Cambridge. There can be no question whatever as to the genuineness of these documents.

In 1604, a Roman Catholic controversialist named Holywood circulated another version of what took place. According to his story consecrations were held in the Nag's Head Tavern in Cheapside, when Scory held a Bible in his hand and laying it on the heads and shoulders of those present as they knelt, said to each: '"Take thou authority to preach the Word of God sincerely." And they all rose up bishops.'

It is now admitted that this story is an absurd fabrication. Quite apart from the fact of its being wholly out of character with what is known of Archbishop Parker, his register meticulously records the successive stages by which his consecration was brought about; the official documents 'forming together an intricate network of independent instruments', still exist, and any suggestion that they are all forgeries is ridiculous. The register shows that: 1. the royal mandate was produced at the consecration and read; 2. Parker took the required oaths; 3. the presiding bishop commenced with the Litany and proceeded to use the service of consecration according to the Second Prayer Book of Edward VI; 4. the Archbishop received the imposition of hands of all the officiating bishops, and 5. with others, received the sacrament; 6. the ceremony was witnessed by Grindal, Bishop-elect of London, two other bishops, the Archbishop's Registrar of the prerogative Court of Canterbury, and two notaries public.

Nor is there any force in the argument that since the Second Prayer Book of Edward VI had been abolished in Mary's reign there was no legally constituted ordinal; or that there was lacking a competent person and a proper intention to make catholic bishops. As to the severing of the link with Rome, that, of course, underlay the whole question of validity, and here there could be no compromise on either side. Those who set store by such things can rest assured that the episcopal succession in the Church of England was fully and canonically maintained.

None of Parker's predecessors was more conscious of the traditional inheritance of his office, nor more determined to stress its continuity with the pre-Reformation past. To this end he gathered around him a group of scholars, and combed both England and the Continent to recover manuscripts dispersed when the monasteries were ravaged by Henry VIII. His decision to write his *De Antiquitate Ecclesiae et Privilegiis Ecclesiae Cantuariensis cum Archiepiscopis Ejusdem* (1579), in which he depicts an unbroken succession from St. Augustine is, in itself, significant. Thus when he comes to the Reformation, at which time 'religion began to grow better and more agreeable to the Gospel', there is little to suggest any violent break in the developing life of the Church of England. In particular, he emphasizes the unique rights that the Archbishop of Canterbury exercised over his suffragans and more widely in his courts. On their death he could claim their seals and second-best rings. The executors of the Bishop of Rochester must furnish him with a silver cup and hunting dogs. Indeed, even the Archbishop of York needed to come to him for confirmation.

To the annoyance of the Puritans, a de luxe presentation volume given to Burleigh was adorned with illuminated coats of episcopal arms, 'his own most prominent of all'. In an accompanying letter he explained that he had written his book in order 'to note at what time Augustine, my first predecessor, came into this land, what religion he brought in with him, and how it was continued, fortified and increased'. Modesty made him add: '. . . ye may relinquish the leaf and cast it into the fire, as I have joined it but loose in the book for that purpose, if you so think it meet; and as ye if it so please you (without great grief to me) cast the whole book the same way.'[98] Puritans were quick to condemn his use without disapprobation of such terms as 'priest regular', 'priest senior', and his failure to condemn the 'wicked lives and gross blindness of Dunstan, Cuthbert, Becket and other fellows of later times'.

In keeping with his desire to preserve traditional practices, Parker, though an abstemious man himself, discharged a lavish hospitality. Here he had the enthusiastic support of the Queen, for she had no desire that the archbishopric should suffer any diminution in prestige because of the severance with Rome. The palace at Canterbury became a centre of the most sumptuous entertainment even if it did not quite vie with the establishment of Cardinal Pole, who had secured a patent to retain a hundred servants as against Parker's patent for forty.

For example, in the year 1565 at Whitsuntide, on Trinity Sunday, and over the July assizes, he provided for the principal clergy and laity a series of splendid banquets. A few years later he was honoured at Canterbury by the Queen herself, who gave him as a souvenir of her visit a massive gold salt cellar valued at two hundred marks. It was on a similar occasion at Lambeth, according to a story told by Sir John Harington, a godson to the Queen, in his *Nugae Antiquae*, that she addressed Mrs. Parker: 'Madam I may not call you; mistress I am ashamed to call you, so I know not what to call you; but yet I thank you.' At least she had risen somewhat in the social scale above her predecessor, Mrs. Cranmer, who seems to have lived with her husband in semi-retirement.

That his primatial office should continue into post-Reformation England without any serious diminution of either its ancient prestige or residual rights was regarded by Parker as of supreme importance. His register, which he kept with more care than either Cranmer or Pole, shows, to quote Dr. Rowse, that 'whatever the changes brought about in doctrine and practice, life and habit continued in the old ways. What is remarkable is how much of the old order and routine remained.'[99] Anthony Hussey continued in the office of Registrar as he had done for the past twenty years. Likewise the machinery of the Archbishop's courts, both metropolitan and diocesan, carried on with business as usual. The Court of Faculties, which issued licences and dispensations, grew in importance since the Archbishop had succeeded in these matters to some of the papal powers, although these were carefully hedged in by Acts of Parliament. The privilege of the Archdeacon of Canterbury to enthrone bishops of the Southern Province went on and has been perpetuated to this day. Thus after Pole's death and during the vacancy, the Dean and Chapter acted according to custom in the discharge of archiepiscopal duties. When he took over, Parker showed himself quietly efficient. There were regular ordinations and institutions to benefices. Licences were issued to schoolmasters, doctors, and midwives. Decrees of excommunication continued to be pronounced.

II

Such a policy, however, of ensuring the continuity of the new with the old was not, in its wider aspects, easy to execute. Quite the reverse. Parker had a fairly clear idea of what he wanted the Church of England to be like, and this was, in the main, shared by Queen Elizabeth—he would never otherwise have been at Canterbury. Yet it was far too early, at the beginning of her reign, to know whether what they both wanted could be achieved. Protagonists of the old faith were regarded as constituting both a religious threat to the emerging Church of England and a political one to national independence. Their position was indeed difficult. Emotionally conditioned to the Latin Mass, they were, apart from a fanatical fringe element educated abroad, probably loyal to Elizabeth. But the menace from Spain, together with the papal bull *Regnans* (1570) which excommunicated the Queen and relieved her subjects from their obedience, made allegiance to Rome in the eyes of the Government synonymous with treason.

Archbishop Parker was aware of this threat, but his energies were largely drawn away in another direction, where, as he conceived it, the dangers were more real because more subtly insinuating. These dangers had to do with the final character or shape of the reformed *Ecclesia Anglicana*. Here views varied. Elizabeth's accession brought home many a Protestant exile, who believed himself to have breathed a much purer air in Strasbourg or Zürich than he had ever done in his homeland. Such enthusiasts found a welcome among God-fearing laymen especially in the Eastern counties. Parker's policy— his *via media* or 'mediocrity' as Puritans contemptuously described it —seemed almost a betrayal of what they had suffered for and come to know. It was certainly not in this direction that they wished the main stream of Anglicanism to flow; and they were determined from inside the structure of the Church of England, in particular from within its beneficed ministry, to direct its current another way.

Insofar as the Puritans constituted a class, they in general wished to establish a presbyterian system. The more moderate among them, in spite of the fact that they did not accept any theory of apostolic succession, saw such a system as not incompatible with a parochial and episcopal establishment, provided that this establishment functioned liberally. More extreme men, however, wanted a root-and-branch change.

The first real challenge to the Puritans came with the appearance of the Elizabethan Prayer Book in 1558, the intention of which, to quote Parker's own words in a different context, was to ensure 'that that most holy and godly form of discipline, which was commonly used in the primitive church, might be called home again'. In its main outlines this Prayer Book was a modified version of the two in use during the reign of Edward VI, and Parker was determined that it should constitute the standard of an enforced uniformity. Its appearance placed the Puritans in a difficult position, since by and large they felt themselves unable to accept Parker's position, namely that there could be a rigid external order without doctrinal oppression.

Elizabeth, as much as Queen Victoria, had an almost pathological horror of 'eccentric' opinions and excessive religious zeal; and had firmly made up her mind that no Puritan Parliament should force through a religious settlement other than the one that she, as Supreme Governor, decided was best. On 25 January 1566 she wrote to Parker—the letter is included in Parker's *Correspondence*—sounding a note of disquiet at the 'growing diversity of opinion and specially in the external, decent, and lawful rites and ceremonies to be used in the churches'. Somewhat unkindly, she scolded him and his fellow bishops for doing so little about this as well as the 'dangerous preaching abuse'. Such an admonition was indeed unfair, because neither the Queen nor Burleigh was yet prepared publicly to back the policy of the Archbishop.

Parker now decided on action. Through his Dean of the Province, Grindal, Bishop of London, he issued directions to his suffragans requiring them to certify any disorders and to use the machinery of the Church courts to secure conformity. By early March, in conjunction with some four other bishops, he had drawn up what was intended to be a definitive standard, 'partly for due order in the public administration of common prayers and using the Holy Sacraments, and partly for the apparel of all persons ecclesiastical'.

Hopefully, the Archbishop looked to the Crown for confirmation of these 'Advertisements', which required the use of copes in cathedrals, and the surplice in parish churches; but such backing was not forthcoming. Undeterred, Parker insisted that there should be no deviation from this required norm, in this respect differing from Grindal who, although he did his best to be co-operative, acted without enthusiasm. Sampson, Dean of Christ Church, refused outright to obey, and was deprived of his office, much to the personal distress of the Archbishop. 'The comfort that these Puritans have, and their continuance is marvellous,' he told Burleigh in 1573, '. . . and but that we have our whole trust in God, in her Majesty, and in two or three of her Council, I see it will be no dwelling for us in England.'[100] The prospect ahead often plunged him into grievous depression.

One result of the 'Advertisements' was the confrontation at Lambeth of Parker, in the company of an embarrassed Grindal, with over a hundred infuriated London clergy, whom the Archbishop somewhat optimistically admonished: 'Be brief, make no words.' This meeting gave no satisfaction to either party. According to a Puritan account, they were urged to acquiesce in the will of the Supreme Governor concerning matters 'ordained and to be ordained'. Thirty-seven declined on the spot and were suspended, and threatened with deprivation unless they conformed within three months. The Archbishop dealt with the London ministers with such rigour that in time few 'radical' incumbents were left.

Parker's position did not become easier as the years went on. He could not have welcomed a Puritan Bill brought before Parliament in 1571—it was not passed—which would have deprived the Archbishop of those powers which, so it was alleged, made him 'as it were a pope', in particular the authority to dispense. Parker's preoccupation with the Puritan challenge was life-long and it did much, to his great regret, to cloud relations with his old university of Cambridge. On the one hand he wished to do his best for his *alma mater*, on the other—to him they were one and indivisible—he wished to prevent it being captured by the Puritans. Thus he suspended George Withers, a fellow of his own college of Corpus Christi, and forced resignation upon Thomas Aldridge. Jointly with Whitgift, Sandys, and Grindal, he imposed new statutes on the University.

Parker did not live to see the *via media*, to which he dedicated his energies, established beyond the possibility of overthrow. His years at Canterbury coincided with a period when Sandys (Bishop progressively of Worcester, London and York) and Leicester, whose sympathy was with the Puritans, were prominent members of the Queen's Council; and when she herself, though acting decisively to support Parker in suppressing 'prophesying' at Norwich, was still curiously reluctant to show her hand publicly and without disguise. Perhaps it was the woman in her which made for such caution: but it cut Parker to the quick. During his latter years he went seldom to court. And in a mood of despondency he once confessed that had he not been so much bound to her mother Anne Boleyn, he would not so readily have consented to serve the daughter as Archbishop. Finally his health began to fail with 'the rheumatic Tempsis' and his letters to Burleigh assume a sombre tone:

> I have of late been shamefully deceived by some young men and so I have by some older men.

Dr. Collinson in *The Elizabethan Puritan Movement* maintains, with a great deal of evidence, that Archbishop Parker (though to a lesser extent than Whitgift) became so obsessed with the Puritan menace that he drove its moderates into more extreme positions, thereby robbing the Church of England of their distinctive contribution. This may be true, but Archbishop Parker inevitably was a child of his own day, and we must not read history backwards. What he did was to give to the Reformed Church of England a balance, and a sense of history which it has retained ever since. Whether he might have given it a better balance, no man can tell.

One lasting contribution Parker made at a critical period. 'I toy out my time,' he wrote in old age, 'partly with copying of books, partly in devising ordinances for scholars to help the ministry, partly in genealogies and so forth.'[101] It was the pull of an early love in which he could well have spent his years. His devotion to it ensured that from its inception the Church of England was cradled in a respect for sound scholarship which was particularly important at a time when the link with Rome had been discarded. Thus he surrounded himself with learned men, among whom his Latin secretary, John Joscelin, proved invaluable in the discovery and editing of ancient manuscripts. To the work of such scholars we owe the earliest editions of Gildas, Asser, Aelfric, and the *Flores Historiarum*. Perhaps the greatest contribution that Parker himself made to theological studies was the publication of the *Bishops' Bible* which he undertook in co-operation with Cox, Bishop of Ely. His handling of this project shows both sensitivity and common sense in requiring contributors to refrain from the marginal comments which marred Tyndale's version. It seems likely that he himself translated the books of Genesis, Exodus, Matthew, Mark, and the Pauline epistles (except Romans and I Corinthians).

It is, perhaps, symbolic of the uncertainty in which the Church of England was to live for many years after Parker's death in May 1575, that the monument erected to his memory in the private chapel at Lambeth was entirely destroyed in 1648 by order of Colonel Scott, the regicide. His remains were disinterred and buried under a dung-hill. But the *Ecclesia Anglicana* survived its eclipse under the Commonwealth, and Archbishop Sancroft had the remains reinterred in Lambeth Chapel with a revised inscription.

# 5

## EDMUND GRINDAL, THE HONEST PURITAN

The choice of Archbishop Parker's successor seems, in retrospect, surprising, not so much because of his character and ability, but because of his known views and sympathies. It was Queen Elizabeth's greatest misjudgement.

Edmund Grindal, educated at Magdalene and Christ's College, Cambridge, and in 1549 appointed Master of Pembroke, had from early years associated himself with the reformers. At a public conference held before King Edward's commission, he was selected out of the whole University to be one of four disputants against the doctrine of transubstantiation. On Mary's accession he fled to Germany, and during her reign resided chiefly at Strasbourg where he came to know many famous continental theologians, in particular attending the lectures of Peter Martyr, and becoming a close friend. In 1554, when serious divisions broke out among the English gathered at Frankfurt, Grindal was called in to act as peacemaker. During his exile, he occupied himself collecting histories of the Marian martyrs, later incorporated into Foxe's *Actes and Monuments*. When Elizabeth followed Mary he was nominated to the see of London, but at first entertained scruples as to the propriety of wearing episcopal attire. It was unfortunate for Grindal personally that he should have gone to a see where Puritanism was at its strongest, and at a time when Archbishop Parker expected him to exercise a measure of rigid control. For this reason he was translated to York in 1570 where, since the most active dissident minorities were Roman Catholic, he could exercise discipline with a good conscience. His translation to the archbishopric of Canterbury was largely engineered by the Lord Treasurer, Burleigh, who wrote to Walsingham that Grindal was 'the meetest man' to succeed Matthew Parker.

There was, however, an interval of some eight months before, at Christmas, Elizabeth signed his *congé d'élire*. She may well have hesitated, for she must have known that he represented a churchmanship for which she herself entertained little sympathy. There were alternatives to Grindal. Cox of Ely was a suitable successor, but he had, in Elizabeth's eyes, committed the unpardonable sin of a second marriage, quite apart from the fact that he had resisted the designs of Hatton, the Queen's favourite, on Ely House. Whitgift, was not yet sufficiently experienced to be seriously considered. What finally tipped the scales in favour of Edmund Grindal was not his impeccable bachelorhood, but a shift in government policy. The international situation had worsened to such an extent that a Roman Catholic sponsored attack upon England appeared imminent. Prudence dictated a conciliatory policy towards the Puritans. Thus the wisest course might well have seemed to be the elevation of a moderate Puritan. Grindal was indeed a new kind of Primate, being 'one of the very few Elizabethan bishops who enjoyed the full approval of the protestant governing class and the equal confidence of all but a small embittered minority of the godly preaching ministers'.[102] Had he continued to exercise an effective ministry at Canterbury for a number of years both the character of the Church of England and the nature of the archiepiscopal office might have developed differently. Hence his importance. The fact that such years were not given him testifies that the Reformation Church of England lived under a royal supremacy which was no fiction.

Any final estimate of Grindal must take full account of the formative years he spent in Germany during the persecution under Mary. This experience engendered in him the psychological responses common to the Puritans of his time. Thus he reacted strongly against what he regarded as 'Romish dregs . . . offensive to the godly', and he determined to put his own house in order. One 'dreg', which Grindal, in company with the majority of Puritans regarded as especially odious was the Archbishop's Court of Faculties, which even Matthew Parker regarded with a degree of disfavour. In this court the Archbishop exercised some of the powers which earlier had been discharged by the Pope, as for example licences to enter into orders under the canonical age, and to marry during the prohibited seasons. So fierce was the opposition to these dispensing powers that a Bill was unsuccessfully introduced into Parliament in 1571 which would virtually have abolished them. Grindal let it be known both to the Queen and the Council that he would not take it amiss if the Court altogether ceased to exist. This was not to happen, but a few months later he made an agreement with the Council under which some of what were thought of as the most objectionable dispensations were 'utterly abolished as not agreeable to Christ's religion'. A list of fees was drawn up to be divided equally between the Queen, the Archbishop, and his officers. But these reforms did not carry.

Such measures were regarded as only the beginning of a more extreme reformation. To this end Grindal appointed a commission of civilians and ecclesiastical judges to propose radical changes in his three remaining courts—those of the Audience, Arches, and the

Prerogative Court of Canterbury. '. . . in your Grace's Court of Audience,' the commission reported, 'as in all your courts, so [many] things be out of order that few things be as they should be.' What would have happened in this field of his jurisdiction had Grindal enjoyed a long and effective reign at Canterbury can only be conjectured. As it was he had no time to bring about the reforms he desired.

Behind such Puritan attacks on jurisdiction there lay a distinctive attitude towards episcopacy, arising out of what was regarded as its Roman character. In this respect Grindal was considerably influenced by Martin Bucer, whom he knew as Regius Professor of Divinity at Cambridge and whose *Scripta Anglicana*, published in Basle in 1577, he helped to collect. Grindal wished to strip bishops of their autocratic character, and to have presbyters assist them in their rule. This policy met a ready response among the gentry newly 'come of age', and these, with Puritans generally, entertained high hopes of the new Archbishop. Thomas Sampson, deprived of the Deanery of Christ Church, but through Leicester's influence appointed Master of Winston's Hospital at Leicester, wrote at the time—the letter is in the Inner Temple Library in London—that Grindal would prove himself a 'Phœnix'; that he would avoid 'lordliness'; and 'keep the humble and straight course of a loving brother and minister of Christ's Gospel'.

Elizabeth was now to find, to her annoyance, that Grindal was not another Parker; and that if he were allowed to direct the life of the Church of England he would move it nearer to the pattern of the reformed churches on the Continent. Hitherto Lambeth had served as a restraint upon the more extreme protestantism of the returned exiles, particularly those who in conscience scrupled as to whether they ought to accept office. Things were now different, and if reform were ever to come from within the establishment the moment seemed opportune. But in desiring reform in a Puritan direction, Grindal found himself in direct confrontation with the royal supremacy. The clash came over his refusal to prohibit 'prophesying.'

To understand Grindal's position a word must be said as to the significance of prophesying within the Puritan movement. Such exercises were regarded not as optional extras, but integral to the whole concept of church order—that is, to a reformed and disciplined ministry. They represented '. . . the most important single phenomenon of the protestant ascendancy over which Grindal presided'; and a contemporary, Thomas Wood, later commented:

> . . . if they had continued they would in short time have overthrown a great part of [Satan's] kingdom, being one of the greatest blessings that ever came to England.[103]

The practice seems to have originated in Zürich, where its general character was academic and biblical. Its Elizabethan counterpart was far more popular and congregational. Usually the clergy assembled in the parish church of a market town, and there engaged in preaching and general discussion, after which they dined together at a local inn. The character of these meetings was in no sense necessarily anti-episcopal. Indeed, some bishops supported them as a means of getting to know their clergy as 'father and brother rather than lord and judge'. Yet there was, undoubtedly, a tendency for such gatherings to form a church within a church. Dr. Collinson has suggested that it would have been possible to combine the best of both worlds, and for the rural deanery to have been used to promote a godly and learned clergy. Certainly Grindal's policy was to direct the energies of the moderate Puritan clergy into constructive channels within the establishment and thereby to revivify 'rustic dumb dog parsons and uninstructed, undisciplined parishes'. He had himself made inquiries of his fellow bishops as to whether they found meetings for prophesying helpful to their clergy. Ten out of fifteen bishops gave them a qualified approval. Grindal thus gained the general impression that though there were defects, these were in the process of being dealt with, to hasten which he issued his *Orders for Reformation of Abuses about the learned Exercises and Conferences among Ministers of the Church.*

It is easy, however, to see why Elizabeth, with her hierarchical convictions, should have reacted strongly against the growth and continuance of these meetings. So far from encouraging preachers, she wished to restrain them as a too unsettling ingredient in a delicately poised politico-religious situation. She summoned Grindal to her presence and ordered the 'utter suppression' of the prophesyings, and the limiting of 'preachers' to three or four a shire. It was a bitter blow for the Archbishop. He made no reply while with her, but later despatched a letter the like of which, we may believe, she never received from any other person in his office.

> I am forced—he wrote—with all humility, and yet plainly, to profess, that I cannot with safe conscience, and without offence of the majesty of God, give my assent to the suppressing of the said exercises; much less can I send out any injunction for the utter and universal subversion of the same. . . . If it be your Majesty's pleasure for this or any other cause, to remove me out of this place, I will with all humility yield thereunto, and render again to your Majesty that I received of the same. . . . Bear with me, I beseech you, Madam, if I choose rather to offend your earthly majesty than to offend against the heavenly majesty of God.

Two requests he must make: that Elizabeth should refer all ecclesiastical matters touching the doctrine and discipline of the Church to her bishops and other divines; and that in matters of this kind she should not 'use to pronounce too resolutely and peremptorily, *quasi ex auctoritate* as ye may do in civil and extern matters; but always remember that in God's causes, the will of God (and not the will of any earthly creature) is to take place.'[104]

Grindal deserved better than to have this notable, if unrealistic, appeal for spiritual independence dismissed by Bishop Frere as 'a particular piece of characteristically puritan crankiness'. Had it come from Archbishop Laud his judgement might well have been different. Yet it is impossible to conceive a document which ran more counter to Elizabeth's conception of her role as a Tudor sovereign, and it does not seem likely that in thus discharging his conscience Grindal anticipated any favourable response. From his own point of view, the timing of this letter was particularly unfortunate, for he was on bad terms with his patron, the Earl of Leicester, over the matrimonial entanglements of the Earl's physician, Dr. Julio, not to mention his refusal to make over to the Earl his 'goodly house and manor of Lambeth'. Hook states in his *Lives of the Archbishops* that Grindal was called before the Star Chamber in March 1577, but there would seem to be no extant supporting evidence, though it is known that he wished to visit the Court in order that he might discuss his disagreement with the Queen, but refrained from doing so on the advice of Burleigh.

Grindal's steadfastness, if not his political realism, must surely evoke admiration. So convinced was he of the rectitude of his course that he refused to countenance a mediating compromise suggested by Burleigh and Bishop Cox, which would have excluded laymen from the exercises. In the eyes of the Queen such a refusal added 'a second offence of disobedience greater than the first'. On 7 May, in her capacity as Supreme Governor, she sent a letter, drafted by Burleigh, —it is quoted by Strype in his *History of the Life and Acts of Edmund Grindal*—direct to the bishops, by-passing the Archbishop altogether, in which she wrote in the most peremptory terms:

> ... furthermore considering ... the great abuses that have been in sundry places of our realm by reason of the foresaid assemblies called exercises ... we will and straitly charge you that you also charge the same forthwith to cease and not to be used.

On Grindal, personally, the Queen's displeasure now fell. He was sequestered for six months, and Dr. Yale—Vicar-General, Official Principal, Dean of Arches, and Judge of the Audience—was required to act for the Archbishop in the legal discharge of his duties. At the end of the period, Grindal received a private letter from the Lord Chancellor telling him that by refusing to comply with the Queen's order he had shown himself disobedient to her supreme ecclesiastical authority. Hence she had no option but to restrain him. He went on to advise the Archbishop as to how he should make his submission, but here Grindal would not budge. On 30 November 1577, he sent Sir Walter Mildmay to the Council with a letter admitting his disobedience, protesting that in conscience he could do no other, asking that intercession be made for him, but making no submission. By this time Dr. Yale had died, and the Queen gave order that Dr. William Aubrey and Dr. William Clark should now exercise the Archbishop's metropolitical jurisdiction, which they did until his death. By 1582 his health had so declined that he expressed a strong wish to resign: but he died in the following year before the Queen had given her consent.

The precise character of the Archbishop's suspension—for this in fact it was—is hard to determine. In the main, during its operative period, he acted (when he did act) on the express order of the Queen or the Council, although occasionally in the last year of his suspension, on his own authority.

Grindal's suspension is significant of a post-Reformation situation. The clergy no longer constituted a separate estate of the realm in the same way as they had done before the break with Rome. The Pope could no longer espouse their rights. Elizabeth was both sovereign and pope. As Supreme Governor she claimed authority to limit the Archbishop's function, if necessities of state, as in the suppression of a 'seditious movement', so demanded. The Archbishop, on his part, did not question that she could suspend but held that she should not. R. E. Head in his *Royal Supremacy and the Trials of Bishops, 1558–1725* concludes:

> His sequestration seems to have been an arbitrary act justified on political grounds. In a situation where political and religious problems were so intertwined it would be difficult to describe it as an invasion of ecclesiastical jurisdiction; rather is it a complicated regulation thereof, in as much as the Crown working through the Privy Council has taken back to itself both his metropolitan and diocesan jurisdiction and gives him permission from time to time to perform certain acts of jurisdiction.

What cannot be denied is that Grindal's suspension for the major part of his primacy was a blow both to the prestige and authority of his office. That he could not make a fight of it is indicative of the fact that the omni-competent sovereign state, embodied at this time in the will of the monarch, had arrived and could command power.

# 6

## JOHN WHITGIFT, ALLY OF THE SUPREME GOVERNOR

The appointment of Grindal had been a disastrous blunder on the part of the Queen. She dared not risk another, for she needed a strong Archbishop in sympathy with her own approach, particularly since she did not, in matters ecclesiastical, always see eye to eye with her own ministers. Leicester's religious affiliations were known to lie more with the Puritan elements in the nation, while Burleigh, although with his usual caution, was not without friends in that quarter. Her own choice had now crystallized around an authoritarian episcopate enforcing the decencies in worship and apparel of the Book of Common Prayer.

This time, in John Whitgift, Elizabeth did not blunder. From her own point of view she could not have done better, and subject to some qualification this is probably true of the Church of England as a whole. Even Grindal seems to have envisaged him as his successor.

Whitgift was then fifty-three years of age, and his formative years had been spent in Queens' College and Pembroke College, Cambridge. He early showed a predilection for the reformed religion, and in his first lecture as Lady Margaret Professor of Divinity had established his position by identifying the Pope with anti-Christ. Theologically he was, and remained, as his Lambeth Articles of 1581 show, a Calvinist, believing in predestination both to salvation and condemnation. But though Calvinist in doctrine, he had no sympathy for Calvinist principles of church order. He became wholly wedded to an episcopal form of government, and to the use of the surplice. His instincts were those of a headmaster—he is by no means unique among archbishops in this respect—and he had the irritability and impatience which can go along with this occupation. He liked everything tidy, without loose ends. As he saw it, it was as much the duty of the clergy to be loyal to their superiors, the bishops, as it was for the bishops, on their part, to administer, under the Crown, the Act of Uniformity. The policy which he later maintained at a national level was earlier tried out in the more closely-knit community of Cambridge. As Vice-Chancellor he determined to insist upon obedience, and by sheer *force majeure* he managed to deprive Thomas Cartwright, the leader of the left-wing Puritans, from the Lady Margaret Professorship of Divinity. There was a storm of protest, particularly when this was followed by Cartwright's deprivation from his fellowship on the grounds that he had not taken priest's orders within nine years. But Whitgift stuck firm, and in spite of an appeal to Burleigh maintained his position. The strength of the Puritan protest was symptomatic of the fact that the attack on the Church of England was now gaining momentum. Two violent tracts appeared in 1572, each entitled *An admonition to the parliament recommending the reconstitution of the Church along Presbyterian lines*. Whitgift was stung into action, and replied setting out his attitude in *An answer to a certain Libel entitled An Admonition to the parliament*. An episcopal form of government was, he maintained, essential if law and order within the realm were to be maintained. In a further *Defence of the Answer to the Admonition* he wrote:

> I do charge all men before God and his Angels . . . as they will answer at the day of judgment, that under the pretext of zeal they seek not to spoil the church; under the colour of perfection they work not confusion; under the cloak of simplicity they cover not pride, ambition, vainglory, arrogancy; under the outward show of godliness they nourish not contempt of magistrates, popularity and baptistry and sundry others pernicious and pestilent errors.[105]

Ecclesiastical preferment was not slow in coming to such a sturdy defender of the Elizabethan settlement. He was made Dean of Lincoln in 1571; Bishop of Worcester in 1577; and nominated, on 14 August 1583, to succeed Grindal as Primate of All England, himself taking part in the enthronement ceremony at Canterbury on 23 October, instead of acting by proxy as in the case of his three predecessors.

Whitgift was destined to hold the archbishopric for some twenty years, during which time his relations with Elizabeth continued to be uniformly easy and co-operative. They needed to be. His good fortune was that they could be so without dissimulation on either side, for his views on church order coincided with hers. Had they differed, he would have been as ineffective as Grindal. According to Walton in his *Life of Hooker* she is said to have treated her unmarried 'little black husband' as her confessor, revealing to him 'the very secrets of her soul'. If this were so he respected her confidence. It was appropriate that he should be with her when she died on 24 March 1603 'as the most resplendent sun setteth at last in a western cloud'.

A. L. Rowse describes him in his *The England of Elizabeth* as 'a man wholly devoted to the interests of the church . . . rather inscrutable as a person, completely sure of himself, resolute and determined, as able a man of affairs as he was intellectually.'

The situation when Whitgift assumed office was in many respects critical. He was opposed to the Roman Catholics on the score of their doctrine, practice, and general ethos, but he saw them as primarily a political menace, to be dealt with appropriately by the government whose penal legislation he fully supported. His life's work, as he saw it, was to ensure the survival of the Church of England, in the mediating form that the Queen and he himself wished, against attack from within. This meant dealing with such abuses as unlearned ministers, pluralism and non-residence. It also meant the stifling of Puritanism in the ranks of the clergy. It is by an assessment of his policy in this field that the final judgement of Whitgift's archiepiscopate must be made. To bring the Puritans to heel, to make them conform to the statutory order of the Church of England, with its royal supremacy, Act of Uniformity, Book of Common Prayer, Thirty-nine Articles—these were the causes which taxed all his resources. How far he overplayed his hand, and, by eschewing conciliation and declining to make distinctions between the less and the more extreme among its ranks, drove Puritanism as a body into a position of non-conformity incompatible with membership of the Church of England, is a moot point. If this charge be true—it has been made often but never with greater force than in Dr. Collinson's *The Elizabethan Puritan Movement*—then Whitgift was guilty of heightening the very menace which he was seeking to minimize, and in the process making the Church of England far less comprehensive and national in character than it might have been. One suspects that there are too many imponderables to hazard a definitive judgement.

The appointment of Whitgift was greeted by the Puritans with both fear and hope. Walsingham's secretary wrote:

> The choice of that man at this time to be archbishop maketh me to think that the Lord is even determined to scourge his Church for their unthankfulness.[106]

Robert Beale, clerk to the Council, found encouragement from the fact that Whitgift while at Worcester had maintained a preaching ministry, and had behaved charitably towards the non-conformists. Such ambiguity, however, was soon resolved. Even before his enthronement he drew up, in consultation with the bishops, a schedule of 'divers articles touching preachers and other orders for the church'; which, the Queen consenting, he served on the dioceses. Under these articles the clergy were required to subscribe to the royal supremacy; to the Book of Common Prayer as containing nothing contrary to the word of God and alone to be used; and to the Articles of 1562. It was the second requirement which made things really difficult for many a Puritan, especially since it was to be served on lecturers as well as on beneficed clergy.

Whitgift was determined to govern, and a new Commission for Ecclesiastical Causes was set up with himself as its head. This straddled across diocesan boundaries and gave to the Archbishop considerable powers. On 17 November 1583, the anniversary of the Queen's accession, Whitgift delivered a forthright sermon at St. Paul's Cross, in which he preached up the royal supremacy and obedience to those in authority—prince, civil magistrates, and bishops. There were, he complained, three classes peculiarly prone to disobedience—papists, anabaptists, and 'our wayward and conceited persons'.

Puritanism, at this time, it needs to be remembered, was not a homogeneous or clearly defined movement either in its doctrine or theory of church government. There were many gradations, from the conformists who wanted more of a preaching ministry and professed a near-Calvinist theology, to those who sought a fully fledged presbyterian system. Even among the latter views varied. Some would have been content with nothing less than a root-and-branch reform and an abandonment of the royal supremacy: others were prepared to accept, for the time being at least, a few minor adjustments within the Church establishment. Puritanism, however, was not only a religious phenomenon. It spilled over into class structures, affected economic attitudes, and had repercussions upon foreign policy, particularly when fellow feeling for Dutch Protestants cut across mercantile interests. Whitgift himself embarked upon no subtle diagnosis, though the Lambeth Articles of 1595, which were 'a check to the attempt to read a full Calvinistic doctrine into the Thirty-nine Articles', owed much to him. Often he dismissed certain forms of Puritanism as 'the natural rebelliousness of youth'. Yet many of its clergy were mature men, responsibly bringing up families in their parishes, and with everything to lose if they were forced out of their livings.

The effect of Whitgift's policy was to impose upon every Puritan preacher 'a clear choice between the ideals of the nascent Puritan movement and obedience to the society from which he derived his livelihood and in which he could alone hope to exercise a national prophetic ministry.'[107]

The story of what happened when the battle over subscription to the Archbishop's Articles went out into the parishes is far too complicated to be told here. In Whitgift's province—'I mean to perform what I have taken in hand to the uttermost'—the Articles were pressed rigorously. Between three hundred and four hundred ministers refused subscription. Many suspensions followed, for example sixty ministers in Norfolk and Suffolk; seventeen in Kent; twenty-three in Lincolnshire; forty-three in Essex; eleven in Ely. In the implementation of this policy, certain aspects of Whitgift's character were seen at their least happy. Thus when a deputation of Kentish ministers 'came to him unsent for, in a multitude', unlearned sots', his reception of them was a mixture of patience—he gave them an afternoon and most of the two following days—and irritability. One interrupter was shouted down with the words: 'Thou boy, beardless boy, yesterday bird, new out of shell.'[108] Yet doubtless they were very difficult. When the Kentish ministers appealed over his head to the Council he let it be known in no uncertain manner that he was answerable only to the Supreme Governor and often he had to defend himself to Burleigh.

A similar scene took place at another Lambeth meeting when some twenty-five Kentish gentlemen descended upon the Archbishop and took the opportunity of showing the 'contempt' which the governing classes at the time entertained for Elizabethan prelates. He had known six Archbishops, Thomas Wootton expostulated, but Whitgift was the first to set himself against the gentry.

Whitgift, in spite of opposition, determined not to retreat from his policy of no concession. Indeed he even declared—the Queen would probably not have agreed with him here—that subscription must be taken 'in that meaning which those that be in authority . . . do set down, and not in that sense which everyone shall imagine'. In a context of this kind, the complaint of John Hammond, a civilian and Master of Chancery, is understandable, namely that 'such a uniformity . . . as shall be void of difference of opinion never yet was, nor never shall be found, but only in ignorance.'[109] Yet in saying this Hammond was ahead of his times. Whitgift was more representative of a contemporary view, although his lack of moderation caused great uneasiness to the more politically-minded members of the Council, especially to Burleigh and Walsingham. Their misgivings certainly had some momentary effect in modifying the rigour of subscription, in that more time was given for second thoughts, and simple assent to the use of the Prayer Book was taken as adequate. But this more accommodating spirit did not last long. In 1584 Whitgift drew up a series of twenty-four Articles which any suspected clergyman was required to answer on oath *ex officio*, thereby incriminating himself. Burleigh complained bitterly that this procedure took advantage of the more simple and that it was 'so curiously planned, so full of branches and circumstances, as I think the inquisitors of Spain use not so many questions to comprehend and trap their preys'.[110] Yet in spite of this alarm, Whitgift was able to persuade the Crown to extend the powers of the Court of High Commission so as to punish heretics and schismatics. The setting up of this court caused great resentment and the matter was raised in Parliament when Whitgift tried to mollify critics by assuring them that it would only be used as a last resort. In fact, however, the powers of the High Commission were increased still further, the general effect being that legal criticism of official religious policy was made almost impossible. No manuscript could be set up in print unless already licensed by the Archbishop or the Bishop of London. Such an intensification of the attack inevitably welded the Puritans together, and this had its effect upon the Parliament of 1584.

The struggle was now on. Its outcome depended on one person: the Queen. In their naïveté, as James I was to experience on his accession, the Puritans believed that if the Queen were only sufficiently informed, she would 'with all speed cut off those abuses'. She herself now realized, at long last, that the time had come for her publicly to declare her hand. She was goaded into this, apart from political expediency, by the repeated contention of some of the Puritans that the government of the Church was subject to the common law and to parliamentary control. Having summoned the Speaker of the House of Commons to Greenwich, she told him firmly that

> she is the Supreme Governor of this Church, next under God.
> . . . Resolutely, she will receive no motion of innovation, not
> alter or change any law whereby the religion or Church of
> England standeth established at this day. . . . For as she found
> it at her first coming in, and so hath maintained it these
> twenty-seven years she meant in like state, by God's grace, to
> continue it and to leave it behind her.[111]

Such a categorical utterance by the Queen, together with the cold reception in the Commons of a bill to establish a Presbyterian system in England, persuaded the Puritans for the time being to abandon any hope of a political victory. Disappointed but not deterred, they turned to implement by their own efforts the 'grand design' of setting up 'a discipline in a discipline, presbytery in episcopacy'.

The time for such an endeavour, with English forces fighting on the Continent and Mary Queen of Scots executed, seemed not unfavourable. But Whitgift stuck grimly to his policy and was fortunate in having as his right-hand man Richard Bancroft, later his successor, whose restless energy and wide knowledge of Puritanism were unrivalled. Not a tract escaped his eagle eye, and with great cunning he appealed to the cupidity of the property-owning classes, claiming that presbyterianism would prove an expensive luxury by burdening every parish with a dozen or so officers. How far Puritanism was established at the local level in various parts of the country either in the form of a *quasi*-congregationalism or presbyterianism—that is, in accordance with *The Book of Discipline* or *The Geneva Form of Prayer*—cannot be told with precision until this period of Church history has been worked over more thoroughly. Often nonconformity would mask itself under a use of the Prayer Book. Many a minister—Edmund Snape is a case in point—regarded his episcopal ordination as a mere civil requirement, and his real commission to derive from the consent of his 'godly neighbour ministers'. It was this secret or illicit nonconformity which explains, if it does not excuse, Whitgift's rigorous and extreme methods. Their effectiveness was increased by the fact that the political tide began to turn against the Puritans. The death of Leicester in 1588 was for them a disaster, since he was the lynch-pin of their political interest. Soon Whitgift was brought on to the Council—it was an indication of his growing authority—and attended its meetings regularly, the first Archbishop to sit there since Pole. 'The Little Faction', consisting of the Lord Chancellor, Sir Christopher Hatton (who had the ear of the Queen), Bancroft, Richard Cosin, Dean of the Arches, and other civil lawyers, applied themselves day in day out to the task of tracking down and subduing Puritans. The Marprelate Tracts, begun in 1588, the year of the Armada, the authorship of which, though not the publishers, still remains a mystery, were brilliant in their political satire but deplorable in their scurrility. Whitgift, Aylmer, and Cooper were their chief episcopal targets, and the intention was to make these eminent ecclesiastics seem ridiculous. The Archbishop appeared as the 'Beelzebub of Canterbury', 'a monstrous anti-Christ', 'a most bloody tyrant', and 'the Canterbury Caiaphas'. Before the Court of High Commission, the Puritan Henry Barrow described Whitgift as 'a miserable compound . . . the second beast spoken of in the Revelation.' Hitherto the Northern province, because of its Roman Catholic sympathies, had been spared any attempt to harry the Puritans but this policy was now abandoned, Archbishop John Piers, newly appointed, insisting on the wearing of the surplice. Prosecutions before the Court of High Commission now reached their maximum, and Cartwright, the intellectual leader of the Puritans, was imprisoned. On the advice of the Lord Chief Justice and the Attorney-General, who counselled that more extreme punishment was necessary 'to the terror of others', trials were transferred, in May 1591, to the Star Chamber. Even corporal punishment was contemplated. Whitgift himself conducted many interrogations, and listened impatiently to many a curious plea. His nerve and tenacity were remarkable. Barrow and Greenwood were executed, Cartwright left England for Jersey. The ambitious attempts to establish presbyterianism which had led to calling a national assembly at Cambridge in 1586, and in London a year later, were now things of the past. The Archbishop, in spite of declining health, became increasingly master of the situation. 'For the remainder of the reign Puritanism was effectively outlawed by a government vigilant against the least overt demonstration of the old radical spirit.'[112] This does not mean, however, that with the disappearance of formal *classis* and synod after 1590, puritanism was extinguished. Subsequent history illustrates that it had been driven underground, waiting to re-emerge if opportunity should offer.

John Whitgift, at the turn of the century, was an elder statesman, vigilant still but resting upon past achievement. His mantle had now fallen on Richard Bancroft, his supporter of many years and destined to succeed him at Canterbury. Yet Whitgift attended the Council in 1603 at which James VI of Scotland was proclaimed James I of England, and immediately dispatched Thomas Neville, Dean of Canterbury, to Edinburgh, carrying with him archiepiscopal congratulations couched in somewhat obsequious terms. In response to a royal request Whitgift drew up a report on the state of the Church, and received an assurance that the King would maintain the Anglican settlement. Age and infirmity did not prevent him travelling to Theobalds to greet James as he approached the outskirts of London.

John Whitgift's archiepiscopate, whatever the final assessment, must certainly be seen as one of the most significant. He it was who, with the Queen, determined the broad structure of the Church of England, which was later to survive suppression under the Commonwealth. If the methods of implementing his policy were at times severe, almost ruthless, with many errors of judgement along the way, they yet led to a Church which the 'judicious' Hooker, author of *The Ecclesiastical Polity*, could commend reasonably to reasonable and religious men. Though not so comprehensive as some might now wish, it was probably as comprehensive as contemporary passion made possible. Perhaps Strype, if a eulogist, may be allowed to have the last word: 'a man born for the benefit of his country and the good of his church'.

# 7

## THE ARCHBISHOP'S ESTATE

At this point it may be well to ask how the office of Archbishop was affected by the major changes brought about by the Reformation and Tudor legislation?

Dr. Churchill is obviously right when she maintains in her *Canterbury Administration* that as a general principle Henry VIII entertained 'no intention of removing from the archbishop any powers hitherto exercised by him if it was in the interests of the King and the realm that he should retain them'. On the other hand there was certainly no desire to build up his office by transferring to the Primate of All England powers hitherto exercised by the Pope.

Central to every aspect of the Reformation settlement was the severance of the link with Rome and its replacement by the Royal Supremacy. The Roman Curia ceased to have any legal, ecclesiastical or spiritual nexus with the Kingdom of Britain. In its place there now stood the King and his courts. Papal licences and dispensations, though now granted by the Archbishop, required confirmation under the King's seal, and if the Archbishop proved recalcitrant two bishops were empowered to act for him.

Without doubt the uncertainty created by the Reformation encouraged bishops, whose predecessors throughout the Middle Ages had disputed certain aspects of the Archbishop's authority, to question it again, though without success. For example, Stokesley, Bishop of London, protested that Cranmer, when visiting as metropolitan, was usurping powers which originally belonged to the Archbishop only as Lord Chancellor or legate.

A little of this uncertainty was seen in a measure of experimentation over the Archbishop's precise designation. Gardiner, angered at Cranmer's proposed visitation of his diocese, complained that his retention of the title 'Primate of All England' was prejudicial to the Royal Supremacy. Cranmer retorted that its use was customary and that generations of popes, claiming a supreme authority, had found no difficulty in accepting this designation. As for himself, he would be prepared for all bishops to abandon their titles and simply to be known as 'apostles of Jesus Christ'. One exceptional style may be mentioned since, somewhat surprisingly, it refers to the Archbishop as Metropolitan 'by the authority of parliament'. More usually he was said to hold his office on the authority of Henry 'supreme head of the Church of England'.

In respect of a great many of the Archbishop's rights, privileges and duties, the break with Rome made no difference. This was particularly true of his metropolitical status. Thus he continued to administer vacant dioceses, and compositions agreed many years before, indeed as early as Archbishop Boniface, operated still. The Archbishop continued to visit his suffragan dioceses, though here his authority, if not his legal rights, was weakened by frequent royal visitations. At a time of so much legislation and revolutionary innovation it was inevitable that customary procedures should be questioned. Even as late as March 1639, William Laud had to fight to maintain his visitatorial powers against the Bishop of Lincoln.

The Courts of Canterbury and of Audience carried on as before, but increasingly laymen controlled their day-to-day business. As to the Pope's appellate jurisdiction, a new court was set up by the Crown to fill its place: the Court of Delegates, which continued till 1832. The royal supremacy also brought to birth such courts as that of the High Commission, from which there was no appeal (except for a short period during the reign of James I). Although the two Archbishops and other members of the episcopate invariably sat on it, the general effect was to undermine the status of purely ecclesiastical courts.

The Priory of Christ Church, Canterbury, was suppressed along with other monastic institutions, including St. Augustine's; but the capitular foundation which arose out of it recovered, under Queen Elizabeth, the right of formal election, the Crown consenting to nominate this way rather than by means of letters patent. During the suspension of Sancroft (1689–91) commissions, such as those for consecrating bishops, were issued in the name of the Dean and Chapter.

One of the most striking features of the post-Reformation administrative system was the tendency to concentrate many offices in the hands of one man. For example, during the archbishoprics of Cranmer and Pole, the jurisdiction of the Arches was held, under a separate commission, by one who was also Vicar-General and Official of the Court of Canterbury. Permanency inevitably added to power and influence. Also, to quote Dr. Churchill again, it freed the Archbishop from a great deal of 'clogging details of mere routine work', and enabled him more effectively 'to direct the fortunes of the Church of England as a whole on its spiritual side'. Administratively, the

Vicar-General could undertake all the duties of the Archbishop which fell into this category.

When from such practical details we turn to ask the effect of the Reformation changes in general on the status of the Archbishop's office no easy answer can be given. If an opinion may be hazarded, it would be that such status was weakened; and it is significant here that Maitland writes of the statutory Reformation beginning 'not with an act against Rome but against Canterbury'.[113] The legislation of Henry's reign, followed by that of Edward VI and Elizabeth, undermined the administrative integrity of the Church's life by cutting radically at its independence. Convocation became entirely subject to the royal supremacy; there was now no jurisdiction, secular or spiritual, which did not end up in the King's Court. Medieval archbishops were exposed to pressure from both pope and monarch; each could at times cancel the other out. The monarch became a pope on the door-step. Elizabeth's suspension of Grindal illustrates the change, for though medieval monarchs exiled and suspended archbishops, the operation could prove difficult and complex.

One other aspect of the Reformation settlement needs to be noted —the end of the Canterbury estates as the Middle Ages had known them.

The determination to dispossess the Church of much of its real wealth in landed property was a chief driving force behind the suppression of the monasteries, and indeed behind a great deal of anti-clericalism. Here Henry VIII, the greatest acquisitor of all, was at one with many of the more sophisticated of his subjects, to such an extent that among churchmen his cupidity aroused alarm. The Venetian ambassador reported home that Henry was on the verge of annexing all ecclesiastical revenues; and the Emperor Charles V received information that Cranmer was prepared to renounce his temporalities to the Crown *pour encourager les autres*. By November 1534 a plan seems to have been drawn up, prior to its securing statutory sanction, which was to have the effect of creating 'stipendiary bishoprics'. Under its terms,

> the archbishop of Canterbury for maintenance of his estate shall have 2,000 marks yearly and not above, and . . . all the residue of the possessions appertaining to the archbishopric may be made sure to the king's highness and his heirs for the defence of his realm and maintenance of his royal estate.[114]

Under these proposals the income of the archbishopric of York was fixed at half this sum. No such act in fact ever came before Parliament, the Crown being content simply to denude the lordship of

Canterbury of many of its estates. Here Cranmer's complete inexperience in secular administration played into Henry's hands, in spite of the fact that he viewed with dismay this royal assault on the historic estates of the see. In fairness to the Archbishop, so his secretary and biographer Morice protested,

> men ought to consider with whom he had to do, specially with such a prince as would not be bridled, nor be gain-said in any of his requests, unless men would danger altogether.

Cranmer did in fact make an effort to save his temporalities by resorting, on advice, to long leases, but this did not prevent his being forced into unequal 'exchanges' with the Crown. Manor after manor was surrendered after 1536: Wimbledon and Mortlake; Otford, with its members of Shoreham, Sevenoaks, Weald, Chevening, and Knole; Maidstone; East Cheam; Aldington; to mention but a few. Cranmer was for many years plagued by debt—he owed money to the King— and perhaps nothing is more pathetic than the following letter of the Archbishop to Thomas Cromwell:

> . . . as concerning such lands of mine as the King's highness is minded to have by exchange at Maidstone and Otford, forasmuch as I am the man that hath small experience in such causes, and have no mistrust at all in my prince on that behalf, I wholly commit unto you to do therein for me as by you shall be thought expedient, not doubting but that you foresee as much for my commodity as you would that I should do for you in such a like matter. . . .[115]

He would have done better to remember the words of the psalmist: 'Put not your trust in princes, nor in any child of man, for there is no help in them.'

In strict law the surrenders of these extensive estates were regarded as exchanges and not forced sales or confiscations. It was, in practice, a distinction without a difference. Certainly Cranmer did not do well out of them; and the final result was that the old medieval lordship belonging to the Archbishop of Canterbury, with the prestige that went along with it, disappeared for ever. It can, at least, be said on the positive side that these 'exchanges' relieved the Archbishop of many onerous responsibilities for local government: but it was a radical break with the past.

*PART IV*

# KINGLY FAVOUR; SUPPRESSION; RESTORATION

*Archbishops*

# 1

## RICHARD BANCROFT, DISCIPLINARIAN

Richard Bancroft, a Lancastrian, who pursued his studies at Cambridge and became Chaplain to Dr. Cox, Bishop of Ely, early distinguished himself as the relentless foe of any form of puritan deviation. Unique among his contemporaries, by dint of sheer hard work, police methods, and assiduous application, he ferreted out the facts about the Puritans and the 'Grand Design'. Indeed in the end he was said to know more about the Puritans than they knew themselves. In the spirit of a Sherlock Holmes and with the venom of a Senator McCarthy he laid bare the activities of such as Snape; tracked down the efforts of Cartwright and his fellows to set up their discipline secretly in the shires of the realm; briefed Queen's Counsel when agents came before the Star Chamber; commissioned satirists to answer the infamous Martin Marprelate tracts whose authors, in spite of a sustained search, he never succeeded in discovering. On his information both Sir Nicholas Hatton and Whitgift depended in their joint efforts to preserve the *Ecclesia Anglicana* as an episcopal and endowed church. Thus Bancroft ended up by becoming indispensable. As to his religious loyalties, he made these abundantly clear in his famous sermon, preached at St. Paul's Cross on 9 February 1589, which may be described as a minor landmark in English Church history. In this harangue he played up episcopacy as a near divine institution, and condemned the Puritans as 'false prophets', seeking after 'singularity' and in sinister alliance with disruptive lay factions. Never had St. Paul's Cross heard a more confident defence of the established Anglican policy.

His appointment as Bishop of London in 1597 increased his influence, the more so as his policy had all the precision which comes from a mind more concerned with the practical working out of a policy than with those nice discussions of doctrinal problems such as James loved.

The accession of James in 1603 did not of itself dramatically change the political scene. James was no fool; or if he was, his foolishness would sometimes generate more common-sense than did the high principles of his son and successor. His main concern was to preserve the royal supremacy and this meant not encouraging south of the border those religious elements which in presbyterian Scotland had invaded his prerogative, and inflicted improving homilies upon him. There is much to be said for the somewhat cynical judgement of Trevor Roper:

> James I has always cut rather a ridiculous figure in English history: and that largely because he was immune from the destructive enthusiasms of his contemporaries.[116]

Neither his Calvinism nor his wooing of Spain diverted him from maintaining the Elizabethan Settlement with its Book of Common Prayer and episcopal order. His pregnant aphorism, 'No bishop, no king', had relevance apart from its prophetic anticipation of the shape of things to come.

Yet the coming of a king, theologically informed, wedded to Calvinism, and nurtured in a country where a 'godly discipline' was already established, filled the Puritans in England with a new hope. What those who presented the Millenary Petition to James could not, or did not, know was that James had escaped with relief from his northern kingdom and had no intention of seeing its near counterpart set up in England. This did not prevent him, however, against Whitgift's advice, calling and presiding over a Conference at his palace of Hampton Court. It was a tactical blunder which Elizabeth would never have committed, for it gave the Puritans, led by John Reynolds, a public platform on which to debate with Anglican churchmen. James, to be fair to him, did his best to appear impartial, but it was clear that he determined to maintain the full rights of his own position as 'Supreme Governor', and to preserve episcopacy. With disarming frankness he admitted to the assembled divines that in Scotland there had been those who questioned his authority; and now some in England, who had at first prayed for him as supreme over all causes and persons, began to 'abate' their terms of his superiority. Whitgift was beyond the cut-and-thrust of debate, and he allowed Bancroft to take over, which he did with such vigour that he brought down upon him a royal rebuke. When Reynolds made the sensible proposal, fortunately accepted, that there should be a new translation of the Bible, Bancroft exclaimed: 'If every man's humour should be followed there would be no end of translating.'

For the Puritans, the Conference proved to be a tragedy. Reynolds put forward the claims of the moderates with tact and forbearance. He asked that the parish minister might examine the faith of his people as to their fitness to receive Holy Communion; and that a class system might be established within the Church of England. James, in spite of his Calvinism, would have no changes in the government of the Church, particularly such as might weaken its episcopal authority. Maybe it was the conciliatory spirit in which Reynolds put forward his proposals which militated against their acceptance. One disadvantage of this restraint was that it gave James little impression of the strength of Puritan feeling throughout the country or in Parliament. Reynolds was no Andrew Marvell, putting the fear of God into his opponents.

Bancroft, as Bishop of London, also deputized for Whitgift at the Convocation which followed the Hampton Court Conference. Through his initiative it issued *Constitutions and Canons Ecclesiastical which embraced various articles injunctions and synodical acts put forth in the reigns of Edward VI and Elizabeth.*

No enterprise was more congenial to his taste or temperament. The Church of England had undergone great changes during the previous century affecting every aspect of its corporate life. The result was uncertainty as to how canons, statutes, common law, and royal injunctions fitted into each other and how far they were enforceable in the courts.

The intention was that this codification—there were 141 constitutions in all—should regulate the religious, and in many respects more than religious, life of the people of England from the cradle to the grave. It was concerned with the ordination of bishops, priests, and deacons; the control of worship; the conduct and attire of the clergy; the regulation of ecclesiastical courts; the licensing of schoolmasters; and the authority of synods. In their precision and comprehensive character, these canons illustrate admirably both the breadth and limitation of Bancroft's mind.

Needless to say the basic assumption of this codification was that every citizen must attend his parish church. James, by his 'prerogative, royal and supreme authority', publicly ratified the Constitutions, and commanded that they be 'diligently observed, executed, and equally kept by all our beloved subjects of this kingdom'. The immediate response of a Puritan dominated Parliament was the passing of a Bill in the House of Commons to secure that no canons enacted in the previous ten years or thereafter should have 'force to impeach, or hurt any person in his life, liberty, lands or goods', unless first confirmed by legislation. The inference was clear. There was a cleavage in the country which went beyond differences of theological view and entered into areas of both law and government. Legalists came to take the view that these canons did not bind the laity; and Bancroft was thereby committed, for the rest of his life, to bitter opposition in the courts of common law. In his *Articles of Abuses*, he protested against the increasing number of prohibitions which by-passed the ecclesiastical courts. Not surprisingly the canons, in their entirety, were never implemented.

Puritans in their anger retaliated by accusing Bancroft of inclining to catholicism. This was unjust, for he himself was responsible for additional measures designed against recusants; but the charge was provoked by his anti-Puritan policy in general. Not content with requiring an external conformity, he even demanded an assent from the heart. His *ex animo* form of subscription, devised by himself, was intended to test how far the clergy gave a full assent to the Book of Common Prayer. In this he went even further than Whitgift. As a result some three hundred clergy were admonished and some sixty probably deprived.

Bancroft became Archbishop of Canterbury in October 1604; and Puritan feeling against him exploded before the Privy Council in November 1606, when Andrew Melville, formerly imprisoned in the Tower,

> burdened him with all these corruptions and vanities and superstitions, with profanity of the Sabbath day, silencing, imprisoning and bearing down, of the true and faithful preachers of the Word of God, of setting and holding up of antichristian hierarchy and popish ceremonies.

Not content with rhetoric, he took Bancroft by 'the white sleeves of his rochet' calling them 'Romish rags and a part of the beast's mark'. James, who regarded kings as 'the breathing images of God upon earth', was cut down to size as 'God's silly vassal.'[117] It was the augury of a bitter harvest to be reaped later.

Bancroft's policy was not, however, confined to a negative hostility to Puritanism. He was equally concerned to build up the day-to-day life and witness of the Church of England. To this end, he fought continually in the Court of High Commission, as did Laud after him, to recover lands lost to the Church. He was unsuccessful, however, in 1610, in securing the passage of a Bill through Parliament which would have made rural praedial tithes payable in kind, and urban ones calculable according to rentals. He was consistently concerned to protect and improve the lot of the parish priest. For these purposes, the courts of High Commission and Star Chamber were invaluable, particularly when it came to disciplining the great offender. A project, dear to his heart, was the founding of a college of controversial divinity at Chelsea, but this was never realized.

The effect upon the archbishopric itself of Bancroft's four years of office is not easy to assess. William Camden, the antiquary, speaks of his 'singular courage and prudence in all matters relating to the discipline and establishment of the Church';[118] and Clarendon pays tribute to his encouraging 'the clergy to a more solid course of study than they had been accustomed to'.[119] Bancroft himself had considerable literary ability and his library still adorns Lambeth. Like his successor but one at Canterbury, he had a passion for order, and was never over nice in his methods to promote it. Politically, maybe, he has much to answer for, since he encouraged James indissolubly to marry the cause of the monarchy with that of episcopacy. True, Elizabeth had come down on the side of the bishops, but she never committed herself to the view that the Crown could not survive without them. Whatever Bancroft achieved, he achieved it, like Whitgift, under the protection of the Crown; but this very dependence was to prove a subsequent cause of danger.

# 2

I

Bancroft died on 2 November 1610, and was buried in Lambeth parish church. It might have been expected that his successor would be of the same school: but things did not work out this way.

Four candidates soon emerged: James Montague of Bath and Wells, Thomas Bilson of Winchester, Lancelot Andrewes of Ely, and George Abbot of London. Of these, Lancelot Andrewes seemed the most suitable and the most likely. He was a personal friend of James, who admired his brilliance in the pulpit; also he was a firm upholder of the royal prerogative, and a churchman after the school of the judicious Hooker. According to Peter Heylin, an ecclesiastical historian, Andrewes's name was put forward by some of the bishops and 'other great men of the court', who felt that they could not recommend either Montague or Abbot, 'both of them being extremely popular and such as would ingratiate themselves with the Puritan faction, how dearly so ever the Church paid for it'.[120] James appeared to warm to such representations, but royal nomination, then as now, was exposed to manipulation by private interests at the last moment. In this case, the intervention came from the Earl of Dunbar, who pleaded Abbot's cause, doubtless reminding the King of the service which he had rendered in introducing episcopacy into Scotland and defending the King in the squalid affair of the Gowrie conspiracy.

> He put it so powerfully in his behalf, that at the last he carried it, and had the King's Hand to the passing of the *Public Instruments*.[121]

In the meantime, the Earl of Dunbar died; but respect for a dead friend worked powerfully on James's temperament. George Calvert, in a letter to Sir Thomas Edmondes, commented that the King had told both Abbot and the Council that

> it is neither the respect of his learning, his wisdom, nor his sincerity (although he is well persuaded there is not any one of

them wanting in him), that hath made him to prefer him before the rest of his fellows, but merely the recommendation of his faithful servant Dunbar that is dead, whose suit on behalf of the bishop he cannot forget, nor will not suffer to lose his intention[122]

—reasons hardly adequate criteria for so responsible an appointment and at such a critical time. On 4 March 1611, Abbot was formally nominated, and on 9 April 'very honourably' installed at Lambeth. So, to quote from a letter of Sir George Calvert, formerly a secretary to Robert Cecil and later the planter of a colony in Newfoundland, it was 'by a strong north wind coming out of Scotland' that Abbot was 'blown over the Thames to Lambeth'.[123] His promotion was said to have left him 'wonder-struck'.

It was in many ways an extraordinary nomination, since it broke continuity in the directing of Church affairs from Lambeth, the more serious as it proved because Abbot was to hold office for some twenty-two years.

Superficially, however, there might seem much to commend it. Both Abbot and the King were theologically Calvinist, while wedded to episcopal government. At a time when puritanism in Parliament constituted an ever-increasing embarrassment to royal policy, such an appointment might well seem an act of conciliation. Nor was Abbot himself without ability or charm. He had a distinguished career at Oxford, culminating in his becoming Vice-Chancellor, in which capacity he conveyed the congratulations of the University to James on his accession. With other scholars he assisted in the translation of the Gospels, the Acts of the Apostles, and the Apocalypse, for the new Authorised Version of the Bible.

Abbot's reign at Canterbury was to illustrate again that the influence of any post-Reformation Archbishop at this period depended on the goodwill of the Supreme Governor. Abbot lost this goodwill, and the effectiveness of his archiepiscopate departed with it.

The reasons for this loss were many, the chief being the fitful and changing nature of his master's political concerns. Among the first to be shed was the royal desire to conciliate the Puritans, which, as we have seen, was the only solid reason for Abbot's elevation. Abbot's strong anti-papism therefore ceased to commend him at a Court where to flirt with Romanism had become fashionable. To make matters worse, his resort to the High Commission for the disciplining of Papists, who could 'expect little mercy when the Metropolitan [was] mediator' incurred the hostility of that doughty champion of the common law, Chief Justice Coke. In addition, the Archbishop made his own position the more difficult by the ambiguity of his theological position. Bishops, in his eyes, were a superintendency pastorate, not a separate order of the ministry; yet as an authoritarian he despised separatists. Such views did not commend him either to episcopalians or Puritans. Moreover, within the Church of England, the austere spirit of Geneva was giving place to the more tolerant and reasonable approach of Arminius.

On one matter Abbot entertained deep feelings. He was determined to use his influence to prevent any alliance with Spain through the marriage of the King's children. Perhaps the great triumph of his archiepiscopate, certainly in the short term, was the marriage of James's daughter Elizabeth to the Elector Palatine Frederick V. Abbot had consistently espoused it, and to this end ingratiated himself with the Elector, giving a lavish banquet, on 29 January 1613, to the German princes. He it was who married the couple on 12 February, using the order of the Book of Common Prayer. The Archbishop little knew what a legacy he was leaving behind him!

In spite of all his difficulties, Abbot's tenure of office might have proved easier, though not necessarily more effective, if he could have shed a stubborn independence which prevented him becoming the tool of either King or Parliament. He never found it easy to give or withhold advice simply to please. Many instances could be quoted. The King's real problem—it became even more urgent under his son—was a shortage of money. To solve this Abbot counselled him in 1615, unpalatable though the advice was, to call Parliament, in spite of its puritan character. He refused to sanction the reading in churches of James's 'Declaration of Sports'. He directly opposed the royal will by declining his support to a divorce for the Countess of Essex to enable her to marry the Earl of Somerset—a matter in respect of which Laud's compliance led to life-long contrition. This latter affair became a *cause célèbre*, and it showed clearly that Abbot was not prepared to accommodate his conscience to the desires of the Supreme Governor. The Countess's petition was referred to a commission of five bishops and six civil lawyers, presided over by the Archbishop, who, however, in an interview with James at Windsor, fell down

> on his knees twice or thrice to entreat his majesty that he might
> be dispensed with being on the commission which he would
> esteem a greater favour than all that he had received from him in
> being raised from a private position, and in so short a time, to
> the highest dignity.[124]

But he was not permitted to wash his hands of this delicate matter. He then drew up a paper for the King's benefit, in which he stressed the evils flowing from divorce—divorce with a view to remarriage was condemned in the canons of 1604—maintaining that the best solution was reconciliation and that no pains ought to be spared to bring this about. James felt his personal honour affronted at such a display of archiepiscopal independence, particularly from one whom he described as his 'creature':

> I must freely confess to you—he wrote to Abbot—that I find the grounds of your opposition so weak as I have reason to apprehend that the prejudices you have of the persons is the greatest motive in breeding these doubts in you.[125]

The last remark, in its reference to the Countess being a niece of Abbot's bitterest enemy, the Earl of Northampton, was ungenerous and almost certainly untrue. When finally the commissioners came to vote on the validity of the marriage, Abbot stood his ground and was one of the minority of five which maintained it. With questionable consistency, however, he was present when the Lady Essex finally married the Earl of Somerset. The Archbishop's own summing up of the case, given in Howell's *State Trials*, goes to the heart of the matter. 'I could not force my conscience which cried upon me that it was an odious thing before God and man to give the sentence the King desired without better warrant.'

Abbot was responsible for the introduction of George Villiers, Duke of Buckingham, to James and the Court. It proved a blunder, for this somewhat shoddy royal favourite became his uncompromising opponent, a contingency which the Queen herself foresaw when she warned him that if this young man were once to be brought in, then the first person to suffer would be the Archbishop himself. And so it proved. While Abbot was advocating war with Spain, indeed war generally with the Roman Catholic powers of the Continent in the interests of the Elector, now King of Bohemia, Buckingham was planning an alliance with Spain, and reopening the question of a Spanish marriage. Let the Elector's war be prosecuted with energy, Abbot urged, 'that it may appear to the world that we are awake when God in this sort calleth to us'.[126] Such words of archiepiscopal exhortation were not calculated to spur the cautious James to action.

As the reign went on, it was clear that Abbot's fortunes were in decline and that the primacy in his hands was becoming increasingly ineffective. He could neither, in conscience, buttress up his waning fortunes by siding with the increasing power of a puritan Parliament, nor commit himself entirely to royal policy. To add to his sense of isolation, he lost the friendship of the Queen, whom he attended on her deathbed, and whose funeral sermon he preached in Westminster Abbey on 13 March 1619.

On 24 July 1621, Abbot went hunting in Bramzil Park, and shot at a buck with a cross-bow. He missed, and killed a gamekeeper, one Peter Hawkins, who had been repeatedly warned to keep clear. The Archbishop was overwhelmed with grief, and ever afterwards observed a monthly fast. Such was his contrition that he granted Mrs. Hawkins a generous pension, which enabled her promptly to secure another husband. The inquest brought in a verdict of 'death by misfortune and his own fault'. The King very sensibly remarked, according to a letter of Sir Dudley Digges preserved among James's *State Papers Domestic*, that 'none but a fool or a knave would think worse of a man for such an occurrence, and that the like had nearly often happened to himself'. There the matter might have ended had Abbot not been a cleric, and surrounded by so much combustible material. 'The fame of that man's death,' Thomas Fuller commented in his *Worthies of England*, 'flew faster than the arrow that killed him.'

Theoretically, it might be argued that the Archbishop had fallen into an irregularity according to canon law and could be suspended from all his ecclesiastical functions. There were, so it happened, four bishops-elect awaiting consecration, two of whom, John Williams, Dean of Westminster, a man whose character it is difficult to under-estimate and who, maybe, had an eye on Canterbury, and William Laud, a life-long enemy, professed conscientious scruples preventing their accepting consecration at his hands.

> . . . for the King to leave a man of blood, Primate and Patriarch of all his churches, is a thing that sounds very harsh in the old Councils and Canons of the Church—so Williams wrote to Buckingham.

Meanwhile Abbot retired to his native Guildford, bemoaning the 'bitter potion' which led to his being 'the talk of men to the rejoicing of the papists and the insulting of the puritans'. James realized that he could not, as Supreme Governor, let the matter rest without some formal judgement, and he set up a Commission on 3 October 1631, which included in its membership the Chief Justice of the Common Pleas, the Dean of the Arches, Laud, and Williams. The opinion of the Sorbonne and other universities was also sought—it was a traditional procedure—and matters of differing degrees of subtlety and irrelevance were raised. John Hacket, author of a biography of Archbishop Williams, wrote that the case 'made work for learned men to turn over their books'. The whole matter is set out at length in *A Short Apology for Archbishop Abbot, touching the death of Peter Hawkins*, written by the legalist, Sir Henry Spelman. Into the intricacies of his argument we shall not follow him. What mattered for the Archbishop was the report that the Commissioners gave to the King on 10 November. While lacking unanimity it was not, on the whole, unfavourable. As to whether he had committed an irregularity, members of the Commission were equally divided. A majority, however, believed that the homicide might conceivably be considered a scandal, particularly 'by the Weak at home and the Malicious abroad'. The Commissioners debated long as to the most appropriate method to reinstate the Archbishop. All agreed that this could only be done by the King, but some felt that he should move by way of instructing four bishops to give formal absolution. Finally this decision was left to the King's discretion. Perhaps, wisely, he decided to act through the bishops. Abbot, however, did not consecrate the bishops-elect, this being done by his suffragans on a commission from him.

It was all a trying ordeal for the Archbishop, and there can be no question but that it permanently lowered his prestige. Thus, not long before his death, his coach was 'incommoded' by a crowd of women who cried: 'Ye had best shoot an arrow at us.'

Back in office, Abbot returned to his endeavours to secure a break with Spain, admonishing the King that the 'honour of England' demanded it. But James unexpectedly died on 5 March 1625. The Archbishop was not with him at his passing, nor was he asked to preach the memorial sermon in Westminster Abbey. Relations between King and Archbishop had never been easy or co-operative, for James soon grew tired of him, and ceased to find his Calvinism a political asset.

II

The accession of Charles, over whose coronation Abbot presided, did not help him to regain favour. The new King had little sympathy either with the kind of churchmanship for which Abbot stood or his desire for a sitting Parliament. Moreover, their relations—Charles was under the domination of the Duke of Buckingham—began badly when Abbot refused to give his *imprimatur* to the printing of a sermon delivered by the extreme royalist Dr. Sibthorpe, Vicar of St. Sepulchre, Northampton. Abbot's objections were fundamental, namely that the preacher gave support to loans not sanctioned by law or custom; that his attitude was conciliatory towards Roman Catholics; and that he lacked sympathy with the plight of foreign Protestants.

It may be that the sermon was sent to Abbot with the deliberate intention of embarrassing him; for on declining his *imprimatur*, it was sent to Laud, Bishop of Bath and Wells, who after correcting some crude errors returned it to the Archbishop. But Abbot determined to stand his ground, and the sermon finally received the blessing of George Monteigne, Bishop of London.

To Charles, egged on doubtless by both Buckingham and William Laud, this non-co-operative attitude seemed a direct affront to his supremacy and a wanton dissociation from his general policy. Feeling his isolation, Abbot removed himself to Croydon, where on 5 July 1627 he received a visit from Lord Conway, Secretary of State, who informed him that it was the King's command that he must withdraw to Canterbury and 'meddle' no more with the High Commission's affairs. No official reason was given, but in private conversation Conway informed him that this order was the result of his failing to license Dr. Sibthorpe's sermon. The Archbishop replied briefly that at the moment he was engaged in a suit with the citizens of Canterbury and therefore his presence among them would be embarrassing. It was agreed that he should retire to his nearby house at Ford, from where he carried on his ordinary jurisdiction through his officials.

This assertion of the royal supremacy was arbitrary. But it could be argued that the Archbishop had no absolute, as distinct from customary, right to sit on the High Commission, which was a court established for ecclesiastical purposes arising out of the royal supremacy. In this respect, the King might claim to be acting constitutionally. However, he now went further, and by an instrument, dated 9 October 1627, the Archbishop's authority was put into a commission to be exercised by the bishops of London, Durham, Rochester, Oxford, and Bath and Wells. The instrument effecting this listed the Archbishop's duties, making a distinction between those that he discharged personally and those which he delegated to others. It then went on:

> . . . we, therefore, of our regal power and of our princely care and providence, that nothing shall be defective in the orders, discipline, government or right of the church, have thought fit, by the service of some other learned and reverend bishops, to be named by us to supply these things which the said Archbishop ought or might, in the cases aforesaid, to have done, but for this present cannot perform the same.[127]

The Commissioners were then named, and the Archbishop's officials continued in their offices. Writs addressed to the Archbishop henceforth took on a different form.

Concerning his parliamentary duties, the King sent him a letter in his own hand forbidding him to attend personally, but allowing him to choose his own proxy. Where Convocation was concerned, he must nominate the Bishops of London and Bath and Wells.

What is significant, in this somewhat extraordinary proceeding, is that there was no mention of any formal charge, nor was the Archbishop called on to give any reasons why his sequestration ought not to stand. The complaint against him, apart from an incompatibility between Abbot's general attitude and the King's policy, was that in refusing to license Dr. Sibthorpe's sermon he had shown himself hostile to the exercise of the royal prerogative in a matter of government—and in the King's eyes nothing could be worse.

His suspension was a political act, and constitutionally an act of tyranny. Not surprisingly, therefore, it became a matter of contention in Parliament, where it added to the armoury of Puritan members who were determined to curb the prerogative of the Crown and in process of drawing up the Petition of Right, which Abbot supported. The Archbishop duly appeared before the House of Lords and—the words are Hacket's, later Bishop of Coventry and Lichfield, taken from *Scrinia Res erata*, his eulogistic biography of Archbishop Williams—

> ... offered his own Case to be considered, banished from his own House of Croydon and Lambeth, confined to a moorish Mansion-place of Foord, to kill him, debarred from the management of his Jurisdiction, and no cause given for it to that time; harder measure than was done to him in Pedagogy, for no Scholar was ever corrected till his fault was told him.[128]

This intervention in Parliament proved finally successful. Charles was persuaded to revoke the Commission for exercising Abbot's jurisdiction and in December he was sent for to the Court, being received from his barge by the Archbishop of York and the Earl of Dorset who escorted him to the King, where he was given the royal hand to kiss and exhorted not to fail in his attendance at the Council twice a week.

The hollowness of such a reconciliation was self-evident, for it could do nothing to change the practical situation which had led to the sequestration. Restored to office, Abbot continued to maintain his independence of the Crown in Parliament; busied himself with his duties as Visitor of All Souls College, Oxford; and on the High Commission used his authority to promote conformity as he, though not always Laud, understood it.

The last four years of his archiepiscopate were a time of near retirement. He had irrevocably lost the King's favour and was out of sympathy with royal policy. Laud, now Bishop of London, who had used the opportunity of Abbot's enforced inactivity to infuse a greater vigour into the policy of Church reform, dominated ecclesiastical affairs, preaching up royal absolutism. It was Laud, not Abbot, who, in co-operation with Archbishop Harsnett, drew up a series of instructions which imposed upon bishops the duty to live in their dioceses; to add to the revenues of their sees; and to give an account of their stewardship to their Metropolitan. Yet constitutional propriety was preserved when Abbot, on the command of the King as Supreme Governor, was required to issue them. On the premature death of the Queen's first child, it was Laud who buried him; and baptized the infant Charles, later Charles II. For Abbot, the knowledge that the Bishop of London would almost certainly be his successor and would reverse his policies, must have been galling. The last account of the condition of his province which Abbot gave to the King has about it, under the guise of a naïve optimism, the sense of a man who has abandoned effective control.

> It is enough to say that the bishops for aught it appeareth to me, have lived at home . . . [that] ordination of ministers for aught that I can learn, are canonically observed . . . and so it may be said of the articles, that I find no noted transgression of them.[129]

Abbot's health was now deteriorating, although it seemed to revive in the last months of 1632 '. . . if any other prelate gape after his benefice', so a Mr. Cory wrote to Sir Thomas Puckering, 'his grace perhaps . . . [may] eat the goose which shall graze upon his grave'. But on 4 August of the following year he was dead. It may be significant that he elected to be buried in his native Guildford, where his noble Charity exists to this day.

Few archbishops have had such a raw deal from subsequent historians as Archbishop Abbot. Maybe he deserved it even if they failed to appreciate, in their condemnation, the impossibility of his position at a time when no archbishop could hope to be effective apart from strong royal support. It was not his fault that to secure such support, he must compromise his conscience, though in discharging this loyalty he might have dealt more tactfully with James. The result was that though division within the Church grew more fierce, he had no effective means to offset it, and his temperament made him too much of a martinet to woo opposition.

Clarendon suggests that had Lancelot Andrewes succeeded Bancroft the Church might well have been spared some of the troubles which later ensued. This is doubtful. Admittedly Abbot neither had the sustained energy, nor could he command the necessary governmental backing, to maintain a practical policy of improving the lot of the clergy, reforming abuses, establishing discipline, and restoring to the Church the financial resources of which she had been progressively despoiled. In these areas of his administration, in spite of the fact that he inherited from his predecessor three able administrators in Sir John Lambe, Sir Charles Caesar, and Sir John Bennett, he lacked a sense of urgency.

# 3

## WILLIAM LAUD, REACTIONARY AND REFORMER

I

Upon the death of Abbot, though a preacher in London implored the Deity 'not to send a Bonner or a persecutor of the Church', little doubt was entertained as to the person of Abbot's successor. On the second day after the Archbishop's death, Charles greeted Laud with the words: 'My Lord Grace of Canterbury, you are welcome.'

The new Archbishop had certainly undergone a long apprenticeship, as he took good care to point out to Lord Saye many years afterwards:

> *Suddenly advanced!* What does my Lord call 'suddenly'? I was eleven years His Majesty's Chaplain in Ordinary before I was made a bishop. I was a bishop twelve years before I was preferred to be Archbishop of Canterbury, that highest place my Lord mentions. When I was made Archbishop, I was full threescore years of age, within less than one month.[130]

With a strongly practical cast of mind, Laud combined a curiously superstitious temperament—he remained throughout life preoccupied with his dreams—and he seems to have entered upon his new office with a sense of foreboding. Even his move to Lambeth complete with two pets—a tortoise and a Smyrna cat—was unfortunate. The ferry over the Thames capsized, so that his coach and horses were submerged. 'But I praise God for it, I lost neither man nor horse.' His health, as so often, worried him, and he did not welcome 'slid[ing] over in a barge to the Court and the Star Chamber' instead of 'jolting . . . over the stones between London house and Whitehall'.

> In truth, my lord—so he wrote to the Earl of Strafford in a letter preserved in his *Works*—I speak seriously: I have had a heaviness hang over me ever since I was nominated to this place, and can give myself no account of it, unless it proceeds from an apprehension that there is more expected from me than the craziness of these times will give me leave to do.

Such forebodings proved well founded.

The significance of Laud's primacy, in the long story of English archbishops, lies in the fact that no successor has ever aspired to play his role. Whether or no we see Laud as an anachronism even in his own time, it was an anachronism which did not recur.

William Laud went up from the Free Grammar School at Reading to St. John's College, Oxford, when John Buckeridge, whose influence upon him proved to be decisive, was its President. Buckeridge had earlier headed the reaction at both Universities against a dominant Puritanism, while condemning the fashionable flirtation with Roman Catholicism. He stood for an Anglican *via media* rooted in an episcopal order.

Laud responded readily to this teaching and never abandoned its essential tenets. A sermon maintaining the visibility of the Church from apostolic times, delivered shortly after his ordination, drawing down upon him the condemnation of Dr. Abbot, then Vice-Chancellor of the University, could still have been preached by him when over seventy.

Laud's theological position, however, was, perhaps, a little more flexible than is sometimes allowed. As he saw it, the twin foundations of faith were the scriptures and the creeds, interpreted by the Apostolic Church. Roman Catholics were members of the true Church in that they 'received the Scriptures as a rule of faith, though but as an impartial and imperfect rule, and both sacraments as instrumental causes and seals of grace.' In the spirit of the 'judicious' Hooker, and influenced maybe by the more radical Chillingworth to whom he was surprisingly tolerant, Laud was reluctant to require too much, or to suppose 'that all points defined by the Church are fundamental'. Indeed, if men were required to subscribe to all 'the curious particulars disputed in the schools', then there could never be unity. What mattered was acceptance of those articles which were of 'soul saving faith'; and when there was genuine doubt as to what these were it was best dealt with by a 'lawful and free general council, determining according to the scriptures'. As to matters 'not necessary for salvation', these could be left to discussion by duly authorized exponents rather than be made subject to *dictats* issued under the authority of an infallible church. This meant that he entertained deep intellectual convictions which kept him away from Rome. Twice in his lifetime he was approached with an offer of a cardinal's hat if he changed his allegiance; but, as he reported to the King, 'something dwelt within me which would not suffer that, till Rome were other than it is'.

By and large Laud's attitude and interests were practical. It was typical that he confessed to being 'the slave of actions not words'. So far from encouraging widespread religious discussion, he wanted to damp it down. Puritanism was anathema to him; anathema in its dogmatism; in its generation of a theoretical religious interest; in its political and economic manifestations. Professor Trevor Roper, whose biography of Laud, if at times a little unsympathetic, is yet a brilliant piece of analysis, writes of puritanism that it was a 'doctrine for the mercantile classes who having acquired wealth looked for power'. Laud was determined, if he could not deprive them of the one, at least to deprive them of the other. Like the bulk of his contemporaries, Laud was no democrat. He did not believe that lawful authority derived from the people, or that there was any peculiar value in election or representation as such. Authority in both Church and State existed by divine decree, and as such constrained obedience. To enforce such obedience both must have power; and in practice this meant wealth and material possessions. Thus he deplored the spoliation of the Church's lands at the Reformation and condemned those bishops who had secured office by consenting to such alienation. He well knew that it was the Puritans, the rising mercantile classes, who now had wealth, and he was determined to redress the balance. Throughout his archiepiscopate he sought to restore to the Church what it had lost; to re-create the clergy once again an estate of the realm; to assert their independence of both local squire and central Parliament. His metropolitical visitation of seven dioceses in 1634 convinced him that there was much crippling poverty among the parochial clergy, and that it existed to such an extent that many 'are scarce able to clothe and feed them[selves]'. He therefore secured the King's co-operation in forbidding bishops to grant leases for life on their ecclesiastical lands. But the better endowed church for which he worked must be efficient and do things decently and in order. Bishops must see to it that the parish church was looked after in a proper manner, by the fencing off of the communion table at the east end; by the wearing of the surplice (and copes in cathedrals); by keeping absenteeism and pluralism within the bounds of the law. 'Thorough' was his watchword, and to this end neither wealth nor privilege must be allowed to stand in the way.

Such a policy demanded constant vigilance and resort to the necessary sanctions. But what were these sanctions, and whence did they derive? The answer to Laud was transparently clear: from the royal governor 'supreme over all causes and all persons ecclesiastical as well as civil'. To discharge his responsibilities the King must have access to financial resources independent of a Parliament dominated by Puritan interests.

Here Laud's basic thinking as to the nature of authority, doubtless subconsciously influenced by practical exigencies, came to his aid.

The King ruled by divine right and was in no way answerable to his people. True, he was a steward who must render up a dreadful account, but to God only. Hence, Laud, unlike Abbot, was prepared to assist in the publication of Dr. Sibthorpe's extreme assertion of the doctrine of passive obedience. The King was God's immediate vice-gerent on earth, '. . . . one and the same action is God's by ordinance and the King's by execution.'

With great unwisdom, so it proved, Laud worked out the logic of this position by arriving at a low view of Parliament. To him it was that 'noise', an assembly meddling with matters too high for it and not really its concern. For eleven years he encouraged the King in its suppression and only inescapable necessity made him counsel its reassembling. Such an attitude goes a long way to account for the extreme hostility felt towards Laud when the Long Parliament met in November 1640. Whereas the House of Commons stood for presbyterianism shading off to independency, the monarchy stood four-square behind episcopacy. A head-on collision, in the long run, was inevitable.

In line with this exaltation of the royal prerogative, Laud took the logical view that all subjects of the Crown, whether in Scotland or Ireland, on the Continent or in the Plantations of America, must conform to the religion of the Supreme Governor.

It was, of course, a constitutional thesis impossible of complete realization: but it was put into practice with varying degrees of success. In Ireland, Strafford, Laud's friend and ally, set about its implementation with energy; but in Scotland the policy proved disastrous and precipitated the Civil War. In this area of royal responsibility Laud regarded himself as properly the King's adviser in spiritual matters, even rebuking Charles when he thought he was being by-passed. North of the border, Laud had no legal status, but here he acted on the assumption that his close relationship with the Crown gave him the right to offer counsel.

To Laud, political, social, and religious philosophy seemed all of a piece: but in fact the royal supremacy encouraged him to adopt a view of his own office which already looked to the past rather than took cognizance of the secular world of the future.

> The Church and the State—he wrote, and Wilkins in his *Concilia* records—are so near united and knit together, that though they may seem two bodies, yet indeed in some relations they may be accounted as but one.

In principle, many Puritans would have agreed.

II

How, at the practical level and against the opposition of a considerable dissident 'nonconformity', did Laud hope to discipline the people of Britain into this Anglican allegiance?

First, he was busily active in using every resource to make the existing machinery of the Church and its personnel work. The keystone in this endeavour was the bishop, a nominee of the Crown, equipped with his own courts and legal officials. Through him parish priests and other clergy within the diocese were to be kept working and loyal. Each diocesan, as we have seen, he required to give an annual account of his stewardship. Here Laud was meticulous in keeping bishops up to the mark, coming back at them when necessary, as in the case of Robert Wright of Lichfield and Coventry who, after a period of four years' silence, eventually apologized for his neglect on the score that it was 'but a slip of forgetfulness'. Perhaps he was too busy amassing a fortune out of episcopal lands. The status of the diocesan bishops had undoubtedly declined with the Reformation, and Laud knew only too well that many of them were more concerned with the enrichment of their families than with the welfare of the Church. Few had his integrity, and they were often, and sometimes justly, the target for scurrilous attack from Puritans, as 'equal commonly in birth to the meanest peasants . . . tyrannising lordly prelates raised from the dunghill'. Selden in his *Table Talk* wrote with greater reserve that they were 'of a low condition, their education nothing of that way' (i.e. as before the Reformation). Such generalizations, however, must be interpreted with caution. Laud hoped that by influencing appointments he would be able to raise the over-all standard.

In this hierarchical episcopal order Laud regarded the authority of the Primate of All England as of great importance, and he determined at all costs to maintain it. Where his metropolitical jurisdiction was resisted, he went to extreme lengths to assert it.

Such was the case in 1634, when Williams, Bishop of Lincoln, determined to resist a provincial visitation, goaded on, perhaps, by the fact that it meant the suspension of the bishop's and six archdeacons' jurisdiction. Williams's case for opposing it was more ingenious than substantial. In a letter to Noy, the Attorney-General, Williams maintained that the diocese of Lincoln originally comprised the Kingdom of Mercia and as such was in no way subordinated to those other kingdoms where the archbishopric was then situated. This independence had never been abandoned. Only in royal or legatine authority had the diocese acquiesced. There had been no

*Matthew Parker*

*Edmund Grindal.*
*A portrait by De Vos, 1580*

*John Whitgift, 1602*

*Richard Bancroft*

*George Abbot, 1610*

*William Laud*

*William Juxon, 1660*

*William Sancroft, 1677*

*The Seven Bishops arriving at the Tower*

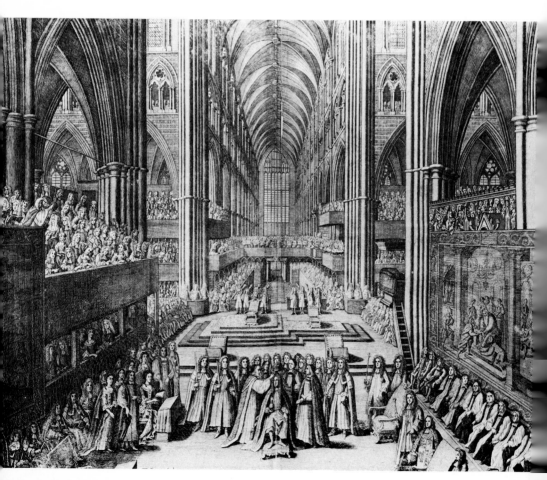

*Archbishop Sancroft crowning James II*

*John Tillotson. A portrait by Sir Godfrey Kneller, 1691*

*Lambeth Palace from the river, 1697*

*The Guard Room, Lambeth Palace*

metropolitical visitation since Cranmer in 1534, and before that since the time of Archbishop Chichele. Thus a visitation should be by royal and not archiepiscopal authority.

Laud was adamant in the face of this opposition, and left Noy in no doubt of his intentions.

> I am resolved to maintain and defend the ancient rights of my archbishopric, as far as in me lieth, to the uttermost: and I doubt not but herein you will give me all just assistance.[131]

He did; for the Attorney-General, after a two-day hearing which commenced on 28 March 1634, and at which both parties were represented, declared against the Bishop of Lincoln on all points. With brief sagacity he pointed out that if former visitations had been resisted, they had been resisted in vain.

Similar opposition was met at St. Paul's Cathedral, but with no more success. In this case, the Dean and Chapter maintained that they held their privileges from the King and were thereby exempt. It was hardly to be expected, in view of Laud's relationship with Charles, that such a claim would be allowed, nor was it. The reply was crushing:

> His Majesty . . . is resolved, for the settlement of peace and good order in the Church, that no place, without special grounds of privilege, shall be exempt from archi-episcopal visitation: and least of all this Church of St. Paul, in regard it appears by their own suggestion that the rest of the diocese hath been visited, and, *de ordinario*, it is known that the Archbishop or Bishop ought to begin his visitation at the Cathedral.[132]

Doubtless it was with some satisfaction that Laud recorded in his diary: 'I visited the Dean and Chapter of St. Paul's, London.'

A third and perhaps more serious attempt to resist his jurisdiction came from the universities, with one of which Laud had close connexions and to which he was a great benefactor.

In the course of his metropolitical visitation, Laud informed these ancient seats of learning that he intended to visit them as parts of the dioceses of Ely and Oxford. Doubtless he was not surprised that this announcement caused a great stir, and that both universities engaged in some private research and time wasting.

> If you think by these delays—the Archbishop warned—to make me forget or forgo the business, you will find yourself much deceived, for I do not intend to do myself or my see that prejudice.[133]

Their resistance made him petition the King, with the result that on 21 June 1635, at Hampton Court and in Charles's presence, counsel was heard on both sides. The arguments on behalf of the universities struck a familiar note. The universities were royal foundations, and as such visitable only by the King or his commissioners. Throughout the Middle Ages they had been exempted by papal bulls from episcopal or archiepiscopal visitation, and if ever they were so visited by the Archbishop, it was as legate or royal representative. The Reformation, in transferring papal jurisdiction to the Crown, did not increase the power of the Archbishop. If Laud would agree to enter upon his visitation as a royal commissioner, then they were prepared to accept him.

Once again the Archbishop would not consider any diminution in the rights of his metropolitical office. 'No, I desire to have my own power,' was his cryptic reply.

The King, as expected, decided for Laud, giving him, as Archbishop, authority to visit whenever he wished on showing adequate reason to the Supreme Governor. The decision was drawn up under the Great Seal; but the 'troubles', so soon to ensue, prevented the Archbishop ever taking advantage of it.

This attempt to assert his metropolitical jurisdiction clouded his relations with the universities; but Oxford certainly owed much to him. As Chancellor, he drew up new statutes, founded a chair in Arabic, and built the Canterbury Quadrangle at St. John's College.

Laud was certainly not nice or squeamish in the assertion of his archiepiscopal authority. His display of it in the suspension of Godfrey Goodman, Bishop of Gloucester, for refusing his assent to the canons drawn up by Convocation in 1640 is described by R. E. Head as 'arbitrary and oppressive'.[134] The motivation of this refusal is obscure, whether it was due to the canons being passed after Parliament had been prorogued or, as Laud alleged, their supposedly antipopish character. Laud insisted that Goodman should make his assent *ex animo*, and though both Houses decided that the Bishop should be suspended *ab officio et beneficiis*, it was Laud who formally passed sentence. Doubtless the Archbishop gained much satisfaction in the exercise of his power this way rather than acting in the capacity of a royal commissioner. Yet he did not hesitate, where his archiepiscopal authority was subject to limitation, to invoke the power of the Crown. When, for example, he was told that there were houses built right up to the Minster at York, and that the wives of members of the Dean and Chapter had seats in the choir, he sent an order in the King's name that both should be removed. More often Laud used the Courts of High Commission and Star Chamber, both of which were bitterly resented by the Puritans because they short-circuited the processes of law and represented an outreach of the royal prerogative. Laud suffered no misgivings. A bishop may sometimes preach the Gospel more publicly and to far greater edification, he used to say grimly, 'in a court of judicature, or at a Council table, where great men are met together to draw things to an issue, than many preachers in their several charges may.' Perhaps this was a case of 'holy worldliness'.

These courts of the Crown were important, since they made it possible for powerful offenders, who might over-awe their local justices of the peace, to be disciplined and punished; men who, for example, enclosed land, sequestered church property, bullied their parson, defied canons. Among these were such 'notorious' Puritans as Prynne, Burton, and Bastwick. The sentences passed were often cruel and degrading. To Laud it seemed fitting that they should be so.

The background of Laud's life was one of constant business. He was without private pleasures, disliked ceremonial occasions, was unattractive to women—a disadvantage at times since Charles was in the pocket of his wife Henrietta Maria—and unimpressive in appearance. His limitations were only too obvious. He knew little of foreign affairs, yet he dabbled in them, anxious that England should not get too involved in vast and visionary commitments, particularly in any pan-Protestant alliance. He sat on the Privy Council for England and Scotland; later for Ireland. When the treasury was put into Commission he was one of the commissioners; and in order to prevent the corrupt Cottingham securing the office, he obtained the treasurership for good William Juxon, Bishop of London. The Bishop's financial integrity, if not his acumen, was absolute, and he was entirely dependent upon his master at Lambeth. Laud wrote jubilantly in his diary:

> No Churchman had it since Henry VII's time. I pray God bless him to carry it so that the Church may have honour and the King and State contentment by it. And now if the Church will not hold up themselves under God, I can do no more.[135]

This manœuvre on the part of the Archbishop caused widespread indignation, and the Venetian Ambassador commented:

> The most conspicuous offices and the greatest authority in the royal Council are falling by degrees into the hands of ecclesiastics, to the prejudice of the nobility and governing houses.[136]

It was a policy of mammoth unwisdom and as the 1630s drew to their close, so the sands were running out both for King and Archbishop. A condition of effectiveness in Laud's governance of the Church, as he well knew, was that he should remain in the King's favour, and that the King should continue in control of the country. The first meant assiduous attendance at Court, and immediate action against those who worked for his overthrow. But what the most time-consuming vigilance could not do was to maintain effectiveness when the King himself no longer had the power to sustain and protect him. It was this latter situation which, when it came, led to the downfall of both Monarchy and Church. Charles, by eschewing foreign wars, had managed to live, though precariously, for some eleven years without Parliament, and to do so by means of benevolences, forced loans, and ship money. But the disastrous attempt, for which Laud must bear a large measure of blame, to impose upon a reluctant people in Scotland an Episcopalian prayer book, made military action imperative. This necessitated money; and on a scale which only Parliament could provide. The Bishops' war led to the end of the road.

The Long Parliament met on 3 November 1640. Strafford was impeached and sent to the Tower. The canons which, most unwisely, Convocation had recently passed, were declared to have no binding force on the laity. Laud could not hope to escape and seems to have anticipated his fate with calm and dignity. A committee was set up to 'investigate' him, one of its members, Sir Harbottle Grimston, declaring that the Archbishop was 'the very sty of all that pestilential filth that had infested the government, and the source of all the miseries which the nation had groaned under.'[137] Laud was committed into the custody of Maxwell, gentleman of the Black Rod, in whose house he was detained for some ten weeks.

On 26 February 1641, Hampden and Maynard presented fourteen articles of impeachment against him at the Bar of the House of Lords. These, as expected, were general in character and included such charges as endeavouring to subvert the constitution; settling justice in his own person under the colour of ecclesiastical law; bringing popish articles into the church, and persecuting those who opposed them; and alienating the mind of the King from his people. On the strength of these charges he was committed to the Tower amidst general reviling. The following two years were for him a time of personal testing as he watched most of what he had striven for being destroyed. He came near to breaking point when on the morning of Strafford's execution he gave his blessing from a window, falling down in a faint as his friend looked up and said fondly, 'Farewell my Lord, may God protect your innocency.' Particularly galling was the humbling experience caused by his old enemy Prynne, publishing a much garbled version of Laud's private diary.

Finally there came the arduous ordeal of his trial, which began on 12 March 1644. For some five months the Archbishop, in spite of his age, defended himself with remarkable intelligence and vigour. As in the case of Strafford, it was decided to abandon impeachment and to proceed by a Bill of Attainder. Even this was not passed without diffculty. A full pardon, signed with the Great Seal of England, and entrusted by Charles to the Archbishop in April 1643, was rejected. The King, as in the case of Strafford, weakly gave way and appended his signature to the Bill. Laud met his death on Tower Hill on 10 January 1645, with serenity and courage.

> So Lord, receive my soul, and have mercy upon me; and bless this kingdom with peace and plenty, and with brotherly love and charity, that there may not be this effusion of Christian blood amongst them, for Jesus Christ, his sake, if it be Thy will ... Lord receive my soul.[138]

Thus he died, as the fourth archiepiscopal victim of violence.

# 4

## THE COMMONWEALTH: 'NOT GOING OUT OF MY SHELL'

There could be no question, in the circumstances following Laud's death, of appointing a successor. Charles, in this period of personal crisis, turned for support to William Juxon, Bishop of London, and to Gilbert Sheldon, Warden of All Souls College, Oxford.

Juxon succeeded Laud as President of St. John's, at Oxford. He was a devoted disciple, totally committed to the cause of the Archbishop and to an extreme assertion of the royal prerogative. He supported Laud in his Scottish policy, and was active, as Treasurer, in raising forced loans and introducing a measure of economy into an extravagant court. At his primary visitation of his London diocese he sought to discipline dissenters into conformity. Yet in spite of this he won universal admiration and respect. Lucius Cary, second Viscount Falkland, who did not view bishops with favour, testified that 'in an unexpected place and power he expressed an equal moderation and humility, being neither ambitious before, nor proud after, either [with] the crozier or the white staff'. Evidence of this is the fact that there was never any question of his impeachment or attainder, either as Bishop or Treasurer, although along with others he was required to pay a fine of £500 for accepting membership of the Court of High Commission. Perhaps the most significant tribute—surprising as to its source—came from Prynne: '. . . his disposition and as a man have been amiable and commendable.'

With the King, Juxon's relations grew more intimate, even affectionate, as the final tragedy came nearer. In the midst of difficult negotiations, and when oppressed by loneliness, the Bishop's presence brought comfort and support. 'This will I say of him,' Charles acknowledged, 'I never got his opinion freely in my life but when I had it I was ever the better for it.' When, in the autumn of 1646, Charles was considering concessions likely to lead to the temporary establishment of presbyterianism, it was Juxon he asked whether he could with a safe conscience give way to this 'proposed compliance'. Juxon advised that in the circumstances this would be a proper expedient, and in this Brian Duppa, Bishop of Salisbury, concurred. The Bishop shared Charles's captivity at Newport, and was with him at his trial, seldom leaving him after his sentence. No man was more fitted to sustain the King in his last moments on 30 January 1649: 'There is but one stage more,' Juxon whispered, 'a stage turbulent and troublesome, but it will carry you from earth to Heaven.' To him, the last enigmatic word was spoken, 'Remember'—a word for which Juxon was later called to give an account before the High Court of Justice and which he said referred to his passing on the George, the jewel of the Order of the Garter, to the young Prince of Wales.

The story of the Church of England, that is, the fate of its 'bishops, and curates and all congregations committed to their charge', during the period of suppression under the Commonwealth —episcopacy was abolished in 1644—has yet to be told *in extenso*. The research needed would include a complete analysis of local records, no easy undertaking. Many clergy went overseas; others underground. Some became schoolmasters, others chaplains to noble families, surreptitiously using the Book of Common Prayer. Some clergy, having made 'friends of the mammon of unrighteousness', abandoned the Prayer Book and retained their benefices. Others committed the proscribed book to memory and continued to use it. In the eyes of the more zealous who adopted an absolutist position, and as a consequence lost everything, these 'time servers' were distrusted and despised. As to the precise number of clergy who were deprived of their livings, polemical treatises must be interpreted with caution. John Walker, in his *Sufferings of the Clergy of the Church of England* (1714), writes of ten thousand ejected, of whom some were incarcerated in gaols and old ships, and others even considered for transportation to Algiers for sale as slaves.

Gilbert Sheldon was particularly sensitive to the plight of those episcopal clergy who were being subjected to persecution 'under a civil authority [which] though not pagan, [was] yet clearly antichristian and such as endeavour to destroy the Church of God'.[139] He himself believed that the deprived bishops ought to agree as to what degree of 'remission' in the use of the Book of Common Prayer could be allowed: or failing this should petition the King in exile to nominate a commission of three to issue directions.

What must be said, if with regret, is that the bishops who survived the Commonwealth did not come out of their ordeal particularly well. It is understandable, perhaps, that a Church built into dependence on the royal supremacy, and with its Supreme Governor a fugitive on the Continent, should feel itself powerless and dispirited. But the bishops, by and large, offered no leadership, and the rank and file of the clergy suffered as a consequence. Dr. Henry Hammond, who himself endured imprisonment, confessed in 1654 that he had been approached by a beneficed clergyman in the diocese of Salisbury 'to petition the Fathers surviving to live in their dioceses, and to act as primitive Bishops'.[140] Henry Ferne, later appointed to Chester, writing in 1655, was forthright in condemnation of episcopal timidity.

> If our Pilots, tired out with the storm, did think it best . . . to let the Ship drive awhile . . . this indeed might be prudence for the then pressing exigency . . . yet now it calls for the more courage and zeal, in providing for that which seems to have been too long neglected (a more regular Church-way of Communion and worship).[141]

A zealous royalist reported to Charles II that 'the inferior clergy and laity much complain' of the lack of episcopal supervision which deprived them of 'a right correspondence and organisation'. True, secret ordinations of priests went on—Thomas Tenison, a future Archbishop of Canterbury, was ordained privately by Bishop Duppa at Richmond—but no attempt was made, after Laud's death, to keep the succession going at Canterbury.

The breach of continuity in the Church of England was not repaired until Charles returned in 1660, thus making an interregnum longer than any which had previously existed even in the darkest days of Anglo-Saxon England. The bishops, by and large, took the view that to remain in obscurity was the only way to avoid persecution. Duppa, although not inactive and probably the most courageous, put it simply: 'I secure myself the same way as the tortoise doth, by not going out of my shell.' Brownrigg never set foot in Exeter during the seventeen years of his episcopate. Only Skinner of Oxford seems to have felt that he retained any responsibility for the continuing life of his diocese. Duppa complained that 'My Lord of London [Juxon] is so remote from me that I shall despair of having any intelligence from him. What he is about I know not.'[142] There was no need to be anxious, for the Bishop was in fact comfortably housed at his manor of Little Compton, Gloucestershire, possessed of a pack of hounds which was the envy of his neighbours. To be fair, he helped financially such clergy as came his way.

# 5

## GILBERT SHELDON AND THE
## RESTORATION SETTLEMENT

I

When Charles II entered London amidst a cheering and near hysterical population on 29 May 1660, it was, constitutionally at least, as if the intervening years of the Commonwealth had never been. According to the law books the new reign began the very moment his father had died at Whitehall; and all Acts of Parliament, subsequently passed without the consent of the King, were automatically null and void.

If this thesis made unexceptionable law, it could not alter the fact that history had gone on, and that there were many practical problems now waiting to be settled. Life is wider than legal logic. In particular the religious settlement was to present peculiar difficulties.

Charles had been brought back to his native land through a working alliance between Episcopalians and Presbyterians, all of whom had grown weary of regimentation, of rule by the army, and the excesses of independency. They preferred a known form of government, if only as the lesser of two evils. Charles himself, by his declaration from Breda, had gone out of his way to encourage the more moderate nonconformists to expect concessions. In the complicated negotiations and trials of strength which followed, it was clear that Juxon, the senior bishop, was too old and infirm to give a lead. His place was taken by Gilbert Sheldon, who had many qualifications for this critical responsibility, not least great strength of character, moral courage, and deep Laudian convictions. Falkland early testified that 'learning, gravity and prudence had in that time . . . raised him to such a reputation that he was then looked upon as very equal to any preferment the Church could yield'. Like Juxon, he had rendered great service to Charles I when his 'troubles' descended, and had suffered the penalty of imprisonment in Oxford. During the period of the Commonwealth he had tried to rally both bishops and clergy, at the same time keeping in touch with the exiled Charles. The general view was that 'none hath his [Charles's] ear more [or is] likely to prevail in his heart more'.

Sheldon, from the beginning, enjoyed the inestimable advantage of knowing what kind of settlement he wanted; and it was significant that on 25 May, the day after Charles landed at Dover, Clarendon, author of *The True Historical Narrative of the Rebellion and Civil Wars in England*, engineered a private meeting in Canterbury between him and the returned monarch. 'Nobody,' he had written earlier to Sheldon, 'is like to do so much good upon him as you are, for sure he reverences nobody more.'[143] What transpired at this 'cabin council' no one knows. Gossip which later circulated in Scotland alleged that it was there that Charles abandoned any thought of establishing presbyterianism in England.

The first few months after Charles's return to London, in spite of a spontaneous resurgence of anglicanism, were not such as to dash the hopes of the Presbyterians. The King himself interviewed a number of their leaders; invited some of them to preach at Whitehall (Sheldon later put a stop to this as Dean of the Chapel Royal); and issued a declaration maintaining in office, for the time being, those who held benefices. Clarendon, whose later personal misfortune it was to have his name associated with a code which he largely condemned, conciliated lay Presbyterians by introducing them to political office. It proved to be an astute move.

The King was a politique, and Clarendon an old-fashioned High Anglican. The news from the shires showed an increasing support for Laudian churchmanship, so strong that it was later to sweep the Cavalier Parliament into power. The Government thought it wise to trim its sails. Appointments to a large number of Crown benefices, which since the reign of Edward III had been in the hands of the Lord Chancellor, were now entrusted to a commission consisting of Sheldon, Earle, and Sir Robert Morey. They saw to it that none but loyal Episcopalians were preferred.

Meanwhile the Lower House of Parliament, in which there was an evident revival of presbyterianism, determined not to be excluded from playing its part in the religious settlement. On 20 July 1660, it petitioned the King to convene a select committee of divines to treat with the problems at issue, and followed this up on 13 September by passing a bill which 'if maintained would drastically modify the traditional requirements of the Church of England'; but Parliament, to the relief of the Laudians, was prorogued.

To Clarendon and Sheldon it seemed important that the ordered life of the Church of England should be restored as soon as possible, and therefore the filling up of the episcopal bench was an over-riding priority. As to the archbishopric of Canterbury, the choice was inevitable. William Juxon, in spite of his seventy-eight years, had unique claims which, in the emotional mood of the moment, were irresistible. He had been the loyal disciple of the Archbishop who suffered; and his pastoral care of Charles before and during his last ordeal gave him an aura to which no one else could aspire. On 3 September a *congé d'élire* was granted to the Chapter of Canterbury; on 13 September he was elected; and on 20 September this was confirmed in the Henry VII Chapel 'amid a great concourse of clergy and laity and every sign of rejoicing'. Juxon was not expected to play a significant part in the grave matters which now called for a decision; nor did he. Almost the only clue to his opinions at this time, and this seems oddly out of character, comes from a Puritan, Robert Dodd, who reports that Juxon, when ordaining him in 1660, remarked that 'he was not for going high against the Presbyterians; but others were of another mind.'[144] On 28 October, in traditional splendour five bishops were consecrated in the Henry VII Chapel, their nomination, according to Izaak Walton, being largely due to Gilbert Sheldon. He himself was among them, being appointed to London.

It was still felt prudent to keep the Presbyterians at least hopeful, and a few days earlier the King had issued a declaration which if implemented would have provided assistant bishops for certain dioceses; enabled presbyters to serve on cathedral chapters as an advisory council to the bishop; and allowed confirmation to be administered 'by the information and with the consent of the minister of the place'. It seemed as if, in some measure at least, the demands of moderate, as distinct from extreme, Presbyterians and Independents, were to be met; but the more percipient recognized in the declaration an interim gesture to secure calm until the Prayer Book was considered by a commission of divines of 'both persuasions'. When the House met on 9 November, the Presbyterians proposed a Bill for 'Making the King's Declaration touching Ecclesiastical Affairs Effectual', which had its first reading on 28 November. The critical moment of the Restoration settlement had now arrived. The Episcopalians rallied their forces, and in a crowded House the second reading was lost by twenty-six votes. When Parliament was dissolved on 24 December, Clarendon did not conceal his satisfaction.

Meanwhile throughout the country, at the parochial level, the re-establishment of the Anglican system continued, unhindered by the King's declaration, which Baxter described as only a 'partial protection'. The newly consecrated bishops set out to restore discipline. In particular, Sheldon addressed himself to this task in the diocese of London, where he was 'resolute and uncompromising' in his policy of insisting on episcopal ordination and rejecting those who refused it. Elections for Parliament, in March 1661, after the 'political freak' of the London results had given the Government an initial shock, returned a Parliament which was Anglican and Cavalier. Reassured by such a resounding victory Clarendon was encouraged, on 10 April, to issue writs for the summoning of Convocation. It was a gamble, and Juxon expressed his anxiety. Sheldon, however, was convinced that Convocation must meet—and meet soon: indeed he took a rather high-handed action to secure its compliance when it did assemble. Baxter and Calamy, who had been elected proctors in the diocese of London, were forbidden to attend ('excused', to quote Baxter's euphemism), the Bishop resorting to an ancient right which empowered him to select two out of the four who headed the poll.

Into this disturbed situation came the coronation of the Merry Monarch on 23 April, St. George's Day, a ceremony which in its careful stage-management was designed to stress continuity with an ancient, episcopal, and monarchical past. Juxon was far too infirm to preside over the whole rite, and it was necessary for Sheldon to help him out; but he managed, clad in a 'rich, ancient cope', to officiate at the unction and blessing of the sword; to place the Crown on the King's head and the ring on his finger; and to deliver to him the two sceptres. A special significance was read into the King's solemn declaration that he would preserve to the Church all her canonical privileges and protect her bishops.

For the aged Primate, the ceremony was the climax of a long career: but his reactions to it must have been mixed. There was no natural affinity between him and the son as there had been with the father; and what he had seen of the new monarch at close quarters did not impress him.

> After some discourses with the K[ing he] was so much struck with what he observed in him that he lost both heart and hope.[145]

What energies the Archbishop could now summon went into the restoring of St. Paul's and the erection of the Great Hall at Lambeth. He died on 4 June 1663. His body lay in state in the divinity school at Oxford, an oration being delivered by the public orator, the irascible Dr. South. The Archbishop had left behind him strict injunctions that his funeral should be unostentatious, but when his body was finally laid to rest in St. John's College these wishes were set aside. Significantly, the remains of his master, William Laud, were brought a few days later from the Church of All Hallows by the Tower to be interred close by him.

It was the misfortune of William Juxon to be caught up in events which were too big for him. Yet perhaps James Shirley's words are a fitting epitaph:

Only the actions of the just
Smell sweet, and blossom in their dust.

That Sheldon should follow Juxon in the primacy was generally expected, and in the circumstances inevitable.

To return. By May 1661, the Church of England was for all practical purposes re-established. What Clarendon and his clerical allies, chief among whom was Sheldon, wished for had been achieved; and it had been achieved without the intervention of Parliament, whose role so far had been negative. On 8 May it met, and on the same day the opening service of Convocation took place at St. Paul's. Juxon was unable to preside, and left it to Sheldon, who 'in excellent latin' addressed the Lower House, desiring them to choose their prolocutor.

So it was that during the summer of 1661 three separate bodies were conferring, and often about the same business: Parliament, Convocation, and the Savoy Conference. They deliberated against a High Anglican background such as Cavaliers had long hoped for. Parliament decreed the burning of the Covenant; required all members of the Commons to receive the Sacrament; and restored to the bishops their seats in the Lords. An attempt to revive the High Commission, however, failed, and a Bill of Uniformity which required assent to the Prayer Book of 1604 was rejected by the Lords, since the conference 'of both persuasions' was in session at the Savoy. On 20 November Parliament was prorogued.

The Savoy Conference met on 15 April at Sheldon's lodgings—he was Master of the Savoy—and for four months pursued its stormy, and finally useless, deliberations. Baxter, not perhaps an impartial witness, wrote afterwards, in the *Narrative of His Life and Times*: 'We spoke to the Deaf; they had other ends [than unity and peace] and were other men, and had the art to suit the means unto their ends.' Archbishop Accepted Frewen of York formally opened the Conference, but immediately gave way to Sheldon who 'knew more the King's mind'. It gave Sheldon the opportunity he desired, and he immediately insisted with great firmness that since it was the Puritans who wished for changes, so it was for them to indicate in writing what their objections to the Prayer Book were and what they wished to be done about it. Such a procedure did not foreshadow the kind of discussion which the Presbyterians desired, although Richard Baxter, for other reasons, approved. The Conference was therefore adjourned to 4 May. On reassembling, it got down to business, but the concessions which the Anglicans were prepared to make were minimal, and no real *via media* proved possible.

Some have questioned whether the Anglicans, led by Sheldon,

really wanted an accommodation; and whether, if they did, the dominance of Baxter at the Conference would have ruled it out. A story, probably apocryphal, since it is second-hand and first appears (1723) in the *Works* of W. Bates, a Presbyterian divine, later circulated that Sheldon, on being asked whether the Presbyterians would subscribe to the Act of Uniformity, replied, 'I am afraid they will.' The truth may be that each side at the Savoy Conference wished for agreement, but on its own terms. Neither felt that there was much room for manœuvre, and Sheldon, by temperament, was not the kind of man to make prolonged efforts at conciliation.

The different roles of the Savoy Conference, Convocation, and Parliament are bewildering. Convocation reassembled in November, and when the King's letter was read, urging them to embark upon a revision of the Book of Common Prayer, it was found that a group of bishops had been busy during the vacation considering 'such alterations in the Book of Common Prayer as they thought would make it more grateful to the dissenting brethren'. The results of these labours were now presented to Convocation. The new Prayer Book which it finally produced differed very little from the old, though incorporating a number of 'small particulars to meet the presbyterians'—in fact it was surprisingly non-Laudian. On 24 February 1662, it was presented to the King by Sheldon.

II

The time had now come for Parliament to take over—and it certainly did so. In May 1662, the Bill of Uniformity, with the revised Prayer Book attached to it, became law. The other 'ingredients' of the Clarendon Code—the Conventicle and Five Mile Acts— followed in due course. With their passing Anglican supremacy became complete.

The interval between the passing of the Bill of Uniformity and its enforcement on St. Bartholomew's Day was an anxious time for all concerned, since there was a widespread fear that there might be Puritan resistance on a massive scale. Pepys reflected more than his own opinion when he commented, that 'the bishops will not be able to carry it so high as they do.' Though the members of the episcopal bench were probably not behind the rigorism injected into the Bill by the House of Commons, they were yet determined on its enforcement, now that it had become law. Sheldon felt this strongly; but Clarendon himself began to have 'cold feet', and to question whether the implementation of the Act would not imperil the whole religious and political settlement, particularly as the reports from the countryside became more alarming. Approaches had already been made by certain Presbyterians, asking that the King should ease their consciences by dispensing them from the penalties under the law. Clarendon now decided, in collusion with the King, to adopt this suggestion—and to do so without consulting the bishops. He therefore advised the Presbyterians to petition the Crown, which they accordingly did on 27 August.

It was at a meeting of the Council, which Sheldon alone among the bishops attended, that the bombshell exploded. His immediate reaction was one of great anger and defiance. The weekly issue of the *Mercurius Publicus* reported:

> . . . his Lordship made it evident how the suspension of this law, at this conjunction, would not only render the Parliament cheap, and have influence upon all other laws, but in truth let in a visible confusion upon Church and State.[146]

This by-passing of the bishops in a matter of such grave importance was not something which Sheldon felt that he could overlook, even though his old friend and ally was mainly responsible. His letter to Clarendon reveals the extent of his distress:

> . . . and now, my Lord, not being able to wait upon you today as I intended, and having this occasion to send, give me leave to complain of your great unkindness upon Thursday in offering to expose me to certain ruin by the Parliament, or the extreme hatred of that malicious party in whose jaws I must live, and never giving me the least notice of it. You cannot blame me if it be sadly resented. . . .[147]

Sheldon's opposition could not be ignored, particularly since it was expected that, if the declaration were issued, he would appeal against it to Parliament. With great courage he sent to Charles an even more forthright letter, reminiscent, though in a very different context, of Grindal's astringent communication to Elizabeth:

> By your Act [of Indulgence]—he wrote—you labour to set up that most damnable and heretical doctrine of the Church of Rome, whore of Babylon. How hateful will it be to God, and grievous to your good subjects . . . that your Majesty . . . should now show yourself a patron of the doctrines which your pen hath told the world, and your conscience tells yourself, are superstitions, idolatry, and detestable. Besides, this Toleration . . . cannot be done without a Parliament, unless your Majesty will let your subjects see that you will take unto yourself liberty to throw down the laws of the land at your pleasure.[148]

It was indeed a remarkable letter, and shows how far the logic of events had led royalists such as Sheldon away from the absurdities of Dr. Sibthorpe. Dr. Richard Boshier, perhaps with this letter in mind, places Sheldon in the tradition of à Becket and Langton, adding that in his 'courtliness and political finesse, driving energy and single-minded devotion to the Church, above all readiness to defy the Royal will—he is reminiscent of the great medieval churchmen'.[149] Perhaps it should be added that this was not the only occasion on which Sheldon rebuked Charles with some sternness. Pepys, on the authority of James, Duke of York, tells how he remonstrated with him over his relations with 'Mistress Steward' who married the Duke of Richmond. 'Sir, I wish you would put away this woman that you keep,' was his terse comment.

The stand which Sheldon took over the proposed toleration made this 'incomparable prelate' the hero of the Cavalier party. As it happened, St. Bartholomew's Day passed off without the incidents which had been feared. Figures are not easily come by but G. Matthews, author of *Walker Revised* (1948), reckons that about 936 were deprived, and that those ejected earlier amounted to some 824. Sheldon, however, did not wish to make matters more difficult for the Presbyterians than they need be, that is if they were willing to conform, and he advertised in their interest a special ordination at St. Paul's for 21 August to which there came many priests and deacons, a number of whom had before been under the hands of the Presbytery.

It is clear that Sheldon played a significant part in the Restoration settlement which was destined to have such long-term effects upon English society in general as well as upon dissent in particular. It is useless to ask what might have happened had the actors in the drama been different. What is fairly certain is that if Charles and Clarendon had had a free hand they would have gone further in conciliating the Presbyterians. Sheldon took a stricter line, and was a strongly contributive factor by sheer force of character in making his view prevail. He was not sensitive to the scruples entertained by sincere Presbyterians, and in a letter (1663) to Ormonde, then Lord Lieutenant of Ireland, he complained that since they would not be governed by 'reason and persuasion' as men, they must be governed 'as beasts by power of force'. Burnet, in his *History of My Own Time*, later maintained that it was the bishops who thwarted a more comprehensive settlement, and he accused Sheldon, unfairly, of not having 'a deep sense of religion if any at all', religion to him being rather 'an engine of government and a matter of policy'.

The effect of what happened in 1662 was to kill finally any hope that the Church of England might be a truly national Church, with only the more extreme and fringe groups outside. Politically it was the House of Commons which came out of these events not simply restored but with its powers increased. The monarchy, the House of Lords, and the Church of England lost influence and this, in the XVIIIth century, was to have repercussions upon the office of Archbishop. Superficially, the Restoration settlement might seem to have realized what Laud had fought for, but one vital element was lacking. William Laud had always worked to make the clergy an independent estate of the realm, independent, that is, of Parliament, and with the Crown the protector of its privileges. The Restoration settlement, finally imposed by the Cavalier Parliament, meant that this hope was banished for ever. Inadvertently, no man did more to promote its passing than Sheldon himself. By a private agreement with the Lord Chancellor, Clarendon, he surrendered the right of the clergy to tax themselves in their own assembly, Convocation. In return they became entitled to vote, though not to sit, in the House of Commons. What this meant was that the Crown no longer had a financial interest in summoning Convocation; and it was this which led to its virtual suppression for well over a century. Also, this concession by Sheldon inevitably affected his own position as Archbishop. It meant that the onerous duty of acting as the King's agent in extracting money from the clergy was an embarrassment no longer, and that thenceforth the clergy's financial burden was no greater than that borne by the rest of the realm. But the shedding of the embarrassment brought with it a loss of power and influence. The political significance of Convocation declined and with it the office of its President. The change represented another step forward on the road to the secular state.

If Sheldon, in response to a new political and social climate, did much to undermine what Laud had striven for, he followed firmly in the steps of his predecessor in trying to discipline the Church into efficiency. Among his papers in the Tanner MSS there is a very severe (undated) letter sent to one of the bishops of his province, insisting that he reside in his diocese.

> I have thought fit—the Archbishop says—by writing to you at this time upon the same subject to shew you how serious I am in that particular, and to tell you once more that I do expect you should forthwith and without any delay go down to your Bishopric and make your Residence there.[150]

The same concern is shown in a letter sent to the bishops of his province, requiring them to give him full particulars as to ordinations, pluralists and their curates, lecturers, instructors of youth, practitioners of physic, and nonconformist ministers. Also among his papers is a missive dated 4 June 1670, requiring prebendaries to perform divine service, since 'our cathedrals are the standard and rule to all parochial churches of the solemnity and decent manner of reading the liturgy, and administering the holy sacraments'.[151]

Such directives are typical of the persistent and routine activities by which Sheldon tried to build up the Church after its suppression during the Commonwealth, and to correct the licence which followed upon the Restoration. His chaplain, Samuel Parker, records of him that though he was a man of 'undoubted piety', and was very assiduous at prayers, 'yet he did not set so great a value on them as others did, nor regarded so much worship as the use of worship, placing the chief point of religion in the practice of a good life'. Thus he would often advise young noblemen: 'Let it be your principal care to become honest men and afterwards be as devout and religious as you will. No piety will be of any advantage to yourselves or anybody else, unless you are honest moral men.'[152] The XVIIIth century was on the way. To posterity Sheldon is remembered as the generous benefactor who gave to Oxford one of its great glories, the Sheldonian Theatre, the gift arising from the Archbishop's dislike at the use of St. Mary's Church for the annual 'Commemorations'. The building was designed by Sir Christopher Wren and cost the large sum of £25,000. It is perhaps ironic that the Archbishop never visited Oxford after its completion.

The last years of his life were marred by increasing physical weakness. He was taken seriously ill in October 1677, when his own physician gave up his case as beyond remedy. Hope revived, however, when a German doctor prescribed his *aurum potabile* which when first applied produced 'wonderful effects and gives a fair promise of recovery'. But it did not work, and he died at Lambeth on 9 November 1677, in his eightieth year.

# 6

## WILLIAM SANCROFT:
## PIETY AND NON-COMPLIANCE

### I

The death of Sheldon led to the usual speculation as to his successor. One candidate seemed, in the eyes of contemporaries, to stand head and shoulders above the rest: Henry Compton, Bishop of London, the youngest son of the Earl of Northampton who was killed in the civil war. Compton was the political ally of the Earl of Danby, and had popularly won acclaim as 'the protestant bishop'.[153] In one quarter, however, he had a very strong enemy, no less a person than the Duke of York, the future James II, whose anger he had incurred through his forwardness in 'persecuting' Roman Catholics, not least the Portuguese Ambassador. Gossip reported that in spite of Danby's optimism, Compton had realistically given up hope, and was trying to engineer the appointment of his former tutor, Richard Sterne, Archbishop of York, since Sterne was older than the dying Sheldon and so might provide him with another chance.

Danby in fact prudently refrained from pressing Compton's claims too forcibly, lest he should compromise his own relations with James. Thus with the duplicity typical of Restoration politics, he played a double game. Until three days before the nomination was made public, he assured Compton that 'he might set his heart at rest, for he would certainly be Archbishop', while at the same time he was 'clandestinely' supporting William Sancroft, the successful candidate —a surprising choice, since, as Dean of St. Paul's, he was not even in episcopal orders. Of one thing we may be sure, Sancroft had done nothing to seek the office. Indeed, when Charles in person offered him this primacy, the good Dean protested 'that he was very unfit for it thro' his solitary life which he had a long time led', and therefore 'fervently desired his Majesty to recommend to it some bishop more worthy of it'.

The reason for Charles's hitting upon Sancroft in particular— except the negative one of keeping a more militant Protestant out—is not at first sight apparent. Maybe in one of those rare moments of insight which occasionally illuminates the mind of the rake, Charles recognized in Sancroft a man of God, who stood outside much of the religious and political strife of the day. Indeed the King long entertained a particular esteem and kindness for him, remarking some time previously that he knew of 'no one more fit to succeed than the Dean of St. Paul's'. Henry Compton will concern us again later. Certainly he deserves a place in a study of the Primates of All England, if only as the supreme representative of the disappointed and rejected candidate—the archbishop *manqué*.

If Sancroft came to Canterbury because he was essentially a churchman, not so involved as others in the complex politics of his day, he could not avoid involvement once he entered upon his office. The time was not yet when an archbishop could live his life more or less independently of governmental changes and national policy.

Up to this point, Sancroft's life had been comparatively undistinguished. Educated at Cambridge, he had held a fellowship there till 1651, in which year he published his *Fur Praedestinatus*, an attack upon Puritanism as undermining the very principles of morality. Together with his *Modern Policies taken from Machiavel, Borgia, and other choice authors*—a satirical work—it constituted his most significant publication. He withdrew to Holland in 1657; went off as a student to Padua; and was at Rome when he heard of the Restoration. Preferment soon came his way once he was back in England. He preached on Episcopacy as a divine order at the consecration of bishops in Westminster Abbey on 2 December 1660, and took part in the Savoy Conference. In August 1662 he was elected to the Mastership of Emmanuel College, Cambridge, where he did a solid piece of work in revising its statutes. Two years later he was appointed Dean of St. Paul's, and became active in its restoration, declining the bishopric of Chester in order to continue the work of repair.

Sancroft's character is not easily delineated. Burnet, who saw his appointment as engineered by the Court in order to secure a 'tool', admitted him to be learned, but commented acidly that he was 'a dry old man, reserved and peevish . . . poor spirited and fearful'. Such a judgement, however, is hardly borne out by subsequent events, or by the more sensitive appraisal of others. Dryden certainly admired him, and distilled this admiration into verse:

> Zadok the priest, whom, shunning power and place
> His lowly mind advanced to David's grace.

Sancroft had not long been Archbishop when he undertook a task, as unsuccessful as uncongenial, which reflected the complexities of the contemporary situation. At the formal request of the King, in conjunction with Bishop Morley of Winchester, he attempted to persuade James to return to the Church of his father. To the Duke, however, apart from his natural obstinacy, this was not an open question. Had Sancroft succeeded, doubtless the history of the next twenty years would have been different.

Charles was blessed with a magnificent constitution, which enabled him to indulge a life of excess likely to have killed a less virile person. True he had suffered one dangerous illness, when Sancroft took alarm and set about drawing up special prayers for his recovery. In the spring of 1685 he was taken ill again, and many hoped that he might once more recover. But it was not to be. After apologizing for being an 'unconscionable time a-dying' and expressing the hope that poor Nelly might not be left to starve, he was, on the initiative of James, received into the Roman Catholic Church by Father Huddlestone, who had saved his life after the battle of Worcester many years before. Sancroft, with other bishops, was present at his deathbed, but his ministrations were not in particular called for.

James's reign and its aftermath were to bring out Sancroft's strength as well as his weakness. They were to lead to his suffering for principles which the Church of England had rashly espoused, while still basking in the sunshine of royal favour. The Archbishop was now, against his natural inclinations, dragged into the maelstrom of national politics. James, though committed to a more serious governmental policy than Charles, lacked that instinctive common-sense which had often saved his brother from disaster. Charles had little difficulty in establishing his priorities—not to go on his travels again; to indulge his private pleasures unhampered; to increase the power of the Crown; and to favour Roman Catholicism—in that order. The new King's objectives were equally to increase the power of the Crown; and to foster the Roman Catholic religion by raising its adherents to full citizenship in spite of the laws of the realm. It was the pursuit of these aims, together and without restraint, which finally spelt the ruin of both, and brought in its train exile for himself and deprivation for Sancroft. James always found compromise abhorrent, and was convinced that resort to it had cost his father the throne.

Not long after the King's accession, Sancroft waited on him, in company with such bishops as were in London, hoping to express appreciation for the royal declaration that he would respect the rights of the established Church. They found him in a threatening mood. He would keep his word, he said, and undertake nothing against the religion established by law, assuming that they did their duty to him; but if they failed in this, they must not expect him to protect them. He would readily find the means of attaining his ends without their help. Such words were not reassuring. It was ominous that at his coronation on St. George's Day, 1685, over which Sancroft presided, he insisted on having the rite curtailed so that it should not be framed within the Anglican service of Holy Communion.

James's brief reign concerns us only in so far as it affected the Archbishop. What is significant is that a man who entertained a natural loyalty to his monarch, and who later showed himself to have taken his oaths in no formal manner, should yet early feel it necessary to oppose royal policies. Such opposition began when James re-established the Court of High Commission and put the Archbishop on it. Sancroft recognized that he was placed in a difficult and embarrassing position, and got out of it by excusing his attendance, on the grounds of age and infirmities; also because his office would not allow him to take part in a Commission over which a layman, Judge Jeffreys, presided. Burnet, in his *History*, later argued that this prevarication shows the Archbishop in bad light:

> . . . he lay silent at Lambeth . . . seemed zealous against popery in private discourse, but he was of such a timorous temper . . . that he showed no sort of course.

These words are too extreme. Sancroft showed enough independence for him to be forbidden the Court; for his advice on preferment to be ignored; and for there to be talk of summoning him before the Commission. In this situation he was forced back on his diocesan duties, in particular the congenial task of concerning himself with the welfare of the parish priest and encouraging him to a proper discharge of his duty.

Sancroft had now little influence upon James, who was determined to follow a policy of 'thorough' undeterred by the advice of wiser men. He enforced Roman Catholic fellows upon Magdalen College, Oxford, against the statutes; he brought Compton, Bishop of London, before the Court of High Commission upon his refusing to suspend, on the authority of a royal order, John Sharp, one of his own clergy; he endeavoured to intrude a papist into the Charterhouse; he peremptorily required Sancroft, who refused, to instruct the clergy to abandon catechizing. The climax to these illegalities came when, on 4 May 1688, the Council ordered all clergy to read, in their parish churches, the new Declaration of Indulgence, issued by James on 27 April, which dispensed with the laws discriminating against those who were not members of the established Church.

It is important, in assessing the attitude of Sancroft and the bishops to the King's declaration, not to judge their reactions by the liberal standards of a later century. It is a complete anachronism to regard James as the enlightened champion of toleration in an intolerant age. The real conflict was not between persecution practised by establishment Whigs and liberty championed by an enlightened monarch; but between respect for law, broadening out into liberty, and an arbitrary despotism obedient to nothing but its own will. It says much for the perspicacity of the more enlightened dissenters that they were able to make this distinction.

The dramatic events following James's Declaration must be briefly told from within the context of the Archbishop's relationship to them. Sancroft took the initiative in summoning a meeting of bishops and London clergy. There was general agreement that the order should be disobeyed, not, in Sancroft's words, 'from any want of tenderness towards dissenters, but because the declaration, being founded on such a dispensing power as may at pleasure set aside all laws ecclesiastical and civil, appears to me illegal'. A petition to this effect was presented at Court, though Sancroft was debarred from being present. On 8 June he, with episcopal colleagues, was summoned before the council. Here they were submitted to long interrogation, but on refusing recognizances to appear at Westminster Hall for the purpose of answering unspecified charges, were committed to the Tower. In this ordeal Sancroft acted with admirable firmness, and won an embarrassing tribute from the Prince and Princess of Orange, who, over in Holland, were watching events with interest not unmixed with concern.

Never had an Archbishop, particularly one of Sancroft's somewhat withdrawn temperament, been more popular. The trial of the bishops at Westminster Hall on the charge of 'uttering' a seditious libel proved from the King's point of view worse than a crime: it was a blunder. Night came before the jury retired, and the bishops' solicitor wisely guarded the door of their chamber. Michael Arnold, one of their number, a brewer, expressed his personal dilemma.

> Whatever I do I am sure to be half ruined. If I say 'Not Guilty', I shall brew no more for the King; and if I say 'Guilty', I shall brew no more for anybody else.

At last the obstinate brewer made up his mind and they were all agreed. At ten o'clock Sir Roger Langley uttered the words, 'Not guilty.' A great shout was immediately raised 'that one would have thought the Hall had cracked'. It was taken up outside and reverberated even in the Palace of Whitehall.

Sancroft immediately after the trial issued instructions to the bishops concerning 'things to be more fully insisted upon in their addresses to the clergy and people of their respective dioceses'. In particular he enjoined that his brethren, in being on their guard against popish emissaries, should at the same time nourish 'a very tender regard to our brethren the protestant dissenters . . . in relation to whom they [were] willing to come to such a temper as shall be thought fit, when the matter shall be considered and settled in Parliament and Convocation'. The common danger of monarchical despotism had brought churchmen and dissenters—that is those who accepted the principle of a national church, the Royal Supremacy, a fixed liturgy and a moderate episcopacy—nearer together than ever before. So was born a scheme in the interest of the less extreme nonconformists—a scheme which William Wake, when Archbishop, recalled in the House of Lords some twenty years later during the impeachment of Dr. Sacheverell. Sancroft was deeply involved; but was overtaken by events. On the very day of the bishops' acquittal, a messenger was sent to The Hague inviting Prince William to come over so as to ensure the calling of a free Parliament. Too late, so it proved, James became seized of the danger to which, in his folly, he had exposed his throne. Sancroft, still hopeful, did his best to use his influence to persuade him to retrace his steps. On 3 October he headed a delegation and in forthright, though earnest and humble, tones implored the King to follow up his recent good resolutions by going even further. Would he not, once and for all, abolish the Court of Ecclesiastical Commission; place the government in the hands of those legally qualified to exercise it; restore their charters to towns; replace the Fellows of Magdalen College; and appoint an Archbishop to York? Also, added the aged Primate respectfully, before whom there now hovered a vision of better things, might not the King, if he desired to be restored to the affections of his people, reconsider the points of difference between the Church of England and the Church of Rome? As a result he might return to the ecclesiastical allegiance of his father and grandfather.

James, however, lacked the temperament to learn even from the most bitter experience, and a series of interviews with Sancroft and the bishops did not dramatically change the situation. Sancroft stood firm in refusing to associate himself with any proclamation of abhorrence at William's declaration from The Hague, although to placate James he issued a declaration in these words:

> Whereas there hath been of late a general apprehension that his Highness the Prince of Orange hath an intention to invade the Kingdom in a hostile manner . . . for my own discharge [I] profess and declare that I never gave him any such invitation by word, writing or otherwise. Nor do I know, nor can believe that any of my reverend brethren, the bishops, have in any such way incited him.[154]

Here Sancroft was mistaken, because although he denied it to James, Compton had in fact put his name to just such an invitation.

William, meanwhile, landed at Torbay on 5 November 1688, and was in process of moving up to London. The Archbishop had another painful interview with James on 17 November, when he urged him to summon a free Parliament: but the same obstinacy which made the King decline to compromise, now led him suddenly to lose nerve. After an attempt at escape on 11 December and a fitful return to London, he finally left the shores of Britain on the evening of 23 December.

II

Sancroft's attitude throughout these testing and traumatic days was constitutionally correct, and he acted in full co-operation with his fellow bishops. But it was for him a terrible ordeal. He inherited from earlier days an attitude to the monarchy which even James's abandonment of the established Church, and his lawless despotism, could not entirely eradicate; indeed had not this despotism been exercised on behalf of Rome, Sancroft might well have played up the royal prerogative as did Laud. But James's 'flight' and William's arrival filled him with dismay, and created a situation which he had never anticipated. One of Sancroft's last public acts was to sign a declaration, on 11 December, exhorting the Prince of Orange to assist in calling a free Parliament. A few days later he saw James in a final interview at Whitehall, and after this he retired to Lambeth. When, on 18 December, the University of Cambridge elected him Chancellor, he declined to serve; and equally when William entered London, he refused either to wait upon him or to attend Parliament. The significance of his office, however, led to his being sought out at Lambeth, and a meeting of bishops and lay peers took place there on 15 January 1689. Sancroft's position was clear, if somewhat naïve politically. He was prepared to declare James unfit to reign, and to appoint William regent or *custos regni*. What he would not do was to go back on his oath to James. Thus he refused to have any relations with the Convention Parliament which declared the throne vacant and offered it to William and Mary. When his chaplain inadvertently prayed for the new sovereigns he was rebuked with great heat, Sancroft admonishing him that he must thenceforward desist from offering prayers for the new King and Queen, or else from performing the duties of his chapel; so long as King James lived no other persons could be sovereigns. Such legalism, however, ran counter to the political fact that William was prepared to acquiesce in nothing but the exercise of effective power, and was known to have declared that he would not be his wife's gentleman's usher—that is, come in exclusively on her rights as the daughter of James II by his first wife, Anne Hyde. His intention was to return to his native Holland unless he were given a real sovereignty.

Politically, what Sancroft insisted upon was not feasible because its concern was to minister to nice scruples of conscience arising from an out-of-date philosophy of the State rather than to secure an effective discharge of the government of the realm. In a paper which he left behind him he set out his own views as to the moral basis of society, and his conviction that no short-term expedients ought to compromise its demands. In this document, typical of his thinking, he laid stress on the fact that it was the mind and opinion of every individual person which contributed to the happiness or ruin of a government, even if this was not always recognized till matters came to erupt in general discontent. That which was just and good should be done irrespective of immediate reward, though in the long run there will certainly be a full return.

Not everyone shared this optimistic view of the workings of Divine Providence, though its Pauline credentials are impeccable.

Such firmly held convictions meant that Sancroft took no part in the Revolution settlement, either in the abortive attempts to secure a 'comprehension' agreeable to the Presbyterians, or in the passing of the Act of Toleration. With doubtful consistency he did, however, issue a commission to his suffragan bishops to enable them to act for him at the Coronation on 11 April 1689, an expedient to which he also resorted for the consecration of Gilbert Burnet to the bishopric of Salisbury. His strictly archiepiscopal duties were discharged by Henry Compton, Bishop of London, who experienced no scruples of conscience at the way events had worked out.

Matters could not be left in this situation of ambiguity, however, and under the terms of an Act of Parliament requiring certain oaths to be taken to the new Government, Sancroft was suspended on 1 August 1689, along with five bishops and some four hundred clergy.

There is little doubt that, left to himself, William would have found a means of preventing Sancroft's subsequent deprivation. Up to the last moment, efforts were made to persuade the Archbishop to come to some accommodation with the Government, but in vain. To Bishop Compton he remarked: 'They'—the non-juring bishops—'could do nothing. If the King thought fit for his own sake that they should not be deprived he must make it his business; they could not vary from what they had done.'[155] Thus his deprivation became inevitable. The period of grace formally expired on 1 February 1690, but even then there was general reluctance to force the pace of events. Sancroft's revenues seem to have been paid him until Michaelmas

1690, and although his successor was publicly nominated on 23 April, he still stayed on at Lambeth. He did, however, pack up his books and tell his chaplains to leave him, which they refused to do though they 'differed from him concerning public matters in the state'. Most of his servants went, and he gave up public entertaining. His principles demanded that he should not leave until forced to do so. On 20 May the Queen ordered him to depart within ten days; and on 12 June he was cited to appear before the Barons of the Exchequer to answer a writ of ejectment; but the Archbishop would not enter any plea which implied recognition of William and Mary. On 23 June judgment was given against him; and that very evening he departed to stay in a friend's house in the Temple. At last, in August, he retired to a small house which he had built in Fressingfield, his birth-place, where he died on 24 November 1693.

The deprivation of Sancroft and his fellow non-jurors has interesting features. It shows how the supremacy of the Crown in relation to the Church of England was now linked up with Parliament. Sancroft had been guilty of no ecclesiastical crime; and he was never accused of connivance in any attempt to reinstate James on the throne. Yet it is difficult to see how an Archbishop of Canterbury who did not recognize the King and Queen could remain in office in an established Church unless that office were permanently in commission. As Archbishop, he exercised responsibilities under the supremacy of the Crown and within a nation-state, and though his status as a bishop remained unimpaired it was the exercise of this office in a defined geographical area which was now removed from him. In reaction against what he regarded as an Erastian view, Henry Dodwell, the learned patristic scholar, maintained that bishops could not be deposed except when they deposed themselves for heresy and that 'those bishops that act anything of common concernment of the national Church without being presided over by the Primate of Canterbury must necessarily divide themselves from the national Head, and hence from the Church that is headed by him.'[156] Such deprivations, he contended, cut at the roots of spiritual independence, and the very nature of a church.

That the primacy of Canterbury was in itself necessary to the functioning of the *Ecclesia Anglicana* was not a thesis, however, which had hitherto commanded either theoretical or practical acceptance. Nor was it held by the non-jurors, who made no effort to appoint a successor to Sancroft after his death, though Sancroft, on 9 February 1691, executed a deed delegating to William Lloyd (1637–1710), the deprived Bishop of Norwich, the exercise of his archiepiscopal authority. The former Archbishop, however, certainly seems to have favoured the continuance of a non-juring episcopal succession.

The fact was that the Archbishop, who drew his inspiration from an earlier age, found himself, for a brief period and under the pressure of exceptional events, the champion of the new. When a dramatic and unexpected twist in national fortunes confronted him with an unexpected situation, he returned to a more congenial loyalty. Sancroft at one end and Burnet at the other, represent, in extreme form, divisions within *Ecclesia Anglicana*, the mutual antipathy of which was to affect its constitutional life, and in the process make the exercise of the Archbishop's office the more difficult.

# 7

## JOHN TILLOTSON, THE LIBERAL

The Revolution settlement won wide support, yet left many rank-and-file clergymen determined to make no further concessions to dissenters. Although not convinced enough to become non-jurors, they yet venerated their cause and the absolutism with which they maintained it. The bishops, however, being royal nominees, were by and large of a different persuasion. They had little sympathy with the views of the non-jurors and were prepared to by-pass the discrimination against the nonconformists written into the Toleration Act of 1689 by sanctioning resort to occasional conformity.

It was inevitable that Sancroft's successor should be an ecclesiastic of this kind. The obvious choice seemed the man who had been passed over in favour of Sancroft some fourteen years earlier—Henry Compton, the most militant of James's opponents. Alone amongst his brethren, he had signed the invitation asking William to come over to England. He had donned military uniform at the time of James's flight, and escorted Anne, the King's daughter, to Nottingham. During the period of Sancroft's isolation in Lambeth he had assumed a position of leadership—the Archbishop's jurisdiction went to the Dean and Chapter of Canterbury[157]—and acted for him at the coronation of William and Mary in 1689. He had presided at Convocation, and in the House of Lords supported legislation in the interests of dissenters. To the uninformed his translation to Canterbury appeared certain.[158] But there were early signs pointing another way.

When the non-juring bishops were replaced, there was one significant omission from the list of nominees: John Tillotson, known to be intimate with William and Mary, of liberal views, and a friend of Burnet, who had the ear of the Queen. What the general public could not know was that William had explicitly told Tillotson, on kissing hands as Dean of St. Paul's, that this was but a stepping-stone to Canterbury. Compton, however, early feared such a possibility, and his instability of character was painfully displayed at the Convocation called to deal with proposals for the comprehension that he had publicly espoused. Here he connived at the election of his old chaplain, Dr. Jane, as prolocutor of the Lower House over against

Tillotson, though he must have known that such a nomination would prove fatal to any hopes of an accommodation with the dissenters. Tillotson was always cautious in his judgements and far removed from petty personal spite, yet recalling these days in a letter to Lady Russell, quoted in Birch's *Life of Tillotson*, he alleged that 'the Bishop of London was at the bottom of that storm which was raised in Convocation last year.' It was all 'on my account' he said ' . . . out of jealousy that I might be a hindrance to him in attaining what he desires, and what, I call God to witness, I would not have.'

The last word was with William and Mary, and they had definitely made up their minds. In October 1690, the Dean was summoned to the royal presence and, as he reported to Lady Russell, the King 'then renewed his former gracious offer in so pressing a manner and with so much kindness that I hardly knew how to resist it'.

Tillotson's sensitive nature shrank from the repercussions of his appointment—the disgust of the non-jurors, and, more especially, the resentment of the Bishop of London, from whose jealousy he had already suffered.

> I told his Majesty—he wrote again to Lady Russell—that I was still afraid his kindness to me would be greatly to his prejudice especially if he carried it so far as he was pleased to speak of . . . for I plainly saw that they could not bear it. and that the effects of envy and ill will towards me would terminate upon him.

But William was not the kind of man to submit to pressure of this kind. With the wisdom of the experienced man of affairs he replied that 'if the thing were once done, and he [Compton] saw no remedy, they would give over, or think of making the best of it'. What particularly carried weight with Tillotson was the King's intimation that 'if he refused he would not fill up any of the Bishoprics during the lives of any of the present Bishops'.

Fear of Compton's malice was not the only factor which made the Dean of St. Paul's hesitate. He particularly disliked the thought, as he himself expressed it, of being 'a wedge to drive out Sancroft': and was reported to have told the King that he 'would with great[er] chearfulness have received his commands to have gone to the Indies than to Canterbury'.

Compton, meanwhile, had not abandoned hope, and in a last desperate bid for office accompanied the King at his own expense to the Congress at The Hague in January 1691, 'the only one of his Dignity and Order that attended him thither'. Perhaps this was why, as late as the end of March, uninformed gossips still asserted that 'the Bishop of London will be Archbishop of Canterbury'.

The announcement of Tillotson's appointment, on 22 April of that year, was a bitter blow to so emotional a man as the Bishop of London. Even Sancroft was moved to pity when he wrote—the letter is included in Dr. Williams's *Collection of Original Papers*—to Lloyd, the deprived Bishop of Norwich: 'Yester night the Bishop of London, knowing nothing of these promotions, was ready to enter the Council Chamber, when a friend pulled him by the sleeve, and showed him the whole scheme; whereupon he retreated.'

There is something pathetically final in these last three words. For a second time one of his own clergy, not in episcopal orders, and again from the Deanery of St. Paul's, had been preferred before him, this second time in even more aggravating circumstances. In 1678 he had been frustrated by James, then Duke of York, an avowed enemy: in 1689 he was disappointed by William, a supposed friend.

Why was Compton passed over and Tillotson preferred? Such questions do not permit of an exact answer. What is certain is that Mary, a woman of genuine piety, did not want Compton at Lambeth, since she told Tillotson that, if he declined, it would be Stillingfleet who would be preferred. Burnet, who had the ear of both King and Queen, regarded Compton as 'weak and wilful'. Tillotson, when seeking to withdraw, suggested Stillingfleet. Perhaps there was some defect of character; perhaps such an appointment was thought likely to exacerbate the non-jurors; perhaps William opted for someone to whom he did not owe so much.

The immediate effects upon Compton were extreme, and he made little effort to conceal the bitterness of his disappointment. When Tillotson was consecrated on Whit Sunday, 1691, in the Church of St. Mary-le-Bow, he absented himself, and his place was taken by Mews, Bishop of Winchester, assisted by Burnet, Stillingfleet, and Hough. Most of the nobility, including Compton's old friend Danby (now Carmarthen) were present, and it was one of the most splendid gatherings since the Coronation. Compton was also a significant absentee when Tillotson was admitted to the Privy Council. Sad to say this private sulk went on for some time. When James Blair came over from Virginia to promote the founding of William and Mary College, he found the Bishop of London ill, resentful, and unwilling to go to Court or to make any approach to the King. Blair's letter to Governor Nicholson, written at the end of the year, is a pathetic commentary on the state of affairs at Fulham, indeed of the vanity of human wishes.

I found myself obliged—he wrote—to take new measures from what I had proposed to myself. The bishop of London was at this time under a great cloud, and mighty unwilling to meddle in any court business, for notwithstanding his great merit from the present government, he had been passed by in all the late promotions, and the two archbishoprics had been bestowed on two of his own clergy, viz Dr. Tillotson and Dr. Sharp, so that notwithstanding the Bishop of London's great kindness to Virginia, yet I found he was not at this time in so fit circumstances as to manage a business at Court, as was expected.[159]

Compton's frustrated experience of disappointment has been told, perhaps, at more length than it deserves. He may be taken, however, as representative of a host of others who felt themselves to have suffered in the same way, but whose anguish spilt over on to an understanding wife where it has remained unrecorded. Compton was unmarried.

If character in itself qualified for office, no man could have had greater claims to Canterbury than John Tillotson. He was intelligent, liberal, and warm-hearted. With a mind singularly receptive and open, he combined great sensitivity and niceness of feeling. The son of a clothworker of Halifax, he went up to Clare College, Cambridge, in 1647, and had little difficulty in adjusting himself to life under the Commonwealth. In 1657 he was a tutor to the son of Sir Edmund Prideaux, of Ford Abbey, Devon, who was Attorney-General to Oliver Cromwell. Years afterwards he told Burnet

> that a week after Cromwell's death he, being by accident at Whitehall, and hearing there was to be a fast that day in the household, went out of curiosity into the presence chamber, where it was held. On the one side of the table Richard with the rest of Cromwell's family were placed and six of the preachers on the other side. There he heard a great deal of strange stuff, enough to disgust a man for ever of that enthusiastic boldness. God was, as it were, reproached for Cromwell's services, and challenged for taking him away so soon.[160]

Although attracted by the intellectual keenness of the Puritans, he came to be much influenced by the more tolerant approach of Chillingworth, author of *The Religion of Protestants*, and Ralph Cudworth, Master of his College, a prominent member of what were known as the Cambridge Platonists.

Tillotson's sympathies were with the Presbyterians at the time of the Restoration, though he was not called upon to appear at the Savoy Conference. In 1663 he was appointed to the living of Keddington in Suffolk, and in the next year was made a preacher at Lincoln's Inn, and in 1670 Dean of Canterbury. It was as a preacher that Tillotson now established his fame. His style was clear, and what he said was meticulously prepared; yet he avoided the conceits and over-elaboration which had tended to make sermons tedious. His delivery gave the appearance of complete ease although he confessed to a friend 'that he had always written every word [and] used to get it by heart', abandoning this method only because 'it heated his head so much a day or two before and after he preached'. Reckoned by contemporary standards, his sermons were brief, and he found a ready and large public in the middle classes. Hithero the pulpit had come to be regarded almost as a Puritan preserve. His aim was to inspire his hearers to practical goodness, and not to weigh them down with over-subtle speculations. Apart from his polemics against Roman Catholics—in this he provided arguments which the deists later used against revealed religion itself—his approach was tolerant and eirenical, the effect being to lower the temper of ecclesiastical debate. Theologically he was among the first of the latitudinarians.

Typical of his liberality was a sermon on 'The Eternity of Hell Torments' preached before Queen Mary in March 1691, in which he tried to draw the teeth of this terrifying doctrine by treating it subjectively in terms of a moral deterrent. In an address given at Whitehall a few years previously he was thought to have gone to excessive lengths when he maintained that liberty of conscience did not extend to making proselytes for the established religion without some miraculous warrant. His lectures on Socinianism and a sermon on the Trinity undoubtedly influenced the metaphysician Samuel Clarke and did something to give rise to the Arian controversy. As to the Athanasian Creed, 'I wish we were well rid of it,' he commented. Frankness was always one of his most endearing qualities.

It has been said of Tillotson that he was the only Primate who took front rank in his day as a preacher. Certainly he believed in the efficacy of the pulpit. 'Good preaching and good living,' he used to say, 'will gain upon people.'

It has been necessary to introduce Tillotson in this way because he represents a kind of Archbishop different from his post-Reformation predecessors. His tenure of Canterbury was short—only three years—and there is no striking achievement to his credit. Certainly he discharged to the full the traditional role of being a friend to the Royal Family. He supported wholeheartedly, after comprehension proved impracticable, the Act of Toleration, declaring that he 'would never do anything to infringe' it. He was happy to connive at the virtual suppression of Convocation, dreading the results of its internal divisions. He took no initiative in political affairs; indeed withdrew from them as uncongenial. The breadth of his humanity is seen in that he was intimate with Thomas Firmin, the Unitarian; and in the last two years of his life was attended by his great friend Robert Nelson, a non-juror, in whose arms he died on 22 November 1694, after being seized a few days before by an apoplectic stroke in the chapel at Whitehall. It was found, after his death, that his extensive charities—he regularly gave away a fifth of his income—left him almost penniless; so that his wife, a niece of Oliver Cromwell and the first lady to reside in Lambeth since 1570, had to be granted an annuity by the Crown. 'Tillotson was a man of a clear head and a sweet temper'—so commented Burnet.

# 8

## THOMAS TENISON, THE PARISH PRIEST

I

On his death-bed Tillotson commended Thomas Tenison, Bishop of Lincoln, as his successor. This advice was in fact followed, though Burnet tried to secure the nomination for Stillingfleet, Bishop of Worcester. To Evelyn, Tenison's appointment was a matter of deep personal satisfaction. 'I had news that my dear and worthy friend, Dr. Tenison, Bishop of Lincoln is made the Archbishop of Canterbury, for which I thank God and rejoice, he being most worthy of it for his learning, piety and prudence'—so runs his diary. Amongst Tories, the appointment was not popular; and Thomas Hearne, in his *Remarks and Collections*, quotes a contemporary rhymester expressing his disgust:

> Tho' his old solid Grace was preferr'd cross the water
> For tacking the Tyde, and well trimming the matter,
> Yet does it not follow that the Church of St. Martin
> Makes her Rectors all Prelates for being uncertain.

Jonathan Swift, disappointed that he had been frustrated in a matter of preferment, described him as 'hot and heavy like a tailor's goose'.

Tenison was by instinct a parish priest, in which capacity he had spent his formative years. It helped him to become a workmanlike Archbishop.

Thomas Tenison was born in a vicarage and ordained by Brian Duppa at Richmond during the Commonwealth; appointed successively to the livings of St. Andrew the Great in Cambridge; St. Peter Mancroft in Norwich; and St. Martin-in-the-Fields. He was no absentee incumbent, but busied himself with his day-to-day duties. In his parishes he left behind him a reputation for a diligent devotion to pastoral care, and at St. Martin's gathered round him a team of assistant curates. While there he founded the first public library in London, and left behind him four schools bearing his name, three of which are still in existence. In his churchmanship, as in his politics, he was liberal, and his piety was practical rather than mystical. He wrote learnedly, if rather laboriously, his best known works being a critique of Thomas Hobbes and a *Discourse on Idolatry*. To Tenison, Roman Catholicism was un-English, incompatible with constitutional monarchy, and his pulpit became a rallying centre for anti-papism. He was early in the councils of those who were corresponding with William. Comprehension in the interests of moderate dissenters found in him a strong supporter, and he was Secretary to the Commission set up in 1689 to revise the Prayer Book with this end in view. In order to bring about a reconciliation he seems to have favoured conditional re-ordination.

Tenison approached ecclesiastical problems with a strong indoctrination of common-sense, and believed firmly in encouraging the clergy to be a disciplined body, caring for their parishioners, and obedient to both statutes and canons. During his short stay as Bishop of Lincoln he conducted a rigorous visitation, necessary since there lingered on a great deal of unsettlement from the Commonwealth. More particularly, as Archbishop, he determined to use fully the powers of his office to ensure an efficient and hard-working clergy. Without Laud's testiness or resort to high-handed methods, he yet believed that ecclesiastical machinery should be set in motion to correct abuses. This meant vigilance on his part, as well as on that of his legal officials. Immediately after his enthronement on 16 May 1695—the first Archbishop to be enthroned in person at Canterbury since the Reformation—he embarked on his primary visitation, beginning at the cathedral, where he confirmed no less than 1,200 people, and in all, throughout his visitation, some 3,674. Thomas Brett, who as a high churchman was not particularly well disposed to the Archbishop, yet says of him that whereas

> our former Archbishops have thought it sufficient once in seven years or thereabouts to send some other Bishop to Visit and Confirm for them, this was done by Archbishop Sancroft; others as Archbishop Sheldon and Archbishop Tillotson have neither come themselves nor sent any other, but his present Grace of Canterbury has almost kept to the strict Letter of the Canon and visited us very frequently, and performed the office of Confirmation with the greatest Order and Solemnity imaginable; not in a hurry or huddle. . . .[161]

His visitation articles were detailed, and through his archdeacon he did his best to follow up what was found amiss.

Among his first acts as Archbishop was to urge upon William 'the great Necessity of Preserving and Restoring the Discipline of the Church'. To this end he drew up a number of injunctions concerned, generally, with the practical ordering of the Church's life, particularly in respect of ordination, conduct of services, duties of bishops, the residence of the clergy, and obedience to the canons. These injunctions were issued on 3 February 1695, by the King as Supreme Governor of the *Ecclesia Anglicana*. The advantage of this procedure, apart from the prestige given to the injunctions by the *imprimatur* of the monarchy, was that they could be sent to both the provinces of Canterbury and York. This was followed on 16 July 1695, by a *Letter* written by Tenison to the suffragan bishops of his own province and subsequently published, 'recommending such Rules and Orders as if well observed, would tend weightily to the Peace and Honour of the Established Church'. These regulations were more detailed and explicit than the Injunctions and dealt with matters of social as well as of ecclesiastical importance. Before issuing them, Tenison consulted his brother bishops, and also John Sharp, Archbishop of York, with whom, in spite of his Toryism, Tenison was anxious to work in harmony.

At one time in his archiepiscopate, Tenison seems to have attempted to keep in touch with special problems in both provinces by drawing up a central register which he called *Notitia Episcopatuum*. This consisted of a vellum book of some two hundred and fifty pages, neatly divided into sections for each diocese. The intention was probably to use it to secure a measure of co-ordination, and he may well have provided it as a result of his promise to the bishops, in 1695, to keep a 'ledger book' containing particulars of the clergy. It is difficult, however, to discover any classification in the matters entered.

Tenison realized, as bishops have realized ever since, that any reform of the Church must begin with the exercise of some discrimination in the selection of ordinands. Here Tenison believed in being practical, and he himself endeavoured to set a standard. Candidates were examined by one of his chaplains, sometimes by himself; and there still exist at Lambeth examination papers set to them, consisting of a number of brief factual questions with the answers given by the candidates. Sometimes a man was failed. Tenison was also concerned that letters-testimonials should be in due and proper form, which meant that they must state categorically that the candidate was fitted for Holy Orders.

One of the great evils in the Church inherited from the Middle Ages and destined to continue until the 1830s was pluralism, with its attendant scandal of non-residence. Pluralities were legal if incumbents conformed to canonical and statutory requirements and received a dispensation from the Archbishop. Only certain people were qualified to hold them, and even then the livings must not be more than thirty miles apart. Tenison took particular care to examine the particulars of each application, and quite a number were refused. On one occasion he stood up successfully to Queen Anne who wished, by royal warrant, to grant a dispensation in a situation which did not justify it. His letter of protest was frank and forthright.

In his policy of reform, Tenison tried to keep in touch with his suffragans through a large correspondence and by Bishops' Meetings in London. In the case of two Welsh bishops whose standard of duty fell lamentably below reasonable expectation—Thomas Watson of St. David's and Edward Jones of St. Asaph—he determined to exercise his archiepiscopal authority.

Thomas Watson was a strong Tory and had been exempted from the Act of Indemnity. In the House of Lords, after the Revolution of 1688, he consistently opposed the Court party and never missed an opportunity to embarrass the ministry. Charges against him of simony, extortion, and perjury began to go the rounds of the diocese; and Robert Lucy, son of the former bishop, who had undoubtedly lived 'in a woeful and culpable omission of many of the direct and important as well sacred as other duties of his office', petitioned Tillotson to inquire into the practices of the bishop. The Archbishop, in July 1694, appointed commissioners to visit the diocese, in the meantime formally suspending Watson. Tenison, when he came into the archbishopric, lifted the suspension but carried on with the investigations, as a result of which he decided to prosecute the Bishop by asserting his own jurisdiction as Metropolitan of the Province. Under a citation dated 23 August 1695 he summoned him to appear before his Court of Audience at Lambeth on Saturday, 24 October. When this day came, six bishops and the Dean of the Court of the Arches as assessors, sat with the Archbishop, and this together with the form of the sentence has led Sir Robert Phillimore, in his *Ecclesiastical Law of the Church of England*, to conclude that though legally the Court was one of Audience, the forms and procedure were those of the Court of Arches.

The story of what happened from this date until Watson, after some ten stormy years, was finally ousted from the House of Lords, makes extraordinary reading. Watson was a born fighter and he contested every inch of the way. His position as a member of the House of Lords, and the freehold possession of his temporal estates, allowed him and his legal advisers to go from one court to another; to accept and then subsequently to question the Archbishop's jurisdiction, although Lord Chief Justice Holt in the Court of King's Bench had no hesitation in stating categorically:

The Archbishop of Canterbury has without doubt provincial

jurisdiction over all his suffragan bishops, which he may exercise in what place of the province it shall please him, and it is not material to be in the Arches, no more than in any other place; for the Arches is only a peculiar consisting of divers parishes in London, where the Archbishop of Canterbury exerciseth his metropolitical jurisdiction, but he is not confined to exercise it there.[162]

Thus encouraged, Tenison proceeded to give sentence of deprivation on 3 August 1699, the bishops concurring.

If the Archbishop's sentence were good in law, then Watson had lost his seat in the House of Lords and also the temporalities of his see. His first and obvious resort was to appeal to the Court of Delegates, a Court created by the Statute 25 Hen. VIII c. 19, for the purpose of securing redress of grievances where there was 'lack of justice at or in any of the courts of the archbishop of this realm'.

Watson, fearing that confirmation of his sentence was inevitable, now fell back on his privilege as a member of the House of Lords, and in this chamber his counsel maintained that deprivation by an Archbishop alone was contrary to precedent. The Archbishop could not claim it as part of his former legatine jurisdiction since this was now lodged in the Crown: and it seemed unlikely according to the 'reason of the thing'—always a difficult thesis to establish in an English court—that 'the House of Lords should submit the rights of peerage to a single man, since a result of deprivation was loss of peerage without possibility of appeal to this House'. Counsel for the Archbishop replied to these submissions at length, making the obvious point that the appeal to the Court of Delegates was itself an admission of the Archbishop's jurisdiction.

Party feeling in the Lords was too strong to allow the Bishop's case to prevail whatever its merits, and it was decided that he could not resume his privilege. Nor was he any more successful when he returned to the King's Bench for another prohibition. Once again the Lord Chief Justice affirmed that the Archbishop had power to deprive.

The way was now clear for the Court of Delegates to confirm the sentence, which it did on 16 February 1700, and for the House of Lords, after an interminable battle, to expel the Bishop from its membership some five years later.

Tenison had shown great determination in prosecuting this case to a successful conclusion. Although contemporary legalists such as Dr. Ayliffe and Edmund Gibson supported this assertion of archiepiscopal authority, pamphleteers maintained that Tenison was motivated by political interests and that if there were to be a deprivation it should have been effected either by Convocation, the House of Lords, or a royal commission.

The political aspect of Watson's case is illustrated in the different treatment meted out to Edward Jones, whose constant 'whiggery' secured for him the see of St. Asaph in 1692. His behaviour in his diocese became such as to cause grave public scandal, reaching a climax in a court case over a presentation to a living. Thirty-eight of the most prominent beneficed clergymen in his diocese laid a full complaint before the Archbishop under thirty-four heads in March 1697. Tenison acted promptly, suspended Jones, and appointed two bishops and his Dean of the Arches to conduct a visitation. Their report was serious, and Tenison once again determined to assert his own jurisdiction. Jones's connexions with the Court party, however, led to many delays, and it was not until 5 June 1700 that the formal hearing began. It was thought by some that Jones, like Watson, must be deprived, and Watson's friends rejoiced that though Tenison and his coadjutors would 'gladly save him', yet they 'could not'. However they proved to be wrong. On 18 June 1701, Tenison suspended Jones for six months *ab officio et beneficio et ultra donec satisfecerit*. Few could help but draw comparisons, and Jones did not make matters easier by declaring that he had only acted in his diocese 'pursuant to the example, or under the directions of his predecessor'. Tenison himself was reported to have confessed that, 'if he had been to pronounce sentence some Weeks sooner, he must have deprived him'. Tenison's own uneasiness showed itself in a refusal to restore Jones to the diocese after the prescribed six months. Jones now proceeded to make a confession in the most abject terms, concluding his document with these words:

> I will sincerely perform my Pastoral Office with a good Con-
> science in all things thereto appertaining; God being my
> helper.[163]

Such humility paid off: he was restored to his office on 5 May 1702.

It is perhaps significant that no charges of not tendering the oaths to the Government were preferred against Jones as they had been against Watson. The probability is that both men deserved sentence and censure; both had fallen lamentably below the standard that ought to be expected of a diocesan bishop. Yet the difference in treatment was almost certainly due to political expediency; an expediency which Tenison regarded as a necessary condition of preserving Protestant liberty. As Edmund Gibson wrote in another context, the Archbishop's policy 'upon which he acted in the whole course of his administration, and from which he could never be driven, by the continual clamours of the Tories about the danger of the Church' was the conviction that 'there was no way to preserve the Church but by preserving the present establishment in the State, and that there was far greater probability that the Tories would be able to destroy our present establishment in the State, than that the dissenters would be able to destroy our establishment in the Church'.

Tenison was not allowed to escape criticism for the seemingly disparate character of the sentences. A rhymester indulged himself in the following doggerel:

> Tho' I were mute, you must confess I've stood
> Fast as a rock against the beating Flood.
> Witness St. Asaph and St. David's Cause,
> Where obstinately I transgressed the Laws,
> And did in either case Injustice show
> Here sav'd a Friend, there triumphed o'er a Foe.[164]

## II

These two cases certainly vindicated, in part helped to establish, the right of the Metropolitan to deprive a suffragan; but while they were *sub judice* a severe attack of another kind was being made on an undoubted constitutional right attaching to the Archbishop's office. This attack arose out of a serious cleavage in the *Ecclesia Anglicana* itself, to which reference has already been made.

The Upper House of Convocation, the more so after the non-juring secession, was wholeheartedly behind the Revolution settlement with its Act of Toleration designed to accommodate the Dissenters. The Lower House, being in the main Tory and High Church was more protective of specifically Anglican interests. Tenison's attitude to Convocation was psychologically determined in 1689, when the Lower House refused even to consider the proposed changes in the Book of Common Prayer which aimed at securing a comprehension. For a time, as Archbishop, so his contemporary biographer writes, he was content to follow 'the steps of Dr. Tillotson and several others of his predecessors and (no licence being granted by the Court for the transacting business) [to] continue the convocations by moderate prorogations without sitting'.

The reasons for this policy were self-evident. Tenison feared lest the factional struggles within Convocation should raise the political temper generally. Tory churchmen, on the other hand, in protesting against the Erastian nature of the Revolution settlement, were forced to split Convocation into two, since they were hardly represented in the Lower House, and by so doing to defy their spiritual superiors, whose episcopal status according to their own theories, was of the *esse* of Church order. By so doing they played fast and loose with undoubted constitutional precedents.

In 1697 there appeared a *Letter to a Convocation Man*, in the main the work of Francis Atterbury, whose dominating personality inspired throughout the attitude taken by the Lower House. This persuasive, though misleading work, asserted that Convocation met 'upon the ground not of grace but of right'. Though Atterbury's constitutional thesis was successfully countered by the more meticulous scholarship of Wake and Gibson, its demand for a sitting Convocation could not be politically resisted. On 10 February 1701 it met to do business, but the years of inactivity had not cooled the passions of its members. The heated disputes which ensued came to centre upon an attack on the right of the Archbishop to prorogue both Houses. Behind the Tory clergy in the Lower House were Tory statesmen, prominent amongst whom was Robert Harley, who accused the Archbishop, in August 1701, of 'trumping up a legatine power'. Though Tenison was firm in maintaining that if the Lower House insisted on the right to adjourn, he equally must maintain his right to prorogue, he yet did his best to be conciliatory, more than once exhorting the Lower House to 'unity and peace'. Political factors, however, kept the dispute going. In 1711, when Toryism was resurgent—it was the period of Sacheverell, and Tenison was now more or less isolated at Lambeth —Atterbury secured his own election as Prolocutor, and effected a change in the licence as a result of which the 'archbishop was not, as was usual on former occasions, nominated president, neither was he consulted prior to its being issued'. To add insult to injury, Sharp, Archbishop of York, was called in to advise the ministry concerning the business to be laid before the Convocation of Canterbury. Tenison's position as a convinced Erastian, who believed, to quote his own words, that 'her Majesty's supremacy over the Synod ought to be asserted more strenuously than has of late been done', was indeed difficult when the Queen herself was dominated by Tory counsels.

What would have happened had this attack been maintained can only be a matter of speculation. As it was, the death of Anne changed the political climate. Atterbury, now Bishop of Rochester, suffered exile in 1724 for treasonable activities entered into on behalf of the 'King over the water'. The disputes in Convocation, whipped up again as a result of the Bangorian controversy, led to its being prorogued in 1717 and (except for an abortive attempt at revival in 1743) not being called again to do business till 1852.

The Archbishop of Canterbury had indeed maintained his constitutional right to preside over the whole Convocation meeting as one body; but the virtual liquidation of a provincial assembly, whose roots went deep into national history, lowered, in the long run, the status and effectiveness of his metropolitan office. It meant that ecclesiastical debate, apart from the proliferation of pamphlets, could only take place in Parliament, where the Archbishop's position, as one among many, lacked the unique significance that was his in his own ecclesiastical Synod. Thus the rise of Methodism and its separation from the Church of England took place at a time when no collective voice could be uttered.

The story of these Convocational struggles goes a long way to explaining Tenison's deep conviction that high preferment in the Church must be confined to those who were entirely loyal to the settlement of 1688. William III, in chastened mood after his wife's death, resolved to encourage 'a pious and laborious clergy', and to this end set up a small commission—as Charles II had done before him—consisting of the two Archbishops and four bishops. Its task was 'to seek out the best and worthiest men they could find that such only might be promoted'. The terms of the Commission—it was reconstituted in October 1699 when John Moore, Bishop of Norwich, replaced the deceased Stillingfleet—were in part drawn up by Tenison. In the absence of the King overseas, it was laid down that minor preferment should be disposed of by the Commission itself; and its 'hands and seals' were to be sufficient under the Great Seal to appoint. As to important preferment, the Commission was to recommend to the King, who was left free, however, to accept or reject such recommendations. What appears to have been restricted was unilateral action by the Crown, since it was explicitly laid down that 'if at any time we'—the King—'be moved in like manner by any Person whatsoever our Pleasure is that neither of our principal secretaries of state shall present any Warrant to us for our Royal signature in such a Case until our Commissioners have been acquainted therewith and have given [their] Opinion and Recommendation as aforesaid.'[165]

The power of the Archbishop of Canterbury on the Commission should be noted. His presence was necessary to constitute a quorum, and to him belonged the right of a casting vote.

The idea was excellent, but the Commission did not survive the reign of William. There were difficulties from the beginning. Many junior appointments were made as a routine operation, but preferment was too valuable a political asset to be controlled even by the King's friends. The Commission, apart from Sharp, wished to promote only Whigs; the Crown at times was anxious to woo Tories, and more so since William did not wish to become a captive of one party.

The political climate changed almost dramatically with the accession of Anne, and for most of her reign Tenison was isolated at Lambeth and his influence on appointments negligible. Her most intimate adviser was John Sharp, Archbishop of York, who succeeded 'alone to the royal confidence and counsel in all affairs relating to the church'. Both Queen and Archbishop were devoted to the interests of the *Ecclesia Anglicana,* and it was this allegiance which controlled their Toryism. Tenison was soon made aware of his changed status when he waited on the Queen in connexion with the Coronation. She insisted that Sharp should preach the sermon, and showed great concern for his personal comfort in making the journey from York to London. Relations between the two Archbishops remained strained, as seen in letters which remain at Lambeth. 'I hope we shall one day agree . . .' Tenison wrote somewhat sadly in 1705. 'If not, I'm sure on my part Charity shall prevail; and I think it will in Yr Grace also.' Appointments soon began to take on a different and more Tory character. Tenison did not lack those who urged him to have things out with the Queen; and under pressure from Lord Somers, he did write a tactful letter on 12 June 1707. In this he reminded Anne that it was 'the good temper of the present Bishops and their appearing for the true interest of their Country' which had 'chiefly gained them respect'. 'But if it should come to pass at any time by any means,' he warned her, 'that such should come upon the Bench as should make it warpt (which may God avert) Episcopacy itself would be in danger of falling.'[166] Such counsel, however, went largely unheeded, except when the political exigencies of the foreign war demanded the placation of the illustrious Duke of Marlborough. From 1710 till the Queen's death, the Whigs, both clerical and lay, found themselves in the wilderness, and Tenison neither possessed influence himself nor had friendly ministers to put his case. The passing of the Occasional Conformity Act in 1711 and the infamous Schism Act of 1714, which was in fact a deliberate attack on the Revolution settlement, showed the strength of the extreme Church–Tory party.

In his relations with his brethren the bishops, it was Tenison's constant preoccupation to encourage them to be good Whigs, and to be zealous in the discharge of their ecclesiastical duties. In this he was handicapped by the bitterness of the disputes in Convocation; by Sharp's influence with the Queen; and by political division within the clergy. Thus his contacts with the bishops, in the main conducted through his chaplains, tended to become formal, the more so as the disabilities of old age crept upon him. Tenison was conscientious almost to a fault, serious and sincere, yet his convictions were too deeply held to enable him to win the confidence of those members of the episcopate who did not share his Whig principles; and this despite his opinion that ''twill be very necessary for the Bishops to meet more often than they do when in Town for the good of the Monarchy and the Ch[urch]'. The Archbishop could not but resent his virtual exclusion from Court where Sharp was always so welcome a visitor.

> It seems to have been our great failure—he wrote to the Archbishop of York—that we have not, by consultations, digested our matters relating to the good of the Church and State before we are to use them.

This did not prevent Tenison trying to see that the Whig element among the bishops was well represented in the House of Lords. If any were to be absent, he expected them to get the consent of the Crown or provide a proxy.

Tenison took an initiative in fostering succour for the Protestant refugees who fled over to England; raising funds for their support; and trying to overcome a national prejudice against them. He was vigilant in Parliament and out to reform contemporary manners and to combat sexual licence. He intervened decisively, as Visitor, in the affairs of All Souls College, Oxford, against Tory attack and established the principle of non-resident fellows. The Primate is still the Visitor of this college. He corresponded with Dr. Jablonski, Chaplain to the King of Prussia and superintendent of the Protestant Church in Poland, with view to closer links and possible lay communion with the Protestant churches of Germany under the leadership of Prussia. Together with Lloyd, Bishop of Worcester, he entered into a lengthy correspondence, but the Archbishop realized the need to prevent a public controversy and nothing came of these tentative negotiations. Tenison helped to found, regularly presided over its meetings, and constantly supported, the Society for the Propagation of the Gospel. He played a considerable part in the setting up of Queen Anne's Bounty, particularly insisting that its finances should not be handled through the Exchequer. He did a great deal to encourage reform in the Church of Ireland, and sought to persuade the bishops in Scotland to take the oaths to the Government so that they might put themselves in the way of receiving help. He was largely responsible for the religious clauses attached to the Act of Union, 1707, clauses which in their open recognition of the Presbyterian Church north of the Border drew down upon him the attacks of high churchmen generally. Four bishops in the Upper House opposed the Bill, but Tenison's mind was clear.

> He had no scruple against ratifying, approving and confirming it within the bounds of Scotland . . . the narrow notions of all the Churches had been their ruin, and he believed the Church of Scotland to be as true a Protestant church as the Church of England, though he could not say it was so perfect.[167]

239

This did not prevent the Archbishop, however, from bringing in a Bill, to be appended to the Treaty of Union, 'for the security of the Church of England', the object being the protection of her rights and privileges.

Tenison's one great objective in the closing years of his life was to promote the Hanoverian succession. To this end he corresponded with the Electress Sophia, and consistently supported her interests, significantly opposing on one occasion an ill-advised scheme to bring her over to England. When Anne died in August 1714, and the son of Sophia—she had died in the preceding year—ascended the throne as George I, Tenison was able, as the Nonconformist Edmund Calamy reported, with a 'peculiar joy' and in spite of great pain and difficulty to crown the new monarch in Westminster Abbey. This he might well do, considering how much he had worked for, and what hopes he set upon, the Protestant succession in the House of Hanover. Almost his last act, in company with the bishops 'in or near London', was to issue a declaration 'testifying their Abhorrence of the Present Rebellion'. It was short lived.

The archiepiscopate of Thomas Tenison, perhaps even more than that of Sancroft, marks the end of an era. Up to the beginning of the XVIIIth century, it is almost impossible to tell the story of the developing life of the English people without reference to Church and Archbishop. These days were now to cease.

# PART V

# 'THE BENIGN AND COMFORTABLE AIR OF LIBERTY AND TOLERATION'

*Archbishops*

WILLIAM WAKE 1716
JOHN POTTER 1737
THOMAS HERRING 1747
MATTHEW HUTTON 1757
THOMAS SECKER 1758
FREDERICK CORNWALLIS 1768
JOHN MOORE 1783
CHARLES MANNERS SUTTON 1805

# 1

## ARCHBISHOPS AND THEIR BACKGROUND

I

Archbishops are the children of their time. Never was this more true than in the XVIIIth century when it may be said, in general terms, that the Church had no history. No longer was its life intertwined with the developing saga of the English people. For this reason it is as easy to be unfair to those who occupied St. Augustine's chair as it is to the *Ecclesia Anglicana* as a whole. For such denigration, protagonists of the Oxford Movement must accept a measure of blame, since their own presuppositions caused them to see these years as the nadir of English church history and to impose this view on posterity.

The XVIIIth century can best be understood as a reaction against the religious, political, and social excitement of the XVIIth. Men had grown weary of absolute systems, whether in Church or State. Ambitious ideologies seemed luxuries which ordinary people, concerned to get on with the business of every-day living, could ill afford. Newtonian science suggested that the universe constituted an orderly system, subject to uniform patterns of behaviour. Must not the same regularity obtain in the world of the spirit?

John Locke helped to shape the character of the century in his epoch-making book *The Reasonableness of Christianity* (1695), the essential argument of which was that 'there were no facts or doctrines of the Gospel or the Scriptures which when revealed were not perfectly plain, intelligible and reasonable'. From such fundamental assumptions came the emphasis on natural religion, and the preaching up of good works as 'the whole duty of man'. The demand was for a faith which would bring together rather than divide, encourage peace rather than breed fratricidal strife. The bloodless revolution of 1688 in its compromising utility and contractual emphasis was itself the product of this calmer spirit. Not surprisingly, therefore, the non-jurors with their transcendental theorizing suffered the fate of the dinosaurs because they, too, failed to adapt themselves to the realities of a new environment. The result was the rise of deism both within and without the Church.

It is within a historic context of this kind that the Archbishops of the period must be seen. Not for them the destructive enthusiasms which tore England apart in more explosive days. Of course, they differed somewhat in their precise theological affirmations. Wake and Secker, for example, thought in high terms of the episcopal office, whereas Herring and Moore saw it as a necessary convenience.

Yet in spite of their various approaches, archbishops shared a common mood; and they shared it with most of the statesmen of their age. Sir Robert Walpole expressed the tone of the century in his guiding principle, *quieta non movere* ('let sleeping dogs lie'). The *rationale* of this passivity ran somewhat as follows.

The happy establishment in Church and State providentially brought about in 1688 might not be perfect, but in a fallible world it is better to enjoy its solid benefits than to put everything to risk by seeking an ideal good. The memory of the Civil War and its attendant evils lingered long, and when it had almost faded, the violence of the French Revolution revived it. 'We must venerate where we cannot comprehend'—so Burke admonished, as he surveyed both the spots which defiled the robe as well as the adornments which enhanced it.

No one expressed this basic philosophy more succinctly than Archbishop Herring in a letter—their correspondence is preserved in the Newcastle papers in the British Museum—to his patron Lord Hardwicke, the Lord Chancellor.

> Nothing in the world is more contrary to my judgment of things than to make alterations in our establishment, of which in one sense the Toleration Act is a part; what I am determined to stick to, is the support of these two in conjunction. I think philosophy, Christianity and policy, are all against changes.

And naturally so, because Herring felt that his age, in comparison with preceding ones, was good, and he congratulated himself that he was

> called up to this high station, at a time, when spite, and rancour and narrowness of spirit are out of countenance; when we breathe the benign and comfortable air of liberty and toleration; and the teachers of our common religion make it their business to extend its essential influence, and join in supporting its true interest and honour. No times ever called more loudly upon protestants for zeal and security and charity.[168]

Sweet reasonableness was the order of the day, and many were the sermons preached on the text 'Be not righteous overmuch'.

As late as 1814, when Archbishop Manners Sutton, a most conscientious Primate, consecrated Dr. Middleton as the first Bishop of Calcutta, he concluded his paternal advice, 'Remember, my Lord Bishop, that your Primate on the day of your consecration defined your duty for you, that duty is to put down enthusiasm and to preach the Gospel.' Admittedly Methodism outside, and Evangelicalism inside, the Church, together with the romantic movement in the arts, represented a protest against this rationalism, this reduction of religion and life to minimal and guaranteed propositions. Sensitive but orthodox theologians, such as William Law the mystic, and Joseph Butler the philosopher friend of Archbishop Secker, early criticized the superficial optimism of their age: but such men were not representative of the ordinary parish pulpit.

Such a background of commonly accepted ideas did not engender a passion to reform such surviving medieval abuses as non-residence and pluralism, which had defied the despotic zeal of Laud, the denunciation of Burnet, and the practical concern of Tenison. Indeed at one stage in their careers most XVIIIth century archbishops were themselves pluralists, and their families stood at the receiving end of the patronage which this made possible. For the most part they died wealthy. Three of Archbishop Moore's sons were joint registrars of the Prerogative Court of Canterbury, and held with this preferment other legal posts, as well, in one case, as two livings.

Moore was not exceptional in such nepotism. Archbishop Potter, earlier in the century, in addition to providing for his family, left, according to the *Gentleman's Magazine*, a personal fortune of some £70,000, none of which came the way of his eldest son, John, Dean of Canterbury, whom he disinherited for marrying a domestic servant.

Archbishops were, of course, expected to be munificent in personal giving, particularly in an age when charity was preached up as the one practical solvent of social ills. As Thomas Tenison put it in a sermon to the Corporation for the Relief of Poor Widows and Children of Clergymen: 'The Public Supplies, as they are managed ... seem not to be sufficient for these things.'

The annual revenue of the archbishopric was reckoned at £7,000 in the time of George III, which compared favourably with, for example, York and London at £4,500, Winchester £5,000, and Bristol, the Cinderella, at £450. By 1831 Canterbury's revenue, largely through the efforts of Manners Sutton reinforced by inflation due to the Napoleonic wars, had risen to £19,182, and the other bishoprics by a comparable percentage. (Durham, due to its coalfields, had leapt to an equality with the primatial see.)

The maintenance of Lambeth Palace constituted a drain on

resources: and often a new arrival found it in a state of disrepair. This could lead to embarrassing disputes between the executors of the deceased Archbishop and his successor. Wake nearly found himself caught up in a lawsuit with Archbishop Tenison's nephew, which to him was particularly distressing as he had been intimate with the uncle and had lived in his family. Hutton was so aggrieved with Herring's executors that he refused to take up residence in Lambeth —he was Archbishop for only a year—but when in London occupied his own house in Duke Street, Westminster. The summer months he spent at the Manor of Croydon given by William the Conqueror to Lanfranc. For centuries this remained a principal residence, and thus acquired intimate associations with a good deal of English history. There for a time Catherine of Aragon hid her grief from the world; and there Queen Elizabeth really did pass a night. Archbishop Herring, a great gardener and lover of natural scenery, preferred Croydon to Lambeth, undertaking the repair of its old buildings and characteristically improving the general layout. On a beam in the Great Hall the brief inscription 'T 1748 H', as well as his initials on some fine lead pipes, still testify to his devotion.

> I love this old House—he wrote—and was very desirous of amusing myself, if I could find means to do it, with the history of its buildings; for the house is not one, but most certainly an aggregate of buildings of different tastes and ages.

Secker, for some reason or another—perhaps because of the delicate health of his daughters—never used Croydon; and Cornwallis seems to have forsaken it altogether because of its neglected condition and the fact that it was too far from London for his society-minded wife. The decision was finally made to get rid of it, and for this purpose a Private Act of Parliament in 1780 (20 George III c. 57) vested the palace in the hands of commissioners. The intention was to erect a new residence at Park Hill on the site of a farm purchased by Archbishop Cornwallis, but though the sale went forward in 1780, it was not until the time of Archbishop Manners Sutton that an estate of some 1,200 acres was bought at Addington, near Croydon.

Successive archbishops in their turn came to love Addington for its beauty and its quiet; and it continued as an archiepiscopal residence for over a hundred years. To Archbishop Tait (1869–82), in the midst of his many illnesses and domestic griefs, it became a place of refreshment and family relaxation. In company with four archbishops, his body rests in the graveyard of the parish church. For practical purposes, as we shall see later, it had few charms for Frederick Temple.

Throughout the XVIIIth and most of the XIXth century, successive archbishops had no residence in Canterbury, much to the chagrin of its inhabitants, though not necessarily to that of the Dean and Chapter. When Moore was appointed to Bangor in 1775 and resigned his Deanery of Canterbury, reference was made in a stanza to the Archbishops' absenteeism from their cathedral city:

> To me you prophesy, our mitred Moore
> Revolving years may probably restore,
> And thus in vain attempt my tears to dry;
> I scarcely know my masters but by name,
> Triennial voices and the choice of fame,
> For ah! my palaces in ruins lie!—Canterbury.[169]

However, an attempt was made to entertain in the city if only on a reduced scale. Both Archbishops Wake and Potter obtained preferment for relatives in the precincts, and Archbishop Secker requested that a similar indulgence might be granted to him, as a result of which his nephew, in 1761, was appointed to the eighth prebend.

## II

If entertaining in Canterbury was restricted, this was most certainly not the case at Lambeth, where the Archbishop was expected by a long-established tradition to maintain a lavish hospitality. Its enormous expense was one of the reasons which made Hutton hesitate before accepting the Crown's nomination. The custom of offering entertainment to all and sundry on public days continued right up to the time of Archbishop Howley in the XIXth century. Any gentleman who had been presented at Court and who wore the appropriate dress could call on Tuesday at the palace and dine there.

An interesting glimpse of such archiepiscopal hospitality is given, in the time of Thomas Tenison, by a German visitor to England, one Uffenbach, who writes that he was one of sixteen persons dining there, for the most part English divines.

> On several days in the week he kept open table, of which both the London clergy and those of the country avail themselves. . . . No health was drunk but the Archbishop's, except any that an individual might himself propose. When the meal was finished we made our bow to the Archbishop. After he had asked what was our native land, and who we were, and enquired after some men of learning in Germany, he dismissed us.[170]

Successive archbishops saw such entertainment as a necessary duty, surviving from an ancient past. Thus the author of the *Life of Bishop Beilby Porteus* (1810), writing from an intimate knowledge, testifies:

> The society of the archbishop is usually made up of the domestic chaplains and the resident and visiting clergy; and in no place in the world is the reception more hospitable and according to clerical decorum more magnificent than in the archiepiscopal palace. . . . To say all in a word, everything at Lambeth usually bears that hospitable magnificence which becomes the wealth and dignity of a British archbishop.

The extent and character of the hospitality varied with the temperament of the Archbishop—and his wife. Tenison and Wake tended to austerity. Cornwallis, who abolished the long-established custom of the chaplains sitting at a separate table, entertained lavishly, his wife adding greatly to the festivities. Throughout the whole of the XVIIIth century the time-honoured practice was maintained of distributing doles at the gate of the Palace to thirty people, each receiving beef, a pitcher of broth, a half quartern loaf, and twopence in money.

The Archbishop's household was necessarily large, comparable with that of a duke. He kept a coach and six horses; also a private state barge with a liveried crew, Wake being the last Archbishop to use it regularly for his attendance upon Parliament. Potter was accused of keeping a 'pontifical estate' and encouraging flattery 'of the grossest kind'. Also, like a duke, the Archbishop was allowed six chaplains, of whom, during the XVIIIth century, many later became bishops, and in two cases—Wake and Potter—Archbishops. The domestic staff was inevitably large, and individuals would often be remembered by archbishops in their wills.

Eighteenth-century archbishops, if their estate was ducal, were by no means ducal in origin. They varied considerably in their social background, though politically most of them were zealous Whigs. It is certainly a mistake to suppose that all bishops of this period were members of great families, though they may have needed their influence to rise.

William Wake sprang from an ancient lineage—there was a tradition that his ancestor was Hereward the Wake—but he made his own way in the world through his industry and ability, which attracted the notice of Archbishop Tenison. From this vantage ground, his preferment followed. Potter was the son of a linen draper, Secker of a solid middle-class dissenter. Cornwallis was the first

Archbishop sprung from the nobility since Cardinal Pole; and as seventh son of Charles, fourth Lord Cornwallis, he could boast of being brother to an earl and uncle to a marquis. John Moore was the son of a grazier, earlier thought to be a butcher, and owed his rise to a chance introduction to the Duke of Marlborough, to whose younger sons he became tutor. Charles Manners Sutton was the grandson of John, third Duke of Rutland. Thus only two of these Archbishops were born into families which could expect promotion almost as of right at a time when Britain was ruled by a small aristocratic oligarchy, the members of which knew each other, and in whose hands resided patronage in Church and State.

The structure of XVIIIth-century society, with its concept of hierarchy and emphasis on being reasonable, affected attitudes to patronage and preferment. For many years Thomas Pelham Holles, first Duke of Newcastle (1693–1768), constituted in his own person a centralized appointments board, ministering royal patronage. He was not, of course, a free agent, but worked within a system which must reward allies and win over potential enemies to the government in power. It was all part of an elaborate system of bribery from which, however, he never enriched himself. The result was that some ecclesiastics toadied to him; others had sufficiently powerful connexions to give as good as they got. Amongst the latter was Cornwallis, who, when disappointed of a bishopric and given as compensation the Deanery of St. Paul's, wrote to Newcastle in December 1766:

> You say you are much rejoiced at my having accepted the Deanery of St. Paul's. For what reason I know not. As to myself I have no joy in it, I am not fond of expedients. Had the recommendation to it come from your Grace by way of atonement I should have rejected the Deanery. After the hard treatment I had met with I could not with honour have accepted it. It is by no means a preferment either agreeable or suitable to me. It would have been kind of your Grace not to have kept me so long in suspense with regard to the Bishopric of Salisbury.[171]

This was the kind of letter which only a member of the oligarchy would venture to write. Yet even those lower down the social scale could, in reliance upon powerful support, balance wishes against expectancies. Plebeian Moore, already Dean of Canterbury and a prebend of Durham, thus weighed up the pros and cons as he saw them:

> How much already in possession must be given up; there are bishoprics and bishoprics—'small', 'middling' and 'pretty good' —what is to be the net gain on a change?[172]

To Eden he confided in 1772:

> It ought to be, I suppose, my Deanery and a small Bishopric, or
> Durham and a middling one, or, if both Preferments are to be
> given up, a pretty good one. . . . Lord North must understand I
> will not be a Bishop unless he contrives I may live with some
> degree of comfort, I mean without such an income as may enable
> me to support my station.[173]

John Potter expressed his own attitude with complete frankness when
reflecting upon an offer of the Deanery of Christ Church:

> There are three considerations which might move me in it.
> These are the profit, the convenience in other respects, and the
> good which may be done it.[174]

Perhaps the order of priorities is unconsciously revealing.

Frankness of this kind was not misunderstood, although Wake
and Secker would probably not have expressed themselves quite so
crudely. Such an attitude certainly does not mean that once in office
duty was neglected. This cannot be asserted of XVIIIth-century
archbishops as a whole, even if by and large they were not men of
outstanding talents or sacrificial zeal. The visitational returns of the
diocese of Canterbury which survive unpublished in Lambeth
Library bear witness to diligence and concern. It does mean, however
that ambition in the Church was not synonymous with a desire for
office as such.

As to the men who came to Lambeth between Wake and Manners
Sutton, only three could claim real distinction in the realms of
scholarship. Wake left behind him a solid corpus of works bearing on
the history and constitution of the Church of England, chief amongst
which were his *The State of the Church of England in those Councils,
Synods, Convocations, Conventions and other Public Assemblies historically
deduced from the conversion of the Saxons to the Present Time; An English
version of the Genuine Epistles of the Apostolic Fathers, St. Barnabas, St.
Ignatius, St. Clement, St. Polycarp, The Shepherd of Hermas, with a
Preliminary Discourse concerning the use of the Father;* and *The Principles
of the Christian Religion.* As a young man he had the temerity, not
without success, to cross swords with the redoubtable French theologian, Bossuet. He also corresponded with Bentley, and gave him
encouragement with his Greek edition of the New Testament. Potter,
his successor, was a technical classical scholar of considerable attain-
ments, whose talents in this field developed remarkably early. At the
age of twenty he had published an edition of Plutarch's *De Audiendis*

*Poetis* and Basil the Great's *Legendis Graecorum*. In 1743 he produced a sumptuous edition of the works of the Greek writer Lycophron; and in the same year appeared his *Archaeologia Graeca*. On the strength of these he gained a European reputation.

The only other Archbishop who could lay claims to serious scholarship—though he himself produced no works of erudition—was Thomas Secker, who as a young man qualified in medicine at Leyden. He developed into an excellent Hebraist, and was of sufficient theological calibre for Butler to seek his advice when writing his classic *The Analogy of Religion*. The *Charges* of Secker, whose sermons the *Gentleman's Magazine* described as 'plain, pathetic [and] practical', constitute a unique source book on the condition of the Church of his day. Manners Sutton, though no scholar himself, showed a practical interest in biblical research. In particular he gave his support to two English scholars who ventured to Mount Athos, returning with a number of early biblical manuscripts, some of which, however, to his own embarrassment, the Archbishop was obliged to return to the Patriarch of Constantinople through the Foreign Office. The curious may care to know that Manners Sutton published a small botanical work on an obscure plant.

Eighteenth-century archbishops, in the main, were therefore neither accomplished scholars nor technically equipped theologians. An odd sermon or two preached on some charitable occasion or a charge to their clergy usually constituted the extent of their literary remains. In this they were not unrepresentative of the bishops as a whole.

# 2

## PREFERMENT AND APPOINTMENT

I

Dr. Johnson, discoursing on the character of the episcopate, on which he had views, observed: 'No man can be made a bishop for his piety or learning; his only chance for promotion is his being connected with somebody who has parliamentary interest.' There was, indeed, a very close connexion between 'parliamentary interest' and Church preferment, this being the particular form that the nexus between Church and State assumed at this time, in distinction from the earlier link with the person of the monarch. No longer did bishops hold great secular offices, or take an immediate lead in directing the affairs of the nation. They were not, however, thereby withdrawn from secular involvement, but rather engaged in a different way. Government was directed by a small group whose over-riding concern was to maintain the Revolution settlement, the linch pin of which was the Hanoverian Succession. This requirement conditioned the selection of archbishops, indeed of the episcopate generally, and controlled their relations with Parliament.

Old Thomas Tenison, staunchly Whig, managed to outlive the Tory Anne in spite of the fact that he was her senior by some thirty years. The result was that William Wake, his own nominee, succeeded him after Hough of Coventry and Lichfield, with genuine modesty, had declined. Wake was less liberal theologically than his predecessor but equally anti-Tory and a strong supporter of the House of Hanover.

John Potter's nomination to Canterbury in February 1737 has a certain cynical interest, if we may trust Lord Hervey, a nobleman whom Pope bitterly satirized as *Sporus* in his *Epistle to Dr. Arbuthnot*:

> Amphibious thing! that acting either part,
> The trifling head, or the corrupted heart;
> Fop at the toilet, flatterer at the board,
> Now trips a lady, and now struts a lord.

Two candidates seemed to have equal claims: Edmund Gibson,

Bishop of London, who had been Wake's right-hand man during his last years, and Thomas Sherlock, Bishop of Salisbury, a rigid churchman of considerable talent. Both, however, had offended Sir Robert Walpole, now first minister, by opposing his Bill to give relief to Quakers. To Queen Caroline, Walpole complained bitterly that if Sherlock were appointed it would mean calling a new Parliament, since feeling against him in the House of Commons, as likely 'to carry Church power very high', ran strong: and the prospect with Gibson was not much better. Left to himself he would have preferred Hare, his old tutor, but such an appointment, he realized, would not be generally acceptable in these circumstances. Hervey stepped in with another suggestion:

> Sure, Sir, you have had enough of great geniuses: why can you not take some Greek and Hebrew blockhead, that has learning enough to justify the preferment, and not sense enough to make you repent of it. . . . Potter is a man—he went on—of undoubted great learning, of as little doubted probity. He has been always, though reckoned a Tory in the Church uninterruptedly attached to this family, without the lure or reward of any preferment but this poor Bishopric of Oxford, where he has stuck for twenty years. The Queen loves him; his character will support you in sending him to Lambeth; and his capacity is not so good, nor his temper so bad, as to make you apprehend any great danger in his being there.[175]

On this negative recommendation Potter became Archbishop, and two men of greater merit were passed over.

Hervey may not be speaking the whole truth, but the story illustrates the concern of the Government to prevent any re-emergence of ecclesiastical independence. The Hanoverian succession was safer when churchmen were reasonably quiet.

What Gibson and Sherlock wished but did not obtain in 1737, came their way on Potter's death some ten years later. But Gibson was now an infirm seventy-eight, and Sherlock—although ten years younger—painfully afflicted with gout. Both unhesitatingly declined the offer, this refusal giving to Sherlock the unique distinction of saying 'no' to both the archbishoprics of York and Canterbury. That two of the most distinguished churchmen should have refused his invitation undoubtedly disturbed the Duke of Newcastle who, with the 1745 rising still a vivid memory, feared 'what malicious interpretation would be put both at Home and Abroad of the King's enemies if his Majesty should find a difficulty in filling up the Archbishopric of Canterbury according to his own inclinations and those of his friends'.[176] The correspondence that followed is set out at length in the author's *Thomas Sherlock 1678–1761*. The very character of the Bishop's handwriting betrays his strong emotion.

Sherlock replied to the invitation with two letters, one formal, the other personal. In the former he wrote candidly: 'At this time of life and in an infirm state of health, what use can I be of to his Majesty, to my country or to my Church? The very attendance of an Archbishop in Parliament, at the Council Board, and on many other occasions is more than I can promise myself to discharge as I ought.' In his private letter, full of a robust common-sense, he added:

> In truth my Lord, I am so infirm that I cannot think myself at all qualified for this laborious station. I will deal openly with your Grace and tell you the distress I have been in; on one side, it was clear to me that I ought not to accept: on the other it went much against me and seemed hardly decent in respect of the King to refuse a second offer of an Archbishopric. But necessity will prevail: and I thought it of more real service to the King to decline this offer, than to fill the greatest office in the Church with an unprofitable servant. . . . I remember the case of Tenison and Wake. They came younger than I am by 10 years or more to Lambeth: they lived long but their latter years were years of forgetfulness and the Archbishopric was in prey to somebody or other who got the management. I am unwilling to begin where they ended, and I have warning from my state of health last winter.

In spite of this forthright letter, Newcastle came back at him again on 15 October, adding the King's strong wishes to his own, and reassuring him that 'younger Bishops' would take a great deal of the labour off his shoulders. Newcastle's brother also sent a persuasive letter. But Sherlock remained adamant, writing finally to Newcastle on 18 October, and to the King three days later.

Such refusals obviously embarrassed the Government, and it was in this situation that Hardwicke, the Lord Chancellor, came forward with his own candidate, Thomas Herring, who as Archbishop of the Northern Province had rallied Yorkshire to the Hanoverian cause during the 1745 rising. The new candidate was considerably younger, but he again had no desire to leave his present diocese where he was comfortably settled.

> [I] am come to a very firm and most resolved determination—he told Hardwicke—not to quit the see of York on any account or on any consideration; and I beg it of your lordship as the most

material piece of friendship yet to be exerted by you to prevent the offer of Canterbury if possible, or to support me in the refusal if the other cannot be prevented. . . . I am really poor. I am not ambitious of being rich, but have too much pride with, I hope, a small mixture of honesty to bear being in debt; I am now out of it and in possession of a clear independency of that sort. I must not go back and begin the world again at fifty five. The honour of Canterbury is a thing of glare and splendour, and the hopes of it a proper incentive to schoolboys to industry; but I have considered all its inward parts and examined all its duties; and if I should quit my present station to take it, will not answer for it that in less than a twelve month I did not sink and die with regret and envy at the man who should succeed me here, and quit the place in my possession as I ought to do to one wiser and better than myself.[177]

Herring was not to be let off the hook so easily, for a third refusal could well have serious political repercussions. Hardwicke came back at him immediately. Both the Pelhams, he wrote, had protested that it was

impossible that a bishop in the vigour of his age, not quite fifty-five, of such a character, so much obliged to the King and so well esteemed and beloved in the world., should decline it . . . that it would have the worst appearance and create the worst impression . . . make people doubt of the stability of His Majesty's Government, give a new triumph to the Jacobites, as if nobody of merit would venture to accept the highest and most important dignity in the Church.

To this the Lord Chancellor added a postscript urging him to accept: 'For God's sake, for the sake of the King, the country and your friends, don't decline.'[178]

Finally Herring gave way, after, so he told Hardwicke, 'stepping to the fire to burn three letters of refusal'. To William Whiston, in reply to a letter of congratulation, he was able to say with truth that he had been 'forced' into Canterbury, and that neither 'pride, nor ambition, nor covetousness' had 'tempted' him 'to desire it'.[179]

*Nolo archiepiscopari*, and there were quite a number of them during the XVIIIth century, suggests an attitude to office which set great store on ease and convenience rather than on success and achievement. Such refusals, if significant, were not of course the rule. Hutton, the friend of Newcastle and 'devoted to the Ministry', moved without difficulty or opposition to Canterbury. The same was true of Thomas Secker, his successor, universally admitted to be an admirable man. On the very day of Hutton's death Newcastle reported to Secker that he had written to George II intimating that it was 'absolutely necessary in the present situation of the King and the Kingdom, His Majesty should make choice for the See of Canterbury of one of the greatest eminence in his profession, of dignity, weight and authority, which person I humbly thought should be the Bishop of Oxford, and I suggested nobody else.'[180]

Secker, without false modesty, replied immediately:

> I received your Grace's letter in the midst of company just going to dinner with me, and have but a moment's time to say that I am quite terrified at the unexpected contents of it, that I shall have great cause to be pleased if His Majesty thinks of some worthier person, that if he should pitch on me I must endeavour thro' God's help to appear as little unworthy as I can.[181]

It is a little ironic to recall that in his farewell, some eight years previously, to the parishioners of St. James's, Piccadilly, published in his *Fourteen Sermons Preached on Several Occasions*, he told them that they had had the best working years, 'the flower and vigour' of his life, and that it was better for him 'not to linger on when he must expect to find [him]self growing less fit every day for the duties of so laborious a life'.

Secker's was the last nomination to Canterbury during the reign of George II, a monarch who, on the whole, the more so after Caroline's death, was content to rely exclusively on the advice of his ministers. George III, however, determined to adopt a more positive role towards ecclesiastical appointments, which meant that he resented the near stranglehold of ministerial control exercised by the 'Venetian oligarchy' over a number of years. It was the King's view that he had a particular reason for asserting his own authority *vis-à-vis* the nomination of the Archbishop of Canterbury with whom he must enter into a unique relationship.

At the time of Secker's death, the Duke of Newcastle was Prime Minister for the second time. Grafton, his first minister, was anxious to secure the primacy for Cornwallis; but the King's preference was for his old preceptor, Dr. John Thomas, Bishop of Winchester. Thomas, however, preferred to stay where he was; and the name of Richard Terrick, Bishop of London, was then put forward, Grafton believing that Cornwallis, Bishop of Lichfield and Coventry, would be as pleased to go to London as to Canterbury. The King now intervened to frustrate this general post by introducing a nominee of his own, much to the annoyance of Lord Gower, since he had his own candidate to succeed Cornwallis at Lichfield and in the Deanery of St. Paul's. The matter was finally straightened out when the King gave his warm assent to Cornwallis.

From Newcastle's point of view things in the end turned out well, for he was anxious to restore amicable relations with the Cornwallis family after the upset over the bishopric of Salisbury. 'No-one,' he wrote to the new Primate, 'rejoices more in your promotion to Lambeth. . . . acquaint the Duke of Grafton how much I approve the measure. I don't mean to take any merit to myself for I have none.' To this 'olive branch' Cornwallis made an eirenical reply:

> I must own I feel myself very unequal to so high a station, and wish I could have declined it with propriety, but found I could not as things were circumstanced. All that can be done now is to exert my utmost endeavours to answer in some degree the favourable expectations my friends have entertained of me.[182]

Contemporaries did not expect very much from this appointment, and they were not disappointed.

George III had played a significant, if not initiating, role in Cornwallis's elevation, and he was determined not to retreat from this position, but rather to assert it more strongly. The next vacancy at Canterbury occurred in 1783. The King, in spite of being pressed by Lord Shelburne for his friend Shipley, Bishop of St. Asaph, immediately let it be known that he wished for the learned Richard Hurd, Bishop of Worcester, whom he described as 'the most naturally polite man he ever knew'. Hurd declined it, so he explains in his unpublished *Dates of some Occurrences in my Own Life*, 'as a charge not suited to his temper and talents, and much too heavy for him to sustain especially in these times'. Disappointed, the King next turned to Lowth, Bishop of London, but found him so much attached to his diocese that he also was unwilling to leave it. Both of these bishops, in declining, suggested John Moore, of Bangor, and George III accepted their advice. A contemporary lyricist sang:

> An impartial and competent judge of desert,
> At such a conclusion must have needs been expert,
> And to baffle distraction I'll venture thus far
> If Moore rose like a meteor he'll shine a true star.[183]

If he did shine it was only as a lesser luminary.

George III's influence upon ecclesiastical preferment, as in other areas of government, was increasing, but so far he had acted in consultation with his ministers. The next vacancy, however, worked out differently, and Pitt, who was then Prime Minister, took such a serious view of what happened that he entered a formal protest. It was the last time the unfettered will of the sovereign realized itself without let or hindrance. The circumstances were as follows.

Archbishop Moore, after a long illness, died on 18 January 1805. Pitt was Prime Minister for the second and, as it proved, the last time; and was anxious that his old tutor, Bishop Pretyman, a mathematician of distinction whom he frequently consulted about ecclesiastical affairs, should go to Lambeth. He made his wishes known to the King, and followed this up with a letter:

> Mr Pitt took the liberty of stating to your Majesty, when he had last the honour of attending your Majesty at Windsor, his anxious wish with a view to the expected vacancy of the arch-bishopric, to be allowed to recommend the Bishop of Lincoln as the fittest person to succeed to that most important station. As there continues to be great reason to suppose that the vacancy will speedily take place, he requests your Majesty's indulgence shortly to state the grounds on which that wish is founded.[184]

A version of what followed after this is set out in a letter in the Croker MSS cited by Jesse in his *Memoirs of George III*. It transpires that the King also had an intimate friend in Manners Sutton, Bishop of Norwich and Dean of Windsor, for whom he had ambitions. As soon, therefore, as he was informed of the vacancy, and knowing that Pitt intended to see him the next morning, he prepared for action. Taking horse, he rode over to Bishop Manners Sutton, who was then residing in the Deanery at Windsor, sending in a servant with a message that a gentleman wished to see him. Manners Sutton at first demurred, but going out found the King standing in a little dressing-room near the hall door. George clasped his friend's hands and greeted him: 'My Lord Archbishop of Canterbury, I wish you joy. Not a word; go back to your guests.'

When Pitt arrived the next morning the King blandly said that he would welcome the opportunity of providing for a friend and relative.

'A friend indeed,' replied Pitt, 'but your Majesty is mistaken as to there being any relationship.'

The King, unperturbed, added that it would be an excellent thing for his twelve children.

'Bishop Pretyman I am certainly most anxious to promote,' ejaculated Pitt, 'but he is not my relative, nor has he such a family.'

'Pho! Pho!' exclaimed the King, 'it is not Pretyman whom I mean but Sutton.'

'I should hope,' was Pitt's retort, 'that the talents and literary eminence . . .'

'It can't be—it can't be,' interrupted the King: 'I have already wished Sutton joy, and he must go to Canterbury.'

There then followed an angry exchange such as (so Lord Sidmouth later told Dean Milman) had rarely passed between a sovereign and his minister.

The King's independent action was a deliberate slight, and Pitt felt that he could not let it pass without a solemn protest. His letter to the King, written on 22 January, the draft of which bears many alterations and corrections, is certainly outspoken.

He confessed frankly 'how deeply his feelings [were] wounded' and how 'his hopes of contributing to your Majesty's service impaired' by this 'apparent disregard of his recommendation'. He reminded the King that such recommendations appeared 'uniformly to have been graciously accepted for a long course of time in every instance' and he concluded:

> The King's refusal to comply with his request can hardly be understood by himself, and will certainly not be understood by the public in any other light than as a decisive mark of your Majesty's not honouring him with that degree of confidence which his predecessors have enjoyed ... Mr. Pitt still flatters himself that when your Majesty is fully aware of these considerations it cannot be your Majesty's intention to reduce him to so mortifying a condition.[185]

George III replied the next day dispelling any hope that there would be a change in the Royal mind.

> The King—he wrote—will certainly this day at the Queen's House hear whatever Mr. Pitt chooses to say on the subject; but His Majesty by no means can view the Archbishopric in the light of a common Bishopric. It is the person on the bench on whom he must depend, and of whose dignity of behaviour, good temper as well as talents and learning he feels best satisfied; the Archbishop as well as the King are for life.[186]

It is significant that George's assertion of power has not been followed by any subsequent Sovereign. No prime minister has since been by-passed in similar circumstances, though Queen Victoria once offered the Deanery of Windsor to Canon Connor of Winchester without reference to Gladstone.

In the above *contretemps* both the King and his Prime Minister sought, for their own comfort and support, to prefer a friend. In fact Manners Sutton, whose archiepiscopate coincided with the beginning of a revival in the life of the Church, proved a conscientious if not outstanding Primate. With his numerous family to support, so *The Times* suggested, his leaving Norwich rescued him from financial embarrassment.

# 3

## 'OUR HAPPY ESTABLISHMENT IN CHURCH AND STATE'

George III's display of royal authority served only to emphasize that, in the main, appointments were in the hands of the Government, and that the Government needed to maintain its authority in the House of Lords. In an upper Chamber, the membership of which was considerably smaller than it is today, the votes of the bishops were important, and ministers were not likely to take too kindly to non-attendance, even when the excuse was that residence in London hampered the proper discharge of diocesan duties. The general practice was for bishops to attend Court and Parliament most of the year and to return to their dioceses during the summer recess. The Archbishop was expected to be active in seeing that, when needed, his brethren were in their place to support the Government, often when they would have preferred to stay in the country. Thus though not always in his later years a regular attendant himself, Wake did his best to keep (for example) Potter, when at Oxford, vigilant in the discharge of his parliamentary duties. For this purpose the Bishop rented a house in London, and promised attendance if he 'could in the least contribute to the service of the Church or of His Majesty's Government and the Protestant Succession'.[187] Instances of archiepiscopal care could be multiplied. In March 1751 Herring wrote to Newcastle, confirming that he had 'desired the bishops to meet here on Friday to consider the Hop, the Quaker, and the Naturalisation Bill so far as concerns the Naturalisation of the Jews'. In respect of the latter, though he was 'constitutionally prone to indulgences', he thought it wise 'to know more of them before we let them into privileges'. If Jews were naturalized why not Mahometans with all the apparatus of Mosques and Mollahs?[188]

At times the Duke could put the pressure on, as the following typical letter to Archbishop Hutton illustrates:

> I lay before your Grace Lord Hardwicke's sentiments and my own upon the conduct we should hold upon the Bill now depending for payment of sailors' wages. . . . If your Grace does us the honour to agree with us in our opinion, I should submit to your

Grace whether it might not be proper for you to give notice to the bishops, such, I mean, as your Grace usually sends to, to attend the House on Thursday next when the Navy Bill comes on. Let your Friends upon the Bench know your thoughts upon the two Bills—Navy Bill and Habeas Corpus.[189]

The Duke was still vigilant in 1762, admonishing Secker 'that the attendance in parliament the beginning of this session would be particularly proper in the present circumstances of the Kingdom and the doubtful state of peace and war'.[190] What Norman Sykes called 'the public station' of the Archbishop of Canterbury meant that he was 'inevitably involved . . . in matters of state, even of purely political import'.[191] Thus Secker, in the summer of 1765, had a hand in the formation of the cabinet of Lord Rockingham.

Archbishops, however, could find themselves in an embarrassing position when they outlived the ministers who appointed them. Thus government changes on the accession of George III led to Secker's being ostentatiously ignored in matters of high ecclesiastical preferment, so much so that he confessed to going seldom to Court where he was not wanted.

The need to keep the bishops up to the mark meant that the Archbishop must contact them individually, as well as call them together in London, to discuss parliamentary business. Such meetings were more important now that Convocation had ceased to assemble —even Secker did not advise its summoning to do business—a deprivation incidentally which meant that bishops got little training for the cut-and-thrust of parliamentary debate. It was the bishops' votes, however, which ministries most wanted, even if on occasions their vocal support could be useful.

Eighteenth-century archbishops varied in the frequency with which they intervened in debates. Wake spoke from time to time when he thought the Church or public morality was involved; but he admitted frankly in his later years that 'in Parliament time I am rather faulty in not going so often as I should to it than in attending constantly upon it'.[192] Potter was not a House of Lords man, and Hutton during his short year of office seems not to have spoken on a single occasion. The reverse is true of Thomas Secker, who developed a particular interest in parliamentary proceedings. As Bishop of Bristol he attended regularly, taught himself shorthand, and kept a record of speeches, these being subsequently drawn upon for the *Parliamentary History* of the period. When he became Archbishop he spoke frequently and well. Cornwallis seldom took part in debates, and Manners Sutton more or less confined himself to matters in which he felt the Church was directly involved.

Just as most archbishops recognized that the episcopate had a duty to support the Government which promoted them, so they in their turn expected the ministry to come to their aid in matters where the Church was itself an interested party—that is where its rights under the establishment were threatened, or the morality of the nation was involved. In this expectation archbishops were at times disappointed. Thus Wake felt that the Government on more than one occasion failed to give him proper support; a disappointment which may have contributed to his voting against the repeal of the Schism Act, although his own *rationale* was that the Church of England had become so comprehensive that dissenters ought to find no difficulty in joining it.

Yet archbishops throughout the XVIIIth century, while approving annual Acts of Indemnity to soften the exclusiveness of establishment, were anxious not to upset its delicately poised balance. In this they had the negative support of successive Governments.

Over a period of years various bills in the interests of dissenters came before Parliament. That of 1773, for example, which would have allowed assent to the Scriptures rather than to the Thirty-nine Articles was thrown out in the Lords, Archbishop Cornwallis remaining silent and the bishops voting against it. When the Bill came up again, the episcopate, by abstaining, allowed it to pass.

In 1787 the dissenters circulated members of the House of Commons with a paper: *The Case of the Protestant Dissenters with Reference to the Test and Corporation Acts*. Pitt was disposed to help them, particularly in view of the valuable support which they had given him at the last election: but he could only do so with the support of the bishops. Moore called his colleagues together, and found that out of the fourteen present only two, Watson of Llandaff, and Shipley of St. Asaph, friend of Burke and Reynolds, were for the proposed Bill. Despite this it was brought into the Commons on 17 March 1787, and Mr. Beaufoy, its mover, with impassioned rhetoric denounced the degradation of the Sacrament by making its reception a condition of civil office. Such, he said, was 'a monstrous attempt, as irrational as it was profane, to strengthen the Church of England by the debasement of the Church of Christ'. Pitt made the speech of a typical politician, having an eye on the bishops' vote in the House of Lords. To pass the measure, he warned, would alarm the Church of England, since there was no way of admitting the moderate dissenters while at the same time excluding the more extreme. The Bill was lost. Moore's comment is revealing:

You will observe—he wrote to William Eden, first Baron Auckland—that the Dissenters are firing away in the papers at

Mr. Pitt. That contest was an ugly thing to happen, and furnished no small uneasiness to me during the suspense of it. Had it ended favourably for them the effects would soon have been serious indeed.[193]

Moore's attitude here was not one of high principle, but arose out of a deep fear of change. When, in 1812, Archbishop Manners Sutton was consulted by Lord Liverpool concerning a further Bill to relieve dissenters from the provisions of the Conventicle and Five Mile Acts (and to a lesser extent from the Act of Toleration), he expressed a wish, unsuccessfully, that its scope could be narrowed. However, he realistically rallied the bishops to its support.

Where Roman Catholics were concerned national sentiment ran higher, and the general feeling lingered that this Church was un-English, and incompatible with the free institutions of Britain. The rising of 1745 whipped up this feeling, and few, till the XIXth century, would basically have disputed the exaggerated opinions of Archbishop Herring, though they might not have used the same language:

No Nation (speaking in the gross) can possibly be happy and flourishing under Popery; because the Influence of it is of so baneful a Nature, that it does not only sink the Spirits of Men, damp the Vigour and Life of Industry, stop every Avenue of Religious Knowledge from the Scriptures, make Princes Tyrants, and their People Slaves; but in a Manner counter-mines the Wisdom and Goodness of Providence, and converts (as it has done in Fact) the more beautiful and fertile Countries into Desolate Wildernesses.[194]

Such remarks go a long way to explain Herring's somewhat extra-ordinary comments on the suggestion that Anselm's bones should be removed from Canterbury to his birthplace at Aosta:

He had no great scruples on this head—he wrote—but if he had, he would get rid of them all, if the parting of the rotten remains of a rebel to his king, a slave to the popedom, and an enemy to the married clergy (all this Anselm was) would purchase ease and indulgence to one living Protestant.[195]

The Archbishop of Canterbury was to experience the extent of this anti-papal feeling during the popular clamour of 1780. A Bill which was designed to bring a small measure of relief to Roman Catholics and to which Cornwallis finally withdrew his opposition, passed through Parliament. It was greeted by 'No Popery' riots in the streets of London, and although the Archbishop was not himself assaulted, his palace at Lambeth came near to destruction. A party of over five hundred marched on it with drums and fifes. The gates were shut, but the mob threatened to return in the evening. The authorities now took precautions and a party of guards was stationed at the Palace while the rioters for nearly a day and a half besieged it. The Archbishop and his family were persuaded to leave, and prudently delayed their return until the disturbances were safely over. Soldiers, sometimes up to the number of three hundred, were stationed in the Palace, the officers being entertained in the best apartments by two of the Archbishop's chaplains. Not the least complaint we are assured, could be made of 'irregular behaviour in any individual'.

It is to the credit of Archbishop Moore that he supported a further Bill in May 1791 to bring an additional measure of relief to Roman Catholics, even if he was careful to point out that he was not prepared to 'destroy wholesome regulations respecting the Protestant Religion'. It is less to the credit of such a liberally minded man as Archbishop Manners Sutton that in 1819 he should have opposed Lord Grey's sensible proposal, seconded by Henry Bathurst, Bishop of Norwich, to relieve candidates for office and Parliament from the necessity to make a declaration that Transubstantiation and the Invocation of the Saints were idolatrous.

> In this dangerous age of experiments—he argued—when so many innovations had been made—when in a neighbouring country, morality, social order, and good government, had been overthrown, and even Christianity, annihilated should this nation, in the pursuit of a political experiment, throw away the blessings of a constitution which had saved us from so many perils?[196]

The speech, in its reference to revolutionary France, is significant of an attitude widely prevalent among the rank and file of the clergy. Not surprisingly, therefore, the Archbishop had opposed a petition in 1805 to bring some amelioration of their lot to the Roman Catholic population in Ireland.

> The substance of the petition—he said—was compressed, for their Lordships' use and convenience, into one short, but pregnant sentence: 'An equal participation on equal terms of the full benefits of the British laws and constitution.' . . . It was no less than a request on the part of the Roman Catholics to legislate for a protestant country. . . . If their Lordships should determine to destroy those fences which the wisdom and experience of their

263

ancestors had, with so much deliberation and care, erected
around the established church, they would do unintentionally,
without doubt . . . all that was in their power to excite and
provoke that bad spirit of animosity and religious intolerance
that marred and disgraced the worst pages of their history.[197]

In taking such a stand he had the episcopal bench behind him.

Attacks on the equilibrium of the establishment did not come only
from those outside who were intent to remove civil disabilities. There
were Anglicans who sought to change its character from within. In
1766 Archdeacon Blackburne published his famous *Confessional*,
which advocated, in the interests of latitudinarian churchmen, a
drastic revision of the Book of Common Prayer. Five years later he
followed this up with concrete proposals for a relaxation of clerical
subscription. At the Feathers Tavern, in the Strand, a petition was
drawn up for presentation to Parliament which demanded liberty for
clergymen to interpret Scripture for themselves 'without being
bound by any human explanation'. Some 250 people, mainly consisting of broad church clergymen, with a sprinkling of lawyers and
doctors, signed the document. On coming before the House of Commons it was negatived by 217 votes to 71. Archbishop Cornwallis
was not directly involved, having courteously declined to further the
cause of the petitioners; but he later intimated that he was prepared
to receive a petition for the revision of the liturgy, and such a petition
was in fact presented to him at Lambeth, signed by so orthodox and
evangelical a clergyman as Porteus, a future Bishop of London.
Whatever his own views, Cornwallis was forced to recognize that the
majority of his brother bishops was not behind any attempt at
revision. The Government also, anxious above everything else to
keep the peace and not to revive old animosities, did not favour a
change. In these circumstances Cornwallis wisely dropped the
matter:

> I have consulted severally my brethren bishops, and it is the
> opinion of the bench in general that nothing can in prudence be
> done in the matter that has been submitted to our con-
> sideration.[198]

It is significant that the Government did not wish to embarrass the
bishops. Their votes were too valuable.

The attitude of the Archbishops towards these various attempts to
make inroads on the established position of the Church of England
was ambiguous. They were not illiberal men, but felt keenly their
own particular responsibilities. To them the establishment was itself

the safeguard of the maximum amount of liberty practically attainable. Hence their reluctance to disturb it.

The rise of Methodism, which was a protest against contemporary Anglican lethargy, was neither hotly opposed by Lambeth, nor approved. Potter's interview with the Wesley brothers certainly suggests an Archbishop of liberal feeling.

> He showed us great affection—Charles wrote afterwards—and cautioned us to give no more umbrage than was necessary for our own defence, to forbear exceptionable phrases and to keep to the doctrines of the Church.[199]

To these cautionary words the brothers replied that persecution must be expected in the Church until her articles and homilies were repealed; an observation which prompted the Archbishop to protest that he knew of no design on the part of the governors of the Church to innovate, and there certainly would be none so long as he lived. In spite of this rebuff John Wesley admitted that that 'great and good man', as he described Potter, gave him advice for which he never ceased to be grateful.

> If you desire to be extensively useful—the Archbishop said—do not spend your time and strength in contending for or against such things as are of a disputable nature, but in testifying against open notorious vice, and in promoting real essential holiness.[200]

These words well express basic XVIIIth-century philosophy, which may account for their giving such great offence to Samuel Taylor Coleridge.

The Methodist 'movement' grew steadily, and Herring, in spite of his liberality, was not so accommodating as Potter. Undoubtedly he found its excesses offensive to his essentially rational approach. On the eve of the appointment of lay preachers, which was the beginning of a real breach with the Church of England, he wrote of John Wesley:

> . . . in my opinion, with good parts and learning [he] is a most dark and saturnine creature. His pictures may frighten weak people, that, at the same time, are wicked, but, I fear he will make few converts, except for a day. I have read his 'Serious Thoughts' (on the earthquakes at Lisbon); but, for my part, I think the rising and setting of the sun is a more durable argument for religion, than all the extraordinary convulsions of nature put together. . . . For myself, I own I have no constitution for these frights and fervours; and if I can but keep up the regular practice of a Christian life, upon Christian reasons, I shall be in no pain for futurity.[201]

265

# 4

The XVIIIth century was in many ways an age of licence, though it could not in this respect vie with the years immediately following the Restoration. Walpole's sexual behaviour was irregular to a degree, and he was not alone in this indulgence. Gambling and gin-drinking permeated all levels of society, even if many a stout Sir Roger de Coverley or a Mr. Hardcastle maintained in the countryside higher standards of personal integrity. The financial speculation centring around the South Sea Bubble undoubtedly lowered national morale. The novelist Smollett, author of *Adventures of an Atom*, a ruthless satire on public affairs during the middle years of the century, writes in somewhat exaggerated terms of the 'scandalous excess' of the 'adventurers, intoxicated by their imaginary wealth', who 'affected to scoff at religion and morality, and even to set Heaven at defiance'. Bishops, no matter how broad or latitudinarian their churchmanship —a rational theology was not thought of as implying a new morality —saw themselves as watchdogs or vigilantes of public behaviour. William Wake felt keenly the scandal of contemporary vice, and believed it was decline in Christian belief and increasing unorthodoxy, which led to it. Thus when it was rumoured that Samuel Clarke, suspected of Arianism, was to be made a bishop, the Archbishop let it be known that 'he would not consecrate whatever the consequences to himself'[202]—a stand later followed by Edmund Gibson, Bishop of London. Many were the letters which poured into Lambeth deploring the prevalent *malaise*, a number calling attention to the gross excesses of 'a company of vile wretches that give themselves the name of the Hell-fire Club'. The Archbishop felt that some action was necessary, and decided to co-operate with Lord Nottingham, though its terms were not quite in the form he would have wished, in a Bill 'for suppressing blasphemy and profaneness'. As always, legislation of this kind presented many difficulties.

The main clauses imposed penalties of up to three months' imprisonment for those, unless they publicly recanted, who spoke against either the Being of God, the inspiration of the Scriptures, or the doctrine of the Thirty-nine Articles; but the Bill never became law, in spite of the fact that Wake was promised in advance the support of the ministry. 'All I propose,' he said in his speech in the Lords, 'is to strengthen the laws already in force; not to look back but forward; not to restrain men's opinions, but their open attempts and actions; to support the religion established against the bold attempts that are made against it.'[203] The bishops themselves, however, to Wake's great disappointment, gave him 'little encouragement to proceed', White Kennett of Peterborough, a close friend, complaining that its effect would be to set up an inquisition. Indeed one member of the bench went so far as to issue a pamphlet, in which, so the Archbishop protested, he 'vilely misrepresented the purpose of the Bill and those who appeared for it'. Wake complained of being 'again deserted by my Brethren, as in the other Bill for Repealing the Act against occasional conformity'.[204]

A particular scandal against which both ecclesiastics and moralists inveighed was the masquerade, or masked ball, an importation from France and notorious for encouraging drunkenness and promiscuity. Here the initiative was taken by Edmund Gibson, Bishop of London. As the result of a sermon of protest on 6 January 1724, followed by an episcopal petition to the King, a proclamation was issued 'that there should be no more masquerades, but what were subscribed for the beginning of the month'. But this prohibition applied only to public masquerades; the private ones continued. Under Wake's presidency sixteen bishops, 'all promoted by his Majesty and every one zealously devoted to his person and government', met in the strictest secrecy at the House of Lords. In a tactful memorial, which was presented to the King through Lord Townsend, the bishops condemned masquerades as offensive to all serious people, while not supposing for a moment 'that all who go to these assemblies have any wicked designs in it'. Yet once there, many were led astray, and though the bishops were sure that the King himself was unaware of their true nature, the fact was that they 'had not been allowed of in any former reign nor were at all suitable to the Temper or Genius of this Nation'.[205]

What happened subsequently is best told in a private memorandum drawn up by the Archbishop.

> This Letter or Memorial being delivered by us to my Lord Townshend, he promised to do his best with the King to satisfy our desires. But what was done by His Lordship I cannot tell; it appeared that no regard was had to our advice and request.[206]

Such a rebuff is indeed remarkable. That the Archbishop of Canterbury, with the unanimous voice of some sixteen bishops behind him, should be treated with such discourtesy as to be kept in total ignorance, to say nothing of their advice being rejected, suggests that those of influence at the Court entertained little sense of social responsibility and resented any interference with their private pleasures.

George III, however, felt a greater concern, and influenced by Lord Bute, son-in-law of Lady Mary Wortley Montagu, saw it as his duty to purge public life. Soon after his accession he told Archbishop Secker that he 'hoped the proclamation against vice and profaneness would be regarded and have a good effect'. The Archbishop assured him that though 'such proclamations had been apt to be considered as matters of course . . . his example . . . would give life and vigour to this'. 'It was his principle duty,' the King replied, 'to encourage and support religion and virtue.'[207]

Masquerades lingered for many a year, surviving the alarms created in 1750 by earthquakes in London and Lisbon. In 1766 an influential appeal was made to Archbishop Secker, as 'the natural patron of the following proposal', to use his influence for one more endeavour to put a stop to them. 'Its authors, after rehearsing their evils particularly in tempting numerous people to squander away their time, health and substance,' suggested a very practical remedy, namely that all such licensed and unlicensed diversions should require tickets stamped by authority and taxable to the extent of four shillings in the pound. What Secker's response to this appeal was has not come to light.[208]

Horace Walpole, writing in 1770 to Cornwallis—incidentally the first Etonian in St. Augustine's Chair, indeed five XVIIIth-century occupants were educated in their local grammar schools—relates how 'that knave, the Bishop of London [Richard Terrick], persuaded that good soul the archbishop to remonstrate against masquerades; but happily the age prefers silly follies to serious ones, and *dominoes comme de raison* carry it against lawn sleeves.'[209] If contemporary gossip is to be trusted, the Archbishop had some experience of masquerades in a mild form in his own home. Fashionable Mrs. Cornwallis was said to hold routs at Lambeth, thus provoking the devout Selina, Countess of Huntingdon, to protest but in vain to the Archbishop. She then secured an interview with the King who promised 'to interpose [his] authority and see what that will do towards reforming such indecent practices'. A royal letter was then dispatched to the Primate:

My good Lord Prelate,—I could not delay giving you the notification of the grief and concern with which my breast was affected, at receiving authentic information that *routs* have made their way into your palace. At the same time, I must signify to you my sentiments on this subject, which hold those levities and vain dissipations as utterly inexpedient, if not unlawful, to pass in a residence for many centuries devoted to divine studies, religious retirement, and the extensive exercise of charity and benevolence; I add, in a place where so many of your predecessors have led their lives in such sanctity as has thrown lustre on the pure religion they professed and adorned.

From the dissatisfaction with which you must perceive I behold these improprieties, not to speak in harsher terms, and on still more pious principles, I trust you will suppress them immediately; so that I may not have occasion to show any further marks of my displeasure, or to interpose in a different manner.

May God take your Grace into His Almighty protection.[210]

This letter is remarkable, but it is not wholly out of character with George III, and certainly bears testimony to contemporary gossip, repeated years afterwards in *The Times*. William Cole, a considerable scholar, wrote in a letter:

No doubt you have seen in the *London Evening Post* of the last fortnight several scurrilous squibs and reflections on our Primate, not for his routs at the palace, but for his endeavouring to bring folks to a sense of their duty and decency. In the last week's paper it is repeated, and the archbishop's lady taxed with routs on a Sunday. Though I had formerly the honour of a decent familiarity with his Grace while at college, and have all the veneration that is due *tanto patri*; yet if the fact is true, and it is boldly and confidently asserted in the Presbyterian manner, I cannot help thinking but all that is said is proper enough for such anti-episcopal carriage.[211]

Whatever be the truth on this matter of routs and masquerades, Cornwallis is certainly known, with Porteus, to have tried to secure a better observance of Good Friday, and for his pains to have called down on his head the cry of 'No Popery' in many a Presbyterian newspaper. Cornwallis also opposed hotly a Bill to license a playhouse in Manchester which was introduced in the House of Lords in 1775. He was convinced that theatres led to idleness, particularly among those destined to live by their toil.

I remember—he said—when I resided in the last diocese I had the care of, I went to a great trading town [Birmingham] to attend an ordination: and having a curiosity to inspect the manufactures carrying on by a Mr. Taylor, upon examining the

works I enquired how many men he employed; he answered
500. 'And where are they? is this a holiday?' 'No,' says he, 'but
we have a playhouse here; the men were at the play last night,
and it is impossible to get them to their business for two or
three days after they have been there.'

The Archbishop concluded:

I am convinced that in trading and manufacturing towns its
effects are immediate and pernicious: I am, therefore, strenuously against committing the Bill.[212]

The Bill, however, passed.

Archbishop Moore supported Wilberforce, in 1787, in securing a
Proclamation against Vice and Immoralities, and in founding a
Society for this purpose in London. His attitude towards the slave
trade, however, which early in his archiepiscopate came under attack
if only from a minority, does not do him overmuch credit. When the
Member of Parliament for Oxford University introduced a Bill to
control the transit of slaves from Africa to the West Indies, Moore,
who dreaded change, admitted that 'it [was] a cursed trade, but
too deeply rooted to be forcibly and at once eradicated'.[213]

Archbishops as a whole shared the commonly accepted view that
the law ought to be severe in order to constitute an effective deterrent
against crime. When Sir Samuel Romilly, in 1810, introduced a Bill
to remove the death penalty for stealing privately in a dwelling house
up to five shillings, Manners Sutton and six bishops voted for its
rejection. With withering scorn Sir Samuel Romilly later wrote:

I rank these prelates amongst the members who were solicited to
vote against the Bill, because I would rather be convinced of
their servility towards government than that, recollecting the
mild doctrines of their religion, they could have come down to
the House spontaneously, to vote that transportation for life is
not a sufficiently severe punishment for the offence of pilfering
what is five shillings value, and that nothing but the blood of the
offender can afford an adequate atonement for such a trans-
gression.[214]

The judges, it must be admitted, did not come out any better,
Lord Ellenborough protesting that if the Bill were to pass, 'there was
no knowing where this was to stop'.

# 5

## THE HANOVERIAN DYNASTY

A traditional function of the Primate, as we have seen, was to act as a personal counsellor to the monarch and his family. Here, of course, much depended on temperament and opportunity. Tenison, for example, was not a Court man, and in his later years seldom went to Whitehall. Its Tory climate made him feel an alien, and Anne more or less ignored him.

Wake did his best to cultivate harmonious relations with George I, and kept in touch with him during his periodical trips to Hanover through Lancelot Blackburne, Dean of Exeter. Blackburne was not always a reliable informant, and it is to be hoped that the Archbishop did not accept uncritically his estimate of the German philosopher Leibnitz.

> Both the Lutherans and Calvinists—he wrote to Lambeth—look upon Leibnitz as an unbeliever, and the Laymen of the Court say he has his religion to choose and was ready to turn Roman Catholic but that they would not come up to his bargain.[215]

Disputes between Hanoverian monarchs and their heirs became an accustomed ingredient in English political life, and it was not easy for archbishops to avoid getting involved. Such family brawls seem hardly worth recording, but they caused many a headache to statesmen at the time, eager to establish and commend the Hanoverian dynasty. Thus, in November 1717, George I embroiled himself in a violent quarrel with the Prince of Wales, whose wife, the intelligent Caroline of Ansbach, had just given birth to a son. The King insisted on the Duke of Newcastle standing sponsor, with the result that, after the christening, the Prince of Wales gave vent to his feelings, and his father retaliated by turning him and his wife out of St. James's. This miserable *contretemps* went on for some time, even after the death of the baby who had been its indirect cause. Wake was called in to arbitrate, and received many episcopal letters expressing grave concern at the repercussions of such a domestic disagreement. Nicholson of Carlisle wrote:

> I shall least of all be able to bear up against Rents and schisms
> in the Royal Family . . . I trust by your Grace's interposition all
> Blackness is already removed from that quarter and that their
> Royal Highnesses are returned to St. James's in perfect
> peace. . . .[216]

It was, however, not until two years later that a reconciliation was
effected, Archbishop Wake, behind the scenes, being active in
promoting it.

> I can't conclude my letter—wrote Trelawney, Bishop of
> Winchester—before I express the great joy I have at the recon-
> ciliation of the King and Prince which must make the Royal
> family happy and the Kingdom easy because I have the pleasure
> to believe you had a hand in it.[217]

Archbishop Potter, in spite of Lord Hervey's scurrilous comments,
was early a member of the intellectual circle that gathered around
Caroline. Indeed he in part owed his rise to her friendship; and it
was through her, while he was Bishop of Oxford, that he preached
the Coronation sermon for George II in June 1727. Among Potter's
first responsibilities after he had become Archbishop was the sad
duty of attending Caroline's deathbed. She was in great pain, but
her integrity and seriousness of purpose shone through her physical
weakness. A few days before the end, friends at the Court felt that
some clergyman ought to be summoned, and through her daughter
Emily she let it be known that she would see Potter. They prayed
together morning and evening, 'at which ceremony', so comments
Hervey in his *Memoirs*, 'her children always assisted'. A contemporary
has suggested that Potter gave her communion, but there can be no
certainty about this, since her own scruples and her unhappy relations with Frederick, Prince of Wales, may have predisposed her
against it.

Secker, on going to Lambeth, already had behind him a long and
intimate association with the royal family through his friendship
with Queen Caroline and the group which she gathered around her.
It was through him that Joseph Butler, author of the one theological
classic of the XVIIIth century, *The Analogy of Religion*, was brought
to her notice. Secker, as Rector of St. James's, Piccadilly, the church
which Frederick, Prince of Wales, attended, was inevitably dragged
into the father–son quarrels to which reference has already been
made.

Frederick, according to the traditional pattern, had been turned
out of St. James's and sought refuge in Norfolk Square. Here the
future George III was born, Potter being the only high officer of

state present at his birth. So weak was the young infant that he was immediately baptized by Secker. Contemporary wits not unnaturally discovered a fund of amusement in these somewhat squalid family upsets. It was said, for example, that on the first occasion Frederick appeared at St. James's, the officiating minister began Morning Prayer with the words: 'I will arise and go to my father . . .,' and that Secker followed with a sermon on the fifth commandment: 'Honour thy father and thy mother.'

In his capacity as a parish priest, Secker baptized all save two of Frederick's many children; but his endeavour to heal the breach between father and son incurred the father's displeasure. Horace Walpole relates that George II refused to go to chapel when Secker was preaching; but not much credence needs to be given to one who described Secker as 'bred a presbyterian and Man-midwife', a reference to his having studied medicine, 'which sect and profession he has dropped for a season'. George's dislike, however, did not prevent Secker being asked to preach the memorial service at Court on the Sunday after Queen Caroline's death. He did so to such effect that the King, who was not present, consented to read his sermon.

George II, whose health had been failing for some time, died in 1760 of a burst ventricle of the heart. According to Horace Walpole the funeral in Henry VII Chapel, impressively illuminated by torch-light, was marred by the Duke of Newcastle's going into hysterics and being ministered to with smelling salts by the Archbishop. It was destined to be the last funeral of a reigning sovereign in the Abbey. Writing to Dr. Johnson, President of King's College, New York, Secker expressed himself as follows:

> We have lost our good old King [George II] a true well wisher to his people, and a man of many private virtues. His successor is a regular and worthy and pious young man, and hath declared himself, I am satisfied, very sincerely to have the interest of religion at heart.[218]

Secker was no stranger to the new King whom he had watched grow up from a baby. It was natural, therefore, that he should be granted an interview some two days after the accession when they discussed the form of the royal prayers.

> The King—he wrote—sent for me into a room where he was alone, and told me that as the Royal Family was numerous and he was unwilling to put in any of his brothers and leave out his uncle, and many names might hereafter make confusion, he thought it would be best to insert only the Princess Dowager of Wales in particular. I assented to it; and then I took the oppor-

tunity of assuring him of my duty and best services. He said very graciously that he had no doubt on that head, and that I was one of his oldest acquaintance, having baptized him on the day he was born after once doubting whether he was alive, as Mrs. Kennon the midwife had often told him.[219]

For Secker, presiding at the 'young man's' coronation was a congenial task, and he himself spent a great deal of time searching out precedents as to procedure. The result was a quickened religious atmosphere, enhanced by the fact that the new King entered into the ceremony with great seriousness. This is illustrated by an incident which Secker himself describes.

> At the Communion the King asked me if he should not take off his crown. I said the office did not mention it. He asked if it would not be more suitable to such an act of religion. I said 'Yes'; but the Queen's crown could not be taken off easily. When I had put on the crown, the ladies pinned it to the Queen's head-dress or hair. The King then asked what must be done? I said as the ladies' heads are used to be covered it would not be regarded. He put off his crown immediately and all the Peers that saw took off their coronets.[220]

Apparently Archbishop Wake's MS. directed that both the King and Queen should remove their crowns but this did not appear in the printed order.

It fell to the lot of Moore to be Archbishop when George III suffered his first attack of mental illness. The situation was complicated at the time by the existence, according to the familiar Hanoverian pattern, of extremely bad feeling between the King and his son, the future George IV. This rupture divided parliamentarians and spilled over into the discussions as to the precise powers to be vested in the Regent. When the King's illness was at its height in November 1788, Moore expressed his feelings thus:

> My anxieties are very great indeed, and every moment increasing from the distance I am from the subject which engrosses my whole heart and from the doubt I feel about the propriety of my attending in person at Windsor. I am led by every principle of attachment and respectful affection, as well as by that duty which peculiarly belongs to my situation, to make a humble offer of my personal attendance and services in any possible situation in which they may be acceptable.[221]

Fortunately the King recovered in January 1789, and Moore took reassurance from a report of Dr. Willis, the physician in attendance on him, that this recovery would be permanent. Such was not to prove the case. Some contemporaries, however, alleged that the Archbishop exercised undue influence over the King at the time of his mental disorder.

It can be well understood that Moore did not relish presiding over the marriage of the Prince of Wales to Caroline of Brunswick, the more so as he had first to satisfy his conscience that George was not legally bound in wedlock to Mrs. Fitzherbert. The Archbishop thus describes the ceremony:

> The crowd at St. James' last night was immense and the heat intolerable. I felt my business a very solemn one indeed, and never said my prayers in my life under more impression and fervency. The Prince's mind was certainly very seriously affected both in the service and after the service, but not in that part of the service from which one might be led to fear he had upon his mind a feeling that he had before bound himself by solemn engagements. There I saw no embarrassment.[222]

Perhaps in thus expressing himself, the wish was father to the thought.

Of all relationships during this period between monarch and Archbishop, that of Manners Sutton and George III was the most intimate. They had much in common. Both were conservative by instinct; both were family men to whom the domestic hearth meant a great deal; both merited the description given of Manners Sutton that he was 'without enough genius or learning to make him angular or unpleasant'. The friendship doubtless developed over the years when Sutton lived at Windsor as Dean. The King used whimsically to say that he was the first monarch whose 'Archbishop of Canterbury and Chancellor had both run away with their wives'. Another anecdote has it that George, who was no Malthusian, speaking to Sutton of his large family, remarked: 'I believe Your Grace has better than a dozen.' 'No, sir,' replied the Archbishop, 'only eleven.' 'Well,' answered the King, 'is not that better than a dozen?'[223]

On the death of George III, Manners Sutton had the most uncongenial task of dealing with the unfortunate situation created by the new King's unhappy relationship with his wife Caroline. Caroline had lived round the Mediterranean for some years, in circumstances which had given rise to reports of scandal. George IV was anxious to marry again: but Caroline, against the advice of her friends, now returned to England. Was her name to be included in the Prayer Book? The King insisted on its omission and Lord Liverpool and his cabinet, apart from Canning, concurred. The Queen's cause, however, was enthusiastically supported by the populace, more in dislike of George than in affection for Caroline. Meanwhile, George wished to hasten on with a divorce, and Lord Liverpool decided to set up a committee to prepare the way. The Government was anxious that the Archbishop should give it respectability by becoming a member, but Lord Dacre, who presented a petition from the Queen against the setting up of the Committee, complained that the Archbishop of Canterbury had already taken a view by consenting to the omission of Caroline's name from the Prayer Book. Manners Sutton was certainly placed in an uncomfortable position. In self-defence he maintained that it was the Ministry which had initiated the change in the royal prayers: all that he had done was to execute the orders of the Council. Still he was willing not to serve on the Committee (this was probably an understatement!) if he could do so consistent with his honour. Finally, following upon the Committee's report, a Bill of Pains and Penalties which proposed both to deprive Caroline of her status as Queen and to dissolve her marriage was introduced into Parliament. Manners Sutton's position was a difficult one, and was made more so by the unpopularity of the proposed Bill. In the Lords he stood his ground, maintaining that the Queen had been shown guilty of adultery, and that this was the one cause for divorce which had Dominical authority. Therefore he had no religious scruple in supporting the Bill. But in this Manners Sutton did not carry all the bishops with him, the Archbishops of York and Tuam, together with eight bishops, voting with the opposition which carried the day. Parliament decided on an annuity of £50,000 for the unhappy Caroline, and Lord Dacre, thus encouraged, asked that her name be reinstated in the Prayer Book. Manners Sutton's speech opposing this petition reads strangely. No religious principle, he maintained, was at stake. It was not a matter of whether Caroline should be prayed for, but of distinction in prayer, since she was necessarily included, though not by name, under the prayers for the Royal Family and, more widely, in the general intercessions of the Church.[224]

In this unhappy affair, it is clear that the Archbishop's over-riding concern was not to offend George IV to whom, as his monarch, he felt bound in public to give support.

# 6

## 'THE CONGREGATION OF CHRISTIAN PEOPLE'

I

The XVIIIth century was no ecumenical period in the history of the Church of England, not through intolerance but simply because of apathy and lack of religious interest. The crisis of the Reformation and its immediate aftermath were over. The necessity for the Reformed Churches of Europe to 'gang up together' which at an earlier time had seemed a condition of survival or a means of imbibing the pure milk of the Protestant word, no longer appeared relevant.

Such general observations must find their exception in Archbishop Wake, whose formative years were spent in the more tempestuous years of the preceding century. He early felt a deep desire to promote the union of the Protestant Churches, his guiding principle, from which he never swerved, being unity in essentials, difference in non-essentials. That principle, however, can sometimes state problems rather than solve them. The ultimate essential of such unity, he believed, though there was room for interim adjustment, was the restoration of episcopacy to those foreign churches which had dispensed with it. For Wake's strenuous efforts in this field the interested reader must turn to Norman Sykes's detailed researches into the life of the Archbishop—his correspondence with continental church leaders such as Ostervald of Neuchâtel; Jablonski of Berlin; Kopijewicz of the Reformed Churches of Lithuania; theologians of the Swiss movement *L'Orthodoxie liberale*. Despite his continuing preoccupation with this cause, the practical result of his labours, apart from the cultivation of personal friendships, was nil. In a letter to Osiander of 28 November 1723 he confessed sadly:

> Each of us believes that the prestige of his own Church turns upon this, that it should attract all the others into its own following, recognising its authority and, as it were, law over all others. Few are willing seriously to consider or honestly to admit in how many and great issues we are all agreed; that in

fact there is no article in fundamental matters of faith in which we do not think alike; and therefore none in which we ought not mutually to tolerate each other. . . . Nor do I desire to stigmatise in this matter any one party more than the rest; rather I think that all are equally to be blamed. For it is plain that we all favour too much ourselves and our own opinions; and that whilst we demand to be granted liberty to defend our own opinions, we are willing to extend this to others only with difficulty, if indeed at all. This has been the beginning of evil. This too is the greatest obstacle to our peace and concord at present, and unless God gives us a better mind, will always be so.[225]

Wake's ecumenical interests were not confined to relations with the reformed churches. As a young man he lived in the French capital as chaplain to Lord Preston, whom Charles II had sent there as envoy extraordinary to the Court of Louis XIV. Thus began a lifelong interest, at a critical period in its development, in the affairs of the Gallican Church. This was the time when, under the impetus of the Jansenist movement, there was a desire in certain quarters to soften the acerbity of the more extreme Roman doctrines in an effort to gain Protestant converts. This general loosening up had protagonists in Dr. Ellis Du Pin, head of the Sorbonne Theological Faculty; and also in Beavoir, chaplain to the English ambassador, Lord Stair, both men of equally advanced views. Such 'modernism' in the Gallican Church was not welcome either to Louis XIV or to the Jesuits, and they persuaded Pope Clement XI to promulgate his famous bull *Unigenitas*, issued on 8 September 1713. Such bald pronouncement condemned Jansenism in general, naming some 110 propositions from Pasquier Quesnel's *Testament en Français* and reaffirming the Ultra-Montane Faith without reserve.

The intervention led to considerable excitement, and it was in this *milieu* that Beavoir, on 11 December 1718, wrote a letter to Wake which included these words:

> Dr. Du Pin, with whom I dined last Monday, and with the Synodic of the Sorbonne and two other Doctors . . . talked as if the whole Kingdom was to appeal to a future General Council &c. They wished for a union with the Church of England as the most effectual means to unite all the Western Churches. Dr. Du Pin desired me to give his duty to your Grace.[226]

Encouraged by a kindly message from Lambeth, Dr. Du Pin proceeded to write to the Archbishop direct:

> One thing I will add with your kind permission, viz. that I earnestly desire that some way might be found of initiating a

union between the Anglican and Gallican Churches. We are not so very far separated from one another in most things as to preclude the possibility of our being mutually reconciled. Would that all Christians were one fold.[227]

Wake replied cautiously, extolling the virtues of the Church of England, and being deliberately anti-papal in tone. He concluded:

Perhaps this may be the beginning of a new Reformation, in which not only the best Protestants but also a great part of the Roman Church may agree.[228]

The matter was now taken up with earnestness in Paris, and other divines began to be drawn in. Du Pin, in co-operation with the Abbés Courayer and Giraudin, drew up a long document which dealt at length with the Anglican Thirty-nine Articles of Religion; declared English orders not invalid; approved the discipline and worship of the Church of England at least negatively; and repudiated extreme views of papal supremacy. The document, which was sent over to Wake, concluded by maintaining that if the Roman Pontiff should object to the two Churches entering into discussions then there ought to be an appeal over his head to a General Council.

Wake was certainly interested, but a natural caution and the responsibilities of his office made him as careful in pressing forward as was Tenison in his dealings with Dr. Jablonski. Wake was particularly anxious to avoid a situation in which he might seem to discard anything vital to the witness of the Church of England. On 30 August 1718, he wrote to Beavoir:

My task is pretty hard, and I scarce know how to manage myself in this matter. To go any farther than I have done, even as a divine only of the Church of England, may meet with censure. And as Archbishop of Canterbury I cannot treat with those gentlemen. I do not think my character at all inferior to that of an Archbishop of Paris; on the contrary, without lessening the authority and dignity of the Church of England, I must say it is in some respects superior. . . . [This] will only expose me to the censure of doing what, in my station, I ought not without the King's knowledge. . . . I cannot well tell what to say to Dr. Du Pin. If he thinks we are to take their direction what to retain and what to give up, he is utterly mistaken . . . they may depend upon it, I shall always account our Church to stand upon an equal foot with theirs; and that we are no more to receive laws from them, than we desire to impose any on them. In short, the

Church of England is free, is orthodox; she has a plenary authority within herself. She has no need to refer to other Churches to direct her what to believe or what to do . . . and therefore if they mean to deal with us, they must lay down this for the foundation, that we are to deal with one another upon equal terms.[229]

The same theme was later expressed by E. W. Benson and Randall Davidson.

Wake thus made it perfectly clear that there could be no question of the Church of England returning to the bosom of the Roman Catholic Church even if on the Gallican pattern. In a series of letters he described for the benefit of Du Pin and his colleagues the formularies of the Church of England, and gave his own mature views on how negotiations might one day go forward:

If we could once divide the Gallican Church from the Roman, a reformation in other matters would follow as a matter of course. The scheme that to me seems most likely to prevail is to agree in the independence (in all matters of authority) of every National Church on any others and their right to determine all matters that arise within themselves; and for points of doctrine, to agree as far as possible in all articles of any moment (as in effect we already do or easily may): and for other matters to allow a difference till God shall bring us to a union in these also. One only thing should be provided for to purge out of the public offices of the Church such things as hinder a perfect communion in the Service of the Church, so that whenever any come from us to them or from them to us we may all join together in prayers and the holy Sacraments with each other.[230]

This exchange of views—we can hardly employ the word 'negotiations'—soon came to an *impasse*, particularly with the death of Du Pin. The Jesuits intervened, and Giraudin, under threat of incarceration in the Bastille, was forced to hand over Wake's letters. When Clement XI read them, he expressed his regret that so profound an author was not a member of the Roman Church. This did not prevent him, however, from forbidding further correspondence.

Any possibility of real negotiations between the two Churches was now at an end (if, indeed, it had ever been possible), but Wake's interest in the Gallican Church remained. It led him to enter into a correspondence with Dr. Peter Francis Courayer, a Benedictine monk who was a Canon Regular and Principle Librarian of the Cathedral Church of St. Geneviève in Paris. Over a space of six years Wake sent him some forty letters which have not unfairly been described as lengthy, learned and laborious. A passage from one of them in which he indulges a little introspection may be quoted for its personal interest:

> I bless God I know my own mediocrity; and am not exalted in any opinion of myself. God has given me an honest mind; desirous to act with integrity in everything, and having long conversed with men of all persuasions, and found some to value in almost every way, I have learnt not only to bear with those who differ from me, but notwithstanding any such differences to love them; to think charitably of them, and to hope that a God of infinite love and goodness will pity and accept of us all. If in this I am mistaken I am sure I err on the best side; and as those thoughts shall never make me either negligent in the search for what is agreeable to God's will or prejudiced against it tho' never so contrary to my present notion; so I am persuaded that by keeping up such a universal charity in my mind for those who in the integrity of their heart differ from me, I shall be always the best prepared to submit to a reasonable conviction and to obtain God's pardon for any involuntary errors I may after all happen to continue in.[231]

In another letter he describes himself as living 'almost a monastic life', with 'the service of God within ourselves and that in public in my chapel and house four times a day'.

> We live orderly and peaceably together—he continues—And tho' the necessity of business draws a great number of persons to me, yet I reduce even that as much as possible to certain times; and then eat openly with my friends two days in the week. To the Court I seldom go, save when obliged to attend my duty either in the public or cabinet Councils.[232]

When Courayer's work, *A Dissertation on the Validity of the Ordination of the English and of the Succession of the Bishops of the Anglican Church*, appeared in 1723, it was in no small measure due to Wake that the author affirmed that 'The validity of the English ordinations stands upon the strongest evidence'. The appearance of this work, not surprisingly, placed Courayer in some jeopardy, which prompted Wake to offer him hospitality in England, where, he assured him, he could enjoy 'a safe and honourable retreat'. Courayer, however, was hesitant to make the journey, and expressed doubts as to whether it was a good place for a religious man to live in. In a lengthy reply Wake admitted that conditions were not ideal, and that our divisions are many; and the liberty taken by men in treating in matters of faith and doctrine is much beyond what either our laws permit or it were wished our government should suffer.[233]

Courayer finally accepted Wake's invitation, and came over to England in 1728. He lived on as a Roman Catholic till 1776, dying at the age of ninety-five, and was buried in the cloisters of Westminster Abbey.

We have lingered over this correspondence because of its unique character. No XVIIIth-century successor took up where Wake left off, or was anxious to do so. The ecumenical interest, sparked off by the fires of Reformation controversy, burnt themselves out; and the European consciousness of the XVIIIth century, shown in its polite use of the French language and the grand tour, was secular in character rather than religious.

Wake's interest in other churches was a legacy from the preceding century, as was his concern for the devoted band of Danish Evangelical missionaries who laboured at Tranquebar. Such was Wake's international reputation, that a letter came to him in Latin from this distant outpost, listing the various difficulties to which the mission was exposed. Wake responded with a personal gift, and also by obtaining a royal letter for collections throughout England. When Zeigenbalq, its leader, came over to England in 1716 Wake presented him at Court, and continued to keep in close touch with the mission through a lengthy correspondence.

Testimony to Wake's lifelong fellow feeling for 'the congregation of Christian People dispersed throughout the whole world' survives in a folio volume of MSS. which contains letters from foreign correspondents in Latin and French. To each Wake wrote a careful and informed reply, always in the language of the writer, the drafts of which remain in his own handwriting.

II

The community at Tranquebar continued to be the main link in England with mission work in India during the XVIIIth century, and financial help to it was channelled through the Society for Promoting Christian Knowledge. When Archbishop Manners Sutton consecrated Dr. Middleton on 8 May 1814 as the first Bishop of Calcutta, responsible people felt that a missionary society should now sponsor this work, and that the time had come for a great effort in this field. Joshua Watson (1771–1855) the leading ecclesiastical layman of his day, and Christopher Wordsworth, Rector of Lambeth, invited the Archbishop's support, and it was readily forthcoming. 'Draw up a

Memorial,' Manners Sutton said, 'and I will present it to the Prime Minister.'[234] As a result the S.P.C.K. handed over its India funds to her sister body, the Society for the Propagation of the Gospel, and the Archbishop secured an allocation of £5,000 for the work of the new Bishop of Calcutta. He also used his influence with Lord Liverpool to prompt the issue of a royal letter authorizing collections for the S.P.G. throughout the country. From the £50,000 obtained, Dr. Middleton set about the founding of Bishop's College.

Perhaps it may be added here that Manners Sutton possessed a flair for making friends among laymen, in particular with such as Joshua Watson, one of the 'Hackney phalanx'; and encouraging them by bringing the authority of his office behind their good causes. Particularly he did much to assist the founding of the National Society, destined to contribute significantly to English education. By securing distinguished patronage, even that of the Prince Regent, he helped to overcome a great deal of initial prejudice. Through thus exercising a fostering care over Church agencies, the Archbishop discovered a role which in his successors was to grow in importance. Yet in relation to the founding of the Church Missionary Society he was cautious, admonishing William Wilberforce in 1800 that he would 'look on the proceedings with candour, and that it would give him pleasure to find them such as he could approve'.

Reference to the Society for the Propagation of the Gospel calls attention to the fact that in so far as archbishops during the XVIIIth century entered into a wider perspective, it came to them, in the main, through their relations with this Society; and their link with the Colonies of the Crown. Tenison, as we have seen, took a great personal interest in the Society's work, chairing the meetings of its board, subscribing liberally to its funds, and corresponding with its workers overseas. Wake took over where Tenison left off, an example followed by his successors, though with varying degrees of zeal.

The work of the Society at that time lay largely in the plantations of America, the ecclesiastical jurisdiction of which was vested in the Bishop of London. It was inevitable, however, that Archbishops of Canterbury should also feel themselves personally involved in this charge, both because the Bishop of London was their suffragan, and also because the welfare of the Church in the plantations could not be promoted independently of governmental policy. Central to this policy was a determination not to allow resident bishops, which meant that the provisions of Tenison's will leaving £1,000 to found two bishoprics in the plantations could not be implemented.

Colonial clergymen, seeking ordination, had therefore to brave the journey to England. Once arrived, it was natural for them to call at Lambeth. In 1721, Carolina sent over two representatives, carrying letters to the Archbishop, in which they reported that though they had many more struggles to contend with than any other colony, yet they were engaged in building a church superior to any yet built in America. Three years later Johnson, the sole clergyman of the Established Church working in Connecticut, wrote to Wake, complaining that 'the fountain of their misery' was 'the want of a Bishop for whom there are many thousands in this country do long'.

In spite of the coolness of the Government, succeeding archbishops, with one exception, uniformly supported the claim put forward by Episcopalians in the plantations to have bishops resident in their own land. Potter wrote specifically to Newcastle on 10 March 1746, reminding him that the bishops as a body in the previous year had urged a resident episcopate in America. By this means the plantations would

> be favoured with an opportunity of receiving Confirmation and Holy Orders in their own country without the necessity of coming to England, which many of them have attempted to do to their great hazard and expense and some to the loss of their lives.[235]

Herring was more cautious, though he did a great deal for the Society for the Propagation of the Gospel, and persuaded Newcastle into membership, mulcting him of an annual subscription of twenty guineas. His reserve *à propos* resident American bishops was partly dictated by his anxiety lest the S.P.G. should get itself embroiled in a controversy with, and hence embarrass, the Government. Writing to Newcastle he declared:

> When the King commands me to consider that affair I will do so with my best judgment and with a principal regard to the tranquillity of his Government, but not before.[236]

Later he reassured Newcastle more explicitly:

> I shall never teaze the Administration on the Foot of Episcopacy in America. . . . I have hitherto endeavoured and shall continue so to do to keep clear of the rancour of high church and govern our affairs so far as in me lies by the gentle methods of Christian moderation.[237]

Bishop Sherlock, on coming to London in 1748, approached the Government with a specific plan, and refused to assume the traditional jurisdiction vested in his see in order to force the ministry's hands. But to no avail. The Earl of Hardwicke, in rejecting Sherlock's proposals, sent a copy of his reply to Secker, who was then Bishop of Oxford. The latter was well aware of the intensity of dissenting opposition, but protested that there was no intention of introducing into the colonies the civil estate of a Church of England bishop. His function would be to superintend, to confirm and ordain, that is to exercise, on the spot, the jurisdiction which now rested remotely in the Bishop of London.

But opposition in America proved too strong, and the dissenters in England sided with them. The general effect was to predispose the Government against action. Perhaps, even if unreasonable, it was understandable that the descendants of colonists who had fled their country to free themselves from 'the mitred, lordly successors of the fishermen of Galilee' should set their face against introducing them into the plantations. Thus Dr. Mayhew, a Congregational minister in Boston, published a pamphlet hotly opposing any such proposal, thereby provoking Secker to issue a lengthy reply in which he maintained that 'the ministers of our Church in America by friendly converse with the principal Dissenters could satisfy them that nothing more is intended than that our Church may enjoy the full benefit of its own institution as all others do'.[238] In England, Francis Blackburne asked why was it that 'in several dioceses there are no Confirmations for several years?' if episcopal ministrations were so necessary to the Church in America.

Secker, when he became Archbishop of Canterbury, was far too good a churchman and too convinced of the need for American bishops to give up the struggle, counselling those who supported him to cultivate perseverance as well as patience. A great development was now taking place in the life of the Anglican Church in the thirteen States fringing the Atlantic seaboard. The demand for bishops thus became more urgent, with the result that Bishops Butler of Durham and Benson of Gloucester emulated Tenison in leaving bequests for this purpose. However, feeling in America continued to make the implementation of any such scheme for the moment impracticable, and Secker, in spite of his 'earnest and continued endeavours' and the assurance of the King's support, could get nothing but promises. As late as 1763 Secker was still writing that 'we must try our utmost for bishops. Hitherto little has been said to ministers and less by them on the subject'.[239]

It was left to the archiepiscopate of Moore, although no initiative came on his part, to see this long struggle brought to a successful conclusion. The hard-won independence of the American Colonies made the situation even more difficult for the clergy in the plantations, since they could no longer take the oath to the Crown which an ordaining English bishop was bound to require. But the American Church now took matters into its own hands and one of their number, Seabury, was ordained by the Scottish bishops on 14 November 1784. On 27 September 1785, a Convention was held in Philadelphia attended by lay as well as clerical representatives, at which the constitution and liturgy of the now independent Episcopal Church came up for discussion. At this Convention the suggestion was made that the Nicene and Athanasian Creeds, together with the phrase 'descended into hell' in the Apostles' Creed, should be deleted in the proposed new Prayer Book. The Convention also drew up a formal petition, dated 5 October 1785, directed to the Archbishops and bishops of the Church of England, asking for the consecration of bishops for the American Churches. Rumours of what was happening at Philadelphia had already percolated into England, and it was freely reported that Presbyterian, even Socinian views, had dominated the proceedings. The English Archbishops and Bishops in their reply expressed their affectionate concern for the Episcopal Church in America but added:

> . . . we cannot but be extremely cautious lest we should be the instruments of establishing an ecclesiastical system which will be called a branch of the Church of England, but afterwards may possibly appear to have departed from it essentially either in doctrine or discipline.[240]

A correspondence followed between the two Archbishops in England and the bishops in America, with the result that finally the Convention, when it met at Wilmington on 10 October 1786, agreed to retain the three Creeds in their existing form. The Convention also decided to send three priests to England—in fact only two came: White and Provoost—to seek consecration as bishops. In the meantime, Moore obtained an Act of Parliament authorizing English bishops to consecrate in these circumstances, and a copy of this Act was duly dispatched to America.

Moore certainly behaved with great courtesy and friendliness when the two American churchmen arrived in England. On 21 December they dined at Lambeth, 'having every reason to be satisfied with their reception and entertainment'; and the Archbishop, after conferring with his fellow bishops, saw them again later at Lambeth. On this occasion he persuaded them to tighten up the regulations which, he thought, made the deprivation of a bishop in America too easy, and on this being agreed, he remarked that the alternative was 'much for the better', at the same time apologizing for being so 'circumspect'. White and Provoost made a further visit to Lambeth on a public day, going from dinner into the Chapel, where two chaplains in surplices said the litany. On 2 February, Moore introduced them to George III when they took the opportunity of thanking him for his co-operation; the King replying that 'His Grace has given me such an account of the gentlemen who have come over that I am glad of the present opportunity of serving the interests of religion'.[241] Two days later, in Lambeth Chapel, Archbishop Moore, assisted by three bishops, consecrated White and Provoost. The two Americans—they were to become bishops of New York and Philadelphia—spent the rest of the day at Lambeth. The leave-taking was 'affectionate on both sides'.

This too long deferred consecration of American bishops shows the significance felt to be associated with the metropolitical see of Canterbury even in an age singularly free from ecclesiastical pretensions. There was a real desire to maintain a link between the new and independent Episcopal Church and the rock from which it had been hewn. Moore took very little initiative in the matter; but it was in the chapel of Lambeth that those bishops of the New World received their commission. Similarly it was Moore who in 1787 consecrated Charles Inglis, who had fled to England during the American War of Independence, as the first English colonial bishop of Nova Scotia.

Moore is an excellent example of a man brought into a particular interest through the office he held. His horizon was limited; but the wider perspective in which Archbishops had perforce to live, even in the XVIIIth century, constrained him to look further afield.

# PART VI

# REFORM; REVIVAL; SECULARISM

*Archbishops*
WILLIAM HOWLEY 1828
JOHN BIRD SUMNER 1848
CHARLES THOMAS LONGLEY 1862
ARCHIBALD CAMPBELL TAIT 1868
EDWARD WHITE BENSON 1883
FREDERICK TEMPLE 1896

# THE REALISM OF WILLIAM HOWLEY

The French Revolution, with its executions and excesses, reacted upon the early years of the XIXth century as had the troubled times of the XVIIth upon the years that came immediately after. The effect was to predispose even naturally progressive people against the very thought of change. The social and economic distress which was the legacy of the Napoleonic Wars pressed most heavily upon the working classes. Their attempts to combine for self-protection and, in blind fury, to destroy the machines which they regarded as the enemy, inevitably led to repressive legislation. The Cato Street conspiracy and the Peterloo Massacre reinforced the opinion of the ruling classes that any tampering with the constitution, or attempt at reform, would open the floodgates to violence and revolution. Burke gave a satisfying intellectual *rationale* for what in most people was unreasoning prejudice. The result was to postpone for three decades necessary reform both in Church and State.

But life was beginning to flow back into the Church of England, and where this was happening it came largely from the more fervent evangelicals such as the members of the Clapham Sect. The energies of these devoted men, however, were not primarily directed towards institutional reform of the Church, or the elimination of long-standing abuses. They were more concerned with mission, education, and the building of churches, each of which activities became associated with a great church society.

William Howley, Manners Sutton's successor, was born in a different stable. The only son of a country vicar, he survived until his eighties, dying in 1848, the 'year of revolutions'. His education was the traditional one of Winchester and New College, which led to a canonry at Christ Church and the Regius Professorship of Divinity at Oxford. Equally important, where preferment was concerned, he became tutor to the young Duke of Orange (afterwards King of Holland) and to the Marquis of Abercorn. His formative years were those of the XVIIIth century. On 10 October 1813, he was consecrated Bishop of London at Lambeth Palace in the presence of

Queen Charlotte, the consort of George III, and two of the princesses, none of whom had ever before witnessed a ceremony of this kind. Howley showed himself a convinced upholder of the establishment, devoted to the interests of the Court. He supported, in the Lords, the Pains and Penalties Bill against Queen Caroline, and expressed an extreme loyalty to George IV, though not in so ludicrous a fashion as his obituary in *The Times* was later to suggest. Howley was known to be opposed to Catholic Emancipation, which commended him to the King, whose 'conscience', inactive in many other spheres, was tender in this. Wellington, as Prime Minister, tried to insist that merit and not political interest should be the criterion for ecclesiastical office; so that though he would have preferred an Archbishop committed to emancipation now that he reluctantly regarded such a measure as inevitable, he could not easily resist the King's wishes. Thus Howley went to Canterbury, and some eight months after his nomination voted against a Bill to relieve Catholics, himself proposing a wrecking amendment in the Lords on the second reading.

Howley, a Tory by instinct, was a man of considerable ability, courteous if shy, and eminently likeable. Brought up a classicist—Charles Wordsworth has a story of his quoting in his carriage Homer's reference to the twinkling motion of the horses' ears—he was fluent in three European languages. He could look objectively at a problem, even if he took time to make up his mind. He possessed the rare capacity of being prepared to follow whither the argument led. To politicians he often seemed weak when he was in fact strong, perhaps because he was a quite deplorable public speaker. 'It could scarcely be said that what fell from his lips ever deserved to be called a speech'—so commented *The Times*.

Inevitably such a man was obliged to recognize that the forces making for change were gaining momentum under the impetus of the new 'Whiggery' which took its cue from the liberalism of Lord John Russell, the radical reformism of Joseph Hume, and the secular utilitarianism associated with Jeremy Bentham. Their first objective was the extension of the franchise to the trading middle classes who, growing in wealth, were determined to secure political power. The 'voteless' included many nonconformists, who were encouraged to hope for better things by the repeal of the Test and Corporation Acts in 1828, a protection, so Sydney Smith had observed some twenty years earlier, 'without which no clergyman [of the established Church] thinks he could sleep with his accustomed soundness'.

Yet William Howley did not rapidly shed the customary responses of a generation which was rapidly passing away—he was the last Archbishop to wear a wig—and the enlargement of the franchise filled him with alarm. In this he was at one with the majority of his brethren, the bishops and the rank and file of the clergy. Earl Grey, the Whig Prime Minister, had to struggle hard to get his Reform Bill through Parliament. Its defeat in committee in 1831 was followed by a dissolution; but back in office, the Whigs piloted the Bill once more through the Commons, only to suffer defeat in the Lords where Howley spoke, and with twenty bishops voted with the opposition. The Archbishop's view was that the Bill pandered to a mischievous modern tendency and that nothing was more dangerous than to upset the delicate balance of the British constitution. Neither Grey, nor William IV in a private interview at the Brighton Pavilion, was able to woo him into changing his mind. Other bishops proved more amenable. But Grey persisted, and after Wellington had proved unable to form a ministry and a reluctant William promised to create new peers, he got the Bill through on 4 June 1832. It was significant that no bishop added his name to the twenty-two peers who registered their dissent.

Never were the bishops more unpopular with the masses, soon to be bitterly disillusioned with the results of the Reform Bill. Riots were widespread throughout the country, and Howley, often designated Herod or Judas Iscariot, fully shared in this collective opprobrium. While the Bill was in the midst of its difficult passage, he was confronted by a hostile mob at Croydon while chairing the annual meeting of the S.P.G., and later applied to the Home Secretary for armed protection at Lambeth. In the following year when he went down to Canterbury for his primary visitation, he was pelted by a furious crowd. One who was present recalled the fierce shout of applause at a large public meeting when one of the speakers suggested that the cathedral should be converted into a stable for the horses of the cavalry. Little wonder that the Archbishop in his charge to his clergy urged vigilance in 'a season when the Church is assailed by so many enemies'. He assured them that

> from the hour in which I was called to an office at all times of most awful responsibility and more especially in these days of rebuke and peril, my attention has been fixed . . . on an earnest desire for the correction of abuses, and the removal of blemishes.

He went on, however, to add cautiously:

> But that which at first sight offends, is not always wrong. Parts, which singly considered, are pronounced to be faulty, may be found on a larger survey to possess a relative excellence, and to contribute by their bearings on the whole of the system to a

beneficial result. . . . A system again, far short of theoretic per-
fection, may be exquisitely adapted to the combination of
circumstances in this mixed state of things. . . . I am unwilling
to hazard its safety by rash innovation; nor could I venture to
act without full consideration of the probable consequences of
any change . . . [but] I have made it my object not only to
devise effectual remedies for real and acknowledged evils, but to
remove all grounds of a dissatisfaction, which whether founded
in reason or not, has a tendency to defeat the success of our
spiritual leaders.[242]

Looking back on these days some fifty years afterwards, Thomas
Mozley commented that it was a time when the Church seemed to be
'folding its robes to die with what dignity it could'.

The Reform Parliament of the thirties, however, equally under
Peel, who followed Lord John Russell, responded to the spirit of the
new pragmatism, whose simple test of utility, particularly where
institutions were concerned, weighed most of them in the balance
and found them wanting. It seemed obvious to those who could overcome the fear of reform and rid themselves of the conviction that all
ecclesiastical property was sacrosanct, that the national Church
stood condemned. Matthew Arnold took such a pessimistic view as to
affirm quite simply that 'no human power could save' it. The extreme
radical, Joseph Hume, referring in the House of Commons to ordinands, used language which might seem to justify the worst fears of
the authors of *Tracts for the Time*:

> For those who enter this body now that it is condemned by the
> country, when its charter is on the eve of being cancelled by the
> authority which gave it, when it is admitted on all hands to be
> not useless only, but absolutely detrimental, neither indulgence
> nor compensation can fairly be expected.

Some, but not all, of the political animosity directed against the
Church of England came, understandably, from those outside who
resented its privilege and patronage. But there were others who,
speaking the truth in love, saw its estate as deplorably unfitted for the
effective discharge of a contemporary duty. It was not difficult to
list its inadequacies: the vast yet maldistributed wealth, seen for
example in the glaring contrast between the capitular revenues of
Durham, enriched by its coal mines, and the crippling poverty of
many incumbents and assistant curates; the prevalence of non-
residence and absenteeism which defied episcopal efforts at control;
the slovenly character of worship and the neglect of church buildings.

This overall picture needs, of course, to be corrected here and there, but in general terms it is substantially true. For a reformed Parliament, intent upon introducing efficiency into the discharge of government at every level, local as well as national, the Church was a sitting target, and must expect drastic treatment. One thing was quite certain: the Church had no machinery to reform itself. The very nature of the Reformation settlement, quite independently of the immediate suppression of Convocation, meant that where change in the institution was needed only enforceable law, that is Parliament, could bring it about. Absenteeism and non-residence, though regulated by canons and statutes, had defied episcopal visitation for centuries; church courts in practice lacked effective powers and were being decreasingly used. As to any redistribution of financial resources, only legislation could over-ride the sacred rights of property.

Fortunately for the future of the Church of England there were some bishops, though a minority, who were well aware both of the need for reform and how to achieve it. Their chief representative was that forceful ecclesiastic Blomfield, Bishop of London, a man of great energy and equal resolution, who saw the contemporary plight of the Church in practical terms. Only a Church radically reformed in its structure could, he was convinced, perform its necessary task of restoring national morale. Equally important, he was prepared to co-operate with the Government in bringing this about.

But other attitudes obtained in the Church. There were those, of whom the Tractarians were the most extreme, who were contemptuous of change, and determined at all cost to resist it, the more so when it was imposed by Erastian legislation. Midway between these and such as Bishop Blomfield stood those who would tolerate moderate reform if only in the hope of preventing anything more radical.

Much depended on what line the Archbishop would himself take. His attitude to the Reform Bill had shown his natural conservatism, but it had also shown that his conservatism was combined with a hard core of realism when matters became really serious. He decided to take his stand with the moderates, that is with the group from whom there emerged 'the slightly mysterious' Scheme, drawn up by Joshua Watson, Christopher Wordsworth, and Van Mildert, which adumbrated a royal Commission of Inquiry. The proposed Commission was to consist exclusively of clergymen, and its terms of reference confined to 'the best practical remedies for the evils of translations, of unseemly commendams, and of offensive pluralities'. Howley himself announced in the House of Lords that he would introduce three bills—to make legal the composition of tithe payments over a short period of years; to facilitate the augmentation, by ecclesiastical persons, of small vicarages and curacies; to restrict pluralities.

Only the second became law, Howley claiming for it that 'some of the small livings will be improved, without resorting to any objectionable measure to obtain that good end'. In the debate on pluralities which roamed widely and angrily over the whole field of ecclesiastical abuses, Howley typically responded to pressure by himself suggesting an investigation of ecclesiastical revenues. 'The Church,' he added, with an optimism which the facts did not warrant, 'has nothing to fear from enquiry; such an enquiry would, I think, be highly beneficial. An ecclesiastical commission for this very purpose, Lord Grey replied, was 'on the way'; and he later announced the setting up of such a body, its terms of reference being to investigate all Church finances. To quote from G. F. A. Best's succinct words in *Temporal Pillars*: 'The serious business of Church reform had at last begun.'[243]

II

It was a critical and challenging time for Archbishop Howley. Perhaps he underwent an intellectual conversion through the contagion of Blomfield's zeal; or more probably saw the way things were going and decided that it was wiser to go with them in the hope of directing their course. Certainly he now brought the authority of his office behind the cause of positive reform. Various factors may also have affected his judgement. First, he was easily swayed by more dominating personalities, and the death in 1836 of Van Mildert of Durham, the most popular bishop with the rank and file of the clergy and a strong opponent of any radical change, removed a constraining influence. Secondly, the drift to Rome associated with Tractarianism made Howley less susceptible to the advice of his High Church chaplains, who were for standing firm. Thirdly, his attendance at meetings of the newly established Ecclesiastical Commission, which required him to read a mass of statistics culled from the answers to countless inquiries, constituted a liberal education in the facts, and facts always counted with Howley.

The detailed story of the reforms of the 1830s, which effected almost a revolution in the constitution of a Church which had hitherto largely retained its medieval structure, lies outside the scope of this work. It began in Ireland where the suppression and amalgamation of a number of sees, which had provoked the bitter protest of John Keble in his famous Assize sermon in 1833, was regarded by reformers as in the nature of a pilot scheme to be later applied to England.

Certainly this was how Peel felt about it on becoming Prime Minister. His first step was to consult both Blomfield and Howley, and with their approval to proceed with the reform of the Church of England by way of a semi-independent Commission, the clerical membership of which he left to the Archbishop. Howley, in addition to himself, proposed Vernon Harcourt of York, Bishops Kaye and Monk, and of course Blomfield. This statutory body, formally designated the Ecclesiastical Duties and Revenues Commission, soon metamorphosed itself into the Ecclesiastical Commissioners. Sir Robert Peel's government did not last long, but long enough for a conservative churchman to complain that in his short administration of 135 days he did more mischief to the Church than 135 years would be able to repair. With the resignation of his ministry, Melbourne took over, and Howley had to use his influence to preserve the balanced lay and clerical membership of the Commission.

The Commission's activity proved to be prodigious. It redistributed episcopal revenues; abolished unnecessary offices, using the money to augment poor livings; adjusted diocesan boundaries; and created new parishes by Orders in Council. Tithe in kind was abolished and converted into a rent charge. Pluralities were suppressed and residence enforced. It is highly to Howley's credit, and this greatly influenced the ordinary run of clergy who were well aware of his natural conservatism, that whatever his earlier misgivings he threw himself with energy into the work of the Commission. Though he lacked Blomfield's administrative drive and grasp of detail, he yet stuck manfully to the necessary task of working out the mechanics of reform. He and Blomfield were the two most regular attenders at the Commission, and since its membership was small— some thirteen—and most of the work was done in the general committee of which three constituted a quorum, they were able to exercise a strong influence upon decisions. No doubt Blomfield produced most of the ideas, but it was Howley's unique authority that ensured their implementation. Moreover, in the House of Lords Howley consistently led the bishops in supporting the work of the Commission; and when he spoke, he spoke, if awkwardly, yet from knowledge.

It is difficult to see how the work of reform could have gone steadily forward apart from his support, particularly in view of much opposition from within the Church.

One by-product of the ecclesiastical reforms which he himself sponsored was that by reducing the income of the see of Canterbury to £15,000 per annum, he permanently deprived the primacy of a great deal of its former magnificence. No more riding in a coach from Lambeth to Westminster flanked by outriders; no more retainers bearing *flambeaux* to escort the Archbishop across the courtyard of the Palace from the chapel (which he restored) to his wife's lodgings; no more public days of general entertainment when the food and wine were served by thirty flunkeys dressed in livery and fifteen waiting outside. It was the end of an age. By contrast, Howley's successor, the simple and pious evangelical John Bird Sumner, lived at Lambeth the life of a country gentleman, walking from the Palace to Parliament with his umbrella under his arm. He lived, however, in a residence to which Archbishop Howley, partly from his own resources, had added an imposing wing which extended eastward from Cranmer's Tower, and converted Juxon's Hall into a library.

Howley's preoccupations were by no means confined to the problems created by the organizational reforms of the Ecclesiastical Commission. His archiepiscopate saw John Keble's Assize sermon on 14 July 1833, in protest against the proposed suppression of twelve Irish bishoprics; the publication of *Tracts for the Times*; and Newman's secession to Rome in 1845. With the Oxford Movement, which in this early university phase had as its main objective the defence of the Church of England as a divine society preserving its apostolic order, Howley was not out of sympathy, and kept in touch with its leaders through Hugh James Rose, his chaplain. Yet he had in fact acquiesced in the Irish Temporalities Bill, and was anxious not to embroil himself or commit his office overmuch. It was a typically archiepiscopal attitude in a comprehensive church. He courteously received petitions from some 6,530 ministers and 230,000 heads of families expressing their attachment to the apostolic constitution of the Church of England, but his welcome was guarded. Equally when Melbourne appointed Hampden—suspected of unorthodoxy—to the Regius Professorship of Divinity at Oxford in 1836, for which Howley had put forward the names of Pusey, Percy, Newman, and Keble, he declined any public controversy; and when some twelve years later Hampden was nominated to the see of Hereford, he did not sign the memorial of the protesting bishops—not surprisingly, since he had assured Russell that he knew of no doctrinal irregularities in Hampden's lectures. Howley died before the consecration.

In co-operation with Blomfield he ignored High Church opposition to the establishment of the Jerusalem bishopric. The general idea of this Anglo-German project was to place a bishop in Jerusalem to look after such Anglicans and German Lutherans as might care to put themselves under his jurisdiction. Friendly relations were to be established with the Orthodox Churches and the conversion of Jews promoted. The bishop might ordain an Anglican if he assented to the Thirty-nine Articles, or a German minister who subscribed to the

297

Confession of Augsburg. The scheme obviously had political implications, and for this reason was supported by Lord Palmerston and the
Queen. English church opinion was divided as to its propriety, even
within the ranks of the Tractarians. Newman voiced his suspicion
that 'there was great reason to suppose that the said Bishop was
intended to make converts from the orthodox Greeks, and the
schismatical Oriental bodies'. Howley felt no reservations, and it was
he who introduced the Bill creating the bishopric into the House of
Lords and consecrated Michael Solom Alexander in Lambeth
Chapel as the first Bishop. To make the position unambiguous,
Howley addressed a letter to the Orthodox Patriarchs dated 23
November 1841 which said:

> In order to prevent any misunderstanding in regard to this our
> purpose, we think it right to make known unto you that we have
> charged the said bishop our brother not to intermeddle in any
> way with the jurisdiction of the prelates and other ecclesiastical
> dignitaries of the East, but to show them due reverence.[244]

Howley was no pioneer, but in his own quiet way he showed a
lifelong interest in the expansion of the Anglican Church. During his
years at Lambeth twelve new bishops were consecrated to British
colonies overseas, which brought the Archbishop into an even closer
relationship with the two great missionary societies which sponsored
them.

The work of the National Society also found in him a steady
champion; the more so as he became increasingly suspicious of the
growing involvement of the State in the education of the nation's
young. In this he was typical of many churchmen who gave a mixed
reception to the setting up of the Committee of Education by Lord
John Russell in 1839 under an Order in Council. The Archbishop
deplored that so great an innovation should be introduced without
an Act of Parliament. Evangelicals and High Churchmen, even
Methodists, from their varying standpoints, came to regard its
activities with grave suspicion. To Lord Ashley it seemed as if the
State were going to take over 'the temporal and eternal destinies of
countless millions'. Archbishop Howley led the Lords as a body in
protest to the Queen, asking her to halt these developments. The
Queen, though receiving the delegation courteously, acted with
impeccable constitutional propriety in refusing to intervene.

Reference to the Queen may serve to introduce Howley's relations
with the Royal Family, which began with the flashy George IV. He
officiated at all baptisms (including that of Victoria), marriages and
funerals which took place during his years at Lambeth. He crowned

the Sailor King who disported himself in the uniform of an admiral
of the fleet for the occasion. He was present at his bedside when, as
'the sun of Waterloo set', William died at Windsor soon after two
o'clock on the morning of 20 June 1837, with the name of Howley on
his lips. Taking horse immediately, the Archbishop, in company with
the Lord Chamberlain and the King's physician, rode through the
darkness to Kensington Palace. Arrived there he and his companions
were admitted to the Princess, who received them alone, having
thrown a cotton gown over her nightdress, and her long hair flowing
free.

The Archbishop presided over her coronation in Westminster
Abbey in the following year, on a brilliant summer day. Many
hitches, for which he was partly to blame, disturbed the smooth running of the elaborate ritual. He forced the ruby ring on to her fourth
finger though it had been intended for her fifth, and only by dowsing
the injured member in cold water could the Queen painfully remove
it. He proceeded to seek for the orb only to find that she had received
it from another's hand; 'and . . . (as usual) was *so* confused and
puzzled and knew nothing and went away'.[245] Howley himself confessed afterwards: 'We ought to have had a full rehearsal.' Fortunately the service was redeemed by the sincerity and artlessness of the
Queen herself, a young girl of nineteen. It is ironic that at her
marriage he tried to make Albert put the ring on her right hand!
Still, she ended up by liking her Archbishop.

Howley was sometimes critical at the influence of the kindly, if
somewhat cynical, Melbourne upon the young Queen. In view of
her subsequent reputation, it seems somewhat out of character that
he should need to take exception to the almost continental gaiety of
her Sundays.

> More than once during the Melbourne ministry—so *The Times*
> wrote—he respectfully tendered to the Crown advice not quite
> in accordance with the wishes of those who at that time sur-
> rounded our youthful and inexperienced sovereign.[246]

Things were to change once the Prince Consort had taken over.

The Archbishop died peacefully at Lambeth on 11 February 1848,
a day before his eighty-third birthday, repeating the words: 'Leave
off from wrath and let go displeasure: fret not thyself, else shalt thou
be moved to do evil.'

He had achieved much.

# 2

## JOHN BIRD SUMNER: CONTROVERSY AND CONVOCATION

I

Howley was succeeded by John Bird Sumner, whose younger brother built up his early fortunes on his friendship with George IV, becoming Bishop of Winchester in 1827. John Sumner rose to high ecclesiastical office in the usual pattern of those days. From Eton he went to King's College, Cambridge; became incumbent of the valuable living of Maple Durham; was nominated to the ninth prebendal stall in Durham Cathedral, which at a convenient season he exchanged for the fifth and then the second stall, each more lucrative than the previous. He was not, however, the avaricious cleric which such a progression might seem to suggest. In many ways he was a good representative of the moderate, sincere, if somewhat limited evangelical churchman. He produced a steady output of theological works, mainly biblical in character, of which *The Evidence of Christianity derived from its Nature and Reception*, published in 1824, bore the marks of the somewhat arid theology of a century earlier, and was reissued in the '60s as a *riposte* to *Essays and Reviews*, the latter being an 'advanced' symposium, to which reference will be made later.

Scholarship, family connexions, political discretion and genuine piety led to Wellington's appointing him Bishop of Chester in 1828, after he had refused the bishopric of Sodor and Man the previous year. If his voting in favour of Catholic Emancipation offended George IV it was not unacceptable to the Iron Duke. To the clergy of his diocese he explained at length his position; his main thesis being that 'the advantages to be expected from the measure are greater than any mischiefs which we have a right to apprehend'.[247] It was unlikely, he pointed out, that the hundred Irish members to be returned to Parliament would all be Roman Catholics, since it was ownership of property which determined electoral rights. True, members of that Church would be admitted to all offices of state except those of Lord Chancellor and the Lord Privy Seal, but 'admissibility' was very different from 'admission'. Even if the worst were to happen and there was a Roman Catholic Prime Minister—

he had unsuccessfully tried to secure that ecclesiastical preferment should be taken out of his hands—he could only nominate to office those who were 'qualified by law to hold such preferment'.[248]

Sumner was one of twelve bishops who voted for the Reform Bill of 1832, and was put by the Government on the Poor Law Commission which Blomfield chaired—a social concern in which he had already shown an interest as is seen in his article in the *Encyclopaedia Britannica* of 1824.

With all his amiability and his anxiety to do the right thing, Sumner was not always perceptive in distinguishing between good and bad advice. He had neither the capacity nor the inclination to offer real leadership, lacking the essential flair. His best work was almost certainly done at Chester, where he showed himself a practical and energetic reformer. He encouraged the erection of schools, and visited his diocese with thoroughness every three years, preparing on each occasion an elaborate charge which was later printed. Before he left he was said to have consecrated over two hundred churches.

William Howley died at a critical moment in the affairs of the Church of England, since Hampden's consecration was imminent. It was therefore necessary for Lord John Russell to nominate an Archbishop who would undertake it, which meant a narrowing of the field since some seventeen bishops had protested against the appointment.

Henry Phillpotts of Exeter talked freely of the Prime Minister going about with a lantern like Diogenes to find a dishonest man who would make a bishop out of one who was equally unworthy. There were rumours, disquieting to high churchmen, that Richard Whately, the liberal Archbishop of Dublin, would be chosen. Connop Thirlwall, a distinguished historian, lacked practical pastoral sense. Samuel Wilberforce had been only three years at Oxford and was unpopular at the Palace. On 17 February, the nomination was announced of John Bird Sumner, who, though condemning Hampden's earlier views, had decided not to join his episcopal colleagues in protest. The Bishop of Hereford, to the relief of some and the chagrin of others, was consecrated in Lambeth Chapel on 26 March 1848.

On his previous record at Chester, Sumner might have seemed admirably suited to the challenge of his age; but his position as a convinced, if moderate evangelical, did not make it easy for him to be objectively eirenical towards the Church of England as a whole, particularly when the Oxford Movement, in the form of ritualism, was beginning to invade the parishes. Certainly an appointment which was acceptable to both Russell and the Prince Consort could hardly be expected to commend itself in high Anglican circles. Nor did it. Sumner's solution, though he made blunders, was to stick as closely as he could to what he regarded as the law of the land. A test came early in the famous case of the Reverend G. C. Gorham, near-Calvinist, antiquarian and botanist, which raised the question as to where authority for doctrine in the Church of England finally lay.

Gorham was a Low Church clergyman, whose views on baptismal regeneration early created a stir, to such an extent, indeed, that Bishop Dampier of Ely had threatened to refuse him ordination in 1811. Though himself a man of extreme views, Gorham yet served to high-light the position of evangelicals within the national Church at a time when the Oxford Movement had introduced a new dimension into theological thinking. It was within this wider context that the attitude of the Archbishop of Canterbury became significant.

The immediate crisis arose when Gorham, in November 1847, was presented by the Crown to the living of Brampford Speke, in the diocese of that doughty fighter and High Churchman, Henry Phillpotts, Bishop of Exeter. Phillpotts declined to institute without first submitting Gorham to an examination, the outcome of which—his 'penal inquisition'—was a firm refusal. Gorham retaliated by applying to the Court of Arches, which directed Phillpotts to institute unless he could show reason to the contrary. The case was then argued, and the Court held that Gorham, in making baptismal regeneration dependent upon worthy reception, had in fact contravened Church of England teaching. Gorham then appealed away from the Canterbury Court of Arches to the Judicial Committee of the Privy Council, which in 1833 had replaced the Court of Delegates. When the case came before it on 11 December, there sat the two Archbishops Sumner and Musgrave, both evangelicals, Blomfield, Bishop of London, and seven lay judges. Dr. Baddeley, one of Phillpotts's counsel, objected to the presence of the Archbishop of Canterbury on the grounds of his having recently given the living of All Hallows the Great, London, to William Goode, who held opinions similar to those of Gorham. Sumner defended himself with some heat, receiving a partial apology, and at the next meeting produced a paper in which he protested 'that the Bishop was not justified' in making his membership a matter for questioning. The Judicial Committee, on 9 March, reversed the decision of the Arches. Gorham's baptismal doctrine, it declared, was 'not contrary or repugnant to the declared doctrine of the Church of England as by law established'. Gorham should therefore not be refused institution. Both Archbishops concurred in this judgement, Blomfield, however, dissenting.

This decision of the Judicial Committee aroused a storm, and led to a number of secessions to Rome, the chaplain of the Bishop of

Exeter, who had examined Gorham, being one of them. In the eyes of such people it now seemed as if even doctrine in the Church of England was to be determined by a purely secular court. It was for them no answer to say that the court merely stated what that doctrine was, but did not attempt to define it.

Not unexpectedly the belligerent Phillpotts still refused to institute. The patron, therefore, appealed for redress to the Metropolitan.

The question now was whether the Archbishop could, as Ordinary, interfere in the jurisdiction of a subordinate diocese. It was at this critical juncture that Phillpotts issued, on 25 March, his famous letter to the Archbishops, which owed much to Pusey. Somewhat unkindly he quoted one of Sumner's own books, *Apostolical Preaching considered in an Examination of St. Paul's Epistles*, detecting there a low view of baptism inappropriate in one who was called upon to advise the lay judges.

> I grieve to think—the letter continued—that, instead of leading, you must have misled those whom you were to instruct not only by mis-stating the matters on which you advised, but also by mis-quoting all, or almost all the authors cited by you in confirmation of your statement.

There then followed these solemn words:

> I have to protest, and I do hereby solemnly protest, before the Church of England, before the Holy Catholic Church, before Him who is its Divine Head, against you giving mission to exercise cure of souls, within my diocese, to a clergyman who proclaims himself to hold the heresies which Mr. Gorham holds. . . . I protest, in conclusion, that I cannot without sin— and by God's grace, I will not—hold communion with him, be he who he may, who shall so abuse the high commission which he bears.[249]

This letter was followed, on 15 August, by an equally solemn warning to the churchwardens of Brampford Speke in which, as Bishop, he 'renounce[d] and repudiate[d] all communion with anyone, be he who he may, who shall so institute the said George Cornelius Gorham as aforesaid.'

Sumner was determined not to be deterred by such public antics, and Gorham was duly instituted by the Dean of the Arches under the Archbishop's fiat.

In this difficult case Sumner had not always given the appearance of strict impartiality, but he sought to stick to the law.

His involvement in the controversy deliberately provoked by that High Church firebrand, the belligerent Archdeacon Denison, Vicar of East Brent in Somerset, was even less happy, and far more ambiguous.

Denison, having failed to persuade Richard Bagot, the decrepit Bishop of Oxford, to prosecute him for his sacramental views, preached three sermons in Wells Cathedral on the Real Presence, hoping thereby to force a public debate. He was not disappointed. In 1855, Joseph Ditcher, vicar of a neighbouring parish and briefed by the Evangelical Alliance, brought the matter before the Archbishop. Sumner, in spite of the fact that two Bishops of Oxford had refused to prosecute, was advised that under a clause in the Church Discipline Act of 1840 (designed, incidentally, to protect an incumbent from a bishop-patron) he had no option but to appoint a commission of inquiry. Such a commission, to which Sumner unwisely nominated five evangelical clergymen, decided after proceedings which have been described as 'ludicrous'—no doctrinal evidence was permitted—that there was a *prima facie* case for the Archdeacon to answer.

Sumner now seems to have had some misgivings, since for a time he did nothing. Ditcher, losing patience, applied to the Queen's Bench to compel the Archbishop to proceed, and in April 1856, secured a writ of mandamus to this effect, Lord Chief Justice Campbell expressing regrets that Sumner had not declined to go forward at an earlier stage.

The scene now changed to Bath, where the Archbishop sat with two anti-Tractarian clergymen as assessors, and with Dr. Lushington, who had years before handled, or mishandled, Lady Byron's divorce, as his legal adviser. This Court declared that the views of Archdeacon Denison were repugnant to the 28th and 29th Articles of Religion. The judgement was anathema to many High churchmen, and Pusey and Keble were among those who signed a protest asking for the matter to be dealt with by 'a free and lawful synod of the Province of Canterbury'. Sumner incurred a great deal of odium from one wing of Anglican opinion for setting up the Articles, in isolation, as the doctrinal norm of the Church of England.

The end of this extraordinary, and in many respects Gilbertian, legal battle was not yet in sight. Denison appealed from the Archbishop to the Archbishop's own Provincial Court of Arches: but the Dean of the Court, regarding this as a nonsense, would not allow it. He was, however, compelled to do so by a writ of mandamus from the Queen's Bench, but by a piece of good fortune discovered that the prosecution was invalid from the beginning in that it had not been initiated within two years of the preaching of the sermons.[250]

304

Sumner did not come well out of these proceedings, and as a consequence the impartial status of his office had been prejudiced as well as the general position of evangelicals living alongside Tractarians in the Church of England. He had made a number of misjudgements and accepted unwise advice from at least one quarter. It is significant that the Government seldom consulted him about the choice of bishops either at home or abroad. Also the whole legal credibility of the establishment in relation to a particular aspect of the Church's life was called in question. Even Sumner admitted that the Judicial Committee of the Privy Council was not a proper judge of matters of doctrine; but when Blomfield suggested that the Committee should accept the collective voice of the bishops as its criterion of orthodoxy, Lord John Russell rejected with scorn any resort to what he described as the 'dogmatic decrees of a dominant hierarchy'. In reverse, when Lord John Russell, egged on by the Prince Consort, contemplated arming the Privy Council with powers to suppress ritualism, the Archbishop protested, and protested successfully.

Sumner's general theological position was undoubtedly suspect to those who, influenced by the Oxford Movement, ascribed great importance to the pre-Reformation inheritance of the Church of England. Phillpotts complained bitterly that the Archbishop even used the weight of his office to involve, against their will, some of his brethren in the view that 'the apostolic succession [was] an empty boast'. Blomfield felt that Sumner wrote too many letters to all and sundry. Also it was rumoured, almost certainly unfairly, that he had conferred with Russell as to omitting certain doctrinal passages from the Book of Common Prayer.

II

Sumner's main concern, and this became occupational with Archbishops who followed him, was to damp down theological controversy and persuade both clergy and laity to direct their energies to more practical pursuits. He regarded his own theological position as biblical. Thus when in the House of Lords he opposed the Bill to legalize marriage with a deceased wife's sister, he appealed simply and solely to scriptural authority.

> It would not, however, be necessary to trouble their Lordships at any length—he said—The argument on which he relied, and on which he grounded his opinion, lay in a small compass; in fact, he considered that the question at issue had been decided for them, being already settled by the law of God. . . . It is no slight advantage that they should be told by authors which

could not err, where the conjugal relationship might and might not exist.[251]

Equally, in voting for the Divorce Act of 1857, he was convinced that the Scriptures allowed divorce for adultery but forbade remarriage to the guilty party. In his visitational charge to the clergy of the same year he stated categorically:

> To doubt or deny the inspiration of Scripture, so as to suppose that it can contain anything inconsistent with the purpose and the mind of God, is to attribute to the Almighty a want of foresight (I speak it with reverence) which we should hardly expect to find even in man's weak and fallible nature.[252]

Such biblical fundamentalism may now strike us as naïve, but it was common in those days and Sumner's own formative years were long behind him. In his eyes the practical problem facing the Church was the reconversion of England, and to achieve this the recovery of its status as the conscience of the nation. But he could not in his office ignore changing theological ideas. The pity was that his own limitations caused him to lack sympathy, where a greater sensitivity to opinions not his own would have made a more creative leadership possible.

Fortunately, there were a number of thinking clergymen who saw that a faith which refused to face up to new climates of thought and scientific opinion could not hope finally to perform its traditional function of interpreting man to himself. It was out of such a concern that *Essays and Reviews* was published in 1860, a symposium in which scholars with varying degrees of insight tried to look at the Christian faith, biblical and doctrinal, within the context of new scientific developments. The essayists included Frederick Temple, a future Archbishop of Canterbury; Benjamin Jowett, Master of Balliol, who maintained that the Bible should be read like any other book; Mark Pattison; and Professor Baden Powell, an unequivocal supporter of the concept of evolution as a key category. What did much to prejudice the essayists was the unsolicited approval given to the volume by Frederick Harrison who, having lost his Christian convictions, had become a disciple of the French positivist Auguste Compte.

The bishops largely took their cue from Samuel Wilberforce, who rallied them with vigour to the defence of the faith. Here the more 'canny' Tait, Bishop of London, and Thirlwall, scholar and Bishop of St. David's, reluctantly fell into line. John Bird Sumner felt keenly his own position as Archbishop, and had little sympathy with the essayists. In company with many of his predecessors, he saw it as one of the functions of his office to reassure public opinion. But his own experience in the Denison case made him realize, as he told a deputation which came to Lambeth, that 'ecclesiastical courts are so encumbered by forms and technicalities, that it is very doubtful whether it would be wise to appeal to them'.[253]

The *furore* aroused by the publication inevitably spilled over into the newly revived Convocation, where Tait endeavoured to remove from the general condemnation the essays of Jowett and Temple. Archbishop Sumner ruled that nothing further could be done until the bishops of the Northern Convocation had deliberated. The result was a joint meeting of the bishops of both provinces over which he presided. By a majority of one it was decided to prosecute some of the essayists individually; but since the Bishop of Salisbury had already instituted proceedings against Rowland Williams, Vice-Principal of Lampeter, who was felt to have treated the Scriptures in a somewhat flippant manner, further action was deferred.

Sumner now became involved personally when, in December 1861, H. H. Wildon, Vicar of Great Staughton, who had pleaded for a relaxation of the formularies, was brought with Rowland Williams before the Court of Arches. The Archbishop, however, died before judgement was pronounced.

It is clear that Sumner himself had little understanding of the new movements in thought which were agitating the minds of many sincere Christians. His over-riding preoccupation, understandably, was to prevent the over-exposure of disagreements within the Church, and it was for this reason that he showed little enthusiasm for the attempt to revive a sitting Convocation. Public debate could be divisive.

That there should develop an agitation for the reassembling of this ancient synod after its long years of suppression was understandable. High Churchmen and Tractarians, in their protest against contemporary secularism, felt that the Church must make its voice heard through its own historic assembly. Practical ecclesiastics such as Blomfield, eager for reform and imbued with a high view of the episcopal office, supported the demand. Laymen like Henry Hoare, who looked forward to the day when such a body would not be exclusively clerical, were equally committed. The 'Society for the Revival of Convocation' worked hard, and a fillip was given to its efforts by the anger which was aroused over Pope Pius IX's Bull of 1850 making England a province of the Roman Church.

Sumner never disguised the fact that he was unhappy at the prospect of a sitting Convocation. Abstract ideas as to what was proper made little appeal to him apart from their utility. Such an attitude had become traditional in archbishops as was seen when

L

Howley quoted with approval Secker's negative words on this subject. On 4 February 1852, Sumner appealed to his episcopal brethren 'to forbear pressing the subject at the present moment, when so few members of Convocation properly understood its functions'. No matter how much synodical action might be desired, he saw little point in petitioning Her Majesty, since 'in the present state of the Church and its multitudinous discussions, their prayer would never be granted'.[254] But the Archbishop proved to be wrong; for Lord Derby thought it prudent to advise the Crown to allow Convocation to meet for business.

The revival of an historic assembly after so many years of enforced inactivity was bound to lead to problems. Sumner, with a long memory stretching back into the previous century, determined that the position of the Archbishop of Canterbury as President of Convocation should be in no way weakened. To this end he declared, on 16 November 1852, that he had 'no idea of surrendering the rights of proroguing Convocation, which had been exercised by all his predecessors'.[255] This and other preliminary difficulties having been disposed of, the Queen was formally petitioned 'to grant Your Royal Licence to order our deliberations', an assurance being added that there existed 'a steadfast endeavour . . . to preserve unimpaired the doctrine and discipline of our Church'.[256]

All was not to be plain sailing, however. Long disuse undoubtedly led to many uncertainties as to correct procedure, and Blomfield, in 1854, moved that a committee be set up 'for the improvement of the Constitution of the Convocation, so as to make it more suitable to the altered circumstances of the Church, and to enable it to discharge its functions in such a manner as to conduce to its increased stability.'[257] Sumner was again apprehensive, fearing what the effect of such a discussion might be on the Establishment as a whole. To his brethren he confessed frankly that

> he had not the same expectation of any great advantage to the more important parts of the Church from any deliberations of this Committee which the Right Reverend Prelates seemed to entertain. He believed that at present they had within themselves quite as much, if not more, beneficial action than any Convocation could give, and he would appeal to everyone of their lordships, whether they did not know many parishes in which they could not expect, by any alteration of rule or doctrinal formularies, a greater amount of [sic] Christian truth or a greater amount of Christian practice.

If the Church wished to have the power herself 'of settling and determining these things' then the whole constitution of the *Ecclesia*

*Anglicana* would need to be changed. As it was, 'it must be settled by Parliament before it could be binding on the Church'.[258]

The Committee met, and the report which the Bishop of London presented to the House raised four important questions affecting the rights of the Archbishop as President:

1. Had he the right to refuse to submit to the Upper House any proposition made by one or more of its members? Here the precedents were not decisive.

2. Had he a casting vote? The answer was 'yes'.

3. Could he, after a resolution had passed both Houses, negative it on his own authority? Once again the answer was 'yes'.

4. Could he prorogue Convocation against the wishes of his brethren? Here the precedents were indecisive.

To Sumner the Establishment was sacrosanct and he was, therefore, anxious to prevent Convocation putting forward exaggerated claims on its own behalf. When, for example, in 1857, a petition was presented from the clergy of the Exeter diocese, asking that a fuller use be made of the Act of Henry VIII which provided for the appointment of suffragan bishops—their own diocesan, Henry Phillpotts, was now over seventy—Sumner commented that he thought the petition was not one which ought to be addressed to the Upper House. When the Bishop of Oxford introduced a motion concerning special services, the President gave his casting vote in favour of an amendment by the Bishop of London to prevent any hasty action. Yet though adamant against revision of the liturgy as a whole he showed himself not entirely averse to some adaptation of the Prayer Book to special needs.

> If we did not imagine that in the end we should adopt these services—he said on 7 June 1860—we had better stop. But I should be well prepared to adopt them, and I do not see how any occasional services are to be adopted but by acting as we are now doing—making the best selection we can; and therefore I think we should send them down as perfect as possible.[259]

It was unwise, so he commented later,

> to enforce any new hymn book on the Church. . . . No doubt a large variety of hymn books is undesirable, but the same hymns are pretty generally chosen, and if any attempt is made to interfere with the liberty of those who have hitherto made the selection, a great dissatisfaction will be felt.[260]

Generally, when John Bird Sumner looked around him at the life of the Church, he saw there much to encourage him. In fact the enterprise of the evangelicals; the witness of the Oxford Movement to the transcendent character of Christian faith and its Catholic inheritance; the sense of national mission which characterized broad churchmen such as Thomas Arnold; the Christian socialism of F. D. Maurice and Charles Kingsley—all these had worked together from within, sometimes in spite of themselves, to invigorate a Church whose organizational structure had been overhauled by parliamentary enactment and the setting up of the Ecclesiastical Commission. Sumner believed intensely that the Church's mission must now reach out to the irreligious masses in England; as well as to the heathen overseas, to whom, he told his clergy in 1857, 'we are bound to hold forth that light, which is designed to lighten every man that cometh into the world'.[261] Thus during the 50th anniversary year of the Church Missionary Society, he actively identified himself with its celebrations. He looked to the future with hope, for he had caught to the full the contagion of Victorian optimism.

> . . . the age is an age of progress. Everything is advancing. Wealth, knowledge, art, science, have advanced, within the last 50 years, in a manner which we cannot contemplate without astonishment. Things which would have once been deemed impossible, are become familiar to our thoughts; things which would have been pronounced incredible, are daily brought before our eyes. It might therefore have been a trial to our Faith if, whilst everything else was making progress, the religion of the Gospel alone remained behind. But let thanks be given to our Divine Head, the Gospel is liable to no such disparagement. Much as there is to be lamented, much as there is to be amended amongst us, no one can compare the present state of religious feeling in this country with its state at the beginning of the century, without a sense of gratitude. . . . The general aspect of Christianity affords just ground for encouragement.[262]

Sumner was undoubtedly more at home in his diocese and in supporting the Church Missionary Society than in presiding over the deliberations of his provincial synod. In his own territory, he encouraged clergy and laity to discuss their problems together, and parish priests to confer in their deaneries. Even Phillpotts commended the Archbishop for allowing that there was nothing to prevent clergy of the diocese from assembling for their common good.

Sumner saw the parish priest as occupying a unique role, and believed that his initiative and energy could bring practical results. His charges to his clergy, therefore, suggested means by which they could allow leadership. Thus he was very keen to encourage district visitors, such as would prove 'a unique help to an incumbent in the management of his parish', and help to keep it under 'discipline' and 'pastoral superintendence'. Each visitor should be allocated forty families, thus making it possible for him to become 'an affectionate friend'.[263]

Sumner knew at first hand the appalling conditions of the poor in the great towns, and though he admitted that religion was 'not more really necessary to them than to every man [yet they] are really more destitute without it who in this world have evil things'. As at Chester, Sumner encouraged the building of churches, and deplored the fact that such a good work was beset with so many legal difficulties, though made somewhat easier under a statute passed in the reign of William IV.

> ... in future times—he said—men will be slow to believe, that the members of our Church were the only parties who were forbidden by law to provide the means of worship for themselves, and so to maintain proper ecclesiastical discipline and order.[264]

John Bird Sumner died at Addington on 6 September 1862, after Bishop Phillpotts had sent him a brotherly message to which the aged Archbishop warmly responded. His tenure of office had not been distinguished. Perhaps the blame, if blame there be, must rest with Lord John Russell, and the exceptional situation within which he was called upon to appoint.

He was succeeded by Charles Thomas Longley, Archbishop of York.

# 3

## CHARLES THOMAS LONGLEY AND THE
## LAMBETH CONFERENCE

I

The last decades of the XIXth century were years of political liberalism, with a militant nonconformity playing an ever increasing role. They were also years of growing secularism. Neither was prepared to acquiesce passively in the privileged position of an established Church, particularly where it affected national education. Thus the *Ecclesia Anglicana* became the target for a great deal of hostile propaganda, which meant, paradoxically, that the Church became news, and this in itself made the Archbishop more of a public figure than he had been for a long time.

The XIXth century, as a whole, witnessed the great expansionist phase in British history, realizing itself in the birth of an Empire upon which—so was the proud boast—the sun never set. The nation of shopkeepers, whose plebeian virtues provoked the contempt of Napoleon, that man of destiny, turned its energy to securing a mercantile supremacy which the Royal Navy protected and industrialists zealously exploited.

This imperial role not only excited the imagination of the romantic Disraeli, but was understood by the more religious as imposing upon the British Raj in distant outposts, as well as upon every citizen at home, a solemn obligation. Tractarian as well as Evangelical discerned the work of divine Providence in this ordering of national affairs. To evangelize the heathen, to bring them out of their ignorance and unbelief into the verities of the Gospel, seemed a clear duty resting upon those on whom the Light had shone in such brilliance. To Britons abroad it was natural to assume that wherever the sovereignty of the Crown extended, there the Church of England with its episcopal government and its Book of Common Prayer should follow. Thus bishops were appointed by Letters Patent under the Crown, took their oaths on consecration, and owed allegiance to the Archbishop of Canterbury. Contemporaries little realized the difficulties which they were laying up for the future in thus identifying the cause of empire with the claims of Christ. Yet problems began early as these dependent territories grew to maturity and set up their own legislatures. Whatever the outcome, this expansion of the Church of England gave an added prestige to the primatial see of Canterbury, and led to its discovering a new if sometimes embarrassing role.

The result was that into Lambeth there began to flow (as Archbishop Longley's correspondence, in some seven volumes, makes evident) a vast flood of letters from overseas bishops asking advice, reporting on the conditions of their churches, and sometimes—in their loneliness—simply seeking encouragement. Secretaries of State for the Colonies, in discharging their difficult role, sought the Archbishop's advice and compliance.

The revival of church life generally, not least in the field of educational involvement, also had its repercussions upon the archiepiscopal office. It meant that the Church of England as the nation's schoolmaster—though it became increasingly unable to maintain this role—represented a political interest which could not be ignored. Legislation such, for example, as Forster's Education Act of 1870, could not be embarked upon without consulting the Church authorities. This, for a harassed government, meant tackling the Archbishop of Canterbury, and leaving him to consult his brother bishops, and, if he wished, to introduce the matter into Convocation, the revival of which traditional assembly brought to its president another field of activity. The drawing up of new canons, first under Longley in 1865, as well as public alarm at ritualistic disturbances in the parishes, brought Parliament into the Church's life. These rubbed off on the Archbishop.

The more leisured days when such as Archbishop Wake could boast of living in privacy were becoming a thing of the past. Archbishops began to feel the strain of their diverse responsibilities and Longley confessed in a visitational charge to his clergy:

> The present state of the Church, at home and abroad, the multiplication of the Colonial Episcopate, and the great uncertainty as to the legal *status* of several of the Colonial Sees, must entail upon me an amount of labour and anxiety which has not fallen to the lot of my predecessors within the last century and a half. . . . Far more congenial to my tastes and feelings are those engagements which bring me into communion with yourselves, enabling me to support and encourage you in the discharge of your parochial duties [than] those matters which demand my presence in the Metropolis.[265]

C. T. Longley came to the Archbishopric of Canterbury at sixty-

313

eight years of age, and held the office for only six years. He felt acutely the burden of his care. Yet he was able to show surprising strength of purpose when need be. Entering into the archiepiscopate at a time of great stress and strain, his consistent policy was to reduce tension; to encourage obedience to the law; and to advocate change only if there were real need. His experience before going to Canterbury was wide. He had held office as a censor of Christ Church and university proctor; he was presented to two livings; became headmaster of Harrow (where a young man, Colenso, was on his staff) and according to *The Times* obituary, would have been more successful had he been stricter.

His first taste of episcopal oversight was at Ripon, when this new see was carved out of the diocese of York. Lord Melbourne saw Longley as a man of liberal views who at the same time would not offend Tory and High Church susceptibilities. It was said that on his doing homage as Bishop of Ripon, William IV shouted: 'I charge you as you will answer before Almighty God that you never by word or deed give encouragement to those d——d whigs who would upset the Church of England.'[266]

Ripon's scattered hamlets and its dense mining and manufacturing populations made his diocesan responsibilities particularly onerous, and certainly somewhat different from his experience hitherto, but Longley threw himself into his work with energy. He encouraged the building of schools and churches, establishing for this purpose a Diocesan Church Extension Fund. He met difficulties—it was an augury of the shape of things to come—from the practice of auricular confession in the City of Leeds, a fact which he recalled some twenty years later in a charge to the clergy of Canterbury. He acted firmly, revoking the licence of the offending clergyman, being upheld in this by the Archbishop of York on appeal.

While at Ripon, Longley stayed in the parsonage at Haworth, certainly not suspecting its posthumous fame. Charlotte Brontë was delighted with their visitor and wrote to a friend:

> The bishop has been and gone. He is certainly a most charming bishop, the most benignant gentleman that ever put on lawn sleeves, yet stately too and competent to check encroachments. It is all very well to talk of receiving a bishop without trouble, but you must prepare for him. The house was a good deal put out of its way as you may suppose. All passed, however, quietly, orderly and well. Martha waited very nicely, and I had a person to help her in the kitchen. Papa kept up too, fully as well as I expected, though I doubt whether he could have borne another day of it.[267]

In 1856 Longley was nominated to the bishopric of Durham, and four years later became Archbishop of York. As Metropolitan he tactfully reversed the decision of his predecessor, and in 1861 summoned the Convocation of the Northern Province to meet for business.

> I cannot but deem it a very wholesome practice—he said—that the members of Convocation should have periodical opportunities of meeting together, of counselling in common for the advancement of the interests of the Church and of religion in the country. I believe that the more frequently such opportunities of mutual conference are afforded to the brethren in the ministry the greater will be the growth of harmony and good feeling which should subsist between those who are engaged in the same holy calling.[268]

It was a positive, if somewhat optimistic expectation. Longley was sympathetic to diocesan synods, and confessed that he would have gone ahead in establishing them were it not for the dissension they might cause in the diocese. This did not prevent his reviving ruridecanal chapters both at Ripon and Durham.

When Longley arrived at Canterbury in 1862 theological controversy was at its height. The stir caused by the publication of *Essays and Reviews* persisted as protagonists awaited the judgment of the Court of Arches. Also the disturbing repercussions, both in England and South Africa, of Bishop Colenso's critical studies of the Pentateuch were assuming every day larger proportions. The invasion of the parishes with the new ritualism brought emotional upset and, on occasions, physical violence.

In his handling of these difficult questions, Longley determined to prevent the clergy taking the law into their own hands whether it was a High Church clergyman in the East End or a distant Archbishop Gray anxious to preserve the faith entire and uncontaminated. This disciplinarian aspect of his responsibilities the Archbishop certainly did not relish. He was no William Laud.

In December 1862, Dr. Lushington declared the judgment of the Court of Arches. Both Wilson and Rowland Williams were condemned on various counts and suspended from their benefices for a year. Both appealed against this decision to the Judicial Committee of the Privy Council on which there sat the two Archbishops and Tait of London, as well as the Lord Chancellor and three law lords. In due course the Committee passed judgment, although in doing so it denied any intention of redefining Church of England doctrine. In a carefully worded document, which was read by the Lord Chancellor, it reversed the decision of the Court of Arches. From this judgment the two Archbishops dissented, although Tait went along with it.

Stanley, the liberal Dean of Westminster, and his fellow broad churchmen were delighted. 'I had not expected anything so clean and clear,' he wrote at the time. On the other hand 11,000 clergymen with 135,000 laymen signed an address of protest, thanking the Archbishops for their dissentient voice.

A somewhat embarrassed Longley decided that he must say something on his own account and for two reasons. First, because he had not felt free to comment at the time of the judgment since he was a member of the court which pronounced it. Secondly, because there was widespread disquiet in England as well as abroad, and he himself had received 'letters of enquiry expressing much perplexity'. 'It was a most painful position to be placed in,' he told his clergy, 'not to be permitted to utter a single word in disapproval of the terms of that judgement,' the more so since, although he had agreed to the conclusions, he had dissented from the premise. Understandably, therefore, 'many members of our Church eminent for their rank, station and talents have urged me to make a statement of my sentiments on these subjects'. The request was a fair one, since as Archbishop 'the Church has a right to know my mind on matters of such solemn interest to each of her members'.[269] The issue was not simply one of doctrine but the nature of the authority which decreed it.

In a primary Charge addressed to the clergy of his diocese, the Archbishop endeavoured to place the controversy and his own attitude in a more general setting. There had existed within the Church during the last two generations, he explained, 'two distinct schools . . . the bias of the one section has ever been rather towards the exercise of individual liberty in the interpretation of the Sacred Writings, with less reference to the principles laid down by Church authority for their guidance; while the other looks to that authority for direction and aid in ascertaining the true meaning of Holy Scriptures'. Both accepted the Bible as 'the very pure Word of God'. Recently, however, a third school had arisen, 'small indeed in number, as I trust, which claims to itself the right of maintaining, that although our Holy Bible contains the Word of God, that Word is not coextensive with the Sacred Volume; so that it is left to the conscience of each individual to decide which is the Divine Element and which the human, and to reject whatever does not approve itself to his verifying faculty'. Such an approach struck at the root of all 'fixed doctrine as deducible from the Holy Scripture', and must lead to undermining the status and binding force of the Articles. Fortunately this 'negative school of theology' would 'before long work out its own condemnation'. He then turned to the nature of biblical inspiration. Here he admitted, with a somewhat obscure logic, that God had ordained 'that men should be the instrument and channel of his revelation' while retaining their 'peculiar characteristics of temperament and talent'. Yet this did not imply that the whole Word of God was not the revealed Word, nor that we can pick and choose. It was important to maintain the 'plenary' inspiration of the Scriptures if not the literal and verbal, particularly in a world increasingly dominated by the controversy between religion and science. Here the Archbishop certainly had wise things to say:

> The Word of God does not pretend to teach us science; the object of revelation is not to instruct us as to the secrets of nature, but to make us wise in matters pertaining to our salvation.

The right course was for 'science to pursue her own investigations'.[270]

In his *Pastoral Letter addressed to the Clergy and Laity of his Province*, published in 1864, Longley stated firmly that the views of Dr. Williams, one of the essayists, were, in his opinion, 'entirely inconsistent with the terms of our formularies'. Of course a minister must have a reasonable liberty, but he was not free to say that any particular part of the Scriptures was *not* the Word of God; and as to the future life 'the Church has [no] more sure warrant for belief in the eternal happiness of the saved, than it has for belief in the eternal suffering of the lost'.

In Convocation, on 21 June 1864, the Archbishop finally set out his views at length. The provincial synod, he declared, had both the right and the power to condemn erroneous teaching. The question was simply whether the publication of *Essays and Reviews* was an occasion to exercise them.

> I do most distinctly state—and I never felt a stronger conviction in my life—that the occasion has arisen and that if ever there was a book which deserved such condemnation it is the book entitled *Essays and Reviews*.[271]

True the bishops had condemned it in their personal capacities, but there would be value in a solemn synodical act. He 'earnestly desired' that they would do this: if it were left undone it would be a clear dereliction of duty.

In this matter Longley clearly knew his own mind, but the driving force behind the condemnation in Convocation was Samuel Wilberforce, Bishop of Oxford, and it was he who at the end of the debate proposed the motion:

> That this Synod . . . doth hereby synodically condemn the said volume, as containing teaching contrary to the doctrine

received by the United Church of England and Ireland, in common with the whole Catholic Church of Christ.[272]

In spite of the Archbishop's confidence as to the lawfulness of this resolution, its propriety was in fact questioned in the House of Lords, although there were impeccable precedents for such action. The Lord Chancellor described the judgment as 'a well lubricated set of words, a sentence so oily and saponaceous that no one can grasp it— like an eel it slips through your fingers and is simply nothing'. Tait's comment was more restrained but equally to the point, namely that the great evil with the liberals was that they were deficient in religion, and the religious in liberality. Perhaps it was a good thing, at this time of religious uncertainty and division, that the Judicial Committee of the Privy Council was there in the background as a final court of appeal, and that serving upon it there were laymen of legal training whose theology was sufficiently inadequate to encourage a measure of detachment—and freedom.

## II

The Colenso case, as it came to be called, was more complicated, since along with debate as to the nature of biblical inspiration, there went such thorny questions as the legal status of the Anglican Church; the writ of the Archbishop of Canterbury in South Africa, and, by implication, in the Colonies generally; the extent of the jurisdiction of the Judicial Committee of the Privy Council.

The Archbishop's position was made more difficult by the character of the main participants.

Colenso was a latitudinarian churchman without much humour, who combined great missionary zeal with a conviction that Christianity was imperilled by the refusal of churchmen to adopt techniques of literary criticism in their approach to the Scriptures. This he proceeded to do without inhibition. Though neither a professional scholar nor a deep thinker, he undoubtedly exercised a profound influence on intelligent lay people who found it difficult to hold faith. The Crown Princess of Germany wrote to her mother, Queen Victoria, in April 1863:

> Dr. Colenso occupies me very much. I admire him, and I hope our Church will not disgrace itself in the eyes of all Europe by doing him any harm.[273]

Colenso was also a convinced Erastian and saw himself exercising his authority as Bishop of Natal under the letters patent granted to him by the Crown at his consecration in 1853.

No man could have been more different from Colenso in character, temperament, and churchmanship, than Gray, Bishop of Cape Town. He believed with great conviction that the opinions expressed by Colenso, particularly in his published work on the Pentateuch, were heretical; that Colenso was in honour bound either to renounce such opinions or resign; and that the Church possessed the inherent power, indeed duty, to bring this about, whether by the bishops collectively or by a provincial synod. To Gray, the royal supremacy and its concomitant the Judicial Committee were anathema, impeding the legitimate freedom of the Catholic Church as a divine institution.

Foremost among English bishops in believing that action must be taken against Colenso was Samuel Wilberforce, Bishop of Oxford and, later, of Winchester. Energetic, a brilliant orator, he entertained a high view of the Church and exercised considerable influence on Archbishop Longley, who, however, moderated his extremism.

Prominent at the other end of the ecclesiastical spectrum was A. C. Tait, Bishop of London, who though he felt little sympathy for Colenso's biblical views, was yet of opinion that law and the royal supremacy must be respected. In this he was supported by the scholar Bishop Thirlwall.

The events which followed after Gray sent a copy of the Bishop of Natal's works to Archbishop Sumner in November 1861 until Macrorie was appointed Bishop of Maritzburg in Cape Town on 25 January 1869, thus leading to schism, can only be suggested in briefest outline. Our main concern is with the policy of Archbishop Longley, who inherited this difficult situation from his predecessor.

Longley had no doubt whatever that Colenso's opinions were heretical and that he ought to resign. In reply to many letters and memorials from his diocese he made his own views plain:

> I cannot be surprised at the feelings of sorrow and indignation with which you view these works, as impugning in your judgement, the authority of the Holy Scriptures, and as derogatory to the Person, the Attributes and the Work of our Divine Redeemer; for happily it is without precedent that such published opinions should have emanated from a Bishop of the Church of Christ. But it is satisfactory to be assured that the principal objections advanced by Bishop Colenso are, for the most part, puerile and trite.[274]

These were strong words, if not scrupulously accurate when applied to opinions which would now be regarded as irrelevant or, after Gore's *Lux Mundi*, commonplace. As Archbishop, he felt he must adopt a policy which would keep the English episcopate together: but whether it was a matter of the continuance of the S.P.G. grant to Colenso; of his preaching in English pulpits; or debating the affair in Convocation, there was no unanimity. Colenso not unnaturally refused a request to resign, and though Longley recognized that as Archbishop of Canterbury he had no power to act judicially, he yet thought that Gray, as Metropolitan, could take proceedings.

This Gray proceeded to do when, under pressure from some of his clergy and in spite of a Privy Council judgment declaring his letters patent invalid, he summoned Colenso to appear before him. Longley watched anxiously the outcome of a trial which was never really in doubt. On 16 December, Gray and his episcopal assessors announced that Colenso had been condemned on all charges and was not fit for his office. Reporting these proceedings to the Archbishop, Gray reiterated:

> We claim the right to decide on matters of faith for ourselves, yielding submission only to the voice of the Church as expressed by the higher authority of her Patriarch, with Bishops of his Dioces [sic] for assessors; or of a National Synod.[275]

It was at this stage that Longley's High Church leanings swayed his judgement and led him away from respect for a strict legality. In company with Wilberforce, Keble, and Pusey he endorsed Gray's trial although, as he must have known, Colenso would appeal away from it to the Crown. Colenso did so, and inevitably his condemnation at Cape Town was declared null and void.

Gray meanwhile was bending his energies, in company with the South African bishops, to secure the appointment of a successor for the diocese of Natal which they had declared vacant.

On this issue Longley was definite, though he did not speak for the whole English episcopate.

> I have no hesitation—he wrote to Colenso on 10 February 1866 —in avowing that, according to my belief, you have been duly and canonically deposed from your spiritual office.[276]

Maybe the use of the words 'belief' and 'spiritual office' introduced a slight *caveat* into the apparently categorical nature of this statement; but the Archbishop was clear that since a recent legal judgment had declared the Church in South Africa to be a voluntary society, the Church in Natal was free to elect a new bishop. Tait and Thirlwall, on the other hand, were adamant in maintaining that Colenso was still legally Bishop of Natal and under the Royal Supremacy would remain so until he was deprived by a fully competent court. Many bishops who were 'middle of the roaders' were also of opinion that a proper means must be found of effectively depriving Colenso before the election of a successor. Often the debates in Convocation constituted an embarrassment to the Archbishop, with the result that he tended to support mediating amendments which robbed resolutions of a great deal of their bite. In practice, therefore, though Longley was anxious to help Gray, no resolutions measured up to the latter's expectations; nor did they vie with pronouncements made by the Anglican Church in America and Canada, churches which were free of any establishment nexus. It was this State connexion which weighed heavily on the Archbishop. Thus, although his sympathies were with Gray, he found it difficult to formulate a consistent policy. Had he been more Erastian like Tait or less Erastian like Wilberforce he might have seen his position with greater clarity. His defence must be that this ambiguity reflected a tension inherent in being Primate of an established Church and at the same time head of an emerging world communion.

In this *impasse* Gray finally returned to what had long attracted him—the summoning of a synod of the Home and Colonial bishops which would give its *imprimatur* to the sentence imposed on Colenso and to the election of a successor. Such a pan-Anglican synod, though not for this purpose, had already been suggested to Longley by the Church in Canada and the Archbishop had written a not discouraging reply.[277] Yet whatever expedient might be resorted to, Colenso, for the time being, was legally entrenched in the bishopric of Natal, a situation which was reinforced when Lord Romilly, the Master of the Rolls, decided that Colenso was still entitled to his salary from the Colonial Bishoprics' Fund. To Bishop Gray, whose over-riding preoccupation remained to secure the appointment of a new bishop, such a decision was starkly and nakedly 'the Church under the government of the Privy Council'. Longley, in conjunction with Wilberforce, declared that there was nothing in Colenso's legal position to prevent the election of a bishop to preside over those of the Anglican Church in South Africa who held him to be canonically deposed from his 'spiritual office'.

At long last—two previous candidates having withdrawn—Gray, who hoped to obtain a royal mandate for this purpose, felt himself in a position to proceed to a consecration. Longley seemed willing to co-operate, although the Dean of Canterbury refused the use of the Cathedral. The proposal stung Tait into action, and on 20 January 1868 he wrote an open letter to the Bishop of Cape Town in *The Times* in which, once again, he contested the assumption that the see of Natal was legally vacant, and pointed out that the bishops, at the recent Lambeth Conference, under the direction of the Archbishop of Canterbury, 'deliberately abstained from affirming that Bishop

Colenso's deposition was valid, either spiritually or in any other way'. Had the Government, he asked, approached the Law Officers of the Crown, and if not had another legal opinion been obtained? There was no precedent for any such action since the time of the non-jurors.

Such a public letter could not be ignored and the Archbishop advised, as a way out of the dilemma, that the Government be asked to issue a mandate for the consecration of a 'Bishop of South East Africa', it being understood that his ministry would be confined to those who 'would be willing voluntarily to submit themselves to him'.

On these terms the Government proved compliant, with the result that the Secretary of State on 30 May, though on Tait's advice refusing a royal mandate, let it be known to the Governors of the Cape and Natal that he did not think it necessary that Her Majesty's Government should interpose any obstacle to such a proceeding or use any influence to prevent it.

The final upshot was that Macrorie was consecrated Bishop of Maritzburg in Capetown on 25 January 1869. The English Government took no part in it, but would not act when Colenso petitioned against it. The unhappy outcome was two bishops operating in and around Natal, and this schism continued until after the death of Colenso in 1883. Not till 1891 was Archbishop Benson able to heal the breach and to persuade both parties to the schism to accept one Father in God.

The story of this controversy now reads sadly—the waste of energy, the heated passions, the misunderstandings. S. C. Carpenter in his *Church and People* takes a comforting view in maintaining that both parties to the dispute finally prevailed. Colenso's biblical ideas 'took root in the Church though in a more sensitive way and not quite as he conceived them'; and Gray's concept of indigenous churches within the Anglican Communion established itself when a provincial synod in 1870, confirmed in 1876, drew up a constitution for the Church in South Africa.

As to Archbishop Longley's role, no man can be expected to transcend the limitations of his own age. The occasional indecisiveness of his policy pointed to the fact that the Archbishop could not see the Colenso affair within the limited perspective of a diocesan bishop. He had wider responsibilities. The issue was a complex one with many ramifications. He could not but be conscious of a divided episcopate at home and the impossibility of bringing together such different attitudes as those entertained by Wilberforce and Tait. It might have been helpful had Longley been a little more sensitive to what Colenso was trying to do, and more effective in restraining Gray from a course which was bound to lead to schism.

Thomas Tenison

William Wake.
A portrait by I. Whood, 1736

*Thomas Secker. A portrait by Sir Joshua Reynolds, 1758*

*Addington Palace*

John Moore.
A portrait by Romney, 1783

William Howley

*John Bird Sumner. A portrait by E. Eddis*

*Charles Longley. A portrait by G. Richmond*

*The First Lambeth Conference, 1867. The bishops photographed on the steps of the palace*

*Archibald Campbell Tait. A portrait by G. Richmond*

# THE RISING TIDE.

MRS. GAMP. "*O you bad, wicked boy! I s'pose you'll be for a washin' away* THAT *Church next!*"

*A Punch cartoon arising out of the Irish Church question, 1868*

*Edward White Benson. A portrait by Sir Hubert von Herkomer*

III

The greatest distinction of Longley's archiepiscopate was the calling of the first Lambeth Conference in 1867, to which reference has already been made. The initiative which brought this about did not spring from Lambeth: on the other hand it can be said with certainty that if the Archbishop had not proved co-operative the Conference would not have taken place. Alan Stephenson, to whose *The First Lambeth Conference* I am indebted, suggests that Archbishop Longley had various 'requisites' inclining him to welcome the novel Canadian proposal for such an assembly:

1. As a moderate High churchman he entertained an exalted view of episcopacy;

2. He was sympathetic towards the establishment of synodical government and had expressed such views to his own clergy;

3. He was, unlike Tait, anti-Erastian, and did not see establishment as in any way necessary to a Church, though he valued it highly in England;

4. He had a feeling for 'Pan-Anglicanism', having long entertained a concern for the Church overseas, not least through his interest in the work of the S.P.G. and the C.M.S.

Perhaps a little ought to be said at this point concerning the outreach of this wider interest.

When the S.P.G. celebrated its 150th anniversary and Archbishop Sumner imaginatively invited bishops from the American Church over to England, Longley took his full share in the celebrations. He was present at a consecration in Leeds Parish Church, when Scottish and American Bishops officiated side by side with English bishops. While still Archbishop of York he made the journey to Inverness, in company with the Bishop of North Carolina, to lay the foundation stone of the Cathedral, and at the banquet which followed referred to the Scottish Episcopalian Church as the 'only representative of the Church of England in Scotland'. This deliberate gesture illustrates his strong feeling for episcopacy, but did not please everyone, as his correspondence at Lambeth shows. *The Times* of 23 October 1866 commented with scorn on the 'extraordinary part' he had played:

> An Archbishop of Canterbury is the very pinnacle of Establishment in the most established Church in the world; and Mr. Spurgeon in the character of an Archbishop would not be a greater anomaly than the ARCHBISHOP in the character of a Dissenter.

The Archbishop also preached at the Annual Church Congress held in York in 1866, a Congress which had a 'Pan-Anglican Flavour' in that the Primus of the Scottish Church attended, together with a number of Colonial and American bishops—the first occasion on which any Bishops from the New World had taken part.[278]

It was out of such a growing consciousness of the Anglican Communion, and within the context of its problems, doctrinal, liturgical, legal, and constitutional, particularly in the Colonies, that the first Lambeth Conference arose. The South African *contretemps* raised the question of the relation of the Colonial Churches to the Crown, a relationship which both Longley and Wilberforce thought should transform itself into the American pattern of independence as soon as practically possible. Also the revival of Convocation, and the changes which it effected in clerical subscription and canon law, posed the problem as to how far what was appropriate for England was equally fitting for Anglican Churches overseas. At a time when diocesan and provincial synods were increasingly establishing themselves, an overall synod of the whole Communion seemed to many churchmen both right and necessary—a view which was given further weight by the Pope's inauguration of geographical dioceses in England in 1850.

The formal request for a Conference, inspired by Bishop Lewis of Ontario, came in 1865 from the Provincial Synod of the Canadian Church. On 16 September 1865, an address was sent to the Archbishop of Canterbury expressing alarm at recent decisions of the Judicial Committee of the Privy Council in connexion with the publication of *Essays and Reviews* and the case of Dr. Colenso. Also a fear was expressed lest the revival of Convocation in England might 'cause us to drift into the status of an independent branch of the Catholic Church, a result which we would at this time most solemnly deplore'.

> In order, therefore—the document concludes—to . . . obviate, so far as may be, the suspicion whereby so many are scandalized, that the Church is a creation of Parliament, we humbly entreat your Grace, since the assembling of a general council of the whole Catholic Church is at present impracticable, to convene a National Synod of the Bishops of the Anglican Church at home and abroad, who, attended by one or more of their Presbyters or laymen, learned in Ecclesiastical law, as their advisers, may meet together, and under the guidance of the Holy Ghost take such counsel and adopt such measures, as may be best fitted to provide for the present distress.[279]

The Lower House of the Provincial Synod produced a separate memorial which was sent to the Convocations of Canterbury and York.

The address and memorial arrived at Lambeth in October 1865, and on 1 November they were published in the *Guardian*. In December the Archbishop sent a reply in which, after having sympathized with the disquiet and the reasons for it, he concluded:

> The meeting of such a *Synod* as you propose is not by any means foreign to my own feelings, and I think it might tend to prevent those inconveniences, the possibility of which you anticipate. I cannot, however, take any step in so grave a matter without consulting my episcopal brethren in both branches of the United Church of England and Ireland, as well as those of the different colonies and dependencies of the British Empire.[280]

Though this letter is cautious, in fact Longley had declared himself. His instincts were for such an assembly, but he was deeply conscious that not all his episcopal brethren would see the matter as he did, which inclined him to believe that the time was not yet. This view he expressed to his fellow bishops when he called them together on 3 February 1866. The Church in Canada, meanwhile, kept up the pressure. John Travers Lewis, Bishop of Ontario, came over to Lambeth and reported that 'Archbishop Longley listened very attentively ... and then said that such a step as he proposed would be without precedent'. 'That may be so,' the Bishop replied, 'but let Your Grace *make* a precedent.' Many interviews followed, and Longley invited him to dine with seventeen of his fellow bishops. He left Lambeth saying: 'Your Grace, do we not all belong to the same family? Why should we not meet?'[281]

Support for such a synod now came from various quarters: from Gray in Cape Town, and at home from Archdeacon Denison, to whom it appealed as a means of definitively combating heresy, and who brought the matter before Convocation. In the debate which ensued some wished to know how the summoning of such a synod fitted into the Royal Supremacy; why the Scottish Presbyterian and Swedish Churches should not be included; whether the laity were to be represented; and what would be the binding force of such canons as it might pass. Underlying the different views, there was an obvious interest. It was finally decided to appoint a committee.

The way ahead was not to be easy, though here it cannot be spelt out in detail. The Lower House of Convocation, on the whole, showed itself more obviously in favour, though there was definite opposition from liberals such as Stanley, and the objects of the synod were differently understood by those who supported it. The idea met a mixed reception when it came, in February 1867, before the annual meeting of bishops, reinforced this time by representatives from

325

America and the Colonies. A conspicuous absentee was Thomson, Archbishop of York—he was absolute in his opposition to such a synod, and questioned its legality—and in this he was followed by four evangelical bishops of his Province. The subject was introduced by Longley reading the letter he had received from the Canadian Church together with others from various colonial bishops. After a lengthy discussion the following resolution, proposed by Wilberforce, was passed:

> We, the Archbishops and Bishops of English, Irish, Colonial, and American Sees, here assembled, pray your Grace to invite a meeting of all the bishops of the various Churches holding full communion with the United Church of England and Ireland.[282]

No mention was made of presbyters or laymen. In response to a later inquiry from Tait, who left early, Longley gave the assurance that he did not intend the proposed meeting to enact canons or make decisions binding on the Church.

That so important a resolution should have been passed with many English bishops absent is remarkable. It can only point to the effectiveness of Longley's leadership and the authority of his office. All present took it as axiomatic that the synod would be summoned on his personal invitation, that he would preside, and that Lambeth was to be the venue.

The Lambeth Conference was now 'on', but much remained to be done both in respect of its planning and the winning over of those bishops who were either lukewarm or positively hostile. Fortunately Tait, though he would not, if Archbishop, have taken the initiative in calling such an assembly, decided, once he knew that it was to take place, to give it his support. Longley now set up a standing committee —Wilberforce was an obvious choice—and very wisely invited Tait to serve on it.

The first task of the standing committee was to approve a letter of invitation drawn up by the Archbishop. This letter made it clear that the invitation came from the Archbishop personally and that he himself would be President of the Conference. It rehearsed the reasons which had led to the invitation, the support that it commanded, and the limitations as well as the scope of its proposed deliberations. In general, its purpose was 'to consider together many practical questions, the settlement of which would tend to the advancement of the Kingdom of our Lord and Master Jesus Christ, and to the maintenance of greater union in our Missionary work, and to increased intercommunion among ourselves'.[283] A hundred and fifty-one bishops were invited.

There was one person towards whom, Longley realized, he must behave with almost excessive tact: Thomson, Archbishop of York; for Longley was going forward without his support, against his wishes and minus the approval of the Northern Convocation. Towards the end of April he wrote to Thomson enclosing an invitation, but adding that he would not serve it on any other Northern bishops until his consent had been given. Longley's letter boldly set out to win Thomson's co-operation. It told the story of the recent episcopal meeting, and went on to assure him that there was no intention of severing the ties between Church and State; that no resolution would be put to the vote; and that the procedure would resemble a church congress, to which Thomson was greatly addicted. He concluded by inviting him to preach the Conference sermon. The Archbishop of York, however, would not relent, though the last paragraph in his letter of reply was generous:

> Let me conclude with a sincere expression of my esteem and respect for you. In any matters where I am forced to take a different course from that which commends itself to your judgment, I should do so with regret and with much distrust of my own opinion.[284]

Thirlwall published a weighty letter, intimating that he would wait to declare himself until he had seen the agenda of the meeting. In the Colonies and in America the synod was widely welcomed, the only criticism being that September did not give adequate time for preparation.

The standing committee meanwhile got on with its task and Longley, on 20 July, issued to the English bishops the first tentative programme, which won over a still not fully convinced Thirlwall. The first day was to be devoted to intercommunion between the Churches of the Anglican Communion; the second to Colonial Churches; and the third to co-operation in missionary action—a restricted agenda which excluded many of the subjects suggested by some of the bishops in their replies to the invitation.

As the day of the Conference drew nearer and the bishops began to assemble, one particular matter loomed large, and it touched the Archbishop keenly for he had given his word that the Colenso affair should not come up for discussion. Not surprisingly, Gray was actively campaigning to reverse this decision, using for this purpose the vantage ground of Archdeacon Wordsworth's house in Little Cloister, Westminster Abbey. On 13 September Gray wrote a courteous but firm letter to the Archbishop pointing out that 'the interest and well being' of his Province was 'entrusted in a measure to my keeping', and that 'nearly everyone expects that this unhappy case will form a chief subject of consultation at the Conference'.[285] The final shape of the Conference was determined at a meeting presided over by Longley, when some thirty bishops were present. Tait avowed that he left this gathering foreseeing 'a very difficult week' ahead. Longley was now particularly anxious that Gray should not discuss the Colenso affair with the other bishops until after the Conference was over. Here he was forced to give way, and such a meeting did take place at the house of Archdeacon Wordsworth. From this Cave of Adullam there emerged a complete scheme for a 'Pan-Anglican Synod' presided over by the Archbishop of Canterbury; a scheme which Longley had publicly disowned, and was contrary to the more Erastian approach of such as Tait and Thirlwall. Longley continued anxious, but grew calm as the great day approached. Canon Benham remembered that as he walked out to the little village of Addington on the evening before the conference assembled, Longley ejaculated several times to himself, 'God is our own God, and He will give us His blessing'.

The Conference began with a service of Holy Communion in Lambeth Chapel at which Longley was the celebrant and one of the overseas bishops the very inadequate preacher. The proceedings proper began in the afternoon with Longley reading a business-like address which rehearsed the preliminaries to the Conference. He repeated once again that it was not a general synod and had no power to make canons. Much to his regret, he was forced to tell the gathering that Stanley had refused permission for the final service to be held in Westminster Abbey; and as it was feared that the Dean of St. Paul's, Milman, would take the same line, preparations were being made to hold it in Lambeth Parish Church.

The bishops then got down to business, and it was clear that there were great divisions of opinion between High Church and Evangelical, with the broad church on the whole tending to side with the latter. Longley's function as chairman was not easy, and he certainly owed a great deal to Wilberforce who (so one present observed) called people to order, set the American bishops right on points of procedure, and hastened the meeting on. But Longley was still in charge.

A dramatic proposal to change the programme came on the second day, to which Longley magnanimously agreed in the interest of the overseas bishops, although Tait and others were hotly against it.

> I think it a great advantage—Longley remarked eirenically—
> that we have had assistance of this Committee in preparing
> resolutions, for I think it will place the subject of the Colonial

Churches and their connection with the Mother Church before us in better order than otherwise might have been the case.[286]

Selwyn of New Zealand, together with Gray, were thus given an opportunity of initiating a long debate on synodical government, which led to a proposal encouraging the setting up of a Pan-Anglican Assembly. This suggestion was hotly contested, Thirlwall in particular protesting that he could see 'no means whatever of carrying it into practical effect'. Longley tried to mediate, for though he had declared himself against the creation of such a body, he felt it necessary to examine the position of the Colonial Churches—which the Government also expected the bishops to do. This contentious topic inevitably led to a discussion as to how far the Archbishop of Canterbury could become the patriarch of the whole Anglican Communion, Bishop Hamilton of Salisbury being of the opinion that the bishops could so nominate him, although by strict ecclesiastical law a patriarchate needed to be created by an ecumenical council. Tait made the typical comment that though there was no one to whom he would more willingly offer the office of Patriarch than Archbishop Longley, yet to do so was quite illegal. The debate dissolved into laughter when Gray reminded his brethren that the title *Alterius orbis papa* had already been used of a former Archbishop of Canterbury.

Finally a general motion was passed, affirming the principle that unity of faith and discipline was best secured by due and canonical subordination of the synods of the several branches to the higher authority of a synod or synods above them—and the matter was then referred to a committee. Though intentionally vague, this resolution encouraged colonial churches to come nearer to the American pattern of self-government.

On the last day there was due to take place the debate on Colenso as envisaged in the revised programme to which Longley had assented. Maybe he thought, on reflexion, that it was wiser to allow the matter to come freely into the open. Thus, when all had spoken, Longley addressed the bishops, admitting that he had not originally intended any such discussion. The Conference was not competent to condemn Colenso, but he believed there would be value in a committee considering what means could be taken to abate the Natal scandal. Longley's last-minute intervention proved decisive. It prevented an attempt at a condemnation; and removed the frustration which the Colonials would have felt had nothing been said. Upon a resolution from Selwyn, which stated that 'the whole Anglican Communion is deeply injured by the present condition of the Church in Natal', such a committee was set up. Two more attempts were made to secure discussion of the Colenso affair, one being ruled out of order by the Archbishop, the other leading to a reaffirmation of the resolution passed in the Canterbury Convocation.

The last act of the assembled bishops was to approve the encyclical, and at the closing service in Lambeth Parish Church the Bishop of Montreal praised Longley for his 'courage and large-heartedness' in sponsoring the Conference. It is significant that when the various committees reported on the morning of 10 December only twenty-eight bishops were present. That on synodical government was shelved because the established position of many provinces of the Anglican Communion made for complication. Here Longley's policy was upheld. No more successful was Wilberforce's attempt to bring into existence a representative tribunal for determining matters of faith and doctrine.

The Archbishop, on the whole, was well satisfied. When it was all over he went off for a holiday in Yorkshire. Letters poured into Lambeth, expressing appreciation for his efforts. Dean Hook told him that he had 'made [his] Primacy the most important since the Reformation by the Episcopal Conference'.[287] Longley himself said:

> For myself, I shall always look back on the Conference as an important era in my life and Archi-episcopate. I trust that it has tended to bind the different branches of the Church in our Anglican Communion more closely together in the bonds of brotherly love.

To his sister he confided:

> If the only fruit of it had been that pastoral which will be translated into Greek and Latin and circulated throughout the whole of Christendom; it would have been enough, when combined with brotherly union of 76 bishops from all quarters of the globe.[288]

One thing is certain. The Conference and its successors did a great deal to enhance the status of the Archbishop's office, and to extend the range of his interests and responsibilities: but it did nothing to increase his legal jurisdiction. *Punch* was not very percipient when its versifier wrote of Longley:

> To grow an Ox the Frog did blow
> Himself in vain to bursting full;
> And Canterbury does just so,
> Trying to match the Papal Bull.[289]

IV

One preoccupation which forced itself upon Archbishop Longley, as it did upon his successor to whom, doubtless, it was equally uncongenial, was the whole question of ritualism.

The 'Anglo-Catholicism' which began at Oxford within the environment of hall and gown had now penetrated into the parishes where devoted priests sought to realize a quickened ministerial vocation. To many such, candle and cross, lights on the altar, chasuble and rochet were not simply psychological gimmicks to provide a colourful interest. Rather they were the outward and visible signs of deep spiritual truths, serving to link the Church of England in the XIXth century with its pre-Reformation past. On the other hand those who smelt Romanism were alarmed at the secessions and, preferring a less ritualistic form of worship, took every opportunity to vent their displeasure. 'High' churches in some cities became centres of riotous behaviour and police protection had to be sought.

No Archbishop could avoid being caught up in this divisive controversy, whether as diocesan bishop, as President of the Canterbury Convocation, or as Primate of All England. The extent of Longley's involvement can be inferred from volume 5 of his correspondence, headed *Official letters and papers relating to ritual controversies*. These show many deputations of protagonists and protesters calling upon the Archbishop at Lambeth. The English Church Union, for example, deprecated 'any alteration being made in the Book of Common Prayer, respecting the ornaments of the Church and the ministers thereof', receiving an archiepiscopal assurance that he had 'already declared [his] determination never to consent to any alteration in any part of the Book of Common Prayer without the full concurrence of Convocation'.[290] The parishioners of Erith, in Kent, complained of certain changes adopted in their services. Viscount Sydney of Chislehurst protested against the Romish tendencies introduced by the Vicar, the Reverend F. H. Murray.

Longley's attitude was uncomplicated, and one that he believed was demanded of him in his capacity as Diocesan and uniquely as Archbishop. Incumbents must behave legally and not flout the provisions of the Book of Common Prayer. In his last diocesan charge he gave his views at large on this explosive subject. The ornaments rubric, he admitted, was 'difficult'.

> . . . it is obvious that if any order or discipline is to be maintained in our Church, it will be impossible to allow each single Clergyman to change the customs and Ritual according to his

331

own private opinion, and to set himself up as a judge of what is lawful and what is not.[291]

Such was equally reprehensible even if some of those who engaged in this kind of 'disobedience' were in fact excellent men and wholly devoted to their calling.

In stressing the duty of being obedient to the law, Longley was, of course, conscious that many Tractarians did not regard decrees of the Judicial Committee of the Privy Council as imposing a moral contraint upon them. The Archbishop himself was certainly unhappy about the composition of this Court, as he confided to his own clergy. The existing situation, he admitted, was more 'unfavourable' to the Church than originally intended under the Statute 24 Henry VIII c. 12. Yet until the present system of law was changed, the clergy were required out of their allegiance to the Crown to pay obedience to the sentence pronounced by the Court. In similar vein he reminded his brethren in the Convocation of February 1867 that 'the whole Prayer Book rests on the authority of Parliament'.

Longley's papers at Lambeth give an interesting picture of the growing preoccupations of an Archbishop in the latter half of the XIXth century. Many are the letters from the Secretary of State for the Colonies, seeking his advice and discussing appointments to overseas bishoprics. The drawing up of special prayers for national occasions continued as an almost routine operation; they show that Longley was no Cranmer. Personal problems sometimes found their way to the Archbishop. One such which demanded a disproportionate amount of his time was that of the Reverend Francis Lyne, self-styled Father Ignatius, who desired to revive the Benedictine Order within the Church of England. The activities of this young man in the course of his campaign were complicated by his relations with a too dominant father. The Archbishop let it be known firmly that the majority of bishops were against any such revival, and that in public Lyne must not wear his cassock, hood, scapular and pectoral cross.

The affairs of St. Augustine's College came before Longley in June 1867, when, on the Warden expelling one of its members, his fellow students promptly petitioned the Archbishop to reinstate him, only to receive a sharp rebuke reminding them that they had no statutory right of appeal. The day of effective student protest was not yet! William Edge, Vicar of Benenden, sent a full report on his visit to Paris and his contacts with the French clergy, probably the first communication of this kind since the time of Archbishop Wake.

Longley never seems to have been on intimate terms with Queen Victoria. His predilection for 'high churchism' did not commend him, and she turned to Wellesley, Dean of Windsor, for guidance, and to the broad church Stanley, Dean of Westminster, for theological enlightenment.

Not long before Longley's appointment to Canterbury, the Queen was plunged into agonizing grief by the unexpected death of her beloved husband the Prince Consort. She was not lifted out of her near despair by Bishop Wilberforce counselling her to make Christ her 'spouse'—advice which she later dismissed as 'twaddle'.[292] Personal unhappiness, however, did not preclude the Queen from asserting herself if she felt the occasion demanded it. When the Prince of Wales's marriage to Princess Alexandra of Denmark was arranged in 1863 for a day in Lent, the Archbishop received a crushing reply when he wrote to the Queen complaining that 'the light in which Lent is viewed by our Church has led her intelligent members generally to refrain from fixing that period for their marriages'. 'The objection rests merely on fancy or prejudice,' she protested, 'and one in this case based on no very elevated view of one of God's holiest ordinances. . . . Marriage is a solemn holy act *not* to be classed with amusements.'[293] So the wedding took place in Lent and Longley officiated. It could not have been welcome to the Archbishop (if he ever knew of it) that 'the patriotic protestants of Colyton' in Devon erected a fountain 'to commemorate the wedding of H.R.H. the Prince of Wales during Lent as a permanent memorial of that national triumph and in vindication of their own loyalty'.

Longley died on 28 October 1868. His archiepiscopate is an interesting example of what can be achieved by an honest man without distinguished talents, who yet acts with courage and determination when a critical decision is imposed upon him.

# 4

## A. C. TAIT AND A NATIONAL CHURCH

During the remaining years of the XIXth century, three Archbishops of very different character but of considerable ability sat in Augustine's chair: A. C. Tait (1868–1882); E. W. Benson (1883–1896); and Frederick Temple (1896–1902). It is, perhaps, fair to claim that neither Benson nor Temple would have entered into their inheritance had the way not been prepared for them by the distinguished archiepiscopate of A. C. Tait. His tenure of office was in many respects remarkable, and his prominence in the life of the nation something unknown since the Primate of All England ceased, after Laud, to discharge a significant political role. This enlargement of influence was in some respects due to the general climate, but it certainly owed something to Tait's own attitude to his office. When Tait died in 1882, at the age of seventy-one, he was universally acclaimed, and immediately offered—though the family declined—burial in Westminster Abbey. The Queen, to whom he was devoted and who was devoted to him, asked for a lock of his hair, a request not even made in respect of Lord Beaconsfield. *The Times*, which had on occasions been among his most bitter critics, paid a magisterial tribute:

> Tait has stood at the helm in troublous times; he has steered the ship past many a storm, and he leaves it in comparatively tranquil waters.

In the Southern Convocation similar compliments, not of a purely formal nature, were made. Jackson, Bishop of London, drew attention to the fact that at the recent enthronement of Tait's successor 'the Cathedral of Canterbury might have been filled twice over with the applications for admission, and those who were not at Canterbury were thinking of it, or speaking of it elsewhere'. This was due

> to the much superior place and the much greater room which the Primacy of All England fills now in the public mind than it did fourteen years ago. It has been said by more than one—

334

Tait came to Lambeth at the age of fifty-eight in the full flood of his powers, the first Primate since Laud to have a clear idea of the function of the archbishopric within the life of Church and nation. Tait recognized that it was a different office from any other in the Church of England; and that what was appropriate, for example, at Fulham was not necessarily so at Lambeth. He must now cultivate a wider view. His temperament fitted the post, and the post drew out the best in his temperament. James Bryce, in a percipient essay, asks what it was about Tait that made him a 'model to his own and the next generation of what an Archbishop of Canterbury ought to be'. His answer was that Tait possessed 'a steady balance of mind', and that his gifts were such as to make him 'more remarkable as an archbishop than as a man'. Had he remained in a junior position 'no one would have felt that fate had dealt unfairly with him in depriving him of some larger career and loftier post'.[306] Tait shared the prejudices, the hopes and the more noble aspirations of the bulk of his fellow countrymen, and gave to them a religious content within the witness of a national Church.

Yet there was nothing 'churchy' about Tait, and he was often called the 'layman's Archbishop'. Indeed he liked to think of himself as a man of affairs, with a deep interest in what was going on around him. He was a sedulous devourer of newspapers, and read widely—novels, verse, history. Though possessing a first-class intelligence he made no pretensions to technical scholarship, most of his theological reading being for practical purposes. He deliberately cultivated what he called the 'spirit of the age'; and had little of the nostalgia which made his successor romanticize the past. He rejoiced to live in the modern age, with its railways and its new science; and his temperament inclined him to optimism in spite of his appalling personal tragedies. This optimism spilled over into his numerous after-dinner speeches, and in charges to his clergy. Like Bird Sumner he welcomed the 'expanding thought and stirring life of an era of freedom, enlightenment and progress . . . in which by God's will our lot is cast'; and he looked forward 'to the time when the whole world shall have been so improved by the blessing of Almighty God that it will be ready for the coming of the Lord'.[307] At a Church Congress in 1877 he declared:

> Some think that I never speak without an undue exaggeration of the brightness of the prospects of the Church over which I am called in God's providence to preside. But they are bright. Look abroad. What other country in the world would you change Churches with? Look at home; which of the denominations would you prefer? Look back: what age are you prepared to say

M

it would have been more satisfactory to have lived in? For my part, I thank God and take courage.[308]

Thus he saw Britain's expanding commercial power as illustrating the superiority of Christian faith, particularly in its Protestant form, over all rivals. Christianity released a moral dynamic, and its rejection, he believed, would lead to national decline. The Christian was 'the best specimen of man the world has yet seen'. Thus he gave his support to all missionary activity, not least in distant outposts of the Empire. Indeed he urged serious consideration as to whether the various missionary societies ought not to join forces under a Board of Missions in order to secure greater co-ordination and prevent wastage.

Yet Tait was no 'enthusiast', in spite of Disraeli's warning to the Queen, and he disliked a great deal of what he saw around him, for example, in Sankey and Moody revivalism. He took his stand on a Christianity shed of its inessentials, simple in its great affirmations, to which the intelligent layman could give a conscientious assent. He was sensitive to the contemporary agnosticism of such as Tennyson, and was convinced that this could not be combated by insisting on the 'over-belief' characteristic of the protagonists of the Oxford Movement. Typical of this concern was his inviting a group of scientists to a discussion at Lambeth, the outcome of which, however, was not very encouraging; and his devoting many of his later charges to a practical *apologia* for Christian faith.

Tait was of opinion that the heart of the English people remained basically Christian; that it was in this faith that they wished their children to be brought up; and that for the majority this more than vestigial faith expressed itself, particularly in times of crisis, through the established Church. The Church of England, he once said in the House of Lords,

> has not only been a part of the history of this country, but a part so vital, entering so profoundly into the entire life and action of the country, that the severing of the two would leave nothing behind but a bleeding and lacerated mass. Take the Church of England out of the history of England, and the history of England becomes a chaos, without order, without life, and without meaning.[309]

Therefore he was against anything that tended to withdraw this Church into a sectarian ecclesiastical enclave, thus removing it further from the life of the nation. He suspected that the Oxford Movement tended to do just this.

Since this national Christianity, in the main though not exclusively, realized itself through the established Church, so Parliament under the royal supremacy was its safeguard. If to High Churchmen, such as Archdeacon Denison and Father Mackonochie, Parliament seemed essentially a secular body interfering in the life of a divine society, to Tait this was almost preposterous. Such an attitude tended to 'de-sacralize' the State. Parliament was still predominantly an Anglican assembly, and even where it was either dissenting or non-believing, it was representative of the nation. It was fitting for the Church of England to recognize that such was the nation with which it had to deal, and which it was trying to serve. The Queen, as an anointed sovereign and Supreme Governor of the Church of England, was not simply a secular person.

Tait did not see himself as an Erastian, for he never envisaged the State as the enemy or the oppressor. Each needed the other. In the Bradlaugh controversy, he opposed any complete abrogation of the oaths; and was prepared to accept the Judicial Committee of the Privy Council with its judges and episcopal assessors as a court which in practice encouraged a reasonable comprehension within the Church of England. Though, as will be seen, he worked loyally with Convocation, he never regarded this body as an alternative to Parliament. He had no wish to see its rights in relation to the Church of England wither away, rights which were rooted in the Reformation settlement. Tait believed positively in an established Church built into the structure of the constitution and accepting a national mission. This did not mean, however, that he was not well aware of the force of the radical nonconformist attack, which led to a succession of bills in the House of Commons to secure disestablishment.

## II

It was from within this general framework of ideas that Tait saw his responsibilities as Archbishop, and established his working order of priorities—nation, province, and diocese. The Church had a responsibility to the nation and this meant that he must give time to its affairs. Integral to this continuing ministry was the care of the sovereign and her family.

The Queen had now been some thirty years on the throne. She was interested in, and particularly well-informed about, ecclesiastical matters, and knew most of the personnel better than some of her Prime Ministers. Never for a moment did she forget that she was Supreme Governor of the Church of England, and she expected people to treat her as such. As a barometer of middle class opinion she was without rival. In his dealings with her, Tait's own tragic history of bereavement, together with his origin north of the border, made for a deep and integrating bond. They had a favourite hymn in common: 'Lead Kindly Light amid the encircling gloom.' Tait was careful to keep her closely in touch with Church affairs, and when ecclesiastical legislation ran into difficulties he would not hesitate to seek her help with the Prime Minister. He took special care to identify himself with the royal family in their domestic affairs. At the time of the Prince of Wales's illness, he was quick in drawing up prayers and circularizing them among the London clergy. He officiated at royal baptisms, and not long before his death, though ill, struggled down to Osborne for a confirmation. The following extract from his diary is revealing:

> Sunday, July 5th, Addington . . . Yesterday we were at the funeral of old Gunner & saw him laid close to his old Master Archbishop Sumner in the beautiful Church Yard. It was a strange contrast to the work of the day before when we had received the Prince & P. of Wales with their two boys . . . with about 600 other guests in the Palace and Gardens at Lambeth . . . Monday we came up early from Lord Pormouth's in time for me to go to Windsor with the Convocation address which was presented by me at 3 to the Queen. . . . I had a private interview with her Majesty afterwards. How full of interest is this busy life and how good to have quiet pauses in it to remind us that it is passing.[310]

To fulfil his national role Tait spoke frequently on public occasions, and here his addresses were usually more effective than his sermons. He was never eloquent, indeed he despised rhetorical brilliance, but he was always earnest, much to the point and well informed. It was part of his basic philosophy that when the Archbishop of Canterbury spoke in public he must know his facts. His appeal was usually to intelligent common-sense and a feeling of duty. That is why he was always listened to, with the result that the Church of England gained in respect. In the House of Lords he probably exercised greater influence than any Archbishop before or since. This did not happen by the light of nature. He deliberately mastered the technique and the most acceptable style of address and regarded constant atten-dance, in order to get the 'feel' of the House, as a paramount duty. Indeed during his early years as a bishop, he made it his business to go into the Peers Gallery of the House of Commons and it was a matter of regret to him that increasing pressure later made this impossible.

Randall Davidson, who knew Tait's practice at first hand, writes:

> From the House of Lords he was scarcely ever absent when anything was going on. Other engagements had to give way to

this, and he used half comically to ascribe his extraordinary influence there to the fact of his regular attendance—'A man can't sit here every night for a quarter of a century without people wanting to know what he comes for and listening to what he has to say'. . . . The Archbishop's robing room became known to public men of every sort who wanted to consult him, and I can recall almost as many interviews of first-rate importance in that room as either at Lambeth or at Addington. . . . It was to him a constant source of regret for the Church's sake that other Bishops made so little of their Parliamentary opportunities.

'If I could only get you to believe,' he once told Bishop Frazer, 'that the House of Lords is a bigger thing than even the *Manchester Guardian*, and that you might be speaking to an Empire instead of to a county!'[311]

Tait's attitude to establishment necessarily meant cultivating right relations with Prime Ministers and those who held political office. Society in the eighteen-seventies moved in a far more limited circle than it does today. Tait frequently met Gladstone and Disraeli at dinners at 10 Downing Street, and on public occasions. 'The Grand Old Man' (with Shaftesbury) was the foremost Christian layman of his day, but paradoxically his own deep interest in the affairs of the Church of England—he was one of those responsible for the revival of Convocation—meant that Tait's influence on ecclesiastical appointments was less during his premiership (though he conscientiously consulted Tait) than under Disraeli whose complete lack of knowledge, in spite of his predilection for a 'church party', was sometimes an embarrassment.

It was not only, however, in matters of ecclesiastical appointments that prime ministers were significant. Tait knew only too well that an established Church, with a final constitutional authority vested in the Queen in Parliament, needed, on occasions, to win the support of the Government in order to adapt itself to changed situations. Also, with a body of opinion actively campaigning to sever the link between Church and State, parliamentary support was indispensable. Here, however, there was a difficulty. Gladstone stood for a greater disengagement of Parliament from ecclesiastical affairs than Tait found palatable. Disraeli's 'Church Party' proved a mixed blessing. In the circumstances, Tait realized the unwisdom of allying the ecclesiastical interest with any one political party. The situation was not as in the XVIIIth century. Thus, during the time that the Bill for Irish Disestablishment was before Parliament, he tried to use Disraeli, who was in the opposition, as well as Gladstone in the Government, to mitigate its terms. Tait was also aware that a disunited Church, a Convocation touchy about its inherent rights, a hostile dissent, would not encourage politicians to embroil themselves in ecclesiastical affairs or find time for legislation.

The first national issue in which Tait became necessarily involved was that to which reference has just been made, the disestablishment of the Church of Ireland. Never was his tact, good sense, persistence and mastery of parliamentary procedure seen to better advantage. Gladstone's Bill to disestablish the Irish Church, introduced in 1868, was not unexpected, and he made it evident that with his majority in the Commons he was determined to see the Bill through.[312]

The case for it was overwhelming. Out of a total population of nearly six million, according to a census of 1861, only some seven hundred thousand belonged to the United Church of England and Ireland created by the Act of Union. Yet Anglicans deliberately resisted the logic of the facts. Thus Archbishop Longley, in his last visitational address to the clergy of Canterbury, published after his death, declared that there could be no established church anywhere if the principle of religious equality were accepted; and that to inflict this principle upon the Church of Ireland would be a 'great act of injustice', and not even in the interests of the peasants.[313] Tait was far too politically percipient to commit himself to such an extreme view. He fully recognized that an Irish problem did exist, and that the Government must do something about it. On the other hand, he believed passionately in established churches. For this reason he appeared first as the strong opponent of the disestablishment of the Irish Church, an attitude which also owed something to his almost instinctive aversion to the Roman Catholic Church, a sentiment which he shared with a vast number of British people, including the Queen. A Church of Ireland, disestablished and disendowed, would not, he maintained, be able to stand up to 'a powerful Roman Catholic body with a foreign Prince at its head, who has the power of . . . placing the chief dignitaries of his Church in a position which no clergyman of a disendowed Protestant Church can possibly assume'.[314] In his opinion, the real troubles in Ireland were due not to the United Church, but to internal disunity. Here the establishment proved itself a stabilizing factor. What Ireland needed was a thorough educational programme, to promote which he had always advocated a system of 'concurrent endowment' for all the Churches of Ireland so that resentment at privilege might be reduced.

Tait, however, as a realist, soon recognized that disestablishment was coming whether he liked it or not, and that Gladstone, even had he wished, could not resist the pressure from within his own party. The practical problem was simply on what terms.

To this question he now bent his considerable energies and

diplomatic skill. Gladstone and the Primate of Ireland were invited to meet him at Lambeth, and he also conferred with the Queen. In all these delicate negotiations his concern was to save as much of the Church's endowments as possible, since he was convinced that if the Church of Ireland went into disestablishment entirely disendowed it would be at the mercy of its wealthy laymen, and the animosity between the Protestant clergy and the Roman Catholic population would thereby be increased. Tait also called together the Irish and English episcopate, so that he might be ready when Gladstone came to him with the terms of the proposed Bill.

These terms, when they appeared, did not please him. Though the Church was to retain its buildings, its schools and burial grounds, not even all post-Reformation endowments were to be retained, and no provision was made for diverting monies to educational uses. Tait sensibly set about securing amendments to the Bill rather than waste his energies trying to secure its rejection. Often this meant walking a veritable tight-rope, and trying to restrain his own bishops. Thus he saw Disraeli with a view to securing amendments in the Commons. To offset the risk of its total rejection in the Lords by the votes of the episcopate, Tait, fortunately, was able to take a more objective view than many of his colleagues, who felt that they could not in conscience do other than vote against the Bill on its second reading, even though they were not unaware of the political wisdom of Tait's approach. It says much for the Archbishop's influence that out of sixty who finally signed a protest against the Bill in the Lords only four were bishops: and that many amendments were passed to the financial advantage of the Irish Church. No one could have secured these improved terms unless he had been familiar with the strategy of the House and willing to accept a real situation for what it was.

### III

The Irish Bill had no easy passage, but the Government found time for it because the impetus came from within its own party.

It was different, however, when the Church itself tried to initiate legislation. One of the most pressing needs, as Tait saw it, was to increase the number of the episcopate through the creation of new sees, and to make it possible for disabled bishops to retire. In the South, the Bishops of Exeter, Salisbury, Bath and Wells, and Winchester were aged and infirm. Gladstone was himself too good a churchman not to recognize the necessity for some such action. In the autumn of 1869 Tait wrote to him, suggesting that there ought to be three new sees, and explaining how they might be financed. As to membership in the Lords, there could be a system of rotation. Gladstone knew, however, the difficulty of securing such legislation, and

345

in spite of a meeting between a committee of the Cabinet with Tait and a few bishops, he decided against going forward at the moment.

Such a rebuff submitted the establishment to strain, and Tait was disappointed, but characteristically told the bishops in the Upper House of Convocation that nevertheless

> we are wise in retaining in every way this distinct connexion between the civil government of the country and its ecclesiastical polity; and that therefore there would be a hesitation no doubt to divest Parliament in any degree whatsoever of its control in reference to the creation of really good officers such as those to whom we are accustomed to regard all Bishops as being in connexion with the Church of England.[315]

In the circumstances the best recourse was to take advantage of the Act under Henry VIII which enabled the appointment of suffragan bishops, and to this the Government was agreeable. Two bishops in a diocese were often better than one, and this expedient, which was thoroughly constitutional, entailed neither cathedral chapter nor archdeacon. If this were tried and found inadequate, then there would be a real case for going back to Parliament. As for himself he had used this Act to create a bishop of Dover, one Parry, in 1870. As the Archbishop's coachman put it: 'We had a hard time of it some years ago. . . . But since we've taken Mr. Parry into the business we've done better.'[316]

An archiepiscopal interjection during the course of this debate in Convocation is worth recording since it illustrates Tait's emphasis on the practical. The Bishop of Llandaff complained that 'the real reason why our spiritual and intellectual work is not done as it might be is that as officers of state, we are completely overwhelmed with secular business. After breakfast you have to sit down to your desk and write letters upon secular business, which might just as well be attended to by a clerk or a lawyer.' 'Why not have one?' was Tait's laconic retort.[317]

In one area in the life of the Church, however, Tait was able to persuade the Government to legislate. It proved to be a sad error of judgement and the greatest mistake of his archiepiscopate. This arose out of the ritualism which has already come before us in relation to Longley. Things had not grown easier, and it was from an increasing unease at what many saw as a most disturbing and 'un-English' phenomenon in the parish churches that the Public Worship Regulation Act came on to the statute book.

To be fair to Tait it needs to be said that bishops were inundated with letters asking them to restrain liturgical innovators. Among

346

those who felt acute alarm was the Queen herself, and she must accept a large measure of responsibility for the legislation which was subsequently passed, though she tried later to exercise a moderating influence.

Tait had already experienced ritualistic excess when Bishop of London, but here his attitude had been, as far as possible, not to get involved, believing that 'each man will best serve God by acting as in God's sight on his own strong convictions'. At Canterbury he felt obliged to take a national view, and to concern himself with the Church as a whole. He thus decided that the eccentricities of a few, even if well meaning, were alienating a large number of ordinary lay people from their loyalty to the Church of England. The nation generally was against ritualism, and the ritualism which they were against was unlawful.

> I do not think—he commented—that there is the slightest danger of this country ever becoming Roman Catholic. But I think . . . that there was a danger lest the foolish conduct of a few might so shake the confidence of the people in their National Established Church that they would consider it no longer worth preserving.
> I have great sympathy with earnestness—he said again—but I have no sympathy with persons who make the Church of England something quite different from that which it was made at the Reformation, and something totally different from that which the great and overwhelming majority of the people of England regard [as] their national Church.[318]

From this position he never wavered.

No matter how misguided Tait's policy proved to be, the Act of 1874 was not engineered in any sectarian spirit of intolerance: rather it was designed to preserve a national, inclusive, and comprehensive Church, and to placate lay opinion. The origins of the Bill are somewhat obscure, but may probably be traced to the annual meeting of bishops at Lambeth in 1874 some few days before Gladstone's unexpected dissolution of Parliament. The question of ritualism was an item on the agenda, and the Queen was pressing for something to be done. 'It is clear,' she wrote to the Archbishop, 'that . . . the liberties taken and the defiance shown by the Clergy of the High Church and Ritualist party is so great that something *must be done* to check it, and prevent its continuation.'[319] The bishops agreed that the two Archbishops should draw up a Bill, which meant in practice that Tait, with the technical help of J. Brunel, Chancellor of the Ely diocese, got on with it. But an unexpected situation now arose. Disraeli, to

347

his own surprise, came back to power at the elections, minus a fully articulated legislative programme. Tait stepped in with his Act to fill the vacuum, the purpose of which was, without great expense and speedily, to secure obedience to the law. At this point Tait's mis-judgement became apparent for, as Lord Salisbury shrewdly com-mented: 'The Archbishop is asking for an impossibility; that it shall be as easy to apply a much disputed law, as if it were undisputed.'[320]

Disraeli himself was in a difficult position. In spite of pressure from the Queen, whose *'earnest* wish' it was that he should go *'as far* as he *can* without embarrassment to the Government',[321] he described the proposed Bill which Tait, to his annoyance, released to *The Times*, as 'the hardest nut to crack that ever was the lot of the minister'.[322] Finally he agreed to give it 'every facility', assuring the Queen that 'if this blow is dealt against the Sacerdotal school it will be entirely through the personal will of the Sovereign'.[323]

The Bill successfully passed through Parliament, though with a number of amendments. The proposed diocesan boards of clergy and laymen were jettisoned; the bishops were given a discretion to veto prosecutions; and a single well-paid judge was appointed to deal with cases in the provinces of Canterbury and York.

Once the Act became law, Tait pleaded with the clergy to accept it in the spirit of mutual understanding.

> . . . no amount of good intentions—he said in Convocation—no amount of self sacrifice can justify a man doing his best to over-throw this great and venerable institution—upon which we all agree the safety of this kingdom so depends.[324]

The bishops also issued an address urging moderation and inferring that they would not interfere with the eastward position.

After preliminary difficulties were overcome in finding a suitable judge, the Act took effect, and before long a number of clergymen suffered imprisonment. Such a consequence had never been con-templated, this lamentable *dénouement* arising from the fact that a forgotten Act of 1813 had changed the punishment for contempt of an ecclesiastical court from excommunication to imprisonment! Other absurdities followed. The Archbishop, to avoid scandal, found himself consuming a consecrated wafer which had been exhibited in court and stamped with the date. 'What Doctors can preserve the Primate's health—if he can be occasionally *forced* to eat wretched Wafer-bread, kept in a Pill box for five months or more!' commented his Registrar.[325] Tait discovered to his embarrassment that what he regarded as an illegal eccentricity was to some clergymen a matter of deeply-felt conviction which they could not abandon even at the price of imprisonment. Though their number was insignificant, yet the publicity they attracted was immense.

P. T. Marsh writes in his *Victorian Church in Decline*:

> In short the Act was a fiasco. It was bound to be so because it relied ultimately on force either in the form of inhibition and deprivation or through imprisonment. As ever in a contest with determined religious conviction, force backfired on those who employed it.[326]

Though Tait's concern was to preserve the unity of the Church and to keep its ethos acceptable to the English people, the Act achieved almost the opposite. It says much for Tait's sagacity that he recognized his mistake, and by 1877 had begun to back-pedal. Bishops were encouraged to use their veto on prosecutions; he himself addressed many clerical meetings, introducing an eirenical spirit, and even humour. Gladstone affirmed that in some respects the Archbishop was a changed man.

One thing, however, the Act did achieve. Never again would a session of Parliament be more or less monopolized by ecclesiastical business. In future Governments were wary of any such legislation, and insisted that the Church should make up its own mind before it was embarked upon.

If the Act of 1874 was the greatest blunder of Tait's archiepiscopate, the Burial Act which he piloted through Parliament was one of his great successes.

The exclusion of dissenters from parish churchyards was rightly felt by them as an unwarrantable deprivation. Now that enforced church rates had been abolished, it remained, apart from the Establishment itself, the grievance which still rankled. Tait was convinced that this exclusion must be brought to an end, but there was no proposal which provoked greater opposition among the rank and file of Anglican clergy, or attracted more odium upon himself. High Churchmen defended the exclusion on doctrinal grounds; others condemned the proposed Act as a clear invasion of the rights of property. Tait began his campaign by holding a conference with the clergy, and taking the public into his confidence. He even made inquiries of various foreign embassies, and was able to point out that the law in England was harsher in this respect than in many continental countries. The Bill, when it appeared, had the effect of permitting any Christian or orderly religious service (or silence) to be held over a person who had a civil right of burial. Fifteen thousand clergy and thirty thousand laymen protested against its terms: but the Bill became law and proved a potent factor in making for

reconciliation. In this respect it helped to preserve the establishment. As Tait put it in the House of Lords:

> I am anxious to detach from the movement for disestablishment
> the agitation which is kept up on the question, and we can so
> detach it by taking the question fairly in hand.[327]

He was right.

It is, perhaps, not unfair to say that Tait found the House of Lords
more congenial than Convocation. Devoted to a comprehensive
Church geared to an inclusive tolerance, he was never fully at ease
with the kind of High Churchmanship which occasionally manifested
itself, particularly in the Lower House. True, he approached Convocation with an initial prejudice, for an established Church, in
Tait's eyes, must find its ultimate constitutional authority in Parliament; and he did not wish it otherwise. Convocation had value as the
sounding-board of a more concentrated Church opinion, but it must
not pretend to set itself up as an autonomous body.

There was, however, a wish even among moderates, to give
greater power to Convocation. Thus Jackson, Bishop of London,
proposed a Bill in the Lords which, if it had gone through, would
have allowed Convocation to alter rubrics, subject to formal ratifica-
tion by Parliament and the Privy Council. The *Quarterly Review*
proposed to get over the difficulty of securing parliamentary legislation by setting up a central agency for the Church of England,
consisting of representatives from Convocation and the Privy
Council. Tait did not view such suggestions with favour, and here
responsible political opinion was with him. In 1881, when he saw
both the Prime Minister and the Lord Chancellor he found that they
decisively discouraged the bringing in of any bill to give legislative or
*quasi*-legislative force to the decisions of Convocation. Only a sad
and realistic acceptance that it would become increasingly difficult
to get legislation through Parliament inclined Tait to favour any
change in the *status quo*. Not surprisingly the suspicion grew that the
Archbishop was not wholehearted in his support of Convocation, and
on occasions he was accused of short-circuiting it. For example, John
Wordsworth complained that his disregard of Convocation was not
reassuring to the clergy and set many good churchmen against it.
Particularly was this the case while the Act of 1874 was passing
through Parliament, when Tait carefully avoided any statement
which might appear to recognize an inherent right in Convocation to
veto or delay Parliamentary action upon a subject of this kind; a
subject, he claimed, not connected with doctrine and on which
Convocation had already reported, even inviting Parliamentary
legislation.

Yet in his capacity as President of Convocation, even Tait's critics allowed that he was firm, friendly, and sometimes humorous. His main concern was to encourage a practical approach. Large, specious, and somewhat doctrinaire schemes usually found in him a caustic critic. When Christopher Wordsworth, Bishop of Lincoln, carried a motion that a joint committee be appointed (9 February 1870) to report upon the laws of the universal church and of the Church of England concerning election, confirmation, and consecration of bishops, Tait remarked that surely this was not a matter which concerned the Church alone. Ought not some lay lawyers to be consulted? He spoke feelingly for, as he went on, he himself had been vilified for the part he had played in consecrating Frederick Temple as Bishop of Exeter.

> I found myself compared—he said—to Judas Iscariot and Pontius Pilate. It was, I believe, myself and my right reverend brother the Bishop of St. David's who were compared to Ananias and Sapphira, although the person who made that comparison did not particularise which was which. I cannot say with truth that those epithets moved me very much.[328]

In some respects Tait would have made a good judge, for he could usually abstract himself from the emotional heat which many contemporary problems engendered. This was both a strength and a weakness—a strength because it led to objectivity, a weakness because it could lead to a lack of sympathy and understanding. Now and again his impatience with the inability of the Upper House of Convocation to come to a decision broke through his normal calm.

This was particularly so in the innumerable debates on the Athanasian Creed which in the interest of sophisticated people he was particularly anxious to remove from the public worship of the Church.

> Is it not natural—he asked—that if the Prelates, after a hundred years of deliberation, cannot make up their minds on one of the most important questions that can be brought before the Church others should say—'If the Bishops are so timid, or can so little gauge public opinion and feeling, then we must assist them in discussing these questions in public meetings.' It appears to me that we may take this lesson from public life—that if a Ministry in public matters does not know its own mind, it finds a greater number of persons who, at public meetings throughout the country, are ready to assist its decisions. . . . What in the world are we here for except to take responsibility on ourselves? And

351

the more serious the responsibility is, the more we are bound to bear it.[329]

Tait was scrupulously careful to maintain the rights of the Upper House of Convocation, as he understood them, and to insist that the bishops, as an order, and because of their special experience, had a unique responsibility. During a debate on the Prayer Book rubrics on 8 July 1872 he declared:

> I do not desire to know, in the first instance, the opinion of the Lower House. I think it most important that we should have perfectly free intercourse with that House, but I think it most undesirable that this House should appear to the public to adopt any course whereby they seem to abandon the functions committed to them as the Upper House and Bishops of the province, and hand over these duties to the Lower House.[330]

It was typical of his chairmanship that he kept a close eye on small details, and did his best to keep business moving. When in a resolution connected with the Bonn Conference the Bishop of Winchester used the phrase 'representative' in connexion with the Eastern Church, Tait asked what precisely *was* the Eastern Church.[331] The same close eye, on another occasion, prompted the question whether it would not be desirable 'to have before us a list of Committees which have never reported to this House'. 'There must be a great many of them,' he commented, and he was right.[332]

Sometimes the Archbishop endeavoured to bring his point home by humorous interjections. In a discussion on the cost of printing the Chronicle of Convocation—some £221 3s.—he suggested that 'every member ought to pay according to the voluminous nature of his speeches'.[333] On another occasion he was asked to find out whether, as Archbishop, he had the power to alter the representation of the Lower House of Convocation, this petition arising from the request of the rural deanery of Burford for greater parochial representation and a wider franchise. Tait was not averse, in principle, to something like this being done, but reported back that all he himself could do was to present an address to the Queen from Convocation for a royal licence to make regulations altering the constitution.

> I have heard a great deal of late—he said—about the desirable-ness of increasing the number of representatives of the parochial clergy in the Lower House. It seems to me that however desirable that may be there is another point to which attention ought to be directed, which is the great advantage that would be derived from the attendance in the Lower House of those who are already members of it—in particular the deans.

There then followed a long dialogue while the President caustically listed a large number of deans who were distinguished by their absence.[334]

Perhaps it was the ecclesiasticism of Convocation which, so far as the Archbishop was concerned, tended to make it not wholly congenial, particularly in the prolonged discussions on ritualism and the Church Courts. Not long before his death, addressing both Houses in College Hall, Westminster Abbey, he asked, somewhat passionately:

> Shall we be engaged longer than is absolutely necessary with the mere outworks of our ecclesiastical situation, when we have the Gospel of God committed to us, and there is a danger lest it be trampled on the ground?[335]

A few days later he returned to the same theme:

> If the Church of England is to maintain itself in the difficult position in which it and the Christian Church throughout the world are now placed, we must make great efforts to encourage real work. Instead of men wasting their time on these subtle and intricate questions, we must endeavour to encourage real theological training.[336]

One effect of the revival of Convocation, as we have already seen, was to bring the Archbishop of Canterbury into close relationship with his brother bishops of the Southern Province. With the episcopate as a whole, Tait kept in touch through a large correspondence and the traditional method of the bishops' meetings which assembled regularly at Lambeth—in the New Year; before sessions of Parliament; and at the annual dinner on Ascension Day. In addition, many *ad hoc* meetings were called for particular purposes. A natural reserve tended to make Tait's relations with the bishops somewhat official even when cordial; but if he did not win deep affection, he always evoked admiration and respect.

IV

Tait's commitment to the Establishment did not prevent his entering into such co-operative relations with nonconformists as events of the day made possible. Here his concern was to cultivate common areas of Christian action rather than to air nice points of theological difference.

In 1876 he incurred a good deal of criticism amongst Anglican churchmen for arranging a conference at Lambeth with twenty leading nonconformist ministers. This arose out of a speech of his in Convocation, leading to a request from outside the Church of England that he would call together a mixed group to discuss contemporary religious thought. Tait warmed to the idea but found that it was strongly opposed by a number of his fellow bishops on the grounds that the nonconformists opposed the educational efforts of the Church of England, and many were members of the Liberation Society. Tait decided to proceed on his own responsibility, and on 24 July 1876 six Anglican bishops, twenty-two English nonconformists, and two ministers of the Church of Scotland assembled at Lambeth. The meeting certainly gave satisfaction to all present, and one member wrote afterwards:

> Your Grace's action has done more than you are least aware of to allay the heart burnings, to disarm antagonism, and to promote the unity of spirit for which we pray.[337]

On occasions like this Tait was at his best. To his clergy Tait repeatedly urged the duty of co-operating with nonconformists wherever possible, particularly on such bodies as the British and Foreign Bible Society.

Once again his aims were immediate and practical. What he wanted was not to engage in Utopian schemes of union but for the established Church of England and nonconformity to get on with their work, no longer handicapped by mutual recriminations. Certainly he did not wish a national Church built upon the lowest common denominator. Though critical in many respects of the way in which contemporary revivalists set about their evangelistic tasks, his attitude is perhaps best expressed in his own words, which did not deserve R. W. Dale's criticism that they were 'complacent' and 'arrogant':

> . . . looking to the vastness of the field that lies before us, and the overwhelming difficulty of contending with the mass of positive sin and careless indifference which resists on all sides the progress of the Gospel, I for my part rejoice that, whether regularly or irregularly, whether according to the Divine, Scriptural and perfect way, or imperfectly, with certain admixtures of human error, Christ is preached and sleeping consciences aroused.[338]

Thus he recognized that General Booth and his militant army had their part to play, and he co-operated in an effort to bring them under the aegis of the Church of England. A committee of bishops, however, set up for this purpose by Convocation in 1882, never got to the stage of sending in a report.

One difficulty in relations with nonconformists arose out of the near monopoly enjoyed by the Church of England in its schools throughout the countryside. Three-quarters of the nation's primary schools were in fact run by the established Church, and of 8,798 schools receiving State aid in 1870, 6,724 were Anglican. Tait had long entertained an interest in national education, and in 1839 went to Prussia to study its system at first hand.

He believed that the vast bulk of the English nation wanted their young people to receive a Christian education, and saw this as the best introduction to responsible citizenship. In practice this meant supporting the Church of England in its role as the nation's schoolmaster. Effective religious education, he was convinced, needed to be doctrinal, and in this respect he did not see eye to eye with those who founded the National Education League in 1869 and who campaigned for a national, compulsory, free and non-sectarian curriculum. Tait consistently encouraged the National Society and the Church of England generally to co-operate with the State system while continuing to make its own contribution within it. Particularly was this important after Forster's Education Act of 1870, under which Church and voluntary schools received State aid, but local authorities were empowered to set up schools and to tax ratepayers to maintain them. Tait entertained the hope that children would benefit from the friendly rivalry between the two systems, and that demands would not be imposed upon Church schools beyond their capacity to pay for them.

As to universities, Tait supported the abolition of religious tests, though anxious to retain, where possible, the rights of episcopal Visitors to colleges. Remembering his own early years, he was concerned to extend the range of entry, and had little sympathy with extremes of social privilege. It is typical, moreover, that he preferred to look to universities for the training of ordinands, rather than to the theological colleges which were then springing up. He would regret the day, he said, when young men ceased to find within the great universities the best possible training for the work to which they had determined to devote their lives.

As to Roman Catholics, Tait was personally friendly, and he would entertain some of their priests at Addington; but he did not, for the present, see any prospect of closer relationships. Many years earlier, when on a visit to Italy, he had written of a religious festival in Perugia:

> The scene was indeed like the worship of some heathen deity.
> This surely is anti-Christ. And this is the city of an archbishop,
> and within the Pope's own territory.[339]

The Roman Church in his eyes seemed corrupt and superstitious; but he avoided controversial warfare with its members. Thus at the time of the Vatican Council of 1870, when many felt that the Church of England ought to take some official notice of its proceedings, Tait thought it far more sensible, as its opinion had not been asked, to say nothing. He took the opportunity, however, to claim that though the Church of England was not necessarily for export to Italy, yet it had 'a great mission in promoting the rational form of Christianity, that true practical Christianity, which we are ourselves privileged to enjoy, and in which may be found the solution of so many of those great questions which at present distress and disturb Europe'.[340]

Tait did, however, show an interest in the Old Catholics in Germany and Switzerland, and invited two of their bishops, Reinken and Herzog, to Addington. It was always one of Tait's contentions that the Church of England ought to be better known in France, and in December 1880 he held a meeting at Lambeth in the presence of Père Hyacinthe, a former Roman Catholic, to discuss how this might be brought about. But always it was the practical which appealed to him. Thus, when Bishop of London and there was published a correspondence between Cardinal Patrizzi and some 198 Anglican clergymen concerning a proposed union of the Roman, Anglican and Eastern Churches, he felt it incumbent on him to take notice of this in what proved his last charge to the clergy of London. Every sincere man, he said, longed for union, but it must be

> no hollow peace, still less a peace which shall be purchased by sacrificing our liberty and God's truth. But when we come to projects of reuniting Christendom, we are not to be hurried on by mere feelings of romance. Of course we are not such children as to suppose that the real unity of Christendom is to be secured by the clergy of Rome, Constantinople and London wearing similarly coloured stoles.[341]

Tait was by no means unaware of the Eastern Churches and kept up an extensive correspondence with them, often within the context of the troubled politics of that part of Eastern Europe. When in August 1876 he received a telegram from the Patriarch of Armenia concerning the Turkish atrocities, he noted in his diary that this 'must be instantly attended to'. With his usual thoroughness he set out to inform himself as best he could of the real situation, and some months later saw the ex-Patriarch in his room at the House of Lords. This concern was typical, and many letters arrived at Lambeth from Jerusalem and Assyrian Christians. Tait saw this personal correspondence with the leaders of Orthodox Churches as important, but he was chary of vaster schemes of union such as High Churchmen in England were anxious to promote. His reservations came out in the debate in the Upper House of Convocation in February 1875, concerning the Bonn Conference. He had a difficulty, he confessed, about these discussions and it was a 'grave one'. Undoubtedly the divisions within Christendom constituted a great 'stumbling block' to the progress of Christ's Kingdom; but he himself felt more disturbed at the moment

> with regard to those divisions which separate us from those with whom we are by nationality and by language and by the country in which we live connected, than with regard to those divisions which separate us from persons who are at a very great distance locally. . . . I think that if I am to begin, I should prefer beginning with union with those who are immediately about our own doors.

Also, what about our Protestant brethren on the Continent of Europe 'with whom it was the custom of our forefathers to unite very heartily and from whom unfortunate circumstances have more or less estranged us in later years'.[342] To Tait, who never forgot his Scottish background, a common Reformation inheritance was as important as episcopal succession.

V

It fell to Tait's lot to preside over the second Lambeth Conference, which met in 1878. He was not a keen supporter of the original proposal, although he co-operated loyally to make the Conference a success. The reason for this caution was simple. There were so many explosive fields of controversy, biblical, doctrinal, and ritualistic, that he questioned the value of their public discussion by a heterogeneous assembly of bishops coming together from all over the world.

Was there to be a second Lambeth Conference? The question was important, for a second must inevitably be regarded as the beginning of a series. Doubt was certainly expressed as to the worthwhileness of another, and the fact that Tait would be the chairman increased the scepticism of some members of the American episcopate. Bishop Kerfoot, however, was able to inform Tait on 3 November 1874 that the bishops in the United States, by a majority of forty-three to three, had asked him to request the summoning of another Conference, though they thought that the period of meeting must be extended and the topics for discussion carefully chosen in advance. The practical Tait had come to the same conclusion, and he raised the matter with his brethren in Convocation and also consulted the Archbishop of York. As a result he wrote to the American bishops on 7 June 1875, suggesting that such a conference should meet in the tenth year after the last, and stressing the necessity 'to exclude all questions which might happen to entrench on the complete independence of the several branches of the Church'. Finally, on 10 July 1877, Tait issued a formal invitation outlining, under six headings, the subjects to be discussed. This time the Northern Convocation co-operated.

For Tait, the Conference took on a solemn and poignant significance. His only son, Crauford, a talented young man, had gone out to the United States as his personal emissary in the months preceding the assembling of the bishops. He returned home only to die.

Tait now saw the Conference as the extension of his son's work, and as having more than earthly significance. His address of welcome from St. Augustine's chair on St. Peter's Day, 1878 to the hundred bishops was impressive, and instinct with that sense of historical occasion to which Tait readily responded. 'The bond that unites us,' he concluded, 'is not the less sacred because so many hopes of earthly joy have withered and disappeared. God unite us all more closely in His own great family.'[343]

Three days later the bishops got down to business in the Great Library at Lambeth. The Archbishop's opening address was a solid performance, though perhaps not over welcome to the more 'catholic' members of the Conference, since he elaborated, in painstaking detail, the difference in the constitutional position of their various Churches, stressing the establishment character of the Church of England with its unique ingredient of the Royal Supremacy. 'I see no symptom of its being changed,' he remarked cryptically, 'until something better be found.' Equally he recognized that each Church had its own relation with the State. Therefore, 'whatever advice we may give in our deliberations in this assembly must go back, before it can have any binding or practical force, to those bodies who are perfectly independent and perfectly competent to act for themselves.'[344]

Tait spared no energy to ensure the success of the Conference. He chaired every public session, and went round the committees. His hospitality left a permanent impression on all those who attended. It was not simply a matter of his presence with them at lunch every day in the Guard Room, but his introducing them in the evenings to the intimate life of his family.

Together with Wordsworth of Lincoln, Fraser of Manchester, and Mitchinson of Barbados, he drew up that part of the report which dealt with such difficult subjects as the attitude of the Anglican

358

Church towards Rome and the Old Catholic Movement; the constitution of the West Indian diocese; and the controversy in England over such matters as ritualism and the use of the confessional. The result was that the report bore the stamp of his robust common-sense. An American bishop later summed up his impressions:

> First and foremost in rank, as he was unquestionably in his presence and 'many sidedness' of character, was the Primate of All England, Dr. Archibald Campbell Tait. . . . Fair and equitable in his address and rulings, and at the same time astute in feeling the temper of his auditors and brethren and singularly adroit in the management of one of the most independent and unimpressible gatherings possible to conceive, the Archbishop's presidency was above praise.[345]

Tait continued to maintain a great interest in the Colonial Churches, and though he recognized that they must inevitably move on to complete independence, he yet felt that this ought to be a gradual process, and that in the meantime there was some value in their maintaining a formal link with Canterbury. The matter often arose at a practical level—this was how Tait preferred it—when bishops who had been appointed by the Crown under letters patent died or resigned and were succeeded by those who possessed no such credentials. Tait took the view that when he consecrated a colonial or missionary bishop, that bishop should take the canonical oath of obedience to Canterbury. Here the Archbishop had the support of the bishops of Australia and Canada, but Archbishop Gray of Cape Town saw it very differently. With his usual disregard of history, he wished the Archbishop to act 'in such a case merely on behalf of the Colonial Metropolitan to whom alone', so he argued, 'could any such oath be legitimately taken'. As to any legal or statutory difficulties, Gray called these a mere 'cobweb which scarce needs brushing aside'. To Tait, however, legality did matter, and he stood firm; indeed he declared that it was not within his powers 'to alter at his individual discretion the oath prescribed in the Consecration service', although he was perfectly happy for a bishop to be consecrated outside England, in which case no such problem arose.

Tait's interest led to a vast correspondence with overseas bishops who often sought his advice in a purely personal capacity, and usually found it shrewd and penetrating. In offering it he showed consummate tact, and Randall Davidson records how on one occasion, in connexion with difficulties in the see of Colombo, he held discussions outside Lambeth Palace 'lest it should be supposed that the archbishop to whom both parties looked for the settlement of the matter, had claimed an official right to intervene'.[346]

# 5

## E. W. BENSON AND THE DIVINE SOCIETY

I

It would be difficult to imagine a greater and more significant contrast than that between Archbishop Tait and his successor Edward White Benson. Admittedly each was, in his own way, distinctively Victorian. Both underwent that almost inevitable experience of the time, harrowing personal bereavement. Benson's eldest son Martin, an intelligent and precocious boy, died at Winchester. Years later, on his sixtieth birthday, Benson confessed that this was 'the inexplicable grief of his life'. 'To see into that will be worth dying,' he commented. Both Archbishops read also providential significance into the growth of Empire.

Benson was brilliant, imaginative, but prone to fits of acute depression. His wife and their family were highly talented, intense, closely knit, yet subjected to great stress and strain. By instinct and temperament he was essentially a priest and a poet, with a great feeling for the universal Church, its liturgy and the beauty of holiness. Greatly influenced by his headmaster, James Prince Lee, later Bishop of Manchester, no other vocation than that of orders ever occurred to him. As a boy he converted a disused room in his father's factory into an oratory. Later in life, when Archbishop, he would 'steal away and shut himself up alone for a while in the place known as Becket's Crown, where is the marble chair of St. Augustine. It was in this contact with the Church's sacred places, and through them with his predecessors and their government, that he examined his own work and formed plans for the future.'[347]

The temperamental differences between Tait and Benson are illustrated in their literary style. Tait writes easily, and if he lacks finesse and subtlety there is a strong and persuasive masculinity. The English of Benson, though more literary and scholarly, is complicated and obscure, but always with a conscious feeling for words, particularly in their more evocative overtones.

Benson had behind him a conspicuously successful career when he came to Lambeth. He was the first headmaster of the newly constituted Wellington College and held the post with distinction, so

360

that the College became not a charity school for the sons of officers, as first envisaged, but a great public school. From Wellington he went on, at the invitation of Bishop Wordsworth, to become canon and Chancellor of Lincoln. There he founded the *Schola Cancellarii*, a theological college for ordinands. He also gave his support to every social movement, establishing night schools for working men, lectures for mechanics, and Bible classes for all. In 1877 he was appointed the first Bishop of Truro, where he was assiduous in visiting his clergy in the remote areas, and identifying himself with Cornish interests, winning the goodwill not only of churchmen but of the great body of Methodists. Benson founded a divinity school similar to that of Lincoln, and co-operated in the revival of the old grammar school. He instituted a high school for girls, to which he sent his own daughters. Most significant, he began the building of the Cathedral to a neo-Gothic design, the foundation stone of which was laid by the Prince of Wales as Duke of Cornwall, on 20 May 1880. While at Truro, he published his work, *The Cathedral, its Necessary Place in the Life of the Church.*

Tait's death in 1882 was not unexpected, for his health had been failing for some time. The nomination of his successor fell to Gladstone, and it is but justice to this great churchman to say that never has a Prime Minister taken more care, showed more personal interest, or been better informed in the discharge of this duty. There were four candidates in the field: the Bishop of Winchester (Harold Browne); the Bishop of Durham (J. B. Lightfoot); the Dean of St. Paul's (R. W. Church)—he would not hear of it; and the Bishop of Truro (E. W. Benson). The intricacies of the appointment are told in detail by G. K. A. Bell in his *Life of Randall Davidson*. Only a few days before his death Tait said:

> I should be truly thankful to think it certain that the Bishop of Winchester would succeed me at Lambeth. He could do more than any other man to preserve the Church in peace for its real work against sin. I pray God he may be appointed and may accept the call.[348]

Tait seems to have regarded such an appointment as almost certain; and Davidson conveyed his desire (coupled with a mention of Benson) to Dean Bradley of Westminster and Dean Lake of Durham, both of whom Gladstone was in the habit of consulting. He also informed the Queen, who commented, in confidence: 'These views . . . will be followed, the Bishop of Winchester's age being perhaps the only difficulty'[349]—a handicap not so serious since she thought Canterbury less exhausting than Winchester. Gladstone, however, had firmly made up his mind to have Benson. Here his greater ecclesiastical knowledge made him more effective with the Queen than the less informed Disraeli. At first she put up a little bit of a fight, and Davidson was sent on an embarrassing errand to find out from Mrs. Browne, at first hand, the state of her husband's health. The verdict was not wholly reassuring. Gladstone, himself aged seventy-three, did some research, and as a result told the Queen that no archbishop since the time of Juxon, and the situation was then exceptional, had been appointed over the age of seventy. With his accustomed frankness he wrote to Bishop Browne, admitting the seeming incongruity of *his* taking this line, but maintaining that their cases differed 'in one vital point, the newness of the duties of the English, or rather anglican or British primacy to a diocesan bishop, however able and experienced, and the newness of mental attitude and action, which they would require'.[350] He might have added that a disillusioned public or a disgruntled party have ways of getting rid of an inadequate Prime Minister!

And so Benson, Tory as he was, and aged fifty-four, was nominated to the primacy. Replying to a criticism that the new Archbishop was giving his support to the Conservative candidate for the University of Cambridge, Gladstone retorted that 'if he had been a worldly man or self seeker, he would not have done anything so imprudent'. Yet surprise was in fact expressed that Gladstone should have found the 'best clergyman in the worst of politicians'.

His offer of the primacy was couched in terms which certainly do Gladstone credit.

> This proposal—he wrote on 16 December 1882—is a grave one, but it is I can assure you made with a sense of its gravity, and in some degree proportioned to it: and it comes to you, not as an offer of personal advancement, but as a request that, whereas you have heretofore been employing five talents in the service of the Church and Realm, you will hereafter employ ten with the same devotion in the same good and great cause.[351]

Benson's nomination was confirmed in Bow Church on 3 March, with 'grotesque ceremonies'—his own comment—and he was enthroned in Canterbury Cathedral on 29 March. On the previous day, the new Archbishop was received by the Mayor and the Dean with a guard of honour of Kent Rifle Volunteers and Yeomanry. He then drove to the Guildhall, where he was greeted with loud blasts upon the Wardmote horn 'irreverently received with loud laughter'. The Mayor presented an address from the Corporation, and the Archbishop replied in a longish speech, in which he noted, to everyone's satisfaction, that the Cornish choughs were included in the city arms.

At the enthronement next day, the Queen was represented by the Duke of Edinburgh, and at a luncheon afterwards in the Chapter House Benson spoke again:

> In contending for spiritual freedom—he said (the reference was to ecclesiastical courts)—we do not seek what some of the greatest of those who have sat in the chair of Augustine have sought and obtained—temporal dominion in the world.

He then turned to the future and struck the note of professional optimism which had become almost an occupational attitude in successive Archbishops.

> The Church of England has no fear. She need never be afraid of education, never afraid of research, or anything that science or philosophy may find out, because science and philosophy have their fountains in the Throne above.[352]

It was a bold thing to say, and it was meant to be significant.

If Benson had an aim as Archbishop, it was to foster the growth of spiritual vitality in the Church of England, thereby releasing its nascent energies. His was essentially a religious approach, and as much as F. D. Maurice he always sought a principle to give coherence to a policy. R. T. Davidson, who knew him well, records:

> I have never seen any man who seemed in the same degree to be able to put the Christian Creed—not in its more general principles but in its details—into practical action in dealing with the passing questions of the hour.[353]

He spent long years researching into, and meditating upon, the works of Cyprian, which finally bore fruit in *Cyprian, his Life, his Times, his Work*, published in 1892. He was deeply influenced by the theology of episcopacy contained in this early father, and felt it was relevant to present needs. Benson entertained a 'high view' of the bishop's office, his work and status. Thus, though he welcomed the revival of energy initiated by Wilberforce which kept bishops busy in their dioceses, he yet deplored that this often prevented their attendance at bishops' meetings. When on one occasion his intimate friend, John Wordsworth, Bishop of Salisbury, excused himself from such attendance on the grounds that he had a prior engagement, he received the following peremptory rebuke:

> . . . do let me remind you that the Bishops' meeting was fixed last July, and that you were supplied with a printed sheet— stating the same. And that if the Bishops set aside these solemn

Church engagements for diocesan ones—there is no wonder that the Church is lacking in corporate life, and that the Parishes follow the example of the Diocesans—and live for themselves. Do excuse me for saying that I think it very sad indeed and fraught with evil omens.[354]

Benson feared that the bishops' increasing preoccupation with business in their own area would end up by making them 'a name without a meaning. . . . Good diocesan bishops—but Bishops of England, no!'[355] 'Diocesanism' needed to be corrected. Benson was much concerned that the bishops should act together as an order, and he called them together for their first 'quiet day' at Lambeth on 20 April 1888. He spent a great deal of anxious thought, and sought advice, as to what the role of a united episcopate (apart from the maintenance of doctrinal truth) ought to be. On Sunday, 19 June 1887, he spent a 'memorable day' closeted at Lambeth with the Bishop of Durham (Lightfoot) and Canon Westcott. They told him frankly that he and the other bishops were slow to speak out and act together on the great moral issues of the day, leaving this to the Pope and Mr. John Bright. Benson agreed that the meetings of bishops were 'so short, so full of matters to discuss (ludicrously full), the speechification so lengthy, the unwillingness to commit ourselves so great, and the finalities so hurried, that though some things are carried through not amiss, yet really grave questions have no hearing, or if they are supposed to come "within the sphere of practical politics", an inadequate one'.[356] The general advice offered by those two eminent churchmen was that some form of 'Cardinalate' seemed absolutely necessary, and that this might be secured by some four or five bishops giving at least a fortnight to an annual conference, with no other duty but to discuss 'matters proposed by the Arch-bishop—or otherwise found necessary'. This was in harmony with Benson's own thinking, though he was sceptical as to whether any of the bishops could find the time from their dioceses to devote to this continuing care.

Yet the need for a small but strong council of wise and statesman-like ecclesiastics, to whom he could refer particular matters and who would be at hand to give him advice at any time, remained, though he did not see how 'this responsibility can really be shared'. In this respect he deplored the reduction in the number of the Westminster canonries, and felt that they might have been used to supply men of the calibre needed. What he never ceased to deplore was that 'as head of a department [he] had often neither the time nor energy left to deliberate widely and closely about the Church's needs; and he thought it impossible to originate wise and fruitful schemes for

Church progress under the severe pressure of official life'.[357] We shall have to return to this theme later and ask whether the need has been met.

In encouraging the bishops to act as a body Benson never lost sight of his own unique status and responsibility as Primate of All England. The history of the see kindled his imagination, and he told the people of Cornwall not long before leaving them, that Canterbury was 'more ancient than the Throne of Queen Victoria', and from earliest days 'has always been the loyal subject and servant of the Sovereign's Throne and of the people'. 'It is a very remarkable office to which I have been called,' he went on, 'and one which ought to and really does crush one to the earth while one thinks of its responsibilities.'[358] This was in line with the remark of Lightfoot, who, at a public dinner, confessed that he regarded the office of Archbishop of Canterbury 'as little inferior even now to that of the Bishop of Rome, and destined at no distant date to be even greater'.

II

It was such an attitude to his office, and his own theological concerns, which determined the part that Benson played in what is now known as 'The Lincoln Judgment', and which he regarded as perhaps the most significant event in his archiepiscopate.

This *cause célèbre* began in 1888 with a petition presented by the Church Association to the Archbishop complaining of certain alleged illegal ritual practices committed by William King, the saintly Bishop of Lincoln, and requiring him to bring the Bishop before his Court. Benson was placed in a real dilemma, since the jurisdiction of the Archbishop's Court of Audience in a matter of this kind was in doubt yet if he declined to act on complaint he might be compelled to do so by a mandamus from the Queen's Bench division of the High Court. Lord Selborne and Gladstone both advised the Archbishop either to use his discretionary powers to veto the proceedings—though this might seem a tacit recognition of jurisdiction—or to decline jurisdiction altogether. The constitutional historian, Bishop Stubbs, declared of the Court of Audience: 'It is not a Court: it is an Archbishop sitting in his library.' Bishop Wordsworth said almost the same thing, though at greater length and more politely, allowing, however, that according to the canons there did seem to be an ultimate jurisdiction resting in the Archbishop which was not exhausted in the judicial authority delegated to the Dean of the Arches and the Vicar-General.[359] Lord Carnarvon thought that the issue of the trial would prove 'disastrous'—*whatever* it be'. Benson felt strongly that he ought not to expose the archbishopric to the risk of asserting a jurisdiction which might later by another court be declared invalid. Therefore, after consulting Randall Davidson, he informed the petitioners that he was uncertain whether in this matter he had any jurisdiction. This led them to appeal, as he had hoped, on this point of law to the Privy Council, which in its judgment delivered on 3 August—here the bishops concurred with the lay judges— declared that he had.

Benson received this verdict with mixed satisfaction, commenting: 'It is a good thing that the Church should have such and so spiritual a jurisdiction—but it is a painful and terrible case to try it upon.' Benson was now convinced, and the advice he sought from the Lord Chancellor confirmed him in this conviction, that he had no option but to hear the case, and that a Court had in fact been 'discovered' which High Churchmen according to their own principles must obey. He wished, therefore, to stress the 'spiritual' nature of this court, and objected, as Tait would not have done, to the Privy Council's judgment including the words that the Queen 'authorises and commands' him to hear the case. 'The authority *exists*,'[360] he maintained, in the Court of the Archbishop of Canterbury.

Benson also entertained a further anxiety, lest Bishop King would turn up in person, unaccompanied by legal advisers.

> This *would* ruin it. He would plead only for *tolerance* and be posed as the martyr. Whereas what is wanted is a clear lucid statement and arguments of all that is to be said on that side as to the practices. Of course the Court could not find arguments for either side.[361]

The Church must now use the opportunity given it through a purely spiritual court, which 'no secular statute has established, or meddled with at any time', to determine whether the practices complained of had a real justification in the history, law, and usage of the Church'.[362]

For these reasons, in spite of the pressures brought to bear upon him, Benson declined to use his veto. So the Bishop of Lincoln was summoned to appear at Lambeth on 4 January 1889. Though the personal background was unhappy, Benson did not see his task as wholly uncongenial. As distinct from the Privy Council, which was 'obliged to go by the merest letter of the Book of Common Prayer, as if they were printers', he 'would be expected to go to Historical and Theological lights and side lights, and to acquaint [himself] even with the *mens* of such a student and compiler as Cranmer'.[363]

At the first hearing, King protested that he wished to be tried before all the bishops of the Province, an appeal in line with many that Benson had received that Convocation might act as a jury or nominate assessors; or that the Archbishop's Court should be converted into a synod. Benson saw, and rightly saw, grave inconveniences in any such procedures, and was determined to assert his own jurisdiction and to follow the precedent set in the case of Bishop Watson by Archbishop Tenison. He himself would constitute the Court—'the most ancient . . . of inherent jurisdiction existing in England probably'—and call to his aid a number of episcopal assessors. On Saturday, 11 May, the Archbishop gave judgment in these terms:

> The Court finds that from the most ancient times of the Church the Archiepiscopal jurisdiction in the case of Suffragans has existed; that in the Church of England it has been from time to time continuously exercised in various forms; that nothing has occurred in the Church to modify that jurisdiction.[364]

The Archbishop's sense of irony came to his aid during this trying time. Four students from Ely Theological College joined in sending a protest to Lambeth. Benson commented:

> I ordained four of those little gentlemen at Advent, and their knowledge of all the *rest* of Church History has yet to be acquired. Their luminosity on this one point is *electrical*.[365]

The case began on 4 February, and ended on 25 February. The Bishop of Lincoln was accused, nominally of ten, in fact of seven, practices in relation to the celebration of the Holy Communion. The Archbishop carefully supervised the 'lay out' of the library for the occasion, taking care that the Metropolitical cross was placed on the table beneath the 'judge' as a symbol of his spiritual jurisdiction. In August he went off, to draw up his judgment, to the Rieder Furca Hotel, near the Bel Alp. How odd, he reflected at the time, that 'one of the earliest *notes* I ever made, when I began to collect topics for a commonplace book, was an extract from Ed. VI. injunctions about Lights. I was about 13 then, and here I am 61 and at the same poor thing still'.[366]

Benson made it clear that he did not feel it right for his court 'to shelter itself under authority, as to evade the responsibility, or escape the labour of examining each of the points afresh'. The effect of his judgment was to make legal certain practices which had hitherto been regarded or declared illegal. The Archbishop decided:

1. that the mixture of water with wine must not be performed as part of the Communion Service;

367

2. that the eastward position was lawful provided the manual acts were visible;

3. that the *Agnus Dei* might be sung;

4. that lighted candles on the altar, if not lighted during the service, were permissible;

5. that the sign of the Cross at the absolution and at the blessing was an innovation and must be discontinued.

Into this judgment, which the Archbishop himself read at Lambeth, there went a wealth of historical scholarship; and all was expressed eirenically and in a spirit of genuine concern. At the end of his judgment he declared, with some emotion:

> The Court has not only felt deeply the incongruity of minute questionings and disputations in great and sacred subjects, but desires to express its sense that time and attention are diverted thereby from the Church's real contest with evil and building up of good, both by those who give and by those who take offence unadvisedly in such matters.[367]

To this Tait would have said a loud 'Amen'.

The overwhelming mass of interested and informed opinion declared that if such work must be done the Archbishop had done it well. Professor Sidgwick described the judgment as 'able, fearless and judicious', indicative that the Archbishop felt himself on his own 'native heather'.[368] Extremists at both ends, of course, inveighed against it, and in practice High Churchmen paid it scant regard. The Church Association appealed away from it to the Privy Council, whose previous judgments the Archbishop had in fact reversed. This appeal was dismissed.

One gratifying aspect of this somewhat sorry business, since one cannot but regret the waste of effort and energy to which it led, was the mutual respect firmly entertained between the saintly Bishop of Lincoln and the Archbishop. Indeed, King accepted the judgment and issued a pastoral letter to this effect to his diocese.

Many who longed for peace from ritualistic disputes were convinced that the Archbishop had uttered the right word; and that, for once, Church and State had been able to come to a common mind because the full facts had been put in a more spiritual and historical context. On the clergy in his own diocese Benson urged tolerance and common sense. To declare that a practice was not illegal did not mean that it ought to be adopted, particularly when it ran counter to the wishes of the majority of parishioners; a distinction which some clergymen find it hard to appreciate. It soon became evident, however, that Benson's judgment was to have little practical effect in the parishes. Conviction and conscience combined to make control almost impossible.

Benson saw the Church in more catholic and apostolic terms than did his predecessor, needing its own organs of government, even if these organs, in matters of legislation, must be reinforced by the authority of Parliament. Writing of his father, A. C. Benson commented that to him ecclesiastical loyalties always came first and that political considerations which, against his will, he was forced to entertain, took a distinctly second place.

In general Benson believed that the State should contribute to the process of church reform by making time available in Parliament. Also he recognized freely that a distinction must be made between an established and a non-established Church. Hence the Church of England never had a clerical court at the head of affairs, and he thought it 'never ought to have'. In the Lincoln case, though Benson acquiesced in an approach to the Privy Council concerning the legality of the Archbishop's Court, he rejoiced that the authority of the Court did not stem from this secular source. He cordially welcomed the publication, on 12 December 1885, of a memorial promoted by the Bishop of Durham and emanating in the main from the Senate of Cambridge University, which asserted that 'the Church of England has long suffered serious injury from the postponement of necessary reforms', and proposing 'most urgently . . . the admission of laymen of all classes who are *bona fide* churchmen to a substantial share in the control of church affairs'.[369]

The practical problem, however, was how to persuade the Church into a common mind as to what these reforms ought to be, and how to get them made into law. The Archbishop accepted the memorial as a challenge and was prepared to do something about it. He himself wished for a church more conscious of its integrity, deploying laymen as well as presbyters and bishops. He both sanctioned and showed initiative in advocating a House of Laymen 'to supplement the clerical Convocations and to form a consultative body of lay Churchmen drawn by a system of election from each diocese of the province'. The grafting of the new on to the old was not to prove easy. The Lower House of Convocation, to quote Benson's words, proved 'timid', and papers 'wandered backwards and forwards'. In the Upper House he was able to reassure his brethren that such a House of Laymen would be consultative only, and be the first to recognize that each 'order' had its particular function within the whole. 'They were no more likely to alter an old Article or to introduce a new one or to change the Liturgy than they were to celebrate the Sacraments.' Insistence on this difference of function was a matter of deep principle with Benson. In February 1892, when Convocation was discussing the issue of a book of family prayers, he declared firmly:

> It is not the part of the assembly of the presbyters of the Church
> to issue in the name of the Church, books of prayer or of doctrine,
> but that is the part of the Bishops of the Church.[370]

Thus the scheme, so dear to Benson's heart, went forward, and at
the request of Convocation, in February 1886, he called the House of
Laymen into existence, formally opening its proceedings.

It was a great moment for the Archbishop. He believed that the
Church of England had rediscovered a structure rooted in the nature
of a Church and going back to primitive times. In a carefully prepared speech, he dealt with the difficulty yet the need to reinforce
Convocation, particularly in that 'which relates to the voice of the
laity in the controlling of Church affairs, whether for the larger or
the smaller areas of administration'. He had always maintained that
the laity needed to play a significant part in the life of the Church,
and he now reaffirmed this in his own distinctive style:

> The consultative bodies of Laymen which are now to be found
> in all branches of the Anglican Communion carry us back long
> ages to the times when, before the Italian Church over-rode all
> such promises, St. Cyprian promised the faithful laity that he
> would without their assent do nothing.[371]

It was with deep satisfaction that Benson attended a great service in
St. Paul's Cathedral in connexion with Church Defence when there
was present, as well as the Convocations of Canterbury and York, the
House of Laymen.

The creation of the House of Laymen, however, did not pass
without critical comment. A question was asked in the House of
Commons as to whether the Archbishop had not in fact set up a third
House of Convocation, without securing a legal opinion from the
Crown lawyers. Was he not liable to imprisonment? Benson promptly
drew up a memorandum which he passed on to the Home Secretary,
and confided to his diary: 'I put together a few things and, of course,
ordered my barge in proper form to be ready when I should be
committed to the Tower.'[372]

The House of Laymen, though it had moral force, left the legal
position of the Church of England unaltered. Church reform still
needed parliamentary legislation, and this was made difficult by
party divisions within *Ecclesia Anglicana*, which disinclined politicians
to use the precious time of Parliament for this purpose. It was not
made easier by the division of England into two Provinces, each with

its separate Convocation. Here Benson was foremost in seeing the need for some closer collaboration, and as a result of a letter in February 1886 from the Archbishop of York, he agreed that there should be mutual exchange of resolutions. In 1887 he went further, and appointed a joint committee of both Houses to consider what more could be done.

III

Benson's views on the establishment are important. As a prebendary of Lincoln in 1871, he preached a sermon in which he argued that the Church of England must prepare itself to lose its link with the State; but as he grew older it was not a prospect which he viewed with relish. If this were to happen, he once said in the jocular vein which he affected to conceal anxious thought, 'I shall head a revolt, seize the principal agitators and hang them at Lambeth out of the windows.'[373] More likely, he added ruefully, it would be the other way round. The question of disestablishment, he believed, was no clerical question. In the main it was the concern of the laymen, and it was up to them to speak for the Church if they were the Church. Doubtless the duties of the archiepiscopal office itself helped in the process of hardening Benson's views on this matter until he believed that the continuance of the relationship between Church and State was a matter of fundamental importance to the English people. So strongly did he believe this that on a public platform he declared that if the *Ecclesia Anglicana* were to lose its unique position he would prefer the establishment of any denomination, holding the essentials of Christian doctrine, to a formally neutral or irreligious State. It was not fear of what might happen to the Church, but to the English people 'which made him resolute to fight every inch of ground in defence of the establishment'. In his *Seven Gifts* he wrote:

> What we believe as Christian citizens is that a Church freely established as it is in England is the best mode of advancing the best interests of Religion. By *freely* we understand that it admits of self-reform such as it has exemplified in its history on a grander scale than any other Church, seldom more actively, continuously, and happily than in the last half century.[374]

Nor did establishment militate against what he called 'apostolic form' or catholic mission. Yet he was never doctrinaire on this subject, and admitted that the Church would secure certain freedoms if the nexus were broken.

Benson's predilection for establishment, however, never made him feel at home in the House of Lords. His son writes that his work there was not congenial to him; he was convinced of the importance of securing prompt and practical Church legislation, but the Parliamentary methods of securing it were distasteful to him. He cared deeply and anxiously for the results of measures, but he was not a good Parliamentary speaker, and he had none of the arts of the Lobbyist.

Apart from his temperamental dislike of the House's way of doing things, Benson also suffered another disadvantage. Unique among Archbishops since the Restoration, apart from Sancroft and Tillotson, he had had no prior parliamentary experience whatever. Truro, as a new see, did not as of right carry a seat in the House of Lords, and he confessed frankly that he always found speaking there somewhat of a strain. In March 1884 he wrote to Westcott:

> It is really a terrible place for the unaccustomed. Frigid impatience and absolute good will, combined with a thorough conviction of the infallibility of laymen (if not too religious) on all sacred subjects are the tone, morale and reason of the House as a living being. My whole self possession departs, and ejection from the House seems the best thing which could happen to one.[375]

Perhaps this uneasiness in the presence of independently minded laymen was made more acute in that as headmaster and bishop it was his wont to take precedence. This dislike, however, was not allowed to stand between him and what he regarded as a clear duty. He attended the House regularly, and did his best, not very successfully, to secure that his suffragans were present. He often lamented that their diocesan duties kept them away. Some critical situations brought the bishops together, as for example the Suspensory Bill designed to disestablish the Welsh Church.

The Archbishop was zealous, even 'touchy', concerning the rights of the bishops as members of the House of Lords. For example, when the Deceased Wife's Sister Bill came before Parliament he took grave exception to an appeal circulated only to the lay lords though it contained a request to the spiritual peers 'not to use their exceptional position'. He realized the importance of Parliament to an established Church, and he certainly endeavoured to use it to promote necessary Church reform. Persistently he laid the needs of the Church before successive governments and claimed their help. From 1886 till his death in 1896 he was at some time or another sponsoring legislation. Unfortunately he lacked both Tait's ability to work through the tortuous paths of parliamentary procedure, and his facility in drawing up statutes. Also his manner of putting his case—he usually spoke from notes which encouraged him to pack in too many ideas—was not very compelling to lay people. For example in 1887 he introduced into the House of Lords his own Patronage Bill, designed to prevent trafficking in livings; but it was far too complicated, Bishop Magee complaining that it was 'overloaded with a number of complicated . . . provisions for a great Diocesan Council of Presentations'.[376]

Again when the Report of the Commission on Ecclesiastical Courts appeared in 1883 Benson was anxious to secure the co-operation of the Government in getting a Clergy Discipline Bill on the statute book, particularly since he had the support of both parties in the Church, of the press, and also of Mr. Gladstone 'who had promised to help its passage'.

> It has long been said—he pleaded—that the Church is safe if she has ten years to reform abuses. The years are passing. United with the state she cannot get rid of *some* abuses without assistance. Those which she can deal with alone are (you will admit) disappearing. And as to the others I trust I am not mistaken in building on the assistance which alone is effective in the House of Commons.[377]

But once again Benson was unsuccessful, and the Bill had to be withdrawn. As a consequence, he became disillusioned with the Conservative Government, complaining bitterly that its members had done nothing to redeem their pledge 'to stand by the Church they love'.

Maybe in this matter Benson underestimated the difficulties of the Government, since many who belonged to the party, in particular the unionists, were hostile to Church reform. Some advised him to get a private member to propose the Clergy Discipline Bill again in the Commons, but he was forced to confess: 'I know so little of how any of these things are done.' In near despair he again asked help of Gladstone, the 'great Churchman of the age', and finally by sheer persistence he was in this instance successful.[378]

It may seem surprising that it was from the Conservative Government that Benson experienced least co-operation. It was something he felt keenly, and it manifested itself over ecclesiastical appointments. As Archbishop he was seldom consulted, and the following is a typical entry in his diary:

> Heard that X is to be Bishop of Y., as we have a Conservative Government and he is a High Churchman, neither he nor the Premier vouchsafe to communicate with me either before or after. (Never did). A Liberal Government . . . always does. Mr.

Gladstone never failed to consult either about Episcopal or lower dignities beforehand with me. The fact is that Erastianism is far more of a Conservative than of a Radical error, and it comes out even thus.[379]

The involvement of the Archbishop in appointments, however, was steadily to increase as the century went on, due not least to the Queen, whose power and influence were undoubtedly factors making for a distinguished episcopate. Her preference was for broad churchmen and scholars; and left to herself she would have excluded Tractarians and extreme Evangelicals, as well as political nominations. By exerting what she regarded as her constitutional right of veto, she kept Prime Ministers on their toes, since to stand their ground they often felt the need to confer with the Archbishop before they confronted the Supreme Governor. She, on her part, in acting as an impartial jury, would also have recourse to Lambeth. The result was to make it more and more difficult for the Archbishop of Canterbury to be by-passed or ignored.

The disestablishment of the Church of England ceased, as the century drew to a close, to be a live option, but in Wales the Church was under attack and many parliamentary candidates were pledged to break its State connexion. Benson paid his first visit as Primate to Wales when he laid the foundation stone of the Canterbury Buildings at St. David's College, Lampeter. His speech, on this occasion, was looked forward to with eager expectancy. He never spoke better. He began with the vivid metaphor of Alpine climbers who pass over a dangerous crevasse in safety only because all are roped together. This, he stressed, was how they must see the present crisis. He yet recognized the need to remove any injustices to which the privileged status of the Church of England in Wales led. Hence he supported the Tithe Act which removed many legitimate grievances. In 1889 at the Church Congress in Cardiff he said:

> I might have travelled much more widely over the history of Wales. I am not concerned to defend the terrible sins, the errors, honest or dishonest, of the past. It would be nearly as difficult a task as it will be 500 years hence to defend today's. But, for good or for grief, the history of Wales is Church history, and Church history is the history of the country. An alien Church! Then whose are those noble names that gild the chronicle from times obscure with distance down to yesterday?[380]

It was meant to be a rallying cry, but it did not prevent the Liberal party from adopting Welsh disestablishment as its official policy in February, 1891. Henceforward this was a matter of acrid debate and feverish controversy, until, in 1895, the Bill to secure it 'perished with the Government that gave it birth'. In spite of his onerous duties, Benson had thrown himself into the fight with tremendous energy. It says a great deal both for the prestige and influence of the office of Archbishop and Benson's untiring will, that he was perhaps the greatest single factor, for better or for worse, in uniting the opposition against the Bill. He lectured; he revised leaflets; he broadened the base of the Church Defence League; he consulted distinguished laymen—all to this end. His speech at the Church Congress at Rhyl (1891) was described by the Bishop of St. Asaph as 'the turning point in the whole controversy'. His concluding words are worth quotation:

> But you, who are our eldest selves, fountain of our episcopacy, the very designers of our sanctuaries, the primaeval British dioceses, from which our very realm derives its only title to be called by its proudest name of Great Britain—I come from the steps of the chair of Augustine, your younger ally, to tell you that, by the benediction of God, we will not quietly see you disinherited.[381]

Benson saw great value in a national Church, yet beyond this his attitude to the person of Queen Victoria evoked an emotional loyalty which took even himself by surprise. On 20 August 1888 he wrote in his diary:

> The sentiment of loyalty is a very independent one. I remember the first throb of it, and I believe it will never grow less and is disconnected with anything touching regard for oneself. I steadily feel readiness to please her and her will, if need were, to the utmost of my power. It seems braggadocio even to say to oneself 'to death', but I think I would die joyfully to defend her from any wrong. What *is* this 'loyal passion' for our temperate kings?[382]

This passion, it is clear, ministered to something deeply embedded in Benson's temperament, not less so because of the sex of the Sovereign. He always got on better with women than with men. Archbishop and Queen had known each other for a number of years. She had visited Wellington; he saw her at Windsor soon after the death of the Prince Consort; he had had an hour's interview at Osborne after his appointment. It was his custom, after he became Archbishop, to send his sympathy on her many bereavements, and he would sometimes discuss with her matters of State. His diary records many such conversations:

At dinner the Queen asked me about the Bishops voting for the Franchise Bill [i.e. that of 1884]. I told her that the Bishops of today were not like the Bishops of 50 years ago or 55. They did such governing as they did through the superior clergy or missives. Now meetings, lectures, temperance gatherings, constant openings of mission rooms and churches, above all schools, familiarise them with the people as well as the people with them. . . . It is not likely that now when all sides agree that the people can use the Franchise properly, the Bishops should be found against their own flocks and unwilling to trust them.[383]

Many letters, of course, passed between Queen and Archbishop on episcopal appointments. The following, of 3 July 1890, from Victoria is typical:

. . . I entirely agree with you in the immense importance of the Selection for Bishoprics. It is a great anxiety and the men to be chosen *must* not be taken with reference to satisfying one or the other *Party* in the *Church* or with reference to any political party—but for their *real worth*. We want people who can be firm and conciliating, else the Church cannot be maintained.[384]

Usually Benson's language about the Queen is extravagant. Describing the opening of Parliament on 21 July 1886, he writes:

After so many tall vast men had trooped in her procession before her into the House one was almost startled by the smallness of the figure which followed them. But it is a remarkable smallness indeed, for there was no figure of them all more stately in demeanour, or more impressive in every way.[385]

His royalism reached the peak of its fervour at the time of the Jubilee celebrated in Westminster Abbey on 21 June 1887, when he drew up the order of service and left behind in his diary a meticulous description of the occasion. At the Jubilee banquet in Windsor Castle he was thrilled to wear a medal which the Queen sent him just before dinner.

I rather suspect that it is the first time that an Abp. has worn a decoration, and I am not sure that I ought—but obedience is the want of our time.[386]

'Everyone feels that the socialist movement has had a check.'[387] So he commented on the celebrations generally.

Yet in spite of this romantic adulation, Benson never became an intimate friend. Religiously Queen and Archbishop lived in different worlds. His mysticism and 'churchiness' were far removed from the practical approach of the Prince Consort.

Benson had many unofficial contacts with the Prince of Wales, although they were never particularly close. The Prince's social and private life, for which his mother, who denied him any real responsibility, must bear a measure of the blame, did not encourage an effective relationship. Benson wrote to the Prince on the death of the Duke of Clarence, and his diary records many occasions when they conversed together, for example on 20 May 1896, when they discussed 'Florence, bicycling [concerning which the Queen used to say that the English were "a little mad"]; education, missionaries.' Much to his embarrassment, and against his will, the Archbishop became involved in the notorious baccarat scandal when the Prince was called upon to give evidence in a case of libel. Its details—they are written up in E. F. Benson's *As We Were*—need not detain us. Enough that the Prince became the centre of a storm of abuse, in which the newspapers, not least *The Times*, joined with a certain degree of relish. Victorian puritanism found a unique outlet. Stead, the well known editor, took some satisfaction in calculating how many prayers had been offered in public for the Prince over the previous fifty years, the assumption being that they had been offered in vain. It was said that the Prince kept bad company; that he always went round with a pocket full of counters; that in this particular case it was he who had insisted on playing cards against the wishes of his host. To make matters worse the Prince was given to understand that the Archbishop, who was known to entertain little sympathy for gambling, 'had been instigator of this campaign'. 'Bertie', in typically forthright manner, asked the Archbishop to meet him at Marlborough House. Benson was soon able to dispose of this rumour, protesting that he had deliberately refrained from making any comment whatever. On the other hand, if the Prince wished to know his opinion, he would give it to him verbally or by letter. The Prince then launched into a defence of his own conduct, maintaining that he was no inveterate gambler; that he carried his counters with him in order to prevent the use of higher stakes; and that his host had not been opposed to such play. On parting, the Prince agreed that the Archbishop should write to him expressing the views of sensible people in relation to a matter which had caused grave public disquiet. 'Very well,' said the Prince, 'we will consider that settled, and we're old friends.'

The letter was duly sent. The Archbishop began by again dissociating himself from the press campaign, which he admitted could have no object but 'low political gains'.

> The Church has—he wrote—I am sure, felt throughout that if there were a word to be said about the Tranby Croft affair it must be said in a perfectly different spirit and manner.

As a friend, however, he must not mince his words.

> . . . I should ill repay your Royal Highness's kindness as regards my own loyalty, if I did not in a few words assure you how keen and anxious has been the feeling in the Church roused by the controversy, and how many and keen have been the representations made to the Bishops and leading men of every order. It is not the way of the Church to be vociferous, but whatever touches the throne and those near it, touches the Church and affects the peace of its best members.

Whereas intemperance had been the great evil amongst the working classes some twenty years before gambling was its counterpart today.

> All alike who, without holding any absurd views as to minute acts, are in earnest on the subject would be encouraged and their hands strengthened, if you would take any natural opportunity which might present itself of saying what you said to me, while fully distinguishing what is innocent from what is bad.[388]

The Prince acknowledged the Archbishop's letter in a friendly spirit, but gave it as his opinion, in reiterating his 'horror of gambling', that since 'the whole matter has now died down . . . it would be inopportune in me in any public manner to allude again to the painful subject which brought such a torrent of abuse upon me'.[389]

In thus declining the Archbishop's request, the Prince was probably wise.

In the 1880s a group of aristocratic ladies, alarmed by the low moral tone of 'society', and headed by the Duchess of Leeds, waited on the Archbishop, urging him to do something to 'stop the moral rot'. He declined to lecture the Prince of Wales, but consented to conduct a series of prayer meetings at Lambeth. They duly took place, but Queen Victoria, although she had no sympathy for the 'smart set', strictly forbade the attendance of the Princess of Wales. 'I can't understand,' she said, 'why Princesses should want to go to Lambeth Meetings. It's all sacerdotal. I can't think what it's all about.'[390]

IV

Tait's decision to call a second Lambeth Conference in 1878 made it nearly certain that such Conferences had come to stay; and that the chairmanship of them was to form a staple ingredient in the life of the Archbishop. Such occasions were destined to owe much to the subtle and sometimes decisive influence of the Primate in spite of steering committees and prepared agendas. The chairmanship of the Conference was an exacting task, made more so both by the range and diversity of 'type' represented among the bishops; also by the fact that all of them had experience of presiding at meetings in their own dioceses. It was a gathering which Benson anticipated with pleasure; and though not an 'easy' assembly, the uncertainty and controversy which had constituted a background to the Conference of 1867 had now in the main disappeared.

In the preparatory work for the Conference of 1888, Benson was fortunate in being able to call upon the unique experience of Randall Davidson, who had written a history of the Conferences of 1867 and 1877, and been Tait's right-hand man. There were initial difficulties, one of which the Archbishop solved by a happy combination of the wisdom of the serpent and the harmlessness of the dove. Some bishops let it be known that they wished to process in their copes both at Canterbury and in Westminster Abbey, an innovation which would undoubtedly have upset some of the more evangelical bishops. Benson made no reference to what he had heard, but issued a circular saying the question had been raised as to whether the red or black chimere should be worn. The Archbishop opted for the black chimere, lawn sleeves, and red hood!

The Conference began with a service in Canterbury Cathedral, which Benson vividly described in his diary, drawing particular attention to the history and associations of the Cathedral.

> The Archbishop's address from St. Augustine's Chair—writes Randall Davidson—was wise and generous if somewhat obscure. Seldom to my mind has the contrast been more remarkable than between the big simplicity of the words *spoken* from the Chair in 1878 and the somewhat eager, apologetic and involved utterance *read* from the same chair in 1888. But it was thoroughly *good* all the same—and no-one is more effective *looking* in a function of this sort, or more genial and kindly as the centre of such a gathering.[391]

Davidson obviously missed the down-to-earth practicality of Tait, as well as the peculiar sentiment which he could inspire. Benson's outreach was wider, less defined, and directed to those whose history loses itself in mysticism. Two days later (2 July) there was a service in Westminster Abbey 'in some ways more impressive than at Canterbury itself'. The Archbishop spoke for three quarters of an hour, and encouraged himself in the belief that 'the interest of the event . . .

kept people awake and *still* in the most marvellous way'. Benson's own summary of the sermon may be quoted:

> I continued to press the Church to keep its Diocesan centres very strong, not comminuting their resources, not reducing the size of the Dioceses so that the strong influence of each ceases to radiate through all. Then I pressed extension of organisation— new religious orders free from the snares of the past, in intimate connexion with dioceses—and thirdly to hold no work true which is not absolutely *spiritual* work. If God give us grace to work these three things out, his Church will not lose strength the next few years.[392]

At the opening session the Archbishop repeated the cautionary note of his two predecessors. 'The Conference,' he said, 'was in no sense a Synod and not adapted, or competent, or within its powers, if it should attempt to make binding decisions on doctrines or discipline.'[393]

Yet the Conference of 1888, as most, was to have its critical moment, this time arising out of a discussion of Presbyterian orders; and a report on the teaching of the Faith, drafted by Temple, Bishop of London, and rejected 'after a stormy and most unfortunate debate'. The final Encyclical was drafted by Bishops Lightfoot of Durham and Stubbs of Oxford, the former being one of an intimate circle with whom Benson often discussed matters of faith and morals. As might have been expected it gave great prominence to social questions; to Home Reunion; and relations with other churches.

> We have realised—the final section states—more fully than it was possible to realise before, the extent, the power, and the influence of the great Anglican Communion. We have felt its capacities, its opportunities, its privileges. . . . Wherever there was diversity of opinion among us there was also harmony of spirit and unity of aim.[394]

Benson was very conscious of the new status of the Chair of St. Augustine as the 'pivot' around which the Anglican Communion revolved. Randall Davidson later referred to this in these terms:

> His 'authority' if we can call it so is almost universally recognized, but it is undefined; it is moral not legal, and its effective exercise depends in no small degree upon the personal weight, tact and courtesy of the Primate . . . therefore, very much turns upon the Archbishop's willingness to concern himself actively as a

counsellor and friend in the affairs of these distant communities. Any unwillingness on his part to take trouble in the matter, or on the other hand any assumption of a definite authority and right to interfere, would probably result in a speedy diminution of his opportunities. . . . Perhaps in nothing did Archbishop Benson show more conspicuously his courteous Christian tact than in his unfailing readiness to be at the call of every Colonial or Missionary Diocese which might need his help, while avoiding every shadow of a claim to assert in autocratic form the rights of *alterius orbis papa.*[395]

To illustrate this informal method of consultation a few typical examples may be quoted. These arose out of the educational difficulties of a mission station in China; the selection of a provost for a colonial university; the ordination examination for missionaries in Africa; and (more officially) the development of an indigenous branch of the Church of England in Africa; the limitation of the jurisdiction of the American and English Churches in Japan.

Benson always entertained a great sense of ecclesiastical propriety. It offended him when the title of 'Archbishop' was precipitously, and not always courteously adopted, without the necessary consultation, in various branches of the Anglican Communion. Since such new archbishops did not take an oath to Canterbury, Benson believed that this 'going it alone' might lead to new provinces becoming, without intending it, separate churches. His knowledge of ecclesiastical procedure often served him in good stead in delicate matters of this kind. It was improper, he told the Bishop of Rupertsland, for a Primate to exercise jurisdiction outside his own Province (1 April 1895). He expressed the hope that when British Columbia became a province, the step would be taken with a proper regard for previous obligations and with all due exercise of courtesy. 'Australia and South Africa,' he commented, 'proceeded regularly. They had decided not to make any alteration in title until the Lambeth Conference.'

V

Benson was a man of far too wide and generous instincts not to be interested in Christian unity. At the end of his life, speaking to his Diocesan Conference, he declared:

A desire for sympathy among classes, for harmony among nations, above all for reunion in Christendom is a characteristic of our time. We recognise the fact. We cannot fail to find in it a call to renewed faith in the mission of the Church, and to more strenuous labour for the realisation of Christ's bequest of peace.[396]

Writing on 29 April 1895 to Lord Halifax, that great protagonist of union with the Roman Catholics, he expressed himself with even more fervour:

> With my whole soul I desire Union. Disunion with Noncon-formists, Foreign Reformers, Rome, Easterns, is the main and most miserable cause of delay in the Christianisation of all men in Christian and Heathen countries alike. The Love of Christ compels a burning desire for Unity.[397]

With the Eastern Churches Benson had a natural affinity and he took 'extraordinary pain and trouble over his communications with their Patriarchs and bishops'. He made a long statement in Convocation on Anglican relations with them in which it was plain that his own devotion to Church history, to architecture and liturgy, prompted and sustained his interest.

His contact with these Churches came in a variety of ways. Largely through his initiative the controversial Jerusalem bishopric was revived but in a different form. This joint project of the Church of England and the Prussian Lutheran Church had run into difficulty, having strayed from its original intention largely, Benson believed, 'through the German alliance'. There had been a vacancy for some five years, and the Prussian Government intimated its willingness to withdraw. Benson, in reviving it, took great care to secure the co-operation of the Greek Patriarch in Jerusalem, who assured the Archbishop in respect of a new appointment that he would 'receive him with much love, and with all [his] power will assist and support him in all his exertions and actions'.[398] With practical common sense Benson insisted that whoever went there must be capable of enduring the rigours of extensive travel, and that his designation should be Bishop *in* and not *of* Jerusalem. In spite of some opposition, G. F. Popham Blyth, formerly Archdeacon of Rangoon, was consecrated to the bishopric, and took with him letters of commendation from Benson to the three Patriarchs which defined clearly the extent (and limitation) of his care and oversight. All was not yet plain sailing, however, and there were difficulties between the new Bishop and the Church Missionary Society which provided the endowment; but the principles which Benson laid down became firmly established.

Perhaps no eastern Church commended itself to Benson more, or excited so strongly his feelings of compassion, as the Assyrian Church, which represented the *ecclesia* of the old Persian Empire, whose bishops were originally dependent upon Antioch. The story of this Church—its determination in spite of enforced migration and persecution to maintain its own Nestorian faith—is an epic. In the XIXth century its members became subject to both Turkey and Persia, and were surrounded in both countries by Islam. The Archbishop's son writes that

> the condition of such a Church, helplessly faithful, would appeal to my father. His strong historical sense, all his aesthetic admiration for Eastern ecclesiasticism and symbolism, his strong admiration for the estate from which it had fallen, would serve to strengthen his compassion for the human weakness, his reverence for the divine life in the fallen Church. The Assyrians appealed to him for help to preserve their existence as a national Church—he was eager to meet them.[399]

He saw it as a special vocation resting upon the Church of England 'to maintain the energies of the more failing Churches of the East, and quietly to aid their own yearnings after more light, and restored discipline'.[400]

Archbishop Benson decided to inform himself as best he could of the situation on the spot. He did so through Athelstan Riley, whose visit in 1884 led to the setting up of a regular mission, which was to remain a life-long preoccupation. 'Hence daily when I wake one of the very first petitions which I offer in the dark is for Assyrian missionaries,' he used to say. Once again he carefully defined their task in commissioning two of their number as

> not touching questions of politics or of governments, or of administration in the very slightest degree, not making one proselyte from Church to Church, nor preaching to those outside, to whom you are not sent; you have to infuse fresh life into that which is faint, courage into that which is afraid, knowledge into those who have but inaccurate rudiments, faith where everything on earth fights against faith.[401]

Benson engaged in an extensive correspondence, raised money, started a magazine, and encouraged the establishment of two schools.

These Eastern Churchmen long remained a preoccupation with successive Archbishops. As late as November 1937, Alan Don, Cosmo Lang's chaplain, was writing in his diary: 'These Assyrians are always with us—a meeting again today to wind up the largely abortive National Appeal.'[402]

383

On the nine-hundredth anniversary of the conversion of Russia, Benson despatched a letter of congratulation to the Metropolitan of Kiev, written with great delicacy of feeling. Coming as it did, quite unexpectedly, from a Church of which the Russians knew next to nothing, it created a great impression. The Metropolitan took the letter so seriously as to ask the Archbishop in reply to 'explain' and 'inform' him under what 'conditions you find it possible to unite our Churches'. Benson now conferred with his fellow bishops, and in a further letter on 5 March 1889, informed him that the first step would be the 'admission of religious believers to Holy Communion in either Church'; and later 'the serious consideration (taking abundant time for the purpose) of whether any impediments, disciplinary or doctrinal, exist, which still render necessary the formal separation to which for strange reasons we find ourselves placed'.[403]

Benson's relations with the Church of Rome were, in the nature of the case, restricted; and there can be little doubt that here his attitude hardened with the passing of the years. As Archbishop he felt keenly that he must not do anything to weaken the status or authority of *Ecclesia Anglicana*. Also, at Lambeth he became more conscious of the wide range of Church of England opinion, one wing of which was positively anti-Roman. His sense of history, his intimate knowledge of the primitive church, and his insistence on the continuity of the post-Reformation Church of England with its pre-Reformation past convinced him of the insubstantiality of Roman claims. Doctrinally he felt that the gulf was wide. 'To render to the Virgin any part of homage, to the Church any part of the trust due to their Lord,' so his son writes, 'struck him with a peculiar horror.' With individual Roman Catholics he could be personally forthcoming, as with his life-long friend Father Burbrick, but the Roman method of religious debate seemed, he felt, to belong to a world where reasoning was 'a mere sequence of words and the Bible has another Gospel in it'. He believed, with Bishop Wordsworth, that the Romans indulged in a falsification of history, and that the Church in this country was justified when it 'repudiated the Pope's supremacy and declared itself truly English by recognizing in all causes the supremacy of the King; then first realising the first words of Magna Carta, "the Church of England shall be free".'[404] He was sometimes a little irritated when in order to secure his presence at a meeting on some social question the convener would add that he hoped to get Cardinal Manning along: 'Just as,' he commented, 'when the dog won't eat his dinner, we call out "Puss, puss".'[405] Still, he was always ready to engage in united action when this was helpful. Thus he joined in a combined delegation of Nonconformists, Jews, and Roman Catholics to the Education Department on the rating of school houses, but was a little chary of extending the range of co-operation in this particular field. When he became Primate, Canon Mason wished him to send formal notice of his election to Rome and to the other great sees of Christendom as had been the custom in early times. Benson's letter of reply is revealing (27 November 1887). The survival of an Italian mission in England, he said, was 'uncatholic and unchristian', and he facetiously concluded:

> It is the Pope's business to eat dust and ashes, not mine to decorate him. Therefore, my dear Mephibosheth, hold thy peace.[406]

Reunion as he saw it could not be a hurried affair: it must be based on truth and integrity, and take account of more than one aspect of the divided Church.

> The aspiration after unity, if it be intelligent, is a vast one—he wrote in a Pastoral Letter of 1895—It cannot limit itself to restoring what is pictured of past outward unity. It must take account of Eastern Churches, of non-Episcopal Reformed Churches and bodies on the Continent, at home, and among the multiplying population of the New World as well as of the Christianity of Asia and Africa under extraordinarily varying conditions.

In all this he saw the *Ecclesia Anglicana*, under God, as having a unique role to play. 'History appears to be forcing upon the Anglican Communion an unsought position,' he continued, 'an overwhelming duty from which it has hitherto shrunk.'[407] Yet in practical terms he was forced to admit 'that the dream of Union is simply inappreciably and infinitely far off'.

It was within the circle of such ideas that Benson was called upon, in 1894, to deal with an attempted *rapprochement* between the Church of England and Rome, brought about through the initiative of Lord Halifax, a great lay churchman whose sincerity was unquestionable, even if not always matched with an equal sagacity. This arose out of a friendship between the noble Lord and a French priest, Abbé Fernand Portal, of the Congregation of St. Vincent de Paul and later Professor in a theological seminary at Cahors. Both men felt the need to foster at least the desire for union, and to let it manifest itself around the discussion of a concrete issue, which for them was the matter of English orders. In the summer of 1894, Portal came over to England, and through Lord Halifax a purely private interview took place with the Archbishop at Addington. There was no formal

385

discussion of any kind, but Benson's record of the interview shows how wide was the psychological gulf between the three men, seen particularly in Portal's contention that the 'truth' ought only to be taught to fit persons. Commenting later Benson wrote:

> I said this was the difference that underlay everything else between England and Rome, that it was alike prudent and right to impart truth. Portal asked me what I thought of the Pope's Encyclical on Scripture, and I was obliged to say that though very beautiful Latin it was full 50 years behind the present state of actual *knowledge*, and that I could not have believed that such a paper could have been written *now* by any theologian.[408]

The story of what happened between the interview and the issue of the papal encyclical *Apostolicae Curae* in 1896 declaring Anglican orders invalid must be briefly told.[409] There was much to-ing and fro-ing on the part of Lord Halifax; many letters between him and the Archbishop; and an embarrassing interview between the Archbishop and Portal in Devonshire. One thing was quite clear, namely that the prospect of a *rapprochement* was not at all congenial to the Roman Catholic hierarchy in England, which in these negotiations had been completely by-passed. The Pope himself was never directly involved, though reported to have remarked: 'How gladly I would say my *Nunc Dimittis*, if I could make the smallest beginning of such a reunion.'[410]

Archbishop Benson's attitude was consistent throughout, and similar to that of Archbishop Wake. He could not and would not, even by implication, concede that either he or the Church of England generally had any doubt as to the validity of its orders, though he allowed that there was nothing to stop the Roman Catholic Church, from its own point of view, examining them. Nor did he regard it as proper that he should deal with secret emissaries and engage in cloak and dagger diplomacy. '. . . the archbishop of Canterbury,' he told Halifax, 'is not in a position to take a private and unofficial line with secret agents from great powers.'[411]

Nor, in his eyes, was the matter of Anglican orders the only issue needing clarification in any scheme for reunion: '. . . the fundamental claim of the Pope's Supremacy would be a bar at once: the oath taken by the clergy of the Queen's supremacy was made in order to bar it.'[412]

Lord Halifax's enthusiasm tended at times to make him gloss over real difficulties, and his draft letters for Benson to send to Rome seldom *in toto* met with the Archbishop's approval. Benson's critical remarks were probably well justified: 'Halifax is like a solitary player of chess, and wants to make all the moves on the board himself on both sides.' On another occasion he told him frankly:

> ... I am afraid that you have lived for years so exclusively with one set of thinkers, and entered so entirely into the usages of one class of churches, that you have not before you the state of religious feeling and activity in England with the completeness with which anyone attempting to adjust the relations between churches ought to have the phenomena of his own side clearly and minutely before him.[413]

For this reason, though Halifax often pleaded to be trusted, the Archbishop was forced to confess that he could not make him 'almost an ambassador'. The personal factor, however, was not the only reason why the 'talks' finally failed. That the Pope could issue his bull in 1896 shows how wide was the gulf separating the two communions.

Benson died suddenly from a heart attack on 11 October 1896, while staying at Hawarden after returning, with his wife, from a preaching tour in Ireland. Gladstone on being told the news exclaimed: 'He died as a soldier. It was a noble end to a noble life.'[414] The *Quarterly Review*, to which he had been a contributor, wrote: 'Archbishop Benson was not only a good man, but a man of rare gifts, extraordinary charm of character and endowed with the strange power of making lives more vivid.'[415] He was the first Archbishop to be buried in Canterbury Cathedral since Cardinal Pole.

It is difficult not to make a comparison between Archbishops Benson and Tait. Tait's greatest care was to assert for the Church of England its position as a national Church; integrating itself with the people's life in the fullest possible way. Benson, though supporting its established position, yet saw this Church more in terms of its place within a definite Christian context, and he welcomed the fact that it was increasingly authenticating its own life.

Both emphases were needed; yet it may prove, if not yet, that Benson, by working to give the Church of England its own organs of government, proved the more percipient. The concept of the national Church, in the cause of which Tait spent himself, still retains a measure of cogency; but its days are clearly numbered. Benson, such is the paradox, in seeking guidance from past history, ended up by glimpsing a more distant horizon.

# 6

---

## FREDERICK TEMPLE, A MAN OF STATURE

---

I

Benson's sudden death led to the usual speculation as to his successor. The Queen had no doubt as to whom she wanted—her favourite clergyman, Randall Davidson, married to the daughter of Archbishop Tait, her favourite Archbishop.

> You will perhaps have guessed what I wished for the Primacy?
> —she wrote later—It was *yourself*, and for the following reasons:
> . . . my opinion is that you possessed the necessary qualities for
> that important Post, and above all because your great intimacy
> with the 2 last great Primates enabled you to know their views
> and their work. In fact I think *their* mantle has fallen upon
> you.[416]

This, however, could not yet be—Davidson was then only forty-eight, and the Queen had to content herself with seeking his views. These, bearing the title 'The qualifications desirable at all times and specially needed at the moment', are worth quoting.

> Farnham Castle, October 18, 1896
> 1. A real devotion of the highest sort to the spiritual part of
> the great Office.
> 2. Such capacity, and knowledge of the world and of men as
> will enable him to take his proper place in the public affairs of
> the Church and Realm.
> 3. Such learning and reputation as shall ensure real weight
> for his words apart from the position he holds.
> 4. A large hearted and liberal sympathy with men of 'other
> schools of thought' than his own, both inside and outside the
> Church.
> It is further clear that, if it be possible, the new Archbishop
> should be a man of ripe years, and of the sort of experience to
> ensure for him the *ready* and not merely the *dutiful* allegiance of
> those who have long been Bishops.

388

Davidson then turned to an assessment of particular candidates and placed 'foremost beyond question both in power and influence' Frederick Temple, Bishop of London; though 'he is 75 years old, and his eyesight is failing'. Then there were the Archbishop of York (Dr. MacLagan), the Bishop of Manchester (Dr. Moorhouse), both aged seventy, and the Bishop of Rochester (Talbot) easily the best of the younger bishops.[417]

The Prime Minister, Lord Salisbury, decided for Temple, and Temple it was. Despite his age, his stature was immense. The Queen agreed to the nomination somewhat reluctantly, for writing to Davidson from Balmoral she confessed: 'I do not like the choice at all, and think the Bishop of London's presence eminently *unsuited* to the post.'[418]

Frederick Temple did not find it difficult to make up his mind. He was not that kind of man, and replied immediately with typical frankness:

> I am very conscious of many deficiencies in my qualifications for such a post as that of the Archbishopric of Canterbury. But I believe that I could do the Church good service in that capacity, and I do not feel that I have any right to refuse the call which Her Majesty has made upon me. I will do my best to carry on the work which the late Archbishop, my most intimate friend for forty years, has been doing with such marked success.[419]

He remarked that he had five more years of work left in him. In fact he lived and worked at full pressure for another six.

Frederick Temple differed in many respects from most other Archbishops. In character he was rugged, austere, and abrupt, yet at the same time deeply compassionate and with a hidden emotional life which could suddenly erupt. He had prodigious energy and would keep going throughout the day almost like a machine. When Principal of Kneller Hall Training College near Richmond in Surrey, he thought nothing of adding an extra lesson at 5 a.m. to meet the needs of those who volunteered to learn Latin. As Headmaster of Rugby School he would work eighteen hours at a stretch. Yet there was something spontaneous about him which made young people, even children, respond to him more easily than adults. No one ever doubted his integrity or uncomplicated piety. His character doubtless owed much to the challenge of his early years. His father was a sub-inspector of the militia and bought a farm in Devon when in 1830 the family returned to England. The venture failed, and the Major departed for Sierra Leone, leaving the family behind him, and died soon after. Frederick Temple went to school at Blundells, and through the kindness of a friend proceeded to Oxford, where he graduated with a double first in classics and mathematics. He became a lecturer at his old college of Balliol; but a growing and passionate interest in social questions, particularly the welfare of the under-privileged, persuaded him to leave Oxford. In 1846 he was ordained by Bishop Wilberforce, and on resigning his fellowship spent ten years attached to the department of the Committee of the Council of Education; first as examiner in the office; then as Principal of Kneller Hall; and finally as one of Her Majesty's Inspectors of Training Schools. The experience thus gained was to prove a unique equipment for a future Archbishop of Canterbury. In 1857 he accepted the headmastership of Rugby in succession to Tait. Here his force and vitality, coupled with sheer goodness, were a powerful and formative influence. 'A beast but a just beast' is by no means a fair estimate. It was while at Rugby that he displayed his theological liberalism by contributing to *Essays and Reviews*; and in the ensuing controversy wrote to Tait the almost classic words:

> Tell a man to study, and yet bid him, under heavy penalties, come to the same conclusions with those who have not studied, is to mock him. If the conclusions are prescribed, the study is precluded.[420]

At the age of 55 he married Beatrice Blanche Lascelles, on her mother's side a grand-daughter of the Earl of Carlisle. The union led to great mutual happiness, and in the companionship of his two sons Frederick Temple 'renewed his youth, and would often share their games like a happy schoolboy'.

To William, aged 6½, the future Archbishop, he wrote:

> The plague of boys
> With all their noise
> Is better than being without them.
> Tell Mother to write
> At once tonight
> And tell me all about them.[421]

In 1869 he was appointed Bishop of Exeter where he vigorously discharged his diocesan duties, making long trips to remote rural areas. At a national level, he brought his specialized experience to bear on matters of education. Forster's Act of 1870 had set up a dual system to operate throughout the nation: Temple was anxious that the Church Schools should not lag behind, and he raised a fund to effect necessary improvements in his diocese. He was also concerned that poor boys should have an opportunity of getting to the universities. He served on a Royal Commission for Education and was mainly instrumental in starting the scheme which afterwards developed into the Oxford and Cambridge Local Examinations.

After a stay of some sixteen years in his Western diocese, Temple was translated to London and entered upon his new duties with unflagging energy. He took the lead in a great deal of social work, and what time he could spare from his diocesan duties he devoted to the cause of temperance, which more and more claimed his attention.

When he was appointed to Exeter in 1869 there was a great outcry in certain circles because of his association with *Essays and Reviews*. It was an indication of the decline in religious interest that nothing comparable now occurred. True at his confirmation in Bow Church (22 December 1896) a protest was lodged on the grounds that the new Archbishop was a confessed believer in the full doctrine of evolution though this was incompatible either with the Book of Common Prayer or the Thirty-nine Articles.

Frederick Temple came to Lambeth with a ripe experience, but his formative years were over. Inevitably he brought with him the same basic attitudes and methods that he had employed in Exeter and London. 'I do not think I shall find the work very new,' he said on his election.

Still, it was not easy to take over a post at seventy-six though 'he towered above all other members of the then episcopate'; and Temple made it the more difficult by his inability to delegate. (The trait was to persist in his son William.) Here Randall Davidson's words are worth quoting:

> His habit of doing everything for himself extended from petty trifles . . . to the biggest things in Church and State. His Chaplains had no knowledge of his correspondence, though a certain number of letters, not many, were given them to write. He told them little or nothing, and they had to pick up facts as best they could.[422]

In a school, this had not proved so serious: indeed it led him to give independence to his staff in their own departments, a boon for which Canon Scott Holland, who worked under him at Rugby, never ceased to be grateful. But Canterbury needed a more corporate approach. Tait confessed that he had never written a single important letter without it being vetted by some other person. Archbishop Benson discussed matters with his chaplains, and entered into long theological dialogues with Lightfoot and Westcott.

Temple's method of working at Lambeth was quite different. He was a lone wolf. Davidson felt keenly being 'out in the cold as regards the central affairs of the Church of England after twenty years of closest knowledge'.

Temple's attitude to Davidson is, perhaps, understandable. Davidson was Tait's son-in-law, had been intimate at Lambeth for many years, and was in the confidence of the Queen. Many an archbishop might well have felt that in order to establish himself in his new office he must look elsewhere for counsel. The criticism of Temple is not that he dispensed with Davidson but that he did not replace him with anyone else of comparable weight and authority.

Temple had only been to Canterbury on some two occasions before his enthronement on Friday, 8 January 1897, but he was given a cordial welcome by the Corporation. It had long been a matter of regret to the citizens of Canterbury, as we have seen, that the Archbishop had no residence of his own among them. The new Archbishop therefore gave great satisfaction when he declared: 'I confess I also regret very much that there is no kind of residence attached to the Archbishopric in this place. . . . I should be very glad indeed if I were able in course of time to make such arrangements as to make it possible to come here very frequently, and particularly on the occasions of great festivals of the Church. . . . I believe that the work of the Church is always best done by the effect of that personal influence which comes from personal contact, producing personal regards.'[423]

In speaking thus, Temple was enlarging on the theme of his predecessor. But Temple, with characteristic decision, determined to do something immediately. There was another reason which prompted him. The diocese of Canterbury had ceased to consist exclusively of the quiet agricultural countryside with which Manners Sutton had been familiar. London had spread out its tentacles; industrial towns clustered along the banks of the Thames; and the coast had become thickly populated. The result was a situation with which the organization of the past was incapable of coping. Also the cost of keeping up Addington as a quiet rural retreat was steadily rising. Frederick Temple immediately obtained the consent of the Ecclesiastical Commissioners to its sale, and asked their architect to look round for a suitable residence in Canterbury.

Temple's intention to get rid of Addington Palace (which was sold in 1897 for £70,000) met with considerable opposition, the Queen herself being approached to intervene when it came up for her signature at the Privy Council. Randall Davidson was not alone in thinking that the Archbishop had been 'rather hasty in his decision', and might have struck a better bargain. But the matter went forward. 'I think the day is past,' Temple commented, 'when Archbishops of Canterbury should appear as country gentlemen.'

In April 1898, he secured occupation of and adapted a house belonging to the Chapter on the site of the ancient archiepiscopal palace. The Chapel, in which the Archbishop took a particular interest, was in part furnished by the women of the diocese. When asked whether he thought his successors would wish to live at Canterbury, he replied with a grim smile: 'No I don't, I want to make 'em.' Yet reflecting on his own frequent residences at Canterbury he later wrote:

> I am beginning to find here something of the homeliness of Exeter nearly thirty years ago. The Cathedral people receive me kindly, and seem to like the idea of my living among them. The City people are even warmer. And my Wife and my Boys are enough to make any home happy.[424]

A residence in Canterbury undoubtedly did a great deal to bring the Archbishop into closer touch with his diocese, not least with the personnel of the Cathedral. During the last Christmas of his life, he entertained the families of the precincts, together with the choirboys. 'You may like to remember, in future years,' he said in farewell, 'that we have all kept this Christmas together.' Subsequent Archbishops have strengthened the links with both city and cathedral.[425]

At the 1888 diocesan conference, postponed to October because of the Lambeth Conference, he admitted the great difficulty for an Archbishop in having so many responsibilities outside his own diocese. He hoped, however, to do as he had done at London, namely to conduct one third of the confirmations, which would enable him to get to know the parishes; and at the same time to accept engagements throughout the province. Nor must he forget, he added, as Primate of All England, that there was a Northern province. His diocesan conferences were usually significant occasions. In 1901, for example, the Archbishop, who was always at his most impressive on his feet, discussed ritualism; the proposed creation of the new diocese of Southwark; and foreign missions, it being the bicentenary year of S.P.G. At his last Conference, he turned to a matter dear to his heart, the education of the nation's young, stressing the duty of churchmen to give liberally to support voluntary schools.

The Archbishop acted with determination in another matter: the disposal of Lambeth fields to the London County Council, thus repeating as Archbishop what he had already done as Bishop at Fulham. The fields were used to provide recreation for the neighbourhood, but though this personal link was greatly valued, Temple felt clear in his own mind that it would be better for everybody if it were made into a public space.

Randall Davidson and a majority of the Commissioners opposed the scheme, but it was found that the Commissioners' consent to a lease during the Archbishop's pleasure was not needed. So it went forward. A letter from Temple to Davidson is characteristic:

> It never occurred to me that what you said was either impertinent or in bad taste. I thought your pertinacity unwise. . . . Do not let us quarrel because we cannot agree on such a matter as this. If you can stop what I propose to do, by all means stop it. I shall be vexed, but I shall not feel any resentment, nor rely less on your friendship.[426]

When Temple took over from Benson there were two immediate matters requiring his attention. First a *Responsio* to Pope Leo XIII's Bull, *Apostolicae Curae*; and secondly the Lambeth Conference.

As to the first, Temple had nothing to do with the original draft which had been drawn up by the Bishops of Oxford, Salisbury, and Peterborough. He now set about going through it, particularly, to quote his own words, 'to cut out all the thunder'. When he had finished, the *Responsio* had lost none of its force, but it read more kindly and appeared less controversial. These words are typical:

> . . . the difference and the debate between us and him [the Pope] arises from a diverse interpretation of the self-same Gospel, which we all believe and honour as the only true one. We also gladly declare that there is much in his own person that is worthy of love and reverence. But that error, which is inveterate in the Roman Communion, of substituting the visible head for the invisible Christ, will rob his good works of any fruit of peace. . . . God grant that even from this controversy may grow fuller knowledge of the truth, greater patience, and a broader desire for peace in the Church of Christ, the Saviour of the World.[427]

The *Responsio* was finally signed by the two Archbishops and issued early in March 1897.

The arrangements for the Lambeth Conference had been more or less completed by Benson before his death. This Conference was specially significant since the bishops had brought forward their meeting to 1897 to mark the fourteen hundredth anniversary of St. Augustine's landing in Kent. Thus, after a quiet day conducted by Temple at Lambeth, the 197 bishops proceeded on 2 July to Ebbs

Fleet where a service was held on the traditional site. On the following day an inaugural service took place in the Cathedral at which the Archbishop preached; and on the Monday, after Holy Communion in Westminster Abbey, the first session began at 11 a.m.

The Conference, for Temple, was certainly a testing time. Benson was a greatly respected figure and had won the confidence of the bishops by a vast correspondence following upon his presidency of the Conference of 1888. Not least, he was highly esteemed by the American bishops whose status was somewhat different from that of the colonials. For some inexplicable reason, Temple began with a gross miscalculation of the Conference's mood. It was assumed that in his opening address there would be some reference to his predecessor in terms similar to those he had most generously used at the time of his enthronement in Canterbury. But Benson's name was not mentioned even by remotest implication. Davidson as episcopal secretary had worked closely in the planning with Benson; but Temple, he complained, 'hardly consulted me about anything, leaving me a perfectly free hand about things that were in any sense within my province and saying absolutely nothing to me, unless under pressure, about the policy or the plans, or the order of proceedings, for which he would have to be, when the time came, technically responsible, but in which I was necessarily closely connected.'[428]

Temple's omission was widely commented upon, and Davidson tactfully asked whether he intended to make a reference to Benson or would he prefer an American bishop to do it. Temple's answer was that he thought nothing of the sort was necessary. But when Davidson protested that some bishops would wish it, he replied, 'Then I will do it.' He did so and did well. Davidson confesses to his mystification:

> It would be easy to give scores of other instances as to his curiously direct way of keeping always to the exact point . . . without the admission of anything of a sentimental or illustrative sort. Whether that element in life was absolutely trampled under foot or was simply ignored because the thoughts were absent from his mind I do not know.[429]

Yet in spite of this initial blunder, Temple undoubtedly gained the admiration of his colleagues, as was seen in the spontaneous gesture of the American bishops in sending him a present when the Conference was over. Temple's direct approach, his complete absence of cant or frills, impressed everybody. In spite of his age his presidency was firm and designed to get on with the business in hand. When one bishop spoke at excessive length Temple interjected cryptically:

395

'Bishop of ——, next time you don't want others to talk, keep your own mouth shut.' To another bishop, somewhat floundering, he said, not unkindly: 'Bishop of ——, what you mean is all right, but what you say isn't what you mean.'[430]

One important matter that came before the Conference is best seen through the eyes of John Wordsworth, Bishop of Salisbury, who believed firmly that the Anglican Communion needed a central co-ordinating council or governing body. In 1895 he had taken the lead in a committee of bishops to consider 'the organisation of the Anglican Communion'. Its report was never published, but came before a meeting of bishops early the next year. Benson was interested, though aware of the difficulties, and the matter was put on the agenda of the Lambeth Conference of 1897, John Wordsworth being made chairman of the committee to consider it.

This item did not find much support among the rank and file of the American bishops. On the contrary, as the Bishop of Albany pointed out in a letter to Randall Davidson written on 19 February 1897, its inclusion on the agenda had led some bishops to decline the invitation to be present. It was one thing for the Colonial Churches to discuss a matter of this kind; quite another for the American, among whom there was 'a very decided objection and very strong opposition to any idea of attempting to establish any authoritative relation to the See of Canterbury'.[431]

But, as Davidson pointed out in reply, it was too late to remove this matter from the agenda. Such opposition meant that John Wordsworth did not get all that he wanted, though a central consultative body for supplying information and advice was set up, but not, as some wanted, a Tribunal of Reference. Archbishop Temple's words in his Encyclical were consequently very restrained.

> This body must win its way to general recognition by the service which it may be able to render to the working of the Church. It can have no other than a moral authority, which will be developed out of its action.[432]

The Conference, in another resolution, while approving the title of Archbishop for Metropolitans, advised that the proposed adoption of such a title should be formally announced to the Bishops of the Churches and Provinces of the Communion; also that when a bishop-elect, not coming under the Archbishop of Canterbury's jurisdiction, was consecrated in England under the Queen's mandate, he should not take a personal oath of obedience to the Archbishop but make a solemn declaration before his consecration that he would 'pay all due honour and deference to the Archbishop of

Canterbury, and will respect and maintain the spiritual rights and privileges of the Church of England, and of all Churches in communion with her'.[433]

The Encyclical issued by the Conference was drawn up by the Archbishop unaided and without consultation during the course of the final night. The style and content were typical of the man: direct, and instinct with a subdued moral passion. On only one matter did the Conference presume to raise an objection, namely on the severe words directed to the Church of England on its neglect of missionary enterprise. Many bishops felt the attack to be unjust and begged the Archbishop to tone it down; but he declined. The next morning, however, although not conceding the point, he came up with a new form of words which was accepted. When one of the bishops sprang up to express his thanks he was sternly rebuked by the President: 'Bishop of ——, you may thank me as much as you like; but you must thank me in silence.' The Conference concluded with a trip to Glastonbury, and a service in St. Paul's Cathedral, at which the Archbishop made an impassioned plea for the Church to awake from its slumber and with zeal to proclaim its Gospel throughout the world.

II

Apart from his necessary work as diocesan and provincial, Archbishop Temple, at the outset of his primacy, declared that there were three causes of paramount concern to the Church to which he wished to devote his energies. They were temperance, education, and foreign missions.

Temple believed that intemperance was the biggest single social evil of his time, and that from it other evils sprang. Experience, while at Exeter, of 'that most degraded of all creatures, a drunken clergyman', determined him to become a total abstainer, although he did not wish to impose this personal discipline on others. He was convinced, however, that this was a cause in which the Church must spend itself; that the Church of England Temperance Society must be supported at diocesan and national level. After the publication of the report of the commission on the licensing laws (January 1901) he circularized his clergy, pleading that since they 'have more influence than any others in producing this effect', they should come behind the bishops in supporting the Commissioners, thereby forming a 'strong public opinion'.

On this cause he spoke in the House of Lords; to the Cambridge Union; and in 1898 to the General Assembly of the Church of Scotland, pleading for more restrictive legislation. One present on the latter occasion described his speech as 'direct, practical and impassioned . . . free from all attempt at rhetorical flourishes of any kind; leaving the indelible conviction that a truly Apostolic minister had spoken and spoken in the power of the Spirit of God'.[434] It was the first time that an Archbishop had addressed such an audience.

Temple maintained a strong educational interest throughout life, not surprisingly since he had spent some of his best years helping to build up what was then known as elementary and secondary education. He brought to it an experience exceptional in an Archbishop, and never lost his concern for the under-privileged. Like Maurice, and later his own son William, he believed that religion must be the foundation of any system which set out to build up the whole person. As Archbishop, without losing sight of a wider spectrum, he recognized a special responsibility for the schools which lived under the aegis of the Church of England. Here there were many problems. Forster's Education Act of 1870, by inaugurating a national system with a State-sponsored sector, gave the Church schools a new standard to live up to, the financial implications of which were serious. The Archbishop's continuing preoccupation was to make Anglicans alive to their responsibilities but to secure that these responsibilities were not so ambitiously conceived as to outsoar the resources to meet them. This meant, for him, public addresses up and down the country; speeches in Convocation; co-operation—where possible—with the Government; and vigilance in the House of Lords in respect of the various Bills which came before Parliament during his archiepiscopate. His great hope was, like Tait's, that the dual system should work fairly and to the mutual advantage of both Church and State.

In 1897 a Bill was brought into the House of Lords which came to the aid of the Church schools by giving them a grant for some five years and requiring their managers to set up Associations to administer it. The Archbishop commended the Bill both in Convocation and in Parliament. In the former he expressed the hope that the great co-ordination of Church and board schools which was bound to follow the passing of the Act would prove mutually beneficial. As to the nonconformist complaint that some of their money from the rates was to be used to subsidize Church of England schools, he maintained that this was no different from members of the Church of England subsidizing board schools. Temple realized clearly, however, that increasing State aid must go along with increasing State control and here he proved invaluable as a mediator between Convocation and the Government. For example, he welcomed the Voluntary Schools Bill as a further extension of partnership; but insisted that the managers of Church schools could not give up the right to appoint their own staff. Only by so doing were they able to ensure that religious instruction should be given with integrity. He approved in the main the Acts of 1899 and 1900, but while making it clear that he wished no preferential treatment for the Church of England, he expressed concern lest under the guise of 'religious equality' religious education should be excluded from public recognition and left to chance operation. In 1900 he spoke at length in the Upper House of Convocation on the general position of voluntary schools. Once again he showed an intimate knowledge, not least in his penetrating analysis of the three schemes then emanating from Birmingham, Manchester, and Leeds, and recently published in the *School Guardian* of 23 December 1899. Of these he preferred that of Leeds, and for three reasons: that it required the Education Department to have regard to the religious belief of the parents; that it set up local authorities with power to grant assistance from the rates or 'imperial' resources; that it proposed that the Cowper Temple clause be repealed, and reasonable arrangements made for separate religious instruction when this was requested by an appropriate number of parents. The Archbishop took the opportunity to urge—it was a perpetual theme—that Church people should be prepared to support their own schools. This was indeed the nub of the problem, since simply to retain them was not enough; they must be efficient. Yet the financial position, in the following year, came near to breaking-point, and Temple told Convocation with his accustomed bluntness, and setting out the arithmetic involved, that the Church just could not afford to maintain the buildings of its schools and at the same time pay the cost of religious education. In these circumstances a joint meeting of the two Convocations decided for the former.

The five-year grant to Church schools expired in 1902, and another Bill came before the House in the same year. It was destined to be the last occasion on which Temple addressed the Lords, and he certainly used the opportunity to the full. The purposes of the Bill, he said, would now be generally accepted, namely to establish a uniform system which should handle all the different branches of education; to do much more for secondary schools; and to deal justly with Church schools. There could be no doubt, and he was here echoing the sentiments of Tait, that the country wished for a religious education, but his interests were by no means confined to this area.

Again and again in this House—he said—have I joined with others in pressing on the Government that our secondary education ought to receive attention, and that we were doing damage by leaving it without organization. The necessity of organization has at last been proved by unmistakable proofs —namely, that the authorities charged with the lower education have been driven . . . to encroach upon the secondary education which stood next above them.[435]

He only wished they could have acted more quickly. The Church was right, he maintained, to complain of the onerous burden that its members had to bear: i.e. 'to perform the double labour of supporting their own schools, which were a necessity, and of supporting the kind of schools which they did not themselves want.' At a point in his speech, the Archbishop suddenly collapsed on to his seat; but struggling up continued:

The Bill is an honest and statesmanlike measure, and I hope your Lordships, in spite of any objections that may be made, will, nevertheless, pass it into law, and let us see how it will act when it begins to work.[436]

He was immediately hurried out of the House and back to Lambeth where he lingered till 23 December. Even more than Chatham he 'died on the floor of the House'.

Temple's passionate concern for the propagation of the faith by active mission was life-long. While at the University, he expressed the hope that England might assume 'the sublimest position ever occupied by any nation hitherto, that of the authoritative propagator of the Gospel over the world'.[437] In a letter to his mother, arising out of a visit of the Bishop of New Zealand (October 1841) he wrote:

I hope we shall soon have done with the littleness of yearly sending out a few individual missionaries at the expense of a private society, and that in future we shall continue the same glorious part. It is not mere momentary enthusiasm with me, mamma; my heart beats whenever I think of it. I think it one of the noblest things England has done for a long time, almost the only thing really worthy of herself.[438]

He was speaking and writing in a similar vein at the Lambeth Conference of 1897. It was a favourite theme in addressing clergy, whether at the rural deanery, the diocesan conference or on a national occasion. The clergy were bound to instruct their people about missions—and inform themselves. He accepted numerous invitations to speak for the S.P.G., and the C.M.S., and was particularly active on behalf of the former during its bicentenary year in 1901. Technological advance, he reiterated, had 'opened the way' for foreign missions 'in a most marvellous manner. All the great difficulties were gone'. Indeed, the opportunities of getting to the world at large and giving the heathen the message of the Gospel had suddenly been 'multiplied by the Providence of God far more than a hundredfold'. Equally significant was the unparalleled increase in the population of Britain which had led to mass emigration.

> With these indications of the will of God manifested by His providential government of the world; with these remarkable indications which he had put before them the more earnestly because they were really new things in human history; with these indications of God's call . . . it was plain enough that the English nation and the English Church had been called to a work in God's name, and that every one of them was bound to listen to that call, and do his share towards working at what our Lord left as His last message to all Christians, 'To go and preach to all nations.'[439]

His final sermon in Canterbury Cathedral, on his birthday which fell on Advent Sunday, preached on the text 'Woe is me if I preach not the Gospel', was a stirring call to a great effort to propagate the faith.

### III

Archbishop Temple was not quite so caught up in ritualistic problems as were his three predecessors, but he did not entirely escape them. As Archbishop, he was inevitably a 'target for tonight', and his correspondence illustrates his cares. There was the man who protested that he could not communicate with fermented wine, to which the chaplain replied that the Archbishop 'knew nothing to prevent the dilution of the wine with water before it is brought into the church to whatever extent may be necessary'.[440]

As a general principle, Temple was anxious that in matters of ritual which were in doubt, the bishops should take advantage of the rubric in the Prayer Book which allowed them to refer such matters to the provincial Archbishop. Thus on 31 July 1899, the two Primates sat at Lambeth in response to a request from the bishops to advise on the use of incense and procession of lights. The formal decision, drawn up entirely by Temple, though approved by his brother of York, called down some criticism upon him. It was, in fact, a closely reasoned argument and shows that at an advanced age

Temple had not lost his mental vigour, even if his was not a subtle mind. As to procession of lights, this was 'neither enjoined nor permitted'. Equally was this the case with the use of incense which, he laid down, 'we are far from saying . . . in itself is an unsuitable or undesirable accompaniment to Divine worship'.[441]

Indeed the Sovereign might on a great occasion with the consent of the Archbishop of Canterbury order it, although this was improbable.

This judgment led to a deputation, representing nearly 140,000 lay communicants, waiting upon the Archbishop to present a 'solemn protest', accusing him of pressing a definition 'upon the dioceses of which Your Grace is not the ruler', and concerning himself with only one party in the Church. In an interesting reply the Archbishop pointed out that the judgement was not based on a parliamentary statute but on the 36th canon: also that he and the Archbishop of York did not constitute a court as they had no coercive power. They had a right, however, to address the bishops and clergy of their provinces and to state their views. After that, it rested with the bishops whether or not to adopt them. True, the ruling did, in the main, affect one party within the Church, but 'it is a very serious thing if men claim that they may pick up here and there practices from the history of the early Church which approve themselves to their minds, and then insist, without any authority, that they may make them part of the worship of the Church of England'. He could not agree that the solution of this or any other problem was disestablishment, which would bring with it a loss to the religious life of the nation greater than they could measure.

> I am quite ready to face Disestablishment and its necessary concomitant, disendowment—he told them—if it be God's will. I am quite prepared in that case still to go on and act as if we stood in the same position as that which we have held for the last 300 years. But [here the voice broke with deep emotion] I dread, with all my soul I dread, what may come, if the Church of England were to break in two.[442]

The Archbishop then gave his blessing, and was characteristically friendly.

This opinion, and another against reservation, show at least that the Archbishop could make up his mind; the one essential, it would seem, in the somewhat rare world of liturgical matters of this kind.

With the Queen and the members of the Royal Family Temple was never on close terms. True, his devotion to the Throne was simple and sincere; but he was not the stuff of which courtiers are made. There was little finesse, or small talk, but a robust independence, and a seriousness which could be uncomfortable. Particular royal occasions, however, moved him deeply. When at the Diamond Jubilee celebrations in 1897 there was an unexpected pause in the ceremonies on the steps of St. Paul's while the Queen awaited the arrival of the royal carriage, the Archbishop stepped into the breach and with great emotion called for three cheers which he himself led with gusto. The Queen's eightieth birthday on 24 May 1899 was marked by a great service of thanksgiving in the cathedral church of London, and the Archbishop distinguished himself by preaching a far more sensible sermon than is usual on such royal occasions. He lamented the fact that great scientific advance had not been matched by equal moral progress, although he thought there had been a genuine advance in sympathy between man and man. It was here, in this area of personal living, that the Queen had made a distinctive contribution.

> Throughout the reign of Queen Victoria, one of the great blessings conferred by the reign had been the example of a woman's sympathy, the sympathy of a genuine and true woman with all that touched her people. . . . It was for this reason that the mention of her name always brought a thrill to our hearts. It was good that we should thank God for all He had conferred upon us in giving us such a ruler.[443]

His speech in the House of Lords on the occasion of her death led to the comment: 'Well, Your Grace, you made us all cry.' He spoke, he said, as a representative of the Church of England which, 'as your Lordships are aware, is connected by closer ties with the Sovereign in this country than in almost any other'. In very simple extempore language he then extolled the Queen not simply because of her 'powers of statesmanship' but because

> her influence, the character of her Court, the character of the domestic life, of which her subjects were allowed to know something, had a penetrating power which reached far beyond the possibility of our being able to trace it. There can be no question that all society has been the better because the Queen has reigned. . . . She was a religious woman. She prayed for her people. She was a good woman. She set up a true standard of such lives as Christians ought to live.[444]

The Archbishop was over eighty years of age at the time of Edward VII's Coronation. Originally fixed for 26 June 1902, it was postponed till 9 August on account of the King's sudden illness. In spite of his age the Archbishop threw himself into the preparations with energetic enthusiasm, playing a significant part in drawing up and shortening the elaborate ritual. He ran into some difficulty when the *Form and Order of Service recommended for use in the Churches of the Church of England on the Coronation Day* was said to be issued by the command of the King, particularly since it contained the phrase, 'The Protestant Reformed Religion established by Law'. A number of parish priests signed a protest stating their inability to use it.

There was some anxiety as to how the King, the Archbishop, and the Dean of Westminster, Dr. Bradley, who was greatly enfeebled, would manage to get through the lengthy procedure. Randall Davidson was so alarmed when he saw the 'tottering gait' of the Archbishop that he offered him a meat lozenge to support him. 'What's the good of that?' Temple rasped. 'My trouble's in my *legs*, not in my stomach.' For Temple it was all a deeply emotional experience, though he kept himself under firm control. Owing to the condition of his eyes, each separate question which had to be addressed to the King was printed in large type on scrolls backed with crimson silk—they are preserved in Westminster Abbey Library—and these were unrolled one by one and held by the Bishop of Winchester on his right side, so as not to interpose between the Archbishop and the King. There were occasional pauses but the Archbishop kept going, and his voice was remarkably clear and strong. An incident which happened when the Archbishop, as the first subject of the realm, paid homage, shows the powerful effect of the ceremony upon him. He knelt but could not rise, until the King helped him. The aged Archbishop laid his hand upon the King's arm and said with deep feeling: 'God bless you, sir; God bless you; God be with you.' The King caught his hand and kissed it. It was the kind of moment which makes traditional rites suddenly come alive.

Archbishop Temple was eighty-one at the time of his death on 22 December 1902. His energy up to the end of his days was remarkable, but certain aspects of the passing of the years manifested themselves only too clearly, particularly in his relations with the Colonial Churches. It had long been a custom for overseas bishops and missionaries to seek the Archbishop's advice. He in his turn would consult the various societies and individual bishops before replying with his opinion. This, however, seems to have ceased when Archbishop Temple took over, for there is no reason to doubt Randall Davidson's somewhat depressing words:

He brushed aside all that help and answered everything of the sort with his own hand, so far as it was answered at all. I fear that generally in his later years the reply was merely that the matter would receive consideration, and nothing more was heard of it.[445]

Perhaps it is to be regretted that a man of such strength of character, deep inward conviction, and high ability, came to Lambeth when creative drive was a thing of the past.

# PART VII

# WAR; WINDS OF CHANGE; ECUMENICITY

*Archbishops*

RANDALL THOMAS DAVIDSON 1903
COSMO GORDON LANG 1928
WILLIAM TEMPLE 1942
GEOFFREY FRANCIS FISHER 1945
ARTHUR MICHAEL RAMSEY 1961

# 1

## RANDALL DAVIDSON, THE LAST OF THE VICTORIANS

I

No man has ever come to high office better prepared by an intimate acquaintance with its workings over a long period of years than Randall Davidson. A Scotsman, quietly yet confidently ambitious, he had waited in the wings since Archbishop Frederick Temple's appointment in 1896 had led to his almost total exclusion from decision-making at Lambeth. His career and basic attitude to church affairs, even his technique of working as Archbishop, were largely moulded by his father-in-law, Archbishop Tait, the more so since he finished with the life of a parish priest after only four years as an assistant curate at Dartford in Kent. The connexion began early, for Randall's father and A. C. Tait had been at school together, and the Archbishop's son was his intimate companion at Oxford.

Tait's death was the occasion of Davidson's introduction to the Queen, who summoned him to Windsor on 9 December 1882, and recorded afterwards that she 'was seldom more struck than I have been by his personality'.[446]

Davidson was a born courtier, and this interview began a friendship which had its effect on the Church at large. Not that Davidson lacked independence, when he thought the Queen's interests demanded it, as in the case of her intention to publish a further volume of her *Leaves from a Journal of our Life in the Highlands*. While Dean of Windsor he became her unofficial adviser in all matters of ecclesiastical preferment. In a private memorandum he set out at length the Queen's manner of procedure. When an ecclesiastical post of 'any importance' in the gift of the Crown became vacant, she would immediately ask his advice as to the kind of person required.

> I say the sort of man—he wrote—for I always deprecated any endeavour upon the Queen's part to shift to her own shoulders the responsibility belonging to the Prime Minister, as representative of the English people.

When the Prime Minister's nomination came to her she would send it on to Davidson, and he would reply with a long memorandum, or on occasions with a simple approval.

> Sometimes I advised her to accept nominations which did not seem to me very good ones, but I never scrupled to advise her to veto nominations if they were really unsuitable or bad, and during my years of advising her the veto was exercised a great many times.[447]

Davidson worked on the principle that the Queen was constitutionally free to use her negative power in this way, but ought not to initiate recommendations.

One admires Davidson's self-confidence, and his document is an admirable illustration of how influence, accountable to no one, and not subject to any public scrutiny, could then work within the system. Fortunately Davidson's judgement was usually perceptive, and if he was a little too nervous of the 'enthusiast' he yet had a real gift for detecting ability and the lack of it.

Davidson's years as Bishop of Winchester, where he went from Rochester in 1895, were energetic and purposeful; and it is not therefore surprising that Bell, in his monumental biography which is more than a biography, writes of him as 'the almost certain successor of Archbishop Temple as he himself could hardly fail to recognise'. Indeed, to a close friend he said: 'I know I am not good enough, but I do know the ropes better than others.'[448]

And so it came to be, A. J. Balfour intimating his intention of making Davidson Archbishop within a week of Temple's death. Edward VII, writing from Sandringham, expressed the hope that 'the friendly intercourse which has existed between us for so long will always continue'. 'I shall always be only too happy,' he assured him, 'to discuss your desires regarding the Church as heretofore.'[449]

The general verdict of the Press was one of satisfaction, and even Lord Halifax, though regretful that the new Archbishop was not animated by the ideals of St. Anselm, St. Thomas, Stephen Langton, or Laud, yet assured him that 'in view of our present circumstances if it had depended on my voice you would be where you are'.[450] Yet no archbishop, he warned him, had ever greater difficulties to contend with.

Thus there began in 1903 a tenure of office which ended in the very different world of the late 'twenties. They were years of great scientific and industrial advance; of the shattering conflict of the First World War with the disappearance of thrones and the painful readjustment to peace; of wide-spread unemployment and the General Strike; of the birth of the League of Nations; of the advent of broadcasting; of the coming of age of the Labour Party and its first Government.

Within the Church of England they were years of the Life and Liberty Movement, the mainspring of which was William, son of Archbishop Temple; of the Enabling Act with its setting up of Parochial Church Councils reaching up to the Church Assembly. They were years of the abortive attempt to secure the revision of the Prayer Book in 1927 and 1928; of the emergence and steady growth of the ecumenical movement; of decline in faith, increasing secularism and the weakening position of the Church of England which Tait's flair had tended to conceal. They were years when the official optimism of late Victorian England began to wear thin.

Davidson's approach to his duties was pragmatic. His over-all policy did not flow from any conscious working out of great theological truths, but from commitment to certain liberal values, temperamentally congenial, which he had acquired across the years. The objectives of such a policy were to maintain for the Church of England its place within the national life, not least in its education of the young; to keep it theologically liberal and comprehensive; to ensure that it worked with other churches for common ends; and to maintain the status of Canterbury as the 'pivot' around which the wider Anglican Communion revolved.

One archiepiscopal legacy which Randall Davidson accepted and became a slave to was incessant work from early morning to late at night—work which Cosmo Lang was later to describe as 'incredible, indefensible and inevitable'. He used to reckon his day at between sixteen or seventeen hours, a mammoth apportionment which began with Tait. One cannot but question whether such complete absorption necessarily adds up to that measure of detachment which leads to wise decisions. Friends often chided him on the score that he had almost come to think that the Church of England would fold up without his continuing presence at Lambeth. Insofar as he indulged such *hubris*—and he was not that sort of man—it was the penalty of living too long in the centre and too briefly at the circumference. The Church of England has the knack of surviving, sometimes in spite of its official leadership.

Yet Davidson's methods of working were very different from that of either of his predecessors. He did not, as did Benson, think in terms of a formal organization like a *curia*; nor was he, like Temple, unwilling to consult colleagues. The Archbishop's own words are interesting in this context:

> To anyone who sets himself to consider what the Cathedral and See of Canterbury now connote, popularly as well as

officially, as the historic centre of a great constitutional system, the enquiry naturally suggests itself: Should there not, for the dealing with these large matters, be a group of officially appointed men, call it by what name you will—Council, Curia, Cabinet, Board, Committee—who might jointly bear the burden, and, speaking with collective voice, increase immensely the weight of what is said, and ensure for it a hearing to which no one man's voice, in a system such as ours, can possibly be entitled? The answer lies in the facts of the case. Such a Council or Curia, if formed, would necessarily be an official body for doing official work. But then no technically official position, bearing relation to the whole Anglican Communion, belongs of right to, or is today, claimed by the Archbishop of Canterbury. To speak of it as his by right, or to claim for him any authoritative voice, beyond the quite limited range of the fifty-seven dioceses subject to his metropolitical jurisdiction, would be a new departure of the gravest and, in my judgment, of the most perilous kind.[451]

Such advice as he needed he could always command.

Amongst his personal counsellors in the early days were Bishop John Wordsworth, a man of great if somewhat restricted ecclesiastical learning; Bishop Francis Paget, a scholar and theologian; Bishop Edward Talbot, a practical Diocesan; Cosmo Lang, a fellow Scotsman who made Lambeth his London home and became almost indispensable; Lord Stamfordham, whom he had known since his Windsor days. Of all his secretaries Arthur Sheppard, who joined his staff in 1899 and retired only in 1923, was pre-eminent. Usually the Archbishop had two chaplains: one to deal with diocesan business; the other with a more general writ, thus becoming almost 'a second pair of eyes'.

II

To preserve the place of the Church of England in the life of the nation meant, as Davidson saw it, cultivating those in the seats of power (a task very congenial to him); taking his place in the House of Lords; and concerning himself, not simply with what affected the Church and its rights, but the wider community. Randall Davidson was interested in social questions, and had shown this over a number of years. Though never doctrinaire, distrustful of ambitious systems, always anxious to get at the facts, reluctant to act precipitately, he did feel with a genuine passion that Christian faith ought to make a difference to the ordering of society. On occasions he was prepared to stand his ground on a matter of principle against popular pressure and, behind the scenes, to push politicians, although always punctilious never to embarrass them in public. Consistently as Prime Ministers entered office during his twenty-six years at Lambeth, he would write a tactful letter placing himself at their service, but taking care to refrain from seeming to encumber them with help. That to Campbell-Bannerman, in 1905, may be taken as typical:

> It has been my high privilege to be on terms of confidential friendship with your *four* immediate predecessors in that office, and with the two younger of them my intimacy has been close and real, although upon a good many public questions I differ pretty widely from the opinion of either. Should the new Prime Minister allow me to stand in a friendly personal relation to himself I shall appreciate it on every ground, and occasions may possibly arise when the maintenance of the confidential intercourse which it has for more than 20 years been my privilege to hold with Downing Street would on public grounds have its advantages. Whether this be so or not, I hope you will let me assure you of my absolute readiness at any moment to place at your disposal, should you desire it, such information as I may be able to furnish upon any of the Ecclesiastical matters, either personal or general, which of necessity claim so frequently the attention of the Prime Minister.
>
> It is I hope needless for me to add that I shall perfectly understand it if for any reason you would prefer to rely wholly upon others for such information with regard to Ecclesiastical facts or folk as you may from time to time require.
>
> My sole anxiety is to make it clear to you from the outset of what will I hope be a great and memorable Premiership, that I am at your service to the best of my power, if and only if, such service may be at any time desired.[452]

This letter is a model, and it met a warm response.

Right relations with Prime Ministers were important when it came to matters of Church appointments.

No one ecclesiastic has exercised a greater influence on preferment than did Randall Davidson when Dean of Windsor. This continued until the Queen's death. The situation changed somewhat when he became Archbishop of Canterbury, since he then had to deal directly with the Prime Minister. Here he was scrupulously correct in not wishing to deprive the head of the Government of his undoubted constitutional rights as the Queen's adviser, though he would be frank in expressing his own views. For example, on his translation to Canterbury, he expressed his preference for Dr. Talbot, Bishop of Rochester, as his successor at Winchester, but took care to list six other names in favour of whom strong arguments could be made. The concluding words of his letter to Balfour are significant:

> I have had my say. I hope it is not too lengthy. Of course it is a mere contribution to your material for decision. It is hard upon you to have so much all at once to decide.[453]

As a matter of fact Ryle, and not Talbot, went to Winchester.

Balfour's successor, Sir Henry Campbell-Bannerman, was much more independent, and it was a common remark of the Archbishop that no one so often sought his advice and so regularly rejected it. It is only fair to say of Campbell-Bannerman, however, that it was a high sense of duty which often made him, as he said of himself, 'finicky and fastidious'. His disadvantage was that like other Prime Ministers he did not really know the field.

With Asquith it was different. He had a wide knowledge and was deeply interested. One of his private secretaries writes that he weighed 'respective claims with the most scrupulous care and, while he was always ready to receive the advice of the Archbishop of Canterbury, with whom he was very intimate, it was invariably on his own unbiassed selection that a name was submitted to the King'.[454] Randall Davidson was the first to admit that Asquith was the best informed and the most thorough of all the Prime Ministers with whom he had to deal. In particular he would scrutinize the academic record of those whose names were brought before him.

No contrast could be more extreme in this respect than that between Asquith and Lloyd George. Lloyd George knew little of Church life or Church leaders, and took over as his ecclesiastical adviser Canon Pearce of Westminster, who had hitherto been consulted only in connexion with minor preferment. To Lloyd George it was preaching ability which commended a man rather than academic expertise or the capacity to enter into mature personal relations. The Archbishop, on the other hand, did not believe that every bishop needed oratory among his gifts any more than a Home Secretary is expected to be 'an admirable Trafalgar Square speaker'. Nor did he share Lloyd George's strong prejudice against headmasters. To be fair to the Prime Minister, he made no secret of his inadequacy and for this reason was prepared to accept help. Some members of Parliament, knowing the situation, proposed the setting up of an advisory committee of three laymen and three clergy. Davidson was not enthusiastic, and gave it as his opinion that they should not constitute a formal committee but should only be consulted individually and not on every vacancy. The experiment was tried but was soon abandoned.

When a similar suggestion was put forward in Convocation—here

the advisory committee was to be confined to the two Archbishops—
he was equally critical. Whatever was decided, he said, could not be
official, since the Prime Minister had a responsibility on behalf of
the nation which could not constitutionally be taken from him. He
did, however, pass on the motion to the Prime Minister, from whom
he received the reply that this was already the Prime Minister's
practice; it would continue; and he was glad to know that in this
procedure he had the support of Convocation.

On one occasion, however, the Archbishop took a strong line.
He was anxious, in June 1921, that Dr. Donaldson, Bishop of Brisbane, should go to Salisbury. Lloyd George approved in principle
but demurred when he understood that the Bishop intended to
remain in Brisbane until the Synod met there in October. Randall
Davidson firmly informed the Prime Minister that although it was
for him to nominate it was for the Archbishop, since he was in
charge of the diocese during a vacancy, to fix the date on which the
new bishop took over his duties.

With Bonar Law, Prime Minister for less than a year, and with
Baldwin, consultation between Lambeth and Downing Street was
constant, and the Archbishop's influence often prevailed. As to
MacDonald, the first socialist Prime Minister, the Archbishop was
determined that nothing should be done to weaken the responsibility
of his office in relation to ecclesiastical appointments. If the Prime
Minister wished, he told him, he could consult the Archbishop or
anyone else that he chose; but the responsibility finally rested with
him. Ramsay MacDonald, in the first flush of his excitement, had to
resist pressure from some of his own party who wished him to
appoint clergy to high office for political reasons. Two of his nominations proved significant for the future: Dr. Barnes to Birmingham and
Hewlett Johnson to the Deanery of Canterbury.

Successive Prime Ministers appreciated that Davidson made it a
principle never to associate himself with a public agitation unless he
was certain as to what the facts actually were. He seldom saw his
office in prophetic terms, and deprecated any suggestion that
churchmen had a monopoly either of wisdom or altruism. Particularly was he chary, perhaps overmuch, of signing or putting his
name to a document. An example of this reluctance, under considerable pressure, may be seen in his response, in the summer of 1903, to
requests for him to rouse the national conscience on behalf of
Christian suffering in Macedonia at the hands of the Turks. In a
letter to A. J. Balfour, written on 17 September 1903, he set out his
own attitude with clarity:

In such emergencies as the present I always shrink from taking such a line as may be likely to hamper the Executive Government upon whom the responsibility rests, and who are, I am persuaded, quite as likely at this moment as any of us clergy can be to be alive to the *horribleness* of what is going on—while their knowledge of details and of possibilities is of course incomparably greater.[455]

The result of this epistle was a long letter, designed for publication, from Balfour to the Archbishop, which gave the latter great satisfaction in that it 'recognized that the Church of England as such has a sort of "status" in the matter and responsibility, though an undefined one, as the religious mouthpiece of England, when any utterance is desirable'.[456] The Archbishop remained cautious, and although supporting a Macedonian Relief Fund, he did not favour a central service in St. Paul's Cathedral.

Particularly galling to many sincere people was their failure to secure his signature to a letter protesting against traffic in opium. In his reply to Mr. Broomhall, leader of the campaign, the Archbishop stressed that he could not think the Royal Commission which had recently reported on this matter was 'either ill-informed or unfair'.

> I have no wish personally—he went on—to promote the continuance of a trade which is undoubtedly productive of much evil, though apparently, in the opinion of many wise observers, it is also productive of a great deal that is wholesome and good.[457]

Mr. Broomhall's bitter riposte was that when he showed the Archbishop's letter to his son, who had spent many years in China, he exclaimed 'Incredible: it's heartbreaking.'[458] It was; and the Archbishop's reply still leaves a somewhat nasty taste in the mouth.

The Archbishop showed the same caution, and seems to have incurred the worst of both worlds, over the agitation which centred around the employment, under wretched conditions, of Chinese labour in the mines of the Transvaal after the South African War. Speaking in the House of Lords in February 1904, he said that from his own inquiries he was convinced that the subject was a complex one, but that

> at all events it is certainly a form of administration a little difficult to reconcile with the liberties and freedom which should exist in a British colony.[459]

This speech, muted though it was, did not please the Government, and many criticized him for setting himself up as 'Political *Censor*

*Morum*'. On the other hand, what he said then and some three weeks later equally upset Bishop Gore and his friends, particularly in the use of such words as:

> . . . if it be a necessity, it is one which I personally feel to be of a very painful kind, of a very lamentable kind and one which is not without its elements of humiliation.[460]

With caution almost second nature, it is not surprising that Davidson exercised it in full measure when approached by the various peace movements which proliferated as the international situation during the first decade of the XXth century progressively worsened. Here his oft-repeated contention was that the Church should enunciate basic principles, but that when it came to what practical action such general principles demanded, then this must be 'guided by what statesmen declare to be possible for the nation's life, and the Church as represented by the clergy cannot take the place which ought to be occupied by statesmen'.[461] Thus he felt unable to sign an 'Appeal from the Churches for Peace', which maintained that the calamities of war were 'very imperfectly realised or understood in the more immediate circles of sovereigns, statesmen and diplomatists'.[462] On the contrary, he himself had found 'the people who surround statesmen and diplomats to be 'the strongest and most outspoken against the dangers of war'.[463] Therefore it was quite improper for clergy to pontificate 'as to what the size and number of our ships should be, or what sort of ships ought to be multiplied and what ought not'. He did, however, write to A. J. Balfour, on 3 January 1905, at the time of the Russo-Japanese War, when Port Arthur had fallen, asking whether any mediation on the part of Britain might not be demanded; and confessing that he would

> not be doing justice to those whose representations and appeals to me have been, as I think you know, both frequent and urgent, or to my own sentiments and anxieties did I not at the moment assure you that to the best of my belief the whole country would be with you or behind you if you found it possible to let England now take some overt step in the direction of bringing about the restoration of peace.[464]

The Prime Minister's reply was perhaps to be expected, namely that it was 'likely to be not only useless but worse than useless, unless and until the combatants are willing to take advantage . . .' etc.[465] —by which time, we may assume, such an initiative would have become unnecessary.

416

Caution, on Davidson's part, often led to misunderstanding. Thus, in 1909, an explosive year when there was a Navy scare and widespread talk of war with Germany, Dr. Scott Lidgett, a Free Church leader, suggested that the two Archbishops should issue a message to the nation. The Archbishop demurred. 'The "plain man" would say,' he replied, 'this talk or pious injunction is all very well but do you mean that we are to have new Dreadnoughts or not?'[466] However, when Dr. Harnack came over to England in February 1911 in connexion with the German Churches Commission for fostering friendly relations between Great Britain and Germany, Davidson presided at a meeting in the Queen's Hall which had as its object the founding of a British section. When on the eve of the First World War the Archbishop was asked to submit a memorial for presentation to Mr. Asquith urging that Britain be kept out of the conflict, the Archbishop replied firmly that he 'could not possibly sign it without an assurance that it was on lines which the Government would find helpful and not harmful'.[467] Asquith, when approached, left him in no doubt as to the answer.

It is understandable that the Archbishop, with his great sensitivity to lay opinion, should entertain an incurable dislike of clergymen —innocent of the real facts—generating moral heat while leaving others to handle the consequences of their zeal. At times, however, he fell a victim to his own logic, since once clergy disclaim any detailed political knowledge, their enunciation of principle needs to take on some prophetic quality or they become platitudinous to a degree. There are occasions for doing right 'though the heavens fall'. It is, perhaps, fair comment that had Davidson been more prophetic in respect of the employment of Chinese labour in the Transvaal he might have altered the practical situation to advantage. Doubtless his reply would be that his caution gave more force to his words on the few occasions when he did utter; not least during the First World War, when on one issue he took a firm line and incurred much unpopularity.

Davidson was convinced that England had no option but to honour her commitment to Belgium and become a combatant, and in the Upper House of Convocation, soon after the outbreak of hostilities, he declared:

> I imagine that there is not one of us who entertains any doubt of this, that our nation could not, without sacrificing principles of honour and justice more dear than life itself, have stood aside or looked idly on. Fearful, devilish, calamitous as a great war must be, there would be something, there is something, yet worse. To stand selfishly aside while vile wrong is perpetrated

in a matter wherein we are concerned would, if I may use the phrase, debase the moral currency of a people more, far more, than to join in warfare, terrible as it is, for rolling the wrong back.[468]

But as hostilities went on, the growing disregard of the rights of civilians and the abandonment of older and traditional restraints distressed him enormously and he took the initiative in sounding a note of alarm. In particular he endeavoured to stem the tide of increasing hatred. In Convocation, on 17 February 1916, he proposed a resolution which after a long debate was carried, that

> This House . . . while recognising that it does not lie within its province to express any opinion on matters purely military, desires to record its conviction that the principles of morality forbid a policy of reprisal which has, as a deliberate object, the killing or wounding of non-combatants, and believes that the adoption of such a mode of retaliation, even for barbarous outrages, would permanently lower the standard of honourable conduct between nation and nation.[469]

To the Archbishop it was a matter of motive and intention, and he did his best to remain faithful to the vestigial remains of the Christian doctrine of the just war. When he had reason to believe that the British armed forces were being equipped with gas, he protested to Asquith that 'as a Christian citizen . . . I confess that I am profoundly disquieted'. He urged that the King let it be known that he was so 'horrified by these barbarities' [i.e. use of poison gas by the Germans] that he desired his army should 'resolutely abstain from any such foul conduct'.[470] But the Archbishop's intervention was unsuccessful, and poison gas was added to the national armoury.

In 1917, as the war situation deteriorated, the agitation for extensive reprisals arose again, and many saw the allied attack on Freiburg as a response to this demand. The Archbishop raised the matter in the House of Lords on 2 May.

> I do know that the Christian judgment of England—and I do not shrink from using that term in its fullest sense—is that when we come out of the war (scarred and wounded yes; bereft of our best and noblest and most hopeful, yes) we mean to come out with clean hands and with the right to feel sure that in the coming years, whatever record leaps to light, we shall never be ashamed.[471]

What effect the Archbishop's attitude had on Government policy, though reinforced by a resolution of the Free Church Federal

Council, is difficult to determine. It certainly brought a great deal of abuse upon himself, as he confessed at the time:

> I am . . . the recipient of a continuous shower of protests, denunciations, and often virulent abuse, from every part of England, especially from London. I am said to be the cause of the Air Raids, to be in league with the Germans, and to be responsible for the death of those who suffered, and so on. Devout prayers are expressed that I (and occasionally my wife, to whom they sometimes write) may be the next person to be blown to pieces.[472]

Davidson also exerted himself in the House of Lords and by letters to ministers to promote a 'large and common-sense attitude' towards conscientious objectors on the grounds that it was both 'politic ana desirable'. Particularly in respect of the 'absolutists' he urged release from prison. After the War he opposed 'as an act of real unfairness' the unwillingness of the Government to re-employ conscientious objectors unless they had served in the non-combatant corps.[473] He spoke often in the Lords and informally approached the ministers to facilitate the exchange of prisoners. He made sustained efforts, although in vain, to save the life of Sir Roger Casement, calling attention to his fine work in the Congo; suggesting that his mental balance had been affected; urging that a reprieve would be far more sensible strategy than an execution; and asking whom it was expected that his death would deter. Maybe he weakened the impact of his own case by admitting that Casement *deserves* hanging', thus basing his plea on expediency.[474] It was the defect of his temperament and often served to rob his representations of a real cutting-edge.

While hostilities were at their height he wrote a long letter to Dr. Adolf Deissmann of the Lutheran Church, replying to charges against Britain, yet at the same time breathing an air of genuine Christian charity.[475] For the most part, however, during the grim years of the War, the Archbishop did his best to identify himself with the various aspects of the national effort. In May 1916 he visited France and Belgium, where he spent some eight days holding consultations, meeting generals and mixing with the troops. With the collapse of Russia in April 1918, the allied situation grew desperate. A Military Service Bill was introduced into the House of Lords and the Archbishop let it be known that he was prepared, in co-operation with the bishops, to consider the clergy becoming combatants; but the Allies finally triumphed before this was implemented.

When President Wilson called for the setting up of a League of Nations, Randall Davidson responded immediately to Lord Robert

Cecil's appeal for support. In an eloquent letter to *The Times* on 28 September 1918, he wrote:

> I can speak for no Government, but I am convinced that the mass of thoughtful Christian folk in England feel with an earnestness beyond words the force of his [President Wilson's] contention that for reasons not of policy but of principle, not of national interest but of righteousness and justice and enduring peace, we want a League of Nations on the very lines which he has drawn.

In order to commend this cause in early and critical days, Davidson spoke to the General Assembly in Scotland, both established and free; and to Convocation. The 'screwing up' of the peace terms caused him great concern as did his sad reflection that 'we have no statesman big enough to handle these problems . . . certainly not Lloyd George'.[476] On 24 May 1919 he wrote to the Prime Minister, calling his attention 'to the many communications . . . reaching me from people who to a large degree eschew ordinary politics', but who were yet 'anxious and disquieted about the terms of Peace'. 'We trust you and your colleagues,' he continued, 'to succeed in securing a Peace which shall correspond with our purposes in entering the War, which shall be such that we can ask God's blessing upon it, and which shall be of the kind that will be lasting and not the beginning of new strife.'[477] Lloyd George in a friendly reply stressed the difficulties of reconciling justice with mercy. Events were to prove that he would have been wiser to take the Archbishop's counsel more to heart; although it must be admitted that dealing with Clemenceau could not have been easy.

It fell to the Archbishop to preach at a service of thanksgiving in St. Paul's to mark the signing of the Peace Treaty. It gave him a further and significant opportunity to urge loyalty to the League of Nations which 'may want, I think it will want, consideration and adjustment here and there as the months and years run on'.[478] In 1922 he accepted an invitation to preach in St. Peter's Cathedral, Geneva, before the opening of the Third Assembly. His great hope remained that the League would avoid large and specious talk and would get down to the practical task of removing the causes of war. He did not live long enough to see it betrayed by the very nations which had set it up.

It will be seen from these glimpses of Davidson during the stern years of war that he took seriously his responsibilities and, although with tact, did not hesitate to let his views be known to those in the seats of power.

In the same spirit it was part of his creed to enter seriously into his duties as a member of the House of Lords, even if attendance was not easily fitted into other demands on his time. He was therefore particularly sensitive when Augustine Birrell, Minister of Education, at the National Liberal Club in 1907 went out of his way to attack the bishops of the established Church.

> I cannot remember—he said—a single great cause they ever advocated. I cannot recall a single victory they ever won; hardly a word they ever said in the cause of humanity.[479]

This outburst, so unqualified in its condemnation, undoubtedly got under the Archbishop's skin, and he took it up on the grounds that when a Cabinet Minister of the front rank 'tells the world that, in what he calls the cause of humanity, the bishops have usually kept silent in Parliament', he, as Archbishop, must reply. He did so by listing the particular Bills which he had either introduced into the Upper House or supported, omitting those connected directly with matters relating to the Church or education. The list was indeed formidable, and included legislation concerning industry, outdoor relief, friendly societies, midwives, and aborigines in Western Australia.[480] In a short reply Birrell explained that he was 'thinking of Pioneers—of Unpopular Causes, Unjust Wars, Contagious Diseases Act, and things of that kind'.[481] Undoubtedly here he had a point.

In respect of their parliamentary duties, Davidson, as his predecessors, was concerned that the bishops as an order should take them seriously, but on principle he felt that he ought not to inspire any block voting, a principle to which he adhered, under pressure, during the debates on the Parliament Bill in 1910. When Lord Salisbury complained to the Archbishop that he understood the bishops would support the Government in this matter, he was sharply informed that he 'absolutely declined to be in any sense a whip in this matter or to bring pressure, direct or indirect, to bear upon the Bishops'.[482]

Davidson maintained his interest in social and political affairs to the end of his archiepiscopate. Perhaps most spectacular was his intervention in the General Strike. This industrial crisis arose out of a dispute in the mining industry, which led the Trades Union Congress, at midnight on 3 May 1926, to 'freeze' the national economy. This breakdown in human relations became a matter of grave concern to the Archbishop, and he consulted widely. He was perceptive enough to appreciate how complex were the causes which had led to the strike, but felt, and expressed this view in the House of Lords, that he must condemn its 'unwisdom and its mischievousness'. It was 'so intolerable that every effort is needed, is justifiably called for and ought to be supported, which the Government may make to bring that condition of things as speedily as possible to an end'.[483] On 6 May two English bishops with a group of leading nonconformists met at Lambeth, and issued a call to prayer, adding that they were 'anxiously considering' how Christian opinion could be harnessed to a settlement. It was suggested that the Archbishop should himself broadcast an appeal for the strike to be called off, for the Government to renew its offer to help the coal industry, and for the employers to withdraw their new wages scale, all these to happen 'simultaneously and concurrently'. To Randall Davidson's deep regret John Reith, the Director-General of the B.B.C., refused this request on his own authority, maintaining that it would 'run counter to his tacit arrangement with the Government about such things'. The Archbishop wrote a long letter to the Director-General, pointing out the seriousness of denying to the Christian Churches the possibility of making their voice heard at such a time of crisis, unless that voice were approved by the B.B.C.[484] The rejected appeal, however, appeared in *The Times*, Winston Churchill refusing to publish it in the official *British Gazette*. Its issue drew a great deal of fire from those who were convinced that the strikers alone were responsible for the situation and therefore that they must go back to work unconditionally. It also led to a flood of congratulatory letters. Gilbert Murray rejoiced that 'the Church had led the conscience of the country'.[485]

It was characteristic of the Archbishop's eirenical spirit that as soon as the strike was over he wrote a friendly epistle to Baldwin paying tribute to his firmness and spirit of conciliation. It is significant of the respect in which Lambeth was then held in left-wing circles that on 13 May Mr. Ben Turner and Miss Margaret Bondfield descended upon the Archbishop to solicit his influence to prevent victimization.

At the head of the nation was the monarch, and Davidson was always very conscious of being intimate with the Royal Family. When he was appointed to Lambeth, he found in Edward VII a man whom he had known many years, and it was natural that he, as friend and Primate, should attend his deathbed as he had that of his mother. 'I have seldom or never seen a quieter passing of the river,' he later commented.[486] At the request of Queen Alexandra he went to Buckingham Palace on 11 May to hold a short and private service over the body of the dead King. The Archbishop conducted the ceremony at the Lying-in-State in Westminster Hall, and spoke impressively:

Here in the great Hall of English history we stand in the

presence of Death. But Death is, to us Christians, swallowed up in a larger life. Our common sorrow reminds us of our common Hope to rise from sorrow to thanksgiving and prayer.

He presided over the interment at Windsor, when he had a talk with the German Emperor and President Roosevelt.[487]

The Archbishop was the first to greet the new King as he came out from his father's deathbed. It was a time when the Archbishop, quietly and without fuss, was able, because of his long experience, to be particularly helpful. He was one of the group who conducted George V into his first Council. It was at his suggestion that, in the Prayer Book, Alexandra should be designated the Queen Mother and not the Queen Dowager.

The Coronation which followed presented a difficulty by reason of the extreme anti-Roman declaration, drawn up in 1689, which the King was required to swear. To members of that Church the terms were simply offensive. On the other hand, any modification too far in the other direction was bound to incur the protest of evangelicals within the Church of England, and certainly of some nonconformists outside it. Asquith, the Prime Minister, to whom it was all 'like the quibbles of the schoolmen', proposed a form of words which the Archbishop could not accept. Finally the Archbishop came up with a formula which declared that the King was a 'faithful Protestant'. It was generally approved.

With George V, Randall Davidson was on terms of more than a conventional friendship. On 23 February 1914, he entertained him and the Queen at Lambeth Palace in the presence of a mixed company which included the editor of *The Times*, two overseas bishops, and Mrs. Benson, a link with former days. It was the first time since the Reformation that a reigning sovereign, together with his consort, had visited and been entertained in this way at the Palace, Queen Elizabeth having had no consort.

Randall Davidson was convinced of the value of a national Church; but it was his lot to be at Lambeth when the historic Church of Wales, which had survived by the skin of its teeth during the primacy of Benson, was finally disestablished. This could not have come as a surprise to him. The Liberals, who were returned to power in the elections of 1906 by an overwhelming majority, included over 150 nonconformists. Mr. Lloyd George took the initiative, and asked the Bishop of St. Asaph whether the Church of Wales would withdraw its opposition to a 'mild' disestablishment bill. Randall Davidson counselled caution, but agreed to the setting up of a Royal Commission to report on existing provisions for the spiritual needs of the Welsh population. The result was the introduction of a

Bill to disestablish the Church in Wales, the effect of which was to sunder its dioceses from the Convocation of the Province of Canterbury, and to remove endowments prior to 1662—no less than one half of its existing revenue. Randall Davidson felt that he must oppose it, although he admitted that what really mattered was the spiritual welfare and shepherding of the people of Wales. Disestablishment constituted a surgical operation on the Province of Canterbury, and disendowment a crippling handicap to the Church in discharging its traditional role. Above and beyond this, Davidson believed in established churches, and the geographical parochial system that went with it. The case for disestablishment was, of course, that the membership of the Church of Wales was less than that of the nonconforming churches, which meant that it had ceased to be, in practice, a national church. On the eve of the Bill's introduction, the Archbishop addressed a meeting of ten thousand churchmen in Caernarvon; he spoke against it in the House of Lords, and later in the year at an excited meeting in the Albert Hall. The Government agreed to appoint a Select Committee to inquire whether the removal of the Welsh dioceses from the Convocation of Canterbury, without provincial consent, was constitutional; also whether nonconformists in Wales were themselves opposed to disendowment. The First World War broke out before the Committee could meet, and in spite of a protest from the Archbishop, the Welsh Church Act was passed under the provisions of the Parliament Act of 1911 (it was three times rejected by the Lords), though a Suspensory Act was passed to postpone its operation for twelve months or at latest to the end of the War. When at last hostilities ceased, the Archbishop wisely bent his energies, not on reopening the whole matter of disestablishment, but to securing better financial provisions. In this he was not wholly without success. There remained the question as to whether the Welsh dioceses, prohibited by law from retaining their membership in the Canterbury Convocation, should voluntarily elect to remain in the Province. Here the Archbishop was asked by the Welsh bishops to give advice. He had no doubt that for the benefit of Wales the Church there ought now to become a separate province. Accordingly he released the Welsh bishops from their oaths, and solemnly in full Synod of the two Houses of Convocation, on 10 February 1920, declared the four dioceses of Wales to be separate from the province of Canterbury as from 31 March, and free to form their own province if they so desired. 'Brothers,' Davidson said, 'solemnly, affectionately, hopefully, we who remain in these Convocation halls will wish you God speed.'[488] On 1 June 1920, the Archbishop enthroned the Bishop of St. Asaph as first Archbishop of Wales in his own cathedral.

It must be admitted that the Archbishop did not show the same objectivity in this matter which he so strikingly displayed on other occasions. He believed too firmly and for too long in established churches to make this possible. Also he was personally sensitive to the feeling of the Welsh bishops, which made him unwilling to try to impose disestablishment upon those who were against it. Yet once the Bill was passed, he was foremost in urging that a practical view be taken and that everything be done to rescue as much as possible from defeat. He was a statesman and always preferred solid results to the satisfaction of indulging in a rhetoric that might damage the cause he had at heart.

### III

Our study of Randall Davidson has dealt so far with his national role, not simply because this was significant to him, but because he was the last Archbishop to be able to play it in this particular manner. After his time, people in the seats of power began to change. They became less clubbable; less cultivated; less nostalgic for a Christianity which, if they now ceased to believe in it, had until recently educated the nation and dominated the universities. Equally important, such people had less time on their hands.

Davidson, however, was not remiss in discharging other roles, all of which he recognized as part of the complex responsibilities of an Archbishop of Canterbury.

In his diocese, Davidson was assisted by the Bishops of Dover and Croydon, whom he took into his confidence and with whom he worked happily. One ticklish diocesan problem came his way which he dealt with wisely and calmly. The creation by Act of Parliament in 1904 of the Diocese of Southwark left the Diocese of Rochester greatly diminished in size. The question was raised as to whether Rochester should be compensated, a suggestion which usually brings opposition from the 'conceding diocese', particularly when, as in this case, part of the proposed transfer-area was affluent. The Dean and Chapter of Canterbury, together with his own suffragan bishops, opposed the scheme. Davidson was, therefore, caught between two fires; but he sensibly allowed the matter to be dealt with by an independent commission which finally recommended that the rural deaneries of East and West Dartford, North and South Malling, Shoreham, and Tonbridge should go to Rochester.

A significant event took place during Randall Davidson's archiepiscopate which was to affect intimately the life of the Church of England. This was the Enabling Act of 1920 which led to the setting up, centrally, of the Church Assembly and, locally, of parochial church councils.

We have already seen that the Convocation of Canterbury was revived in 1852 and that of the Northern Province some nine years later; that there were occasional joint meetings of both Convocations; and that under Benson a House of Laymen was established. In 1903 there came into existence an informal Representative Church Council of some seven hundred members. The Church of England had, therefore, over a period of years, been feeling its way towards a greater autonomy within the over-all legal status of its establishment.

Davidson, who in company with many others had scant esteem for a doctrinaire independence, yet recognized that Parliament had little time and less inclination to embark upon ecclesiastical legislation. Lord Halifax, as might have been expected, and other distinguished lay churchmen, were eager to effect a remedy. The result was a resolution passed through the Representative Church Council in July 1913, requesting 'the Archbishops of Canterbury and York to consider the advisability of appointing a Committee to inquire what changes are advisable in order to secure in the relations of Church and State a fuller expression of the spiritual independence of the Church as well as of the national recognition of religion'.[489] This resolution led to the setting up of the Archbishops' Commission on Church and State with Lord Selborne as its Chairman. Its proposals, which were designed to give legal status to parochial church councils, diocesan synods, and a central assembly, were warmly received by Convocation although the Archbishop warned the more ardent spirits against expecting too much too soon. The warning was directed in particular against the leaders of the Life and Liberty Movement, not least the brilliant and effervescent William Temple, who throughout the country were rousing the consciences of churchmen to desire a greater spiritual independence. In the opinion of the Archbishop, its members underestimated the difficulties ahead and the preoccupation of ministers as the war situation seemed to worsen. Thus when he and the Archbishop of York (Cosmo Lang) received a deputation from the Life and Liberty Movement, he was a little nettled, although he took it with his accustomed calm, at the charge that 'no leadership had been given in the last four or five years'. The fact was, he reminded them, that there simply was no chance at the moment of getting legislation through Parliament.

But the War at long last came to an end and in February 1919, when the Representative Church Council met, the Archbishop left the chair and made his own position, which was now for going forward, perfectly clear. He admitted frankly that if he believed the consequences of what was proposed to be as Hensley Henson, Bishop of Durham, supposed, namely the end of the Church of England as the Church of the nation, then he could not for a moment support it. But this was not so. The burden of Davidson's argument was the sober, factual one, that Parliament could now no longer give time to ecclesiastical legislation, and that therefore necessary reform was delayed, even prevented altogether. When he had brought before the ministers in power during the last quarter of a century matters which needed attention 'they did not say "We are opposed to it," or "We are objecting to what you do," but rather, "You are asking a machine to do it, which is already so clogged with work, and work of a different kind, that you are asking an impossibility." '[490]

The Archbishop's intervention did a great deal to reassure the doubters, and on 28 February the scheme and the Enabling Bill were adopted by the Council without dissent. Even Bishop Gore, on the eve of his resigning the Bishopric of Oxford, congratulated the Archbishop.

The intricacies and the amendments which accompanied the introduction of the Enabling Bill into Parliament need not detain us. Its passage was accompanied by a lengthy correspondence in the Press on the relations of Church and State, in which Hensley Henson sounded a sombre note of warning as to what would happen if the Bill were passed. *The Times* expressed the simple hope that the Bill 'will not become law'. But it did. The Archbishop moved the second reading in the House of Lords in one of his most effective speeches— definite, practical, and to the point; though in terms which did not commend themselves to the more enthusiastic and 'ideological' of the Bill's supporters, particularly Gore. They were not dealing with deep spiritual things, he said, but with 'the outer secular rules within which our work has to be done'.[491]

This major constitutional change in the structure of the Church of England went through Parliament with remarkable speed. What was then decided had been some seventy years in gestation; but the Bill owed its passing as much to the restraint and sagacity of the Archbishop as to the enthusiasm and energy of the Life and Liberty Movement. Davidson's known caution, his refusal to present the case in abstract, ideological terms, reassured many members of the House of Commons. Perhaps he may be pardoned for saying to the Librarian at Lambeth: 'My dear Jenkins, if people would only let me do things in my own way, the Church of England would get on all right.'[492]

One of Randall Davidson's prime concerns, and it was bound up with his archiepiscopal office, was to preserve the comprehensive character of the Church of England which he believed it to have acquired at the Reformation. This meant holding a balance between parties and not allowing them to devour each other. He was just old enough to remember the *furore* over *Essays and Reviews*, and this persuaded him into a life-long reluctance to over-define, and there-fore to resist those who wished 'error', as they saw it, to be officially condemned. Among these Charles Gore was pre-eminent. Though Gore welcomed modern biblical criticism, he believed that where this led to a denial of such key doctrines as the Virgin birth and the Resurrection then authority must act. The publication by Dr. J. M. Thompson of *The Miracles of the New Testament*, and later of *Founda-tions*, edited by Dr. Streeter, led to Charles Gore and Dr. Winning-ton-Ingram, the Bishop of London—an uneasy alliance—drafting a resolution for introduction into the Upper House of Convocation. Its general effect was to commit the Church of England to the historic facts of the Nicene and Apostles' Creeds and to question the sincerity of those who publicly recited such creeds but would not *ex animo* affirm them. The Archbishop's reply to the Bishop of London, on 31 March 1914, is worth quoting as illustrating his general attitude. It is Tait brought up to date:

> I could not, even at your and his request, join in the issue of a declaration the outcome of which would, I honestly believe, be that we should render intolerable the position of quite a large group of our best and most thoughtful clergy, not because they themselves differ from you or me in their beliefs, but because they could not stand the issue of a new and authoritative declaration.[493]

The Archbishop prudently sponsored a mediating resolution, being supported in so doing by the fact that counter-petitions were being sent into Convocation, including one from a number of university professors headed by Dean Inge, sounding a note of alarm. Davidson was particularly anxious not to deter scholars from their legitimate pursuits and that the Church should not fail to face up to modern problems. This concern expressed itself in his solemn words to the Upper House:

> We do not, as I understand your words, say to students or seekers after truth, as such, 'Stop; that path is barred, that conclusion is forbidden; you must not go there.' To the student we must say: 'Follow the truth; do your utmost to find it, and let it be your guide whithersoever it may lead you.'[494]

There was, however, a distinction to be drawn between the student and the accredited clergy in their parishes, in respect of whom the 'denial' of the historical facts of the Creed was more serious.

Here Davidson's manner of working was typical. First, to secure a far less rigid resolution once he saw that a resolution was going to be passed; then to explain carefully how he understood its terms and have this put on record. It was his way of helping to preserve comprehension. Reflecting on this policy he wrote:

> Bishop Gore of Oxford regards me as perilously lax in what I teach and practise as regards the national character of the Church of England, a phrase to which he has a special anti-pathy. I am increasingly certain that the rigorist attitude is a mistaken one, and that we rightly inculcate and use an elasti-city in these matters.[495]

For this reason he was at first suspicious of a proposal put forward by a number of theologians for a doctrinal commission to consist of Anglo-Catholics, Liberals, and Evangelicals. For a group of men to get together, as in the case of the contributors to *Lux Mundi*, and to 'stand on their own merits as scholars' was one thing; for a body to be officially appointed and subsequently to issue an authoritative report was another. His first reaction, therefore, was 'critical and un-welcoming'; but the 1921 Conference of the Modern Churchmen at Cambridge, where the subject was 'Christ and the Creeds', led to a violent controversy. Convocation became disturbed, and in May 1922 passed a resolution affirming belief in the Nicene Creed, but with an addendum, partly due to Davidson's work 'behind the scenes', commending 'reverent' inquiry.

The Archbishop was now slowly coming round to see some ad-vantage in people of different schools of thought getting together, provided that they were temperamentally tolerant and inclined to be constructive; yet he still demurred at any attempt at 'securing a unity of belief' and any drawing up of 'an unambiguous statement of the doctrines [of the Church of England] to which they could give general adherence'.[496] Finally, however, in co-operation with the Archbishop of York, he nominated a group of men of different schools of theological thought to meet as a commission 'to consider the nature and grounds of Christian Doctrine with a view to demon-strating the extent of existing agreement within the Church of England and with a view to investigating how far it is possible to remove or diminish existing differences'.[497]

The report of the Commission—*Doctrine in the Church of England*—was not published until 1938, some eight years after Archbishop Davidson's death. It was an excellent, if unequal, piece of work, and would doubtless have had more influence had not the nation again been plunged into war so soon after its appearance. When peace came, the intellectual, social and religious climate had dramatically changed; so much so that the theological liberalism, endemic in the Report, no matter what the particular view of the members of the Commission, ceased to appeal. It may yet be found to have a more permanent value. Certainly Dr. Davidson would have approved of its title: *Doctrine in* [not *of*] *the Church of England.* No attempt was made to give it episcopal sanction.

Similarly cautious in approach was the Archbishop's response to an 'open letter' by Bishop Barnes which appeared in *The Times* on 20 October 1927.

Bishop Barnes was a scientist and mathematician of distinction; an active exponent of biological evolution, and a strong opponent of high sacramental claims. In propagating his opinions he displayed, like Bishop Colenso, the spirit of the crusader, being convinced that it was the refusal of the Church to take modern science seriously which prevented intelligent laymen from committing themselves to the Faith. His attitude to theology was pragmatic; and he shocked contemporaries by suggesting that such false views as transubstantiation should be tested by submitting a consecrated wafer to trial by experiment. The nub of his 'open letter' was to invite the Archbishop 'to consider what steps can be taken to help those of us who are giving of our best to fit the Church to be in the future the spiritual guide of an educated nation'.[498] The Archbishop did not reply publicly to this letter or to a second which the Bishop sent to the Press. His own view, expressed privately to Barnes, was that the Bishop exaggerated the resistance of churchmen to evolutionary theories; and that it was his own somewhat crude attitude to the sacraments which caused such great offence. To the Archbishop, Barnes's belligerent approach, together with the scorn which he poured on lesser mortals, was equally inimical as High Church intolerance to comprehension.

Comprehension, however, was not easily maintained when passions ran high, as Davidson well knew. Those who feel their deepest insights affronted tend not to be tolerant. Such proved to be the case in the abortive attempt at Prayer Book revision which was rejected by the House of Commons in 1927 and again in 1928. This rejection concerns us here only insofar as it relates to the policy of the Archbishop.

Before the First World War, the bishops had authorized changes in public worship of a minimal kind, that is in respect of eucharistic vestments, the use of the Athanasian Creed, and reservation of the sacraments. The exigencies of the battlefield, however, led many chaplains to adopt a high sacramentalism. Prayer Book revision began to be seen in more ambitious terms—a new communion rite affecting the prayer of consecration; and a permitted use of reservation. These demands came at a time when the Enabling Act had created what was felt to be an easier way of realizing the mind of the Church. The first revision of the Prayer Book was long in the process of gestation; when it appeared, the opposition consisted chiefly of evangelicals, modernists, and those obsessed with a fear of Rome. However, on 6 July 1927, the Prayer Book passed through the three Houses of the Church Assembly with considerable majorities. Davidson's general attitude was characteristic, but lacked some of its usual flair, in part because of a fear that the extreme Anglo-Catholics might secede if the revision failed. Basically, however, the Archbishop was not interested. His mind did not work that way and he could not summon up the enthusiasm necessary for leadership in this field.

> I have found it very difficult—he wrote frankly in January 1926
> —to know what, speaking generally, ought to be my own line
> in regard to proposals for changing the Communion Office. On
> the one hand my own instinct would have been for leaving that
> Office alone and adhering to what has satisfied English people
> for more than three centuries. And I am certain that such
> is the view of the overwhelming majority of English Church-
> men throughout the country. The average M.P. or County
> Councillor, or local squire or man of business, says emphatically
> 'let it alone'. Ought it to be one's policy to fall in with that wish
> or give leadership in that direction, and practically refuse what
> the ecclesiastically minded folk want in the way of change or
> reform or reversion to older usage? The answer is not easy.[499]

These are significant words. To his brother bishops he confessed with almost pathetic candour that he found it 'very difficult to attach the importance that some attach to questions like the order of the paragraphs in a long prayer'—particularly when 'the outstanding thing dominating all else [was] the strike—first general, then coal-field'.[500] In Convocation, on 13 February 1927, he repeated:

> In my heart I cannot honestly say that I very greatly long for
> any of the changes, or that they are of supreme deep-down
> importance.[501]

What in practice he decided to do was loyally to support the will of the Church as it declared itself both in the Convocations and the newly established Church Assembly.

With the Ecclesiastical Committee having given the all-clear on 24 November 1927, the Measure was introduced into Parliament, and on 12 December the Archbishop moved in the Lords 'that the

Prayer Book Measure be presented to His Majesty for Royal Assent'.

The Archbishop never performed better. His speech was meant to reassure, and to appeal to the calm voice of reason. There were some, he began disarmingly, who asserted that this was not really a matter for Parliament; that the Church had spoken its own mind clearly, and that the duty of Parliament was merely to endorse this utterance. He totally dissented from this view: the matter was brought forward under the Enabling Act and 'every member of this House has, in my view, his absolute right to vote freely upon a matter of this kind and it would be impertinent on my part to suggest anything else'. He then gave a history of the revision; explained what precisely the changes were, and the benefits which would result from the passing of the Measure; in particular the freeing of the Church from party strife which had gone on for too long, thereby releasing its energies to perform the rightful task of the 'bettering of English life'. With deeply controlled emotion he said:

> I am an old man. I have been a Bishop nearly 35 years and an Archbishop for nearly 25 years and my life has not been lived in private or silently or unrecorded. Standing here I assure your Lordships today that I am absolutely unconscious of any departure from the principles of the reformed Church of England to which I declared allegiance at my ordination 52 years ago and I have striven to maintain them ever since.[502]

The Measure passed the Lords: but was shipwrecked in the Commons, where Joynson Hicks played on the emotional fear of Rome with telling effect. The Bill was lost by 238 to 205 votes.

The Archbishop maintained his customary good temper, but he felt he had been badly let down. It was the first Measure of substance to be introduced under the Enabling Act, and it had failed to secure a passage. The matter now was not simply the fate of a Prayer Book for which, as an individual, the Archbishop had little enthusiasm, but whether, even after the Enabling Act, the Church had any final independence. The Archbishop and bishops decided not to abandon the Book, but to give it a second chance in the House after amending it in the Church Assembly. They did so, but once again the Commons refused to endorse perpetual reservation. In spite of a competent speech by the Solicitor General, Sir Boyd Merriman, the voting was 266 against, 220 for.

It was for the time being the end of a very long road. The Archbishop—Gore said it was one of the few occasions when Randall Davidson clearly enunciated a principle—led the bishops in issuing the following declaration:

It is a fundamental principle that the Church—that is, the Bishops together with the Clergy and the Laity—must in the last resort, when its mind has been fully ascertained, retain its inalienable right, in loyalty to our Lord and Saviour Jesus Christ, to formulate its Faith in Him and to arrange the expression of that Holy Faith in its forms of worship.[503]

Davidson still adhered to establishment, and in a dignified speech in the Church Assembly expressed the hope that when passions had had time to cool a capable committee of churchmen and statesmen might consider 'whether any readjustment is required for the maintenance, in the conditions of our own age, of the principles which we have here and now reasserted'.[504] His own attitude was paradoxical. He did not question the right of Parliament under the terms of the Enabling Act to act as it had—indeed, in the Lords he had affirmed this right—but maintained that in declining to 'respect the wishes of the solid central body of Church opinion' it had 'departed lamentably . . . from the reasonable spirit in which alone the balanced relationship of Church and State in England can be satisfactorily and harmoniously carried on'.[505] The Archbishop may perhaps have now regretted his earlier statement when introducing the first revised Prayer Book in the Lords.

Was Davidson himself in part responsible for this failure? We cannot tell how far the usual tactics of the Archbishop, successful in other fields—in the Enabling Act, for example—were a handicap in this. My own view is simply that the time, so far as members of the House of Commons were concerned, was not yet. It is significant that the majority against was greater the second time.

IV

Randall Davidson certainly attained a unique status throughout the Anglican Communion. One of his first tasks on coming to Canterbury was to restore the lines of communication which Temple's old age had sundered. He had not been more than six years in office when a great Pan-Anglican Congress, organized by the Central Board of Missions, and including representatives literally from all over the world, took place in London, to be followed by the fifth Lambeth Conference. The purpose of the former was educational and there were no resolutions. The Archbishop presided over some of its meetings, but he confessed that never again ought the two Conferences to meet in the same year, and he himself found the physical strain tremendous.

The procedure adopted at the Lambeth Conference conformed

to precedents; and the subjects dealt with included: 'The Faith and Modern Thought'; 'Supply and Training of Clergy'; 'Religious Education'; 'Foreign Missions'; 'The Book of Common Prayer'; 'Ministries of Healing'; 'Organisation of the Anglican Communion'; 'Reunion and Intercommunion'.

If the themes were not original, yet the chairmanship of the Archbishop gave a practical slant to the discussion which was reflected in the resolutions. It is significant that a cautious advance was made in giving greater cohesion to the controversial Central Consultative Body. Its membership, drawn from the churches of the whole Anglican Communion, was fixed at eighteen, and direct reference to it was made possible.

The hospitality of the Archbishop and Mrs. Davidson was warm and gracious. Throughout the summer a succession of overseas bishops with their wives stayed two nights at the Palace. The Archbishop used this unique opportunity not only to get to know the bishops personally but also the conditions obtaining in their dioceses, for which purpose he saw that those from common areas had ample opportunity to meet each other. The Bishop of Albany (W. C. Doane), the senior member, spoke of the Archbishop as combining the 'shrewd and businesslike insight of Archbishop Tait, the gracious and courteous consideration of Archbishop Benson, and the strength and power of Archbishop Temple'.[506] Eulogy, doubtless, but an exaggeration based on a not inaccurate appraisal.

The next Conference should have been in 1918, but the War was still ravaging Europe. It met as soon after the end of hostilities as possible. There were contemporary problems such as race, marriage, the ministry of women, and modern cults such as Christian Science and Theosophy, which seemed to need long and earnest consideration. Within the Church there was the upsurge of modernism and the gathering momentum behind plans for reunion. On both of the latter Bishop Gore felt strongly, and it was he who probably persuaded the Archbishop to see them somewhat more dramatically than a sober appraisal really required. Once again the Archbishop's primary concern was that the Conference should get down to something useful. If the Bishops were to proclaim 'mere platitudinous statements that this or that heresy (Spiritualism, Christian Science, etc.) has a basis of truth, but that one must safeguard Catholic Order,' so he commented, 'any of us could say that, and we should be a laughing-stock if we bring people from the ends of the earth to put that on paper.'[507] In the interest of 'some of the best and most devout among the younger men and women of today, who are intellectually keen, religiously earnest, and wholesomely progressive in thought', he was opposed to getting bogged down in long credal discussions. The temptation then would be 'to stiffen the obligation incumbent on a Christian believer, and encourage the clergy to such action and influence'.[508]

Reunion had been discussed and reported on in the last three Conferences, but now the subject took on a new urgency. The World Conference on Faith and Order had been established some ten years before, and war conditions had tended to blur denominational distinctions. The East African bishops were preoccupied with the Church in Kikuyu; a union scheme was in embryo in South India; the American bishops were considering a scheme whereby Congregational ministers could be ordained without giving up their own orders.

As a reaction against this general climate there were those who felt that the very basis of catholic order was being threatened by the impetus of this new ecumenism.

It was in the Reunion Committee, largely through the imagination of its chairman, Cosmo Lang, Archbishop of York, that there was conceived and worked out *The Appeal to All Christian People* to which reference will be made later.

Fortunately this Conference, more than any previously, had the advantage of a mass of material circulated in advance. Also, episcopal secretaries for the various committees had been carefully chosen and briefed.

In his chairmanship the Archbishop, wisely, went to almost excessive lengths to see that each bishop had the fullest opportunity of expressing himself, independently of the value of his contribution. The respect in which he was held enabled him to do this while retaining a right degree of order. He himself went the round of the committees, but it was that on reunion which commanded most of his attention.

True to the tradition of Tait and Benson, Randall Davidson made much of the Archbishopric of Canterbury as the 'pivot' of the Anglican Communion; and he took up again the correspondence which Temple, through age, had neglected. Overseas bishops found gracious hospitality in the archiepiscopal palace. Letters poured into Lambeth, and were answered in meticulous detail. Davidson always remained strongly opposed to any 'papalistic' attitude to the See of Canterbury or any attempt to make it into a patriarchate. 'History affords us abundant reasons to the contrary,' he commented, a view which was confirmed by the report of the Committee on Organisation within the Anglican Communion which recorded its conviction that 'no supremacy of the See of Canterbury over Primatial or Metropolitan Sees outside England is either practicable or even desirable.'[509] Often, indeed, Davidson was able to play a significant

P

role just because he had no legal authority. Thus he was called in by both sides when in 1913, at a conference in Kikuyu, a scheme was put forward for the federation of different missionary bodies working in British East Africa. Bishop Weston of Zanzibar smelt heresy, and demanded that the Archbishop should require from the Bishops of Mombasa and Uganda 'a complete and categorical recantation of their errors which they have taught in word and action'.[510] This the Archbishop wisely refused to do; but he felt that the Kikuyu Conference, both in the nature of its proposals and the united communion service used at its close, was a proper matter for examination by the Lambeth Consultative Body. Doubtless he was encouraged to make this suggestion by the fact that the authority of this body was moral and not legal. The Bishop of Zanzibar at first found difficulties in accepting this proposal; but the Archbishop managed to bring the three bishops together in London, and against the background of imminent war drew up an eirenical and states-manlike memorandum similar in character to the shorter one issued by the Consultative Committee. The scheme was in a measure irregular, Davidson wrote, even if the intention of those who had taken the initiative was excellent. What had happened in Kikuyu was not a matter of merely local interest, but properly concerned the whole Anglican Communion.

v

For the Russian Orthodox Church, the Archbishop entertained a deep sympathy, and he was genuinely distressed when the Bolsheviks, at the end of the First World War, subjected it to spoliation and persecution. The Metropolitan of Odessa dispatched to Canterbury an appeal for help, receiving the reply that Davidson would do what he could and assuring him that 'the terrible persecutions and martyrdoms detailed by your Eminence awake profound emotions in the hearts of Christian people in this country'.[511] The Archbishop was as good as his word. He launched an Imperial War Relief Fund, and corresponded with Lloyd George. He brought before the House of Lords the plight of the imprisoned Tikhon, Patriarch of all the Russias, and he took the initiative, in the name of representative churchmen in this country, of writing to President Lenin. The Soviet authorities denied all charges of oppression, but the Archbishop refused to withdraw anything from the speech he delivered in the House of Lords on 25 May. Rather, he asked that permission be given for a representative group of Churchmen to go to Russia on a mission of inquiry.

Little, of course, came from such efforts. Soviet ideology made this impossible, apart from the fact that the Russian Church in its hierarchy had been too integrated with the repressive Tsarist regime to expect any preferential treatment.

The Russian Church long remained a preoccupation with the Archbishop, and the increasing persecution of religion made him convinced that the time had come for ecclesiastics in England to show their hand. Thus, on 13 April 1923, a massive declaration was issued, signed by the leaders of all the churches, in which the attack on religious liberty was condemned in forthright terms. 'Such a policy cannot be tolerated in silence,' it declared, 'by those who value religion or liberty.'[512]

The protest raised a stir in Britain, and there were not lacking those who pointed out to the Archbishop—Asquith was one of them —that 'through all the long dark years of bloody tyranny which preceded the Revolution, the Church in Russia lent its countenance to the unspeakable horrors of wholesale deportation and private execution of persons suspected of holding enlightened political opinions'.[513] It is only fair to the Archbishop, however, to add that he had tried to use his influence with the Orthodox Church in Russia, before the Revolution, in the interests of liberty.

It was typical of the personal approach which Davidson liked to cultivate that when Patriarch Tikhon died, on 8 April 1925, the only tribute sent by a religious leader outside Russia was a wreath from the Primate of All England.

Where the Orthodox Churches were concerned, the days were long past when a Supreme Primate of the Greek Church needed to ask: 'Who is the Archbishop of Canterbury?' In the 'twenties the tragic consequences of the First World War drove successive Patriarchs of Constantinople, as well as other Eastern prelates, to travel to Lambeth to solicit help, optimistically believing that its occupant exercised far more political influence than in fact was the case. True, this did not prevent Randall Davidson frequently using his good offices with the Government to protect the rights of the Orthodox at a time when there was a lamentable delay in the Turkish Peace Settlement and the Allies were going their separate ways. Political and religious considerations were inextricably interwoven, and it seemed as if the physical survival of countless Christians would be jettisoned as a consequence. Dorotheos, in appealing to the Archbishop and through him to the Church of England, pleaded that 'there can be only one safeguard for us; it is the dislodgment of the Sultan from Constantinople'.[514] On 17 December 1919, the Archbishop brought the plight of these menaced populations before the House of Lords, carefully informing himself from Lord Bryce's official report. Davidson's championship of their cause was vigorous and earned great respect in Constantinople; but he remained bitterly disappointed with the seeming impossibility of getting anything done. In June 1920, the aged and infirm Dorotheos came to Paris and twice visited Lambeth—he was the first Patriarch of Constantinople to come to the West since Joseph, the Patriarch of Constantinople, attended the Council of Florence in 1439—but the journey proved too much for him and he died in London, after having seen the King and Lord Curzon. The Archbishop attended the funeral and recorded in his diary:

> For the first time in history the Archbishop of Canterbury officiated by reading the Gospel in English at funeral rites in the Greek Church in Bayswater.[515]

The prestige of the See of Canterbury was displayed in a remarkable way when Meletios, elected in 1922 to succeed Dorotheos, and Chrysanthos, Metropolitan of Trebizond, head of the anti-Meletios party, both came over to London to win Davidson's support. The Archbishop, who was ill at the time, realized that this was a situation in which he must not act the partisan; but when, through French help, Meletios finally got to Constantinople, he dispatched a telegram to Lambeth on his enthronement, expressing his greetings and his gratitude.

Persecution, however, went on, and the situation of the Eastern Christians continued to be a matter of grave anxiety. Davidson never ceased to be active. He brought up the matter in Convocation; and had a long talk at Lambeth with Venizelos, the great Greek statesman, who poured out his feelings in impassioned utterance. When Lloyd George's coalition Government gave way to that of Bonar Law and pressure was being brought to bear on the Government to retreat from its commitments in the Middle East, the Archbishop wrote to the Prime Minister, on 24 October 1922, expressing clearly his own views and those of the bishops. He had kept in close touch with representatives of the Greek Orthodox Church, and assured the Prime Minister that a great weight of religious opinion would be behind him if he stuck to the pledged word of the British Government. When, at the Lausanne Peace Conference in 1922, the Turkish delegation demanded the removal of the Patriarch from Constantinople, the Archbishop telegraphed Lord Curzon; and in the end the Patriarch remained in his traditional home. It was a triumph for the Archbishop, who could never have acted so effectively had he not known so many of the political personnel—and shown so much persistence.

When it came to more specifically theological relations with the Orthodox Churches, particularly where Anglican orders were con-

438

cerned, the Archbishop was cautious and circumspect, on the whole leaving the initiative with Archbishop Lang.

In 1922 the Metropolitan of Thyatira was nominated to represent the Patriarch of Constantinople to the Archbishop of Canterbury and took up residence in London. This was followed by a letter from the Patriarch to the Archbishop, as 'The Chief Hierarch of the whole Anglican Church', declaring that the Church of Constantinople, having taken the matter into consideration, found that Anglican orders 'possess the same validity as those of the Roman, Old Catholic, and Armenian Churches'.[516] This declaration, of course, did not commit the other Orthodox Churches, although similar judgments were to come later. The Archbishop was naturally pleased; but following good archiepiscopal precedents he was careful to let it be known in the full synod of Convocation in February 1923 that he had not sought such a declaration, and his glad acceptance of it did not imply that there had ever been any doubt as to such validity. The link with the Eastern Churches was emphasized when the sixteen-hundredth anniversary of the Council of Nicaea, because of the confused political situation in the Middle East, was celebrated in London. Invitations were sent to the ten autocephalous Churches, most of whom sent delegations. The Archbishop preached at a service in Westminster Abbey on St. Peter's Day, and made the most of the dramatic contrast between Nicaea in A.D. 325, a 'City of Victory', and London, 'a little Roman-British citadel protecting the roadway on the north bank of the Thames'; and Nicaea today, a 'deserted and poverty-stricken hamlet in a swamp'.[517]

The archiepiscopate of Randall Davidson, though through no positive steps on his part, saw renewed 'conversations' with Roman Catholic churchmen. The Lambeth Appeal of 1920 aroused great ecumenical interest, and the Conference itself had affirmed that should the Church of Rome at any time desire to hold talks on the conditions of reunion, 'we shall be ready to welcome such discussions'.[518]

The initiative came, once again, from that venerable protagonist of reunion, Lord Halifax, now eighty-two years of age, and the Abbé Portal, now sixty-six. The former got into touch with the Archbishop and received from him a very guarded letter of introduction to Cardinal Mercier, to whom Davidson had sent both the Report of the Lambeth Conference and the *Appeal to All Christian People*, making it clear that Lord Halifax was acting in a purely personal capacity. From this meeting there resulted the famous Malines Conversations, four in number, which continued until the death of the Cardinal, to whom they became a matter of deep personal concern; and of whom it was said that his greatness was 'likely to be better recognized in the next world than it is in this'. Randall Davidson, in order to restrain Lord Halifax, insisted that he be joined by (among others) Armitage Robinson, Dean of Wells. On one matter of principle Randall Davidson would not budge. In giving approval to such discussions (he always maintained that they were not 'negotiations'), he insisted that the Pope must do the same. He gained his point, if only formally.

As so often happened, Randall Davidson brought fire upon himself from extremists at both ends. Addresses poured into Lambeth. There were those who condemned his sanctioning any such meetings at all; while others felt that he displayed an excessive timidity. Not all the bishops approved the conversations: and Davidson himself was a little apprehensive of repercussions upon Prayer Book revision. In view of these attacks, Davidson made a formal statement in the Upper House of Convocation, declaring that he could have 'stamped out the very suggestion of such a conversation', but this would have been opposed 'to every principle which I have entertained in religious matters'.[519] To have imposed conditions on the Roman representatives would have precluded the very possibility of the two Churches getting nearer together. Where Davidson was open to criticism—and the point was forcibly put by Hensley Henson—was in choosing as the Church of England representatives only those whose ecclesiastical affiliations tended exclusively to be more 'Catholic' or 'High Church'.[520]

The course of the conversations undoubtedly caused him anxiety, and he sent a briefing to those whom he had chosen:

> Don't detract from the importance of the XXXIX Articles. Don't budge an inch as to the necessity of carrying the East with us in ultimate Reunion steps. Bear constantly in mind that in any admission made as to what Roman leadership or 'primacy' (?) may mean, we have to make quite clear too that which it must not mean.[521]

The Catholic hierarchy in England, as before in the time of Benson, were known to be opposed in principle to the conversations; but the death of Cardinal Mercier, whose grace and courtesy added a unique ingredient to the discussions, brought them to an end.

The motto 'more haste, less speed' was felt by the Archbishop to apply equally to relations with the Free Churches, although these, understandably, were more easy than with the Roman Catholics. The response of the Free Churches in Britain to the Lambeth Appeal was cordial, the Anglican leadership here being mainly in the hands of Cosmo Lang. Randall Davidson recognized the need for discussion at parochial and congregational level; and believed that growing personal intimacy would lead to greater mutual under- standing. In this spirit he addressed the Conference of Wesleyan Methodists at Bristol on 21 July 1923 on the theme of 'Reunion', suggesting that they were 'just now standing together at a junction in human history, so vast in its import, so measureless in its possi- bilities'.[522] In an informal speech later in the day he said: 'If you want your roads to last they must be made slowly.'

Of his relations with the Free Churches generally, the *Congrega-tionalist* wrote:

> Not tolerance but good will has been ushered into ecclesiastical relationships during Dr. Davidson's regime at Canterbury.[523]

Relations with the Free Churches could not, even yet, be with- drawn from the general question of the nation's education of its young.

Randall Davidson was at University when Forster's Education Act introduced the 'dual system' which brought with it problems that successive Archbishops had learned to live with. In this general field of education, the Archbishop followed his temperamental policy of seeking a *via media* and cultivating good relations with the Government of the day. Thus he wrote a conciliatory but frank letter to Augustine Birrell on his becoming minister, and it was widely expected that the Liberal Government would introduce a new Education Act. To prevent misunderstanding, Davidson informed the Government of Convocation's view, on 22 February 1906, that

> no scheme of national education can be established with justice, or accepted as permanent, unless full recognition is given to the right of parents to obtain for their children, so far as is possible, instruction in their own faith . . . by those who can give it with genuine belief.[524]

The draft of the new Bill, which, in brief, required that after 1 January 1908 only schools provided by the local educational authority should be recognized as public elementary schools, was submitted by the Archbishop to extreme criticism. He followed this up by seeing the Prime Minister and members of the Cabinet, but his policy of seeking to amend the Bill rather than promote its outright rejection exposed him at both ends. The hostility to the Bill among Church people was extreme. The National Society opposed it *in toto*; and Dr. Knox, the voluble Bishop of Manchester, described it as 'pure robbery and confiscation', declaring his intention of bringing thirty-two train-loads of Mancunians to London and camping them in the grounds of Lambeth Palace.

> Do all those who speak so vehemently—Davidson asked—and with such obvious truth, about the value of our Church Schools realize what has been the transfer taking place in recent years? Some 550 Church of England Schools closed in the last three years, with accommodation for more than 160,000 children.[525]

Behind the scenes the Archbishop was active. He stayed at Belmont with Campbell-Bannerman and at Whittinghame with Balfour. He discussed the Bill with the bishops, always seeking to engender a spirit of reasonable compromise. When it finally came up for its second reading in the Lords in August 1906, the Archbishop began by placing the Bill in a wide historical context; accepted that the nation had declared in favour of popular control; but maintained that the terms were one-sided.

> What does the bill do?—he asked—It takes 14,000 existing schools, with their trusts, and demolishes, not the mere wording of the trusts, but the very essence and pith of them.[526]

He expressed the hope that the Bill would not be thrown out but amended, and he suggested six ways in which this ought to be done. His intervention helped to carry the second reading, and when the debate was later resumed certain amendments were in fact agreed.

The situation now developed into a constitutional crisis between Lords and Commons, but despite many informal meetings in which the Archbishop, much to the disgust of some churchmen, was prominent, all was to no avail and the Bill was finally abandoned by the Government.

Nor was Runciman's Bill, two years later, any more successful, though it conceded some of the points which the Archbishop had insisted upon. It failed because, although it allowed Church schools to contract out of the 'provided system', the financial provisions, in spite of assurances to the contrary, were such as to make it impossible for the Church to take up the option. The Archbishop felt bitterly what he regarded as this betrayal—he was accused by some churchmen of being a 'simple Simon'—and when the Representative Church Council met to consider the terms of the Bill, only the House of Bishops voted in its favour. The Archbishop's calm assessment of the situation, his emphasis again on tailoring the Bill to preserve as many Church interests as possible, was in vain.

The war years calmed passions by turning the thoughts of governments to other matters, and the Education Act of 1918 did not upset the religious *status quo*. H. A. L. Fisher, however, when he was appointed to the Board of Education, determined to make one last attempt to get rid of the dual system, while at the same time meeting the legitimate requirements of both Church of England and Free Churchmen. He was the more hopeful because the war years had gone a long way to weaken denominational prejudices and the whole tone of the Lambeth Appeal had met a co-operative response from non-Anglicans. He therefore invited the Archbishop and Dr. Scott Lidgett to sponsor a joint conference of members of the Church of England and Free Churchmen under his chairmanship. The Archbishop and Dr. Scott Lidgett co-operated willingly, there being agreement that religious teaching was an essential element in right education; and that to be worth having it must be given by competent teachers, properly qualified and conscientiously wishing to undertake it.

Nothing concrete, however, came out of Fisher's efforts. The National Society, at its annual meeting, carried an amendment to the official motion, thus declaring its intention to keep its Church schools.

Different views may still be held as to who was right. Certainly the Archbishop had tried hard; but the fact was that his approach was more objective, maybe more far-seeing, than that of those who opposed him.

In 1928 the Archbishop reached the age of eighty, and two years ahead loomed another Lambeth Conference. He had always said that he would never face another. He was aware within himself of failing powers, and of being no longer able 'to grasp six or seven [things] almost simultaneously'. He was conscious also that the Church was moving into a new era which needed a different kind of leadership. He had said of his office that it was an impossible job for one man but only one man could do it. He had geared the arch-bishopric to tremendous labour. He had in fact contemplated resignation in 1925. Now he was certain it was right, independently of the rejection of the revised Prayer Book.

No Archbishop before him had ever resigned. Indeed, to some people the office seemed a sacred trust which so long as life lasted ought not to be laid aside. The decision to resign must have been costly. Public life had been the breath of his nostrils. Without children, he had found his friends in his work, and his peculiarly personal way of doing things brought such friends in abundance.

The date of his resignation was fixed for the day of his golden wedding, a delicate tribute to his wife who had been so solidly behind him, though discreetly and in the background, throughout his long years of ecclesiastical office. A commission on which there served the Archbishop of York and the three senior bishops was set up by royal warrant, and as an act of courtesy, the Archbishop also wrote formally to the Dean and Chapter of Canterbury.

His departure from the scene was received with genuine regret by so many people that the Archbishop was bemused and overwhelmed. To an intimate friend he confessed:

> I honestly don't understand it . . . if I was describing myself I should say I was a funny old fellow of quite mediocre, second rate gifts and a certain amount of commonsense—but that I had tried to do my best.[527]

Dr. Hensley Henson, whose nomination to the bishopric of Hereford in 1918 had needed all Davidson's diplomacy to ride the storm, wrote of him as still 'astonishingly alert and vigorous', although during the last two years he had given 'many evidences of senectitude at the helm'. He was created a peer, taking the title Lord Davidson of Lambeth, thus creating a precedent which has been followed by two subsequent Archbishops.

We have lingered long over Randall Davidson, but this has been deliberate. His tenure of office marked the end of an age. No subsequent Primate of All England has so adroitly discharged that role, nor will those archbishops that come after.

# 2

## COSMO LANG AND HIS SEVEN FACES

There was little doubt as to who would follow Randall Davidson. Cosmo Lang, Primate of the Northern Province, had for many years been in his closest confidence, indeed affection, though their characters were markedly different. The Archbishop of York had lodgings in Lollard's Tower and came up to London before each Bishops' Meeting and helped to draw up the agenda. Often there would be an urgent demand which prompted Lang to say: 'The Archbishop does not always remember that the distance from Bishopsthorpe to Lambeth was the same as that from Lambeth to Bishopsthorpe.'

> I could not but have a foreboding—Lang wrote later—that it might fall to me to be his successor. . . . It became clear that a big trial would await me—either to accept a *very* difficult position if some other Bishop were appointed and to try in the circumstances to play the game rightly and honourably; or to face, knowing my shortcomings, the tremendous responsibilities of the office. [528]

On 26 July 1928, when Lang journeyed to London for a garden party at Buckingham Palace, he received a request from the Prime Minister to go to Lambeth the next evening. Perhaps Cosmo Lang may be left to take up the story at this point.

> He told me that he proposed to recommend me to the King as the next Archbishop of Canterbury and that the King had given his ready assent . . . certainly no Prime Minister had ever conveyed such an offer smoking a pipe. . . . I asked whether I might have some time to consider his proposal. He at once said: 'No, it is inevitable. I won't hear of any refusal. You are the only man.' [529]

After this Randall Davidson was ushered into the study and the triumvirate settled the other appointments consequent upon his

445

resignation, including Temple's going to York. It was quick work, though doubtless Davidson had thought long and hard about it.

The new Archbishop's appointment was 'confirmed' in St. Mary-le-Bow, Cheapside, with the customary protest from the extremely Protestant Mr. Kensit and his friends. His enthronement was given a new look and a heightened contemporary relevance through the initiative of George Bell, Dean of Canterbury, who organized a series of independent processions to bring in the world of the arts. St. Augustine's chair was removed from the *Corona* in order to give it greater prominence and placed on a special platform on the steps at the east end of the nave. One change of a more academic interest was calculated to please the constitutional pundits. In order to emphasize the Archbishop's link with his cathedral, the mandate was issued to the Dean and Chapter instead of to the Archdeacon. Representatives of the Church of Scotland, the Free Churches, and the Churches of the Continent were present.

The enthronement, in its pageantry and traditional setting, was an occasion admirably suited to the temperament, the bearing, and the voice of the Archbishop; but some, who had known Lang for a long time, could not but notice that his sermon lacked the vigour of his address in York Minster on a similar occasion some twenty years earlier. The ceremony was followed almost immediately by a serious illness, the first Lang had known. It took him by surprise, for he had earlier written to Dick Sheppard: 'I think I have some invincible youth hiding within me and a late lark singing.'

Cosmo Gordon Lang was sixty-four when he came to Canterbury. The son and grandson of Scottish ministers, he went from the University of Glasgow to Balliol College, where he took a first in history. Intending to go into politics by way of the law, his plans changed when he felt a compulsion to ordination, and as a result, went to what became his beloved Cuddesdon, to which he used to return annually with a growing nostalgia. Ordination was followed by a curacy at Leeds Parish Church; by a period as Dean of Divinity at Magdalen College, Oxford; and as Vicar of the parish of Portsea, which brought him to the notice of Queen Victoria and her family. His next appointment was to a canonry at St. Paul's, and shortly afterwards to Stepney as its suffragan bishop. In 1909 he was nominated to the primacy of the Northern Province at the comparatively young age of forty-five.

Such bare bones of his *curriculum vitae* give no indication of the man. They might suggest a conventional and highly successful ecclesiastical careerist. Lang was undoubtedly ambitious; but he was far from being an ordinary man, and it is perhaps not too much to claim that in character he is by far the most fascinating of recent

Archbishops. He was highly imaginative, at heart a romantic, given to dramatizing himself and seeing persons and things in exaggerated terms. Spiritually he may be described as schizophrenic, except that his was not a personality split into two but into a number of seemingly disparate parts. It is understandable that the Duke of Windsor should have mistaken a part for the whole and described him as 'too polished, too worldly'.[530] 'I see seven Archbishops,' Sir William Orpen is reported to have said when getting to work on his portrait; 'which of them am I to paint?' Cruelly he selected that which was 'proud, prelatical and pompous'. Of this portrait Archbishop Söderblom commented: 'That is what the devil meant him to be, but thanks be to God it is not so.'[531]

Lang cultivated the company of royalty; delighted in the ancestral homes of old families; accepted the ostentatious hospitality of the wealthy; and took a deep satisfaction in his rise from Woodlands Road to Lambeth Palace. One of his chaplains, Alan Don, related to the author how on one occasion the Archbishop held a luncheon party exclusively for dowager duchesses. Afterwards Don remarked, in a spirit of disillusion: 'They didn't seem any different from anybody else.' 'That just shows, Alan, how mistaken you can be,' replied the Archbishop gravely.[532] To him they *were* different, and it was this difference, together with the comfort, which persuaded him every year to embark northward on his self-styled 'snob's progress'.

Lang reacted against humanity in the mass, though when he braced himself for the ordeal, he would think nothing of beginning an address in the Albert Hall to an audience of dedicated women: 'Dear Sisters in Christ.' His attitude was generally patrician.[533] He disliked waiting for trains, and on one occasion, when forced to travel from Victoria to Canterbury, was heard to mutter at the platform barrier: 'Never again! Never again!' He insisted that his barber should come to him: shopping and ordinary matters of finance eluded his grasp and he left them to others. He had no wife.

There was, however, a side to his deeply complex character which was intensely spiritual, which sought fulfilment in the 'flight of the alone to the alone'. The intense struggle of Cosmo Lang's inner life is revealed in his diary through outpourings so intense that they might have led to breakdown. That they did not, shows a quality of dedication which ended by attracting grace. He was often oppressed by a great sense of personal failure; and in his Scottish retreat at Ballure would indulge in a veritable orgy of self-recrimination which in its more extreme expression could not decently be used by his biographer.

The logic of his mind took fire from his imagination. Copes, mitres, ritual, deference to hierarchical office, these meant a great

447

deal to him since they clothed the dense world of physical reality with 'majesty and honour'. Although prone to a natural irritability and unable to suffer fools gladly, his ultimate integrity, even his personal idiosyncrasies, won the affection of his friends. Those who knew him best liked him most, which is high praise. Those who saw him only at a distance were more critical.

In estimating the significance of his archiepiscopate of thirteen years, it is perhaps fair to say that his tragedy, although tragedy is a too hysterical word, was not only the Second World War, which prevented his assembling the Lambeth Conference of 1940 which could have proved the climax of his work for reunion; but also the fact that he came to Lambeth too late. Temperamentally and by natural endowment he was quite a different person from Randall Davidson; but he had acted the understudy so long and had such great admiration for his preceptor, that his own aptitudes were blighted and never found full expression. His charismatic approach might have encouraged him to pioneer new ways—and others to follow him. As it turned out, when he entered into office he settled down to deploying his brilliant gifts—and they were brilliant—for the thing in hand without contemplating the more distant scene. This was in character for Davidson; it did not suit Lang.

## II

At the time of his ordination, Cosmo Lang listed as one of his chief ambitions 'to promote the unity of the Church in Great Britain'. It remained his greatest interest, and this sphere of his activities ought, therefore, to be given pride of place.

His archiepiscopate was not destined to see any spectacular advance in this field; but in relation to the Orthodox Churches of the East he more than maintained the progress initiated by his predecessors. The glamour of the East; the sense of history which its ancient churches, even in grinding poverty, enshrined; their long oppression under the Ottoman Empire; the relaxed spirituality of their liturgy—all these made an immediate appeal to him, as they had to Benson, in spite of the fact that he never quite got over his embarrassment, when ceremonially greeting patriarchs, of burying his face in their lavish beards.

It was this known concern which persuaded Randall Davidson to make Lang Chairman of the Reunion Committee at the Lambeth Conference in 1920. The times seemed propitious for progress, not least because the churches felt a collective shame that each had supported its own nation in the most bloody conflict known to history; and the birth of an international idea in the League of Nations seemed to suggest that Christians should get together.

448

As a preparation for the Lambeth Conference, the Eastern Committee was appointed under the chairmanship of Bishop Charles Gore in 1919, and in the following year a delegation came over from Constantinople. Lang was not at first optimistic of anything of real value coming out of the Conference, because of the diversity of view among the bishops, from Weston of Zanzibar to Henson of Durham. That something other than mere platitudes on reunion did emerge was almost entirely due to his own imaginative leadership.

> For the first week—Lang wrote to his mother—I seemed like a skipper, sitting at the tiller attempting to keep his boat going on a bit of water where cross tides and currents moved it to and fro and prevented it from making any headway; then after a week there came a puff of a fair wind and I put on all sail and finally reached the harbour of a unanimous Report.

That was the famous *Appeal to All Christian People*.[534]

Undoubtedly this document had a flexibility not always discernible in ecclesiastical pronouncements, particularly in its recognition that all were Christians 'who believe in our Lord Jesus Christ and have been baptized into the name of the Holy Trinity as sharing with us membership in the universal Church of Christ which is his body'.[535]

The *Appeal* evoked an unexpectedly warm response in England. Lord Halifax wrote that no event had given him such pleasure; Dr. Scott Lidgett affirmed that it was the most remarkable document of its kind since the Reformation; the secretary of the Baptist Union saw in it 'the finger of God'. Even the Bishop of Zanzibar declared that it must constitute the guiding vision for the years ahead.

The effect of the *Appeal* was in fact cumulative; it created an atmosphere in which conversations could take place with Presbyterian and Free Churchmen; and it helped to encourage the Faith and Order Conferences at Lausanne in 1927 and Edinburgh in 1937.

The immediate result of the *Appeal* was that over a period of four years, twenty meetings were held between nonconformist leaders and Anglicans. The work of these conferences was controlled by a sub-committee of which Archbishop Lang was chairman. Though he was often disappointed at what he regarded as the failure of nonconformists generally to glimpse the ideal of visible organic unity, he was perceptive, patient, and conciliatory. Equally, if not more important, he stumped the country speaking on the *Appeal* and challenging Anglicans and Free Churchmen to act together in response to it. Perhaps the high-water mark of his achievement in

449

this field was the acceptance by the Joint Conference of his *Points of Agreement* on the nature of the Church, the Ministry, and the Creeds.

More widely, the *Appeal*, together with Lang's sustained initiative, encouraged the Orthodox Churches, by using their principle of economy, to move closer to, and to regularize their relations with, the Church of England. The result was the progressive recognition by their various churches of the validity of Anglican orders.

In 1930 there came the seventh Lambeth Conference, always a great test, even physical ordeal, for any archbishop. The general expectation was that relations between churches with reunion as the ultimate goal would constitute its main preoccupation. This was as well, for the rejection of the Prayer Book could have led to excessive introspection around matters domestic to the Church of England and its peculiar form of establishment. Lang determined that whatever happened this should not be the case, particularly as he had recently availed himself of the opportunity of making contact with many Eastern Churchmen. In 1929 he visited Athens, where he was received by Chrysostom, attended by fifteen of the Metropolitans and bishops of Greece. He was back in Athens again a year after the Lambeth Conference, and received an affectionate welcome. From there he went on to the Holy Land, entering Jerusalem in his 'purple silk cassock, cape and cap', and was received at the Church of the Holy Sepulchre by Timotheus on behalf of the Orthodox Patriarch of Jerusalem, together with representatives of the Armenian and Coptic Churches.

In his quest for reunion Lang, though imaginative, was no bold revolutionary. His ambition to bring the churches nearer together, and to use the Anglican Church as a bridge to this end, demanded, he was convinced, a disciplined and intelligent approach. The guiding principles needed to be laid down with care; and undue haste must be avoided. In going forward, it was important not to alienate any one Church, no matter how far removed it might seem from Anglicanism. Equally, in any negotiations the comprehensive character of the Church of England must not be compromised, which meant that Evangelicals ought to be in on the discussions with Catholics; similarly the more Catholic elements with the continental churches. Differences must be frankly faced, yet not pressed in such a way as to hinder progress in mutual understanding.

Not surprisingly a delegation from the Orthodox Churches attended the 1930 Lambeth Conference, and entered into discussions with the Committee on Relations with Episcopal Churches over which A. C. Headlam, Bishop of Gloucester, presided. The Committee decided to set up a Joint Theological Commission to

*Frederick Temple.*
*A portrait by Sir Hubert von Herkomer*

*The Archbishop's Palace, Canterbury*

*Randall Thomas Davidson. A Spy cartoon, 1910*

*Cosmo Gordon Lang. A portrait by Sir William Orpen at Bishopthorpe*

*William Temple. A portrait by Philip de Laszlo, 1934*

*Geoffrey Francis Fisher. A portrait by Middleton Todd, 1953*

*Archbishop Fisher crowns Queen Elizabeth II*

*Arthur Michael Ramsey*

*Lambeth Palace*

*Cardinal Heenan, Archbishop of Westminster, Dr. Immanuel Jakobovits, the Chief Rabbi, and Dr. Ramsey, Archbishop of Canterbury, in the St. John's Wood Synagogue before the meeting of the Council of Christians and Jews, June 1971*

examine the 'theological relations' between the two communions. Archbishop Lang did not repeat Davidson's mistake *vis-à-vis* the Malines Conversations, but saw to it that Evangelicals were well represented on this Committee, which met in London in 1931. Once again nothing spectacular was achieved, but misunderstandings were removed.

One significant break-through of a general nature, however, did occur in the setting up by the Archbishop, at the request of the Church Assembly, of the Council on Foreign Relations. Archbishop Davidson had tended to resist any encroachment on what he regarded as a personal responsibility. He preferred to seek advice where he wished rather than in an officially constituted body. Lang at first took the same view, but bowed to the wish of the Assembly, insisting, however, that 'it [i.e. the Council] could not take the place of that personal action or advice on the part of the Archbishop which these overseas Churches always particularly valued'.[536] Lang certainly had a point here, for it was unlikely that an overseas church would send an inquiry direct to a committee of the Church Assembly. Still the Council on Foreign Relations proved helpful to the Archbishop in giving advice, and has firmly established itself.

In 1935, the Archbishop sent a delegation to Romania, under Hicks, Bishop of Lincoln, and himself entertained its Patriarch at Lambeth in 1936. Other delegations were sent out to Sofia, Athens, Belgrade, Estonia, and Latvia—visits which were unfortunately interrupted by the War. For the first time since the Reformation the Church of England, in 1932, through the Old Catholics, entered into full relationship with a continental Church.

Lang wisely recognized that any enterprise such as the Malines Conversations was not yet practical politics. Yet he managed to establish friendly relations with Cardinal Hinsley, and the 'private wire' between Westminster and Lambeth proved a great help in mutual understanding.

Not least important, *The Lambeth Appeal* encouraged Dr. John Whyte of the Presbyterian Church of Scotland to pay two visits to Lambeth. As the representative of an established Church, he understandably wanted to deal directly with the Church of England and not to enter into discussions through the Episcopal Church of Scotland. If, deep down, Lang appreciated this point of view since 'the kirk was in his bones', he knew that he could not sanction negotiations on these terms. What he did was to secure a compromise by which the Episcopalians in Scotland and the Presbyterians in England were also included. Meetings were held, and Lang went to Edinburgh to address the Assembly, not very successfully as it turned out. The Assembly declined to appoint a commission to negotiate, and at its next meeting decided by a narrow majority to go no further until each Church admitted the validity of the other's ministry.

'Am I *persona grata?*' asked the proposer of the motion, Dr. Fleming, of Lang some years later at Lambeth.

'*Persona grata*, my dear Fleming,' was the reply, 'but not *persona gratissima.*'[537]

Once again the war came to halt further exchanges.

Of his work for reunion Dr. Bell, who was in a position to know, writes:

> There is no man in the whole Anglican Communion who has left a deeper impression on the Unity movement in that Communion between 1920 and 1947 than Lang. Temple in certain respects extended its influence more widely, for he went far outside the *Ecclesia Anglicana*; but Lang, especially by his promotion of the *Appeal* of 1920, by his leadership in the Joint Conference with Free Churchmen, and by setting his seal on the Oecumenical Conference in 1937, took the significant decisions for the Church of England and its sister Churches. And certainly it was Lang, rather than Davidson, who gave the principal impetus while the two were Archbishops together.[538]

As a diocesan bishop, Lang was assiduous in the discharge of his duty so far as his other commitments would allow. It was his usual practice to go to Canterbury every weekend, and to do this by car so regularly that he was, as he confessed, entirely unknown on the railway station at Canterbury. After twenty years in Yorkshire he found the countryside in Kent less stimulating, but as the years passed he grew attached to it. By the time he resigned, he had visited, at least once, every parish in his largely rural diocese.

Fortunately he worked easily with others. Usually the suffragans and assistant bishops with the archdeacons met the Archbishop at least once a month at the old Palace in Canterbury. It was through their eyes that he was kept informed of the life of those parishes which lack of time prevented his visiting with any frequency. Four deans —Wace, Bell, Dick Sheppard, and Hewlett Johnson—served the Cathedral during his archiepiscopate. They were all men of considerable talent in their way. Referring to the last Lang said:

> I had to make it plain that the Dean and the Archbishop were not the same person and that the Archbishop had no control over the opinions of the Dean. But my own personal relations with him were always most cordial; there was never a trace of

the faintest friction between Bishop and Dean within the Cathedral. I only wish that the Chapter had been always immune from that strange disease which I was accustomed to call 'the Cathedral blight'.[539]

Hewlett Johnson survived to embarrass successive Archbishops and to witness with force and courage, if not always with sagacity, to his own particular brand of Christian Socialism. No matter what estimate may be made of his views, the Church sorely needs men of such independence.

Lang's capacity for work never ceased to surprise even his own staff. In the personnel of the latter he was fortunate, and in spite of a deep-seated irascibility which sometimes erupted, they were devoted to him. Like his predecessor, he preferred to seek help where he could get it whether it was from the great missionary societies, the Ecclesiastical Commissioners, Queen Anne's Bounty, or a committee to deal with difficult constitutional problems which he himself set up under the chairmanship of the Bishop of Gloucester.

> There has been the grandiose conception of a sort of 'Abbey of Cardinals'—Lang wrote—a precedent which I don't think would commend itself to Anglican Churchmen . . . experts in various branches of the work of the Church at home and abroad to assist the Archbishop with their knowledge and counsel.
>
> On questions of policy, it would have been very unfortunate in my judgment if it were considered that they were decided, or even strongly influenced, by particular individuals and not the Archbishop himself. On legal questions there were always ready to hand and in frequent consultation my legal secretary, and, in exceptional matters, the Vicar General. . . . Thus there was always a Headquarters Staff in fact, if not in form, and one much wider in range and abler in *personnel* than any ever suggested by 'reformers' whose fertility of suggestion was greater than their acquaintance with the facts. Anyhow, I seemed to get on well without the apparatus of any of those fancy schemes.[540]

Some of his necessary duties, although he did them efficiently, he entered upon without relish. This was largely the case with his presidency of the Southern Convocation and of the newly established Church Assembly. He found the Canterbury Convocation far less intimate than that in the North, where the bishops always stayed with him at Bishopthorpe. Also he was not convinced that the constitution of this ancient ecclesiastical assembly made it suitable to discharge a contemporary vocation.

453

Certainly there could not be a more cumbrous proposition than one which requires any major matter affecting the spiritual life of the Church to secure the assent of two separate independent bodies, the Convocations of the two Provinces, and of the separate Houses of Bishops and Clergy within each. Something has been done, and more could be done, to mitigate this grievous practical inconvenience. Thus within each Convocation the two Houses have often met together in full Synod, as it is called.[541]

He admitted that his relations with the Lower House were not always easy, particularly when Dr. Kidd was prolocutor, 'and certain officious and insistent Proctors (whom I shall not mention by name) made it their business and pleasure to show a meticulous jealousy of the privileges of the House'. 'Clergy are very troublesome people,' he would complain: and in light-hearted vein would often greet the Prolocutor: 'What mischief has your House been up to today?'[542]

On the whole, not least because of its lay clientele, he found the Church Assembly more congenial. Here he tried to maintain Davidson's guiding principle that this Assembly was on the whole concerned with legislation and finance while Convocation had as its writ the spiritual life of the Church, a surprising distinction in an Archbishop nurtured on Lightfoot and Westcott. In spite of the Assembly's intricate rules of procedure, which Lang did his best to interpret with a degree of liberality, he found it a 'fairly businesslike body'.

Of course—he said—like all such Assemblies, it suffered from its bores; but it suffered them if not gladly, at least even with excessive patience. The chief sufferer was the Chairman, who had to sit through all their tedious speeches and interruptions, but I hope I kept any signs of irritability in due check. On the whole I thought the level of speaking was high, higher than in Parliament.[543]

He admitted to some difficulty in reconciling the role of chairman, whose duty it was to keep business moving, with that of the Archbishop who ought to give leadership. On the whole he felt he tended to over-emphasize the latter. It was a fault on the right side. His general view, wrung from an experience of many years, was expressed as follows:

I fear the Church is not at its best in these ecclesiastical assemblies; and though I always tried to take them seriously and to do my duty to them, the fact that they were never really congenial seems to show that I have never been an ecclesiastic in the narrow sense of the word—at heart.

Fortunately he was able to bring to his aid his 'habit of taking a humorous view of my fellow creatures'.[544]

### III

Cosmo Lang was as anxious as Randall Davidson that the Church should play a national role, and therefore that he himself, as Archbishop, should seek to involve himself in its affairs. His temperament, however, was different, and times had changed. He did not appreciate hanging around the House of Lords as had Tait and Davidson, nor did he nor could he know successive Prime Ministers with such intimacy. Speaking in Parliament he found comparatively easy, for, to quote his own words, he had become 'independent of applause and satisfied with attention'. He was usually to be found in his place when he felt that he ought to speak or that Church interests were involved. He made repeated protests in the Lords against the persecution by the Soviet Government of Russian Christians, and greatly objected when the War Office tried to forbid the use of prayers for the Russian Church at parade services. The Russian Government regarded him as a great enemy and did him the honour, in conjunction with the Pope, of a somewhat insulting cartoon in the Museum of the Godless in Leningrad. He early protested against the rise of Nazism, and condemned the whole Aryan policy as exemplified in the writings of Rosenberg. When the German Ambassador, von Hoesch, called on him at Lambeth, Lang bluntly told him that Christian opinion was outraged by the way in which the unification of the Protestant Churches had been carried out. He even warned von Hoesch that unless within a week there were some 'effective signs of a change of policy', he would bring the whole matter before the English bishops and Protestant leaders on the Continent.[545] With von Hoesch's successor, von Ribbentrop, Lang had many brushes, in particular when he protested against the persecution of both Protestants and Roman Catholics, and the imprisonment of Pastor Niemöller. Equally he condemned the Italian invasion of Abyssinia; and consistently befriended the Emperor Haile Selassie, even allowing him, so Alan Don records, to place some of his valuables in a safe in Lambeth, and appealing to Lord Halifax to negotiate with Mussolini his return home.

In 1933 the Archbishop spoke, and with wisdom, on the constitutional problems facing India.

> To govern India—he said—has been the greatest achievement this country has ever attempted. . . . It will be an even higher achievement, an even nobler task, to assist India to govern herself.[546]

His interest encouraged Sir Samuel Hoare to invite him to serve upon a joint committee set up to consider the Indian Constitution, telling him that his acceptance would be 'very reassuring to thousands of men and women in this country who are not looking at this question through the spectacles of any party'. There were some who thought it improper for the Archbishop to be asked to serve, amongst them Lord Salisbury, but Lang accepted.

The work proved onerous, and he came to describe it as his 'chief tyranny': but he found it absorbing and the general verdict was that he had done well.[547]

As Hitler's vast ambitions became the more evident, so general alarm throughout Europe increased. While the Munich crisis was at its height, he transmitted, through Cardinal Hinsley of Westminster, a telegram to the Pope urging him to send a personal entreaty to Hitler to hold his hand. After the reprieve, engineered by Neville Chamberlain, the Archbishop, in company with most of his fellow citizens, breathed a sigh of relief and expressed over the B.B.C. the hope, naïvely it now seems, that the era of tension might pass. While 'appeasement' was seen by the Government as a viable policy, Lang, according to a diary of Dr. Alan Don, under the date 24 November 1938, met Cardinal Hinsley in the Athenaeum to discuss what should be done to safeguard Christian missions in the event of any of the German colonies being handed back to Germany. The mind boggles at the prospect of the Nazi Government having bases in the continent of Africa in 1939! But the ruthless persecution of the Jews, which Lang condemned in forthright terms in a letter to *The Times*, showed that Nazism was irredeemable and when war was declared he never doubted that Britain was right to stand up to Nazi aggression. It was his second experience, as Archbishop, of a vast and more than European conflict.

War, in its beastliness, was abhorrent to Lang.

> I was harried with anxiety—he wrote of the first 'breaking of the nations' in 1914—as to the rightfulness of the Church in any way supporting war; and I well remember the real torture of mind when I tried to think out the problem in September while in retreat at Cuddesdon. But I was driven to the conclusion, right or wrong, that we were bound in honour to enter it, and that the Church could not rightly oppose it.[548]

He consistently took the view that the task of the ordained clergy was to continue their ministry of Word and Sacrament either as parish priests, as chaplains, or in non-combatant duties. The hate campaign against the Kaiser in the First World War seemed to the Archbishop particularly offensive, and in a public speech at York he recalled his 'sacred memory' of the German Emperor keeping watch, with Edward VII, over the coffin of Queen Victoria. Such an experience convinced him that the Kaiser 'could not lightly have embarked upon a war with England'.[549] The torrent of abuse that greeted these words now seems almost unbelievable. He was described as a sycophant of the German Emperor, pro-German, and twenty-four Iron Crosses were sent him. The suspicion he thus aroused remained for many years, and even Buckingham Palace was, surprisingly, said to be a little cool for a time. To a sensitive man this cut deeply. When in Middlesborough he found a meeting he was due to address boycotted, he remarked bitterly: 'I have tried hard to be of service to the nation and this is my reward. . . . I think I must give up this public work.'[550] It was a harrowing experience which he never forgot and which left him prematurely aged.

The physical strain of the Second World War was greater. He endured its rationing, its air-raids, and its closing down of Lambeth Palace with fortitude; but it was the war situation which convinced him that he must retire.

Lang was a great royalist. The whole paraphernalia of monarchy at the summit of a hierarchical society ministered to something very fundamental in his nature. His relations with the Royal Family began early when, as Vicar of Portsea, he preached twice a year before the old Queen, and was frequently at Osborne. 'I shall ever,' he wrote, 'regard these visits to the great Queen as among the highest privileges of my life.' Recalling the first time he dined with her he wrote:

> I can never forget the impression made when, before dinner, the door opened, the page announced in a loud voice, 'The Queen', and she entered, so small in stature, yet clothed with such unconscious but unmistakable dignity. I have been present at many great State occasions during the last half century, but I do not think that I have ever been so immediately and deeply impressed by that simple entry of 'The Queen'.[551]

As for the rest of the evening, he commented:

> The dinner was exactly like any private friendly party, except that, of course, the Queen did not actually speak except to the royalties next her.[552]

The 'of course' is very revealing.

457

The Queen, if she did not resort to the superlatives which she employed on her first encounter with Randall Davidson, was obviously impressed. 'He is a very interesting man and clever man, a Scotchman, and was at Oxford.'[553] This meeting led to his being a frequent guest, and he records long conversations not only with the Queen but, among others, with Princess Beatrice, the Duchess of Connaught, and the Empress Frederick. He was present at Osborne when a telegram of fervent loyalty came to the Queen from besieged Kimberley.

> I can never forget the tone and manner with which she said: 'It [the South African War] was not only necessary: it is just. It must, it shall be fought out to the end. These brave fellows shall not be allowed to suffer in vain. There is no place for panic.'

He remembered how she stamped her foot as she said: 'I will hear of no complaints against my generals till the war is over. They have my confidence. They will do their utmost.'

> It was touching indeed—he went on—to look down on this simple little old lady and to feel that here was *Britannia at bay*! All the strength and self control and determination of the Empire seemed really and literally to be personified in her. She dealt very faithfully with President Kruger. 'The man's parade of religion annoys me. I don't think much of a religion which is used to justify self-aggrandisement and wilfulness and corrupt government.'[554]

Read in the light of subsequent history, these remarks strike a somewhat pathetic note.

As Vicar of Portsea and a Royal Chaplain, Lang made the acquaintance of Prince Edward, later King Edward VII, which led to his often staying at Sandringham. The fascination which such visits exercised upon him may be seen in the lengthy account of his introduction to the Princess of Wales, the Duke and Duchess of York, and their children. 'I have rarely enjoyed a country visit more . . .'[555] was a typical comment. Equally his life-long friendship began at this time with the future George V, although their relationship started with a praiseworthy display of independence on Lang's part. Lang was preaching at the Dockyard Chapel on an occasion when the collection was allocated to the Korean Mission. While preparing his sermon, he was privately advised that the Duke of York had expressed himself violently against the worthwhileness of

Christian missions. Lang decided to devote himself to their defence. Afterwards the Duke tackled Cosmo in his usual blunt manner. 'I believe you preached that sermon at me. I don't agree with it.' Lang tactfully suggested that commitment to world evangelism seemed to him bound up with being a Christian. 'Then, you tell me that with my views I can't be a Christian.' Lang replied that he could only state the premise: it was for the Duke himself to draw the conclusions. 'Well, I call that damned cheek,' he snorted as he walked off.[556]

This incident, unimportant though it may seem, shows that Lang could stand his ground when his Christian allegiance seemed really threatened. It did not long impair their developing friendship, though the future Duke of Windsor found it difficult to see what they had in common. Soon royal letters to Lang were signed 'your sincere old friend G.R.I.' In 1923 the King awarded him the Royal Victorian Chain and in 1933 made him Lord High Almoner, only one Archbishop having held the office before him. When in January 1936, following upon a serious illness some years previously, the King developed a condition of acute cardiac weakness, the Archbishop telephoned Lord Wigram telling him that 'I hoped that, if the anxiety grew, I might be allowed to come as, apart from the call of personal friendship, I felt the country would expect it'.[557] The Queen agreed, and the Archbishop left for Sandringham. On Monday 20 January he was admitted to the King, when they spoke together of their long friendship. Dressed in his cassock, Lang solemnly recited the 23rd Psalm and some verses of scripture, ending with St. Paul's triumphant proclamation, 'I am persuaded . . .' As the end drew near, he gave the final benediction: 'Go forth upon thy journey from this world, O Christian Soul . . .', then withdrew so that the Queen and her family might be alone with the King at the moment of his passing. Later in the day, he recorded:

> After saying goodbye to the Queen—her fortitude still marvellous—I went to the King's room alone: there was no one there. I lifted the veil from his face and looked upon it for the last time. It had a light upon it of most beautiful serenity and peace. So with a final silent commendation of his soul to God I left.[558]

The death of George V inaugurated a new reign which Lang admits that he anticipated with apprehension. He had heard a great deal of the Prince of Wales's affairs, and his diary records, under Balmoral, September 1935, that he had had a 'long and intimate talk' with the King on 'certain family troubles'. [559]

Incidents, small in themselves, made him uneasy, as when, within five minutes of George V's death, the new King ordered all the clocks at Sandringham, which had been kept half an hour fast—a vain effort originally to secure some degree of punctuality from Queen Alexandra—to be put back. Nor was he reassured by his first brief interview:

> I spoke a few hasty but deeply felt words about his great responsibility and my desire to give him loyal service. He was very cordial.[560]

A second talk at Buckingham Palace somehow did not go better:

> I told him frankly that I was aware that he had been somewhat set against me by knowing that his father had often discussed his affairs with me. But I assured him—which was true—that I had always tried to put the most favourable view of his conduct before his father. He did not seem to resent this frankness.

The King then changed the subject by saying that he understood he must now appoint bishops, and asked how this was done, at the same time mentioning vaguely some two clerics whom he had met. Finally Lang spoke to him again of his great responsibilities and promised his loyal support. Even in his own short summary of this interview Lang's approach seems somewhat patronizing:

> . . . I feel that a long and greatly valued chapter in my life, associated with the constant kindness and friendship of King George, is closed. There is not only a new reign but a new régime. I can only be most thankful for what has been, and for what is to be, hope for the best. God guide the King.[561]

The Archbishop, to be fair, had no desire to be hostile to one whose charm, vitality, and social concern he admired; but he did not like the company he kept. The King, on his part, genuinely regarded the Archbishop as the embodiment of a rigid ecclesiastical code which lacked personal sensitivity; and, as he put it in *A King's Story* 'more interested in the pursuit of prestige and power than the abstractions [*sic*] of the human soul'.

Not surprisingly, the summer of 1936 saw no customary visit to Balmoral, although the Duke and Duchess of York invited the Archbishop to their Highland home at Birkhall, where he was entranced by their two children. His anxiety, however, concerning 'the King's matter' grew, the more so as it was rumoured that the King intended to marry Mrs. Simpson after she had secured her second divorce. To Lang the Coronation of a monarch carried with it a deep mystical significance, and he saw the whole nation as being lifted through it into a higher dedication, which he hoped would lead to an evangelistic 'Recall to Religion'. He was deeply anxious to prepare the King for his anointing; but somehow just could not bring himself to approach it. The months slipped by.

> ... the thought of my having to consecrate *him* as King weighed on me as a heavy burden. Indeed, I considered whether I could bring myself to do so. But I had a *sense* that circumstances might change. I could only pray that they might, either outwardly or in his own soul.[562]

To carry through the Coronation as things were would be 'unreal and meaningless', like 'pouring all those sacred words into a *vacuum*'.[563]

The situation, however, was to change dramatically; and the Archbishop has often been blamed as a major agent in bringing this about. The facts, however, do not point this way; although he did feel that if the King should insist on marrying Mrs. Simpson, abdication was the only way out.

In the events which were to follow, it should be said that no subsequent accounts of the abdication, in spite of differences of approach, have broken the substantial accuracy of the version put forward by J. C. Lockhart in his biography of Lang.

News of the 'King's matter' was already common knowledge in America and on the Continent, and before long was to 'break' upon the public in England. The Archbishop meanwhile made repeated endeavours to see the King who, with complete constitutional propriety, insisted that he would discuss the affair only with the Prime Minister. Later Lang regretted that he had not put his views and feelings into a letter; though it is quite untrue that this was due to his wishing to hurry the monarch off the throne. The Prime Minister did in fact see the King, who left him in little doubt that he intended to marry Mrs. Simpson, come what may. Baldwin then plainly told him that any resort to a morganatic marriage would require legislation, and that neither his Government nor the Opposition was prepared to embark upon it. On 1 December 1936, the whole matter became news headlines in England through an address given by Dr. Blunt, Bishop of Bradford, at his Diocesan Conference. This had been written some six weeks earlier, and referred not to any possible marriage with Mrs. Simpson but to the King's neglect of church-going. Subsequent accusations of connivance between the Archbishop and the Bishop of Bradford were unfounded.[564] On 3 December, the Prime Minister passed on to the

461

Archbishop the substance of a conversation he had had with the King the previous day, in which he reiterated that the Cabinet, the Opposition—Winston Churchill claimed that to consult the Opposition was unconstitutional—and all the Commonwealth countries, were opposed to any legislation to allow a morganatic marriage. It now became clear that if there were a marriage then there must be an abdication, unless the King was prepared to defy the Government and endeavour to go above their heads to the country. The Archbishop saw the Moderator and Secretary of the Federal Council of Evangelical Free Churches, and the same evening appealed to the clergy, both on the radio and in the Press, 'to refrain from speaking directly on the King's matter, but simply to pray for him and his ministers'. On Sunday, 6 December, the Prime Minister summoned the Archbishop to London in order to discuss a new proposal put forward by the King, namely to hasten Mrs. Simpson's divorce. The Archbishop received a hostile reception from the crowd in Downing Street, and on the following day his picture appeared in the Press under such captions as 'The Archbishop Objects'. It was the only occasion when his opinion was definitely sought. The end of this agonizing ordeal was now in sight. The King signed a deed of abdication on 10 December: it was announced in Parliament on the same day, and the Archbishop made a short speech in the Lords. On the next day, the Abdication Bill passed both Houses. The King made a dignified broadcast from Windsor Castle in the evening—a broadcast which Lang admitted, contained some 'real pathos', although he detected one jarring note.

On 13 December the Archbishop himself broadcast to the nation. It was a difficult and unenviable task. Perhaps the Archbishop's heightened sense of the drama of history constituted a dangerous temptation. Alan Don remembered bringing his Shakespeare to him on request, from which there came 'The pity of it, O the pity of it'. As for himself, the Archbishop felt that he could not speak only of the King's charm and what he had done for the country:

> . . . in my position I was bound to say something about the surrender of a great trust from the motive of private happiness and about the social circle in which he had thought that that happiness could be found.[565]

So the broadcast placed the main blame for what had happened on the King's circle of friends.

> Even more strange and sad it is that he should have sought his happiness in a manner inconsistent with the Christian principles of marriage, and within a social circle whose standards and ways

of life are alien to all the best instincts and traditions of his people. Let those who belong to this circle know that today they stand rebuked by the judgment of the nation which had loved King Edward. I have shrunk from saying these words. But I have felt compelled for the sake of sincerity and truth to say them.[566]

Re-reading his speech after the lapse of years, one cannot but feel that the same thing could have been said without provoking the kind of resentment that filled his postbag for some time. William Temple, the Archbishop of York, used the opportunity perhaps with more discretion to draw the distinction between *eros* and *agape*, though not entirely to Lang's liking. Hensley Henson, always one of the Archbishop's critics, though full of personal esteem, expressed in his journal what many felt:

> There was a growing sentiment that this eager zeal to 'improve the occasion' and point the moral was not only rather mean, but also altogether useless. After all the King did abdicate with dignity and go away without fuss.[567]

Even Alan Don felt that Lang had been 'a little unfair to the poor King', and regretted that he had not 'submitted his address . . . to one of us beforehand'. It was, of course, the Archbishop's high view of monarchy and his concern for its continuing status that prompted his censorious and somewhat unctuous words. Had he been a little more sensitive to ordinary human feeling, he would have known that to give the appearance of 'kicking a man when he's down' would be offensive. Four lines of verse which came through the post to Lambeth, and which his chaplains mercifully never allowed him to see, expressed cruelly what many felt:

> My Lord Archbishop, what a scold you are!
> And when your man is down how bold you are!
> Of Christian charity how scant you are!
> And, auld Lang swine, how full of cant you are![568]

Lang's touch was perhaps surer when, at her request, he drew up a statement which was issued to the press under the name of Queen Mary, and which *The Times* published with the heading 'A Mother's Heart'.[569]

Maybe it should be added that to his private diary Lang confided: 'My heart aches for the Duke of Windsor . . . I cannot bear to think of the kind of life into which he has passed.'[570]

463

With the advent of a new King the atmosphere, so far as Lang was concerned, suddenly changed. Without the resilience and the obvious gifts of his elder brother, George VI was more like his father, and the Archbishop turned to preparations for the Coronation with dedicated enthusiasm. Lang now recalled that when he had discussed the occasion with Edward VIII, the King had called in his brother, the Duke of York, passing the service book to him with the words: 'I think you had better follow this.' When the Archbishop called on George VI and Queen Elizabeth at 145 Piccadilly he wrote ecstatically that 'it was indeed like waking after a nightmare to find the sun shining'.[571] In a broadcast, he seized the opportunity to urge a recall to religion in line with the reality of the King's own dedication. Lang proceeded to study the Coronation rite—it was a congenial task—and introduced a few changes. The Litany was made introductory; the Oath was put back in its old place immediately after the Recognition and before the Communion Office; the Sermon was omitted, against the wishes, incidentally, of Winston Churchill; the old order of Anointing from the hands to the head was revived; representatives of the Church of Scotland and Free Churches were allocated places in the Great Procession. Perhaps most important, a new oath was devised, after great difficulty, which included all the Dominions within its terms of reference. The Archbishop took a great personal interest in the rehearsals, and decided what parts of the service should be broadcast. At Windsor Castle over Easter he went through the ceremony with King and Queen, and nearer to the Coronation led them, at Buckingham Palace, in a more spiritual preparation, going from the Palace to Broadcasting House where he spoke to the nation. On 12 May, Coronation Day, the Archbishop, who seemed to have shed his years, lifted the ceremony into a dimension of mystery which was the result of more than technical efficiency, or even of the quality of his voice and the dignity of his demeanour.

> And now the Great Day itself, Wednesday May 12th—to me, I suppose, in a sense the culminating day of my official life, the day on which the Archbishop of Canterbury fulfils his highest office in the national life, on which through him the Church of God consecrates that life in the person of its King.[572]

What, if any, were the long-term effects of the Coronation on the national life? One of Lang's chaplains thought that 'without doubt coming when it did, the Coronation did much to stabilise the British Commonwealth under the new King'.[573] Hensley Henson, on the other hand, confessed to being unhappy at 'this unprecedented parade of pageanted piety'[574] and was not alone in being sceptical of its value. Perhaps Lang did not realize that most people were not so moved as he was by symbolic ceremonial and nostalgic recollection—and that even when they registered, the effects soon wore off. Randall Davidson, with his more matter-of-fact approach, was nearer to a common humanity. Recalls to religion, he used to say, based on royal events or the exigencies of war never get very far.

It was the oft-repeated intention of Cosmo Lang to retire at the age of seventy-five; but the outbreak of war frustrated this proper resolve. Not until the bombing began, coupled with his recognition that the post-war years would need a fresh approach, did he bring himself to the point of resignation in 1942. His closing years were spent in a grace-and-favour residence at Kew, where he felt keenly his isolation from public affairs. To Prebendary Saywell, Rector of St. Michael's, Cornhill, he confessed to being lonely, and said that had he known how short would be his successor's tenure of office, he would not have retired.

Lang's reign at Lambeth was disappointing to those who paid him the compliment of hoping a great deal from it. Randall Davidson saw his task as one of allowing the nascent energies of the Anglican Church to find expression without cancelling each other out. Lang was not cast to play this role: but a too-protracted apprenticeship, added to war and old age, constrained him to follow it, yet without conviction. It was in the field of reunion that he did well. Bishopthorpe and Lambeth, in spite of the fact that eight northern Primates have gone on to Canterbury, are very different assignments. Each has its own possibilities: but maybe Cyril Garbett was unique in realizing the particular opportunities offered by the Archbishopric of York as Canon Smyth's excellent biography suggests.

# 3

## WILLIAM TEMPLE, A WORLD CHURCH AND CHRISTIAN SOCIALISM

I

Archbishops of Canterbury seldom now come to office through any form of popular acclaim as, for example, did Dunstan in Anglo-Saxon England. Before radio and television they were shadowy figures to the vast majority of Englishmen whose lives were untouched by them. William Temple, Cosmo Lang's successor, is a notable exception.

The claims of William Temple, Archbishop of York, for Canterbury were so considerable that no Prime Minister could easily ignore them, even amidst the preoccupation of war. Writing to his brother on 27 January 1942, Temple confessed that he would be surprised 'if just at this moment the "powers" select me for Canterbury. . . . Some of my recent utterances,' he went on, 'have not been liked in political circles, and it would be thought by some that to choose me now is to endorse them.'[575]

Temple was probably right in supposing that he was not particularly *persona grata* with Winston Churchill, the Prime Minister, upon whom the final burden of choice lay. Yet politicians respond to pressure, and to have passed William Temple over would have been manifestly to prefer the lesser man and to call in question the whole appointing system. Indeed it would have created an embarrassing situation for whoever went to Canterbury. Such was the status of William Temple. Thus he was nominated as the ninety-eighth Archbishop, the first son to follow a father in this office.

To Bernard Shaw the arrival of such a person at Lambeth was 'a realised impossibility'.[576] The tragedy was that he held office for only two and a half years, dying at the comparatively early age of sixty-three when, although terribly fatigued, he seemed still in the full flood of his powers.

William Temple admitted that his father had done his most creative work prior to his coming to Lambeth. The son did not have time to do otherwise, particularly since his brief archiepiscopate was spent during the exceptional years of the Second World War.

But there was one great difference in that the tremendous contribution which William had already made to the life of Church and nation was of such a significance that the unique office he held was given a new dimension and outreach through his tenure of it.

For this reason our short study of Temple must suggest the quality of the man, the variety of his interests, and therefore what it meant to ordinary people to have this kind of person at Canterbury. For good or ill, the Primate of All England is a representative figure. What he is many assume the Church to be.

William Temple was a larger-than-life person, prodigal in his gifts, lavish in his generosity, wide in his interests, abundant in his energy, holy in his dedication; so fulfilled and integrated as to defy the efforts of so skilled a writer as Dean Iremonger to produce a graphic biography. Oliver Cromwell is said to have urged the painter to put in his warts; in the Protector's case it was hardly necessary advice. Temple seemed to have none, unless errors of judgement be included in this category. The letters of Temple which have survived irradiate goodness and intellectual concentration, but they lack the introspection which makes for interest. There were, it is true, critics who disapproved his socialism, retreated before his larger horizons, and complained that the systems he erected were not always geared to practical reality. But even these never doubted his integrity, the expansiveness of his sympathy (if he did not always express this with warmth), his unfailing good humour, and his profound humility. The sad fact is that all-round virtue, in retrospect, does not excite curiosity as does, for example, the more passionate, schizophrenic spirituality of Cosmo Lang. Indeed it is Temple's very wholeness, the clarity of his vision, and his preoccupation with ideas (maybe a legacy of his early idealism) which make it difficult to come to grips with him. The astonishing thing, however, is that this philosopher and theologian, this peripatetic preacher and lecturer, this churchman and socialist, this man who never talked down to an audience, ended up by 'registering' with ordinary people in the sense that he became the embodiment of a vision—the vision of a caring Church which believed that social justice mattered. The significance of his all too brief archiepiscopate lay in the fact that such a man, devoted to humane and progressive causes, was at Canterbury; that in spite of establishment prejudice he had been appointed by that establishment to a position of unique responsibility. For all too brief a space, the remote office of Primate of All England was caught up in an aura which seemed as if it might give a new direction to the discharge of an ancient role. The reason for this hope was that Temple, uniquely among archbishops—and here he is utterly different from Tait—did not need office in order to exercise influence and to be able to play a national role. From the beginning of his adult life he had given himself to good causes and served ends not because his particular post required such service but because of an inner constraint to be up and doing. By sheer force of character and brilliance of gifts he made the Archbishop of Canterbury a figure to be reckoned with in the seats of power, at a time when the general drift of public secular life was moving the other way.

Undoubtedly the most powerful and formative factor in Temple's development was his own father. Their relationship was close, and the son used to say that the father would not always reveal his own views 'because he knows how much I am tempted to accept them without thinking'.[577] Frederick was sixty years of age when William was born, and this helped to make William an essentially XIXth-century character. His philosophic standpoint, for example, if it moved considerably from that which was dominant in the last decades of the previous century, never lost its imprint. It was largely because of Frederick that William's natural bent for metaphysical study did not lead to the pure scholar but to the more practical reformer. His ability showed itself early. From Rugby School he went to Balliol College, Oxford, where he secured a first in classical moderations, and at Queen's College took a first in Greats. He was much influenced both by Caird's idealism and Cook Wilson's realism. Perhaps it is significant of his general approach at this time, and it dates him, that he fell under the spell of Browning, whose 'completeness' he admired. His social interests and his bent for public speaking, which remained with him throughout life, led to his being elected President of the Union. A fellowship at Queen's seemed to be right, and a visit to the Continent introduced him to German scholarship; but he was already finding Queen's too 'strait' for him. His father had given some of the best years of his life to the cause of education at the grass roots, particularly to helping the underprivileged, and through the influence of R. H. Tawney, William Temple attended the first National Conference of the Workers' Educational Association. He was immediately attracted, and caught by contagion an interest which for some years dominated his busy life. On behalf of the W.E.A. he roamed the country and for some years was its president. He believed in education and the liberation of the mind which went with it. Concern for adult education brought him into close contact with trade union leaders and with many whose over-riding interests were directed towards securing social justice. To Temple, as to Maurice, they were complementary objectives.

> You can have no justice at the basis of your social life until education has done its full work.[578]

Indeed, what appealed to Temple about the W.E.A. was that for him it combined, in one harmonious whole, a social and an educational ideal.

> Education—he said—should remain primarily corporate rather than individual, primarily spiritual (that is, effective through influence, and through an appeal to sympathy and imagination), rather than primarily intellectual (that is, effective through an appeal to intelligence and memory), primarily concerned with giving people the power to pronounce judgment on any facts with which they may come in contact rather than supplying them simply with the facts. It should be primarily co-operative and not primarily competitive.[579]

His link with W.E.A. induced in him a persisting tendency to see every worker in terms of those whom he had come to know in the refined atmosphere of the lecture room. It was a factual mistake, but it was a mistake on the right side.

> Are you going to treat a man—Temple asked—as what he is, or what he might be? Morality requires, I think, that you should treat him as what he might be, as what he has it in him to become; and business requires that you should treat him as what he is; and you cannot get rid of that strain except by raising what he is to the level of what he might be. That is the whole work of education. Give him the full development of his powers; and there will no longer be that conflict between the claim of the man as he is and the man as he might become.[580]

Temple's educational interests, however, were by no means confined to W.E.A. He had a concern for university reform, and shocked some of the bishops by his more Erastian attitude to Birrell's Education Bill of 1908, which, as we have seen, was shipwrecked in the Lords. It seemed fitting that he should be asked by H. A. L. Fisher, President of the Board of Education, to be Chairman of a new Committee on Adult Education. The purpose of the committee was to co-ordinate work in this field at the national level, and to sponsor local effort. Temple felt it was a good thing that the Church should be involved in such an enterprise.

The pattern of his life was now being set—the ubiquitous propagandist on behalf of such societies as the Young Men's Christian Association, and the Student Christian Movement and the Church of England Men's Society: ceaseless lecturing; constant travelling; omnivorous reading; and a book always on the stocks.

469

But all these diverse interests were, in Temple, the expression of a deep and Christo-centric faith, which permeated the whole of his life and constituted a regulative loyalty. He had never really thought of any profession but that of a clergyman, even at a time when he contemplated spending his life as a professional philosopher. True, he was hindered for a short time in moving forward to ordination by doubts as to the Virgin birth and the physical resurrection; but these were doubts within faith. From them he was rescued by the paternal solicitude of Randall Davidson.

At the early age of twenty-nine he was appointed headmaster of Repton. There, under the stimulus of his intellectual enthusiasms, the sixth form sprang into life; but the actual job of being a head-master was not temperamentally congenial. He liked young people, but the mechanics of keeping a timetable and the maintenance of school discipline proved irksome. His time at Repton saw the appearance of *Foundations*, a symposium consisting of nine essays, two by himself, and concerned as its sub-title indicates with 'A Statement of Christian Belief in Terms of Modern Thought'. The essays do not show Temple in the full maturity of his thought, but on the way to it, and with a facility for easy expression which never left him and which could constitute somewhat of a snare. He was still feeling after his 'vocation of the moment'.

From Repton Temple went off to become Rector of St. James's, Piccadilly. As a preacher, in the centre of London, he drew a large and intelligent congregation, but he did not possess, for all his deep spirituality and human concern, that something elusive which goes into the making of a parish priest, not least the small talk; the con-suming interest in the arthritic knee; the sensitivity to the idio-syncrasies of ordinary people whose potential needs to be imagina-tively discerned before it can be creatively elicited. But he was on the eve of finding causes big enough and challenging enough to consume his thinking and his energies. An entry into journalism as editor of the *Challenge* showed his flair and virtuosity, but it failed because there was not as yet a large enough educated clientele to keep such a publication going.

II

The decisive break came for Temple with his resignation from St. James's in order to devote himself full time first to The National Mission and then to the Life and Liberty Movement which grew out of it. Both were born in the fires of war, as the result of a wide-spread feeling that the Church was losing its hold on the nation. Neither Gore, who poured scorn on the whole idea of a mission, nor

Davidson, who reacted with his usual caution, protesting that one of his functions as Archbishop was to say 'no', could prevent things going forward. Responsible laymen got to work on the Archbishop, who appointed a commission of twelve men to go into the whole question of a mission and finally came up with a plan of campaign. Temple was one of the twelve. Randall Davidson laid the matter before the Bench of Bishops, and it was decided to launch a National Mission of Repentance and Hope in the autumn of 1916. Temple's fear, as secretary of the enterprise, was lest the official leadership should rest content with a few meetings culminating in a gathering at the Albert Hall.

Once begun, the Mission developed momentum, became more highly organized, and Temple was swept along with it. His resilience was remarkable. But even his lively optimism was not, in the long run, justified, as he felt bound to report to the tenth meeting of the Council. People were not returning to their national Church; and those affected by the mission were, in the main, those already committed. In the light of such disillusion the continuation committee, of which Temple was a prominent member, became convinced that the 'follow up' must be directed to the Church itself.

'Don't you think, William dear,' said Dick Sheppard of inimitable fame, 'that there ought to be a "ginger" group in the Church?'[581] So the Life and Liberty Movement was conceived, geared to the conviction that the Church could not speak to the nation until it had put its own house in order, and was in a position to control its own affairs. This did not necessarily entail disestablishment, but it certainly supposed the possibility of it if a proper freedom could not be secured any other way. It was significant that no bishops were admitted to membership of the movement. Inevitably William Temple was its acknowledged leader, and the most energetic crusader on its behalf. At an enthusiastic meeting in the Queen's Hall, which William Temple addressed with restrained yet moving eloquence, a resolution was carried by acclamation, Hensley Henson alone dissenting. It condemned the 'intolerable hindrance' under which the Church worked, and urged the Archbishops to find out on what terms Parliament was prepared to grant the Church its freedom, 'so that it may the better fulfil its duty to God and to the nation and its mission to the world.'[582]

Temple followed this up, on behalf of the Council of the Life and Liberty Movement, with a vigorous letter to the Press.

> We are weary of perpetual deliberations—he wrote—A disturbance would be better than a continuance of inactivity. Need we calculate much longer? We are clear that the Church

just now has her greatest and possibly her last opportunity of vindicating her Catholic and national character.[583]

The passing of the Enabling Act was for Temple a great milestone, and he can be pardoned for momentary exultation; but he was careful to remind his followers of the need to be up and doing. 'We have been given our chance,' he said, 'now we have to take it.' That he was later disappointed with the results which flowed from the setting up of a representative system within the Church is undoubted. But this disappointment may in part have been due to the exaggerated hopes widely entertained at the end of the First World War. Also the rejection of the Prayer Book in the House of Commons was an unhappy initiation leading Temple to complain of Davidson's 'lack of defiance'. Yet in spite of this he was not prepared, as he would have been earlier, to advocate disestablishment as the remedy.

### III

To Temple the Christian Church was essentially a supranational society, and its fragmentation a matter of deep personal concern. The story of the ecumenical movement is a thrilling one—the great conferences of Mission at Edinburgh, Jerusalem, and Madras; of Life and Work at Stockholm and Oxford; of Faith and Order at Lausanne and Edinburgh, leading to the inauguration of the British Council of Churches, marked by a service in St. Paul's Cathedral on 25 September 1942. These were not only landmarks in ecumenicity but milestones in the life of William Temple, so intertwined as to be inseparable from the 'swelling theme'. For him it meant constant travel abroad, with a memorable trip to the Holy Land in 1928; a vast correspondence with leading churchmen on the Continent; attendance at innumerable conferences; and the drawing up of countless reports for which he had almost a magical flair.

In this great enterprise he worked alongside that remarkable American, John R. Mott, a layman who pioneered the Fellowship of the World Christian Federation, from which the modern ecumenical movement may be said, in part, to have sprung.

The story of Temple's involvement can only be briefly referred to, but it is central to any estimate of William Temple's contribution to the life of his time. Like Moses he did not live to see the realization of the hope which he had steadily kept before him. It was not until some four years after his death that the World Council of Churches was formally inaugurated in Amsterdam on 23 August 1948; but he had helped to pioneer the way.

472

Such pioneering work meant overcoming a great deal of initial prejudice, if not outright hostility, due largely to fear lest the emergence of a 'World Christianity' might blur, indeed compromise, what some regarded as the essentials of Catholic Order. To such, the title-deeds of the World Council—a 'Fellowship of Churches which accept our Lord Jesus as God and Saviour'—were not reassuring. During the course of its constitutional revolution, Arthur Headlam, Bishop of Gloucester, wrote to Temple:

> You are practically destroying the Faith and Order Movement and very probably destroying a great deal of the Reunion Movement.[584]

This opposition spilled over into the Church Assembly. But Temple was not to be deterred and he succeeded in carrying a motion in this body: 'That this House welcomes the establishment of the World Council of Churches constituted in accordance with the scheme submitted to the Assembly and accepts the invitation to be represented.' This was real leadership, and he had the stature to give it.

Ecumenically, Temple held a unique place in world Christianity, not simply because of the offices which he held, but because of what he was in himself. It was his enthusiasm, his competence, his theological insight, his integrity, not least his ability as a chairman which made him so great a force. His most effective contribution was made in the early days, when to launch the ecumenical movement was not easy. To overcome difficult clashes of temperament which derived as much from diverse cultural and religious backgrounds as from personal idiosyncrasies, and to bring out of them some sort of common mind, demanded flair, patience and persistence. Temple undoubtedly possessed them, together with the gift of lifting such human diversity, while being true to it, into higher dimensions of a unified purpose. In himself there were knit together many of the different responses for which the totality of Christendom stood— the theological; the worshipful; the ecumenical; the social; the political. In this respect he was a 'representative man'.

With the Orthodox Churches of the East, Temple had long made contact through the ecumenical movement generally. The havoc of war, combined with the shortness of his own Canterbury archiepiscopate, made any real advance impossible during his tenure of office. But he had a great deal to do with the sending of a delegation from the Church of England to the Russian Orthodox Church in 1943, which was headed by Dr. Garbett, Archbishop of York, who carried a personal letter from the Primate of All England. Temple also began negotiations for a return visit in 1945, but died

473

before it took place. Insofar as he himself was able to advance relations with the Orthodox, it was in an intimate and personal way. He met many of their leaders at working conferences, and got to know them. They on their part respected his genuine fellow-feeling and his understanding of their problems. It was a mark of esteem that on his death a memorial service was held in the Greek Cathedral of St. Sophia, Bayswater.

Temple's eirenical outreach was not only world-wide; it included a concern for the separated churches of Britain. The *Appeal to All Christian People* had undoubtedly opened windows. It was followed by a series of meetings called by Archbishop Davidson to Lambeth to which reference has already been made. At the Lambeth Conference of 1930 Temple was chairman of the Committee on Unity. For once in his life he seems to have disappointed the Free Churchmen and to have rather dismissed them in the *Report* by suggesting that 'no memorable advance' had been made. Temple himself across the years came to the conclusion that abstract discussion around concepts of validity and authority got nowhere. Negotiations would only be fruitful when 'concentrated on some definite proposal'. He therefore welcomed the appearance in 1938 of *An Outline of a Reunion Scheme* which described 'the kind of Church in which the Churches might find themselves united without loss of what is specially valuable in their distinctive traditions'. The document did not hit the headlines, but interest in it was revived when Temple in 1943 addressed the full synod of Canterbury on 'Christian Unity and Church Reunion'.

Conversations also took place with the Church of Scotland which had as its goal entering into 'unrestricted Conference', but after a tentative start these negotiations unfortunately broke down, much to the chagrin of Temple, who was chairman of the Church of England delegation.

He inevitably became involved in the scheme for union between a group of non-episcopal churches and the Anglican dioceses of India, Burma, and Ceylon. Temple himself saw the scheme as arising out of a situation of 'pastoral urgency' and as such gave it his blessing. But the proposals met resistance in England, and by the time he had gone to Lambeth this opposition became so serious that a number of superiors of religious orders threatened to secede if the proposed union went through as planned. Among his last acts in Convocation, in response to inquiries, was to give an assurance that the Church of England would not break off communion with the Church of India, Burma, and Ceylon if it allowed four of its dioceses to go forward into the new Church of South India; but that there would not for the present be full communion with the new Church.

The statement was vague and lacked the decisiveness necessary for true leadership. Doubtless Temple was feeling the strain and preoccupation of the war years and had lost his sureness of touch. It was left to Dr. Fisher to make the matter more clear.

William Temple could not but be mindful of the vast communion which owed allegiance to the Pope of Rome, and which was holding aloof from what Temple regarded as the most significant religious fact of his day—the rise of a 'world church' which he believed divine providence was calling into being at a time when other forces were tearing the world apart.

He felt keenly for the Pope during the years of the Second World War, and on two occasions expressed sympathy at the restrictions imposed by the Italian Government on his liberty. He informed the Holy See of the formation of the World Council of Churches, expressing the hope that it 'should have the help from time to time of unofficial consultation with Roman Catholic theologians and scholars', and that there should be a mutual 'exchange of information'.[585]

But there was much in the ethos of the Roman Catholic Church which in the last analysis was uncongenial, probably because he prized religious and intellectual freedom too highly and was at times suspicious of the Curia's political influence.

To a chaplain in the forces he wrote:

> I . . . think it is true that an authoritarian organisation or religion is always bound to find itself lined up on the whole with authoritarian politics. I think the Church of Rome will always stand in its support of democracy in politics for emphasis on the rightful power of the majority, without which no doubt there is no democracy, but will make very little of the moral rights of the minority, without which democracy cannot be wholesome.
>
> Their whole attitude to freedom of thought is, to my mind, quite unsatisfactory. They acknowledge that compulsory faith is a contradiction and useless; but they also take the view that if, as in Italy or Spain, only the Roman Church exists on any substantial scale, they are entitled to use the arm of the State to prevent propagation of any other form of belief. The faith of the people in those countries is, therefore, not compulsory; it is just what they have grown up in and their wills consent to it; but neither is it a deliberate choice because alternatives have been shut away from them. In other words, the Roman Catholics treat grown-up people permanently as children and that is a

475

frame of mind which inevitably overflows into politics. I think this is really the source of the trouble.

I believe that all the doctrinal errors of Rome come from the direct identification of the Church as an organised Institution, taking its part in the process of history, with the Kingdom of God. This is just as bad, theologically, as the view which regards the Church as a mere instrument in preparation for the Kingdom of God.[586]

William Temple did not live long enough to witness the changed mood introduced by that remarkable man, Pope John XXIII. The suspicions which he entertained made him more at home with the Roman Catholics whom he met in the movement known as 'The Sword of the Spirit', an organization which co-operated with Anglicans and Free Churchmen in the more specifically social spheres, especially in the 'Religion and Life' weeks.

With Cardinal Hinsley, Temple was on terms of friendship, and this doubtless would have continued under his successor had Temple lived. One of his great ambitions, when the War was over, was to make a personal approach to the Pope 'in the hope that Roman and Anglican theologians might be encouraged to undertake some joint study of the Natural Law as the basis of Christian living'.[587] He did not live to prosecute the idea; though he may well have decided anyhow that the terms of reference had ceased to attract.

Little has been said so far of William Temple as Archbishop. This is deliberate, since, apart from the shortness of his stay at Lambeth, the most important fact about him was not the offices which he held but the causes which he espoused. Certainly he discharged his episcopal duties at Manchester, York, and Canterbury with conscientious diligence: and wherever he went he left his mark.

At Manchester he identified himself closely with the life of that great city, and was largely responsible for the creation of the Diocese of Southwell. His methods of administration were perhaps individual and not necessarily to be copied. He did not divide up the diocese between his suffragans, but left them to roam over it. Nor did they meet regularly as a team, although they were constantly consulted and used as chairmen of various diocesan committees according to their line of interest. Very much in character was his setting up a Board of Women's Work, with the intention of enhancing their status. In the city, Temple was a force to be reckoned with, even if there was felt to be a slight lack of personal warmth and intimacy.

For the northern see of York he came to have a great affection, and broke down the somewhat patrician style of living that Cosmo

Lang had maintained. Like Lang he found the northern Convocation more of a family affair than its southern counterpart. While at Bishopthorpe he kept no permanent domestic chaplain; delegation was certainly not his flair. 'Very well, I can see to that quite easily,' was his usual comment—and he usually could. But it was not the way to build up a team or to bring out the best in others. Maybe it was a family failing. Often those who worked with him found difficulty in his carrying in his head so many things which they would have preferred committed to paper. As a judge of men he was at times far too charitable to be discerning, and for this reason some of his appointments were poor. It was the defect of his virtues.

IV

Yet to the average person in Britain, not particularly concerned either with the future of the Church of England or with the more distant vistas of Christian reunion, it was not as an ecclesiastic that he registered or became the embodiment of a living hope. Rather, it was an outreach of another kind which made the impact. Temple was passionately convinced that Christianity had to do with international relations, with economics, indeed with the whole life of man in society, individual and corporate. It was the most materialistic of all religions. To harness this faith to securing social justice seemed to Temple an obvious duty, and he was a pioneer of the Conference on Christian Politics, Economics and Citizenship (COPEC) which was launched at Birmingham in 1920. Temple was by nature emotionally drawn to the underdog, and as a young boy he would be moved to tears if he saw another in pain. His reading of Maurice, Westcott, and Gore helped to make him a lifelong, if not doctrinaire, socialist, and a member of the Christian Social Union. As early as 1918 he announced in the Lower House of Convocation that he had joined the Labour Party; and he justified himself in an article in the *Daily News* on the ground that 'the Labour Movement is essentially an effort to organize society on the basis of freedom and fellowship'. From this view he never really deviated.

> It is the system—he maintained—which is foul and rotten. Producer, capitalist—all are entangled in the meshes of its net, while we prate about the spread of refinement; and while we pride ourselves on the spread of education; while we glory in an Empire whose flag is said to stand for Justice—we are condemned by the facts at our own doors, of stupid coarseness, of ignorant insensibility, and of a wanton oppression.[588]

477

When William Temple was seized with an idea it was inevitable that he should actively prosecute it, and on its behalf make himself widely available. Consequently he addressed and chaired numerous meetings and he was never over-discriminating about the respectability of the inviting organization if it seemed to offer a worthwhile audience. He worked closely with Prebendary Kirk in the Industrial Christian Fellowship; he wrote innumerable articles and books on this social theme. His method was to seek a principle and to apply it to the actual situation which was the subject of investigation. For example, in the light of what he understood as a theology of the Incarnation, he submitted the profit motive and private property to a systematic critique. Nor would he hesitate to do this in establishment circles. Such forthrightness did not commend him to everybody, particularly when his competence was questioned. A great deal of his own social thinking across the years was brought into focus and was given publicity at the Malvern Conference which met in 1941.

The purpose of this conference was 'to consider from the Anglican point of view what are the fundamental facts which are directly relevant to the ordering of the new Society that is quite evidently emerging, and how Christian thought can be shaped to play a leading part in the reconstruction after the war is over'.[589] It was an ambitious agenda. The Conference was attended by invitation, and a very mixed assembly was brought together, including such diverse personalities as Middleton Murry, T. S. Eliot, Dorothy Sayers, Richard Acland, Kenneth Ingram, and Maurice Reckitt. Thirteen diocesan bishops, two suffragans and four hundred clergy gave balance. Discussion roamed widely; but there seemed to be no unanimity of view, although much genuine concern. It was a situation made for Temple. With great virtuosity he produced what he used to describe as one of his 'parlour tricks', spending the last evening in drawing up a list of 'conclusions' which substantially was accepted by the conference in the morning.

From the point of view of the publicity which it attracted, the conference was a success, but once again Temple was anxious that there should be an effective follow-up. The 'conclusions', he stressed, were not designed to 'require' assent but to challenge thought, and so carry forward the general process that went on in the Conference. He himself gathered a number of Christian economists around him at Lambeth; and having first submitted the manuscript to Keynes, published in 1942 his *Christianity and the Social Order*, which sold some 140,000 copies. We are not here concerned with a critique of Temple's social philosophy. What counted was that an Archbishop should insist that religion had to do with the general life of the community; that economics was a branch of ethics even though it had its own specialization; and that politics was concerned with the Kingdom of God. *Christianity and the Social Order* ends with six objectives which it suggests governments ought to pursue, and an appendix outlines a practical programme to this end. Temple was accused of being an amateur intruder in a highly technical field, but it needs to be remembered that he consulted Keynes (and also Tawney) as to whether the appendix ought to be included. Both insisted that it should; but Temple still took care to add these words:

> Let no one quote this as my conception of the political programme which Christians ought to support. There neither is nor can be any such programme. I do offer it as *a* Christian social programme, in the sense of being one which seeks to embody Christian principles; but there is no suggestion that if you are a Christian you ought to think these steps wise or expedient. [590]

Fortunately Temple's unfailing good humour never forsook him when, as so often, he became the subject of virulent and unfair attack. Thus when Neville Chamberlain accused him of 'interference' because he maintained that the unemployed ought to have the first claim on any tax remission, he replied by asking whether it was such a grievous offence for a body of responsible persons who thought as he did to say to the Government, 'please don't put us first'. He felt deeply the terrible effects of unemployment upon the whole outlook of the men so deprived, and in 1933 he was responsible, with the help of the Pilgrim Trust, for sponsoring an inquiry into their situation. Its findings led to practical and remedial steps, such as the setting up of occupational centres, and the provision of educational facilities.

Not long before his death, William Temple came into prominence, indeed attracted to himself a great deal of abuse, through a public utterance at a meeting in the Albert Hall, when he shared the platform with the Archbishop of York, the Bishop of Bristol, and Sir Stafford Cripps. The Church, he affirmed, had a duty 'to declare its judgment upon social facts and social movements and to lay down principles which should govern the order of society';

> I should like—he said—to see the banks limited in their lending power to sums equivalent to that which depositors have entrusted to them, and all new credit to be issued by some public authority.

It was up to the State to 'resume the right to control the issue and cancellation of every kind of money'. [591]

For an Archbishop of Canterbury to step down into the technical arena of finance in this way—he addressed the Bank Officers' Guild in similar vein—was almost certainly without precedent, although Temple used to say that Bird Sumner's first book was on economics! (It was, in fact, an article in the *Encyclopaedia Britannica* on the Poor Laws.) His utterance produced a *furore*. The city talked of an 'invasion'. His thoughts were not, of course, original, for he was greatly influenced by the academic economist R. H. Tawney; but if vested interests and some specialists were critical, the general effect of this 'invasion' was to create a new 'image' for the Church by identifying what some regarded as an establishment office with economic reform and the cause of the under-privileged. In this respect he did much to engender a climate of opinion in which the Welfare State was born, and socialism was made to appear respectable. The value of such a transformation is not weakened by the fact that the kind of Christian socialism which he espoused seems to-day over-simplified, too systematic, too logically inferred from first principles, and not always sensitive to the complexity of real situations. Yet if Temple erred in always seeking a principle rooted in some theological truth, modern political thinking may seem to have rushed to the other extreme in its naked pragmatism. Insofar as the Church of England cannot now avoid engaging a social concern it owes much to its ninety-eighth Archbishop.

Temple came to Lambeth in 1942 during the most critical phase of the War when, as Churchill told him, the 'burden' was 'heavier' than for most of his predecessors 'in the long succession from St. Augustine'.[592] It was not a situation that he would have chosen any more than the younger Pitt wished to be a war minister. The appointment was universally approved. *The Times*, as well as the *Daily Herald*, which referred to him as the 'Red Archbishop', gave him a warm welcome. That great critic, Hensley Henson, wrote enthusiastically:

> Temple will garner the harvest of his manifold labours and journeyings. His appeal is beyond all parallel many-sided. The philosopher, the theologian, the social reformer, the party politician, the religious worker, the missionary, the advocate of reunion, the champion of oppressed minorities, the educationalist, the pacifist—all will feel that they have a title to look hopefully to the advent of a sympathizer in the Head of the Church of England.[593]

In a letter to Temple he said he would have made the same choice, though they differed widely in their views.

In spite of Henson's words the Archbishop was himself convinced that the War had to be fought and had to be won. It was the lesser of two evils, and though he accepted that no deployment of force could advance the Kingdom of God, yet he believed its use could offset the forces of evil and help to preserve patterns of elementary justice. Such force must be scaled down to a minimum adequate to secure the ends for which it was deployed. Unnecessary suffering must be avoided, and to indulge it was a sin. Temple, however, had little sympathy with those who would fight a soft war. That way lay defeat, and useless travail. But he never forgot that he was the Archbishop of a Church ministering a universal faith. Thus he declined to give his sanction or authority to prayers for victory as such. This was to presume. Prayer should be directed, in a fallen world, to the doing of God's will: and its character should be such, at public worship, that any right-motivated Christian could join in it, no matter to what nation he belonged. As to individual pacifists, with many of whom he entered into a sensitive correspondence, he sought for a civilized treatment of them by the Government; and went so far as to maintain, with questionable logic, that God constrained some Christians to witness to this minority view in order that during the ambiguities of war the more excellent way of God's Kingdom should not go by default. Doubtless, from Temple's point of view, the logic of this argument would entail that God did not constrain too many! With men in the forces, surprisingly, Temple established a position perhaps unique in an Archbishop. He was not, and never could be, in spite of his inimitable and infectious laugh, hail-fellow-well-met. He was too intelligent, of too great an integrity, to wish to put himself over in this way. To play down to an audience was utterly foreign to his nature. But to members of the forces, looking forward fearfully but in hope to the new world that was to emerge out of the horrors of war, he came to stand for the idea of a more just and more caring society. As such he may well have contributed to the Labour victory in 1945. Although he lacked facility for easy confrontation with individual people he yet appealed, in the mass, to their incipient idealism. Never once during the war did he speak other than for an informed Christian conscience. Crude ideas of vengeance or the view that the war had been sent as a divine judgment he combated in season and out of season. He was also careful to point out that the duty to engage in warfare was civic and did not arise out of a specific Christian obligation. To the chaplains he was a constant inspiration, and his personal letters to them are instinct with wisdom and understanding. The work of the chaplains, he recognized, was never easy; and Temple was only too well aware that in the early days of the war some of them were not recruited from men of the highest calibre. Also the chaplains' department was hampered by its appearing a cog in a vast administrative machine. Temple decided to break through this officialdom by appointing Dr. Leslie Owen, Bishop of Jarrow, as his personal liaison with the Services.

From its inception, Temple was well aware of the power inherent in broadcasting. He accepted the chairmanship of the Central Council for Broadcast Adult Education and also of the Advisory Council from its first meeting in 1935 until the spring of 1937. His own style as a performer, if not calculated to win popularity on this new medium, was clear, intelligent and honest; as he showed when he conducted a service on D Day, 6 June 1944.

During his archiepiscopate Temple was often in touch with ministers of state, usually to try to mitigate some of the inevitable hardships of war so far as they bore in upon individuals or particular classes of persons. Sometimes he was distressed at official caution approaching to 'woodenness'; and he complained on one occasion of Herbert Morrison to the Prime Minister.

> In face of what is happening—he wrote—the kind of arguments addressed to a recent deputation by the Home Secretary seemed so trifling as to be almost profane.[594]

Sometimes he would himself head delegations to ministers, often on behalf of the Jews. In the House of Lords he moved a resolution deploring their massacre in Germany, stressing the terrible urgency of the situation and calling for practical action. His concluding words were impressive in their force and sincerity.

> We know that what we can do is small compared with the magnitude of the problem, but we cannot rest so long as there is any sense among us that we are not doing all that might be done. We have discussed the matter on the footing that we are not responsible for this great evil, that the burden lies on others, but it is always true that the obligations of decent men are decided for them by contingencies which they did not themselves create and very largely by the action of wicked men. The priest and Levite in the parable were not in the least responsible for the traveller's wounds as he lay there by the roadside, and no doubt they had many other pressing things to attend to, but they stand as the picture of those who are condemned for neglecting the opportunity of showing mercy. We at this moment have upon us a tremendous responsibility. We stand at the bar of history, of humanity, and of God.[595]

It was fitting that the World Jewish Congress should, on William Temple's premature death, express its deepest grief.

He never wished, however, to embarrass ministers without real cause, and he understood their sensitivity, maybe over-sensitivity, lest displaced Europeans might be Nazi agents. He always took the view, however, that whether his words were effective or not, the word 'ought to be said for the sake of the principles of justice itself, and I shall continue the advocacy which I have endeavoured to offer hitherto'.[596]

One piece of legislation was passed while Temple was at Lambeth which related to an area of the national life in which Archbishops had become traditionally involved. This was the Education Act of 1944. Here the Archbishop took a realistic approach, and accepted that power was steadily passing from the Church to the State.

> Our main business—he affirmed at his first Diocesan Conference in July 1942—is not, surely, to be fighting a rearguard action in perpetual retreat till we are driven off the field by the competition of the resources of the State, but to take care that we are interpenetrating with our influence all that the State itself is doing.[597]

He was convinced that religion must form a part of any mature education; and although he was no last ditcher, his practical view was that the dual system should for the time being remain, and that the Church must not stampede itself into giving up its own schools. When, in July 1943, the White Paper on educational reconstruction was published, the Archbishop welcomed it as 'a glorious opportunity'. The 1944 Act was not the Bill he himself would have drawn up, yet he was certain that it would be unwise to threaten its passage through the House by numerous amendments. True, many nonconformists remained unhappy with their situation, particularly in small villages which were dominated by the Church school: here the Archbishop did his best to woo them into acceptance. His own speech in the Lords commending the Bill was powerful, perhaps his best performance in a chamber where, curiously, he did not always do himself justice. Maybe his general approach was too intellectually clinical, even for an aristocratic assembly.

v

William Temple moved far from his early ambitions to be a professional philosopher, but he never lost his interest. His predilection, however, was for the philosopher King rather than for the more detached attitude of those who must philosophize simply because they have an itch to do so.

Temple went up to Oxford when Victorian idealism of the Green–Caird vintage was still a lively force: he lived until the reaction against it came in linguistic analysis and logical positivism. His most significant works (in my judgement) are *Mens Creatrix* and *Christus Veritas*; although his most ambitious and inclusive is *Nature, Man and God*, delivered as the Gifford Lectures of 1932. It must be confessed that none of them strikes a vibrant chord in these days. It is not simply that his statement of theism represents an attempt to combine an early idealism with a later realism; but that the psychological climate within which philosophical inquiry is pursued has changed so drastically that its mood now seems alien. Between us and him there is a great gulf fixed. Temple today strikes us as too self-confident; indeed, the very clarity of his statement creates today a curious remoteness, as if at the deeper levels which his thought penetrates things ought not to be so plain. Also it must be confessed that Temple failed to do justice to, or come to grips with, the 'monotonous uniformity' of scientific methodology. He was not basically interested. Such criticisms may mean no more than that when the present fashion in philosophy changes and the dogmatism of logical positivism as well as the limitation of attention inherent in linguistic analysis cease to exercise a near absolute constraint, then his position will again become at least intelligible.

Temple freely and frankly admitted that he was too devout a believer in the Christian revelation to hold in suspended judgement certain basic convictions, which in the nature of the case must constitute question-marks to the philosopher. He did not wish to, nor could he, make his mind a *tabula rasa*; nor did he regard the manufacture of artificial doubt, after the fashion of Descartes, as the sure way to knowledge. 'The primary assurances of religion are the ultimate questions of philosophy.'

> Theology—he wrote in the preface to *Christus Veritas*—accepts [its doctrines] from Religion and shows them to be probable by exhibiting them as the springs of a conception of Reality which, when reached, commends itself as the most satisfying conception which is in fact available. The method of Theology is thus precarious, and is only justified by the result; in the result it is justified, but not on grounds acceptable to Philosophy. The method of Philosophy is secure, but its results comparatively barren. One day, perhaps, the two will perfectly coincide; but that day is not yet; both theologians and philosophers are concerned to hasten it, but meanwhile the motto of Theology must be *Credo ut intelligam*.[598]

Temple's position is personalistic through and through. His key category is the Divine purpose for good 'as realised in the relations of persons with the Absolute Person and with one another'. This deeply held conviction conditions his entire ethical system, and leads to his suggesting in *Nature, Man and God* that the right act is that which on the whole promotes the most good; good being understood as an increase of love and trust between persons. Final reality in the world, and beyond the world, consists of a Society of Spirits constituting a Commonwealth of Value—a view reminiscent of McTaggart. In spite of his idealism, however, Temple never surrendered himself to a Hegelianism which rationalizes the processes of history and sees them as a self-evidently coherent and valuable system. Though strongly drawn to Plato, particularly in his preference, over against Aristotle, for the 'good man' rather than the 'good citizen', he was yet critical of Plato's lack of any real conception of progress. Christianity *makes* sense of the world, which is not the same thing as saying that the world, as it is, is transparently 'sensible'. As much as Marxism, Christianity seeks to change what is, and thereby changes the data from which valid inferences may be drawn.

Here Temple tries to bridge the gulf between the ideal and the actual, and to reconcile intelligible structures with brute facts. Typical of this inclusive approach is his affirmation:

> I do not for a moment believe that our belief in the inherent value of the human person can be maintained except on the basis of the conviction that he is himself the focus of that principle which gives to history its meaning.[599]

Ought Temple, with his rare gifts, to have opted for a vocation to philosophy rather than to the busy life of affairs? It might be said, of course, that action is not incompatible with such a cultivation. Indeed General Smuts asserted that it thrives on it. Yet some have maintained that Temple, a man who might have achieved really high distinction, became at best a most gifted amateur in a specialized field. Perhaps, like Anselm, he ought to have gone into exile! If the philosophers, in the long run, vie with the poets in being 'the trumpets which sing to battle, the unacknowledged legislators of mankind'; and if Christianity urgently needs in the XXth century what Aquinas attempted for it in the XIIIth century, a living rationale, would Temple have done better to limit his territory of interest to a more definite and astringent intellectual quest? Is not the philosopher so much the *rara avis* that one who had the 'feel' and the flair ought wholly to have devoted himself to it?

Questions of this kind, however, have no meaning. In practice William Temple gave his answer and that is the end of it. With his temperament and the ever remembered example of his father, a university chair in philosphy would not have brought permanent fulfilment. Nor, maybe, with all his brilliance did he possess the sustained intellectual curiosity which goes into the making of the true philosopher. He never knew doubt. Thus from his prolific output of some forty odd books, it is the *Readings in St. John's Gospel* (1939, 1940) which still interest and inspire. They are instinct with a devotion to Christ as Lord, and in this devotion reveal the hidden springs of William Temple's life.

> We cannot too strongly or harshly drive this truth into our souls, however eager we may be to trace 'the grace of Jesus Christ' in others, even in atheists. Apart from Him, I can do nothing. All fruit that I ever bear or can bear comes wholly from His life within me. No particle of it is mine as distinct from His. There is, no doubt, some part of his whole purpose that He would accomplish through me; that is my work, my fruit, in the sense that I, and not another, am the channel of His life for this end; but in no other sense. Whatever has its ultimate origin in myself is sin: 'O God, forasmuch as without thee we are not able to please thee, mercifully grant that thy Holy Spirit may in all things direct and rule our hearts, through Jesus Christ our Lord.'

Perhaps it is significant that Frederick Temple should have written to William many years earlier while he was at Oxford:

> I am obliged to confess that from seventeen to five-and-twenty . . . I felt all along like a swimmer who sees no shore before him after swimming, and at last allows himself to be picked up by a ship that seems to be going his way. . . . My passing ship was S. John.[600]

# 4

## GEOFFREY FISHER, THE HEADMASTER
## WITH AN OUTREACH

I

The death of William Temple, on 26 October 1944, was unexpected and devastating. He was then sixty-three years of age; the war was approaching its end; and it was confidently expected that he would lead the Church of England into the post-war years of necessary reconstruction. At his funeral service in Canterbury a rebellious young clergyman, Joseph McCulloch, reflected somewhat sadly: 'We are burying the hopes of the Church of England.' Others now believe that he would not have been at home in the vastly changed world which succeeded the war. Perhaps he should have gone to Lambeth in 1928.

It fell to Winston Churchill, who knew next to nothing about ecclesiastical personnel, to nominate his successor. Three names were widely canvassed. Garbett, Archbishop of York, who had solid virtues, wide experience (he was approaching seventy), coupled with a reputation for sound common sense, and a capacity for hard work; Geoffrey Fisher, Bishop of London, who had won the affection of his clergy and had shown marked powers of administration; and George Bell, Bishop of Chichester.

Geoffrey Fisher relates that he and Garbett discussed the possibility of one of them going to Lambeth. Both confessed to not seeking it; Fisher, in particular, because he disliked making pronouncements, his main interests being pastoral. Each assured the other of his co-operation if he were chosen.

It was George Bell, however, who was generally, if uncritically, assumed to be the most likely. As Davidson's chaplain and author of his monumental biography, he knew Lambeth and its ways with an intimacy which no contemporary could rival. He had also fostered the cause of Christian union; and had thrown himself energetically into the work of the World Council of Churches. Before and during the war, he had bravely championed the cause of the refugees. In the House of Lords he had strongly opposed obliteration bombing, and behind the scenes involved himself in an effort, through Scandinavian mediation, to secure a negotiated peace with the anti-Nazi elements in Germany. No bishop of the Church of England, with the single exception of Temple himself, enjoyed such a reputation on the Continent. He was sixty-one years of age.

But it was Geoffrey Fisher, not Dr. Bell or Cyril Garbett, who went to Canterbury. The general view, almost certainly the correct view, was that Bell's forthrightness in criticizing Government policy in respect of the war strategy did not commend him to the Prime Minister, and had moreover given offence at the Palace. As Alan Don confided to his diary: 'The Prime Minister admires courage and deplores indiscretion; and George has been both courageous and indiscreet in his speeches about the war. . . . He has paid the penalty of his conscientious opposition to the more fire-eating patriots in the House of Lords.'[601] Bell himself was not surprised: 'I have no illusions,' he wrote, 'about Churchill's attitude to me—he is the last person to put me in any position of greater influence.'[602]

This does not mean that these were necessarily the only reasons for his being passed over. Dr. Jasper, in his biography of Bishop Bell, has suggested others, and William Temple seems to have thought of Fisher as his successor. It does, however, raise questions as to the nature of the limitation involved in the process of nomination by the Crown on the advice of the Prime Minister. Constitutionally, of course, the situation is no different from that which obtains in respect of diocesan bishops; but it becomes more obtrusive in relation to the Primate of All England. The Archbishop holds a unique place in English society. He is regarded as the representative mouthpiece of the Church; what he says is news. If his views run counter to governmental policy he can become an embarrassment.

Some might argue that whatever the limitation it is all for the good of Church and nation in that it frankly recognizes facts of power, and is more than compensated for by the other benefits which establishment confers. Yet the fact remains that the State is in a position to refuse as Archbishop one who is likely to prove a too disturbing occupant of St. Augustine's Chair. No committed pacifist could ever find himself at Canterbury—unless it were at a time when war was regarded as an impossibility.

Geoffrey Fisher has given us an account of his interview with Winston Churchill at 10 Downing Street not long after his appointment, an encounter which recalls Tait's in similar circumstances with Disraeli. Both Prime Ministers were innocent of any intimate knowledge of ecclesiastical affairs or persons. In the course of their talk Churchill—perhaps it was a little display of 'one-upmanship'— expressed surprise that the Archbishop had never read Renan's *Vie de Jésus*! Years later, when preaching after his retirement in a village church near Sherborne, Fisher made this shrewd assessment of the faith of the great war leader:

> Churchill had a very real religion, but it was a religion of the Englishman. He had a very real belief in Providence; but it was God as the God with a special care for the values of the British people. There was nothing obscure about this; it was utterly sincere, but not really at all linked on to the particular beliefs which constitute the Christian faith and the life which rests on it.[603]

The new Archbishop, who was enthroned at Canterbury on 19 April 1945, was not well known to the British public except to those who had a particular interest in Church affairs. This was typical of the man. Essentially he made his contribution *through* his job, and it was the needs of the job which conditioned his interests and stimulated his imagination. While Temple was stumping the country on behalf of 'Life and Liberty' and campaigning for social justice, Fisher was quietly adjusting the timetables at Repton School, preaching in the chapel, immunizing sixth-formers against the political enthusiasms of the dedicated Victor Gollancz, and cultivating those intimately pastoral relations with the boys which he found deeply satisfying and did so well. He was, in fact, the sixth Archbishop, out of the last eight, to have been a headmaster. On Fisher's own admission, he preferred not to glimpse the too distant scene: the task in hand commanded his full attention. Always his main interests were personal, pastoral and administrative. He had an excellent memory for people, and as headmaster, bishop, and Archbishop, he was free from pomposity, did everything without fuss, and was uniformly friendly. His limitation was that he tended to see things too clearly; and to do this by restricting his field of interest and attention. The result was that when others dithered as they sorted out priorities, he had little apparent difficulty in making up his mind and acting accordingly.

At Oxford he secured a triple first, yet he had neither the instinct nor the intellectual curiosity of the scholar. His own approach was pragmatic and he wrote of himself:

> I have never tried to think out a considered plan of what I ought to do through the years; I have never tried to formulate a policy that I ought to follow; I have just gone forward and taken up each task, or group of tasks, as they appeared to demand attention, and no doubt there came to be some kind of pattern forming in my mind into which they all fitted.[604]

For this reason the following short study will turn from one subject to another as the Archbishop engaged himself in it.

Though naturally tolerant, disagreement with his undoubtedly reasonable views always surprised him. Maybe this was partly due to his being appointed headmaster of Repton, in succession to William Temple, at the age of twenty-eight, so that he missed the early struggle to arrive and the chastening lessons which subordination engenders. Canon Purcell in his *Fisher of Lambeth* writes that he was unfortunate in coming to one office after another at times when there was a 'clearing up' operation to be done—at Repton after the permissive Temple; in London after the near liturgical anarchy of Winnington-Ingram; at Canterbury after the devastation and havoc of war. Such situations were not of his own choosing, but the challenge they presented was not uncongenial. Being a bishop, he himself used to say, was not unlike being a headmaster.

After beginning to feel that he was a forgotten man at Repton—he was there eighteen years—he was appointed Bishop of Chester in 1932. There he was active in getting about his diocese, and worked vigorously with Prebendary Kirk on an industrial mission in Birkenhead. He became Bishop of London in 1939, succeeding the saintly but not very efficient Winnington-Ingram who had been there for nearly forty years. War conditions were doing much to unsettle and disrupt the diocese, and Fisher determined to make it generally more disciplined than it had been for many years. This was not unreasonable, for even Archbishop Temple had maintained that the Church of England needed a greater degree of internal order. Yet Fisher's efforts in London, in particular to secure liturgical conformity, probably indicate that here he was living in a world which was in process of passing away. His chaplain, F. C. Synge, shrewdly suggests that Dr. Fisher was unaware of new movements making for reform, and therefore failed to realize that 'liturgical conformity was never again going to be obtainable within the framework of Cranmer's scholarship and presuppositions'.[605]

## II

When Fisher became Archbishop, he characteristically decided to take stock of the situation around him by asking certain questions. How were the clergy paid? Here, with Trustram Eve (now Lord Silsoe), First Church Estates Commissioner, he did much to improve what were almost impossible conditions. What were the clergy preaching? Which theological colleges were in a healthy state? How could order and discipline be secured in the parishes?

If the clergy, however, were to be law-abiding, so Fisher's mind worked, they must know clearly what the law was, and this law must be relevant and reasonable. Hence the revision of the canons of 1604, into which Fisher threw himself with real dedication, and which he himself described as 'the most absorbing and all-embracing topic of my whole archiepiscopate'. The idea of such a work was not new. It had been considered by Convocation over a period of years, and engaged the attention of a commission under Archbishop Garbett which produced a revised set of canons in 1947. From the beginning Dr. Bell, Bishop of Chichester, was sceptical as to the worthwhileness of the undertaking and wrote to the Archbishop of York:

> I should not be in favour of attempting to secure a comprehensive Code, for I do not think that it is in accordance with the history and genius of the Church of England.[606]

Dr. Fisher, however, thought otherwise.

> I had no doubt whatever—he commented later—that this report must be at once acted upon, even though it would be an enormous undertaking; first because here, after years of hesitation, a great commission had at last brought a proposal into practical politics. But, more than that, because (with the instincts of a headmaster) I knew that it was absolutely essential to the well-ordering and self-respect of the Church of England to have Canons which could and should be obeyed. The lack of order had become quite dreadful.[607]

If the idea of such a revision was not new, it was yet Archbishop Fisher's patience and persistence which finally carried this mammoth enterprise to near completion.

Was he wise to give this matter such an over-riding priority? A case may be made that in the challenging years after the war, when great institutions were being submitted to reappraisal, what the Church of England needed was the steadying influence which a known law, constitutionally passed through Convocation and Assembly, could alone bring. The opposite conclusion can equally be drawn, namely that a time of change and necessary experimentation does not provide the *milieu* within which it is proper to impose a fixed law upon so subtle an institution as *Ecclesia Anglicana*. Such a criticism was not met by the setting up of a permanent committee to secure subsequent revision when needed. Nor does the present nexus of Church and State make any fully coherent body of canon law attainable, even if it were desirable. This was clearly seen in the failure to regulate canonically the seal of the confessional.

Dr. Walter Matthews, Dean Emeritus of St. Paul's, believes that though there might have been a real need for some clarification, a fatal mistake was made when the detailed legislation of 1604 was taken as a model for 1950. The kind of discipline which might have worked happily was a series of principles laying down in a broad way the purposes and ideals of the pastoral office, as understood in the Anglican branch of the Catholic Church, and beyond that almost nothing.[608]

In the opinion of the author, the revision of canon law consumed a great deal of Convocation's time to very little purpose.

In such an exercise, Geoffrey Fisher's skill as President of Convocation and Chairman of the Church Assembly was seen at its most expert. Unlike the majority of his predecessors, he thoroughly enjoyed these sessions and followed everything that happened with rapt attention. He took care to master the rules of procedure, thereby getting the better of his only rival in this field, J. K. Douglas.

By temperament he was a born committee man, interested in the ways that institutions function, and concerned to make them efficient. He enjoyed the authority and the personal involvement which being in the chair gave him; and he kept business going forward steadily. What bored Lang gave him interest.

It was very often in the dull moments or in the casual asides, that one got the best glimpses of where people's thinking was going. I thoroughly enjoyed every minute of it. There was nobody who didn't contribute something in his speech, and they on their side felt, I think, all of them, that I was a real member of the Church Assembly, not presiding, but in with them, in all the matters and business that they had to handle. And there was, I'm quite sure, a trust between us which had a very great positive value.[609]

When Geoffrey Fisher first presided over the Church Assembly it suffered from one overriding defect. It was a democratic assembly but lacked anything analogous to a cabinet committed to getting measures through. To introduce a piece of legislation into the Assembly was like launching a paper boat on to the Whitestone Pond at Hampstead. It usually ended becalmed in the centre or drifting aimlessly around the periphery. An attempt to deal with this practical problem was made under Geoffrey Fisher when the Standing Committee, in addition to being responsible for ordering the business, was also required to advise on policy. Fisher was hopeful, and later commented:

This was a grand step forward; it gave a new feeling to the Church Assembly, to have this amount of central direction. It

might have been the beginning of a curia around the Archbishop but, I think very wisely, after my time the Archbishop
of York was made chairman of the Standing Committee, thus
relieving the Archbishop of Canterbury, and giving the Standing Committee a valuable sense of independence. Matters of
great importance came up, and if there had not been a Standing
Committee to review them, and keep them together in a single
survey I don't know where one could have got; and the fact
that there were bishops, clergy and laity on the Standing
Committee was a protection against it becoming a curia.[610]

A traditional responsibility of the Archbishop's was to preside at
the Bishops' Meetings, which Hensley Henson earlier described as an
'extra-legal . . . normal and recognized part of the ecclesiastical
system'.[611] These go back a long way, certainly to the XVIIth
century. Some of his colleagues felt that Geoffrey Fisher tended to be
dictatorial and to give too direct a lead. Though he himself admitted
that in his later years he became excessively talkative—it was this
among other things which persuaded him that he ought to retire—
he would not admit to this particular charge.

I have no doubt that I was thought to be driving them too
much because, as a matter of fact, inevitably, there are things
in which one has to give a lead if one is to get anywhere at all.
I never did try to drive them too much. Far from it.[612]

His usual custom was to introduce a subject with a brief historical
preamble; and after each bishop had spoken he (to quote his own
words) 'summed up and, no doubt, in the summing up, I pointed to
what was my own conclusion as to the best next step. That was what
I was there for as chairman. . . . Archbishop Lang did far too much
of it.'[613]

The proceedings at Bishops' Meetings were always regarded as
confidential. Many were the occasions, however, when Archbishops
across the years found it necessary to reproach individual bishops for
apparent breaches of the rules. Archbishop Davidson, who was
himself a veritable oyster, administered a sharp rebuke to Moule of
Durham for referring in a letter to his clergy to a decision agreed at
such a meeting concerning the *English Hymnal*.

I have been trying almost *ad nauseam*—he wrote—to reiterate
the necessity of our observing as absolutely confidential everything that passes within these walls on such occasions.[614]

The propriety of an attitude of this kind on a matter of public concern to the Church must surely be questioned. It was this secrecy,

particularly with the growth of a representative system of government in the Church Assembly, which has increasingly made Bishops'
Meetings subject to grave suspicion. With typical openness, Geoffrey
Fisher called together a group of Assembly critics, showed them past
agendas, and explained the nature of the meetings, stressing that
their purpose was to secure co-ordination of episcopal action. The
problem, however, remains, since the relation of the Bishops' Meetings to the new General Synod has yet to be worked out. Perhaps
there will prove to be an inherent, if not inbuilt, resistance to
'democratizing' the English episcopate.

Dr. Fisher was no speculative theologian, and his entry into this
sphere was dictated by his office in response to practical needs. His
own faith was essentially simple, sincere and uncomplicated.

Reference has been made earlier to Dr. Barnes, Bishop of Birmingham—to his intellectual integrity, his preoccupation with the
religion and science controversy; his deep (and justifiable) conviction
that many cultivated people had unnecessary intellectual obstacles
put in their way by obscurantist churchmen. In 1947 there appeared
Bishop Barnes's *The Rise of Christianity*. It was not one of his best
books, nor was it a field in which he had mastered his materials.
Even his transparent honesty could not disguise the fact that into an
allegedly historic thesis too much *a priori* thinking had been uncritically injected. Lambeth was inundated with protests and with
calls for the Bishop's resignation. The consequent publicity led to the
Bishop writing a series of popular articles in the *Sunday Pictorial*,
which Dr. Fisher endeavoured to counter by persuading the editor
to allow Dr. Blunt, Bishop of Bradford, to reply. The Archbishop,
however, in the face of a great deal of pressure, felt that he must
himself deal with the matter in his Presidential Address at the
October Convocation. Had he not done so, there would almost
certainly have been a proposal in the Lower or Upper House for
some more drastic action to be taken. It was precisely this that the
Archbishop wished to avoid—as did Archbishop Ramsey some sixteen years later in relation to the Bishop of Woolwich and his
*Honest to God*. Perhaps what Fisher said may best be summarized in a
quotation:

> A bishop from the nature of his office, by reason of his responsi-
> bilities to the Church and to its members, is, I think, called upon
> to judge himself by, and to be judged by, stricter standards
> than may be allowed to others. So long as he retains that office,
> he must satisfy himself, and seek to satisfy others, that he is
> adequately and faithfully expressing in his teaching the general
> doctrines of the Church and their scriptural basis which he is

494

placed by his office to defend and promote. The Bishop of Birmingham may be satisfied that his teaching in this book conforms to those requirements. I would have no trial in this matter: but I must say, for my part, that I am not so satisfied. If his views were mine, I should not feel that I could still hold episcopal office in the Church.[615]

If justification is needed for the double standard which such words might seem to suppose, it may be found in the fact that no further move was taken against the Bishop in Convocation.

I trust—the Archbishop said—that what I have said, with the full sense of the responsibility of my office, may serve to minimize the harm and give to members of the Church such reassurance as they may need.[616]

To give reassurance and to resist any erosion of the faith is one of the traditional roles of the Archbishop's office, not always easily discharged when at the same time he wishes to preserve the comprehensive character of the Church of England. The Archbishop wisely did not say that Bishop Barnes *ought* to resign.

With Hewlett Johnson, Dean of Canterbury, Fisher's relations were somewhat of a piece with those of Cosmo Lang, except that more heat and mutual irritation were engendered. The causes of friction multiplied as the Dean's travels behind the Iron Curtain and throughout the Commonwealth became more extensive. The Archbishop vented his displeasure on a number of occasions—when 'the Red Dean' visited Hungary in 1948; when he quoted a remark made by Jan Mazaryk on the evening of Munich, 'Halifax, that lackey, that errand boy of Hitler!'; when he escorted Mr. Malik, the Soviet Ambassador, 'an unbeliever', around the Cathedral on Easter Day; and when he published a pamphlet accusing the Americans of resorting to germ warfare in China.[617] Following the precedent of Lang, Dr. Fisher issued a declaration that 'The Archbishop of Canterbury has neither responsibility for what the Dean may say or do, nor the power to control it'.[618] On one occasion he wrote to the Dean suggesting that he resign, but it is not true, as Hewlett Johnson alleged, that in the House of Lords he seconded a motion that the Crown 'should withdraw my charter as Dean of Canterbury and discharge me'.[619]

Such constant but unsuccessful efforts to control the Dean undoubtedly clouded relations between the Archbishop and the Cathedral, though Hewlett Johnson writes in his *Searching for Light*:

Fisher and I were diametrically opposed in our outlook on politics; he was a very kind man personally.[620]

495

Dr. Fisher in retirement recalls him as 'a charming, gracious, friendly, pastoral man, once he was off his main subject of socialism and Russia'.[621] Perhaps the pity was that they never conversed frankly with each other as man to man, at least that is how the Dean saw it. It was a typically English situation, not without its comic side.

Barnes and Hewlett Johnson illustrate how far removed (mercifully) the *Ecclesia Anglicana* is from a papal system of authority. Long may this continue!

Geoffrey Fisher's influence on episcopal nominations was not wholly salutary, the more so since his power here was probably greater than that of his immediate predecessors, and certainly greater than that of XIXth-century archbishops, when the position of Parliament in ecclesiastical affairs was stronger, the Prime Minister better informed, and the Sovereign more involved. Unexpectedly the increased significance of the Prime Minister's Patronage Secretary, which began with Gladstone's appointment of E. W. Hamilton, has served to increase rather than diminish the Archbishop's influence.

The usual practice was for the Archbishop to put two or three names before Downing Street with his own order of preference. On occasions the Prime Minister might suggest a name not on the list, but did not proceed to nomination without the full concurrence of the Archbishop. Indeed Lord Attlee admitted that he never made a recommendation to a bishopric unless it had archiepiscopal approval. While Geoffrey Fisher was at Lambeth the practice sprang up of consulting the Archbishop about deaneries. Dr. Fisher was undoubtedly well informed and a man of great conscientious application; but the opinion may be hazarded that the position of dominance which he established had its effect upon the character of the episcopate. This certainly was the view of Dr. Bell. The gifts required in a bishop are not necessarily those expected in a good housemaster. Excessive influence exercised by one man in ecclesiastical appointments, especially when that one man happens to be Archbishop of Canterbury, can weaken the subsequent independence of those appointed.

III

When Geoffrey Fisher became Archbishop one of his first tasks was to determine the date of the Lambeth Conference which had been postponed from 1940 by reason of the War. He decided that 1948 was the earliest possible year for it to assemble. There was some doubt, however, as to how many, particularly among the American bishops who had felt somewhat outsiders at the 1930 Conference, would wish to attend. Fisher had developed a close friendship with Sherrill, Presiding Bishop of the Episcopal Church, and on his advice paid a visit with Mrs. Fisher to the United States in 1946, the intention being to put the Lambeth Conference on the map. He certainly succeeded. His first stop was Winnipeg, where he addressed a synod of the Church of Canada; and then on to Philadelphia for the General Convention of the American Episcopal Church. Here he dilated at length on the Anglican Church in this new phase of its history, particularly its international character.

> The Anglican Communion—he said—embraces many national churches, provincial in name or character, and a large number of dioceses not yet organized as separate provinces or national churches. They are spread all over the world. The name Anglican is already a misnomer; it indicates their remote origin, but it does not at all describe their present condition. They are indigenous churches, not only here and in England and in the British dominions, but in India, China, Japan, Ceylon, and Africa, East and West.[622]

So the 1948 Lambeth Conference met, and it produced, probably, one of the most weighty and informed of all reports. The devastation of war introduced a note of realism; the determination to create a more purposeful world conditioned a great deal of its corporate thinking. It was not the fault of those who deliberated that the vast theological changes which were destined later to approach explosion point were then only in process of fission; and, equally, that the fuller implications of the advance of scientific technology were then only on the way. Some of its resolutions in the social sphere still have value, and its over-all attitude to communism, if adopted more generally, would have saved churchmen from the crudities of the stark alternative, 'Christ or Communism'. The Archbishop gave to the Conference warmth and friendliness, high expertise in chairmanship, and a practical approach. He was anxious to avoid time-wasting and the discussion of nice points which could not lead to concrete action. As a result certain practical decisions were taken. The South India reunion scheme was given an over-all, if limited, blessing; the Anglican Congresses were to be summoned mid-way between the ten-yearly meetings of the Lambeth Conference; the Anglican Advisory Committee for Missionary Strategy was set up, one of its tasks being to establish at Canterbury a central college for the Anglican Communion, which, alas, has not survived. No particularly profound theological thinking came out of the Conference, or, indeed, was to be expected. Yet it did try to keep its feet firmly on the ground.

The Lambeth Conference was followed by the Archbishop's second visit to America for the General Convention of the Episcopal Church in 1952, on which occasion the sermon that he preached in Christ Church, Boston, was broadcast on radio and television throughout that vast country. It was an opportunity not to be missed. Fisher made much of the common heritage which the United States shared, with England in particular and with Europe in general. Yet he gave a solemn warning that the civilization of the West, painfully built up over the centuries, could 'fail [as] the casual result of ordinary people letting their absorption with the cares and riches and bustle of this world shut their eyes to God'.

The next trip was to the General Assembly of the World Council of Churches in Evanston, and to the newly established Anglican Congress at Minnesota, where the Archbishop sat beside Bishop Henry Sherrill, who, as presiding Bishop of the Episcopal Church of America, acted as chairman.

His last American trip was to the Central Committee of the World Council of Churches in 1957. Fisher admired the exuberance and the questing spirit of the Americans. Equally they appreciated his resilience, his unaffected friendliness, and his wit. His visits were great personal triumphs. Their long-term effects in strengthening the links between the two Churches is more open to question. In part this was due to his friendship with Bishop Sherrill who was distrusted by the main body of American bishops as aiming to establish a Primacy in their own country corresponding to Canterbury. Canon Max Warren, formerly secretary of the Church Missionary Society, writes:

> Much that has happened in the relation between the Churches derives from this friendship! What I think can be said about the relationship of the Church in North America and the Archbishop of Canterbury is that the intrusion of our Archbishops into the American scene has not been calculated to enhance the position of *Alterius Orbis Papa*.[623]

However, be this as it may, the immediate effect of Geoffrey Fisher's visits was to help the Archbishop to take his second Lambeth Conference of 1958 in his stride. He knew the personnel and they, for the most part, knew him. The subjects dealt with still had a familiar ring; but there was an even greater sense of urgency.

Reconciliation was the general theme, as it applied to relations between the Churches and within the wider comity of nations.

Church unity was therefore discussed, and a more tidy distinction made—the Archbishop was fertile, sometimes almost fatally so in making distinctions of this kind—between full communion and inter-communion.

Nuclear weapons had now been added to the armoury of war, and a statement about them duly found its way into the Encyclical Letter.

> The use of nuclear weapons is repugnant to the Christian conscience—it declared—Some of us would go further and regard such use in any circumstances as morally indefensible, while others of us, with equal conviction, would hold that so long as such weapons exist there are circumstances in which to use them might be preferable to political enslavement. We believe that the abolition of nuclear weapons of indiscriminate effect and destructive power by international agreement is an essential step towards the abolition of war itself. So we appeal to all Christians to press through their governments for the banning of such weapons, accepting such limitations of their own sove-reignty as may be required to ensure inspection and control, so that no government may make them.[624]

Particularly significant was the report on the home and family with its resolutions on contraception, which were to assume an added significance after the issue by Pope Paul VI of his ill-fated encyclical *Humanae Vitae*. One practical decision emerged from the Conference representing the growing self-consciousnesness of the Anglican Communion: the appointment of Stephen Bayne as Anglican Executive Officer. The choice was indeed a happy one, though the office proved a difficult one to discharge. At the last session, Bishop Sherrill made a presentation, referring to the fact that, earlier in life, the Archbishop had had 'something to do with a boys' school'. In reply Fisher defended headmasters, his closing words being 'Class dismissed'.[625]

Of all Archbishops of Canterbury, Fisher was by far the most travelled, which led to his being a familiar figure throughout the whole Anglican Communion. This was a matter of temperament and inclination allied to increasingly fast aircraft. A brief list of such journeys gives some idea of the vast distances he and Mrs. Fisher covered. In 1950 he went to New Zealand and Australia (thus becoming the first Archbishop to visit the Antipodes); in 1951 to West Africa; in 1955 to Central Africa; in 1959 to India, Japan, and Korea; in 1960 to Nigeria (for its Independence Day celebrations, by request) and East Africa. The specific purpose of these extensive tours varied, but all were in a measure good-will missions. They

R

enabled the Archbishop to meet many people and to offer friendship and understanding. With him the human interest always pre-dominated. In Sydney he was able to be of practical help and to speak his mind freely on the party divisions which had so far pre-vented, over a period of forty years, the setting up of a self-governing constitution. The visit to New Zealand had particular significance, for it was a hundred years earlier that Archbishop Sumner had given his benediction to the pilgrims from Canterbury on their departure for the southern hemisphere. The visit to West Africa was under-taken at the Archbishop's own suggestion in order to inaugurate the new province. Four years later he was back again to discharge the same responsibility in respect of Central Africa. The Archbishop was percipient enough on these African tours to become aware of certain things which did not augur well for the future. At Zomba or Blantyre, for example, some of the settlers were caught up in what he later described as 'the schizophrenia present among the white population', and refused their club-house for an inter-racial gather-ing.[626] In 1960 he was back to inaugurate the Province of East Africa.

Constitution-making was for him a congenial occupation, and he did it well. This was fortunate, since all the new provinces of the Anglican Communion which came into existence after the Second World War—West Africa, East Africa, Uganda—the jurisdiction of the Archbishopric in Jerusalem, and the East Asian Episcopal Conference, belong to his archiepiscopate. Wisely, he appreciated the need to divest himself of authority for the African and Asian areas of the Communion, and it is probably here that historians will see his most enduring work, maybe confirming Archbishop de Mel's description of him as a modern Theodore in the wider context of the Anglican communion. This is high praise.

The most spectacular of all Dr. Fisher's journeys was that under-taken not long before his retirement. The inspiration for it came entirely from within himself 'in one flash . . . in my study'. He saw it as 'a whole thing exhibiting in one manner the unity of the Churches in the Church Militant already existing'.[627]

The idea was to visit Jerusalem as the guest of the Anglican Arch-bishop; and while there to call on the Orthodox Patriarch of Jerusalem and the heads of the other churches in the Middle East; then to move on to Constantinople and call on his All Holiness, Athenagoras I, Oecumenical Patriarch of the Orthodox Church; and finally to spend a few days in Rome and to make a courtesy call on His Holiness, Pope John XXIII.

Such a journey, no matter how spontaneous, could not have been conceived independently of contemporary trends working within

Christendom. With the Orthodox Churches, Fisher had made an intimate relationship through his friendship with Archbishop Germanos, who was the representative of the Oecumenical Patriarch in London. Pope John XXIII had already indicated a willingness to open windows. A Roman Catholic observer, Monsignor Willebrands, Secretary of the new Secretariat for Christian Unity, attended the Central Committee of the World Council of Churches at St. Andrews, as an observer.

Geoffrey Fisher carried himself on this exhausting journey with his usual poise and 'openness'. Unemotional as he usually was in public, and, indeed, suspicious of excessive display, he was visibly moved in Jerusalem. Describing his reception in the Church of the Holy Sepulchre he employed (for him) somewhat unusual language:

> I cannot describe the church. I hardly saw it. I remember the first place I knelt—a stone on which Our Lord's body was supposed to have rested after being taken down from the cross. Why can I not recall this with exactitude? Because throughout, in a strange way, I became mentally passive; feeling a kind of victim with Our Lord. For from the moment I entered the church, I was engulfed in a great crowd of Orthodox monks and Franciscans and others, who surrounded me and, almost literally, carried me from place to place. . . . The whole thing was an astonishing outpouring of every kind of excited motion, all flowing round and over me, not me as a person, but as a kind of centre point of that triumphal showing forth of Christian fellowship.[628]

At Istanbul he greeted the Oecumenical Patriarch and the Patriarch of the Armenian Church, and had a talk with the Apostolic Delegate, an office which Pope John had held many years previously.

As the grand climax of the tour came the courtesy call on Pope John. The significant interview with the Pope took place on 2 December 1960.

> . . . We greeted each other at once in the ordinary, friendly way. We shook hands and smiled at each other. . . . He began the conversation with a rather elaborate story, designed, I think, to ease the opening of the conversation. It seemed to me it was going on a long time; so at a convenient moment I broke in by saying: 'Yes, Your Holiness, that reminds me of—' something that invited a reply. As soon as he realised that this was a to and fro conversation, going wherever the winds or the Holy Spirit took it, he delightedly played it like that. So we talked as two

happy people, who had seen a good deal of the world and of life, and of the Churches, glad to talk together I cannot remember how the conversation went, except that it flowed without the slightest difficulty.[629]

He did remember, however, that when the Pope read in English a passage from an address he had given and used the phrase '. . . the time when our separated brethren should return to the Mother Church', he interjected, 'Your Holiness, not *return.*' Puzzled, the Pope replied: 'Not return? Why not?' To which the Archbishop said: 'None of us can go backwards. We are each now running on parallel courses; we are looking forward, until, in God's good time, our two courses approximate and meet.'

After a moment's hesitation the Pope replied, 'You are right.'

'From that moment,' the Archbishop commented, 'as far as I know, he and the Vatican never talked about our returning to a past situation, and looking backwards for our objective.'[630]

It was the first time an Archbishop of Canterbury had visited the Holy See since Archbishop Arundel made the journey in 1397. Owing to the caution of the Vatican no official photographs were taken. Even the *Daily Mirror* regretted this embargo. The visit constituted a significant break-through, the end of which is not yet.

It was part of the Archbishop's general approach to turn his attention, almost prosaically, to the matter in hand. In one such matter he showed a timely initiative. The reference is to his well-known Cambridge sermon.

We have already seen how the *Letter* issued after the Lambeth Conference of 1920 led to the *Outline of a Reunion Scheme*, which delineated from one point of view the future Church which 'would have a ministry fully unified for its own internal life on the basis of episcopal ordination'. In 1941 there was issued *A Reply of the Free Church Federal Council* which, while friendly, was yet critical of the *Outline*, and suggested that the approach it envisaged was not the way to union. With the end of hostilities, Archbishop Fisher asked both the Congress of the Free Church Federal Council and the Methodist Conference whether they wished the matter to be re-opened. He also requested two groups, catholic and evangelical within the Church of England, to give an opinion as to the fundamental differences between their two positions. Before any of these could report, he preached his sermon in Great St. Mary's Church before the University of Cambridge on 3 November 1946.[631] Canon Purcell describes it as 'seminal, of lasting importance' and as opening 'the way towards far-reaching discussions and explorations.'[632] The timing was not accidental.

The Archbishop confessed to a feeling that there was a certain reluctance to carry on with the work of unity. Indeed, a distinguished scholar had recently affirmed that schemes for reunion should be postponed until there was time for further theological thinking and corporate prayer. He himself, however, questioned the wisdom of thus beginning all over again; and believed that the real difficulty lay in the fact that the way ahead had been conceived in constitutional terms, 'by acceptance of which they become one'. What he now proposed was that

> while the folds remain distinct, there should be a movement towards a free and unfettered exchange of life in worship and sacrament between them as there is already of prayer and thought and Christian fellowship—in short, that they should grow towards that full communion with one another, which already in their separation they have with Christ.[633]

This process would best be fostered if, accepting that in the reunited church of the future there must be provision for episcopacy, for a Council of Presbyters, and for the Congregation of the Faithful, each Church should try to take into itself these characteristics of a fully authentic *Ecclesia*. By this means the stalemate which he feared would be avoided, and in a moving passage he concluded:

> Have we the wisdom, the humility, the love and the spirit of Christ sufficient for such a venture as I have suggested? If there were agreement on it, I would thankfully receive, at the hands of others, their commission in their accustomed form and in the same way confer our own; that is the mutual exchange of love and enrichment to which Lambeth, 1920, called us.[634]

The General Purposes Committee of the Free Church Federal Council immediately responded to the Archbishop's plea. In company with Alfred Rawlinson, Bishop of Derby, Geoffrey Fisher received representatives of the Free Churches at Lambeth on 16 January 1947; and as a result it was agreed that the individual Free Churches should be invited to hold conversations with the Church of England along the lines of the Archbishop's suggestions. Such conversations took place over the next five years, the Archbishop being kept in close touch with them through the Bishop of Derby and Stephen Neill. Of particular significance were the conversations with the Methodist Church, during the course of which the Archbishop was often consulted by Dr. Harold Roberts and Harry Carpenter, Bishop of Oxford. They led to the publication of a report in 1963, proposing that union should be achieved in two stages. It was not a scheme which Geoffrey Fisher, now retired, felt able to approve, and its rejection by the Convocations of York and Canterbury, when Dr. Ramsey had become Archbishop, shows how difficult it is for a Church, distinguished by its comprehensiveness, to come to a common mind. Wisely or not, Dr. Fisher made public his own opinions on developments in *Covenant and Reconciliation: A Critical Examination* (1967), in which he condemned making the choice for amalgamation before there was full communion. This particular chapter in ecumenical relations, however, still awaits its conclusion.

Dr. Fisher's predecessor had made it inevitable that no Archbishop could live his life, or order his days, independently of the World Council of Churches. Its existence, together with its national counterparts, gave a new dimension to the archiepiscopal office. On 23 October 1948, there took place the first Assembly of the World Council of Churches at Amsterdam, where the widest possible ecumenical outreach was represented, though the Roman Catholics and the Orthodox Churches within the Russian orbit were conspicuously absent. It so 'happened', to quote Dr. Fisher's own words, 'that the Archbishop was in the chair'. His reaction to the occasion can be best given in his own words:

> It was a great moment. Some chairmen would at that time have become emotional in their prayers, their thanksgivings, their loud *Te Deums*. Being myself a very restrained person, I had to say something, and said a few words of unpremeditated prayer: but it was all on a very quiet and deep, and unostentatious note.[635]

Fisher was fearful, however, lest the World Council should seek to initiate any doctrinal changes. 'If the Council tried to force any changes in our Church we should clear out,' he said. The sentiment, if not the language, was that of Randall Davidson, and it reflected the mood of many bishops at the time of the first Lambeth Conference.

> The World Council of Churches—he summed it up—is not a Church. It is none of its business to negotiate a union between Churches.[636]

But he worked hard for it.

Behind the World Council of Churches, as its constituent members, were the National Councils. Fisher became chairman of that in Britain when he was appointed Archbishop. As a chairman he was anxious for all to have their say; though at the same time concerned, perhaps over-concerned, to prevent the Council straying too widely, and involving itself in political activities as such. It was a truly archiepiscopal reaction.

> Various views were possible among Christians—he commented after his retirement—and in any case we on the British Council of Churches did not bear the responsibility for political action. It was not for us to say 'This shall be' or 'That shall be'. Only those with the full range of responsibilities and knowledge could do that in the political sphere. And therefore all we ought ever to do was to provide for a report by those who were specially knowledgeable, discuss the report, and then to commend it to the Churches, and possibly direct that it be brought to the notice of the responsible Government department.[637]

Maybe there was reason, particularly in the early days, for the B.C.C. to be cautious: but in matters of political decision one may be cautious overmuch. There can be no more dangerous delusion than that 'the Government knows best'. Often it does not.

IV

As Archbishop of Canterbury, and through no choice of his own, Dr. Fisher inevitably became, for the first time in his life, a national figure. Though he had confessed earlier to Garbett that he did not like making public pronouncements, he certainly overcame this inhibition, commenting widely, often wisely, on public affairs both at home and abroad—learning the art as he went along. Opportunities, sought and unsought, came his way in abundance. In Australia, for example, he made some percipient remarks on the rigorous demands which the Welfare State makes on its citizens:

> In fact, the Welfare State calls at every point for a far higher level of citizenship from all of us than ever before. It requires citizens who put what they do for others before what they get for themselves; who are keen to put more into the common pool than they take out of it. This higher level of citizenship is essential if the Welfare State is to work: and if it does not, the successor State will almost certainly be some sort of tyranny. In this field of citizenship, the plain Christian has his plain Christian duties.[638]

The opening of the Festival of Britain and the General Election of 1951 saw him preaching at special services in St. Paul's Cathedral.[639]

On 2 September 1956, he gave a sermon at a Trades Union Congress in Brighton, his theme being 'Partnership in Industry'.[640] An outstanding success was the speech at the dinner given in his honour by the Pilgrims on 16 November 1954. It was an occasion when he was particularly sensitive to his audience. In lighter vein, he recalled how on one occasion, when he had the privilege of welcoming President Eisenhower, the General turned to him and said: 'I don't suppose the Archbishop of Canterbury has ever read the Declaration of Independence,' to which there came the instant reply: 'And I am sure that the President has never read Magna Carta.'[641]

On various social questions where ethical issues seemed to be involved he often made pointed comments, if of unequal merit. When the Wolfenden Report appeared in 1957 he issued a critique in his Canterbury Diocesan Notes, making a distinction between a crime and a sin, the latter, so he claimed, being 'objective, outside and beyond man's fallibilities and self illusions, not, like the law, man-made'. In co-operation with the Archbishop of York, he set up a commission which reported on the moral aspects of artificial insemination, and himself commented on it in his Presidential Address to Convocation in January 1958. In harmony with the Commission's report he maintained that A.I.D. was a breach of marriage, and that legislation should make resort to it a criminal offence. He also gave evidence before a Home Office Inquiry.

Though he was anxious that the British Council of Churches should not offer political advice which could embarrass the Government, he proved himself by no means a 'yes-man'. During the War, as Chairman of the Public Morality Council, he opposed the giving of instruction on contraceptives to young troops without at the same time urging moral discipline. In the House of Lords, in connexion with the Small Lotteries and Gaming Bill, on 26 April 1956, he expressed himself in the most forthright terms against the institution of Premium Bonds.

> Private gain—he said—divorced from responsibility in management or workers or anywhere else is anti-social. The Government's great concern must be that money gained shall be truly earned and that money earned shall be used reasonably, thoughtfully and for the general good.[642]

At the time of the Kabaka's deportation from Uganda, the Archbishop was active behind the scenes, writing several letters to the Colonial Secretary, thus exercising a decisive influence on Government policy. In this way he showed how an Archbishop of Canterbury, through his links with the great missionary societies, is able to bring a specialized knowledge to bear on problems which politicians have to wrestle with from a different angle. Examples could be multiplied. Geoffrey Fisher made a direct personal approach to Mr. Harold Wilson on the British Government's policy in regard to aid to under-developed countries. Canon Max Warren writes:

> I think it can be fairly claimed that the fact that Britain's aid in this connexion has not been reduced, despite our economic crisis, owes something to the force with which the Archbishop made his point.[643]

On some matters of quite major political importance, Fisher found himself in opposition to the Government. This was not due to any particular political affiliation; but because he weighed each situation on its merits, and when he had made up his mind, usually declared it. Sometimes, as was inevitable, he blundered. The controversy arising out of his invitation to Archbishop Makarios to attend the Lambeth Conference as an observer was not handled very well. It was certainly proper for such an invitation to be sent, and not to have done so would undoubtedly have offended the Orthodox Churches. The result, however, was one of those unreasoning outbursts of public resentment which an Archbishop of Canterbury is in a unique position to attract, especially when a patriotic drum can be struck. *The Times*, innocent of the real facts, pontificated that

> although the Government were informed about the Archbishop of Canterbury's invitation to Archbishop Makarios to visit the Lambeth Conference, there is reason to think that it has deeply embarrassed and displeased them.[644]

The popular press was even more unkind, stressing that Makarios, if he had not condoned, had not condemned the use of violence against British troops in Cyprus. The Archbishop, genuinely distressed, lost, for once, his sureness of touch, and gave evident indications of strain. In a television interview with Richard Dimbleby, perhaps to retrieve his position, he condemned the general political behaviour of Makarios and said that he was 'a bad man'. The Greek Church was not unnaturally enraged, and the Archbishop sent off a cable:

> Archbishop Makarios's ecclesiastical office highly honoured by me. My remarks expressly excluded reflections on his personal character. Criticism confined strictly to certain political aspects.[645]

It was hardly a distinction rooted in an incarnational Christian theology. Not unexpectedly, Makarios announced his inability to visit Lambeth.

It was all very unfortunate, and showed how, in spite of much-vaunted ecumenicity, national sentiment still forces churchmen apart. Archbishop Fisher, it must be confessed, was not alone among English ecclesiastics in finding it hard to understand the political involvement of a church which for centuries has constituted a rallying point for patriotic resistance against the Turks. On the other hand, some two years earlier the Archbishop had spoken with great understanding about Cyprus in the Lords when he had stressed the seriousness of deporting the head of the Orthodox Church on that island.

On the Suez issue the Archbishop again adopted a position of more or less forthright condemnation of the Government's inept intervention. In principle, he believed that this 'invasion' was a violation of British obligations to the United Nations. The Government 'had not only lost a very good opportunity of doing the right thing but . . . had done the wrong thing'.[646] In the Lords he engaged in a merciless interrogation of the Lord Chancellor, Lord Kilmuir, which gave the latter a most uncomfortable, if deserved, five minutes.

The Archbishop also came up against the Government concerning the Protestant liberties to be written into the new constitution for Malta. This was a matter on which he felt keenly and concerning which he addressed the British Council of Churches on 24 April 1956, and the Church Assembly at its Spring session some two years later. The Government, however, for political reasons, would not budge. Fortunately the advent of John XXIII, if it did not change the constitutional situation, led to a new psychological approach and practical changes.

The Archbishop, as his predecessors, inevitably had dealings with members of the royal family. In this subtle area of human encounter, office and precedent cannot of themselves constrain effective relations. Unfortunately we have little knowledge of the royal family's reactions to the Archbishops. Fisher was no courtier, nor was he in any way obsequious. Rather his tendency was to be a little patronizing. It fitted in with his temperament to take this aspect of his responsibilities seriously. His semi-official contacts, which made a personal relationship possible, were numerous, as in the case of every Archbishop. During his archiepiscopate Princess Elizabeth and the Duke of Edinburgh were married in Westminster Abbey; Prince Charles and Princess Anne were baptized; and Elizabeth II crowned on 2 June 1953. On all these occasions the Archbishop officiated, conducting the ceremonies with intelligence and efficiency, and preparing for them with great care. He possessed a fine and eminently audible voice, though he lacked Lang's rare quality of lifting a ceremony into a world of drama and mystery. What he could do was to introduce a straightforward spiritual intention. Supremely was this the case with the Coronation. The Archbishop, following a former precedent, determined to use the event for a national call to rededication. To this end, he used every means of mass communication to make the public aware of the Coronation's ancient history, and its present relevance. He welcomed bringing it into every home through television. Still today the ancient ritual retains the elements of election, of confirmation of the people's choice, of self-dedication and consecration. A small and expert committee was established to advise on the elaborate ritual, and as a result the presentation of the Bible was introduced at the beginning of the service, thus enabling the Moderator of the Church of Scotland to be brought into the ceremony. On his own personal initiative the Archbishop drew up a small volume of prayers to be used daily by the Queen during the preceding month. On the eve of the Coronation, following the precedent set by Lang, he went to Buckingham Palace and conducted a short meditation. The Archbishop worked easily with the Earl Marshal, and the Coronation itself went off smoothly and seemed to make an impression at the time on the nation.

Geoffrey Fisher had his one occasion when relations with a member of the royal family led to hostile treatment by certain sections of the press, reminiscent of what Archbishop Lang had undergone at the time of the abdication of Edward VIII.

Princess Margaret was widely reported as intending to marry Group Captain Peter Townsend, who prior to his leaving the Queen Mother's Household to become an air attaché in Brussels had been the 'innocent' party to a divorce. Speculation increased, and Princess Margaret's secretary felt it necessary to appeal to the Press, with its 'customary courtesy and co-operation', to respect her 'privacy'. On 28 October 1955 there appeared the announcement:

> Princess Margaret went to Lambeth Palace yesterday afternoon and was received by the Archbishop of Canterbury, Dr. Fisher. She stayed nearly an hour.[647]

This was followed on 1 November by a further public statement from the Princess announcing that she had decided not to marry the Group Captain. In arriving at this decision, she was 'mindful of the Church's teaching that Christian marriage is indissoluble'—a not entirely accurate statement of the Church of England's total view. She had acted alone on the grounds of conscience, and she thanked those who had prayed for her, and the help given throughout by the Group Captain himself.

It was at this stage that the Archbishop came under fire from the Press: and he did not make matters easier for himself when, interviewed by Richard Dimbleby, he said somewhat testily that he did not care 'two hoots' what people might be saying, and that much of it represented 'a popular wave of stupid emotionalism'. Such language evoked a further reaction, which paradoxically went far to justify the words which the Archbishop had used. The popular Press talked of a 'crisis' and 'a rising tide of anger'; of the Princess's romance being 'broken by ecclesiastical influence'. This was certainly not true, at least so far as any direct intervention by the Archbishop was concerned. The fact was that the incident had everything about it to bring out latent anti-church feeling, particularly since by indulging in this *odium ecclesiasticum*, genuine sympathy with a distressed young lady could find an outlet.

Perhaps the fact is that the Archbishop must expect on occasions to be a national scapegoat. Doubtless thereby he ministers to a deep psychological need!

One thing that the incident high-lighted was the exposed position in which Archbishops stood *vis-à-vis* the Press generally. This was no new situation. Following Tait's example, Randall Davidson had some years earlier, in somewhat magisterial way, rebuked *The Times* for grossly biased and inadequate reporting. Lang suffered on two specific occasions from journalistic attacks. Archbishop Temple on the whole was more fortunate, though his socialist pronouncements often drew sharp criticism. Some of Archbishop Fisher's difficulties were personal, and derived from his own exuberance, frankness, the vestigial remains of the headmaster, and sheer inexperience in this field. One who was present in the Press Club on a rather unhappy occasion records:

> In my judgment—and I speak from personal reaction on the occasion in question—he himself is wholly responsible for creating the 'schoolmaster' image. It was the press conference immediately after his return from Central Africa, where he had made the famous remark, 'All men are not equal in the sight of God but all are equal in the love of God.' The newspapers had sent top staff to probe him on this. Had he said it? Did he mean it? These were the first questions. To which he answered 'Yes' in both instances, and then followed up with a positively brilliant exposition. . . . He then went on with equal brilliance for forty minutes or so answering every question. I, as an Anglican, felt immensely proud of him. Then there was a pause in the questions. Fisher put his hands together, elbows on the table, rested his chin on his finger-tips, looked round the room at

every face there, and said: 'Well, the headmaster is waiting, has the sixth form nothing more to say?' It was not only the words but the snide way in which he said it. One could mentally hear every notebook snap shut and an icy chill descend. . . . The legend had been well and truly launched.[648]

But Fisher, deep down, was far too sensitive a man not to be concerned with the image that he presented *via* the Press. Here the Archbishop himself ingenuously confessed:

I have no doubt that I said rash things about the press, in public, when I ought not to have done so. But if I did, it was because I thought then, and I still think, that the press uses its freedom very often in ways that are damaging to the morale of the nation. However, if I did, I was fair game for them to hit back at.[649]

By no means all of Dr. Fisher's difficulties flowed from his own temperament. They also derived from the fact that there was no organization of any kind at Lambeth capable of dealing with the Press at any level of competence or expertise. In other words, there was no professional liaison officer to make the task of the Press easier. All this changed when, somewhat late in the day, Colonel Robert Hornby, formerly Director of Public Relations for the British Army, was appointed Chief Information Officer of the Church Assembly. From then on Press relations with Lambeth were handled in a fully professional manner and Dr. Fisher co-operated to the full.

Another appointment which led to easier relations between Lambeth and the lay world outside was that of Mr. Robert Beloe as a lay secretary. This was a new office and owed its creation to the initiative of the Archbishop himself. Reference will be made later to its scope and significance.

On 17 January 1961, an announcement from Downing Street told of Archbishop Fisher's resignation. He was seventy-three years of age, some years younger than either Davidson or Lang at the time of their retirements. It took people by surprise but it was typical of the man. He felt it was the right time to go and that was all there was to it.

If the image of the headmaster was sometimes in the forefront and he endeavoured to keep a far too vigilant eye on too many things, he yet also left behind him a genial and democratic image. This can be seen in the progressive diminution of archiepiscopal estate at Lambeth. Lang once said to Fisher: 'When people come to see me in this study, they realize that the Church of England is a great institution.' 'Well, that's not the way I feel about anything,' Fisher later commented.[650] Yet even Cosmo Lang was forced to abandon his former estate under the exigencies of war. Archbishop Temple cared for none of these things. Geoffrey Fisher, by inclination, preferred something less elaborate and more domestic. Upon him and his wife fell the responsibility of restoring the fabric of the Palace after the devastation of war. Lady Fisher has given a vivid picture of their task:

> Up to Archbishop Fisher's time, each succeeding archbishop was himself the landlord of the Palace, and out of his income bore all the expenses of its upkeep. In former days when taxation was negligible and wages low, it was possible to maintain a very large staff and live on a large scale. . . . By the time we came to Lambeth taxation was reducing the income to barely a quarter, and wages and all other expenses had increased in proportion as the net income decreased.[651]

Fortunately, as Lady Fisher says, the Church Commissioners have largely dealt with this problem,

The restoration of Lambeth Palace—it was the palace which Howley had rebuilt in 1830, replacing a 'muddle of old rooms and passages and corridors which had come down from early time'—took place during the years 1945–1955. Archbishop Fisher, who had known the former building in Lang's time, described it as a 'forbidding place . . . overwhelmingly Victorian'. The reconstruction made possible the provision of a hostel consisting of fifteen bedrooms and a sitting-room, which could be used by bishops and visitors, lay and clerical, from Britain and overseas. This has proved a tremendous asset. The XIIIth-century chapel was also restored, the Queen and members of the royal family being present at a simple service of rededication.

So was Lambeth Palace shaped and equipped to serve a new era in the developing life of the Church of England.

The time is not yet, while he is happily engaged as an assistant priest in rural Dorset, to make a real assessment of the archiepiscopate of Dr. Geoffrey Fisher. Perhaps posterity will confirm Archbishop de Mel's appraisal.

When Dr. Ramsey was enthroned as the hundredth Archbishop on Tuesday, 27 June 1961, he did not enter into his estate as a Melchizedek without ancestry. Far from it. Behind him, as this book has endeavoured to show, there lay over 1,300 years of continuing and sometimes eventful history. The office has on the whole stood up to the test well. The Archbishop of Canterbury is still with us; he is regarded as a national figure whose public utterances are news; he is widely respected throughout the Anglican Communion; he is still seen abroad as something more than a little bit of old England which has providentially survived to feed a traditional nostalgia. As I write these words there lies on my desk *The Times* leader for 13 November 1970, which in reference to Archbishop Ramsey's visit to the centenary celebrations of the Province of Cape Town comments:

> He is the highest authority in the Anglican Communion, and it is appropriate, to use a neutral word, that he should be in South Africa to state the Church's position on the inescapable question: should the Church resist the State on apartheid.

We must be careful, however, not to paint too rosy a picture, for the Archbishop's office, because of its representative character, is not exempt from, indeed may principally bear, the stresses, the strains, and the questionings to which Christian faith is itself now subject. What of the present and the future?

In his palace at Lambeth, newly equipped with a hostel, the Archbishop still lives surrounded by his *familia*, his household, which retains a curious blend of the domestic and the official. Daily worship continues to be part of its life. This staff consists, at present, of three principals—the senior chaplain, the personal, and the lay secretary —and the domestic chaplain, to which there needs to be added three 'specialists' who are frequently called in for consultation.

The senior chaplain deals with correspondence, particularly that which concerns diocesan bishops, the General Synod, Convocation, and overseas provinces. He needs to be a mature person, sufficiently senior to elicit and deserve trust.

The personal secretary in consultation with the senior chaplain, goes through the forty-odd letters which flow daily into Lambeth— the Archbishop having seen them at breakfast—and deals with the follow up, conferring widely in the process.

The lay secretary, an excellent innovation by Dr. Fisher, deals mainly with episcopal involvement in the House of Lords. He is responsible for arranging a rota—today twenty-six diocesan bishops have seats in the Upper House—and without breaking in upon the independence of individual bishops, or encouraging them to 'gang' up together, he does his best to ensure that in debates of national importance they are represented. This is no easy task since the House of Lords' timetable is often determined by the Commons, and the bishops are more than fully employed in their dioceses. The lay secretary also makes contact with government departments, and handles matters of general interest to Lambeth, such as, for example, race relations.

These three members of staff do not work in isolation, but each, with his own secretary, is in daily consultation.

A fourth person, heir to a long tradition, who is continuously with the Archbishop, at home and on his travels, is the domestic chaplain. In particular he undertakes secretarial duties in connexion with diocesan visits, and generally looks after the Archbishop's comfort.

Three other 'officers' who regularly confer with the Primate, thus providing a measure of expertise in their respective spheres, are the General Secretary of the Church of England Council on Foreign Relations; the Archbishop's Registrar and Legal Adviser; and the Press Officer.[652]

This small group of some seven people act in a personal capacity to the Archbishop, which means that most of them do not necessarily carry over into the regime of a successor, who may well feel that he ought to select his own staff. Indeed, he need not necessarily organize his *familia* this way at all. In this respect the Archbishop stands in a different relation to his staff from that of the Prime Minister to the civil servants who advise him. The latter are highly trained, have an independent status, and watch ministers come and go. It has been suggested that something analogous to this would be appropriate at Lambeth in order to preserve continuity and to place at the disposal of the Archbishop a long experience with established methods of working. Modern Archbishops have on the whole preferred to surround themselves with men of their own choosing. Perhaps this is right, but it ought not to be taken for granted.

The desire of A. C. Benson for a *curia*, however, has not entirely gone by default. The development of the Church Assembly, now the General Synod, and to a lesser extent the British Council of Churches, has, through their specialized agencies, provided an informed personnel which is at the Archbishop's disposal. The Board of Social Responsibility, the Advisory Council of the Church's Ministry, the Missionary and Ecumenical Council, the Board of Education, are cases in point. Certainly the position of solitariness, which Benson deplored, no longer exists in quite the same way. The change has been brought about by a process of evolution, though with occasional mutual suspicion on the way.

What of the traditional spheres of responsibility which occupy so much of an Archbishop's time?

The diocese of Canterbury continues under his pastoral care. The peculiar of Croydon, where the Archbishops used to have a palace, still remains an island within the diocese of Southwark. The Archdeacon of Canterbury and the suffragan Bishop of Dover have for some time been supplemented by two further archdeacons, two suffragan and three assistant bishops. The traditional visitation of the diocese goes on. The legal officials remain. The link with the Cathedral and City of Canterbury which Archbishop Ramsey inherited has become more intimate since Frederick Temple established a house in the precincts. Regular visits at the weekends and at the great Festivals have made him more of a local figure.

There are those who maintain that the perennial cares of discharging a diocesan duty, even if considerably delegated, make life unnecessarily difficult for an Archbishop and demand too much of his time, that is if he is to fulfil his wider responsibilities, particularly throughout the Anglican Communion. The Reverend John Heuss, sometime Rector of Trinity Church, New York, expressed doubts in a sermon in Westminster Abbey, as to whether the head of such a Communion can, with his local duties, be peripatetic on the scale needed. Whatever the future holds in this respect, it is probably true to say that the Archbishops as a class would regard the severing of the traditional diocesan link with profound dismay; and this applies to the diocese. Still the problem is a real one.

The Archbishop is still Metropolitan of the Province of Canterbury, and as such presides over its Convocation. He still administers the spiritualities of vacant dioceses in his province, and constitutes the authority behind all their official acts; but he no longer holds formal visitations and has not done so since the time of Archbishop Laud. He still confers degrees, if with more caution.

As Primate of All England his office has been affected by the development of the Church's own structures of government at a national level. The suppression of Convocation between the years 1717 and 1852 meant that during this period such central direction as the Church received, apart from parliamentary control, came through Queen Anne's Bounty (founded during the archiepiscopate of Thomas Tenison) and the Ecclesiastical Commissioners. With both of these the Archbishop was intimately associated, and in this respect his unifying presence filled a void. The revival of Convocation if it restored one area of the Archbishop's provincial authority, required an adjustment to a new situation. The establishment of the General Synod will bring the Northern and Southern Provinces together under his presidency, as previously in the Church Assembly, but the fact that he is not always to be in the chair will enable him more easily to offer leadership. Yet the way ahead is not clear, complicated as it is by the Church's nexus with the State (which includes the role of the Church Commissioners) and the nature of the historic episcopate.

One detects here a conflict of principle, more subtle than a simple confrontation of the hierarchical with the democratic. Is the Archbishop of Canterbury to be wholly contained within the structures of the Synod, and is the Synod, under God, to constitute the *fons et origo* of the Church's authority, not least in its faith and worshipful life? Benson would probably have said yes—and no. Or is there a residual authority inherent in the episcopate in general and the Archbishop in particular, which cannot be delegated or shunted off? This is not a purely academic question, and for this reason is probably better left to sort itself out in practice. An illustration of the way it could arise may be offered.

The members of the Church of England Council on Foreign Relations, though set up in response to a resolution of the Church Assembly, are nominated by the Archbishop and paid for largely by the Church Commissioners. This way of doing things had point so long as relations with the Orthodox Churches remained at the level of Patriarch to Archbishop; but when this phase passes will the Council be absorbed into the Synod? Does not the same apply to the Archbishop's Council, concerned as it is with Roman Catholics, particularly now that the Curia has set up its own Secretariat for Unity?

The Synod is itself too large a body to originate policy or to provide the executive thrust to implement such policy when decided. True, this has been foreseen and provision is made for standing and executive committees: but will the Archbishop's relation to these be of such a kind as to make possible a really creative leadership?— a question which becomes the more important at a time when the future of the Convocations is uncertain. In respect of the latter, my own guess is that they will wither away, a process which could well be hastened if a metropolitan see of London were established, as was proposed by a member of Convocation as early as 1905.

Dr. Michael Ramsey inherits a unique position as 'head' of the Anglian Communion, a status which the Crown has ceased to occupy since the XVIIIth century. Yet this position is in a process of radical change, due, apart from a different social and political climate, to the gradual evolution, across many years, of an organizational structure for the Communion as a whole. A Consultative Body of the Lambeth Conference was, as we have seen, established in 1897, and its character strengthened by successive Conferences. That of 1958 produced the Executive Officer, a pioneering appointment which has presented the holders with some difficulties, largely due to their relations with Lambeth suffering from an ambiguity of status. Yet in this movement towards greater cohesion there is a feeling in certain parts of the Anglican Communion that the Church of England is dragging its feet. Such a view was expressed by George Luxton, Bishop of Huron, in his *Unity in Mission*, published in 1967, and obviously intended to stimulate discussion at the Lambeth Conference in the following year. In particular, he suggested that the Conference should set up a central authority for the purposes of mission, general study, research, planning, administration and finance. Progress in this direction was certainly made at the Conference presided over by Dr. Ramsey in 1968, though care was taken to safeguard the position of the Archbishop and to prevent the Consultative Council which it established becoming too much of an executive body. The Archbishop was made its president and an *ex officio* member of all its committees. Its chairman and vice-chairman hold office for six years, and the council is to meet every other year.

It is interesting to notice, in view of earlier history, that this drive towards greater definition came from a bishop on the other side of the Atlantic. *Unity in Mission* further maintained that the appointment of the Archbishop of Canterbury by the British Crown constituted a stumbling block to the discharge of his wider role.

> Your Archbishop of Canterbury—the Bishop of Huron writes—is, in a special sense, *our* Archbishop. We should like to know that his appointment comes out of the Church at its best and clearest and fullest. This would be immensely satisfying to many of us.

Indeed the Bishop wrote, 'My prayer is that some day . . . (perhaps when my grandchildren are on the stage) an Anglican from India or Pakistan or Africa or China may be seated on the chair of St. Augustine'.[653] The speculation is an interesting one, but it illustrates how different, in this respect, is the Pope from the Primate of All England. A non-Italian may in a matter of years ascend the papal throne; but an Archbishop of Canterbury who has not come up through the diocesan structures in England is far less likely.

If a question mark hangs over the Archbishop's office where the Anglican Communion as a whole is concerned, this is equally the case with the World Council of Churches. Archbishop Fisher, representing the Anglican Communion, was one of the five members comprising the *Praesidium*, though a faint effort was made behind the scenes at the Assembly of the World Council of Churches in 1954 to put forward the name of the Presiding Bishop of the Episcopal Church in America. Dr. Michael Ramsey enjoyed a period of office on the *Praesidium*, but today the Anglican Communion is represented by Alphaeus Zulu, Bishop of Zululand and Swaziland.

What seems likely to happen is that the Archbishop of Canterbury will lose real power, as distinct from honourable status, both within the Anglican Communion and in the World Council of Churches, that is unless he shows a particular interest and takes a real initiative: but will his other commitments give him the time to do this?

## II

How is the Archbishop's historic role *vis-à-vis* the nation likely to develop in this secular and pluralistic age? No precise answer in political terms is possible, because since the time that the Archbishop ceased to hold governmental office his effectiveness here has been a matter of indirect influence rather than of direct power—an influence dependent upon his own skill and temperament as much as on the strength of the religious interests which he could command. The established status of the Church of England is being increasingly eroded and its built-in educational outreach diminishing. This process will undoubtedly continue. Certainly no modern Prime Minister, to quote the somewhat exaggerated words of a former Archbishop, is likely to go to such as Randall Davidson 'to advise [him] as his chief confidant and his friend in almost everything . . . not only in Church but in State'. Yet the Archbishop is still one of a number of bishops in the House of Lords, and any Prime Minister, it may be confidently assumed, and this would apply equally to members of his cabinet, would make himself available for a private interview if this were asked for. Behind the scenes the Archbishop can, and does, make representations; and sometimes more publicly as was the case in October 1970, when Dr. Ramsey wrote to the Prime Minister, on behalf of the bishops, concerning the sale of arms to South Africa. It is not without significance that the present Archbishop was appointed as the first chairman of the National Committee for Commonwealth Immigrants.

Certain traditional functions remain. The Archbishop is called on to baptize and marry members of the Royal Family, and has opportunities of getting to know the Sovereign personally. He is still

Visitor of All Souls College, Oxford, a Trustee of the British Museum, and exercises other *ex officio* responsibilities.

In one respect, *vis-à-vis* the community as a whole, an almost dramatic change has been brought about by the advent of broadcasting and television. Through the initative of John Reith, Director General of the British Broadcasting Company (as it then was), Randall Davidson early in 1923 was consulted as to the principles on which religious broadcasting should be based, and a small advisory committee representative of the various churches was set up. Canon Adam Fox once said to the author that the television personality is the contemporary equivalent of the medieval saint in that he is introduced into every home. The effect of radio and television has undoubtedly been to make the Archbishop known to the rank and file of the population in a way quite impossible before the coming of this mass medium. His face and voice are familiar, and successive Archbishops have not been slow to recognize the significance of this new means of communication, though their technical ability to use it themselves has varied. Dr. Ramsey disarmingly confessed to a group of I.T.V. personnel: 'I have no other ambition but to be your pupil, and I hope I will continue to be that.' Integrity, however, and Dr. Ramsey certainly has it, always 'comes over'.

The Archbishop does not nominate to the Governing body of either B.B.C. or Independent Television. He is consulted informally before the B.B.C. appoints a Head of Religious Broadcasting, and this is doubtless true with the other Authority. It is unlikely that such a nomination would go forward if the Archbishop were known to be against it. The Archbishop of Westminster and the President of the Free Church Federal Council are informed. The Archbishop is also consulted as to the Chairman of the Central Religious Advisory Committee which acts for both B.B.C. and Independent Television. To the broadcasting authorities the Primate is doubtless regarded as the spokesman of 'official Christianity in this country', and as such has a *quais*-right to speak at times of national crisis. However, Randall Davidson, as we have seen, was frustrated in his desire to do this during the General Strike. Usually such facilities are provided, but difficulties can still arise as, for example, when Mr. Ian Smith made his Unilateral Declaration of Rhodesian Independence and some were of opinion that a distinction ought to be made between the Archbishop of Canterbury acting in his representative capacity and the Archbishop expressing his own views.

III

What kind of person is needed as Primate of All England? The answer must surely be that this will depend on time, place and circumstance. A catalogue of virtues or particular gifts does not really help. Dean Hook in his monumental *Lives of the Archbishops* writes in typical XIXth-century style:

> Among the Archbishops there are a few eminent men distinguished as much for their transcendent abilities as for their exalted station in society; but, as a general rule, they have not been men of the highest class of mind. In all ages the tendency has very properly been, whether by election or by nomination, to appoint 'safe men', and as genius is generally innovating and often eccentric the safe men are those who, with certain high qualifications, do not rise much above the intellectual average of their contemporaries. They are practical men rather than philosophers and theorists, and their impulse is not to perfection but *quieta non movere*.[654]

As a general factual statement this is probably true, though there have undoubtedly been conspicuous exceptions to it. Whether it ought to be so true is another matter. Once again it depends what the immediate situation is. Certainly the method of appointment and the age at which Archbishops come to office—the average age since the Reformation is about sixty, the youngest being Cranmer at forty-four—do not encourage charismatic or pioneering gifts; and one can appreciate the retort of Dr. Wand, formerly Bishop of London, to John Betjeman's contention that the only thing which mattered in an Archbishop was 'holiness'—'That is a typical layman's heresy.' Of course one is right to expect holiness; sincere and informed conviction; intellectual gifts; but, whether he likes it or not, administrative responsibilities do at present fall the way of the Archbishop, and though, in the nature of the case, he discharges them through delegation, he must still be aware of them. If he is not, other people, accountable to no one, will step in and take over. Whether the arrival of the General Synod will radically change this situation remains to be seen.

It is perhaps significant that though state education has existed in England since 1870, no Archbishop so far has passed through it. The first Prime Minister to do so was Lloyd George. Nor has anyone sat in St. Augustine's Chair, since the Reformation, who was not a student at Oxford or Cambridge. Understandably nominations to Lambeth have been conditioned by the contemporary social climate, but such a limitation of the field of intake is doubtless on the way out. It is inconceivable that either talent or suitability can be so narrowly confined.

Mention of the Prime Minister prompts the reflection that whereas it is unlikely that any politician could arrive at 10 Downing

Street without being driven there by some elemental ambition, this is not equally true of Lambeth. Many ambitious men have indeed sought to sit in St. Augustine's Chair, and some have succeeded; but there have been those who so far from seeking it have tried to avoid it, and have said 'yes' only from a sense of duty. Others have declined the invitation, though not always from the highest motives.

Yet in spite of what has been said, leadership is expected of an Archbishop. True, leadership is something indefinable; but whatever its character it must bring out the best in others by fostering initiative. Writing in 1902, Father Dolling deplored 'the destruction of all individuality on the part of the diocesan [Bishops]',[655] which he ascribed to the distinguished archiepiscopates of Tait, Benson and Frederick Temple. Such a danger, however, would only become real if the Archbishop's influence on appointments were to become excessive. This was certainly not the case during the reign of these three outstanding ecclesiastics.

The Church of England, it must be admitted, is not an easy body to 'direct', whatever this somewhat loaded word may mean. It penetrates deeply into history; it is comprehensive in character; it has never given to the Primates of All England the *aura*, the theological status, or the authority which the Supreme Pontiff in Rome has attracted to himself. Even their places of burial are scattered. The Archbishop's view does not always constrain either Convocation or the Synod. Archbishop Ramsey was known to support the proposals for Anglican–Methodist Union but they foundered. The Archbishop sometimes finds bishops voting against him in the House of Lords, and, like Randall Davidson, willingly accepts this. The eleven thousand or so parish priests in the Church of England are neither homogeneous nor are they easily led. One sees point in the comment of an Archbishop who said at the annual bishops' dinner in the Mansion House, maybe in somewhat lighter vein: 'I hope to go down to history as the Archbishop who left the clergy alone.' It was not an entirely dishonourable ambition.

What this entails in practice is that the leadership which Lambeth can offer must be sensitive to the ethos of the Church of England. It must endeavour, through kindling the imagination, to move the Church towards its vocation of the moment; to lift it out of its lethargy when it is lethargic; and to inspire it to tread new paths. Yet at the same time this leadership must recall that Church to the rock whence it was hewn, and lay bare the treasures of its inheritance. Here is the paradox inherent in an ancient yet continuing office. The response of an Archbishop to this challenge will depend on the quality of his dedication, as well as on the way the Church generally measures up to the high demands, intellectual and personal, which go along with living in the seventies. St. Augustine came to Britain bearing a faith relevant to a people whose northern gods were no longer adequate to its changed estate. In the present crisis of culture and civilization, which could prove the birth pangs of a new era or the death struggles of an old, the Archbishop of Canterbury still occupies a strategic position from the vantage ground of which he has the opportunity of discharging a distinctive role.

It would be tragic indeed if, 'at such a time as this', he were to shrink into a merely local figure presiding over an inward-looking community preoccupied with its own life. *Dei gratia* this need not happen. The present is a call to wisdom, to integrity, and to greatness.

1. Colgrave and Mynors, *Bede's Ecclesiastical History of the English People*, 1969, I. 25, p. 75
2. Deanesly, M., *Augustine of Canterbury*, 1964, p. 43
3. Colgrave and Mynors, *op. cit.*, I. 29, p. 105
4. *Ibid.*, I. 27, p. 87
5. *Ibid.*, I. 27, p. 89
6. *Ibid.*, II. 4, p. 147
7. *Ibid.*, II. 3, p. 143
8. *Ibid.*, II. 3, p. 145
9. *Ibid.*, II. 6, p. 155
10. For Theodore's work see Bede, Eddius, *Vita Wilfridii* (ed. Colegrave, 1927) and *The Anglo-Saxon Chronicle*, Everyman Library, reprinted 1967
11. Stenton, F. M., *Anglo-Saxon England*, 1950, p. 131
12. Colgrave and Mynors, *op. cit.*, IV. 2, p. 335
13. *Ibid.*, IV. 2, p. 333
14. For this section I am indebted to J. W. Lamb's *The Archbishopric of Lichfield*, 1964, and *The Archbishopric of York*, 1967.
15. See article by Stubbs in *Dictionary of Christian Biography*, ed. Smith and Wace, London 1877–87: also Wilkins, *Concilia* I. 166
16. Haddan and Stubbs, *Councils and Ecclesiastical Documents relating to Great Britain and Ireland*, Oxford, 1870, III. 587
17. *Encyclopaedia Britannica*, 11th ed. 1910–11. Vol. 7–8
18. Stubbs, W., *Memorials of St. Dunstan Archbishop of Canterbury*, Rolls Series, introd. lxxxvii
19. Stenton, F. M., *op. cit.*, p. 362.
20. Stubbs, W., *Memorials of St. Dunstan*, p. cv.
21. Florence of Worcester, *Chronicon ex Chronicis* ed. Thorpe (Eng. Hist. Soc., 1848–9). Quoted McKilliam, A. E., *A Chronicle of the Archbishops of Canterbury*, 1913, p. 99
22. *The Anglo-Saxon Chronicle*. Everyman Library, p. 162
23. *Ibid.*, p. 164
24. Barlow, F., *Edward the Confessor*, 1970, p. 78
25. See Kemp, E. W., *An Introduction to Canon Law in the Church of England*, 1957
26. Churchill, I. J., *Canterbury Administration*, 1933, I. 254, 255
27. William of Poitier's *Vie de Guillaume le Conquérent* (ed. Guizot), p. 414. Quoted McKilliam, A. E., *op. cit.*, p. 127
28. Macdonald, A. J., *Lanfranc*, 1926, p. 68
29. Southern, R. W., *St. Anselm and his Biographer*, 1963, p. 145
30. Quoted Winston, R., *Thomas Becket*, 1967, p. 43
31. *Ibid.*, p. 116
32. *Materials for the History of Thomas Becket, Archbishop of Canterbury*, ed. James Craigie Robertson, Rolls Series 1875ff. IV. 19. Quoted Winston, *op. cit.*, p. 125

33. *Materials* III. 36. Quoted Winston, R., *op. cit.*, p. 126
34. *Materials* V. 498. Quoted Winston, R., *op. cit.*, p. 117
35. *The Historical Works of Gervase of Canterbury*, ed. Stubbs, W., 2 vols. Rolls Series 1879–80. I. 518, 519. Quoted Cheney, C. R., *Hubert Walter*, 1967, p. 47
36. Richardson and Sayles, *The Governance of Medieval England*, 1963, p. 341
37. Knowles, M. D., *The Monastic Order in England*, 1949, p. 268
38. Patent Rolls 1381–1385, p. 33. Quoted Dahmus, J., *William Courtenay*, 1966, p. 75
39. Hook, W. F., *Lives of the Archbishops of Canterbury*, 12 vols, 1860–76. II. 140
40. Ordericus Vitalis, *Historia Ecclesiastica* (ed. Bohn). VII. 16 (iii pp. 247–8). Quoted Macdonald, *op. cit.*, p. 232
41. Macdonald, A. J., *op. cit.*, p. 210
42. Southern, R. W., *op. cit.*, p. 123
43. *Ibid.*, p. 158
44. Quoted Richardson and Sayles, *op. cit.*, p. 294
45. Quoted Stenton, D. M., *English Society in the Early Middle Ages*, 1967, p. 42
46. *Materials* IV. 15. Quoted Winston, R., *op. cit.*, p. 116
47. Wendover, Roger, *Flores Historiarum*, Rolls Series. Quoted Cheney, C. R., *op. cit.*, p. 102
48. *Gervase of Canterbury*, II. 95. Quoted Cheney, C. R., *op. cit.*, p. 110
49. Giraldus Cambrensis, *De Invectionibus* (ed. W. S. Davies), in Y Cymmrodor XXX (1920). Quoted Cheney, C. R., *op. cit.*, pp. 4, 5
50. Holt, J. C., *Magna Carta*, 1965, p. 188
51. Warren, W. L., 'A Reappraisal of Simon Sudbury'. *Journal of Ecclesiastical History*, X, p. 144
52. *Ibid.*, p. 150
53. McKissack, M., *The Fourteenth Century*, 1959, p. 291
54. Dahmus, J., p. 166
55. Higdon, *Polychronicon*, Rolls Series 3X. 58, 59. *William Courtenay*, 1966
56. Dahmus, J., *op. cit.*, p. 78
57. *Ibid.*, p. 105
58. Hook, W. F., *op. cit.*, V. 476
59. Southern, R. W., *op. cit.*, p. 194
60. Du Boulay, F. R. H., *The Lordship of Canterbury*, 1966, p. 239
61. See Pugh, R. B., *Imprisonment in Medieval England*, 1968
62. Du Boulay, F. R. H., *op. cit.*, p. 255
63. *Ibid.*, pp. 263, 264
64. Douie, D. L., *Archbishop Pecham*, 1952, p. 276
65. Canterbury College, III, 43–5 *Reg. Courtenay*, fol. 42 V. Quoted Dahmus, J., *op. cit.*, p. 203
66. Thorne, W., *Chronicle of St. Augustine's Abbey, Canterbury*. Quoted McKilliam, A. E., *op. cit.*, p. 229
67. *Historiae Anglicanae Scriptores*, X. p. 2194, London, 1652. Quoted Dahmus, J., *op. cit.*, p. 211
68. *Ibid.*, p. 211
69. *Historiae Anglicanae Scriptores*, X. p. 2194. Quoted Dahmus, J., *op. cit.*, p. 212
70. Churchill, I. J., *op. cit.*, I. 54
71. *Ibid.*, I. 41
72. *Reg. Courtenay*. Quoted Dahmus, J., *op. cit.*, p. 158
73. Douie, D. L., *op. cit.*, p. 192
74. Godfrey of Malmesbury, p. 42. Quoted Macdonald, A. J., *op. cit.*, p. 92
75. Macdonald, A. J., *op. cit.*, p. 94

76. Southern, R. W., *op. cit.*, p. 137
77. *Ibid.*, p. 137
78. *Ibid.*, p. 138
79. *Materials* V. 87. Quoted Winston, R., *op. cit.*, pp. 169, 170
80. *Materials* VII. 217. Quoted Winston, R., *op. cit.*, p. 297.
81. *Chronica Rogeri de Hoveden* (ed. Stubbs, W., 4 vols., Rolls Series 1868–71). III. 239. Quoted Cheney, C. R., *op. cit.*, p. 53.
82. Southern, R. W., *op. cit.*, p. 140
83. William of Newburgh, II. 44. Quoted Cheney, C. R., *op. cit.*, p. 53
84. Cheney, C. R., *op. cit.*, p. 53.
85. *Reg. Courtenay*, fols. iv–2. Quoted Dahmus, J., *op. cit.*, p. 239. Also Wilkins, *Concilia*, III. 154, 155
86. Jacob, E. F., *Henry Chichele*, 1967, p. 47
87. *Ibid.*, pp. 58, 59
88. Quoted McKilliam, A. E., *op. cit.*, p. 291
89. Pollard, A. F., *Wolsey*, 1929, p. 57
90. *Ibid.*, p. 193
91. Scarisbrick, J. J., *Henry VIII*, 1968, p. 242
92. For the text see Wilkins, *Concilia*, III. 746
93. This draft of a speech is calendared L.P.V., No. 1247. It is printed in the *Dublin Review*, April 1894, CXIV. 401–4. Extracts are quoted in Hughes, P., *The Reformation in England*, 1950, I. 240–1
94. Pickthorne, K., *Early Tudor Government*, II. 192
95. Ridley, J., *Thomas Cranmer*, 1962, p. 66
96. Cranmer, *Works*, II. 460. Quoted Ridley, J., *op. cit.*, p. 56
97. McKilliam, A. E., *op. cit.*, p. 308
98. For a discussion of *De Antiquitate* see Brook, V. J. K., *A Life of Archbishop Parker*, 1962, p. 323
99. Rowse, A. L. *The England of Elizabeth*, 1950, p. 405
100. Collinson, P., *The Elizabethan Puritan Movement*, 1967, p. 146
101. Parker, *Correspondence*, IV. 473. Quoted Rowse, A. L., *op. cit.*, p. 401
102. Collinson, P., *op. cit.*, p. 159
103. *Letters of Thomas Wood*, p. 23. Quoted Collinson, P., *op. cit.*, p. 167
104. See Strype, J., *The History of the Life and Acts of Edmund Grindal*, 1821, Book II. 569–72
105. Quoted in *Dictionary of National Biography*, Vol. LXI
106. Lambeth Palace Library MS. 647, ff. 151, 162
107. Collinson, P., *op. cit.*, p. 248
108. *Ibid.*, p. 254
109. *Ibid.*, p. 257
110. *Ibid.*, p. 270
111. *Ibid.*, p. 285
112. *Ibid.*, p. 431
113. Maitland, F. W., *Roman Canon Law*, p. 122. The reference is to the Archbishop's legatine status.
114. Du Boulay, F. R. H., *op. cit.*, p. 318
115. Cranmer's *Letters*, II. 348. Quoted Du Boulay, F. R. H., *op. cit.*, p. 323.
116. Trevor Roper, S., *Archbishop Laud*, 2nd ed., 1962, p. 26
117. McKilliam, A. E., *op. cit.*, p. 332. See also Babbage, S. P., *Puritanism and Bancroft*, 1962, p. 332. Melville was reported as having called James 'God's silly vassal', and 'taking him by the sleeve'.
118. Camden, W., *Britannia* (ed. Gibson, E.), I. 242. Quoted *Dictionary of National Biography*, III, 108.

119. Clarendon, Earl of, *The History of the Rebellion and Civil Wars in England*, 1826, I. 125
120. Heylyn, P., *Cyprianus Anglicus*, 1668, p. 63
121. *Ibid.*, Quoted Welsby, P. A., *op. cit.*, p. 36
122. Calvert to Edmondes, 10 March 1611; Birch, T., *Court and Times of James I*, 1849, I. 110. Quoted Welsby, P. A., *op. cit.*, p. 36
123. *Ibid.*
124. Quoted *Dictionary of National Biography*, I. 13. Article by F. L. Lee
125. See Cobbett, W., *State Trials*, 1809, pp. 860 ff.; also B.M. Sloane MSS., 3828 ff. 1, 2
126. Welsby, P. A., *op. cit.*, p. 78
127. Rymer, T. *Foedera*, London, 1816. Tom. XVIII, 941. Quoted Head, R. E., *Royal Supremacy and the Trials of Bishops, 1558–1725*, 1962, p. 52
128. *Scrinia Reserata*, II. 72. Quoted Head, R. E., *op. cit.*, pp. 54, 55
129. Lambeth MSS. 943, f. 105.
130. Laud, *Works*, VI. 91. Quoted Trevor Roper, S., *op. cit.*, p. 32
131. Wilkins, *Concilia*, IV. 487. Quoted Trevor Roper, S., *op. cit.*, p. 190
132. Wilkins, *Concilia*, IV. 524. Quoted Trevor Roper, S., *op. cit.*, p. 204
133. Laud, *Works*, V, p. 564. Quoted Trevor Roper, S., *op. cit.*, p. 207
134. Head, R. E., *op. cit.*, p. 71
135. Laud, *Works*, III, 226. Quoted Trevor Roper, S., *op. cit.*, p. 227
136. Cal. Ven. XXIII, 531. Quoted Trevor Roper, S., *op. cit.*, p. 227
137. Quoted McKilliam, A. E., *op. cit.*, p. 344
138. Heylyn, P. *Cyprianus Anglicus*, 1688, London, Lib. V. p. 55
139. Quoted Bosher, R. S., *The Making of the Restoration Settlement*, 1951, p. 19
140. Harleian MSS. B.M. 6942, f. 97
141. Bosher, R. S., *op. cit.*, p. 25
142. Duppa, B., 10 November 1657, *Correspondence*; Northamptonshire Record Society, Lamport Hall. Quoted Bosher, R. S., *op. cit.*, p. 26
143. Scott, G., *The Travels of the King*, 1907, p. 475. Quoted Bosher, R. S., *op. cit.*, p. 136
144. Matthew, A. G., *Calamy Revised*, 1934, p. 166
145. Contemporary accounts of the Coronation are to be found in the diaries of Samuel Pepys and John Evelyn. The former is much more lively
146. *Mercurius Publicus*, 1662, no. 35, p. 579. Quoted Bosher, R. S., *op. cit.*, p. 261
147. Clarendon MSS. Bodleian Library, 77, f. 319
148. Airey, O., 'Notes on the Reign of Charles II', *British Quarterly Review*, lxxvii, 1883, pp. 332, 333. Quoted Bosher, R. S., *op. cit.*, pp. 264, 265, note 3
149. Bosher, R. S., *op. cit.*, p. 264
150. Staley, V., *The Life and Times of Gilbert Sheldon*, 1913, p. 119
151. *Ibid.*, pp. 131, 132
152. *Ibid.*, p. 194
153. *Diary of Edward Lake* (ed. Elliott, G. P.), Camden Society, 1846, p. 19. The foregoing account of the passing over of Compton and the appointment of Sancroft is related at length in Carpenter, E., *The Protestant Bishop*, pp. 37–42
154. Macpherson, *Original Papers*, I. 279
155. *The Correspondence of Henry Hyde*, 1828, p. 299
156. For an exchange of letters between Dodwell and Tenison see Carpenter, E., *Thomas Tenison*, pp. 197–202
157. Compton had tried to curtail this jurisdiction on the grounds that the present was not a normal vacancy, but on consulting Stillingfleet, Bishop of Worcester, he decided to take the matter no further

158. This account of Compton's being passed over for the second time is documented in Carpenter, E., *The Protestant Bishop*, pp. 161–5
159. Pennington, E. L., *Commissary Blair*, 1936, p. 8.
160. Burnet, G., *History of my own Time*, Clarendon Press, part I, p. 147
161. Brett, T., *Account of Church Government and Governors*, 2nd ed. 1710, p. 244
162. Phillimore, W. G. F., *The Ecclesiastical Law of the Church of England*, I. 67
163. *A Short Narrative of the Proceedings against the Bp. of St. A.*, 1702, p. 74
164. Shippen, W., *Faction Display'd*, 1704, p. 3
165. S. P. D. William III, 28 October 1699, 8D, p. 27
166. Tenison to Queen Anne, 12 June 1707, Lambeth MSS. 930, f. 195
167. Carstares, W., *State Papers and Letters*, 1774, p. 760
168. *Letters from the late Most Reverend Dr. Thomas Herring, Lord Archbishop of Canterbury to William Duncombe, Esq., deceased, from the year 1728–1757*, pp. 110, 111
169. Nicholls, J., *Literary Anecdotes of the Eighteenth Century*, 1812, VIII. 94
170. Quarrell and Mare, *London in 1710*, p. 149
171. B.M. Add. MSS. 32976, f. 458
172. Quoted Rowden, A. W., *The Primates of the Four Georges*, 1916, p. 350. The Auckland Correspondence in the British Museum contains many revealing letters from Moore to Lord Auckland (formerly Sir William Eden) whose sister became Moore's second wife
173. Auckland Correspondence. B.M. Add. MSS. 34412, f. 281
174. Quoted Rowden, A. W., *op. cit.*, p. 138
175. Hervey, *Memoirs of the Reign of George II*, 1848, ii, 108, 110
176. Newcastle to Herring, 19 Oct. 1747, S. P. D. Geo. II, 102, p. 134. The account which follows of Sherlock's declining Canterbury is taken from Carpenter, E., *Thomas Sherlock*, pp. 136–40. The two letters quoted are: Sherlock to Newcastle, 14 Oct. 1747, B.M. Add. MSS. 35589, f. 315; and Sherlock to Newcastle, 14 Oct 1747, B.M. Add. MSS. 35519. f. 317
177. Quoted Rowden, A. W., *op. cit.*, p. 194
178. Quoted Rowden, A. W., *op. cit.*, p. 195
179. Herring to Whiston, 28 Jan 1748, *Letters from the late Most Reverend Dr. Herring to William Duncombe, Esq., deceased*, p. 108
180. Quoted Rowden, A. W., *op. cit.*, p. 275
181. *Ibid.*, p. 276
182. B.M. Add. MSS. 32990, f. 419
183. Quoted Rowden, A. W., *op. cit.*, p. 355
184. Quoted *ibid.*, pp. 386, 387
185. *Ibid.*, p. 388
186. *Ibid.*, p. 389
187. Potter to Wake, 14 April 1721. Quoted Rowden, A. W., *op. cit.*, p. 139
188. B.M. Add. MSS. 92724, f. 161
189. B.M. Add MSS. 32878, f. 177
190. Newcastle to Secker, 16 Oct 1762. B.M. Add MSS. 32943, f. 242
191. Sykes, N., *Church and State in England in the XVIIIth Century*, 1962, p. 86
192. Quoted Rowden, A. W., *op. cit.*, p. 95
193. B.M. Add. MSS. 34424, f. 284
194. Herring, *A Sermon preached at Kensington on Wednesday the 7th of January; by the Most Reverend Father in God Thomas, Lord Archbishop of York*, London, MDCCXLVII, p. 19
195. Herring to Dean Lynch, 23 Dec 1752, H.M.C. Various Collections, I. 226
196. Parliamentary Debates, 1st Series, vol. 40, col. 1056, 10 June 1819
197. Parliamentary Debates, 1st Series, vol. 4, cols. 777–8, 13 May 1805

198. Quoted Rowden, A. W., *op. cit.*, p. 330
199. *Ibid.*, p. 156
200. Southey, R., *Life of Wesley*, I. 190
201. *Letters from the late Most Reverend Dr. Thomas Herring to William Duncombe Esq., deceased*, p. 173
202. *The Christian Remembrancer*, III. June 1881, p. 337a. Quoted Sykes, N., *William Wake, Archbishop of Canterbury*, 1957. II, 159
203. Quoted Rowden, A. W., *op. cit.*, p. 72
204. *Ibid.*, p. 73
205. *Ibid.*, p. 107
206. *Ibid.*, p. 108
207. *Ibid.*, pp. 277, 278
208. *Ibid.*, p. 287
209. Walpole, H., *Letters* (ed. Toynbee), 1903, VII. 381
210. *Life and Times of Selina, Countess of Huntingdon* 1839, I, 285 ff.: also *The Letters of King George III*, ed. Dobrée, p. 139
211. Quoted Rowden, A. W., *op. cit.*, p. 331
212. Parliamentary Debates, vol. 18, 15–17 Geo. III, 1774–1777, col. 640, 12 May 1775
213. Quoted Rowden, A. W., *op cit.*, p. 369
214. *Memoirs of the Life of Sir Samuel Romilly, Written by Himself*, ii, 325
215. Quoted Rowden, A. W., *op. cit.*, p. 49
216. Nicholson to Wake, December 1717. Quoted Rowden, A. W., *op. cit.*, p. 51
217. Trelawney to Wake, 28 April 1718. Quoted Rowden, A. W., *op. cit.*, p. 52
218. Rowden, A. W., *op. cit.*, p. 278
219. Court Papers MSS., Lambeth No. 1130
220. Stanley, A. P., *Memorials of Westminster Abbey*, p. 101
221. B.M. Egerton MSS. 2182, f. 58
222. B.M. Add. MSS. 34453, f. 230
223. Quoted Rowden, A. W., *op. cit.*, p. 384
224. See Rowden, A. W., *op. cit.*, pp. 415–17
225. Quoted Sykes, N., *William Wake, Archbishop of Canterbury* II. 87
226. Beavoir to Wake, 11 Dec 1718. Quoted Rowden, A. W., *op. cit.*, p. 79
227. Du Pin to Wake. Quoted Rowden, A. W., *op. cit.*, p. 79
228. Wake to Du Pin, 24 Feb 1718. Quoted Rowden, A. W., *op. cit.*, p. 80
229. Sykes, N., *William Wake, Archbishop of Canterbury* I. 266
230. Wake to Beavoir, quoted Rowden, A. W., *op. cit.*, pp. 83, 84
231. Wake to Courayer, 9 Dec 1721. Quoted Rowden, A. W., *op. cit.*, p. 88
232. Wake to Courayer, 7 Dec 1726. Quoted Rowden, A. W., *op. cit.*, p. 95
233. *Ibid.*
234. Churton, E., *Life of Watson*, p. 173. Quoted Rowden, A. W., *op. cit.*, p. 406
235. Potter to Newcastle, 10 March 1746. Newcastle B.M. Add. MSS. 32706, f. 282
236. Herring to Newcastle, 20 June 1750. Newcastle B.M. Add. MSS. 32721, f. 132
237. Herring to Newcastle, 24 July 1754. Quoted Rowden, A. W., *op. cit.*, p. 206
238. Chandler, T. B., *Life of Johnson*, p. 176. Quoted, Rowden A. W., *op. cit.*, p. 283
239. Rowden, A. W., *op. cit.*, p. 285
240. *Ibid.*, p. 363
241. *Ibid.*, p. 367
242. Howley, W., *A Charge delivered at his Primary Visitation in August and September 1833*

243. Best, G. F. A., *Temporal Pillars*, 1964, p. 277
244. McKilliam, A. E., *op. cit.*, p. 397
245. Longford, E., *Victoria R.I.*, 1964, p. 81
246. *The Times*, 12 Feb. 1848
247. *A Letter to the Clergy and Diocese of Chester, occasioned by the Act of Legislature, Granting Relief to His Majesty's Roman Catholic Subjects*, by John Bird, Lord Bishop of Chester, 1829
248. *Ibid.*
249. Davies, G. C. B., *Henry Phillpotts*, 1954, pp. 251, 252
250. See Chadwick, O. *The Victorian Church*, I. 491, 495
251. *Speech of His Grace, the Archbishop of Canterbury in the House of Lords on February 25, 1851*
252. *The Charge of John Bird, Lord Archbishop of Canterbury, to the Clergy of the Diocese at his Visitation 1857*, p. 6
253. *The Times*, 14 March 1861. Quoted Chadwick, O., *op. cit.*, II. 79
254. *Chronicle of the Convocation*, Upper House, 4 Feb 1852
255. *Ibid.*, 16 Nov 1852
256. *Ibid.*, 17 Nov 1852
257. *Ibid.*, 1 Feb 1854
258. *Ibid.*, 1 Feb 1854
259. *Ibid.*, 7 June 1860
260. *Ibid.*, 18 June 1861
261. *The Charge of John Bird, Lord Archbishop of Canterbury, etc., 1857*, p. 19
262. *Ibid.*, p. 19
263. Best, G. F. A., *op. cit.*, p. 165
264. *The Charge of John Bird, Lord Archbishop of Canterbury, etc, 1857*, p. 12
265. *A Charge intended for Delivery to the Clergy of the Diocese of Canterbury at his 2nd Visitation 1868 by the Most Reverend Charles Thomas, late Lord Archbishop of Canterbury*, 1868, p. 3
266. McKilliam, A. E., *op. cit.*, p. 405
267. Arnold, F., *Our Bishops and our Deans*, I. 163. Quoted McKilliam, A. E., *op. cit.*, p. 406
268. *A Charge addressed to the Clergy of the Diocese of York at his Primary Visitation in August, 1861 by Charles Thomas, Lord Archbishop of York*, 1861, p. 8
269. *A Pastoral Letter addressed to the Clergy and Laity of his Province by Charles Thomas, Archbishop of Canterbury*, 1864
270. *A Primary Charge addressed to the Clergy of his Diocese by Charles Thomas, Archbishop of Canterbury*, 1864
271. *Chronicle of the Convocation*, Upper House, 21 June 1864
272. *Ibid.*
273. Crown Princess to Queen Victoria, 11 April 1863. Quoted *Dearest Mama* (ed. Fulford, R.), 1968, Evans, p. 194
274. Stephenson, A. M. G., *The First Lambeth Conference, 1867*, p. 128. Lambeth Library, Longley Letters III, p. 192
275. Stephenson, A. M. G., *The First Lambeth Conference, 1867*, p. 138
276. *Ibid.*, p. 140
277. See *Cantuar*, p. 325
278. The sermon is included in the official report of the Congress
279. Stephenson, A. M. G., *op. cit.*, p. 151
280. *Guardian*, 21 Feb 1866. Quoted Stephenson, A. M. G., *op. cit.*, p. 159
281. *The Life of John Travers Lewis*, pp. 67. Quoted Stephenson, A. M. G., *op. cit.*, pp. 159, 160
282. Sumner G. H., *Life of Charles Richard Sumner*, p. 451. Quoted Stephenson, A. M. G., *op. cit.*, p. 182

283. Lambeth Library, Longley Letters VI. 6
284. Stephenson, A. M. G., *op. cit.*, p. 192
285. Lambeth Library, Longley Letters III. 91
286. Stephenson, A. M. G., *op. cit.*, p. 256
287. Lambeth Library, Longley Letters VIII. 39
288. Longley to Catherine Longley, 12 Oct 1867. Quoted Stephenson, A. M. G., *op. cit.*, p. 304
289. See Stephenson, A. M. G., 'The First Lambeth Conference and Punch', in *Church Quarterly Review*, January–March 1959, pp. 99–105
290. Lambeth Library, Longley Letters II. ff. 85–86
291. *A Charge intended for Delivery to the Clergy of the Diocese of Canterbury*, 1868
292. I cannot trace the authority for this well-known story, given to me by a colleague at Westminster Abbey.
293. Battiscombe, G., *Queen Alexandra*, 1969, Constable, pp. 42, 43
294. *Chronicle of the Convocation*, Upper House, 10 April 1883
295. *Ibid.*
296. Davidson and Benham, *Life of Archibald Campbell Tait*, 1891, II. 556 note 1
297. *Ibid.*
298. Buckle, G. E., *The Life of Benjamin Disraeli* V. pp. 61–71
299. *Ibid.*
300. Morley, J., *Life of Gladstone*, 1903, III. 93
301. *Church Times*, 31 Oct 1868
302. Ashwell and Wilberforce, *The Life of Samuel Wilberforce* III. 267
303. Kirk-Smith, H., *William Thomson, Archbishop of York*, 1958, p. 155
304. Derby to Disraeli, 3 Nov 1868. Buckle, G., *op. cit.*, V. 68
305. *Ibid.* V. 70
306. Bryce, J., *Studies in Contemporary Biography*, 1903, p. 108
307. Davidson and Benham, *op. cit.*, II. 488
308. Church Congress Report, 1877
309. Quoted Davidson and Benham, *op. cit.* II, 488
310. Tait's Diary for 5 July 1874. Lambeth 53 ff. 21–3
311. Davidson and Benham, *op. cit.*, II. 562
312. For a detailed account of Gladstone's Irish legislation see Bell, P. M. H., *Disestablishment in Ireland and Wales*, 1969
313. *A Charge intended for delivery to the Clergy of the Diocese of Canterbury*, 1868
314. Parliamentary Debates, 3rd Series, vol. 192, cols. 2128–9, 25 June 1868
315. *Chronicle of the Convocation*, Upper House, 3 Feb 1873
316. Quoted Chadwick, O., *op. cit.*, II. 345
317. *Chronicle of the Convocation*, Upper House, 11 Feb 1873
318. *Church Association Monthly Intelligencer*, 1 July 1869. Quoted Marsh, P. T., *The Victorian Church in Decline*, 1968, p. 116
319. Queen to Tait, 15 Jan 1874. See Buckle, G. E., *The Letters of Queen Victoria*, 2nd series, II. 300
320. Buckle, G. E., *The Life of Benjamin Disraeli* V. 317.
321. Marsh, P. T., *op. cit.*, p. 170
322. *The Letters of Disraeli to Lady Bradford and Lady Chesterfield*, I. 63. Quoted Marsh, P. T., *op. cit.*, 164
323. Disraeli to Queen, 11 July 1874, Royal Archives, D5/19. Quoted Marsh, P. T., *op. cit.*, p. 185
324. Quoted Marsh, P. T., *op. cit.*, p. 219
325. Lee to Davidson, 18 Dec 1879. Tait Papers f. 389. Quoted Marsh, P. T., *op. cit.*, p. 232
326. Marsh, P. T., *op. cit.*, p. 233

327. Parliamentary Debates, 3rd Series, vol. 229, col. 625, 15 May 1876
328. *Chronicle of the Convocation*, Upper House, 9 Feb 1870
329. *Ibid.*, 9 Feb 1872
330. *Ibid.*, 8 July 1872
331. *Ibid.*, 15 Feb 1875
332. *Ibid.*, 19 April 1875
333. *Ibid.*, 12 Feb 1873
334. *Ibid.*, 6 May 1873
335. *Ibid.*, 8 Feb 1881
336. *Ibid.*, 11 Feb 1881
337. Davidson and Benham, *op. cit.*, II. 503
338. *Ibid.*, II. 510–12
339. Tait's Diary, Lambeth 17 f. 190
340. *Chronicle of the Convocation*, Upper House, 16 June 1871
341. See Charge of 1866, pp. 55–61. Quoted Davidson and Benham, *op. cit.*, I. 485
342. *Chronicle of the Convocation*, Upper House, 15 Feb 1875
343. Davidson and Benham, *op. cit.*, II. 370
344. *Ibid.*, II. 371
345. *Ibid.*, II. 376
346. See *ibid.*, II. Chap. XXVIII *passim*
347. See also Benson, A. C., *The Life of Edward White Benson*, 1900, ii. 124
348. Bell, G. K. A., *Randall Davidson*, 1935, I, 53
349. Queen to Davidson, 5 Dec 1882. *Letters of Queen Victoria*, 2nd series, III. 367. Quoted Bell, G. K. A., *op. cit.*, I. 55
350. Morley, J., *op. cit.*, III. 96
351. Gladstone to Benson, 16 Dec 1882. Quoted Benson, A. C., *op. cit.*, I. 548
352. Benson, A. C., *op. cit.*, II. 7
353. *Ibid.*, II. 674
354. Benson to Wordsworth, 8 May 1887. Quoted Watson, E. W., *Life of Bishop John Wordsworth*, 1915, p. 165
355. See Benson's letters to Davidson, 5 Jan 1887 (Benson, A. C., *op. cit.*, II, 226) and again 12 March 1888 (Benson, *op cit.*, II. 202)
356. Benson, A. C., *op. cit.*, II. 557
357. *Ibid.*, II. 557
358. *Ibid.*, I. 570
359. Watson, E. W., *op. cit.*, p. 249 and Benson, A. C., *op. cit.*, II. 334
360. See Benson, A. C., *op. cit.*, II. 331
361. Benson to Westcott, 13 Nov 1888. Quoted Benson, A. C., *op. cit.*, II. 332
362. See Archbishop Benson's 'The Duty of the Archbishop's Court to entertain the Cause', reproduced at length in Benson, A. C., *op. cit.*, II. pp. 332–4
363. Benson, A. C., *op. cit.*, II. 339
364. *Ibid.*, II. 347
365. *Ibid.*, II. 353
366. *Ibid.*, II. 356
367. Benson, A. C., *op. cit.*, II. 363–4
368. *Ibid.*, II. 378–81
369. Benson, A. C., *op. cit.*, II. 73
370. *Chronicle of the Convocation*, 17 Sep 1892, p. 371
371. Benson, A. C., *op. cit.*, II. 111
372. *Ibid.*, II. 112
373. *Ibid.*, I. 607
374. Benson, E. W., *Seven Gifts*, 1885, p. 107
375. Benson to Westcott, 22 March 1884. Quoted Benson, A. C., *op. cit.*, II. 66

376. Benson, A. C., *op. cit.*, II. 75 note i
377. Benson to W. H. Smith, undated, *c.* 1888. Quoted Benson, A. C., *op. cit.*, II. 77
378. Benson to Gladstone, 21 April 1891. Quoted Benson, A. C., *op. cit.*, II. 81
379. Benson's diary. Quoted Benson, A. C., *op. cit.*, II. 100
380. Church Congress 1889. Official Report p. 8
381. *Ibid.*, 1891, p. 42
382. Benson's diary, 20 Aug 1888. Quoted Benson, A. C., *op. cit.*, II. 216
383. Benson's diary, 11 July 1884. Quoted Benson, A. C., *op. cit.*, II. 30
384. Queen to Benson, 3 Jan 1890. Quoted Benson, A. C., *op. cit.*, II. 293
385. Benson's diary, 21 Jan 1886. Quoted Benson, A. C., *op. cit.*, II. 107
386. Benson's diary, 25 June 1887. Quoted Benson, A. C., *op. cit.*, II. 134
387. Benson's diary, 21 June 1887. Quoted Benson, A. C., *op cit.*, II. 133
388. Benson, E. F. *As We Were*, 1930, p. 217
389. Prince of Wales to Benson, 13 Aug 1891. Quoted Benson, E. F., *op. cit.*, p. 218
390. Benson, E. F., *op. cit.*, p. 103
391. Bell, G. K. A., *op. cit.*, I. 120
392. Benson, A. C., *op. cit.*, II. 213
393. Benson, A. C., *op. cit.*, II. 214
394. *Conference of Bishops of the Anglican Communion, 1888.* S.P.C.K., p. 19
395. See *Cantuar*, pp. 410, 411
396. Benson, A. C., *op. cit.*, II. 619
397. *Ibid.*, II. 617
398. *Ibid.*, II. 173
399. *Ibid.*, II. 178
400. Benson, E. W., *The Seven Gifts*, p. 214
401. Benson, A. C., *op. cit.*, II. 183
402. Alan Don, private diary.
403. Benson, A. C., *op. cit.*, II. 156–61
404. Benson, E. W., *Seven Gifts*, p. 208
405. Benson, A. C., *op. cit.*, II. 585
406. Benson to Canon Mason, 27 Nov 1887. Quoted Benson, A. C., *op. cit.*, II. 586
407. *Ibid.*, II. 587
408. *Ibid.*, II. 593
409. *Ibid.*, II., 581–624
410. *Ibid.*, II., 597
411. Benson to Halifax, 15 Oct 1894. Quoted Benson, A. C., *op. cit.*, II. 604–5
412. *Ibid.*, II. 600
413. Benson to Halifax, 14 Dec 1894. Quoted Benson, A. C., *op. cit.*, II. 611
414. McKilliam, A. E., *op. cit.*, p. 425
415. *Quarterly Review*, October 1897, p. 320
416. Queen to Davidson, 24 Oct 1896. Quoted Bell, G. K. A., *op. cit.*, I. 284
417. Davidson to Queen, 18 Oct 1896. Quoted Bell, G. K. A., *op. cit.*, I. 283
418. Queen to Davidson, 24 Oct 1896. Quoted Bell, G. K. A., *op. cit.*, I. 284
419. Temple to Salisbury, 23 Oct 1896. Quoted *Memoirs of Archbishop Temple* by Seven Friends (ed. Sandford, E. G.), 1906, II. 246
420. Temple to Tait, 25 Feb 1861. Davidson and Benham, *op. cit.*, I. 291
421. Temple to William Temple, 25 May 1888. Quoted Sandford, E. G., *op. cit.*, II. 678
422. Bell, G. K. A., *op. cit.*, I. 291
423. Sandford, E. G., *op. cit.*, II. 210

424. See the tribute of Sir George Collard, Mayor of Canterbury. Quoted Sandford, E. G., *op. cit.*, II. 236
425. Sandford, E. G., *op. cit.*, II. 216
426. Temple, F., to Davidson, 23 Oct 1900. Quoted Bell, G. K. A., *op. cit.*, I. 299
427. Quoted Sandford, E. G., *op. cit.*, II. 262
428. Bell, G. K. A., *op. cit.*, I. 303
429. Bell, G. K. A., *op. cit.*, I. 304
430. Sandford, E. G., *op. cit.*, II. 277
431. Bishop of Albany to Davidson, 19 Feb 1897. Quoted Bell, G. K. A., *op. cit.*, I. 300
432. Official Report, Lambeth Conference, 1897
433. *Ibid.*
434. Sandford, E. G., *op. cit.*, II. 283
435. Parliamentary Debates, 4th Series, vol. 115, cols. 1221–2, 4 Dec. 1902
436. *Ibid.*, col. 1225
437. Temple to his sister, 13 Nov 1841. Quoted Sandford, E. G., *op. cit.*, I. 54
438. Temple to his mother, Oct 1841. Quoted Sandford, E. G., *op. cit.*, I. 55
439. Sandford, E. G., *op. cit.*, II. 228
440. *Ibid.*, II. 292
441. *Ibid.*, II. 301
442. *Ibid.*, II, 304
443. *Ibid.*, II. 366
444. Parliamentary Debates, 4th Series, vol. 89, col. 16, 25 Jan. 1901
445. Bell, G. K. A., *op cit.*, I. 291
446. *Letters of Queen Victoria*, 2nd Series, III. 367. Quoted Bell, G. K. A., I. 55
447. Bell, G. K. A., *op. cit.*, I. 164, 165
448. *Ibid.*, I. 383
449. The King to Davidson, 11 Jan 1903. Quoted Bell, G. K. A., I. 386
450. Lord Halifax to Davidson, 20 Jan 1903. Quoted Bell, G. K. A., *op. cit.*, I. 388
451. See Davidson's 2nd Visitation Charge to Canterbury Diocese, Feb. 1912. Quoted Bell, G. K. A., *op. cit.*, I. 711
452. Davidson to Bannerman, 11 Dec 1905. Quoted Bell, G. K. A., *op. cit.*, I. 502, 503
453. Davidson to Balfour, 5 Jan 1903. Quoted Bell, G. K. A., *op. cit.*, II. 1239
454. Bell, G. K. A., *op. cit.*, II. 1240
455. Davidson to Balfour, 17 Sep 1903. Quoted Bell, G. K. A., *op. cit.*, I. 421
456. Davidson to Balfour, 21 Sep 1903. Quoted Bell, G. K. A., *op. cit.*, I. 422
457. Davidson to Broomhall, 24 Oct 1903. Quoted Bell, G. K. A., *op. cit.*, I. 436
458. Broomhall to Davidson, 12 Aug 1904. Quoted Bell, G. K. A., *op. cit.*, I. 437
459. Parliamentary Debates, 4th Series, vol. 129, col. 1005, 11 Feb. 1904
460. *Ibid.*, vol. 131, col. 190, 4 March 1904
461. See his speech in Convocation, 30 April 1901
462. Bell, G. K. A., *op. cit.*, I. 549
463. *Ibid.*
464. Davidson to Balfour, 3 Jan 1905. Quoted Bell, G. K. A., *op. cit.*, II. 482
465. Balfour to Davidson, 6 Jan 1905. Quoted Bell, G. K. A., *op. cit.*, II. 482
466. Davidson to Scott Lidgett, 23 March 1909. Quoted Bell, G. K. A., *op. cit.*, I. 590
467. Bell, G. K. A., *op. cit.*, II. 733
468. *Chronicle of the Convocation*, Upper House, 9 Feb 1915
469. *Chronicle of the Convocation*, Upper House, 17 Feb 1916
470. Davidson to Asquith, 7 May 1915. Quoted Bell, G. K. A., *op. cit.*, II. 758

471. Quoted Bell, G. K. A., *op. cit.*, II. 832
472. Davidson to Horton, 11 Oct 1917. Quoted Bell, G. K. A., *op. cit.*, II. 837
473. Rae, J., *Conscience and Politics*, 1970, p. 235
474. Bell, G. K. A., *op. cit.*, II. 786–9
475. Davidson to Deissmann, 22 Sep 1915. Quoted Bell, G. K. A., *op. cit.*, II. 921
476. Bell, G. K. A., *op. cit.*, II. 947
477. Davidson to Lloyd George, 24 May 1919. Quoted Bell, G. K. A., *op. cit.*, II. 947
478. Bell, G. K. A., *op. cit.*, II. 949, 950
479. *Ibid.*, I. 541
480. Davidson to Birrell, 20 Feb 1907. Quoted Bell, G. K. A., *op. cit.*, I. 542
481. Birrell to Davidson, 21 Feb 1907. Quoted Bell, G. K. A., *op. cit.*, I. 581.
482. Bell, G. K. A., *op. cit.*, I. 628
483. *Ibid.*, II. 1306.
484. Davidson to Reith, 8 May 1926. Quoted Bell, G. K. A., *op. cit.*, II. 1306
485. Murray to Davidson, 20 May 1926. Quoted Bell, G. K. A., *op. cit.*, II. 1315
486. Bell, G. K. A., *op. cit.*, I. 608
487. *Ibid.*, I. 609–11
488. *Chronicle of the Convocation*, Upper House, 10 Feb 1920
489. Bell, G. K. A., *op. cit.*, II. 957
490. *Ibid.*, II. 968, 969
491. *Ibid.*, II. 975
492. *Ibid.*, II. 979
493. Davidson to Bishop of London, 31 March 1914. Quoted Bell, G. K. A., *op. cit.*, I. 676
494. *Chronicle of the Convocation*, Upper House, 30 April 1914
495. See Gore to Davidson, 15 March 1919. Quoted Bell, G. K. A., *op. cit.*, II. 470 ff.
496. Davidson to Gore, 15 Feb 1922. Quoted Bell, G. K. A., *op. cit.*, II,, 1147
497. Same to same, 28 Dec 1922. Quoted Bell, G. K. A., *op. cit.*, II. 1150
498. Barnes to Davidson. Quoted Bell, G. K. A., *op. cit.*, II. 1321
499. Bell, G. K. A., *op. cit.*, II. 1332
500. *Ibid.*, II. 1333
501. *Chronicle of the Convocation*, Upper House, 13 Feb 1927
502. Parliamentary Debates, 4th Series, vol. 69, col. 773, 12 Dec. 1927
503. Bell, G. K. A., *op. cit.*, II. 1351
504. *Ibid.*, II. 1352
505. *Ibid.*, II. 1353
506. *Ibid.*, I. 571
507. *Ibid.*, II. 1003, 1004
508. Davidson to the Bishop of Gloucester, 15 May 1920. Quoted Bell, G. K. A., *op. cit.*, II. 1005
509. Bell, G. K. A., *op. cit.*
510. *Ibid.*, I. 694
511. Davidson to Metropolitan of Odessa, 8 Jan 1919. Quoted Bell, G. K. A., *op. cit.*, II. 1068
512. *Ibid.*, II. 1080
513. *The Nation and the Athenaeum*, 21 April 1923: also Asquith to Davidson, 22 April 1923. Quoted Bell, G. K. A., *op. cit.*, II. 1081
514. Bell, G. K. A. *op. cit.*, II. 1089
515. *Ibid.*, II. 1091

516. Patriarch of Constantinople to Davidson, 28 July 1922. Quoted Bell, G. K. A., *op. cit.*, II. 1006
517. Bell, G. K. A., *op. cit.*, II. 1113
518. Official Report, Lambeth Conference, 1920
519. *Chronicle of the Convocation*, Upper House, 6 Feb 1924
520. Henson, H. H., *Retrospect of an Unimportant Life*, 1942, 1943, 1950. II. 139
521. Bell, G. K. A., *op. cit.*, II. 1260, 1261
522. *Ibid.*, II. 1123
523. *The Congregationalist*, U.S.A. 30 Aug 1923. Quoted Bell, G. K. A., *op. cit.*, II. 1124
524. *Chronicle of the Convocation*, Upper House, 22 Feb 1906
525. Bell, G. K. A., *op. cit.*, I. 538
526. Parliamentary Debates, 4th Series, vol. 162, col. 934, 1 Aug. 1906
527. Bell, G. K. A., *op. cit.*, II. 1364
528. Lockhart, J. G., *Cosmo Gordon Lang*, 1949, p. 310
529. *Ibid.*
530. *A King's Story: the Memoirs of H.R.H. the Duke of Windsor*, 1951, p. 273
531. Lockhart, J. G., *op. cit.*, p. 290
532. Private information
533. Private information
534. Lockhart, J. G., *op. cit.*, p. 268
535. Official Report, Lambeth Conference, 1920
536. Lockhart, J. G., *op. cit.*, p. 329
537. *Ibid.*, p. 370
538. *Ibid.*, p. 273
539. *Ibid.*, p. 332
540. *Ibid.*, pp. 329, 330
541. *Ibid.*, p. 332
542. *Ibid.*, p. 334
543. *Ibid.*, p. 334
544. *Ibid.*, p. 335
545. *Ibid.*, p. 382
546. *Ibid.*, p. 382
547. *Ibid.*, p. 383
548. *Ibid.*, p. 246
549. *Ibid.*, p. 248
550. *Ibid.*, p. 251
551. *Ibid.*, p. 130
552. *Ibid.*, p. 130
553. *The Queen's Journal*, 30 Jan 1898. Quoted Lockhart, J. G., *op. cit.*, p. 132
554. Lockhart, J. G., *op. cit.*, p. 136
555. *Ibid.*, p. 143
556. *Ibid.*, p. 144
557. *Ibid.*, p. 390
558. *Ibid.*, p. 392
559. *Ibid.*, p. 390; and p. 386
560. *Ibid.*, p. 392
561. *Ibid.*, p. 395
562. *Ibid.*, p. 398
563. *Ibid.*, p. 399
564. See Peart Binns, J. S., *Blunt*, pp. 151ff.
565. Lockhart, J. G., *op. cit.*, p. 404
566. *Ibid.*, p. 405

567. Henson, H. H., *op. cit.* II. 378
568. Lockhart, J. G., *op. cit.*, p. 406 n.
569. Private information
570. Lockhart, J. G., *op. cit.*, p. 406
571. *Ibid.*, p. 408
572. *Ibid.*, p. 417
573. Alan Don, Private Diary
574. Henson, H. H., *op. cit.*, II. 382
575. Temple, W., to his brother, 27 Jan 1942. Quoted Iremonger, F. A., *William Temple*, 1948, p. 474
576. Iremonger, F. A., *op. cit.*, p. 475
577. *Ibid.*, p. 3
578. Quoted *ibid.*, p. 79
579. Quoted *ibid.*, p. 83
580. Quoted *ibid.*, p. 79
581. *Ibid.*, p. 219
582. *Ibid.*, p. 233
583. *Ibid.*, p. 246
584. Headlam to Temple. Quoted *ibid.*, p. 412
585. *Ibid.*, p. 412
586. *Ibid.*, pp. 419, 420
587. *Ibid.*, p. 424
588. See Temple's address to the Pan-Anglican Congress of 1908
589. *Ibid.*, p. 429
590. Temple W., *Christianity and Social Order*, Penguin Special, 1942
591. See Iremonger, F. A., *op. cit.*, p. 57; also *William Temple: An Estimate and Appreciation*, 1946, p. 73
592. Iremonger, F. A., *op. cit.*, p. 595
593. Henson, H. H., *op. cit.*, III. 234, 235
594. Temple to Eden, Dec 1942. Quoted Iremonger, F. A., *op. cit.*, p. 565
595. House of Lords Debates, vol. 126, col. 821, 23 March 1943
596. Iremonger, F. A., *op. cit.*, p. 567
597. *Ibid.*, p. 571
598. *Christus Veritas*, Temple, W., 1924 Preface
599. Temple, W. *Christianity as an Interpretation of History*, 1945, p. 12
600. Temple, W., *Readings in St. John's Gospel*, 1945, p. 261: also Sandford, E. G., *op. cit.*, II. 690
601. Alan Don, Private Diary
602. Jasper, R., *George Bell*, 1967, p. 285
603. Purcell, W., *Fisher of Lambeth*, 1969, p. 110
604. *Ibid.*, p. 149
605. *Ibid.*, p. 87
606. Bell to Garbett, 21 Dec 1945. Quoted Jasper, R., *op. cit.*, p. 194
607. Purcell, W., *op. cit.*, p. 207
608. Matthews, W. R., *Memories and Meanings*, 1968, p. 306
609. Purcell, W., *op. cit.*, p. 202
610. *Ibid.*, p. 203, 204
611. Henson, H. H., *op. cit.*, I. 284
612. Purcell, W., *op. cit.*, p. 205
613. *Ibid.*, p. 205
614. Davidson to the Bishop of Durham, 10 Nov 1906. Quoted Bell, G. K. A., *op. cit.*, I. p. 509
615. *Chronicle of the Convocation*, Upper House, 15 Oct. 1947

616. *Ibid.*
617. Johnson, H., *Searching for Light*, 1968, p. 272
618. *Ibid.*, p. 263
619. *Ibid.*, p. 326
620. *Ibid.*, p. 402
621. Purcell, W., *op. cit.*, p. 141
622. *Ibid.*, p. 179
623. Private information
624. *The Lambeth Conference, 1958*, S.P.C.K., 1958, p. 1.21
625. Purcell, W., *op. cit.*, p. 199
626. *Ibid.*, p. 229
627. *Ibid.*, p. 270
628. *Ibid.*, p. 277
629. *Ibid.*, p. 283
630. *Ibid.*, p. 283
631. See *The Archbishop Speaks* (ed. Carpenter, E.), 1956, pp. 63–71
632. Purcell, W., *op. cit.*, p. 160
633. Carpenter, E., *The Archbishop Speaks*, p. 68
634. *Ibid.*, pp. 70, 71
635. Purcell, W., *op. cit.*, p. 189
636. *Ibid.*, p. 188
637. *Ibid.*, p. 191
638. Carpenter, E., *The Archbishop Speaks*, pp. 124, 125
639. *Ibid.*, pp. 208–12, 213–15
640. *Ibid.*, pp. 114–21
641. See Carpenter, E., *The Archbishop Speaks*, pp. 200–7: also Purcell, W., *op. cit.*, p. 211
642. House of Lords Debates, vol. 196, col. 1304, 26 April 1956
643. Private information
644. *The Times*, 23 May 1958
645. Purcell, W., *op. cit.*, p. 259
646. *Ibid.*, p. 261
647. *Ibid.*, p. 244
648. Private information
649. Purcell, W., *op. cit.*, p. 253
650. *Ibid.*, p. 130
651. *Ibid.*, p. 119
652. The Archbishop also has a special relationship with the First Church Estates Commissioner and with the Secretary of the General Synod. Also with the heads of the great missionary societies, particularly U.S.P.G. and C.M.S.
653. Bishop of Huron, *Unity in Mission*, 1967, pp. 8, 9. It is interesting to notice that the Church and State Commission in its Report (1970) suggests that if a particular method of appointment were adopted for the Archbishop of Canterbury, the Executive Officer of the Anglican Communion should be a member of the Vacancy in See Committee of the diocese. The Archbishop of Canterbury would be on the Vacancy in See Committee for the Diocese of York, but not the Executive Officer (Appendix C.3).
654. Hook, W. F., *Lives of the Archbishops of Canterbury*, 12 vols, 1860–76, I. 40
655. *Theology*, Vol. LVIII. No. 415, Jan. 1955 Editorial

ABBEY, C. J. *The English Church and its Bishops*. Longmans, 1887.

ABBEY and OVERTON. *The English Church in the Eighteenth Century*. Longmans, 1878.

ADY, C. M. *The English Church*. Faber & Faber, 1940.

*The Anglo-Saxon Chronicle*. Ed. Whitelock with Douglas and S. I. Tucker, EHD, vol. i, and independently 1961; also Everyman Library, trs. Garmonsway, G. N., reprinted 1967.

ASHWELL, A. R. *Life of Bishop Samuel Wilberforce*. John Murray, 1880–2.

BABBAGE, S. B. *Puritanism and Richard Bancroft*. S.P.C.K., 1962.

BARLOW, F. *Edward the Confessor*. Eyre & Spottiswoode, 1970.

BATTISCOMBE, G. *Queen Alexandra*. Constable, 1969.

*Materials for the History of Thomas Becket, Archbishop of Canterbury*. Ed. J. C. Robertson. Rolls Series. 1875ff.

*Bede's Ecclesiastical History of the English People*. Ed. Colgrave and Mynors. O.U.P., 1969.

BELL, G. K. A. *Randall Davidson, Archbishop of Canterbury*. O.U.P., 1935.

BELL, P. M. H. *Disestablishment in Ireland and Wales*. S.P.C.K., 1969.

BENSON, A. C. *The Life of Edward White Benson*. Macmillan, 1900.

BENSON, E. F. *As We Were*. Longmans, 1930.

BENSON, E. W. *Seven Gifts*. 1885.

BEST, G. F. A. *Temporal Pillars*. C.U.P., 1964.

BETHELL, D. *William of Corbeil and the Canterbury York Dispute*. J.E.H. XIX. October 1968.

BEVAN, G. M. *Portraits of the Archbishops of Canterbury*. Mowbray, Oxford, 1908.

BINNS, J. S. P. *Bishop Blunt, 1879–1957*. Mountain Press, 1969.

BIRCH, T. *Life of Tillotson*. 1753.

—— *Court and Times of Charles I*. 1848.

BOSHER, R. S. *The Making of the Restoration Settlement*. Dacre Press: A. & C. Black, 1951.

BOWEN, D. *The Idea of the Victorian Church*. McGill University Press, Montreal, 1968.

BRETT, T. *Account of Church Government and Governors*. 2nd ed., 1710.

539

BROOK, V. J. K. *Life of Archbishop Parker*. O.U.P., 1962.

BROOKE, Z. M. *The English Church and the Papacy*. C.U.P., 1931.

BROSE, O. J. *Church and Parliament. The Reshaping of the Church of England, 1828–1860*. O.U.P., 1959.

BROWNE, J. C. *Lambeth Palace ad its Associations*. Blackwood, 1882.

BRYCE, J. *Studies in Contemporary Biography*. Macmillan, 1903.

*The Canon Law of the Church of England being the Report of the Archbishops' Commission on Canon Law*. S.P.C.K., 1947.

*The Canons of the Church of England*. S.P.C.K., 1969.

CARMICHAEL, J. D. and GOODWIN, H. S. *William Temple's Political Legacy*, Mowbray, 1963.

CARPENTER, E. F. *Thomas Sherlock*. S.P.C.K. (Church Historical Society), 1936.

—— *Thomas Tenison, His Life and Times*. S.P.C.K. (Church Historical Society), 1948.

—— *The Protestant Bishop*. Longmans, 1956.

CARPENTER, S. C. *Church and People, 1789–1889*. S.P.C.K., 1933.

CARSTARES, W. *State Papers and Letters*. 1774.

—— *The Catholic Encyclopaedia*. 15 vols, published between 1907 and 1914.

CHADWICK, N. *Studies in the Early British Church*. C.U.P., 1958.

CHADWICK, O. *Victorian Church*. Part I, 1966; Part II, 1970. A. & C. Black.

CHENEY, C. R. *From Becket to Langton*. Manchester University Press, 1956.

—— *Hubert Walter*. A. & C. Black, 1967.

*Chronicle of the Convocation of Canterbury*.

*Church Assembly Report of Proceedings*.

*Church Congress Reports*.

CHURCHILL, I. J. *Canterbury Administration*. S.P.C.K., 1933.

CLARENDON, EARL OF. *The History of the Rebellion and Civil Wars in England*. Oxford, 1826.

COBBETT, W. *Parliamentary History*. 1806.

*Colenso, Letters from Natal*. Ed. Wyn Rees. Shuter & Shooter. 1958.

COLLINSON, P. *The Elizabethan Puritan Movement*. Jonathan Cape, 1967.

*Concilia Magnae Britanniae et Hiberniae*. Ed. Wilkins. 1737.

COULTON, G. G. *Medieval Panorama*. C.U.P. & Collins, 1938.

*The Works of Thomas Cranmer, Archbishop of Canterbury, Martyr, 1556*. Ed. J. G. Cox. Parker Society, 1844–6.

*Life and Letters of Mandell Creighton, D.D.* by his wife. 2 vols. Longmans, 1906.

CROSS, A. L. *The Anglican Episcopate and the American Colonies*. Longmans, 1902.

DAHMUS, J. *William Courtenay*, The Pennsylvania Park U.P., 1966
DARK, S. *Seven Archbishops*. Eyre & Spottiswoode, 1944.
DAVIDSON, R. T. *Five Archbishops, a Sermon*. S.P.C.K., 1911.
—— *The Five Lambeth Conferences*. S.P.C.K., 1920.
DAVIDSON and BENHAM. *Life of Archibald Campbell Tait*. 2 vols. Macmillan, 1891.
DAVIES, G. C. B. *Henry Phillpotts, Bishop of Exeter, 1778–1869*. S.P.C.K., 1954.
DEANESLY, M. *The Pre-Conquest Church in England*. A. & C. Black, 1961.
—— *Augustine of Canterbury*. Nelson, 1964.
—— *Sidelights on the Anglo-Saxon Church*. A. & C. Black, 1962.
*Dearest Mama*. Ed. Roger Fulford, Evans, 1968.
*Dictionary of Christian Biography during the first eight Centuries*. Ed. Smith and Wace. 2 vols. Murray, 1880.
*Oxford Dictionary of the Christian Church*. Ed. F. L. Cross. O.U.P., 1966.
*Dictionary of English Church History*. Ed. Ollard, Crosse, Bond. Mowbray, 1948.
*Dictionary of National Biography*. O.U.P.
Digest of S.P.G. Records, 1701–1892. Published by the Society. 1893.
DOUIE, D. L. *Archbishop Pecham*. Clarendon Press, 1952.
DOWNEY, J. *The Eighteenth Century Pulpit*. O.U.P., 1969.
D'OYLY, G. *Life of William Sancroft*. 1821.
DU BOULAY, F. R. H. *The Lordship of Canterbury*. Nelson, 1966.
DUCKETT, E. S. *Saint Dunstan of Canterbury*. Canterbury, 1955.
EVERY, G. *The High Church Party, 1688–1718*. S.P.C.K., 1956.
*Encyclopaedia Britannica*. 11th Edition, 1910–11, vols. 7–8.
FLORENCE OF WORCESTER. *Chronicon ex Chronicis*. Ed Thorpe. English Historical Society, 1848–9.
FULLER, M. J. *The Throne of Canterbury or The Archbishop's Jurisdiction*. Griffith Farran & Co., 1891.
*The Historical Works of Gervase of Canterbury*. Ed. William Stubbs. Rolls Series. Longmans & Trübner, 1879.
GODFREY, C. J. *The Church in Anglo-Saxon England*. C.U.P., 1962.
*The Remains of Edmund Grindal D.D.* Ed. Nicholson, W. 1843.
HADDAN and STUBBS. *Councils, and Ecclesiastical Documents relating to Great Britain and Ireland*. Oxford, 1870.
HANSARD. *Parliamentary Debates*.
HART, A. T. *John Sharp, Archbishop of York*. S.P.C.K., 1949.
HAUGAARD, W. P. *Elizabeth and the English Reformation*. C.U.P., 1968.
HEAD, R. E. *Royal Supremacy and the Trials of Bishops, 1558–1725*. S.P.C.K., 1962.

HENSON, H. H. *Retrospect of an Unimportant Life.* 3 vols. O.U.P., 1942, 1943, 1950.

HERRING, T. *A Sermon preached at Kensington on Wednesday the 7th of January.* London, 1747.

*Letters from the late Most Reverend Dr. Thomas Herring, Lord Archbishop of Canterbury to William Duncombe, Esq., Deceased, from the year 1728–1757.*

HERVEY. *Memoirs of the Reign of George II.* John Murray, 1848.

HINCHLIFF, P. *The One Sided Reciprocity.* Darton, Longman & Todd, 1966.

—— *John William Colenso: A Fresh Appraisal.* Journal of Ecclesiastical History, Vol. XIII, 1962.

HOLT, J. C. *Magna Carta.* C.U.P., 1965.

HOOK, W. F. *Lives of the Archbishops of Canterbury.* 2nd ed. rev. and new series. Bentley & Son, 1861–1876.

HOWELL, T. B. *State Trials.* 1809–15.

HOWLEY, W. *A Charge delivered at his Primary Visitation in August and September 1833.* 1833.

—— *A Charge delivered at his Ordinary Visitation in September 1840 by William, Lord Archbishop of Canterbury.* 1840.

—— *A Charge delivered at his Ordinary Visitation 1844 by William, Lord Archbishop of Canterbury.* 1844.

HUGHES, P. *The Reformation in England.* 3 vols. Hollis & Carter, 1950, 1953, 1954.

INGE, W. R. *Diary of a Dean.* Hutchinson, 1949.

INGLIS, B. *Abdication.* Hodder & Stoughton, 1966.

IREMONGER, F. A. *William Temple.* O.U.P., 1948.

JACOB, E. F. *Henry Chichele.* Nelson, 1967.

—— *Introduction to the Register of Henry Chichele.* Vols. I and II. O.U.P., 1943, 1938.

—— *The Fifteenth Century, 1399–1485.* Oxford History of England. O.U.P., 1961.

*James I, by his Contemporaries.* Ed. Robert Ashton. Hutchinson, 1969.

JASPER, R. C. D. *George Bell, Bishop of Chichester.* O.U.P., 1967.

JESSE, J. H. *Memoirs of the Life and Reign of George III.* Tinsley Brothers, London, 1867.

JOHNSON, HEWLETT. *Searching for Light.* Michael Joseph, 1968.

KEMP, E. W. *An Introduction to Canon Law.* Hodder & Stoughton, 1957.

*A King's Story: The Memoirs of H.R.H. the Duke of Windsor, K.G.* Cassell, 1951.

KIRK-SMITH, H. *William Thomson: Archbishop of York.* S.P.C.K., 1958.

KNOWLES, DOM D. *The Monastic Order in England.* C.U.P., 1949.

—— *Thomas Becket.* C.U.P., 1970.

—— *Episcopal Colleagues of Archbishop Thomas Becket.* C.U.P., 1970.

LAMB, J. W. *The Archbishopric of Lichfield.* Faith Press, 1964.

—— *The Archbishopric of York.* Faith Press, 1967.

LATHBURY, T. *A History of the Convocation of the Church of England.* 2nd edition. J. R. Smith, 1853.

*Laud's Works.* Library of Anglo-Catholic Theology, Oxford, 1847–60. J. H. Parker.

LE NEVE, J. *The Lives and Characters of the Protestant Bishops of the Church of England.* 1720.

LEE, SIR S. *King Edward VII, a Biography.* Macmillan, 1925.

LLOYD, R. *The Church of England in the Twentieth Century.* Student Christian Movement, 1966.

LOCKHART, J. G. *Cosmo Gordon Lang.* Hodder & Stoughton, 1949.

LONGFORD, E. *Victoria R.I.* Weidenfeld & Nicolson, 1964.

LONGLEY, C. T. *A Primary Charge addressed to the Clergy of his Diocese by Charles Thomas, Archbishop of Canterbury 1864.* 1864.

—— *A Pastoral Letter addressed to the Clergy and Laity of his Province by Charles Thomas, Archbishop of Canterbury 1864.* 1864.

—— *A Charge intended for Delivery to the Clergy of the Diocese of Canterbury at his 2nd Visitation 1868 by the Most Reverend Charles Thomas, late Lord Archbishop of Canterbury.* 1868.

LOYN, H. R. *Anglo-Saxon England and the Norman Conquest.* Longmans, 1962.

LUXTON, G. *Unity in Mission.* 1967.

MACDONALD, A. J. *Lanfranc.* O.U.P., 1926.

MAITLAND, F. W. *Roman Canon Law in the Church of England.* Methuen, 1898.

MARSH, P. T. *The Victorian Church in Decline.* Routledge, 1968.

MATTHEWS, A. G. *Walker Revised.* 1945.

MATTHEWS, W. R. and others. *William Temple: an Estimate and an Appreciation.* James Clarke, 1946.

*The Life of Frederick Denison Maurice.* Ed. Frederick Maurice, 4th edition. 2 vols. Macmillan, 1885.

MAYR-HARTING, H. *Henry II and the Papacy, 1170–1189.* J.E.H., Vol. XVI, April 1965.

McKILLIAM, A. E. *A Chronicle of the Archbishops of Canterbury.* J. Clarke, 1913.

McKISSACK, M. *The Fourteenth Century, 1307–1399.* Oxford History of England. O.U.P., 1959.

MONYPENNY and BUCKLE. *Life of Disraeli.* 6 vols. John Murray, 1910.

MOORMAN, J. R. H. *Church Life in England in the Thirteenth Century.* C.U.P., 1945.

—— *A History of the Church in England.* A. & C. Black, 1953.

MORLEY, J. *The Life of William Ewart Gladstone.* Macmillan, 1903.

543

MYERS, A. R. *England in the Late Middle Ages*. Pelican History of England. Penguin, 1966.

NEWSOME, D. *Godliness and Good Learning*. John Murray, 1961.

NICHOLLS, J. *Literary Anecdotes of the Eighteenth Century*. 1812.

PERKINS, J. *The Crowning of the Sovereign*. Methuen, 1937.

PHILLIMORE, W. G. F. *The Ecclesiastical Law of the Church of England*. Sweet & Maxwell and Stephens & Son, 1895.

POLLARD, A. F. *Wolsey*. Longmans, 1929.

POOLE, A. L. *From Domesday Book to Magna Carta, 1087–1216*. O.U.P., 1951.

POWICKE, F. M. *Stephen Langton*. O.U.P. and Spearman, 1928.

POWICKE, SIR M. *The Thirteenth Century, 1216–1307*. Oxford History of England. O.U.P., 1951.

PROTHERO, R. E. *Life and Letters of Dean Stanley*. 2 vols. Murray, 1893.

PUGH, R. B. *Imprisonment in Medieval England*. C.U.P., 1968.

PURCELL, W. *Fisher of Lambeth*. Hodder & Stoughton, 1969.

RICHARDSON and SAYLES. *The Governance of Medieval England*. Edinburgh University Press, 1964.

RIDLEY, J. *Thomas Cranmer*. Clarendon Press, 1962.

ROPER, H. TREVOR. *Archbishop Laud*. 2nd edition. Macmillan, 1962.

ROWDEN, A. W. *The Primates of the Four Georges*. Murray, 1916.

ROWSE, A. L. *The England of Elizabeth*. Macmillan, 1950.

RUDGE, P. F. *Ministry and Management*. Tavistock, 1968.

SAYLES, G. O. *The Medieval Foundations of England*. Edinburgh University Press, 1966.

SCARISBRICK, J. J. *Henry VIII*. Eyre & Spottiswoode, 1968.

SEEBOHM, F. *The Oxford Reformers*. Everyman Library, 1929.

SOUTHERN, R. W. *Saint Anselm and his Biographer*. C.U.P., 1963.

—— *Western Society and the Church in the Middle Ages*. Pelican History of the Church. Penguin, 1970.

STALEY, V. *The Life and Times of Gilbert Sheldon*. Wells, Gardner, Darton & Co., 1913.

STANLEY, A. P. *Historical Memorials of Canterbury*. Murray, 1883.

STENTON, D. M. *English Society in the Early Middle Ages*. Pelican History of England. Penguin, 1967.

STENTON, F. M. *Anglo-Saxon England*. 2nd edition. Oxford History of England. O.U.P., 1950.

STEPHENSON, A. M. G. *The First Lambeth Conference, 1867*. S.P.C.K., 1967.

STOCK, E. *A History of the Church Missionary Society* (C.M.S.). 1899–1916.

STRYPE, J. *Memorials of Thomas Cranmer*. Oxford, 1840.

—— *The Life and Acts of John Aylmer*. Oxford, 1821.

—— *The History and Life and Acts of Edmund Grindal*. Oxford, 1821.

—— *The Life and Acts of John Whitgift*. London, 1822.

STRYPE, J. *The Life and Acts of Matthew Parker*. Oxford, 1821.

STUBBS, W. *Memorials of St. Dunstan*. Rolls Series. 1874.

SUMNER, J. B. *A Letter to the Clergy and Diocese of Chester Occasioned by the Act of the Legislature granting Relief to His Majesty's Roman Catholic Subjects*. 1829.

—— *The Speech of His Grace, the Archbishop of Canterbury in the House of Lords, Feb. 25, 1851*.

—— *The Charge of John Bird Sumner, Lord Archbishop of Canterbury to the Clergy of the Diocese at his Visitation 1857*.

SYKES, N. *Edmund Gibson*. O.U.P., 1926.

—— *William Wake, Archbishop of Canterbury, 1657–1737*. C.U.P., 1957.

—— *From Sheldon to Secker, 1660–1768*. C.U.P., 1959.

—— *Church and State in England in the XVIIIth Century*. C.U.P., 1962.

—— *Queen Anne and the Episcopate*. English Historical Review, Vol L.

TANNER, L. E. *The History of the Coronation*. Pitkins, 1952.

*Memoirs of Archbishop Temple by Seven Friends*. Ed. E. G. Sandford. Macmillan, 1906.

TEMPLE, W. *Some Lambeth Letters, 1942–44*. F. S. Temple. O.U.P., 1963.

—— *Christus Veritas*. Macmillan, 1924.

—— *Natuure, Man and God*. Macmillan, 1940.

—— *Christianity and the Social Order*. A Penguin Special, 1942.

THOMPSON, H. P. *Into All Lands*. S.P.C.K., 1951.

WARREN, W. L. *A Reappraisal of Simon Sudbury, Bishop of London, (1361–75) and Archbishop of Canterbury (1375–81)*. J.E.H., Vol. X, 1959.

WATSON, E. W. *Life of Bishop John Wordsworth*. Longmans, 1915.

WELSBY, P. A. *George Abbot*. S.P.C.K., 1962.

WENDOVER, R. *Flores Historiarum*. Rolls Series. 1886–9.

WHITE, J. L. *Abdication of Edward VIII*. Routledge, 1937.

WHITELOCK, D. *The Beginnings of English Society*. Penguin. Revised ed. 1966.

WHITNEY, J. P. *Earlier Growth of Papal Jurisdiction*. 1932.

WILLIAM OF POITIERS. *Vie de Guillaume le Conquérant*. Ed. Guizot.

WILLIAMS, N. *Elizabeth Queen of England*. Weidenfeld & Nicolson, 1967.

WINSTON, R. *Thomas Becket*. Constable, 1967.

# LIST OF ARCHBISHOPS OF CANTERBURY

| | | | |
|---|---|---|---|
| AUGUSTINE | 597 | THEOBALD | 1139 |
| LAURENTIUS | 604 | THOMAS À BECKET | 1162 |
| MELLITUS | 619 | RICHARD (OF DOVER) | 1174 |
| JUSTUS | 624 | BALDWIN | 1185 |
| HONORIUS | 627 | HUBERT WALTER | 1193 |
| DEUSDEDIT | 655 | STEPHEN LANGTON | 1207 |
| THEODORE | 668 | RICHARD LE GRANT | 1229 |
| BEORHTWEALD | 693 | EDMUND RICH | 1234 |
| TATWINE | 731 | BONIFACE OF SAVOY | 1245 |
| NOTHELM | 735 | ROBERT KILWARDBY | 1273 |
| CUTHBEORHT | 740 | JOHN PECHAM | 1279 |
| BREGUWINE | 761 | ROBERT WINCHELSEY | 1294 |
| JAENBEORHT | 765 | WALTER REYNOLDS | 1313 |
| AETHELHEARD | 793 | SIMON MEPEHAM | 1328 |
| WULFRED | 805 | JOHN STRATFORD | 1333 |
| FEOLOGILD | 832 | THOMAS BRADWARDINE | 1349 |
| CEOLNOTH | 833 | SIMON ISLIP | 1349 |
| AETHELRED | 870 | SIMON LANGHAM | 1366 |
| PLEGMUND | 890 | WILLIAM WHITTLESEY | 1368 |
| AETHELHELM | 914 | SIMON SUDBURY | 1375 |
| WULFHELM | 923 | WILLIAM COURTENAY | 1381 |
| ODA | 942 | THOMAS ARUNDEL | 1396 |
| AEFSIGE | 959 | ROGER WALDEN | 1398 |
| BEORHTHELM | 959 | THOMAS ARUNDEL | 1399 |
| DUNSTAN | 960 | HENRY CHICHELE | 1414 |
| ATHELGAR | c.988 | JOHN STAFFORD | 1443 |
| SIGERIC SERIO | 990 | JOHN KEMP | 1452 |
| AELFRIC | 995 | THOMAS BOURCHIER | 1454 |
| AELFHEAH | 1005 | JOHN MORTON | 1486 |
| LYFING | 1013 | HENRY DEAN | 1501 |
| AETHELNOTH | 1020 | WILLIAM WARHAM | 1503 |
| EADSIGE | 1038 | THOMAS CRANMER | 1533 |
| ROBERT OF JUMIÈGES | 1051 | REGINALD POLE | 1556 |
| STIGAND | 1052 | MATTHEW PARKER | 1559 |
| LANFRANC | 1070 | EDMUND GRINDAL | 1576 |
| ANSELM | 1093 | JOHN WHITGIFT | 1583 |
| RALPH D'ESCURES | 1114 | RICHARD BANCROFT | 1604 |
| WILLIAM DE CORBEIL | 1123 | GEORGE ABBOT | 1611 |

| | | | |
|---|---|---|---|
| WILLIAM LAUD | 1633 | JOHN BIRD SUMNER | 1848 |
| WILLIAM JUXON | 1660 | CHARLES THOMAS | |
| GILBERT SHELDON | 1663 | LONGLEY | 1862 |
| WILLIAM SANCROFT | 1678 | ARCHIBALD CAMPBELL | |
| JOHN TILLOTSON | 1691 | TAIT | 1868 |
| THOMAS TENISON | 1695 | EDWARD WHITE | |
| WILLIAM WAKE | 1716 | BENSON | 1883 |
| JOHN POTTER | 1737 | FREDERICK TEMPLE | 1896 |
| THOMAS HERRING | 1747 | RANDALL THOMAS | |
| MATTHEW HUTTON | 1757 | DAVIDSON | 1903 |
| THOMAS SECKER | 1758 | COSMO GORDON LANG | 1928 |
| FREDERICK CORNWALLIS | 1768 | WILLIAM TEMPLE | 1942 |
| JOHN MOORE | 1783 | GEOFFREY FRANCIS | |
| CHARLES MANNERS | | FISHER | 1945 |
| SUTTON | 1805 | ARTHUR MICHAEL | |
| WILLIAM HOWLEY | 1828 | RAMSEY | 1961 |

547

# INDEX

Names of Archbishops of Canterbury are printed in **bold type**, with dates of consecration in brackets. Popes and Prime Ministers are grouped alphabetically under 'Popes' and 'Prime Ministers' respectively. Figures in **bold type** indicate principal references. '*p*' means '*passim.*'

CANTUAR

Keble, John, 304, 320; his 'Assize' sermon (1833), 295, 297
Kemp, Canon, 42
Kemp, Cardinal, Archbishop of York, 121
**Kemp, John** (1452), 75
Kent: Earl of, 57; gentlemen and ministers of, and Whitgift, 167; Kingdom and Kings of, 4, 5, 10–14 *p*, 16, 17, 20, 24–30 *p*, 39; Men of, 26, 27
Keynes, John Maynard, 478, 479
Kikuyu: Church in, 435, 436; Conference, 436
**Kilwardby, Robert** (1273), 52, 69, 92
King, William, Bishop of Lincoln, 365, 366–7, 368
Kingston-upon-Thames, 32; Council (838), 31, 36
Knox, Dr., Bishop of Manchester, 441–2

Lake, Dean of Durham, 361
Lambeth Conferences: I (1867), 321, 323–30, 379, 504; II (1878), 335, 357–9, 378, 379; III (1888), 378–81; IV (1897), 394–7, 400, 517; V (1908), 433–4; VI (1920), 434–5, 448–50, 502, 503; VII (1930), 450, 451, 474, 497; VIII (1948), 496–8) IX (1958), 498–9, 517; X (1968), 517
Lambeth Palace, 81, 82, 85–6, 92, 124, 142, 143, 146, 149, 154, 156, 159, 167, 179, 181, 182, 197, 206, 219, 223, 228, 237, 244–5, 266, 268, 283, 286–7, 290, 292, 340, 343, 356, 422; hospitality at, 246–7; attacked by mob, 263; 'routs' at, 268–9; annual bishops' meetings at, 347, 353, 445, 493–4; meetings of Anglicans and Nonconformists (1876), 354; bishops' 'quiet day' at, 364; King George V and Queen Mary entertained, 423; Free Churches' representatives at (1947), 503; and the Press, 511; and the Archiepiscopal Estate, 511–12; restoration of, 512; today, 513–14
**Lanfranc** (1070), 32, 34, 38, 44–5, 56–8, 65, 78, 83, 84, 88, **104–16**, 126, 245; quoted, 44; and primary of Canterbury, 106–8, 109, 113; and the *pallium* and Papal legates, 115–16
**Lang, Cosmo Gordon** (1928), 383, 411, 426, 435, 438, 440, **445–65**, 467, 509; his enthronement, 446; personal details, 446–8; his 'tragedy', 448; and Queen Victoria, 446, 457–8; and Christian unity at home and abroad, 448–52; and Lambeth Conferences (1920 & 1930), 448–50, 450, 451; visits Athens and Holy Land, 450; his 'delegations' to foreign churches, 451; and Cardinal Hinsley, 451, 456; and diocesan duties, 452; and Hewlett Johnson, 452–3, 495; his methods, 453; and Convocation, 453–4; and the Church Assembly, 453, 454–5; and 'national role' of the Church, 455–7; and India, 455–6; and wars, 456–7; and the Royal Family, 457–65; and Edward

VII, 458; and George V, 458–9; and Edward VIII (Duke of Windsor), 459–60, 460–3; and 'the King's Matter' and Abdication, 460–3; and George VI and Queen Elizabeth, 460, 464; and Queen Mary, 463; and the Coronation, 465; his reign at Lambeth, 465; and the Press, 510; and Lambeth Palace and Estate, 511–12
**Langham, Simon** (1366), 94, 95, 97
**Langton, Stephen** (1207), 50–2 *p*, 67–8, 100, 102, 118–19, 210
Lateran Council, Third (1179), 51, 65, 66, 88, 101
Latimer, Hugh, 142
**Laud, William** (1633), 161, 172, 183, 185–9 *p*, **190–9**, 206, 211, 244, 515; personal details, 190–1, 197; his theological position, 191–2; and the royal authority, 192–3, 196, 198; and Parliament, 193; his policies, 194; his visitations, 194–6; and the universities, 195–6; and Juxon for Treasurer, 197; his impeachment, trial and execution, 198–9
**Laurentius** (604), 9, 11
lay investiture, 59–60, 127
laymen in Church government, 369–71, 426
League of Nations, 419–20, 448
Lee, James Prince, Bishop of Manchester, 360
Leicester, Earl of, 161, 163, 169
*Letter to a Convocation Man* (Atterbury and others, 1697), 236
Lewis, John Travers, Bishop of Ontario, 324, 325
Liberation Society, 335, 354
Lichfield: Archbishopric (See) and Province (*temporary*) of, 22, 24–8 *p*; Cathedral, 26
Life and Liberty Movement, 410, 426, 427, 470, 471–2, 489
Lightfoot, J. B., Bishop of Durham, 361, 364, 365, 380, 391
Lincoln, battle of (1141), 60
Lincoln: Bishop of, 102, 103; Cathedral, 360; Diocese of, 102; *Schola Cancellarii*, 361
'Lincoln Judgment' (*see also* ritualism), 365–71; Benson's decisions, 367–8
Lindisfarne, 14
Lindsey, Diocese of, 19
'Little Faction, The', 169
Lloyd, William, Bishop of Norwich (deprived), 221
Locke, John (*The Reasonableness of Christianity*, 1695), 242
Lollard doctrines (*see also* Wycliff), 74
London, Bishops of (*unnamed, see also under names*), 10, 11, 38, 49, 54, 55, 62, 71, 95, 102, 104, 115, 104, 115, 283, 285
London, City of, 6, 22, 27–30 *p*, 40, 48; St. Bartholomew's Priory, 100
London, Councils of: (1075), 108; (1283), 104
London, Diocese and See of, 12, 17, 26, 97, 100

556